Introduction to Modern Information Retrieval

Second edition

G. G. Chowdhury

facet publishing

© G. G. Chowdhury 1999, 2004

Published by
Facet Publishing
7 Ridgmount Street
London WC1E 7AE

Facet Publishing (formerly Library Association Publishing) is wholly owned by
CILIP: the Chartered Institute of Library and Information Professionals.

G. G. Chowdhury has asserted his right under the Copyright, Designs and Patents
Act 1988 to be identified as the author of this work.

Except as otherwise permitted under the Copyright, Designs and Patents Act 1988
this publication may only be reproduced, stored or transmitted in any form or by any
means, with the prior permission of the publisher, or, in the case of reprographic
reproduction, in accordance with the terms of a licence issued by The Copyright
Licensing Agency. Enquiries concerning reproduction outside those terms should
be sent to Facet Publishing, 7 Ridgmount Street, London WC1E 7AE.

First published by Library Association Publishing 1999
Reprinted 2001
Reprinted by Facet Publishing 2002
This second edition 2004

British Library Cataloguing in Publication Data
A catalogue record for this book is available from the British Library.

ISBN 1-85604-480-7

Typeset in 10/12pt Times and Arial by Facet Publishing.
Printed and made in Great Britain by MPG Books Ltd, Bodmin, Cornwall.

To Sudatta, Avirup and Anubhav

Contents

August 24 - Sept 19   Chs 1-3
September 19 - Oct 3 Chs 4+5
October 3 - 24   Chs 6 + 7; 20-21
Oct 24 - Nov 7   Ch 9
Nov 7 - Nov 21 Chs 10-14
Nov 21 - Dec 5 Chs 15-19

Preface		**xi**
Coverage		xi
Acknowledgements		xiii
1	**Basic concepts of information retrieval systems**	**1**
	Introduction	1
	Purpose	2
	Functions	3
	Components	3
	Kinds of information retrieval systems	4
	Design issues	5
	Design phases	8
	References	11
2	**Database technology**	**13**
	Introduction	13
	Data	13
	The database	13
	Records and fields	14
	Properties of databases	14
	Kinds of databases	15
	Database technology	16
	The development of databases in an information retrieval environment	18
	Discussion	22
	References	23
3	**Bibliographic formats**	**24**
	Introduction	24
	Bibliographic records	25
	Integrated database approach	27
	ISO 2709: Format for Bibliographic Information Interchange	28
	MARC format	31
	UNIMARC format	36
	The Common Communication Format	38
	Discussion	40
	References	40

4	**Cataloguing and metadata**	**42**
	Introduction	42
	Cataloguing	42
	Metadata	50
	Summary	54
	References	55
5	**Subject analysis and representation**	**57**
	Introduction	57
	Classification	58
	Bibliographic Classification	65
	Classification of internet resources	66
	Subject analysis	70
	Subject indexing	72
	Exhaustivity and specificity	72
	Manual indexing	74
	Pre-coordinate indexing systems	76
	Post-coordinate indexing systems	84
	Problems of manual indexing	86
	Theory of indexing	86
	Discussion	87
	References	87
6	**Automatic indexing and file organization**	**91**
	Introduction	91
	The process of indexing	91
	Automatic classification	94
	Index file organization	96
	Inverted file	97
	Sequential access	102
	Alternative text retrieval structures	110
	Discussion	119
	References	120
7	**Vocabulary control**	**123**
	Introduction	123
	Controlled vs natural indexing	124
	Vocabulary control tools	126
	Guidelines for developing a thesaurus	142
	Criteria for evaluating a thesaurus	143
	Use of thesauri in online information retrieval	143
	References	148

8 Abstracts and abstracting   153
Abstracts   153
Types of abstract   153
Qualities of abstracts   155
Uses of abstracts   156
The art of abstracting   157
Automatic abstracting   160
Recent works on text summarization   165
Discussion   166
References   166

9 Searching and retrieval   169
Introduction   169
The search strategy and its prerequisites   169
The pre-search interview   170
The searching process   170
Retrieval models   171
Alternative information retrieval models   182
Search facilities offered by most text retrieval systems   183
Discussion   189
References   190

10 Users of information retrieval   192
Introduction   192
Users and their nature   192
Types of information needs   193
Information needs in different areas of activity   195
Information seeking behaviour of users   200
What we need to know about users   201
User studies   205
Possible sources of information about users   210
References   212

11 User-centred models of information retrieval   214
Introduction   214
Information seeking   214
Human information behaviour models   216
User-centred information search models   219
Discussion   223
References   224

12 User interfaces   227
Introduction   227
The four-phase framework for interface design   227

Information seeking and user interfaces   230
User interfaces and visualization   231
User interfaces of some information retrieval systems   232
References   240

13 Evaluation of information retrieval systems   243
Introduction   243
The purpose of evaluation   244
Evaluation criteria   244
The steps of evaluation   252
New retrieval parameters   253
References   253

14 Evaluation experiments   255
Introduction   255
The Cranfield tests   256
MEDLARS   261
The SMART retrieval experiment   262
The STAIRS project   266
Limitations of early evaluation studies   267
TREC   269
References   278

15 Online and CD-ROM information retrieval   280
Introduction   280
Online searching   280
CD-ROM databases   292
Summary   296
References   298

16 Multimedia information retrieval   299
Introduction   299
Multimedia information retrieval   299
Standards   311
Summary   312
References   312

17 Hypertext and markup languages   315
Introduction   315
Hypertext   316
Markup languages   323
Discussion   327
References   328

18 Web information retrieval   330
    Introduction   330
    Traditional vs web information retrieval   330
    Web information: volume and growth   332
    Access to information on the web: the tools   335
    Web information retrieval: evaluation studies   347
    References   349

19 Intelligent information retrieval   352
    Introduction   352
    Intelligent retrieval systems   353
    Artificial intelligence   353
    Expert systems   354
    Kinds of expert systems   355
    Components of expert systems   355
    Historical development of expert systems   357
    Development methodology and approaches   357
    Knowledge elicitation and representation
        methods   359
    Inference strategies   360
    End-user modelling and interfaces   360
    Development tools   362
    Expert systems for library and information services   362
    Discussion   367
    References   368

20 Natural language processing and information
    retrieval   372
    Introduction   372
    Natural language understanding   372
    Syntactic analysis   373
    Semantic analysis   381
    Pragmatic knowledge   390
    References   394

21 Natural language processing systems   396
    Introduction   396
    Literature on natural language processing systems   397
    Natural language text processing systems   398
    Natural language user interfaces   408
    Internet, web and digital library applications of natural
        language processing systems   412
    Machine translation and cross-language information
        retrieval   413

Summary   415
References   416

22 Information retrieval in digital libraries   425
Introduction   425
Information resources in digital libraries   426
The basic design of a digital library   426
Interoperability   428
Information retrieval features of selected digital libraries 428
Common features of information retrieval in digital libraries 436
Special IR features in DLs   437
Problems and prospects   437
Summary   441
References   442

23 Trends in information retrieval   445
Introduction   445
Evaluation of information retrieval systems   447
Developments related to the input subsystem   448
Searching and retrieval   450
User studies and user modelling   452
User interfaces   454
Information retrieval standards and protocols   454
Information retrieval in the context of web and
    digital libraries   455
Intelligent information retrieval   457
Evaluation of natural language processing systems   459
Machine translation   459
Conclusions   461
References   462

Index   467

Preface

The rapid growth and development of the internet, the world wide web and digital libraries since the first edition of this book have brought about many significant changes in the world of information retrieval. While the original aim of this book to provide a blend of traditional and new approaches to information retrieval remains the same, this second edition has been revised to incorporate some of the wider perspectives – and the latest developments – of information retrieval.

The book aims to cover the whole spectrum of information storage and retrieval in a way that is relevant to an international readership. The primary audience I have in mind comprises students of library and information science programmes, both at undergraduate and at postgraduate levels. Written from a relatively non-technical perspective, this book is expected to meet the requirements of students undertaking courses in information retrieval, information organization, information use, digital libraries, etc. It will also help practising library and information professionals to brush up their knowledge in different areas of information retrieval.

Coverage

While the content and coverage of Chapters 1 and 2 have remained the same, they have been updated to incorporate wider perspectives of information retrieval ranging from the shelf to the web. Chapter 3 has been revised considerably by dropping discussions on the less well-known bibliographic formats in favour of new sections on the MARC21 format.

In the first edition Chapter 4 covered the areas of cataloguing and classification, and consequently the discussions on both these areas were rather brief. In this edition a chapter has been devoted to each of them. Beginning with the basics of cataloguing and AACR2, Chapter 4 discusses the implications of using AACR2 in automated cataloguing. There follow sections on the cataloguing of internet resources, and on metadata and the various metadata standards. Chapter 5 discusses the basic concepts of classification and subject indexing, which are considered to be the traditional approaches to information organization and retrieval. However, this chapter also describes the various approaches to the use of these traditional tools for organizing web information resources.

Chapter 6 discusses various automatic indexing and file organization techniques. Chapter 7 discusses the issues of vocabulary control in information retrieval. This chapter has been revised by adding new sections on the use of vocabulary control tools in online information retrieval. While the basic concepts of abstracts and abstracting remain the same, Chapter 8 updates the sections on automatic abstracting to include some recent studies in this area. Chapter 9 discusses the information search process and the various information retrieval models. This chapter now also discusses various alternative information retrieval models, and provides some illustrations for the process of query expansion as part of an online information search process.

The first edition had only one chapter on information users. In this edition, Chapter 10 covers the basic issues of information users and the various approaches to user studies, while Chapter 11 discusses the various user-centred information retrieval models. Chapter 12 covers the topic of user interfaces, an essential component of an information retrieval system.

Chapters 13 and 14 cover discussions on the evaluation of information retrieval. These chapters have been revised significantly to include discussion of the TREC (Text Retrieval Conferences) series of evaluation experiments. Discussions on online and CD-ROM information retrieval have been merged to form only one chapter, Chapter 15. While some theoretical discussions on online and CD-ROM retrieval technology have been dropped, more examples have been provided to illustrate the information retrieval process.

Chapter 16 covers discussions on multimedia information retrieval, which appeared in Chapter 15 in the first edition. This chapter has been significantly revised to include discussions on image, audio and video information retrieval. Chapter 17 covers discussions on hypertext information retrieval. New sections on hypertext markup languages, including SGML, HTML, XML and XHTML, have been added.

Chapter 22 of the first edition has been completely revised to form the new Chapter 18, which covers various aspects of web information retrieval. A number of screenshots have been added to illustrate the features of various web information retrieval tools, and recent studies analysing various web information retrieval studies. Chapter 17 of the first edition has been updated to form the new Chapter 19, covering discussions on intelligent information retrieval, with new sections describing some recent studies in this area.

Four chapters (18 to 21) in the first edition have been merged and updated to form the two new Chapters 20 and 21 on natural language processing. Chapter 20 discusses the theoretical issues of natural language processing, while Chapter 21 discusses various studies on the applications of NLP techniques to the different areas of information retrieval. Chapter 22 is a new chapter in this edition that covers various aspects of information retrieval in digital libraries. Information retrieval features of selected digital libraries have been discussed here, along with discussions on some digital library research in the areas of information access and retrieval. The book ends with Chapter 23, which analyses the trends in information retrieval.

Acknowledgements

In order to illustrate the content of the various chapters in this book, I have included a number of screenshots of various information sources and services, acknowledged here:

Figures 5.1, 5.2, 5.3 and 12.3: Reproduced with permission of CDLR, Centre for Digital Library Research, **http://cdlr.strath.ac.uk/**.
Figures 7.1 and 7.2: Reproduced with permission of the Library of Congress.
Figure 7.4: Reproduced with permission of OECD Publishing.
Figure 12.1: Used with permission of California Digital Library. The content, both textual and graphical, of systems provided by the California Digital Library is copyrighted by the Regents of the University of California, unless otherwise noted.
Figures 12.2, 12.7, 12.8 and 12.9: Reproduced with permission of ProQuest Information and Learning Company. Further reproduction is prohibited without permission.
Figures 12.4, 12.5 and 12.6: NCBI Entrez and Taxonomy are freely accessible resources from the National Center for Biotechnology Information, US National Library of Medicine.
Figure 18.1: Reproduced with permission of Google, **http://www.google.com**.
Figure 18.3: Reproduced with permission of Lycos Network; HotBot® is a registered service mark of Wired Ventures.
Figure 18.4: Reproduced with permission of Kartoo, **http://www.kartoo.com**.
Figure 18.5: Reproduced with permission of Vivisimo Inc, **http://www.vivisimo.com**.

Many individuals and institutions have directly or indirectly helped me in preparing this edition. Those whose resources have been used as illustrations and discussions in this book are acknowledged with thanks. I am also indebted to various information retrieval specialists who have given their comments, in the form of both formal and informal review of the first edition.

I am especially indebted to my wife, Sudatta, who has provided constant direct and indirect support, while I have been working on this edition. I am also deeply indebted to my two wonderful sons, Avirup and Anubhav, who have been my source of inspiration throughout this period. Finally, I must express my gratitude to the staff of Facet Publishing, without whose constant help and support this book would not have seen the light of day.

G. G. Chowdhury

Chapter 1

Basic concepts of information retrieval systems

Introduction

The term information retrieval was coined in 1952 and gained popularity in the research community from 1961 onwards.[1] At that time information retrieval's organizing function was seen as a major advance in libraries that were no longer just storehouses of books, but also places where the information was catalogued and indexed.[2] Subsequently, with the introduction of computers in information handling, there appeared a number of databases containing bibliographic details of documents, often coupled with abstracts, keywords, etc., and consequently the concept of information retrieval came to mean retrieval of bibliographic information from stored document databases. These information retrieval systems were, truly speaking, document retrieval systems, since they were designed to retrieve information about the existence (or non-existence) of bibliographic documents relevant to a user query. Lancaster[3] comments that an information retrieval system does not inform (i.e. change the knowledge of) the user on the subject of his enquiry; it merely informs him of the existence (or non-existence) and whereabouts of documents relating to his request. However, this notion of information retrieval has changed since the availability of full text documents in bibliographic databases. Modern information retrieval systems can either retrieve bibliographic items, or the exact text that matches a user's search criteria from a stored database of full texts of documents. Although information retrieval systems originally meant text retrieval systems, since they were dealing with textual documents, modern information retrieval systems deal with multimedia information comprising text, audio, images and video. While many features of conventional text retrieval systems are equally applicable to multimedia information retrieval, the specific nature of audio, image and video information have called for the development of many new tools and techniques for information retrieval. Modern information retrieval deals with storage, organization and access to text, as well as multimedia information resources.

The concept of information retrieval presupposes that there are some documents or records containing information that have been organized in an order suitable for easy retrieval. The documents or records we are concerned with contain biblio-graphic information which is quite different from other kinds of information or data. We may take a simple example. If we have a database of information pertaining to an office, or a supermarket, all we have are the different kinds of records and related facts, like names of employees, their positions, salary, and so on, or in the case of a supermarket, names of different items, prices, quantity, and so on. The retrieval system here is designed to search for and retrieve specific facts or data, like the salary of a particular manager, or the price of a perfume, and so on. The major objective of a bibliographic information retrieval system, however, is to retrieve the informa-tion – either the actual information or the documents containing the information – that fully or partially match the user's query. The database may contain abstracts or full texts of documents, like newspaper articles, handbooks, dictionaries, ency-clopaedias, legal documents, statistics, etc., as well as audio, images, and video information. Whatever may be the nature of the database – bibliographic, full-text or multimedia – the system presupposes that there is a group of users for whom the system is designed. Users are considered to have certain queries or information needs, and when they put forward their requirement to the system, the latter should be able to provide the necessary bibliographic references of those documents con-taining either the required information, or the actual text in the case of a full-text retrieval system. Alternative models of (knowledge-based) information retrieval seek to provide the user with the information directly rather than just the citations, the abstract or the full text.

We can now narrow down our discussion to three major areas that constitute an information retrieval system: items of information, users' queries, and matching of these queries with the document database. An information retrieval system thus has three major components – the document subsystem, the users subsystem, and the searching/retrieval subsystem. These divisions are quite broad and each one is designed to serve one or more functions, such as:

- analysis of documents and organization of information (creation of a document database)
- analysis of users' queries, preparation of a strategy to search the database
- actual searching or matching of users' queries with the database, and finally
- retrieval of items that fully or partially match the search statement.

Purpose

An information retrieval system is designed to retrieve the documents or informa-tion required by the user community. It should make the right information available to the right user. Thus, an information retrieval system aims at collecting and orga-nizing information in one or more subject areas in order to provide it to the user as soon as asked for. Belkin[4] presents the following situation which clearly reflects the purpose of information retrieval systems:

1   a writer presents a set of ideas in a document using a set of concepts

2   somewhere there will be some users who require the ideas but may not be able
to identify those. In other words, there will be some persons who lack the ideas
put forward by the author in his/her work
3   information retrieval systems serve to match the writer's ideas expressed in the
document with the users' requirements or demands for those.

Thus, an information retrieval system serves as a bridge between the world of creators or generators of information and the users of that information.

Functions

An information retrieval system deals with various sources of information on the
one hand and users' requirements on the other. It must:

- analyse the contents of the sources of information as well as the users' queries,
and then
- match these to retrieve those items that are relevant.

The major functions of an information retrieval system can be listed as follows:[5, 6]

1   to identify the information (sources) relevant to the areas of interest of the target users' community
2   to analyse the contents of the sources (documents)
3   to represent the contents of the analysed sources in a way that will be suitable
for matching users' queries
4   to analyse users' queries and to represent them in a form that will be suitable
for matching with the database
5   to match the search statement with the stored database
6   to retrieve the information that is relevant, and
7   to make necessary adjustments in the system based on feedback from the users.

Components

It is evident from the above discussion that on the one side of an information retrieval
system there are the documents or sources of information and on the other there are
the users' queries. These two sides are linked through a series of tasks. Lancaster[5]
mentions that an information retrieval system comprises six major subsystems:

1   the document subsystem
2   the indexing subsystem
3   the vocabulary subsystem
4   the searching subsystem
5   the user-system interface, and
6   the matching subsystem.

The broad outline of an information retrieval system is shown in Figure 1.1.

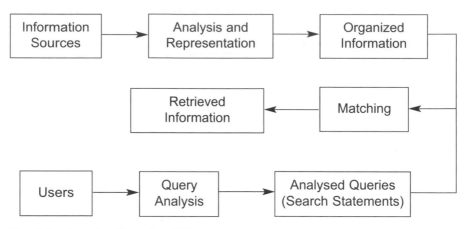

Fig. 1.1   *Broad outline of an IRS*

All the tasks mentioned in Figure 1.1 can be brought under two major groups – subject/content analysis, and search and retrieval. Subject or content analysis includes the tasks related to the analysis, organization and storage of information. The process of search and retrieval includes the tasks of analysing users' queries, creation of a search formula, the actual searching, and retrieval of information. The major emphasis of this book is laid on these two areas. Researchers in the information retrieval world are engaged in developing suitable methodologies for both sets of operations. Developments in the technological world, especially in computer and communication technology, have provided an additional impetus to the development of information retrieval systems. Researchers who are working on the storage side of the information retrieval system are engaged in designing sophisticated methods for identification and representation of the various bibliographic elements essential for documents, automatic content analysis, and text processing, and so on. On the other hand, researchers working on the retrieval side are attempting to develop sophisticated searching techniques, user interfaces, and various techniques for producing output for local as well as remote users. The recent emergence of the Internet, particularly the World Wide Web (discussed in Chapter 18), has made a significant impact on the information retrieval environment.

Kinds of information retrieval systems

Two broad categories of information retrieval system can be identified: in-house and online. In-house information retrieval systems are set up by a particular library or information centre to serve mainly the users within the organization. One particular type of in-house database is the library catalogue. Online public access catalogues (OPACs) provide facilities for library users to carry out online catalogue searches, and then to check the availability of the item required.

By online information retrieval systems we mean those that have been designed to provide access to remote database(s) to a variety of users. Such services are available mostly on a commercial basis, and there are a number of vendors that handle this sort of service. With the development of optical storage technology another type of information retrieval system appeared on CD-ROM (compact-disc read-only memory). Information retrieval systems based on CD-ROM technology are available mostly on a commercial basis, though there have been some free and in-house developments too. Basic techniques for search and retrieval of information from the in-house or CD-ROM and online information retrieval systems are more or less the same, except that the online system is linked to users at a distance through the electronic communication network.

Recent developments in computer and communication technologies have widened the scope of online information retrieval systems. The Internet and World Wide Web have made information available for use by anyone virtually anywhere with access to the appropriate equipment. This has led to the concept of a digital global library system where information can be generated and made available in electronic form on the Web for use by any user from any corner of the world. This of course involves a number of technical and management issues that need to be resolved in order to make the global digital library concept a reality.

Design issues

A system can be defined as a set of interacting components, under human control, operating together to achieve an intended purpose; thus a system carries out processing on inputs to produce required outputs; the agents of this processing are people and machines.[7, 8] Vickery and Vickery[8] represent the input, processing, and output of a system as shown in Table 1.1.

System design may be viewed as a series of choices from which the designer selects each element and tries to fit it with the proposed objective of the system. Therefore, if a system is designed carefully, the designer must be aware of the choices that are to be made, and he or she must consider the consequences of making any available choice. The life-cycle approach to system design suggests the following basic stages in the life of a system:[9]

Table 1.1 *Inputs and outputs of a system in general*

Input	Processing	Output
Source data	By people and machines	Results
Policies		Reports
Funds, fees		Demands on sources
Recipient demands		Feedback to sources
Recipient feedback		Requests to recipients
Source requests		General publicity
Environmental information		Profits/losses

1   an analysis has to be conducted in order to establish the requirements of a system, and to learn the various options available

2   next comes the design phase, which eventually gives rise to a specific system to match the requirements

3   next comes the implementation stage, which leads into the operating evolution during which the system fulfils its objectives and is modified from time to time to match the minor changes in requirements, and eventually

4   the system becomes less effective, due to several reasons such as mechanical faults, arrival of new technologies, major changes in the requirements and environment, and so on. This stage leads to decay which finally leads to replacement of the system, i.e. starting at step 1 again.

Liston and Schoene[10] suggest that an effective information retrieval system must have provisions for:

1   prompt dissemination of information
2   filtering of information
3   the right amount of information at the right time
4   active switching of information
5   receiving information in the desired form
6   browsing
7   getting information in an economical way
8   current literature
9   access to other information systems
10   interpersonal communication, and
11   personalized help.

Vickery[7] suggests that before the system design begins, the designer should examine the various performance requirements of the system. Kent[6] mentions the following performance criteria to be taken into consideration:

1   subject coverage; that is, what subjects are to be covered by the proposed system
2   depth of analysis required for the source documents
3   precision of service required; that is, the acceptable limit of the service measured in terms of relevance of the retrieved output
4   speed of service acceptable to the system users
5   form and type of input and output involved
6   any special requirement, like compatibility with other systems, available equipment, personnel skills, etc.

Liston and Schoene[10] suggest that an information retrieval system should be user-oriented, that is, it should give primary emphasis to the convenience of the users. Such a system should meet the following functional requirements:

1   it should identify the specific information requirement of the user community
2   it should provide for interaction between the system designer and the users
3   it should provide information in a form suitable for ready use

4 its scope should be broad enough to cover all kinds of requirements of the user community
5 it should be capable of providing the right information at the right time
6 it should provide information that is easily accessible
7 it should be adaptable to environmental changes
8 it should maintain standards for protection of data
9 it should devise ways for facilitating oral communications, and
10 it should be easily accessible and convenient to use as a whole.

Vickery and Vickery[8] suggest that the designer of an information retrieval needs the following information:

1 a specification of the user group to be served, its characteristics, size and location
2 a knowledge of the information needed by the group, the forms in which it is required, its urgency and the frequency of demand
3 an understanding of the system's requirements consequently expected, and the services to be delivered
4 a grasp of any existing system that is to be developed, replaced, or competed against
5 the coverage of the system, that is the content and size of the stock
6 the nature and volume of items to be input to the system, and
7 a knowledge of appropriate alternative storage and retrieval procedures.

The system being designed may have a number of parameters that need to be considered. Liston and Schoene[10] suggest that the following points are to be kept in mind while designing an information retrieval system:

- the fixed parameters of the system
- the variable parameters
- identification of the available options within each variable
- identification of the factors that affect the choice among the various options available within each variable
- identification of the factors that will be affected by a choice among available options, and
- analysis of the variables and the factors affecting and affected by each choice in order to determine the sequence in which decisions should be made and how decisions should be made.

The different parameters of an information retrieval system might be summarized as follows:[10, 11]

1 general parameters:
   - purpose
   - scope
   - functions

- form of organization
- financial resources

2   input parameters
- coverage
- types of input
- acquisition
- input processing
- subject analysis and indexing

3   output parameters
- services
- products
- users
- preparation of information products
- marketing and distribution
- user feedback
- standardization

4   internal parameters
- document storage
- index data storage
- vocabulary control
- level of mechanization
- centralization of operations
- staff aspects.

Design phases

Designing an information retrieval system involves a number of steps. Vickery and Vickery[8] suggest that we must ask the following questions:

1   what are the functions of the proposed system?
2   what information is to be transferred or transformed?
3   what is the objective?
4   what wider systems are concerned?
5   what are the functions and objectives?
6   in what ways are these functions and objectives likely to change?
7   what is the general environment of the system?
8   what kind of service output should the system have?
9   what kinds of documentary inputs should be made available to the system?
10   what processes are necessary to transform the inputs to the desired outputs?
11   what are the expected volumes of input, output, and transaction rates?
12   what are the foreseeable constraints that might affect the system design and its performance?
13   what are the available options to accomplish the stated objectives of the proposed system?
14   how is the performance of the system going to be measured?, and so on.

Several different methodologies have been suggested for the development of information retrieval systems. Weisman,[11] as early as 1972, suggested a methodology comprising the following four interdependent phases:

Phase I deals with the basic requirements of the system. The tasks involved in this phase help the designer determine the basic requirements upon which the system would work. This phase actually sets the basic objectives of the system. An information retrieval system is designed to meet the information requirements of its users. Hence, identifying the users and determining their basic needs are the two most important tasks, and these are accomplished at this phase. This phase is not only useful in the design of a new system, but also helps to find out whether any change is required in the design aspects of an existing system.

Phase II deals with the actual design aspects. The system designer has to take a number of decisions at this stage. Two major determining factors are the coverage of the system and the available resources. Here the designer determines the coverage regarding the subject, the nature of publication, time period, range of users to be covered, range of services to be provided, and so on. The designer has also to identify the different functions of the proposed system and then should determine the sequence of those functions which will optimize the performance of the system. This actually requires detailed systems analysis and the performance of the resulting system largely depends on how perfectly the system has been analysed and how the operations of each subsystem are interlinked. Each operation and related factors must be defined clearly in relation to others and to the environment as a whole. In fact this phase produces the basic framework on which the actual tasks of design rest. The pilot system is designed through all these analyses and observations. Once the pilot system is designed, it is tested in the next phase.

Phase III involves the tasks of pilot system installation and its evaluation. It is at this stage the pilot system is tested, not only to determine how it works but also to identify under what constraints it works. Each subsystem of the pilot system is evaluated to determine how and in what way it is affected by different factors. Using these observations the designer recommends necessary changes and/or adjustments in the final system. It is necessary to determine at this level what the optimum performance level should be, that is beyond which the ratio of enhanced cost and improved performance will be too high. Thus the basic motto of this phase is not only to debug the newly designed system but also to define the unavoidable constraints that are too difficult to overcome.

Phase IV involves the task of implementing the system. It is at this stage that the pilot system is revised, if necessary, based on the observations from the third phase. Once the final system has been designed, it is installed and is tested in the real-life situation. Another major task of this phase relates to the training of staff members. Whenever a new system is designed and installed, it is necessary that the persons who will operate the system are trained adequately. The system designer is probably the right person to propose the best way to train the people. After all these tasks are performed, a final report on the system is prepared.

A number of methodologies have been suggested in the recent literature for development of information systems. Rowley[9, 12] suggests that the following five main stages are commonly featured in any system development project:

1   Definition of objectives. This phase involves the following activities:
    • preparation of terms of reference
    • initial needs analysis as a study proposal
    • feasibility study
    • evaluation of options and analysis of existing systems.
2   Definition of systems requirements. Detailed specification of the systems requirements are prepared.
3   Design. This stage involves the following activities:
    • creation of a logical and physical systems model, and
    • choice and ordering of hardware and software configuration.
4   Implementation. The activities involved here are:
    • planning and preparation
    • education and training
    • database creation
    • system installation, and
    • switch-over.
5   Evaluation. There could be several activities, such as,
    • initial evaluation
    • ongoing monitoring
    • maintenance, and
    • evolution.

Various information-systems methodologies (i.e. mathematical approaches to systems planning, analysis and design) such as structured systems analysis and design (SSADM), holistic methodologies and prototyping, object-oriented methods have been described by Rowley.[13] Frants, Shapiro and Voiskunskii[14] suggest that proper understanding of a system's function, structure and the nature of interaction among its various components is essential to reduce the cost of development, and to avoid mistakes. Korfhage[15] suggests that an information system is composed of an *ectosystem* and an *endosystem*. An ectosystem consists of those factors that are not under the control of the system designer, such as people who are involved in the system, the forms in which the information is available, and the equipment and technology available for the system. The endosystem, on the other hand, consists of those factors that can be specified and controlled by the designer, such as the equipment, algorithms and procedures used. The performance of an information retrieval system is largely dictated by the designer's choice of media, devices, algorithms, and structures, i.e. by the endosystem design, whereas the evaluation of the performance of the system resides within the ectosystem.

    Developments in information retrieval can be viewed from two different perspectives:

- The computer-centred view that deals with building efficient computer systems for storage, organization and access to information, and focuses on areas like building up efficient access mechanisms, query processing, ranking algorithms, display and delivery of search results, etc.
- The user-centred view that focuses on the study of human information behaviour, understanding of human needs, information context and use, etc.

This book aims to focus on both these views of information retrieval, since successful information retrieval systems should take both views into account. It also covers the broader scope of information retrieval that ranges from library OPACs to the web and digital libraries. Alongside the latest developments in computerized information retrieval, this book discusses the traditional library tools and techniques, like classification, cataloguing and vocabulary control, as well as the traditional manual indexing systems. It is believed that today's information professionals should know about these traditional tools and techniques because of at least two reasons. Firstly, they show the process of the evolution of information retrieval, from the shelf to the web; and secondly, many recent developments in information retrieval in web and digital library environments have their roots, explicitly or implicitly, in traditional bibliographic tools and techniques. In some cases the wheel has been re-invented, perhaps because inventors were not aware of the tools and techniques built and used by libraries over a long period for organization and access to information resources.

References

1 Sparck Jones, K. and Willett, P., 'Overall introduction'. In: Sparck Jones, K. and Willett, P. (eds.), *Readings in information retrieval*, San Francisco, Morgan Kaufmann Pub. Inc., 1997, 1–7.
2 Parsaye, K., Chignell, M., Khosafian, S. and Wong, H., *Intelligent databases: object-oriented, deductive hypermedia technologies*, New York, John Wiley, 1989.
3 Lancaster, F. W., *Information retrieval systems*, New York, John Wiley, 1968.
4 Belkin, N. J., 'Anomalous states of knowledge as a basis for information retrieval', *Canadian journal of information science*, 5, 1980, 133–43.
5 Lancaster, F. W., *Information retrieval systems: characteristics, testing, and evaluation*, 2nd edn, New York, John Wiley, 1979.
6 Kent, A., *Information analysis and retrieval*, 3rd edn, New York, Becker and Heys, 1971.
7 Vickery, B. C., *Techniques of information retrieval*, London, Butterworth, 1970.
8 Vickery, B. and Vickery, A., *Information science theory and practice*, London, Bowker-Saur, 1987.
9 Rowley, J., *The basics of information systems*, 2nd edn, London, Library Association Publishing, 1996.
10 Liston, D. M. and Schoene, M. L., 'A systems approach to the design of infor-

mation systems'. In: King D. W. (ed.), *Key papers in the design and evaluation of information systems*, New York, Knowledge Industry, 1978, 327–34.

11   Weisman, H. M., *Information systems, services and centers*, Los Angeles, Becker and Hays, 1972.

12   Rowley, J., 'Aspects of a library systems methodology', *Journal of information science*, **20** (1), 1994, 41–5.

13   Rowley, J., *The electronic library*, fourth edition of *Computers for libraries*, London, Library Association Publishing, 1998.

14   Frants, V. I., Shapiro, J. and Voiskunskii, V. G., *Automated information retrieval: theory and methods*, San Diego, Academic Press, 1997.

15   Korfhage, R. R., Information storage and retrieval, New York, John Wiley, 1997.

Chapter 2

Database technology

Introduction

Database technology emerged in the late sixties as a result of a combination of various circumstances. There was a growing demand among users for more information to be provided by the computer relating to the day-to-day running of the organization as well as to planning and control purposes. This demand coincided with advances in computer technology and in expertise in computer data processing. The technology that emerged to process and manipulate data of various kinds is broadly termed as database management technology, and the resulting software packages are known as database management systems (DBMSs). DBMSs do just what the name suggests: they manage a computer-stored database or collection of data.

Basic concepts of database systems, their growth, and recent trends in database technology are discussed in this chapter. Our main concern is with bibliographic or text databases which form the basis of information retrieval systems. Different kinds of bibliographic/text databases are mentioned by way of examples. Finally, measures to be taken to develop databases in an information retrieval environment are briefly discussed.

Data

The word data refers to a set of given facts. Information in a form that can be processed by a computer is called data. Data has for long been used to refer to scientific measurements, but words constitute data just as numbers do. A list of names is data, a set of keywords is data, a doctor's record of his patients is data, and figures relating to temperature, humidity, etc., or sales of a company, are data.

The database

A database can be conceived as a system whose base, whose key concept, is simply a particular way of handling data. In other words, a database is nothing more than a computer-based record-keeping system.[1] The overall objective of a database is to record and maintain information. The *Macmillan dictionary of information technology*[2] defines a database as 'a collection of interrelated data stored so that it may be accessed by authorised users with simple user-friendly dialogues'. The *Chambers science and technology dictionary*[3] provides a more simple definition of a database: 'a collection of structured data independent of any particular application'.

It may be noted from the above definitions that a database contains some data that are structured and integrated. Ellingen[4] defines a database as 'a collection of information that can be searched as a single entity'. According to Oxborrow,[5] a database can be considered as 'an organised collection of related sets of data, managed in such a way as to enable the user or application program to view the complete collection, or a logical subset of the collection, as a single unit'.

From the above definitions we can simplify the definition of a database as 'an organised collection of related sets of data that can be accessed by more than one user by simple means and can be searched to reveal those that touch upon a particular need'. In the computer world we frequently deal with files, which are the outer identifying boundary or a sort of folder containing data. Thus, a file is equivalent to an ordinary address book, if we are talking about names and addresses. A file in a computer is given a unique name by which it is addressed.

Records and fields

A *record* is a collection of related information.[4] A database is an organized collection of units of information, and each unit of information in a database is called a *record*. A record is generally what a user wants to find while searching a database. An example of a record is a book card in a library's catalogue, which describes the book's title, author, subject, etc. A collection of database records constitutes a database file.[6] Identifying what the record is to be is one of the early tasks in designing a database. If the database is a bibliographic one, the bibliographic information about each document is the unit of information or record.

A stored record is a named collection of associated stored fields.[7] Each record is made up of particular segments or elements of information, each of which is called a *field*. A field holds a particular type of information within a record that can be separately addressed. The different items of information in a bibliographic record may be author, title, etc. Thus, the different fields in a bibliographic record can be the 'author field' containing name(s) of author(s), the 'title field' containing the title, and so on. A field may be subdivided into still smaller units called *subfields*. For example, if 'imprint' is regarded as a field in a bibliographic database, then the different components of the imprint – the publisher's name, place of publication, and date of publication – can be called subfields.

A record is thus composed of fields and subfields. Identifying what fields and subfields are to be included in each record is an important task in the database design process. Each field is given a unique identifier, called *field tag*, at the design stage, which is then used throughout for data input, editing, searching, printing, and so on.

Properties of databases

A database is designed to avoid duplication of data as well as to permit retrieval of information to satisfy a wide variety of user information needs.[8] Major properties of a database can be summarized as follows:[9]

- it is integrated with provisions for different applications
- it eliminates or reduces data duplication
- it enhances data independence by permitting application programs to be insensitive to changes in the database
- it permits shared access
- it permits finer granularity, and
- it provides facilities for centralized control of accessing and security control functions.

Kinds of databases

In discussing databases it is sometimes useful to classify them by the type of data record contained and sometimes by subject coverage. The two major divisions are *reference databases* and *source databases*. Reference databases lead the users to the source of the information: a document, person or organization. They can be divided into three categories:

1   *bibliographic databases*, which include citations or bibliographic references, and sometimes abstracts of literature
2   *catalogue databases*, which show the catalogue of a given library or a group of libraries in a network, and
3   *referral databases*, which offer references to information such as the name, address, specialization, etc., of persons, institutions, information systems, etc.

Source databases provide the answer with no need for the user to refer elsewhere.[10] These databases contain the information sought for in machine-readable form and, therefore, may be regarded as a kind of electronic document. Source databases can be grouped according to their content, for example,

1   *numeric databases*, which contain numerical data of various kinds, including statistics and survey data
2   *full-text databases*, which contain the full text of documents
3   *text-numeric databases*, which contain a combination of textual and numerical data, such as a company annual report and handbook data.

Bibliographic databases form the basis of most of the information retrieval systems available today, be they home-grown or available on CD-ROM or through online access. Bibliographic databases can be divided into five broad categories:

1   large discipline-oriented databases
2   interdisciplinary databases with coverage based on key or core journals
3   cross-disciplinary databases
4   smaller, more specialized databases serving a particular technology or application area, and
5   databases covering specific types of publication.

However, there could be many more kinds of bibliographic databases, such as:[11, 12]

Specific subjects/disciplines: CASearch, BIOSIS, ERIC, MEDLINE, ENERGY-
LINE, FOREST, PIRA ABSTRACTS, and so on.
Multidisciplinary: SCI SEARCH, SOCIAL SCISEARCH
Mission-oriented: NASA
Problem-oriented: ENVIROLINE, TOXLINE
Referral: Foundations Directory, Fine Chemicals Directory, Ulrich's International
Periodicals Directory
Factual: PTS Forecasts, CARIS/FAO (Ongoing Research)
Textual references: DRUGLINE, and so on.

Many of these databases are available in online and CD-ROM versions.

Database technology

The historical development of database technology has been closely related to the
development of computer hardware and software. With respect to hardware development, it is now common to talk about 'computer generations', and in a similar way
several 'database system generations' can be distinguished.

The history of database systems to date can be divided into five generations, which
roughly follow the five decades of computing from the 1950s, the first two of which
were concerned with the predecessors of database systems.[13] A central role in this
development was played by the ongoing evolution of hardware and software on the
one hand, and a continuous change and increase in the user requirements for data processing on the other.

The *first generation* concerns the 1950s. In those early days, the major task of any
computer system was to process data under the control of a program, which primarily
meant calculating, counting, and so on. Each program was either directly provided
with the data-set it operated upon, or it read its data from some secondary memory
into the main memory of the computer, processed it, and finally wrote the modified
set back to the secondary memory. Secondary memory then referred to punched cards
or to magnetic tapes, both of which allowed sequential processing only. Thus, the first
file systems exclusively allowed sequential access to the records of a file.

The *second generation* (the early sixties) was different from the first one in several
aspects. On the one hand it became possible to use computers in online mode and
batch mode. On the other hand, the development of magnetic disks as fast secondary
memory led to the arrival of more sophisticated file systems, which now rendered
multiple access possible. A direct access file allows access to a record in that file
directory via its address (on the disk). Such an address can be located, for example, in
a special index file, or found by using a hash function (see p. 115).

Both these generations were thus characterized by the availability of file systems
only, which strictly speaking are the forerunners of database systems. Of central
importance for the use of a file system is the static association of certain data-sets
(files) with individual programs that operate on these. As an example, consider a

library that stores data on the books it owns, on the readers who may use the library, and on the books that are currently checked out. In this case, all possible events (recording of new acquisitions, etc.) are handled by a particular program where each is provided with a copy of the files it needs for the appropriate time period. Thus individual files must exist in multiple copies, since different events may occur simultaneously and are hence processed in parallel. In addition, if the programs are written by distinct programmers, it might be difficult to enforce a uniform formatting when the individual files are being created. It is obvious that there will be problems of redundancy, inconsistency, inflexibility, etc.

The *third generation,* which roughly coincides with the 1970s but actually started in the late sixties, is characterized by the introduction of a distinction between logical and physical information, which occurred parallel to an increasing need to manage large collections of data. During that time data models were used for the first time to describe physical structures from a logical point of view. The then emerging approaches such as the hierarchical or the network model are classified as 'implementation-oriented'.13

Starting from this distinction between the logical meaning of data, that is, the syntax and semantics of its description, and its current physical value, systems were developed that could integrate all the data of a given application into one collection with only a particular 'view' to it.

The *fourth generation*, which generally reached the marketplace in the 1980s, saw systems (now called DBMSs), that, in addition to storing data redundancy-free under a centralized control, make a clear distinction between a physical and a logical data model, which is particularly true for the relational model of data. Systems based on this model are typically provided with a high degree of physical data independence and the availability of powerful languages. The former aspect means that any physical storing of data is transparent ('invisible') to users, and that in principle both the physical and logical side may be changed without the other being affected. The latter aspect primarily results from a transaction from record-oriented to set-oriented management and processing of the data in a database. The language that users have for working with a relational system to a considerable degree frees them from questions of 'how' to manage data; they may instead concentrate on the 'what'.

While the third generation may be termed 'pre-relational' and the fourth 'relational', the *fifth generation*, which began to emerge in the 1990s, can be termed 'post-relational'.13 The most significant achievements of this generation are the object-oriented database systems, multimedia systems and knowledge-based systems.

A significant characteristic of modern day database systems is that they are web-based, i.e., they work in a web environment: users can use common browsers to search and retrieve records from a database, add or edit records, etc., and all this can be done remotely through the internet without any knowledge of the software and hardware characteristics of the database systems concerned. We all do these things through our day-to-day activities involving online shopping, holiday and airlines booking, and so on. A great many technologies, standards and protocols are involved in making databases work through the web, but database access and retrieval through common web browsers has become so easy that we, as users, can do the database searching, editing, etc., without having even basic knowledge of databases and networking, let alone the underlying complex technology.

The development of databases in an information retrieval environment

An information retrieval system may contain various kinds of databases. The data may be factual, containing information required for research, planning, management, and for all kinds of day-to-day activities. Such databases may include information related to drugs, patients, etc., in a health-care information system; information related to various chemicals, pollutants, plants, parks, etc., in a pollution-control environment; forests, plants, and so on, in a forestry-management environment; vehicles, spare parts, etc., in an automobile information system; and so on. Several attempts have been made by information scientists to developing methods for designing these factual databases as part of information retrieval systems. For example, Neelameghan[14] discusses a new approach to database development by applying the postulates, principles, and techniques formulated by Dr S. R. Ranganathan within the framework of his general theory of knowledge classification at various stages in the design and development of specialized databases, such as in conceptualizing, structuring, and organizing information as perceived by specialist users and preparing databases therefrom.

However, in most cases the databases in an information retrieval environment are bibliographic or referral in nature. There are now integrated approaches to database development which allow the development of both the bibliographic and referral databases on a single (integrated) database structure.

There are several steps that a database designer has to follow in order to develop databases in an information retrieval environment. Basic considerations relating to the design and development of a text retrieval system have been discussed by Chowdhury.[15]

Basic considerations

In most general terms, to run an information retrieval system we need the following:[16]

1   a software (text retrieval) package
2   a processor to execute the programs
3   memory to hold intermediate working
4   disk storage to hold the data files
5   devices for archiving data files to recover from accidental damage or loss of data
6   printer(s) to produce hard copy for different purposes, and
7   terminals for data input and for controlling the whole process.

Information retrieval software packages can be simple ones that work on stand-alone systems, or quite complex ones that work on large networked databases and on the web. However, like other application programs, information retrieval programs need a processor for their execution, data storage facilities on disk, and terminals and printers for output. The programs are stored in files on disk, the user gives commands to load the text retrieval program, the program is read into the memory and begins to work. In a single-user, single-tasking system, the operating system allows only a single stream of operations – one user doing a single application. Multi-user systems allow independent users to access the computer without regard to the operations of other users.

There are a number of factors that are to be considered when developing an information retrieval system. Some of these issues are independent of any specific text retrieval software. Once these issues are settled, software-specific issues need to be considered. The first question that should be taken into consideration is the functionality of the proposed system. At this stage, the objectives of the proposed system are to be determined. It is important to determine the purpose for which the system is being developed. Is it:

- an information retrieval system?
- an online public access catalogue?
- a system for resource sharing?, or
- for any other specific purpose?

It should also be determined whether it will be a standalone system or will be working in a network environment.

Once the designer is certain about the functionality of the system, the next questions concern:

- the nature of the documents/records to be incorporated in the system
- the maximum number of documents/records to be incorporated in the system, and so on.

These questions are very important because they help the designer choose an appropriate text retrieval software; software packages impose a limit on the total number of records that can be created and stored in a particular version. An understanding of the nature of the records also helps the designer identify the different fields that are to be created. This has also an impact on the choice of the appropriate software because text retrieval software also impose a limit on the length of individual fields and the total number of fields that can be included in a given database.

The nature and number of users are also important factors to be considered. The performance of the proposed retrieval system can reach a satisfactory level only if the requirements of the users are kept in mind right from the beginning of the design stage. In a typical library environment there are two broad categories of user, the library/information personnel, and the end-users. Library and information personnel often act as intermediaries, but they may also act as end-users – seeking information from the system for their own use or for taking a decision. For example, library personnel may assist end-users in locating a given book by searching the online catalogue, or may provide an answer to a reference query, in which case acting as an intermediary. On the other hand, the librarian may consult the online catalogue to ascertain the availability of a book in the library's collection and, using that information, decide whether to place an order for the book or not; in this case the library staff acts as an end-user. The interests of the user should be given due importance at the stage of database design. The structure of a database should be made complex only if the user's requirements call for that; the basic guideline should be the utilitarian principle.

Finally, the designer must pay due attention to the availability of resources, including that of both hardware and software as well as the necessary staff. Each text retrieval software program prescribes a minimum hardware requirement, and before choosing software one must ascertain that the necessary hardware is available. Similarly, it must be ascertained what kind of training will be required to make optimum use of the software and, in case trained staff are not available to begin with, what training facilities are available.

Two types of information retrieval software packages are available: one that allows the user to design the database by going through the various stages of database design and development, and the other that only asks the user to specify the source, which will then be automatically indexed and ready for searching through a standard or customized search interface. Inmagic DB/TextWorks (**www.inmagic.com/prod_ data_ dbt.htm**) is an example of the former type, while DtSearch (**www.dtsearch. com/**) is an example of the latter type of software. Whichever type of software is used, it is always best to think about the design features carefully, since the success of the information retrieval system chosen largely depends upon the design of the database.

Database design

Designing the database constitutes the first step of developing a text retrieval system. This step involves a number of important decisions and the performance of the resulting system will depend largely on these. A text retrieval system may be used for a variety of operations – preparation of library catalogues, bibliographies, current awareness lists, biographical lists, and so on. In each of these cases, the nature of the database and consequently the nature, content, and number of fields will differ.

The first step in database design relates to the determination of the different fields and subfields, their nature, content, length, and various other attributes. The designer should also know how the users would approach the database for the purpose of retrieving information, how they would like to see the records displayed or printed, and so on.

Thus, we can list the following functions to be considered at the stage of database design:

- the nature of the data
- the nature and number of fields and subfields
- the nature of the database indexing
- the format for display and printing of data
- the sorting of data while printing
- the entry/editing of data, etc.

Depending on the nature of the data/records to be incorporated into the database, the designer lists the various fields and subfields. For example, the designer may decide to use the following fields for a simple library catalogue:

Author
Title of book
Publisher's name
Place of publication
Date of publication
Price
Call number
Accession number
Keywords.

The designer may wish to bring some items of information under one umbrella, given a common field name, while keeping each item of information in different subfields. For example, the designer may create a field called 'Imprint' having three subfields, one each for 'Publisher's name', 'Place of publication', and 'Date of publication'. The steps involved in defining the structure of the database include defining field tags and various attributes and parameters for all the fields and subfields to be incorporated into the database. Each type of text retrieval software has its own way of doing these things, and thus the actual steps vary from program to program (for more details see Chowdhury[15], and Chowdhury and Chowdhury[16, 17]).

Database indexing

This is an important step in any text retrieval system because it will generate the index file on which searches can be performed. Most text retrieval systems create an inverted index file (see Chapter 6). Software packages have different mechanisms to indicate which of the fields would be indexed and how they would be indexed, and a database designer has to follow those steps. In some software packages, the index file is generated and updated as soon as new records are added or existing records are deleted, while in others, creation and updating of the index file have to be done by a batch mode. Thus, again this process is software-dependent.

Data entry form/worksheet

Another important task involved in the database design stage relates to the creation of the data entry form or worksheet, which is like a blank form used for entering data in the database. In some text retrieval packages, the designer has to create a data entry worksheet which is used by the data entry operators to enter data into the database. However, some text retrieval software allows data to be entered directly without the need to create any form or worksheet for the purpose.

Output format

The database designer has to consider how the user will expect the records to be displayed when the database is browsed or when records are retrieved by a given search. Some software allows the designer to produce one or more output formats for displaying the retrieved records. However, the facility of displaying records in a chosen format is not available in all text retrieval systems.

Data entry, searching, and printing

The job of database design ends with the tasks mentioned above. The next job is the creation of records. This involves entering data elements in the appropriate columns in the worksheet or form for data entry. This can be done in one of two ways. Records can be created by keying-in the data elements in each field and subfield in the data entry form/worksheet, or a number of records can be downloaded from other, already existing databases.

Discussion

In the previous section the various steps that one has to follow to develop a database using text retrieval software were described. The specific steps and measures prescribed for each operation differ from program to program, but some points may be generalized.

The first step obviously relates to an understanding of the functionality of the proposed system. Once this is ascertained, that is the functions to be performed by the system are known, the next questions relate to the nature and number of documents to be incorporated into the database, and the nature and number of target users. This information is of help in the design task.

With these basic considerations in mind, one has to follow the specific prescriptions of the chosen software. The major issues involved here are:

1   design of the database structure
2   decisions regarding the generation of the index file
3   decisions regarding the format of data display
4   design of the worksheet or form for data entry
5   creation of records
6   generation of the index file
7   searching the database
8   displaying, sorting, and printing records.

Some information retrieval systems have certain built-in facilities for performing some of the above-mentioned tasks, and therefore they need not be performed by the user (designer). One important step, not discussed above, is monitoring the performance of the system. This is important because an information retrieval system may not perform the desired functions at a given stage, or one may want to improve the performance of the system to a certain level. This calls for close observation of the performance of the system, and finding out the reasons for failure, if any. Thus, points for improvement may be noted down for necessary modification at one or more stages of the system.

Over the past few years, information retrieval systems have improved significantly in terms of database design as well as search and retrieval features, and most information retrieval software nowadays supports the handling of multimedia information, in addition to full-text (Chowdhury and Chowdhury[16,17], Gillman[18], and Losee[19]).

References

1 Deakin, R., *The database primer*, London, Century, 1983.
2 Longley, D. and Shain, M. (eds.), *Macmillan dictionary of information technology*, 3rd edn, London, Macmillan, 1989.
3 Walker, P. M. B., *Chambers science and technology dictionary*, Cambridge, Chambers, 1988.
4 Ellingen, D. C., 'Database design', *Database*, **14** (3), 1991, 104–6.
5 Oxborrow, E., *Databases and database management systems: concepts and issues*, 2nd edn, Chichester, Chartwell-Bratt, 1989.
6 Eddison, Betty, 'Database design', *Database*, **12**, 1989, 88–90.
7 Date, C. J., *An introduction to database systems*, 3rd edn, Reading, MA, Addison-Wesley, 1981.
8 Cortez, E. M. and Kazlauskas, E. J., *Managing information systems and technologies: a basic guide for design, selection, evaluation and use*, New York, Neal-Schuman, 1986.
9 Claybrook, B. G., *File management techniques*, New York, John Wiley, 1983.
10 Gillman, P. and Peniston, S., *Library automation: a current review*, London, Aslib, 1984.
11 Tedd, L. A., *An introduction to computer-based library systems*, 3rd edn, Chichester, John Wiley, 1993.
12 Rowley, J., *The electronic library*, fourth edition of *Computers for libraries*, London, Library Association Publishing, 1992.
13 Vossen, G., *Data models, database languages and database management systems*, Wokingham, Addison-Wesley, 1991.
14 Neelameghan, A., 'Application of Ranganathan's general theory of classification in designing specialised databases', *Libri*, **42** (3), 1992, 202–26.
15 Chowdhury, G. G., *Text retrieval systems in information management*, New Delhi, New Age International, 1996.
16 Chowdhury, G. G. and Chowdhury, S., *Searching CD-ROM and online information sources*, London, Library Association Publishing, 2001.
17 Chowdhury, G.G. and Chowdhury, S., 'An overview of the information retrieval features of twenty digital libraries', *Program,* **34** (4), 2000, 341–373.
18 Losee, R. M., *Text retrieval and filtering: analytic models of performance*, Boston, Kluwer Academic Publishers, 1998.
19 Gillman, P., 'Text retrieval', *IT link*, **10** (6), 1998, 10–12.

Chapter 3

Bibliographic formats

Introduction

An information retrieval system should create and maintain one or more databases containing records pertaining to the requirements of the user community. In any organization different kinds of information may be required. A large proportion of information required is factual: the contents of the database, i.e. the records, contain various facts, e.g. features of a particular chemical element or compound, a metal, a tool, a piece of equipment, an automobile, a spare part, a drug, a patient, a plant, a forest, an agrochemical, a national park, and so on. Creation and maintenance of such a factual information retrieval system requires a background knowledge of (i) the subject field, (ii) the actual and potential users and their activities vis-à-vis their information requirements and interests, and so on. Such a database system is usually developed for use by people within an organization/institution or in a group of organizations/institutions, but the data are not expected to be accessible to everyone as happens in the case of library databases. Decisions relating to the database structure, format, and data exchange mechanism are governed in such cases by several factors, such as the chosen database management software, the database design principle, and moreover the needs and access rights of the user community.

The second large category of information required in any organization is bibliographic or textual in nature. A bibliographic or textual information retrieval system will contain details of bibliographic items, with or without abstract and/or full text.

The third category of information that may be required in an organization includes personal and institutional information, project information, and so on. All these categories of information quite often need to be shared among a number of users and institutions and therefore the format chosen for creation of the databases is of paramount importance. Several attempts have been made over the last three or more decades to develop mechanisms for the exchange of bibliographic data, and consequently a number of bibliographic exchange formats have been developed. Most of these formats were designed to hold bibliographic data, though some formats can also accommodate other kinds of data (such as project information). Given the variety of bibliographic formats available, it can be difficult for the designer of an information retrieval system to choose the one that would suit the needs of a particular user community. This chapter presents some insights into this problem and attempts to provide some guidelines.

Bibliographic records

The term 'bibliographic record' is relatively new, having entered the information vocabulary mainly as a result of automation.[1] It has been defined as 'the sum of all the area and elements . . . which may be used to describe, identify or retrieve any physical item (publication, document) of information content'.[2]

Gredley and Hopkinson[1] define a bibliographic record and a bibliographic item as follows:

> Bibliographic record:
>> A collection of data elements, organized in a logical way, which represent a bibliographic item.
> Bibliographic item:
>> Any document, book, publication or other record of human communication; any group of documents, or part of a document, treated as an entity.

For effective retrieval and use, bibliographic data must be organized properly. The creation of bibliographic records in a way that facilitates search and retrieval, locally as well as through electronic networks, and exchange of bibliographic information among libraries/information centres calls for standard formats governing the process of record creation and exchange. Bibliographic formats have been created for this purpose. However, it is important to distinguish between exchange formats, also known as interchange or communication formats, and local or internal processing formats.

Internal formats are internal to a software system. In contrast to the exchange format, they can be tailored specifically to the needs of the local system and do not have to conform to any external standards. Internal formats can be structured in an infinite variety of ways which depend on the software used. Exchange formats are intended for the exchange of records between systems. They should, therefore, be acceptable to the exchanging agencies, hospitable to the type of materials that are the subjects of the records being exchanged, and sufficiently flexible to cope with the needs of many different software systems.[1] In fact, exchange formats should facilitate the exchange of data to be used in a wide range of different bibliographic applications, from the production of traditional catalogue cards to records in databases for providing online access to local as well as remote users.

A bibliographic data format, which can be accepted as a means of exchanging data, should have three basic components as follows:[1]

1   *Physical structure*: rules for the arrangement on a computer storage medium of data to be exchanged. This may be considered as a container or carrier into which data may be placed. The carrier remains constant although the data change from record to record.
2   *Content designators*: codes to identify the different data elements in the record (e.g. author, title, scale of map, starting date of a journal, and so on).
3   *Content*: contents of the record, governed by rules for the formulation of the different data elements, are very closely tied up with content designators. The

data elements separately identified by the codes in the exchange formats have to be defined, not only in terms of content but also in form, if the records are to be suitable for use by another agency.

Effective exchange of bibliographic data between agencies can be accomplished only if the records of agencies exchanging data conform in respect of all the three components: the structure, the content designators, and the data element definitions.[2] The universal acceptance of ISO 2709 on record structure[3] as a basis for exchange formats has enormously benefited the information community. It is accepted for the exchange of bibliographic data on magnetic tape, and in its logical aspects it is also being used for the formatting of bibliographic data sent online and stored on other media such as floppy disk and CD-ROM.

The second component relates to the content designators, which are represented in most bibliographic formats by tags, indicators, and subfield codes; in short, codes that define the different elements in the record. There are several bibliographic formats that can be used to create and exchange bibliographic records, such as MARC (Machine-Readable Catalogue), and its family (various national versions of MARC including MARC 21 and the UNIMARC – the universal MARC), CCF, IDIN, MIBIS, etc. They all embody different schemes of tags and other identifiers. However, it must be mentioned that many of the differences between the formats are sometimes superficial: bibliographic records, regardless of source, all tend to contain much the same data elements, and it is possible to convert designators automatically in order to convert data from one format to another.

The third component – the form and content of data elements – varies according to the 'catalogue code' used as well as to the way the different data elements, prescribed by the rules, are divided up and separately identified by the format. This part is governed by the information retrieval software used. All bibliographic information retrieval systems need to follow some cataloguing rules in order to ensure consistency in data presentation – in display as well as in printed output.

Within an information system, the records that form the database will usually exist in a number of separate but highly compatible formats. Typically there will be:[4]

- format in which records will be input to the system
- format best suited to long-term storage
- format to facilitate retrieval
- format (though more often several) in which records will be displayed.

In addition, if two or more organizations wish to exchange records between one another, it will be necessary for each of these organizations to agree upon a common standard. This is true in any network of organizations. Each must be able to convert to an exchange-format record from an internal-format record and vice versa. If in any network of organizations, whether national or international, there is a single standard exchange format, information interchange within the network will be greatly facilitated, both technically and economically. However, many national standard exchange formats exist. Although there is a great deal of similarity among these formats, they are not identical and therefore records cannot be exchanged directly from one format to the other.

In order to resolve the lack of uniformity among national standard formats, international standard exchange formats have been developed. Within the community of national libraries the UNIMARC format, which was developed to provide a single common denominator for exchange purposes, assumes that ISBD (International Standard Bibliographic Description) is the standard for the form of data elements that describe the item, and the community of abstracting and indexing services is served by the UNISIST *Reference manual*,[5] which prescribes its own content designators to be assigned to bibliographic descriptions of various types of materials. Both of these formats were designed to serve a limited range of institutions, and therefore it has not been possible to mix in a single file bibliographic files from different types of organizations and services; consequently, an organization receiving records from various agencies needs a separate set of computer programs to handle each type of record.

Integrated database approach

An information retrieval system may create and maintain several different databases. Various attempts have been made over the past few years to developing novel approaches to designing databases for information retrieval. Neelameghan[6] has shown that the postulates, principles, and techniques of Ranganathan's general theory of knowledge classification may be applied to the different stages of designing specialized databases for information retrieval. Neelameghan[7] has been advocating the benefits of having an integrated database structure for any information retrieval system that would, within one structure, be able to hold bibliographic as well as non-bibliographic data. Neelameghan and his associates [8, 9] have proposed an integrated database structure for efficient information retrieval. An integrated database system, called ABNCD+, has been developed by Neelameghan and his associates[9] using Micro-CDS/ISIS software. Before this some international agencies had already come up with models for developing bibliographic database systems using this software,[10, 11] but they did not advocate an integrated database structure like that of Neelameghan.

One of the major objectives of designing an integrated database is that the user can conduct concurrent search and retrieval of different types of records (bibliographic documents, profiles of institutions, information systems, experts, projects, etc.) for a given query. This means that with a single query the user will be able to retrieve all the relevant bibliographic records along with profiles of projects, institutions and information systems, and persons on the same subject. Therefore, information centres will not have to design databases for each of these kinds of records: a single database structure capable of holding all kinds of records will be sufficient. However, difficulties may arise because the size of an integrated database will be considerably large, and therefore any problem in one part of the database may damage the whole database. Nonetheless, the advantage from the user's point of view is enormous: he or she will not have to spend time formulating separate queries for each database (i.e. in order to retrieve each kind of record).

Integration in a database system can be achieved in a number of ways, such as:[9]

- integration of different databases containing different types of records into a single database
- functional integration: the output at one stage is used as input to another stage in the system; for example, document selection record can be used to create the acquisition record, it in turn the catalogue entry, which can then be used to generate information products and services
- through networking – e.g. via a local area network (LAN) or wide area network (WAN)
- using software capable of linking records from different databases concurrently
- a combination of two or more of the above types of integration.

Features and proposed fields of some bibliographic formats are discussed in this chapter with a view to identifying those that would best suit the requirements for establishing an integrated database system.

ISO 2709: Format for Bibliographic Information Interchange

ISO 2709 is an international standard that specifies the requirements for a generalized machine format that will hold any type of bibliographic record. It may be noted that this standard does not define the content of individual records or the meanings assigned to tags, indicators or identifiers, rather it only prescribes a generalized structure that can be used to transmit records describing all forms of material capable of bibliographic description between data processing systems.[3]

According to ISO 2709, the general structure of a bibliographic record can be shown schematically as in Figure 3.1.

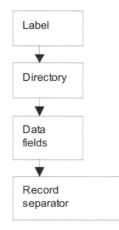

Fig. 3.1 *General structure of a bibliographic record*

A bibliographic record should include the following fixed and variable-length fields:[3]

- *a record label*: this is a fixed-length field holding basic information related to a record, such as record length, record status, implementation codes (e.g. record type, bibliographic level, etc.), identifier length, and so on
- *a directory*: this is a variable-length field that holds two types of information – a directory map indicating length of the 'length of datafield' in each directory entry, and the length of 'starting character position' in each entry, and a directory entry for each field in the record, where each entry gives information on field tag, length of data field, starting character position of each field, and occurrence of the field and the number of segment containing the field. The directory entry ends with a terminating symbol
- *a record identifier*: this is a variable-length field that indicates the record identifier
- *reserved fields*: these are variable-length fields used to hold some reference data related to the given record
- *bibliographic data fields*: these are variable-length fields holding the actual bibliographic data along with indicators
- *field separators*: each data field has to be terminated with a field separator
- *record separator*: each record has to be terminated with a separator symbol.

The following are the examples of a label, directory, and data field according to ISO 2709 (the example has been taken from a CCF – common communications format – record).

Label

    00101a_m__2200067___452_

The characters in the label indicate the following items in sequence:

00101 = total number of characters in the records
a = record status (here it indicates that it is a new record)
_ = blank space (one)
m = bibliographic level: monograph
__ = blank spaces (two)
22 = indication that the data in each field other than '001' begin with a two-character indicator and each subfield begins with a two-character identifier
00067 = length of the label and directory: the first character of the record is numbered 0, and therefore the label and the directory expand from character position 0 to 66, and the first character of the data starts at character position 67.
___ = blank spaces (three)
452 = Indication that the second, third, and fourth elements of each entry in the directory consist of four, five, and two characters respectively. The first element, i.e. the tag, always consists of three characters in any implementation of

ISO 2709, and is therefore not indicated
_ = blank space (one).

It may be noted that labels are always 24 characters long.

Directory

001000700000**200001000023**300001600007**#

The directory consists of an entry for each of the three fields present in the given record. The characters in the directory indicate the following items (in sequence):

001 = tag of the first field
0007 = length of the field
00000 = starting character position of field
** = occurrence of the field and number of the segment containing the field (here not used)
200 = tag of the second field
0010 = length of the field
00023 = starting character position of the field
** = occurrence of the field and number of the segment containing the field (here not used)
300 = tag of the third field
0016 = length of the field
00007 = starting character position of the field
** = occurrence of the field and number of the segment containing the field (here not used)
# = end of the directory.

It may be noted that the second item in each directory entry (indicating the field length) is four characters long, the third item (indicating the starting character position of each field) is five characters long, and the fourth item (indicating occurrence of the field and number of the segment containing the field) is two characters long, as indicated in the label (the last three characters but one).

Data field

A12345#00@AJones@BJohn#00@AFruit#%

The characters in the data field indicate the following items (in sequence):

A12345 = data
# = field separator
00 = indicator
@A = subfield identifier
Jones = data

@B = subfield identifier
John = data
# = field separator
@A = subfield identifier
Fruit = data
# = field separator
% = record separator

It may be noted that the data field contains the actual data on three fields with tags 001, 200, and 300. It may be seen from the first directory entry that the first field has a tag 001 and the data is seven characters long, starting from character position 00000. The data along with the field separator (please note that the field separator and sub-field identifiers and indicators are included in counting the number of characters in a data field) in the first field is indeed seven characters long (six characters for 'A12345' and the '#' sign). the second field in the record has a field tag 300 which is sixteen characters long, starting at character position seven. Thus the second block starts with '0' and ends with '#':

00@AJones@BJohn#

where there are two subfields, one containing the data 'Jones' and the other 'John'. The third field in the record has a tag 200, which holds data ten characters long, start-ing at character position 23. This is the third item in the data field (the first item is seven character long, starting at character position 00000 and continuing up to 00006, and the second item is sixteen characters long, starting at character position 00007 and continuing up to 00022) starting at character position 00023 and continuing up to 00032. The last character, at position 00033, is a record terminator.

Thus if we take a look at the complete entry the record will look something like this:

00101a_m__2200067___452_001000700000**200001000023**300001600007**#
A12345#00@AJones@BJohn#00@AFruit#%

MARC format

MARC is an acronym for MAchine-Readable Catalogue or Cataloguing. This general description is somewhat misleading because it is neither a kind of catalogue nor a method of cataloguing. In fact, MARC is a short and convenient term for assigning labels to each part of a catalogue record so that it can be handled by computer. MARC format was primarily designed for meeting the needs of libraries; however, the con-cept has since been embraced by the wider information community as a convenient way of storing and exchanging bibliographic data. Gredley and Hopkinson[1] describe MARC as a group of formats employing a particular set of conventions for the iden-tification and arrangement of bibliographic data for handling by computer. The orig-inal MARC format was developed in the United States (by the Library of Congress) in 1965–66, and since then a number of formats have appeared that have the following common characteristics:[1]

- They adhere to ISO 2709 record structure,[3] or its equivalent national standard.
- Most are national formats based in a national library or national bibliographic agency and are the designated communication formats for exchange of bibliographic records with other similar organizations.

It may be noted that USMARC, UKMARC, and other national MARC formats have some differences in content designations, though all are meant for representing bibliographic items. There are three USMARC communication formats: USMARC format for bibliographic data, USMARC format for authority data, and USMARC format for holdings and locations; all are implementations of ANSI Z39.2, the American national standard for bibliographic information interchange on magnetic tape,[12] which conforms to ISO 2709.[3] The physical structure of the USMARC format is similar to the structure of the UKMARC record, which is based on ISO 2709 and BS4748.[13, 14]

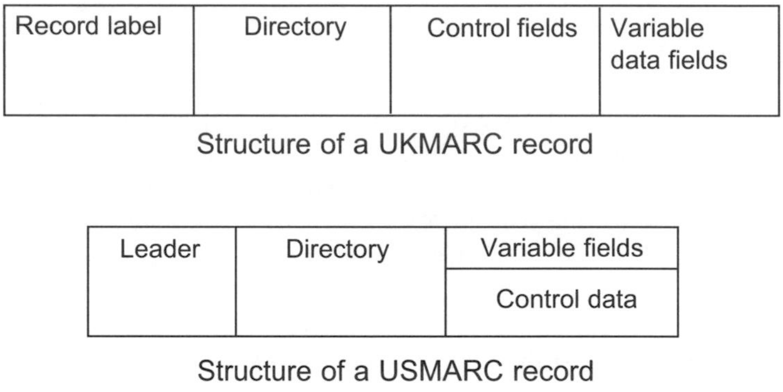

Record label	Directory	Control fields	Variable data fields

Structure of a UKMARC record

Leader	Directory	Variable fields
		Control data

Structure of a USMARC record

Fig. 3.2   *Basic structure of UK and USMARC records*

However, there are some differences in terminology and in definition of fields (see Figure 3.2).

MARC 21

The Library of Congress and the National Library of Canada harmonized the USMARC and CAN/MARC formats in a single edition in early 1999 under a new name: MARC 21. The Network Development and MARC Standards Office at the Library of Congress and the Standards and Support Office at the National Library of Canada maintain the MARC 21 formats. The British Library in 2001 decided to discontinue the UK MARC format and adopt MARC 21 [15] (Bowman). Features of the MARC 21 format are discussed below.

MARC 21 format is a set of codes and content designators defined for encoding machine-readable records. Formats are defined for the following five types of data:

- *MARC 21 Format for Bibliographic Data*: contains format specifications for encoding data elements needed to describe, retrieve and control various forms of bibliographic material including books, serials, computer files, maps, music, visual materials and mixed material.
- *MARC 21 Format for Holdings Data*: contains format specifications for encoding data elements pertinent to holdings and location information for all forms of material.
- *MARC 21 Format for Authority Data*: contains format specifications for encoding data elements relating to bibliographic records that may be subject to authority control.
- *MARC 21 Format for Classification Data*: contains format specifications for encoding data elements related to classification numbers and the associated captions.
- *MARC 21 Format for Community Information*: provides format specifications for records containing information about events, programs, services, and so on, so that this information can be integrated into the same OPAC as data in other record types.

A MARC 21 record contains fields, each designated by a three-character tag, which can store information of two types: (1) about the type of material, its physical characteristics, specific bibliographic aspects, and so on, which is required to process the record, and (2) about the bibliographic data elements required for cataloguing such as the author, title, publisher, etc. Some of the fields have been marked as repeatable (denoted as R), meaning that a MARC record may contain more than one occurrence of the field in question, while certain fields have been marked as non-repeatable (denoted as NR). The MARC 21 [16] format for bibliographic data has the following fields:

- *control fields 001–006*: contain control numbers and other control and coded information, which are used in processing MARC bibliographic records, for example, date and time of processing as well as the type of material (books, electronic resources, maps, music, and so on). Each control field is identified by a field tag and contains either a single data element or a series of fixed-length data elements identified by relative character position.
- *control field 007*: contains special information about the physical characteristics in a coded form.
- *control field 008*: contains 40 character positions (00–39) that provide coded information about the record as a whole and about special bibliographic aspects of the item being cataloged.
- *number and code fields (01x–04x)*: contain control and linking numbers, standard numbers and codes that relate to the bibliographic item described in the record.

- classification and call number fields (05x–08x): contain classification and call numbers related to the item described in the bibliographic record
- *main entry fields (1xx)*: store a name or a uniform title heading used as a main entry in bibliographic records. The following are the various fields for storing main entry fields:
  - 100 – main entry – personal name (NR)
  - 110 – main entry – corporate name (NR)
  - 111 – main entry – meeting name (NR)
  - 130 – main entry – uniform title (NR)

For example, a work of Sir Winston Churchill will be entered as:

100 1#$aChurchill, Winston,$cSir,$d1874-1965

(where the subfield $a is used to denote personal name, $c is for title and $d for dates associated with a person such as deaths of birth, death, and so on; 0, 1 and 3 are used as indicators – 0 for the forename, 1 for the surname and 3 for the family name – and # is an undefined character).

- *title and title-related fields (20X–24X)*: store the title of the item described in the bibliographic record and also information on variant titles, if applicable. Different codes are used for storing title information, for example 210 – Abbreviated title; 222 – Key title; 240 – Uniform title; 245 – Title statement. For example, a typical MARC entry for the title of the book *Information sources and searching on the world wide web* is:

222 #0$a Information sources and searching on the world wide web

(where 0 denotes that there is no non-filing character and $a denotes that it is the key title of the concerned book).

- *edition and imprint fields (250–270)*: store information on the edition, imprint, address and other publication source information, and data related to specific forms of material that apply to the item in question. Different tags are used for storing edition information, for example 250 – Edition statement; 256 – Computer file characteristics; 260 – Publication, distribution, and so on.

    A typical MARC entry for the edition statement of a book is:

250 ##$a2nd ed.

(where the two # signs denote undefined fields and $a denotes edition statement).

It may be noted that field 256 holds important data for electronic records. A typical example of field 256 holding data for computer programs is:

256 ##$aComputer programs
(2 files: 4500, 2000 bytes)

- *physical description fields (3XX)*: store information on the physical character-istics, publication frequency, price and physical arrangement of the item. Information about the dissemination of bibliographic items and the security sta-tus of bibliographic data relating to them is also recorded here. Different tags are used to store specific physical description, for example 300 – Physical description; 306 – Playing time; 310 – Current publication frequency (NR); 340 – Physical medium, and so on.

  A typical MARC entry for the physical designation of a book and a computer file will be as follows:

300 ##$a149p. ;$c23cm.

300 ##$a1 computer disk :$bsd., col. ;$c3½ in.

(where $a denotes the extent, such as pages, volume, $b denotes other physical details such as colour or playing speed and $c denotes the dimension).

- *series statement fields (4XX) (R)*: fields 440 and 490 contain series statements. A typical example of a MARC record holding a series statements is:

440 #0$a Library and Information Science series$n No. 5

(where $a denotes the title of the series and $n denotes the number of item in the series).

- *note fields: part 1 (50X–53X) and part 2 (53X–58X)*: designated for storing dif-ferent types of notes associated with different types of documents. A typical example of the note field is:

500 ##$a Based on an Indian folk tale

- *subject access fields (6XX)*: used to store information on subject headings or access terms that provide additional access to a bibliographic record. Thirteen fields have been designed to store different types of subject access information, for example field 600 is used to store subject added entry for personal names, 650 for topical terms, 651 for geographic names, and so on. The following is a typical example of a MARC record for a subject added entry field:

650 #0$aArchitecture, Modern$y20th century

(where $a denotes topical term and $y denotes chronological subdivision).

- *added entry fields (70X–75X)*: contain information that provides access to a bibliographic record that is not provided through any of the following: main entry (1XX), subject access (6XX), series statement (4XX), series added entry (8XX) or title (20X–24X) fields.
- *linking entry fields (76X–78X)*: contain information that links related bibliographic items.
- *series added entry fields (80X–830)*: contain a name/title or a title used as a series added entry when the series statement is contained in field 490 (series statement) or field 500 (general note) and a series added entry is required for the bibliographic record.
- *holdings, location, alternate graphs etc. fields (841–88X)*: contain descriptions for data elements that may appear either in bibliographic records or in separate MARC holdings records. Field 856 is important for electronic records, especially the internet and web resources. This field contains the information needed to locate and access an electronic resource. A large number of subfield codes and indicators have been proposed for this field. Here is a typical example of information stored in the field for a web page:

856 40$uhttp://www.ref.oclc.org:2000$zAddress for accessing the journal using authorization number and password through OCLC FirstSearch Electronic Collections Online. Subscription to online journal required for access to abstracts and full text

(where the first indicator 4 denotes that the item can be accessed through HTTP (hypertext transfer protocol, used to access web pages, for details see Chapter 18); the second indicator 0 denotes that the electronic location in field 856 is for the same resource described by the record as a whole; $u denotes the URL (uniform resource locator or the address of a web page (for details see Chapter 18); and $z denotes a note).

UNIMARC format

Several versions of MARC formats emerged, for instance, UKMARC, USMARC and CANMARC, whose paths diverged owing to different national cataloguing practices and requirements. Since the early 1970s, an extended family of MARC formats has grown up. The differences in data content in these formats mean that editing is required before records can be exchanged. One solution to the incompatibility was to develop an international (universal) MARC format that would accept records created in any MARC format: records in one MARC format could be converted into UNIMARC and then be converted into any other MARC format. This would require each national agency to write only two programs – one to convert to UNIMARC and another to convert from UNIMARC – instead of having to write a separate program for each MARC format.

In 1977 IFLA brought out UNIMARC (the UNIversal MARC) format, its primary purpose to facilitate the international exchange of data in machine-readable form between national bibliographic agencies.[17] This was followed by a second edition in 1980 and a UNIMARC handbook in 1983. All these focused primarily on the cataloguing of monographs and serials and incorporated the international progress towards the standardization of bibliographic information reflected in ISBDs.[18] The latest edition of the UNIMARC Manual (2nd edition) was published in 1994. Details of the UNIMARC, including the updates are available on the web.[19]

A field in a UNIMARC record comprises the following components:[19]

*   *a tag*: a three digit number, e.g. 700, which defines the type of bibliographic data
*   *indicators*: two single digit numbers right after the tag, e.g. 700#0, which either refine the field definition or show how the field should be treated for catalogue production, for instance by signalling that a note should be made; blanks are shown by the hash sign (#) to distinguish them from a space
*   *subfields*: within each field, data is coded into one or more subfields, e.g. 700#0$a ... $b ..., according to the kind or function of the information; the effect of the subfield coding is to refine further the definition of the data for computer processing; the subfield identifiers consist of a special character, represented by a dollar sign ($) in the examples, and a lower case alphabetic character or a number 0–9
*   *an end of field mark*: represented by the 'at' sign (@) in the examples.

UNIMARC consists of the following nine blocks:

*   *0XX Identification block*: stores information that is needed to identify the record, e.g. 001 0192122622@ (this field holds an identification number for the document) or 010##$a0-19-212262-2$d£12.95@ (this field holds the ISBN at $a and price at $d).
*   *1XX Coded information block*: field 100 stores general processing data; field 101 stores language information, e.g. 1011#$aeng$cfre@. This field gives details of the languages involved. The value of the first indicator (1) shows that the item is a translation. It is a translation into English ($a) from French ($c), and so on.
*   *2XX Descriptive information block*: stores information to describe the item, title and statement of responsibility, e.g. 2001#$a{NSB}The {NSE}lost domain$fAlain-Fournier$gtranslated from the French by Frank Davison$gafterword by John Fowles$gillustrated by Ian Beck@. Here the title field (200) has first indicator (1) showing that the title is significant: in a browsable list – printed, microform or electronic – there would be an added entry for 'Lost domain'. To avoid having the title file in the 'T' part of an alphabetical listing, the 'The[space]' is preceded and succeeded by a special character (represented here by {NSB} and {NSE}) to show where the non-sorting characters begin and where they end. These characters would not appear in any list or on a computer screen.

    $f indicates the first statement of responsibility; subsequent statements are coded $g; other fields in the 2xx series hold other specific items of information, for example, field 210 holds details of publication and distribution (e.g. 210##$aOxford$cOxford University Press$d1959@); field 215 holds information on the physical description of the item (e.g. 215##$aix,298p,10 leaves of plates$cill, col.port$d23cm@).

- *3XX Notes block*: stores specific notes, e.g. 311##$aTranslation of: Le Grand Meaulnes. Paris: Emile-Paul, 1913@ (a note pertaining to linking fields produced by the computer rather than input by the cataloguer; for details see field 454 below).
- *4XX Linking entry block*: holds information on the linking item, e.g. 454#1$100ldb140203$150010$a{NSB}Le {NSE}Grand Meaulnes$1700#0$a Alain-Fournier$f1886-1914$1210##$aParis$cEmile-Paul$d1913@. This is a linking field, pointing to the original of which the item is a translation. Each $1 subfield holds the contents of a field: 001 record identifier, 500 uniform title, 700 author and 210 publication details
- *5XX Related title block*: contains information on related or uniform titles, e.g. 50010$a{NSB}Le {NSE}Grand Meaulnes$mEnglish@. Here it denotes a uniform title. The first indicator serves the same function as that for the 200 field. The $m (language) subfield allows the catalogue to group together all English translations of this work.
- *6XX Subject analysis block*: e.g. 676##$a843/.912$v19@. This field holds a Dewey Decimal Classification number from the 19th edition of DDC (denoted by $v). The '/' is a 'prime mark': libraries with little French literature could drop it and everything beyond it – giving a class number of 843) and 680##$aPQ2611.O85@ (which denotes the Library of Congress class number).
- *7XX Intellectual responsibility block*: e.g. 700#0$aAlain-Fournier,$f1886-1914@. This stores information on the person primarily responsible for the work; the second indicator is 0 as this is a name entered under forename rather than under surname; the $f subfield holds the author's dates of birth and death). This example 702#1$aDavison,$bFrank@ denotes the secondary responsibility; the second indicator is 1 as this is a name entered under surname; the forename is in the $b subfield.
- *8XX International use block*: e.g. 801#0aGBbWE/N0A$c19590202$g AACR2@. This is the 'Originating source' field, which gives details of the creation of the record; subfield $a holds the code for the country and $b the code for the agency creating the record; $c is the date of creation and $g holds details of the cataloguing code used – in this case AACR2.
- *9XX National use block*: holds information for local use, e.g. 98700$aNov.1959/209@ where the field stores the shelf-mark.

The Common Communication Format

The Common Communication Format (CCF) was developed in order to facilitate the exchange of bibliographic data between organizations, and was first published by Unesco in 1984.[4] The following principles apply:

- The structure of the Format conforms to the international standard ISO 2709.
- The core record consists of a small number of mandatory data elements essential

to bibliographic description, identified in a standard manner.
- the mandatory elements are augmented by additional optional data elements, identified in a standard manner.
- A standard technique is used for accommodating levels, relationships and links between bibliographic entities.

A second edition of CCF was published in 1988 and subsequently it was decided that the scope of CCF would be extended to incorporate provisions for data elements for recording factual information that are used most often for referral purposes. As a result, the third edition of CCF was divided into two volumes: CCF/B for holding bibliographic information and CCF/F for factual information. CCF (B and F, taken together) has been designed to provide a standard format for three major purposes:[4]

- to permit the exchange of records between groups of information agencies, including libraries, abstracting and indexing services, referral systems and other kinds of information agencies
- to permit the use of a single set of computer programs to manipulate records received from various information agencies regardless of their internal record-creation practices
- to serve as a basis of a format for an agency's own bibliographic or factual database by providing a list of useful data elements.

The data elements prescribed in CCF for recording bibliographic and factual information in databases are presented in Figure 3.3.

001	Record identifier	085	Segment linking field: horizontal relation
010	Record identifier for secondary segments	086	Field to field linking
011	Alternative record identifier	088	Record to record linking
015	Bibliographic level of secondary segment	100	International Standard Book Number (ISBN)
020	Source of record	101	International Standard Serial Number (ISSN)
021	Completeness of record		
022	Date entered on file	102	CODEN (for serials)
023	Date and number of record version	110	National bibliography number
030	Character sets used in record	111	Legal deposit number
031	Language and script of record	120	Document number
040	Language of item/entity	125	Project number
041	Language and script of summary	130	Contract number
050	Physical medium	200	Title
060	Type of material	201	Key title
061	Type of parent document	210	Parallel title
062	Type of factual information	230	Other title
063	Type of standard	240	Uniform title
080	Segment linking field: vertical relation	260	Edition statement
		300	Name of person

Fig. 3.3 *CCF (B and F)*   *(continued)*

310	Name of corporate body	480	Series statement
320	Name of meeting	490	Part statement
330	Affiliation	500	Note
340	Countries associated with parent	510	Note on related items/entities
400	Place of publication and publisher	520	Serial frequency note
410	Place of manufacture and manufacturer	530	Contents note
		600	Abstract/description
420	Place of distribution and distributor	610	Classification scheme notation
430	Address	620	Subject descriptor
440	Date of publication	650	Services provided
441	Date of legal deposit	700	Human resources
442	Dates related to patent	705	Equipment and other resources
444	Dates related to standard	710	Financial resources
446	Dates related to thesis	715	Income components
448	Start and end dates	716	Expenditure components
450	Serial numbering and date	800	Nationality
460	Physical description	810	Educational qualifications
465	Price and binding	820	Experience of person
470	Mathematical data for cartographic material	860	Project status

Fig. 3.3   (*continued*)

It may be noted that CCF makes provision for holding in one (integrated) database system a number of different kinds of records, for instance books, periodicals, reports, theses, cartographic materials, patents and standards, as well as profiles of projects, institutions and persons.

Discussion

A comparative study of various bibliographic formats has been reported by Chowdhury.[20] Although many bibliographic formats have been developed over the past few decades, MARC 21 is the one most widely used today. CCF is used in some small scale bibliographic and text databases especially in many applications built using the Micro-CDS/ISIS and WINISIS text retrieval software.

References

1   Gredley, Ellen and Hopkinson, Alan, *Exchanging bibliographic data: MARC and other international formats*, Ottawa, Canadian Library Association, 1990.
2   *Standard practices in the preparation of bibliographic records*, rev. edn, London, IFLA UBCIM Programme, 1989.
3   ISO 2709–1981. Documentation: format for bibliographic information interchange on magnetic tape, 2nd edn, Geneva, International Organization for Standardization, 1981.

4 Peter Simmons and Alan Hopkinson (eds.), *CCF/B: the common communication format for bibliographic information and CCF/F: the common communication format for factual information*, Paris, Unesco, 1992.

5 Dierickx, H. and Hopkinson, A. (eds.), *Reference manual for machine-readable bibliographic descriptions*, 2nd rev. edn, Paris, Unesco, 1981.

6 Neelameghan, A., 'Application of Ranganathan's general theory of knowledge classification in designing specialized databases', *Libri*, **42** (3), 1992, 202–26.

7 Neelameghan, A., *Designing an integrated database using CDS/ISIS mini/micro version: a case study and brief guide to LIST: a prototype for an integrated database*, Paris, Unesco PGI, 1987.

8 Neelameghan, A., 'Concept categorization and knowledge organization in specialized databases: a case study', *International classification*, **18**, 1991, 92–7.

9 Rorissa, Abebe, Bamuhiiga, B. B., Chisenga, J., Nxumalo, C. S., Sekimanga, D. A. and Neelameghan, A., 'ABNCD+: a prototype for an integrated information storage and retrieval system', *Microcomputers for information management*, **9** (3), 1992, 137–59.

10 Di Lauro, A., IDIN manual for the creation and management of a bibliographic database using Micro-CDS/ISIS, Paris, OECD, 1988.

11 Di Lauro, A., *Manual for preparing records in microcomputer- based bibliographic information systems*, Ottawa, IDRC, 1990 (IDRC-TS67e).

12 *Z39.2: 1979, ANSI, American National Standard for bibliographic information interchange on magnetic tape*, New York, American National Standards Institute, 1979.

13 *UKMARC manual*, 2nd edn, London, British Library Bibliographic Services Division, 1980–7.

14 Crawford, Walt, *MARC for library use: understanding the USMARC formats*, New York, Knowledge Industry Publications, 1984.

15 Bowman, J. H., *Essential cataloguing*, Facet Publishing, 2002.

16 *MARC 21 Concise format for bibliographic data*, Network Development and MARC Standards Office, Library of Congress, 2002 concise edn. Available at **www.loc.gov/marc/bibliographic/ecbdhome.html**.

17 *UNIMARC manual: bibliographic format*, 2nd edn, London, K. G. Saur, 1994.

18 *ISBD(G): general international standard bibliographic description: annotated text*, London, IFLA International Office for UBC, 1977.

19 IFLANET Universal Bibliographic Control and International MARC Core Programme. Available at **www.ifla.org/VI/3/p1996-1/unimarc.htm#DESIGNATE**.

20 Chowdhury, G. G., 'Record formats for integrated databases: a review and comparison', *Information development*, **12** (4), 1996, 218–23.

Chapter 4

Cataloguing and metadata

Introduction

For centuries libraries have been organizing reading materials on shelves for easy access. However, systematic methods that have been widely adopted for the organization of library materials and their recording for use by readers came into being little more than a century ago. In 1876 Melvil Dewey developed a systematic scheme of library classification, which became a unique tool for organizing library materials on the shelves, and in the same year Charles A. Cutter brought out *Rules for a dictionary catalog*, which enabled librarians to record systematically the library holdings in the form of catalogue entries that could be consulted easily by the user community. Since then a number of schemes of library classification and catalogue codes have been developed to aid the process of organizing library materials systematically.

Details of bibliographic classification appear in the following chapter. This chapter discusses the basic principles of cataloguing and gives guidelines related to the cataloguing of internet resources. This chapter also discusses the concept of metadata with reference to various metadata standards.

Cataloguing

A catalogue is said to be the key to a library's collection as each catalogue entry, containing the bibliographic details of a particular document, informs the user about the holdings of the library. Although the popular definition and use of the term catalogue differ, in the library world a catalogue is essentially an organized list of documents in a library with entries representing the documents arranged for access in some systematic order (Rowley and Farrow).[1] The art of preparing catalogues is cataloguing. Systems thinking was introduced into the discipline of information organization in 1876 by Cutter who was the first to recognize the importance of stating formal objectives for a catalogue.[2]

Why cataloguing?

Svenonius[2] lists the following major objectives of a catalogue, identified by Cutter, as being:

- to enable a person to find a book by:
  - author
  - title
  - subject
- to show what the library has:
  - by a given author
  - on a given subject
  - in a given literature
- to assist in the choice of a book:
  - by edition
  - by character.

The objectives of a catalogue as stated by Cutter were slightly modified by Lubetzky and then formally adopted at an International Conference on Cataloguing Principles held in Paris in 1961. In 1997, the objectives of a catalogue were reformulated as follows by an IFLA (International Federation of Library Associations and Institutions) study group to suit the automated cataloguing environments:[2]

- to find entities that correspond to the user's stated search criteria
- to identify an entity
- to select an entity that is appropriate to the user's needs
- to enquire or obtain access to the entity described.

AACR2

In order to help librarians identify which parameters are required to denote a document and how to represent them consistently (their sequence, punctuation, indentation, capitalization, and so on), several catalogue codes have been developed. A document containing rules for the compilation of printed catalogues of the British Museum was prepared as early as in 1841, but the forerunner of the present-day catalogue code was devised by Cutter in 1876, called *Rules for a dictionary catalog*. The first catalogue code, the *AA Code*, appeared in 1908, followed by the *Classified catalogue code* (CCC) of Ranganathan in 1934, the *ALA code* in 1949, the first edition of the *Anglo-American cataloguing rules* (AACR1) in 1967, the second edition of AACR (AACR2) in 1976, and a revised edition of AACR2 in 1988. Of these, AACR2 has become the most popular catalogue code and is used all over the world.

In each catalogue entry AACR2 allows for up to eight areas, each containing a specific set of information about the document concerned, as shown below:[3]

- *area 1*: title, other title information and statement of responsibility, subsequent statements of responsibility
- *area 2*: edition
- *area 3*: material (or type of publication) specific details
- *area 4*: publication, distribution, etc.
- *area 5*: physical description

- *area 6*: series
- *area 7*: notes
- *area 8*: standard number and terms of availability.

The process of cataloguing involves four different, but interdependent, processes:

1   *Description of the information resource*: At this stage information is gathered about the information resource. The types of information varies from one type of information resource to another, but the cataloguer mainly aims to gather information on the eight different areas mentioned above. The chief source of information for an information resource is the item itself, for example the title page (and the verso of the title page) of a book.
2   *Choice of access points*: At this stage the cataloguer has to decide the various access points (e.g. author, title, publisher or ISBN) that the user may use to find the given information resource.
3   *Choice of headings*: At this stage the cataloguer has to decide the format for the headings. This is done to ensure standardization, and the cataloguer has to decide on various issues, for instance whether to use the heading in its natural order or in a reverse order; which heading to use among the variant names, if any; whether to use the singular or the plural form; and so on.
4   *References*: At this stage the cataloguer provides links for various other access points that are deemed to be used by the users to access the same information resource.

The code describes rules for each of the activities involved in cataloguing, as shown in Figure 4.1. Chapters 1 to 12 of AACR2 provide general guidelines for the cataloguer about the type of information to be entered in each section of a catalogue record. Chapter 1 provides the general structure of a catalogue record and describes what type of information each section should contain. Chapters 2 to 12 provide guidelines for type of information resource. In order to help the cataloguer, the code follows the same section numbering system, for example, section 1.4 in Chapter 1 discusses the section on publication information, and in subsection 4 of each subsequent chapter (section 2.4, 3.4, etc.) there is discussion of how to enter publication information for a specific type of information resource.

In AACR2, three levels of description for catalogue records are prescribed.

1   The first level is brief cataloguing (see Figure 4.2). The cataloguer has to include only the title proper, omitting the other title information. The statement of responsibility may also be omitted if it is the same as the main entry heading. The edition statement is included but not the accompanying statement of responsibility. Material-specific details are provided for cartographic materials and serials. Publication data include only the name of the first publisher and the date of publication. The other items of information to be given include pagination (for books), notes and standard number, if available. First level description is sufficient to identify items in a small library collection.

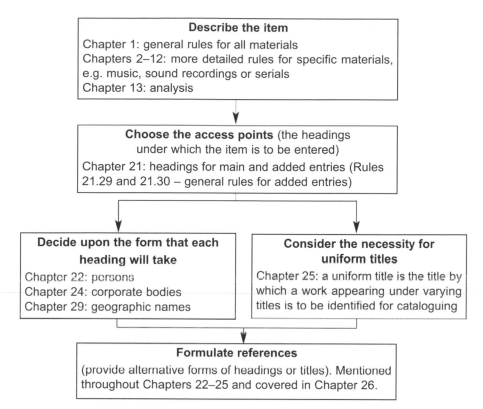

Describe the item

Chapter 1: general rules for all materials
Chapters 2–12: more detailed rules for specific materials,
e.g. music, sound recordings or serials
Chapter 13: analysis

Choose the access points (the headings
under which the item is to be entered)

Chapter 21: headings for main and added entries (Rules
21.29 and 21.30 – general rules for added entries)

**Decide upon the form that each
heading will take**

Chapter 22: persons
Chapter 24: corporate bodies
Chapter 29: geographic names

**Consider the necessity for
uniform titles**

Chapter 25: a uniform title is the title by
which a work appearing under varying
titles is to be identified for cataloguing

Formulate references

(provide alternative forms of headings or titles). Mentioned
throughout Chapters 22–25 and covered in Chapter 26.

Fig. 4.1 *Workflow chart for AACR2*

2   The second level of description includes all the information given in the first
level (see Figure 4.3). In addition, the cataloguer has to include general material designation after the title, parallel titles and other title information; these
will be followed by all the pertinent statements of responsibility. The edition
statement together with its first statement of responsibility, if found in the work,
has to be included. The first place of publication, name of publisher and date of
publication have to be given. The physical description area will include all the
items specified in the applicable rules except for any accompanying material.
The series statement is recorded and notes and standard numbers are included
as appropriate. Second level is sufficient to identify items in a medium-sized
library collection.

3   The third level of description includes all the rules applicable to the item being
catalogued (see Figure 4.4). This level of description is appropriate to large
libraries and research collections.

A typical catalogue entry is shown below with the three different levels of description.

Kingsley, Charles
  Madam How and Lady Why. – Dent, [1976]
  229 p.

  "List of the works of Charles Kingsley": p. x

  I. Title

Fig. 4.2 *First level description of a catalogue record*

Kingsley, Charles
   Madam How and Lady Why : lessons in earth lore
for children / by Charles Kingsley. – London : Dent,
[1976]
   xix, 229 p. : ill. ; 18 cm. – (Everyman's library ;
no. 777. For young people)

   "List of the works of Charles Kingsley": p. x.

   I. Title.

Fig. 4.3   *Second level description of a catalogue record*

Kingsley, Charles
   Madam How and Lady Why : lessons in earth lore
for children / by Charles Kingsley. – London : Dent ;
New York : Dutton, [1976]
   xix, 229 p. : ill. ; 18 cm. – (Everyman's library ;
no. 777. For young people)

   "List of the works of Charles Kingsley": p. x.

   I. Title.

Fig. 4.4   *Third level description of a catalogue record*

Implications for OPACs

Online public access catalogues (OPACs) are the interfaces that help users communicate with the collection(s) of a library. Typically OPACs allow users to search the library's catalogue, and also provide some other facilities, such as checking borrower records, reserving reading materials, library news bulletins, and so on.[4] Although OPACs were first used in the mid 1970s, it was only at the beginning of the next decade that a significant number of libraries switched from card catalogues to automated catalogues.[5, 6] However, those first catalogues were usually modules linked to the automated circulation system and had brief catalogue records and very limited functionality. Several changes have taken place and OPACs have improved significantly since then.

OPAC development went through three stages:[7, 8]

1   *First generation*: OPACs at the beginning were searchable typically by author, title and control number. Each record contained short and often non-standard bibliographic records.
2   *Second generation*: The search functionalities increased during this period, including providing access by subject headings, Boolean search capabilities, and browsing facilities. At this stage users could choose from more than one display format, and some OPACs developed different interfaces for novice and expert users.
3   *Third generation*: Some of the problems and confusions of the second generation OPACs, such as the lack of assistance, non-availability of integrated vocabulary control tools, and so on, were overcome in the third generation. Third generation OPACs incorporate features that are characterized by the facilities of the world wide web.

So, what are the implications of the cataloguing rules on the OPACs? Although catalogue codes were originally devised for manual cataloguing they are very much used in the environment of automated cataloguing. However, in the context of OPACs the concept of main and added entries does not apply, although the distinction is usually maintained in catalogue codes. In OPAC databases a user can use any one or more search parameters, such as the author, title, keywords, ISBN, and so on, to search the catalogue, and the complete catalogue entry may be displayed as a result of the search. Again, one of the justifications for proposing the three different levels of cataloguing was to help cataloguers in a manual cataloguing environment where catalogue entries were prepared on cards and hence there was a restriction of the amount of space available on the cards. Cataloguers were advised to determine the level of information required by potential users and to choose the level of cataloguing on the basis of that information. This is no longer an issue in the context of OPAC since only one catalogue entry is prepared for each information resource with as complete information as possible; moreover this catalogue record is available to the cataloguers of a particular library in a machine-readable form. Guidelines related to the choice of access points are also of less importance in the context of

OPACs. These rules were formulated to help cataloguers in a manual cataloguing environment where they had to keep the access points to a minimum number because of the restrictions of space and number of card catalogues, as well as the manual labour involved in preparing the card catalogues with different headings, arranging them in an appropriate order, and so on. These restrictions do not apply to OPACs. Virtually any individual word or section of a catalogue record can be made an access point and the cataloguing software, at least in principle, can allow users to access the catalogue record through any of those points.

Modern day OPACs also include internet resources. Catalogue codes were not originally devised to deal with internet resources, which have some characteristics that are unique and different from conventional information resources, so cataloguing of internet resources has become an important issue.

Cataloguing of internet resources

Internet resources have some specific characteristics that call for some special rules for cataloguing. AACR2 provides some guidelines for cataloguing computer files but they are not sufficient, for several reasons. Internet resources vary significantly in terms of their content (text, numeric, audio, image video, etc.), file format, availability, URL (uniform resource locator) or the address of a web page (discussed in Chapter 18), and so on. Hence, while some parts of AACR2 can be used to catalogue internet resources, some new rules and guidelines are required to help cataloguers.

With this end in view, OCLC produced a manual for cataloguing internet resources.[9] The guidelines follow the *Anglo-American cataloguing rules*, 2nd revised edition, as well as the *International standard bibliographic description for electronic resources (ISBD (ER))*. In addition to the file type and format description, internet resources need specific information for access. Some information is carried in special MARC fields. Subscription information and local access information are entered in field 856, for electronic location and access, a field developed especially for this kind of information.[9]

For the first two areas of a catalogue record of an internet resource, title proper and statement of responsibility, and edition, the guidelines for AACR2 (Chapter 9) may be followed. However, determining who is responsible for an internet resource may often be a challenging task, since a particular web page may contain several pieces of information that are created or owned by different users. Similarly, the content of web pages changes frequently, and often different versions are not specifically marked. Hence, determining the edition information is often a difficult job. Nevertheless, the OCLC manual provides guidelines for entering information in the first two areas of a catalogue and provides references to the appropriate AACR2 rules.

The third area of an internet catalogue provides the file characteristics. There are two parts to the area: the designation and the number of records or statements. AACR2 restricts the file characteristics to computer data, computer program(s) and computer data and programs(s). However, the ISBD (ER) (International Standard Bibliographic Descriptions, Electronic Resources) provide a long list of file types:[9]

- computer data
- computer numeric data
  - computer census data
  - computer survey data
- computer text data
  - computer bibliographic database
  - computer journal(s)
  - computer newsletter(s)
  - computer document(s) (e.g. letters, articles)
- computer image data
- computer representational data
  - computer map(s) data
- computer sound data
- computer font data
- computer program(s)
- computer utility program(s)
- computer application program(s)
  - computer CAD program(s)
  - computer database program(s)
  - computer spreadsheet program(s)
  - computer word processor program(s)
  - computer desktop publishing program(s)
  - computer game(s)
- computer system program(s)
  - computer operating system program(s)
  - computer programming language(s)
  - computer retrieval program(s)
- computer data and program(s)
- computer interactive multimedia
- computer online service(s) (e.g. bulletin boards, discussion groups and lists, world wide websites).

The OCLC manual provides guidelines for the second part of the file characteristics section, which specifies number of records, statements, and so on. It recommends that information related to the number of files, file size, format and compression should be entered in MARC field 856. Field 856 contains information required to locate an electronic item. It also contains information needed to retrieve the item by the access method identified by the first indicator position. A complete description of the field 856, and guidelines for its use, are available online at **http://lcweb.loc.gov/marc/856guide.html**.

For the publication and distribution area of the catalogue, the manual suggests that a formal statement denoting the publication details of an internet resource, such as place, publisher and date, is to be provided. The guidelines provided in the AACR2 code (Chapter 9) are to be followed for this purpose. For an internet resource a physical description is not required and hence this section does not appear in the catalogue.

The series information contains specific information on the series, if any, and the AACR2 guidelines (Chapter 9) are to be followed for the purpose.

The notes section contains all other information that could not be provided in any earlier section of the catalogue record, and yet is deemed to be of relevance for the given internet resource. The guidelines provided in the OCLC manual combine notes from *AACR2* (Chapter 9: Computer Files; Chapter 12: Serials; and Chapter 1: General). The OCLC manual recommends cataloguers to use a specific MARC note field when available or the 500 field for general notes.

Cataloguing and metadata

Different measures are currently taken for informing users about the various materials accessible through a given digital or a hybrid library. In many cases users are pointed to separate lists, or web pages, providing information about various digital collections, such as online databases, electronic journals and internet resources. However, all these resources are selected and entered manually onto the lists or web pages by library staff. Having a centralized catalogue of all the digital resources available on the web would greatly reduce the burdens of individual digital or hybrid libraries, because they could simply download the catalogue entries, as libraries do for printed information materials. However, there are many problems in cataloguing digital information resources. First, digital – especially internet – resources are so huge in number and grow so rapidly that it is practically impossible for human cataloguers to cope with each and every item. Second, the characteristics of digital information resources demand that a different standard be followed for each major type of document. Bibliographic formats (such as the MARC family and others) and catalogue codes (such as AACR2) are not adequate for representing all the useful characteristics of digital resources. Various metadata standards have been developed over the past few years for representing different types of digital information resources.

Metadata

Schwartz[10] mentions that the term metadata, thus far used primarily in the field of database management, began to appear in the LIS literature in the mid-1990s. However, within a short period the topic became very popular and an important area of research concentration, giving rise to several hundred publications, including an ARIST chapter in 1998.[11] Lange and Winkler [12] traced the history of the term metadata back to the 1960s, but noted that it began to appear more frequently in the DBMS literature in the 1980s. Vellucci [11] notes that the term metadata transcends boundaries among various stakeholders in the development of the internet and provides a common vocabulary to describe a variety of data structures. Speaking simply, metadata is data about data, but this definition does not say much about its purpose. Better definitions of metadata include the following:

- 'Data which describes attributes of a resource' (Dempsey and Heery)[13]
- 'Meaningful data describing another discrete data object' (Gill)[14]

- 'Data associated with objects which relieves their potential users of having to have full advance knowledge of their existence or characteristics' (Dempsey and Heery).[15]

Metadata supports a variety of operations and the users of metadata may be human beings or computer programs. The primary functions of metadata are to facilitate the identification, location, retrieval, manipulation, and use of digital objects in a networked environment.[11]

Libraries have long been used to create catalogue records, as metadata, of their collections, which have been used by library users and librarians for a variety of purposes including the searching and retrieval of records. Such metadata produced by libraries consist of some item-specific information, as well as headings and so on, which has associated rules for further processing, such as the creation of headings, rules for filing, relationship with other records, and so on. In 2003, however, while the term metadata does not exclude non-electronic data, it is applied most often to data in electronic form.[11]

Internet and digital libraries have led to an increased awareness of the need for metadata for diverse categories of items available in digital form. Various subject experts have developed, or are engaged in developing, metadata formats for materials in specific domain and format, for example, internet resources, museum objects and archival records. Weibel, Iannella and Cathro[16] comment that there are two distinct schools of thought that influence the development of metadata standards:

- the minimalists' camp, whose point of view reflects a strong commitment to the notion of the simplicity of metadata for creation by authors and for the use of the metadata by tools
- the structuralists' camp whose members emphasize the greater flexibility of a formal means of extending or qualifying elements such that they can be made more useful for the needs of a particular community.

Dempsey and Heery[15] have identified three groups of metadata:

- *Band one*: proprietary formats used by web indexing and search services. Data is gathered by robot programs and automatic records are created which are typically searched using the basic HTTP protocol with CGI (Common Gateway Interface) scripts.
- *Band two*: formats used for resource description. Examples are Dublin Core and IAFA/WHOIS++ templates (ROADS templates). Services that use this type of format include the OCLC's NetFirst, subject gateways created under the eLib programme, and so on. Metadata records may be created manually or automatically.
- *Band three*: formats used for location, analysis, evaluation, documentation and so on. These formats are more complex and detailed, and require specialist knowledge to create and maintain. They may also be domain-specific. Examples are MARC, FGDC (Federal Geographic Data Committee's content

standard for digital geospatial metadata), TEI (Text Encoding Initiative) Header, EAD (Encoded Archival Description),[17] ICPSR (Inter-university Consortium for Political and Social Research) initiative, and so on

Gilliland-Swetland[18] classifies metadata into five categories on the basis of their use:

*   administrative metadata used in managing and administering information resources
*   descriptive metadata used to describe or identify information resources
*   preservation metadata related to the preservation management of information resources
*   technical metadata related to how a system functions or metadata behaves
*   use metadata related to the level and types of use of information resources.

Metadata standards have been built by experts in different subject areas with different understandings of their domain, information resources, users and use behaviour, and the overall requirements for resource discovery and description on their specific domains. Some of these metadata formats, such as MARC and the Dublin Core, are general in nature and can accommodate descriptive information about digital information resources of different types coming from different disciplines, while others, such as FGDC and EAD, are more specialized and apply to information in a specific discipline or domain.[11]

The Dublin Core

The Dublin Core Metadata Workshop Series began in 1995 with an invitational workshop, which brought together librarians, digital library researchers, content experts and text-markup experts to develop discovery standards for electronic resources. The first meeting took place at Dublin, Ohio, and gave rise to a metadata format called the Dublin Core. It is a 15-element set of descriptors intended to promote author-generated description of internet resources (see Table 4.1). The elements fall into three groups, which roughly indicate the class or scope of information stored in them: elements related mainly to the content of the resource, elements related mainly to the resource when viewed as intellectual property and elements related mainly to the instantiation of the resource.[19,20]

The Dublin Core Metadata Editor[21] is a service that retrieves a given web page and automatically generates Dublin Core metadata suitable for embedding in the <head>...</head> section of the page. In addition to generating instantly the Dublin Core tags for a given web page, the DCDot service also provides an editor for users to edit the tags or add or edit contents, which can then be resubmitted to create metadata. Figure 4.5 shows the Dublin Core metadata for a sample web page.

lin Core standard has the following characteristics:[22]

core set can be extended with further elements, as necessary, for a partic-
domain.

Table 4.1 *Dublin Core data elements*

Group	Element	Description
Content	Title	Name of the resource
	Subject	Topic describing the content of the resource
	Description	About the content of the resource
	Type	The nature or genre of the content of the resource
	Source	A reference to a resource from which the present resource is derived
	Relation	A reference to a related resource
	Coverage	The extent or scope of the content of the resource
Intellectual property	Creator	Who is primarily responsible for creating the content of the resource
	Publisher	Who is responsible for making the resource available
	Contributor	Who makes contributions to the content of the resource
	Rights	Information about rights held in and over the resource
Instantiation	Date	Date the resource was first manifested
	Format	The physical or digital manifestation of the resource
	Identifier	A unique reference to the resource within a given context
	Language	A language of the intellectual content of the resource

```
<link rel="schema.DC" href="http://purl.org/dc">
<meta name="DC.Title" content="Gobinda Gopal Chowdhury">
<meta name="DC.Creator" content="Gobinda Chowdhury">
<meta name="DC.Subject" content="Gobinda Gopal Chowdhury; Department of Computer and Information
Sciences; University of Strathclyde">
<meta name="DC.Description" content="Personal webpage">
<meta name="DC.Publisher" content="University of Strathclyde">
<meta name="DC.Contributor" content="Sudatta Chowdhury">
<meta name="DC.Date" content="31/01/2002">
<meta name="DC.Type" scheme="DCMIType" content="Text">
<meta name="DC.Format" content="text/html 10377 bytes">
<meta name="DC.Identifier" content= "http://www.dis.strath.ac.uk/people/gobinda">
<meta name="DC.Source" content="Personal files">
```

Fig. 4.5 *Dublin Core metadata for a sample web page*

- All elements are optional.
- All elements are repeatable.
- Any element may be modified by a qualifier.

Several metadata standards have been developed over the past few years to deal with some specific types of digital materials. Dempsey[23] describes some metadata and resource discovery initiatives in the UK's Electronic Libraries Programme (eLib) and within the European Union's Fourth Framework Programme for research and technological development. Dempsey and Heery[13] provide an excellent review of several metadata standards, while Cromwell-Kessler[24] maps several metadata standards to one another.

Metadata systems differ in content and structure.[24] Content may differ in terms of the rules that govern them and the language. Different metadata standards create an obvious problem of interoperability. Each metadata system may comprise diverse data elements functioning at different levels. A simpler way for integration may be to translate one system to another as necessary. UKOLN and OCLC jointly organized a conference in 1996 to examine the various general metadata issues and the Dublin Core metadata in particular. The meeting took place at Warwick, and gave rise to a new proposal, called the Warwick framework.[25] While there was a consensus among the participants that the concept of a simple metadata set is useful, there was a fundamental question as to whether the Dublin Core really qualifies as a standard that can be used for all types of digital documents. It was agreed that a higher-level context for the Dublin Core has to be formulated, which should define how the Core can be combined with other sets of metadata in a manner that addresses the individual integrity, distinct audiences and separate realms of responsibility of various distinct metadata sets. The result of the Warwick Workshop was a *container* architecture, known as the Warwick Framework – a mechanism for aggregating logically, and perhaps physically, distinct *packages* of metadata (Lagoze).[26]

EAD

Encoded Archival Description (EAD) is a standard used internationally in an increasing number of archives and manuscript libraries to encode data describing corporate records and personal papers.[17] From its inception, EAD was based on SGML and, with the release of EAD version 1.0 in 1998, it is also compliant with XML. The EAD DTD (Document Type Definition) contains three high-level elements: the <eadheader>, <frontmatter> and <archdesc>. The <eadheader> is used to document the archival description or finding aid, while the <frontmatter> is used to supply publishing information such as a title page and other prefatory text. The <archdesc> contains the archival description itself and thus constitutes the core of the EAD.[17]

Summary

While cataloguing remains highly relevant in the modern information retrieval environment, many parts of the catalogue codes specifying rules for several activities have become redundant in the context of OPACs. AACR2 was not specifically designed to handle internet resources, and additional measures are required to catalogue them. Nevertheless, AACR2 has played a key role in standardizing IR activities (especially for OPACs) throughout the world for over four decades.

Metadata has become an important issue for information organization since the advent of the internet and the web. Several metadata standards have been developed over the past few years. The Dublin Core metadata standard proposed a set of 15 data elements that are thought to be necessary for cataloguing internet resources. The Dublin Core data elements were devised with the expectation that the creators of internet resources would fill in the various columns. However, tools are now widely available that can automatically fill in many of the 15 prescribed data elements for a given internet resource.

It may be noted that catalogues are meant to provide guidelines for creating records that can help users get access to information resources through known data elements such as author, title, publisher and ISBN. They do not provide specific guidelines to support subject access to information. Libraries and information systems have over the years used various classification and indexing systems for organizing information resources on the shelves and for providing subject access to these resources. Chapter 5 discusses the basic principles of classification and subject indexing, and discusses their relevance to the modern world of information retrieval environment.

References

1 Rowley, J. and Farrow, J., *Organizing knowledge: an introduction to managing access to information*, Aldershot, Gower, 2000.
2 Svenonius, E., *The intellectual foundation of information organization*, Cambridge, MA, MIT Press, 2000.
3 *Anglo-American cataloguing rules, 2nd edn, 1998 revision*, Joint Steering Committee for Revision of AACR, Library Association, American Library Association and Canadian Library Association, 1999.
4 Chowdhury, G. and Chowdhury, S., *Searching CD-ROM and online information sources*, London, Library Association Publishing, 2001.
5 Su, S., 'Dialogue with an OPAC: how visionary was Swanson in 1964?', *Library quarterly*, **64**, 1994, 130–61.
6 Large, A. and Behesti, J., 'OPACs: a research review', *Library and information science research*, **19**, 1997, 111–33.
7 Hildreth, C. R., 'Online library catalogues as IR systems: what can we learn from research? In Yates-Mercer, P. A. (ed.), *Future trends in information science and technology*, Taylor Graham, 1998, 9–25.
8 Rasmussen, E., 'Libraries and bibliographical systems'. In Baeza-Yates, R. and Ribeiro-Neto, B., *Modern information retrieval*, ACM Press, 1999, 397–413.
9 Olson, N. B. (ed.), *Cataloging internet resources: a manual and practical guide*, 2nd edn, 2003. Available at **www.OCLC.org/support/documentation/worldcat/cataloguing/internetguide**.
10 Schwartz, C., *Sorting out the web: approaches to subject access*, Westport, Ablex Publishing, 2001.
11 Vellucci, S. L., 'Metadata'. In Williams, M. (ed.), *Annual review of information science and technology*, Vol. 33, Medford, NJ, Information Today Inc., 1998, 187–222.

12   Lange, H. R. and Winkler, B. J., 'Taming the internet: metadata, a work in progress'. In Godden, I. (ed.), *Advances in librarianship*, Vol. 21, San Diego, Academic Press, 1997, 47–72.

13   Dempsey, L. and Heery, R., *A review of metadata: a survey of the current resource description formats*. Work package 3 of Telematics for Research project DESIRE (RE1004), 15 May 1997. Available at **www.ukoln.ac.uk/ metadata/desire/overview**.

14   Gill, T., 'Metadata and the world wide web'. In Baca, M. (ed.) *Introduction to metadata: pathways to digital information*, Getty Information Institute, 1998, 9–18.

15   Dempsey, L. and Heery, R., 'Metadata: a current view of practice and issues', *Journal of documentation*, **54** (2), 1998, 145–72.

16   Weibel, S., Iannella, R. and Cathro, W., 'The 4th Dublin Core metadata workshop report. DC4, March 3-5, 1997, National Library of Australia, Canberra', *D-lib magazine*, 1997. Available at **www.dlib.org/dlib/june97/metadata/ 06weibel.html**.

17   Pitti, D. V., 'Encoded archival description: an introduction and overview', *D-lib magazine*, **5** (11), 1999. Available at **www.dlib.org/dlib/november99/ 11pitti.html**.

18   Gilliland-Swetland, A., 'Defining metadata'. In Baca, M. (ed.) *Introduction to metadata: pathways to digital information*, Getty Information Institute, 1998, 1–8.

19   Weibel, S., 'Metadata: the foundations of resource description', *D-lib magazine*, 1995. Available at **www.dlib.org/dlib/July95/07weibel.html**.

20   Weibel, S., Kunze, J., Lagoze, C. and Wolf, M., Network Working Group Request for Comments: 2413, 1998. Available at **www.ietf.org/rfc/rfc2413.txt**.

21   DCDot: Dublin Core metadata editor. Available at **www.ukoln.ac.uk/ metadata/dcdot/**.

22   Taylor, A., *The organization of information*, Englewood, Col, Libraries Unlimited Inc., 1999.

23   Dempsey, L., 'ROADS to Desire: some UK and other European metadata and resource discovery projects', *D-lib magazine*, 1996. Available at **www.dlib.org/dlib/ july96/07dempsey.html**.

24   Cromwell-Kessler, W., 'Crosswalks, metadata mapping, and interoperability: what does it all mean?' In: Baca, M. (ed.), *Introduction to metadata: pathways to digital information*, Getty Information Institute, 1998, 19–33.

25   Dempsey, L. and Weibel, S. L., 'The Warwick Metadata Workshop: a framework for the deployment of resource description', *D-lib magazine*, 1996. Available at **www.dlib.org/dlib/july96/07weibel.html**.

26   Lagoze, C., 'The Warwick Framework: a container architecture for diverse sets of metadata', *D-lib magazine*, 1996. Available at **www.dlib.org/dlib/july96/ lagoze/07lagoze.html**.

Chapter 5

Subject analysis and representation

Introduction

One of the major functions of an information retrieval system is to match the contents of documents with users' queries. Thus the content of each input document in the collection is to be analysed and represented in such a way that it becomes convenient for matching. In other words, the system personnel have to prepare a surrogate for every document, and all such surrogates must be maintained in an organized manner. The process of constructing document surrogates by assigning identifiers to text items is known as indexing.[1] When the task of indexing is based on the conceptual analysis of the subject of the documents, it is called subject indexing.

Indexing operations have been performed intellectually by human indexers for quite a long time. Automatic systems have been developed comparatively recently where text analysis and indexing are performed by computers. However, the basic tasks involved in indexing are the same, that is to analyse the content of the given document and represent this analysis by some content identifiers or keywords. Lancaster[2] mentions that the process of subject indexing involves two quite distinct intellectual steps, conceptual analysis and representation. Although the methods for representing the contents of documents vary from system to system, the first task, that is the analysis of the subject, is the same in each case. In subject classification, the basic objective of which is to arrange documents according to their subject contents, the result of the conceptual analysis is represented by some artificial language or notational symbols. A number of such systems – Dewey Decimal Classification, Universal Decimal Classification, Library of Congress Classification, Colon Classification, etc. – have been in use for some time. In subject indexing, however, the basic objective is to match the contents of documents with users' queries, and thus the product of the conceptual analysis of the subject is represented in a natural language form. A number of systems – Chain, PRECIS, POPSI, Relational Indexing, etc. – have been developed over the years for preparing subject index entries of documents.

One basic problem involved in the process of subject indexing relates to the choice of appropriate keywords or descriptors through which the index entry is to be represented. The indexer prefers to use keywords that not only represent the subject clearly, but are also likely to be chosen by the user looking for that subject. In order to standardize the task of choosing appropriate keywords for the generation of index entries, a number of vocabulary control devices have been developed. Examples of such devices include the thesaurus, classaurus, thesaurofacet, etc. These tools help the indexer choose the most appropriate term to represent the subject at the indexing stage, and also help the users pick up the most appropriate terms while formulating a query. However, all these tools and techniques, being based on the intellectual capability of human indexers, have been proved inefficient in many places. To avoid the total dependence on human intellect, researchers have attempted to automate the whole process of subject indexing and classification. Most of the systems developed so far for automatic content analysis are based on the statistical calculation of the occurrences of keywords in the documents. Given the obvious shortcomings of such statistically based systems, some researchers have suggested the need for syntactic and semantic analysis of text statements by using computational linguistics in the process of content analysis.

This chapter discusses the basic issues relating to the process of subject analysis and introduces the basic ideas behind automatic indexing processes.

Classification

The first library classification scheme was developed by Melvil Dewey in 1876. Universal Decimal Classification (UDC) was the second major classification scheme to appear. Like DDC, UDC is basically an enumerative scheme but it has many synthetic devices grafted onto its main core, which resulted in a great deal of flexibility. The following are some examples that show how class numbers are built using some of the synthetic devices of UDC:

53(038) – Dictionary of physics
[Here, 53 stands for Physics, and (038) stands for Dictionary. Please note that the notation (0…) is used to denote a form division.]

622 + 629 – Mining and metallurgy
[Note that '+' is used to link the notation representing two subjects]

[23/28:294.3](540) – Christianity in relation to Buddhism in India
[Here, 23/28 denote the Christian religion (Note that '/' is used to denote a range of subjects)]
':' denotes combination of notations implying relationships between subjects
294.3 denotes Buddhism
'[…]' is used for subgrouping
(540) denotes India (Note that a place notation is always used in parenthesis)]

The Colon Classification (CC) of S. R. Ranganathan is an example of an analytico-synthetic classification scheme, which allows the classifier to identify the various facets of the subject in hand and then build the class number through synthetic devices. The seventh edition of Colon Classification provides extreme flexibilities in building class numbers of compound and complex subjects. The following are some examples:

Mathematics B
Chemistry E
Fire (physical chemistry) E:2131
Building NA
Fireplace (in a building) NA,3,94.

The Library of Congress Classification (LC) is an example of a semi-enumerative scheme of classification which provides a long list of all the classes in the universe of subjects; it allows less flexibility for preparing class numbers by synthesis. The following are some examples:

Chemistry QD
Selections from Shelley PR5403
Selections from Wordsworth PR5853
Labour HD8039
Engineers HD8039.E5
Love BF575.L8
Hate BF575.H3.

Examples of other classification schemes include the Bibliographic Classification (BC) of H. E. Bliss, which is an example of enumerative scheme, the Subject Classification (SC) of J. D. Brown, Rider's International Classification, and so on.

Dewey Decimal Classification (DDC)

In 1876 the first edition of Dewey Decimal Classification, entitled *A classification and subject index for cataloguing and arranging the books and pamphlets of a library*, was published. (Dewey's name did not appear on the title page, but it was stated in the copyright notice on the verso of the title page.) The first edition of 1000 copies consisted of 42 pages – 12 pages of introduction, 12 pages of schedules, and 18 pages of index. It made use of three novel features:

1   relative location, instead of the more usual fixed location, in which books were always filed in the same physical place. Fixed location can be difficult to maintain with a growing collection.
2   relatively detailed specification, which was made possible because of the change from fixed to relative location, and
3   the relative index, which became necessary once a reasonable number of subjects had been enumerated.

Over the years new editions of DDC have regularly made their appearance, incorporating a number of improvements over previous editions; currently DDC is available in its 21st edition in its printed form[3] while the 22nd edition is available on the web, and its printed counterpart is due to appear in 2003. The 19th edition, published in 1979, provided a completely new schedule for sociology, the 20th edition, published in 1989, provided a completely revised schedule for music, and the 21st edition, published in 1996, made major revisions in three schedules viz. public administration, education and life sciences. Both the 20th and 21st editions came out in four volumes, the first of which provides an introduction to DDC followed by tables; volumes 2 and 3 contain the schedule and volume 4 includes the relative index and a manual. The latter provides guidance on how to classify difficult areas and how to choose between related numbers.

DDC is the most widely used library classification system in the world. It is used in more than 135 countries, and has been translated into over 30 languages. In the US, 95% of all public and school libraries, 25% of all college and university libraries, and 20% of special libraries use DDC.[3]

General guidelines for classification in DDC

There are systematic steps to the classification of documents. Before beginning to classify documents according to DDC, a classifier should follow the rules below.

1   Place a document where it will be the most useful to the user and to permanent order.
2   Class a document by subject and then by form of presentation, except in the field of literature. For example, a dictionary of library science will be classed with library science and not with dictionaries. Here the subject, library science, is more important than the form, dictionary.
3   Class a work of literature first by its language and then by its form. For example, English drama will be classed first by English language literature (because specific literature is classified according to its language), and then by form (e.g. poetry, drama, fiction, essays, speeches, and letters), in this case drama.
4   When two or more subjects are treated in a work, follow the guidelines stated below:

   • Class a work that covers two subjects with the subject that has been given more emphasis. For example, if a book dealing with physics and chemistry emphasizes the latter, then class it with Chemistry.
   • If two subjects are given equal emphasis and are not used to introduce or explain one another, class the work with the subject coming first in the schedule. This is called the 'first-of-two rule'. For example, a document entitled *A history of South Africa and Ethiopia* will be classed with the history of Ethiopia, though the history of South Africa is discussed first in the document and appears first in the title, because the class number 963 (history of Ethiopia) precedes 968 (history of South Africa) in the DDC schedule.

- Class a work on three or more subjects that are all subdivisions of a broader subject with the number that includes them all, unless one subject is given more emphasis. This is called the 'rule of three'. For example, a document entitled *A history of Ethiopia, Kenya, and Ghana* will be classed with the history of Africa, because its schedule number (960) covers 963 (history of Ethiopia), 967.62 (history of Kenya), and 966.7 (history of Ghana).
- Class a work dealing with interrelated subjects with the subject that is being acted upon. This is called the 'rule of application'. For instance, a document entitled *Shakespeare's influence on Keats* will be classed with Keats, not with Shakespeare, because the influence of Shakespeare is acted upon Keats.
- Class a work in the most specific number in the scheme. For example, a document dealing with the history of the American Civil War will be classed in a specific number (the Civil War, 973.7), not in a broad number (history of America, 973).
- In general, class a work first by subject if there is a choice between subject and geographical region. For example, a work on Indian architecture is classed in the number for architecture, not in the number for geography of India.

The first volume of the DDC scheme consists of seven tables. Each contains a sequence of dependent notations indicating various special concepts used repeatedly with a variety of subjects and disciplines. The notations of these seven tables cannot be used independently but can be used along with the main class numbers given in volumes 2 and 3 of the schedule.

In DDC, the universe of knowledge is divided into ten main divisions, each called a *main class*, as shown below, and each class is again divided into ten main divisions, and this goes on successively, leading to divisions and subdivisions of various disciplines, subjects, and concepts; hence the term *decimal classification.*

Main classes
000 Generalities
100 Philosophy and related disciplines
200 Religion
300 The social sciences
400 Language
500 Pure sciences
600 Technology (applied sciences)
700 The arts
800 Literature
900 General geography and history

Main divisions of the technology class
600 Technology (applied sciences)
610 Medical sciences
620 Engineering and allied operations

630 Agriculture and related technologies
640 Home economics and family living
650 Management and auxiliary services
660 Chemical and related technologies
670 Manufactures
680 Manufacture for specific uses
690 Buildings

Main divisions of the engineering class
620 Engineering and allied operations
621 Applied physics
622 Mining and related operations
623 Military and nautical engineering
624 Civil engineering
625 Railroads, roads, highways
626 [not used]
627 Hydraulic engineering
628 Sanitary and municipal engineering
629 Other branches of engineering

The seven tables are used in different ways according to the instructions given. The following are some examples showing the use of tables in combinations of main class numbers.

Table1: standard subdivisions

This is a table of notations designating certain frequently recurring forms or methods of treatment applicable to any subject or discipline.
Examples:

Study and teaching of library and information science 020.7
[020 – Library Science + -07 – Education, research and related topics (from Table 1)
Note that the '0' from '07' has been dropped according to the instructions given under 020 in the schedule]

Philosophy and theory of physics 530.01
[Note that this number appears as it is in the schedule]

Chemistry periodicals 540.5
[540 – Chemistry + -05 – Periodicals (from Table 1)
Note that the '0' from '05' has been dropped according to the instructions given under 540 in the schedule]

Dictionary of human anatomy 611.003
[611 – Human anatomy + -03 – Dictionaries (from Table 1)
Note that the extra '0' has been added according to the instructions given under 611 in the schedule]

Military education 355.0071
[355 – Military science + -071 – Education (from Table 1)
Note that the extra '0' has been added according to the instructions given under 355 in the schedule]

History of social science 300.9
[300 – Social science + -09 – History (from Table 1)
Note that the extra '0' from '09' has been dropped according to the instruction given under 300 in the schedule]

Table 2: area

This is a table of notations designating geographical areas. Notations in this table can be used with notations elsewhere in the schedules and tables.
Examples:

Foreign policy of Ethiopia 327.63
[327.3–.9 – Foreign relations of specific nations
-63 Ethiopia (from Table 2)
Note that the number has been constructed according to the instructions given under 327.3–.9 in the schedule]

Sheffield university library 027.742821
[027.73–.79 – Libraries of specific institutions
-42821 – Sheffield (from Table 2)
Note that the number has been constructed according to the instructions given under 027.73–.79 in the schedule]

Table 3: subdivisions of different literatures

This table is used with notations from the literature class (class 800).
Examples:

History of German literature 830.9
[83 – German literature + -09 – History (Table 3B)]

Collections of French literature 840.8
[84 – French literature + -08 – Collections of literary texts in more than one form (from Table 3B)]

Description of English literature of the early twentieth century 820.900912
[82 – English literature
-09 – Description (from Table 3B)
-09001–09009 – Literature from specific periods
912 – 1900–1945 (as given under 820 in the schedule)
Note that the number has been constructed according to the instructions given under 09001–09009 in Table 3B]

Note that the numbers for each literature above comprise two digits (though according to the general rule of DDC, each main class number should comprise at least three digits). These two digit numbers in the 800 class are called the base numbers.

Table 4: subdivisions of individual languages

This table is used with notations from the language class (class 400).
Examples:

Alphabets of Amharic language 492.8711
[492.87 – Amharic language
-11 – Alphabets (from Table 4)
Note that the extra '0' has been added according to the instructions given under 420–490 in the schedule as well as those in Table 4]

Pronunciation of Finnish words 494.54181
[494.541 – Finnish language
-81 – Words (meaning, pronunciation, spelling) (from Table 4)]

Phonology of English language 421.5
[42 – English language (this is the base number for English language, and it comprises two digits instead of three) + -15 – Phonology]

Table 5: racial, ethnic, national groups

Examples:

Cross-cultural psychology of Japanese 155.84956
[155.84 – Cross-cultural psychology of specific racial and ethnic groups
-956 – Japanese (from Table 5)
Note that this number has been constructed according to the instructions given under 155.84 in the schedule]

Ceramic arts of Chinese 738.089951
[738 – Ceramic arts
-089 – Racial, ethnic, national groups (from Table 1)
-951 – Chinese (from Table 5)
Note that this number has been constructed according to the instructions given under 738 in the schedule and under -089 in Table 1].

Table 6: languages

Notations from this table can be used with those numbers from the schedules and other tables to which the classifier is instructed to add notation from Table 6.
Examples:

Translation of the Bible into the Dutch language 220.53931
[220.53–.59 – Translation of the Bible into other languages

-3931 – Dutch (from Table 6)
Note that this number has been constructed according to the instructions given under 220.53–.59 in the schedule]

Egyptian literature 893.1
[893 – Non-semitic, Afro-Asiatic literatures
-931 Egyptian (from Table 6)
Note that the number has been constructed according to the instructions given under 893 in the schedule]

Political conditions in English-speaking countries 320.917521
[320.9 – Political conditions
-175 – Regions where specific languages predominate (from Table 2)
-21 English (from Table 6)
Note that the number has been constructed according to the instructions given under 320.9 in the schedule, and under -175 in Table 2]

Table 7: persons

This table is used to denote groups of persons. Its notation can be used with notations from elsewhere in the schedules or tables only when there is an instruction (in the schedule or table) to do so.

Examples:

Children as artists 704.054
[704.04–.87 – History and description of arts with respect to specific kinds of persons
-054 – Children (from Table 7)
Note that the number has been constructed according to the instructions given under 704.04–.87 in the schedule]

Paintings by pre-school children 750.880543
[750 – Painting
-08809–08899 – Specific occupational and religious groups (from Table 1)
-0543 – Pre-school children (from Table 7)
Note that the number has been constructed according to the instructions given under -08809–08899 in Table 1].

Bibliographic Classification

Bibliographic Classification (BC) was originally devised by Henry Evelyn Bliss and was first published in four volumes in the USA between 1940 and 1953.[4] The original classification was essentially enumerative in structure, though it had many synthetic features. In 1967 the Bliss Classification Association was formed in Britain and it was suggested that 'a new and completely revised edition of the full BC should be made available'.[4] The new, revised edition (BC2) was initiated by Jack Mills and was to be produced in 22 parts, comprising one or two subjects per volume. The first volumes were published in 1977. Further revisions have been made to some of the BC2 volumes in order to retain subject currency by its publisher Bowker-Saur and updates appear in the *BCA Bulletin*. BC2 is a fully faceted classification scheme and its major features are:[4]

- The main class order is based on the principle of gradation.
- Based originally on the five fundamental categories (Personality, Matter, Energy, Space and Time) of Ranganathan, BC2 has 13 categories in the following order: thing – kind – part – property – material – process – operation – patient – product – by-product – agent – space – time.
- A comprehensive and consistent citation order is observed throughout, making the position of any compound class highly predictable, based on the facet analysis and the citation order mentioned above.
- The filing order consistently maintains general-before-special.
- The notation is fully faceted and synthetic, and the notational base consists of 35 characters 1 to 9 and A to Z. BC2 does not use any other symbol or punctuation mark. For example, the class number for a work on 'nurse as a caregiver for terminal patients and their families' is HPK PEY FBG K.
- Alphabetical indexes to all classes are provided, using the principles of chain procedure of Ranganathan.

Classification of internet resources

Although classification schemes were mainly designed for organizing bibliographic items on the library's shelves, many researchers have also used library classification schemes for organizing information resources on the web. Some typical examples are described below.

BUBL LINK

BUBL LINK provides access to a catalogue of over 11,000 selected internet resources, catalogued according to DDC, on all academic subjects.[5] Users can search the catalogue by selecting a Dewey class, for example, '300 Social Sciences', or by selecting a term/phrase from the alphabetical index. The subject terms used in BUBL LINK were originally based on LCSH (Library of Congress Subject Headings) but have been heavily customized and expanded to suit the content of the service.[5] If the users opt to search the catalogue by Dewey class, they get a page that lists the main classes of DDC. The users may select a particular Dewey class that will in turn lead to a subclass, sub-subclass and so on. Finally, users may select a specific topic. Figure 5.1 shows the classified list of items on digital libraries, and Figure 5.2 shows the results of a search on a specific topic. Instead of going through the classified list, the user could go through the alphabetical index. Figure 5.3 shows the section of the BUBL Link index on digital libraries. Thus users can gain access to the digital resources by a classified list or through an alphabetical list of subjects.

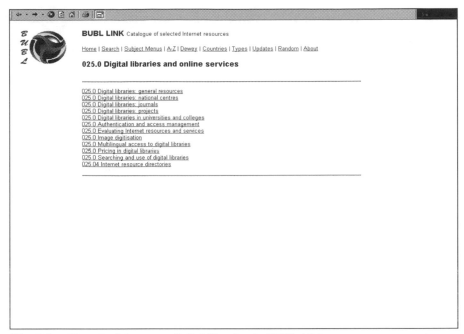

Fig. 5.1   *Classified items on digital libraries in BUBL Link*

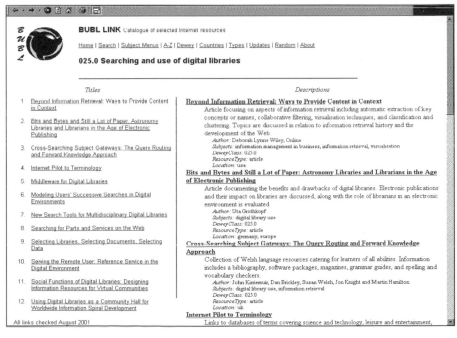

Fig. 5.2   *BUBL Link output on 'searching and use of digital libraries'*

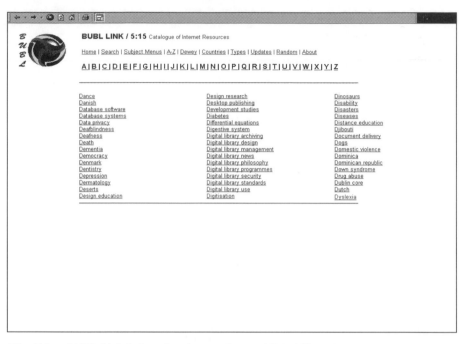

Fig. 5.3   *BUBL Link index showing entries on 'digital library'*

CyberDewey

CyberDewey is another example of the use of DDC in organizing digital information resources[6] and dates from 1995 when David Mundie used DDC to organize internet information. CyberDewey allows users to select a specific Dewey class or select a term or phrase from the alphabetical index. Selection of a Dewey class from the first screen takes the users to the subdivisions of the class with items listed against each subclass. Users can select a subclass or topic to get access to the listed digital information resource. Instead of using a Dewey class, the user may choose to go through the alphabetical index. The corresponding Dewey class number appears against each entry in the index. The user may select any topic, which will lead them to a classified list of topics, the same place that they could reach through the Dewey classes from the first screen.

Scorpion

Scorpion is a project of the OCLC Office of Research exploring the indexing and cataloguing of internet resources. Its objective was to build tools for automatic subject recognition by combining library science and information retrieval techniques. It began as a research project with a view to:

- building tools to perform automatic subject assignment
- building tools to reduce the cost of human cataloguing

- having a better understanding of what cataloguing concepts can be automated
- furthering use and enhancement of Dewey Decimal Classification
- finding means for improved retrieval.

Scorpion assigns subject codes to a document, and the document can then be treated as a query against a DDC database using ranked retrieval; and the results of the search can then be treated as the subjects of the document.[7]

CyberStacks

CyberStacks(sm) is a *centralized*, *integrated* and *unified* collection of selected digital resources categorized using the Library of Congress classification scheme.[8] Using an abridged Library of Congress call number, *CyberStacks*(sm) allows users to browse through virtual library stacks containing monographic or serial works, files, databases or search services to identify potentially relevant information resources. Resources are categorized first within a broad classification, then within narrower subclasses, and resources are listed under a specific class .

Scout Report

The Scout Report Signpost was a US National Science Foundation funded research project from 1996 to 2000.[9] The primary goal of this project was to demonstrate that internet resources could be catalogued, classified and arranged using existing controlled vocabularies and taxonomies such as the Library of Congress Classification (LCC) scheme and Library of Congress Subject Headings (LCSH) in concert with the Dublin Core metadata standard (discussed in Chapter 4). The project ended in 2000 and the materials are now available in the Scout Report Archives, which is a searchable and browseable database containing 12,711 critical annotations of selected internet sites and mailing lists. Users can conduct a search or browse the database by using the LCSH. The index page shows the index entries according to LCSH. Users may select any heading to display the corresponding items on the screen.

EELS and EEVL

EELS (Engineering E-Library, Sweden) is a gateway for quality assessed engineering information resources on the internet.[10] The main part of EELS is structured according to the EI (Engineering Information) subject classification scheme. Users can conduct a search or can browse for engineering information resources according to the various EI class numbers as shown in Figure 5.4. They can select any class and move down the hierarchy, and finally can get a list of items that belongs to a specific class. Recently EELS has been discontinued as a manually indexed subject gateway to be replaced by a new service consisting of automatically harvested records in engineering.

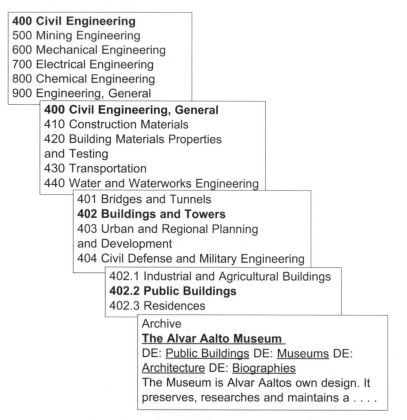

Fig. 5.4 *Browsing categories in EELS*

Another engineering subject gateway, EEVL (Enhanced and Evaluated Virtual Library), also uses the EI classification scheme.[10] It is created and run by a team of information specialists from a number of universities and institutions in the UK to provide access to digital information in engineering, mathematics and computing. From the main web page of EEVL users can select a subject – engineering, mathematics or computing – and once a subject is chosen a list of subclasses appears; the user can go down the hierarchy and finally gets a list of items on a specific class or topic.

Subject analysis

By the term subject analysis we mean the analysis of the thought content embodied in a document. Authors put forward their ideas in documents, and subject indexers must determine the essence of what they have said. Subject analysis means the presence, identification and expression of subject matter in document texts, databases, controlled and natural languages, information requests and search strategies.[12, 13] The most difficult part of subject indexing or classification is in that phase where the indexer, who is not necessarily a subject expert, tries to summarize the content of the whole document in a few words.

Certain guidelines have been put forward in the literature[11-13] that guide an indexer in determining the content of a document for the purpose of indexing. These guidelines take the form of questions that the indexer has to keep in mind while examining a document. Once these questions are answered, the indexer should be more able to index the document.

The following are the questions set by BS 65296 that illustrate the general factors to be considered while determining the subject of a document:

- Does the document deal with a specific product, condition or phenomenon?
- Does the subject contain an action concept, an operation or a process?
- Is the object or patient affected by the action identified?
- Does the document deal with the agent of this action?
- Does it refer to particular means for accomplishing the action, e.g. special instruments, techniques or methods?
- Were these factors considered in the context of a particular location or environment?
- Are any independent or dependent variables identified?
- Was the subject considered from a special viewpoint not normally associated with that field of study, e.g. a sociological study of religion?

However, it may be noted that most of these steps require the intellectual involvement of the indexer; therefore it is possible that two different indexers may analyse the content of a given document in two different ways, resulting in two different index entries.[14] In fact, this is a serious drawback of manual indexing. The following observations of Cleverdon[14] show two of the shortcomings of manual subject analysis systems:

- If two people or groups of people construct a thesaurus in the same subject area, only 60% of the index terms may be common to both thesauri.
- If two experienced indexers index the same document using the same thesaurus only 30% of the index terms may be common.

Salton[1] mentions that the need to use a variety of indexing experts in manual indexing environments introduces unwanted variabilities and uncertainties that may adversely affect retrieval effectiveness. He adds that in automatic indexing environments the lack of human expertise can be overcome by intelligent use of free-text vocabularies in stored records and information requests.

Different aspects of subject analysis and indexing have been considered in the *Annual reviews of information science and technology*[12, 15] Lancaster et al.[12] mentioned in 1989 that although much had been written on various aspects of indexing a comprehensive book on the subject was still needed. Since then Lancaster himself has since written such a book, currently available in its third edition.[11] In the following sections we shall discuss the different aspects of subject indexing in general.

Subject indexing

In the ideal document retrieval environment, a document or a query statement is represented by a group of distinct index terms as well as the semantic relationships between these terms, so that retrieval could be conducted on a structure of semantic relationships.[16] Documents are retrieved on the basis of the correspondence between search terms expressed in a query and the index terms of the document.[17] Subject indexing systems, that is indexing systems based on the analysis of the contents of the documents, have been in practice in the retrieval world for quite a long time. Indexing systems designed to assist in the retrieval of documents operate by assigning index terms to the analysed subject of each document – either manually or automatically.

Subject indexing systems have been classified broadly as pre-coordinate and post-coordinate systems. It has already been mentioned that the major objective of any indexing system is to represent the contents of documents through keywords or descriptors. In post-coordinate systems, one entry is prepared for each keyword selected to represent the subject of a given document, and all the entries are organized in a file. When a user puts forward a query, it is analysed and some keywords are selected that are representative of the user's query. These query terms are then matched against the file of index terms and relevant documents are retrieved. Uniterm, Peek-a-boo, etc., are examples of post-coordinate systems. In pre-coordinate systems, as the name implies, keywords chosen at the subject analysis stage are coordinated at the indexing stage, and thus each entry represents the full content of the document concerned. PRECIS, POPSI, Chain procedure, Relational Indexing, NEPHIS, etc., are examples of pre-coordinate indexing systems. Thus, for a document discussing the application of computational linguistics to the indexing of periodicals, entries prepared according to any of the pre-coordinate systems will represent the full context in which the entry word occurs, whereas in the post-coordinate system each term is generated without any context, i.e. unless all the corresponding entries are found the content of the document cannot be learnt. However, both systems have certain merits and demerits which are amply discussed in the literature.[11, 12, 15, 18–22]

Exhaustivity and specificity

The effectiveness of an indexing system is controlled by two parameters, called *indexing exhaustivity* and *term specificity*. By exhaustivity we mean the degree to which the subject matter of a given document has been reflected through the index entries. An exhaustive indexing system thus is supposed to represent the contents of the input documents fully. However, to attain this objective, the system has to select as many keywords as possible to represent the idea put forward in the document. In a non-exhaustive system, only a few keywords are chosen which give a broad representation of the subject. Term specificity refers to how broad or how specific are the terms or keywords chosen under a given situation. The more specific the terms, the better is the representation of the subject through the index entry.

Before going on to discuss the impact of these two factors on the effectiveness of an information retrieval system, we should introduce two parameters that are used to measure the effectiveness of such a system, i.e. *recall* and *precision*. These are discussed at length in Chapter 13, but for the moment we shall try to develop a basic idea about them.

Recall refers to the proportion of relevant materials retrieved by a system, and can be represented thus:

$$Recall = \frac{Number\ of\ relevant\ documents\ retrieved}{Number\ of\ relevant\ documents\ in\ the\ collection}$$

Precision refers to the proportion of retrieved documents that are relevant, and can be represented as:

$$Precision = \frac{Number\ of\ relevant\ documents\ retrieved}{Total\ number\ of\ documents\ retrieved}$$

These parameters are expressed in percentage terms, that is both recall and precision may vary between 1 and 100%. The objective of any information retrieval system is to retrieve all the documents relevant to a query and simultaneously withhold all those that are not relevant. Thus, a system will always attempt to attain both high recall and high precision.

Now let us try to understand how these two parameters, recall and precision, are affected by indexing exhaustivity and term specificity. Suppose we are looking for information on the Internet. We may simply conduct a search for the term 'Internet'. We may also like to use other related terms, such as 'Net', 'information superhighway', 'World Wide Web', and so on, for the given search. By doing so, we may retrieve more information and therefore will increase the possibilities of having a greater number of relevant items. In other words, by making the search term more exhaustive, we tend to get higher recall. We can say that a higher level of exhaustivity of indexing tends to ensure high recall. However, by increasing the level of exhaustivity, we tend to decrease the level of precision. This happens due to the fact that as we go on increasing the number of keywords, it may so happen that we choose such concepts that are very narrowly discussed in the given documents. Therefore, although we are able to retrieve a large number of documents, the user may find very few among them discuss the subject matter at the desired level. In other words, the system will retrieve a large number of non-relevant documents. Thus, an increase in indexing exhaustivity tends to increase recall but reduce precision.

On the question of term specificity we may note that the more specific is the chosen term the better is the precision (i.e. it can better sift out the non-relevant documents). This can be illustrated by taking a simple example. Say we want to retrieve materials on PRECIS. If we choose a broader term like 'documentation', or the still broader 'library science', we shall end up retrieving a large number of documents, many of which will not discuss the desired topic. If we choose a term such as 'indexing' that is only slightly broader, the number of retrieved items will come down significantly, but the retrieved items will still contain some documents where the desired topic has not been discussed. Thus a high level of term specificity tends to ensure high precision. However, by increasing the level of specificity, we decrease the level of recall. For example, there may be a number of documents indexed under the term 'indexing' where PRECIS has been discussed along with other index languages, but these may not be retrieved if a more specific term, 'PRECIS' is chosen for searching.

It may be noted that there is a trade-off between recall and precision. In fact, one has to reach a compromise, because optimizing both the recall and precision simultaneously is not normally achievable.[1] Lancaster[2] mentions that an intermediate performance level at which both recall and precision vary between 50 and 60%, is most satisfactory to the average user. We can thus conclude that in order to satisfy the average user we should try to achieve an intermediate level of both indexing exhaustivity and term specificity. A moderate level of exhaustivity and specificity might prove economical as well, because as we go on increasing these parameters, the system becomes more expensive in terms of operational costs.

Manual indexing

The basic steps in the manual subject indexing process are:

1   analysis of subject
2   identification of keywords
3   standardization of keywords
4. choice of an indexing system:
4.1 if the chosen system is a post-coordinate one then
    – preparation of entries under each term with reference to the document identification number
    – preparation of reference entries
4.2 if the chosen system is a pre-coordinate one then
    – preparation of an entry (main entry) using all the keywords organized in a way prescribed by the system
    – preparation of index entries by using each significant term as an entry element and the full entry (main entry) as the context, or by rotation/permutation of the significant terms in the main entry according to the rules prescribed by the system chosen
    – preparation of reference entries
5   filing of entries.

These steps are shown schematically in Figure 5.5. It may be noted that the first task in the process of indexing – be it manual or automatic – is to determine exactly what the given document is about, which has been termed as deciding the 'aboutness' of the document. The subject content of a document is sometimes referred to as 'intrinsic aboutness'.[12] However, once the indexer collects information on the 'aboutness' of the document, his or her next task is to represent the same in a way suitable for matching users' queries. While doing so the indexer has to choose the appropriate keywords. We have already seen that the effectiveness of an indexing system and thus the per-

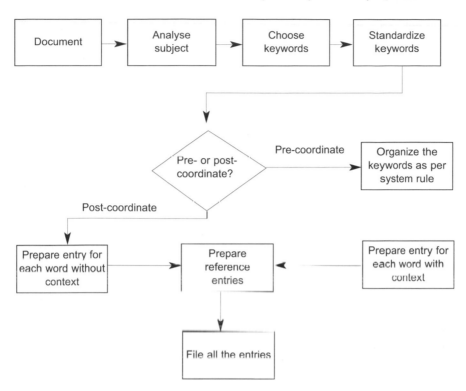

Fig. 5.5   *Steps in a manual indexing system*

formance of the total retrieval system depends on the exhaustivity and specificity of the index terms. A number of vocabulary control devices are available to guide the indexer in choosing the most appropriate index terms.

Some pre-coordinate systems prescribe the use of vocabulary control devices that have been specifically designed for that system, e.g. PRECIS prescribes the use of an online/inbuilt thesaurus, while POPSI prescribes the use of a classaurus. The tasks involved in post-coordinate systems are fairly simple after choosing the keywords. The only task the indexer has to do is to put an index entry under each term separately along with the necessary reference entries ('see' and 'see also' entries). All the entries are then arranged in a file. The tasks involved in pre-coordinate systems are, however, much more complex. The major problem relates to the coordination of index terms to produce meaningful index entries. Each pre-coordinate system prescribes a number of guidelines that are to be followed for preparing the index entries. All these systems are based on some sort of categorization principle, that is the index terms are first categorized, and then they are coordinated or arranged according to some rules prescribed for arranging the categories. It may be noted that choosing an appropriate category for a given keyword is often a difficult task and calls for an intellectual decision. Again, for the purpose of coordination of terms and actual choice of index entries, the indexer has to follow a number of rules and in many cases has to make decisions, especially in the case of conflicts between the choice and applicability of rules.

As may be seen below, in PRECIS the task of term categorization is governed by a table of role operators which prescribes certain categories and their connotations; in POPSI, in the same way, the task is guided by a table of elementary categories, while in relational indexing this is governed by the table of relational operators. In each case the syntactical ordering of the categorized terms depends on a set of prescribed rules. Once the terms are categorized, an entry (called the main entry in PRECIS, the entry for organizing classification in POPSI, and so on) is prepared by organizing the constituent terms with the help of the prescribed rules for coordination. Index entries are then prepared by using each desired term as the entry element along with the main entry as the context. Each system again prescribes rules for generating index entries (by a process called 'shunting' in PRECIS, by permutation in POPSI, and so on). Reference entries are also prepared in the pre-coordinate systems. Once all the entries are prepared, they are filed in one sequence. The basic difference between a file prepared according to a post-coordinate system and that of a pre-coordinate system is that in the former each entry will consist of only one term without reference to the whole context, while in the latter case each entry term will be represented in relation to the whole context. In this way, an entry in a pre-coordinate system shows the subject of the document concerned, while the same in a post-coordinate system does not. Basic features of some pre- and post-coordinate indexing systems are briefly discussed in the following sections.

Pre-coordinate indexing systems

Basic features of some pre-coordinate indexing systems are discussed in the following subsections. It may be noted that the discussions provide only a basic idea about each system; for detailed discussions on each system, readers are advised to consult the sources referred to.

Chain indexing

Dr S. R. Ranganathan developed a method of pre-coordinate indexing, called chain procedure or chain indexing. The principle behind chain indexing is that it attempts to represent, in natural language, the chain of concepts that constitutes a subject. While classifying a document the steps that we follow are the same as those required for subject indexing, the only difference is that instead of representing the subject in natural language we use an artificial (notation) language. Thus, if we can represent the subject in natural language, and can represent all the terms/concepts in the chain forming the subject statement in a systematic manner, then users can access the subject matter by any of the constituent concepts. This is the essence of chain indexing; it is controlled by the nature and structure of the classification scheme used to classify the documents.

The basic steps in chain indexing may be represented as follows.

1   Take the class number prepared for the given document.

2   Consult the corresponding classification schedule and write the notation at each step and the corresponding term or phrase (from the schedule). This will produce a chain of concepts from the general to the specific.

3   Identify the sought, unsought, and false links. Sought links denote the concepts (at any given stage in the chain) that the user is likely to use as access points; unsought links are those that are not likely to be used as access points, and false links are those that really do not represent any valid concept (mostly these are the connecting symbols).

4   Invert the chain (this process is called *reverse rendering*), and this will generate the index entries.

The process can be illustrated by the following example:

Subject statement: Culture of pearls
1   *Class number* (according to DDC, 19th ed): 639.412
2   *Analysis of class number*
       600 Technology
       630 Agriculture
       639 Non-domesticated animals and plants
       639.
       639.4 Fisheries and culture of molluscs
       639.41 Oysters
       639.412 Pearl
3   *Identification of links*
       600 Technology (USL)
       630 Agriculture (SL)
       639 Non-domesticated animals and plants (USL)
       639. (FL)
       639.4 Fisheries and culture of molluscs (SL)
       639.41 Oysters (SL)
       639.412 Pearl (SL)
4   *Index entries*
    Pearl: Oysters: Fisheries and culture of molluscs: Agriculture 639.412

    Oysters: Fisheries and culture of molluscs: Agriculture 639.41
       See also
       Pearl: Oysters: Fisheries and culture of molluscs: Agriculture
    Fisheries and culture of molluscs: Agriculture 639.4
       See also
       Pearl: Oysters: Fisheries and culture of molluscs: Agriculture

    Agriculture 630
       See also
       Pearl: Oysters: Fisheries and culture of molluscs: Agriculture

In some cases a given concept may need to be qualified to denote the domain, for example,

Food: Agriculture
Food: Animal husbandry
Food: Cookery
Food: Medicine, and so on.

If the subject includes a space or a time isolate or a form, then during the reverse rendering stage, the chain just before the part denoting time, space or form must be inverted and the rest of the chain appended to it. For example, if the subject is 'Culture of pearls in India', the class number would be 639.4120954. If we analyse the number, identify the links, and generate index entries, we shall get an index entry, in addition to those shown above, as follows:

Pearl: Oysters: Fisheries and culture of mulluscs: Agriculture: India 639.4120954

For further discussions on Chain indexing consult the literature, such as Foskett,[20] Chakraborty and Chakraborti,[21] and Rajan.[22]

Relational indexing

J. E. L. Farradane devised a scheme of pre-coordinate indexing known as relational indexing. The system was developed first in the early 1950s and has been modified several times since then. The latest changes may be noted from Farradane's own papers that appeared in 1980.[23, 24] Farradane identified nine relational categories which can be represented in a matrix (see Table 5.1).

Table 5.1   *Relational operators*

Discriminatory mechanisms	Associative mechanisms ⟶		
	Awareness association	Temporary association	Fixed
Concurrent conceptualization	/θ Concurrent	/* Self-activity	/; Association
Non-distinct conceptualization	/= Equivalence	/+ Dimensional	/(Appurtenance
Distinct conceptualization	/) Distinctness	/- Action	/: Functional dependence (causation)

According to Farradane, any subject can be represented by identifying and representing, in the form of what he called *analets* (pairs of terms interposed by an operator), the relationship between each pair of the constituent concepts, and he suggested that any possible relationship can be represented by either of these nine relational operators. He proposed the connotation of each of the nine relational operators which have been extended and clarified by Chowdhury[25] and Chowdhury and Mahapatra[26–29] for the preparation of linear index entries. Table 5.1 gives an example of index entries generated according to the principles of relational analysis:[23, 24]

Examples

Subject statement: Statistical techniques for measuring the information seeking behaviour of scientists and engineers in developing countries

Index entry

Information /- Seeking /;⎰Scientists⎱/; Behaviour /- Measuring /; Statistical techniques
⎰ Engineers ⎱
/+
Developing countries

A scheme for drawing linear index entries based on relational analysis was developed by Chowdhury as part of his first doctoral thesis.[25] The following is a simple example of title-like phrase, analet and the resulting index entries.[27]

Title-like phrase: chemical properties and structure of alumina produced by the leaching of clay in hydrochloric acid

Analet:
    Clay /: Alumina /(⎰ Chemical properties
    /-   ⎱ Structure
    Leaching /; Hydrochloric acid

Primary index statement:
    Clay [Leaching *by* Hydrochloric acid] *causing* Alumina. Chemical properties & Structure

Index entries:
    CLAY
    [Leaching *by* Hydrochloric acid] *causing* Alumina. Chemical properties & Structure
    LEACHING. Clay
      [*by* Hydrochloric acid] *causing* Alumina. Chemical properties & Structure

HYDROCHLORIC ACID *in* Leaching. Clay *causing* Alumina
  Chemical properties & Structure
ALUMINA *caused by* Clay [Leaching *by* Hydrochloric acid]
  Chemical properties & Structure

Further details on relational indexing may be obtained in the literature, such as Farradane,[23, 24] Chowdhury[25] and Chowdhury and Mahapatra.[26–29]

PRECIS

PRECIS, the PREserved Context Index System, was developed by Derek Austin and first came out in 1974,[30] a revised version appeared in 1984.[31] This indexing system became very popular not only in the United Kingdom, but also in other parts of the world such as in Canada, Australia, and so on, and it has been widely discussed in the literature (for example, see Chowdhury,[32] Curwen,[33] and Dykstra[34]). Major tasks involved in indexing according to this system are:[31, 32]

- analysing the document concerned and identifying key concepts
- organizing the concepts into a subject statement based on the principle of context dependency
- assigning codes ('operators') which signify the syntactical function of each term
- deciding which terms should be the access points and which terms would be in other positions in the index entries, and assigning further codes to achieve these results
- adding further prepositions, auxiliaries or phrases which would result in clarity and expressiveness of the resulting index entries
- making supporting reference entries from semantically related terms taken from a thesaurus.

Stages 2 to 4 of the above deal with syntactic relations and are governed by (i) a schema of role operators (see Table 5.2) and (ii) the associated rules for dealing with each role operator and making index entries. In PRECIS there are two kinds of operators – *primary operators* and *secondary operators*. The former, which were earlier called *mainline operators*, perform the primary task in the syntactical side. There are seven primary operators for three sets of concepts: (0) is for the 'environment of core concepts'; (1), (2) and (3) are for the 'core concepts'; and (4), (5), and (6) are for the 'extra-core concepts'.

Secondary operators, or interposed operators as they were called earlier, perform secondary functions. These operators are used for three sets of concepts: (f) and (g) are for 'coordinate concepts'; (p), (q) and (r) are for 'dependent elements'; and (s), (t) and (u) are for 'special classes of action'.

Table 5.2 *PRECIS: schema of role operators*

Primary operators		
Environment of core concepts	0	Location
Core concepts	1	Key system; object of transitive action; agent of intransitive action
	2	Action; effect of action
	3	Performer of transitive action; intake; factor
Extra-core concepts	4	Viewpoint-as-form
	5	Selected instance, e.g. study region, sample population
	6	Form of document; target user
Secondary operators		
Coordinate concepts	f	'Bound' coordinate concept
	g	Standard coordinate concept
Dependent elements	p	Part; property
	q	Member of quasi-generic group
	r	Assembly
Special classes of action	s	Role definer
	t	Author-attributed association
	u	Two-way interaction
Codes		
Primary codes		
Theme interlinks	$x	1st concept in coordinate theme
	$y	2nd/subsequent concept in theme
	$z	Common concept
Term codes	$a	Common noun
	$c	Proper name
	$d	Place name
Secondary codes		
Differences		
Preceding differences		1st and 2nd characters:
	$0	Non-lead, space generating
	$1	Non-lead, close-up
	$2	Lead, space generating
	$3	Lead, close-up
		3rd character – number in the range 1–9 indicating level of difference
Date as difference	$d	
Parenthetical differences	$n	Non-lead parenthetical difference
	$o	Lead parenthetical difference
Connectives	$v	Downward-reading connective
	$w	Upward-reading connective
Typographic codes	$e	Non-filing part in italic preceded by comma
	$f	Filing part in italic preceded by comma
	$g	Filing part in roman
	$h	Filing part in italic preceded by full point
	$i	Filing part in italic, no preceding punctuation

In PRECIS there are various types of codes that are used to bring expressiveness in the resulting index entries. There are two sets of *primary codes*: one set (theme inter-links) involves three codes used to link common or related themes in the subject statement, while the other (term codes) also involves three codes, used to denote the status of a term in the subject statement. There are also some *secondary codes* which are mainly divided into two sets: the first set, *differences*, involves three kinds of differences, such as: 'preceding differences', 'date as a difference', and 'parenthetical differences'. The second set involves *connectives* which are used to connect any two or more consecutive terms in the input string. There are also some *typographic codes* which are used to bring the desired typographic form of a given term in the resulting index entry.

Index entries in PRECIS are generated in a two-line, three-part format. The first line, consisting of two units – the *lead* and the *qualifier* – is called the *heading*, while the other line is called the *display*. The lead is the user's access point to the index; the qualifier contains the terms that set the lead into its wider context; and the display contains the terms that rely upon the heading for the context. Index entries are generated with any of the constituent concepts as the lead term, as desired, by a procedure called *shunting*. The process involves moving each term from the display to the heading in turn (clockwise), while the lead term in the previous entry is shifted by one unit to the qualifier. This process continues until all the terms in the display appear in the heading. There are three kinds of format in PRECIS – *standard format*, *inverted format*, and *predicate transformation*. Each format is related to one or more role operators and is used while dealing with the appropriate role operator(s). Rules for each role operator and for generating index entries according to these formats are discussed in detail in the literature (for example, see Austin and Dykstra,[31] Chowdhury,[32] and Dykstra[34]). The following are some sample PRECIS entries:

1   *Subject statement*: Management of libraries in India
     Entries:
        Management
           Libraries. India

        Libraries. Management
           India

        India. Libraries. Management

2   *Subject statement*: Financial aspects of the application of computers in library
     management
     Entries:
        Libraries
           Management. Applications of computers. Financial aspects

        Management. Libraries
           Application of computers. Financial aspects

Computers
Applications in management of libraries. Financial aspects

Financial aspects. Applications of computers in management of libraries

POPSI

POPSI, POstulate-based Permuted Subject Indexing, is a pre-coordinate indexing system developed by G. Bhattacharyya.[35] It uses the *analytico-synthetic* method for string formulation and permutation of the constituent terms in order to satisfy different approach points to the document.[36]

There are two parts in a POPSI index entry – the lead heading, which contains the index term or the access term, and the context heading, which generally appears in the line following the lead heading and contains the subject words, with auxiliary words, denoting the context in which the lead term has been discussed in the given document. As a basis of categorizing the concepts in a subject, Bhattacharyya proposed four elementary categories, discipline, entity, property, and action (DEPA, in short), and a special component called the modifier.

According to POPSI, a *discipline* is an elementary category that includes conventional fields of study or any aggregate of such fields or artificially created analogous fields, such as mathematics, physics, library science, computer science, etc. *Entity* includes manifestations having perceptual correlates, or only a conceptual existence, and distinct from properties and actions performed by them or on them, for example, patent, lung, plant, and so on. *Property* includes manifestations denoting the concept of attribute – qualitative or quantitative, for example, specific gravity, disease, efficiency, and so on. *Action* includes manifestations denoting the concept of doing, either as self action or as external action, for example, evaluation, examination, migration, etc.

In relation to the manifestation of any one of the elementary categories the modifier qualifies the manifestations without disturbing their conceptual wholeness: for example, 'subject' in 'subject classification'.[36] A modifier can modify any of the fundamental categories or a combination of fundamental categories. Modifiers can be common modifiers, like form, time, environment, and place, and special modifiers, which are discipline-based, property-based or action-based.

The basic rule of syntax associated with the deep structure (DS) of a subject indexing language (SIL) is that discipline should be followed by entity (either modified or unmodified) appropriately interpolated or extrapolated wherever warranted by property and/or action (either modified or unmodified). There are other rules that govern the syntactical structure of POPSI, such as:

- a manifestation of property follows immediately the manifestation in relation to which it is a property
- a manifestation of action follows immediately the manifestation in relation to which it is an action
- property and action can have another property and/or action directly related
- a species or part follows immediately the manifestation in relation to which it

is a species or part (the 'species' here is used to denote the genus–species relationship (such as Flower and Rose), and 'part' is used to denote the whole–part relationship (such as, Human Body and Lungs)
- a modifier follows immediately the manifestation in relation to which it is a modifier.

In general, the rules of syntax give rise to the following syntactical structure.[36]

> DISCIPLINE followed by ENTITY followed by PROPERTY and/or ACTION. PROPERTY and/or ACTION may further be followed by PROPERTY and/or ACTION, as the case may be. Each of the above components may further admit of, and be followed immediately by, their respective SPECIES/TYPES and/or PARTS and/or SPECIAL MODIFIERS. The COMMON MODIFIERS generally occur last in the sequence.

Examples of POPSI entries:

Subject statement: Administration of libraries
Index string: Library Science, 6 library, 6.1 management

Subject statement: A history of library associations
Index string: Library Science. 6 learned^body professional^association

Subject statement: A physical bibliography for librarians
Index string: Library Science. 6 document bibliography.
              physical^bibliography

Post-coordinate indexing systems

Two post-coordinate indexing systems, Uniterm and Optical coincidence/Peek-a-boo, are discussed in the following subsections. These systems are not used nowadays, but some of the principles behind them are still valid and hence are useful.

Uniterm

Uniterm, developed by Mortimer Taube in 1953, is a simple post-coordinate indexing system.[20] As the name suggests, it creates index entries for each unit term identified by the indexer. In fact, a card is prepared for each term that is considered to be an appropriate index term for a given document. The term is posted on top of the card. The card is divided into ten columns, 0 to 9. The document number (i.e. the accession number or number of the given document being indexed) is written on the card by a technique known as 'terminal digit posting' – the number is written in a column based on the right-most digit in the document number. Figure 5.6 illustrates the entries that would be generated by indexing the following two subjects: automation of libraries in India (document number 13) and management of libraries in England (document number 45).

At the time of searching, a user has to pick up all the cards relating to his/her search request, and has to identify those numbers that appear in all the cards. The job of an

Automation

0	1	2	3	3	5	6	7	8	9
			13						

India

0	1	2	3	3	5	6	7	8	9
			13						

Libraries

0	1	2	3	3	5	6	7	8	9
			13		45				

England

0	1	2	3	3	5	6	7	8	9
					45				

Management

0	1	2	3	3	5	6	7	8	9
					45				

Fig. 5.6   *Uniterm entries*

indexer, at the input stage, is quite simple in the sense that all he/she has to do is to prepare a card for each term, if it does not already exist, and write the document number by following the principle of terminal digit posting. However, the job of the searcher is rather difficult, because he/she has to pick up all the cards pertaining to the query and then has to compare each number in a given card with all the numbers in all the other cards. This process of comparing numbers may prove to be quite difficult if each card contains quite a few numbers written on it, which is bound to happen for a large collection of documents.

Optical coincidence/peek-a-boo cards

Searching a Uniterm file is difficult because it relies on the ability of the searcher to notice matching numbers on the cards that are retrieved in response to a given query.[20] A mechanism that uses optical coincidence or peek-a-boo cards was devised to overcome the problem of manual searching. This process is based on a simple principle: each card is divided into small units of numbered squares, each unit bearing a specific number, and a document number is punched on the appropriate position on the card. Thus a number of small holes are produced on each card, each hole representing a particular document number in which the term, written on top of the card, appears. At the time of searching, the user has to pick up all the cards matching a given query. The cards are then placed in a box against a source of light. Light will pass through those cards that have punches at the same position: the numbers represented by these positions will contain all the terms present in the query, and thus will be the output.

A peek-a-boo card contains space at the top of the heading for posting of a term/phrase, like a Uniterm card, and the body of the card is divided up into numbered squares ranging from 500 to 1000 or up to 10,000. This system removed some of the problems involved in searching Uniterm cards, but if there were a large number of punches on a card, it could easily become mutilated after being used a number of times.

Problems of manual indexing

Salton[1] and Salton and McGill,[37] mention two major shortcomings of manual indexing systems. First, it is not quite clear that all the complexities and refinements, exemplified by the categorization of terms and assignment of relations between terms, are really beneficial. On the contrary, too much professional time and intellect are wasted in cataloguing and indexing. The second shortcoming of manual indexing is that even if the indexing process is carried out accurately, and at the right level of detail, it is not possible to maintain consistency since more than one indexer will be needed in practice. In other words, the same document might be indexed differently by different indexers, and similarly, queries in a given subject area might be analysed differently from those of documents. These inconsistencies affect retrieval performance and impair the usefulness of the intellectual decisions that control the indexing process.[1] Over the last three decades investigators have therefore sought ways to replace human intellectual efforts by computer processing. Major areas of investigation include methods for extracting terms for the purposes of indexing, automatic organization of terms, automatic approaches to thesaurus construction, and so on. The major issues related to automatic subject analysis and indexing are introduced in the following chapter.

Theory of indexing

The lack of an indexing theory to explain the process of indexing has long been considered as a blind spot in the theory of classification and indexing.[38] However, some theories for explaining the process of indexing do exist though information scientists differ in accepting those views *in toto*. Some researchers (for example, see Quinn,[38] Jones[39] and Fugmann[40]) suggest that there are five levels in the process of indexing.

The first level is the concordance, which consists of references to all words in the original text arranged in alphabetical order.

The second level is the information theoretic level, which calculates the likelihood of a word being chosen for indexing based on its frequency of occurrence in a given text document.

The third level is the linguistic one, which attempts to explain how meaningful words are extracted from large units of text. Some indexers propose that some sections such as the opening paragraphs, chapters, sections, and opening and closing sentences of paragraphs are good sources for choosing indexing terms.

The fourth level is the textual or skeletal framework. The basic underlying tenet here is that the text is prepared by the author in an organized manner and held together by a skeletal structure. It is the job of the indexer to identify the skeleton and those markers that are useful for determining the content of the given text.

The fifth level of indexing theory is the inferential level. An indexer should be able to make inferences about the relationships between words and phrases by observing the sentence and paragraph structure, and by stripping the sentence of extraneous details.

Fugmann[40, 41] proposes a theory of indexing that is also based on five general axioms.

1   *The axiom of definability* proposes that compiling information relevant to a topic can only be accomplished to the degree to which a topic can be defined.
2   *The axiom of order* suggests that any compilation of information relevant to a topic is an order creation process.
3   *The axiom of the sufficient degree of order* posits that the demands made on the degree of order increase as the size of a collection and frequency of searches increase.
4   *The axiom of predictability* says that the success of any directed search for relevant information hinges on how readily predictable or reconstructible are the modes of expression for concepts and statements in the search file.
5   *The axiom of fidelity* equates the success of any directed search for relevant information with the fidelity with which concepts and statements are expressed in the search file.

Discussion

This chapter has covered the basics of organization of information in an information retrieval environment. Three major activities, viz. cataloguing, classification and indexing, have been described and the tools and techniques used in such activities are briefly discussed. Continuous efforts are being made to improve the traditional tools and techniques as can be noted from the latest editions of such tools as the DDC21[3] and BC.[4] While cataloguing, classification and indexing have remained essential activities in traditional information retrieval environments, their usefulness in the digital information environments are now being tested by a number of researchers (see for example, Oddy,[42] Younger,[43] Dempsey and Heery,[44] Ballard,[45] Tennat,[46] Subramanian, Srivdhya and Shafer,[47] and Shapiro and Yan[48]).

References

1   Salton, G., *Automatic text processing: the transformation, analysis and retrieval of information by computer*, Reading, MA, Addison-Wesley, 1989.
2   Lancaster, F. W., *Information retrieval systems: characteristics, testing, and evaluation*, 2nd edn, New York, John Wiley, 1979.
3   Mitchell, J. S., Beall, J., Mathews, W. E. and New, G. R. (eds.), *Dewey Decimal Classification and relative index*, 21st edn, Albany, New York, Forest Press, 1996.
4   The Bliss Bibliographic Classification. Available at **www.sid.cam.ac.uk/bca/bcahome.htm**.
5   BUBL Link. Available at **www.bubl.ac.uk**.

6   CyberDewey: the fast well organized internet directory. Available at **www.anthus.com/CyberDewey/CyberDewey.html**.

7   Shafer, K., Scorpion helps catalog the Web, 1997. Available at **http://orc. rsch.oclc.org:6109/b-asis.html**.

8   Welcome to CyberStacks (sm). Available at **www.public.iastate.edu/ ~CYBERSTACKS/**.

9   Scout Report Signpost. Available at **www.ilrt.bris.ac.uk/mirrors/scout/ addserv/signpost/help.html#01**.

10 Engineering E-Library, Sweden: the Swedish Universities of Technology Libraries. Available at **http://eels.lub.lu.se/**.

11 Lancaster, F. W., *Indexing and abstracting in theory and practice*, 3rd edn, London, Facet Publishing, 2003.

12 Lancaster, F. W., Elliker, C. and Colonell, T. H., 'Subject analysis', *Annual review of information science and technology,* **24**, 1989, 34–84.

13 BS 6529:1984 *Recommendations for examining documents, determining their subjects and selecting indexing terms*, British Standards Institution.

14 Cleverdon, C. W., 'Optimizing convenient online access to bibliographic data-bases', *Information services and use*, **4**, 1984, 37–47.

15 Schwartz, C. and Eisenmann, L., 'Subject analysis', *Annual review of information science and technology*, **21**, 1986, 37–61.

16 Xin Lu, 'Document retrieval: a structural approach', *Information processing and management*, **26** (2), 1990, 209–18.

17 Macleod, I. A., 'Storage and retrieval of structural documents', *Information processing and management*, **26** (2), 1990, 197–208.

18 Craven, T. C., *String indexing*, Orlando, FL, Academic Press, 1986.

19 Borko, H. and Bernier, C. L., *Indexing concepts and methods,* New York, Academic Press, 1978.

20 Foskett, A. C., *Subject approach to information*, 5th edn, London, Library Association Publishing, 1996.

21 Chakraborty, A. R. and Chakraborti, B., *Indexing: principles, processes and products*, Calcutta, World Press, 1984.

22 Rajan, T. N. (ed.), *Indexing systems: concepts, models and techniques*, Calcutta, IASLIC, 1981.

23 Farradane J. E. L., 'Relational indexing: part 1', *Journal of information science*, **1**, 1980, 267–76.

24 Farradane, J. E. L., 'Relational indexing: part 2', *Journal of information science*, **1**, 1980, 313–24.

25 Chowdhury, G. G., *Nature and applicability of Farradane's relational analysis with particular reference to the reparation of linear index entries*, PhD thesis, Calcutta, Jadavpur University, 1989.

26 Chowdhury, G. G. and Mahapatra, M., 'Genesis and scope of Farradane's relational indexing', *Librarian,* **3**, 1988, 10–20.

27 Chowdhury, G. G. and Mahapatra, M., 'Expressiveness of relational index entries: a report on the use of relational indexing in different subjects', *IASLIC bulletin*, **34** (1), 1989, 21–34.

28 Chowdhury, G. G. and Mahapatra, M., 'Scope of relational analysis in studying the concept of interrelationship in subject literature', *INICAE*, **10** (1), 1991, 67–74.

29 Chowdhury, G. G. and Mahapatra, M., 'Applications of the theory of relational analysis in information retrieval', *Journal of library and information science*, **14** (1), 1989, 1–12.

30 Austin, D., *PRECIS: a manual of concept analysis and subject indexing*, London, Council of BNB, 1974.

31 Austin, D. and Dykstra, M., *PRECIS: a manual of concept analysis and subject indexing*, 2nd edn, London, British Library, 1984.

32 Chowdhury, G. G., *PRECIS: a workbook*, Calcutta, IASLIC, 1995.

33 Curwen, A. G., 'A decade of PRECIS, 1974–1984', *Journal of librarianship*, **17** (4), 1985, 244–67.

34 Dykstra, M., *PRECIS: a primer*, London, British Library Bibliographic Services Division, 1985.

35 Bhattacharyya, G., *A general theory of subject indexing languages*, PhD thesis, Karnataka University, Dharwad, 1980.

36 Aptagiri, D. V., Gopinath, M. A. and Prasad, A. R. D., 'A frame-based knowledge representation paradigm for automating POPSI', *Knowledge organization*, **22** (3/4), 1995, 162–7.

37 Salton, G. and McGill, M. J., *Introduction to modern information retrieval*, New York, McGraw Hill, 1983.

38 Quinn, B., 'Recent theoretical approaches in classification and indexing', *Knowledge organization*, **21** (3), 1994, 140–7.

39 Jones, K. P., 'Towards a theory of indexing', *Journal of documentation*, **32**, 1976, 121.

40 Fugmann, R., 'On the practice of indexing and its theoretical foundations', *International classification*, **7** (1), 1980, 13–20.

41 Fugmann, R., *Subject analysis and indexing: theoretical foundation and practical advice*, Frankfurt, Indeks Verlag, 1993.

42 Oddy, P., *Future libraries, future catalogues*, London, Library Association Publishing, 1997.

43 Younger, J. A., 'Resources description in a digital age', *Library trends*, **45** (3), 1997, 462–81.

44 Dempsey, L. and Heery, R., 'Metadata: a current view of practice and issues', *Journal of documentation*, **54** (2), 1998, 145–72.

45 Ballard, T., 'Online catalogs: finding the weakest link: maintaining Web links in MARC records requires quality control decisions', *Information today*, **15** (4), 1998, 56.

46 Tennant, R., '21st century cataloging', *Library journal*, **123** (7) 1998, 30–1.

47 Subramanian, Srividhya and Shafer, Keith E., *Annual review of OCLC research 1997*, Online Computer Library Center Corpn., Dublin, OH, February 1998.

48   Shapiro, C. D. and Yan, P. F., 'Generous tools: thesauri in digital libraries',
     Proceedings of the 17th National Meeting 1996. Edited by Martha E. Williams.
     Information Today Inc., New York, 14–16 May 1996, Medford, NJ,
     Information Today Inc., 1996, 323–32.

Chapter 6

Automatic indexing and file organization

Introduction

Salton[1] gives the following lucid definition of automatic indexing: 'when the assignment of the content identifiers is carried out with the aid of modern computing equipment the operation becomes automatic indexing'. Borko and Bernier[2] suggest that the subject of a document can be derived by a mechanical analysis of the words in a document and by their arrangement in a text. In fact, all attempts at automatic indexing depend in some way or other on the original document texts, or document surrogates. The words occurring in each document are listed and certain statistical measurements are made, like word frequency calculation, total collection frequency, or frequency distribution across the documents of the collection.

The process of indexing

Before going into much detail of the process, we should try to understand the advantages of automatic indexing. Salton[3] mentions the following:

1   level of consistency in indexing can be maintained
2   index entries can be produced at a lower cost in the long run
3   indexing time can be reduced, and
4   better retrieval effectiveness can be achieved.

Harter[4] points out that automatic analysis by means of word frequency analysis can be viewed as a two-tiered problem. In the first stage the problem relates to the identification of a technical vocabulary characteristic of a given subject field. Once the vocabulary or index terms have been chosen, the second problem arises, which relates to the representation of the document with the help of keywords.

As far as the first problem is concerned, the idea of analysing the subject of a document through automatic counting of term occurrences was first put forward by H. P. Luhn in 1957.[5] He proposed that

1   the frequency of word occurrence in an article furnishes a useful measure of word significance
2   the relative position of a word within a sentence furnishes a useful measurement for determining the significance of sentences, and

3   the significance factor of a sentence will be based on a combination of these two requirements.

The basic idea behind Luhn's theory was that the more frequent the occurrence of a term in a given document, the more significant is that term in denoting the subject content of the document. Therefore, by counting the frequency of occurrences of all the words in a given document one can identify the most significant words that can represent the subject of the document. The steps for preparing indexes based on frequency counts are as illustrated by Salton,[1] therefore,

1   choosing all the words in a document
2   eliminating common function words by consulting a stop-word list
3   computing the frequency of occurrence of all words in each document, and
4   choosing a threshold frequency, and selecting all the terms above this threshold frequency as the index terms.

However, such a system tends to produce better recall while neglecting the aspect of precision. This happens due to the underlying principle that says that if a term occurs several times in a document then it should be regarded as a significant term. This may not always be true. For example, in all the documents in a collection on library science, say, the term 'library' will occur quite frequently, but there is no need to use this term as the index term or a search term, because this may retrieve the whole collection. The objective of a good indexing system is to isolate all the relevant documents in a collection from the others, in the same collection, that do not discuss the desired topic. In other words, one has to choose such words for indexing that can differentiate a given document or group of documents from all the others in the same collection. Sometimes this is denoted by the term discrimination. In this connection the guidelines suggested by Harter[4] for automatic selection of indexing terms are worth mentioning:

1   the keywords selected for representing a document should name the subject that is treated in the document.
2   the keywords selected for the index record of a document should name the subjects that are most heavily treated in the document.
3   the keywords selected for the documents should maximize the probability of retrieving the document.

All these points suggest that, when terms are being chosen for indexing, the frequency of a given term should not be high in all documents. In other words, one should choose those terms that occur frequently in one or a few documents but not in all. The precision function is better served by the terms that occur rarely in individual document collections, because such terms distinguish the few documents in which they occur from the rest where they do not.[3]

Karen Sparck Jones[6] is the proponent of the idea of preparing indexes based on *inverse document frequency* (*idf*): if the document frequency (*df_i*) is defined as the number of documents in a collection of N documents in which a term T occurs, then the inverse function of the document frequency of the term can be taken as an indication of the term value as a document discriminator. The inverse document frequency factor (*idf*) can be calculated as log N/df_i.

In an information retrieval environment the contents of a user's query are matched against the contents of the stored documents. Therefore, the objective should be to retrieve items in a ranked order, with those that best match at the top of the list. One way of achieving this might be to apply some sort of weighting to the index terms. This suggests that while determining the importance of a given index term one has to consider the term characteristics within a given document. Salton[1] suggests that the importance of a given term k in an individual document i can be measured by the frequency of occurrence $FREQ_{ik}$ in the document. The usefulness of the term in the collection as a whole may be reflected by the term discrimination value, *DISCVALUE*, or by an inverse function of the document frequency $DOCFREQ_k$. Two possible weighting functions are thus

$$WEIGHT = \frac{FREQ_{ik}}{DOCFREQ_k}$$

$$WEIGHT = FREQ_{ik} \times DISCVALUE_k$$

Salton combines the idea of Luhn and Sparck Jones and proposes that the best indexing terms are those that occur frequently in individual documents but rarely in the rest of the collection. Salton and Young[7] recommend the following formula for the calculation of weight to an index term:

$$W_{ij} = tf_{ij} \times \log N/df_i$$

where W_{ij} is the weight of a term T_j in a document D_i, tf_{ij} is the term frequency for term T_j in document D_i and df_i is the number of documents in a collection of N documents in which term T_j occurs.

The steps for preparing an automatic index will be:

1   identification of all the words occurring in all the documents in a given collection;
2   deletion of function words by consulting a stop-word list
3   preparation of word stems by suffix stripping method, which helps decrease the number of words by producing a common stripped form for the words that have the same root (e.g. COMPUT for COMPUTING, COMPUTER, COMPUTATION, COMPUTATIONAL, etc.)
4   Computation of the value of W_{ij} for each term T_j in each document D_i.

After assigning the weight to the terms the indexer can eliminate those terms that have a low weight. Deletion of high-frequency terms causes losses in recall and elimination of low-frequency terms may affect precision. Thus, a compromise is to be reached. The automatic indexing system developed for the SMART retrieval project[8] followed the steps shown in Figure 6.1.

A number of other approaches to the generation of automatic indexes have been reported in the literature. Croft[9] in his method based on the probabilistic approach suggests that term dependencies derived from queries, and incorporated into a probabilistic retrieval model, can improve performance. Probabilistic methods also consider relevance feedback, which implies the ability of the searcher to locate relevant items in a database.[10, 11]

Automatic classification

While term weighting lies at the heart of modern information retrieval, many other techniques continue to be of interest in information retrieval. Among them document and term clustering have drawn much research attention. Automatic classification or clustering is a multivariate statistical technique that groups together similar objects in

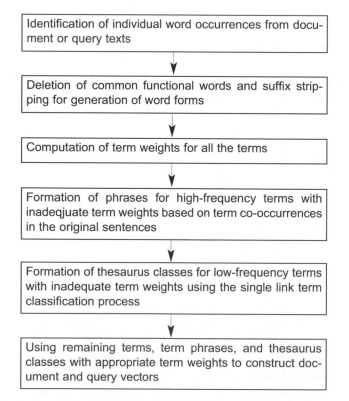

Fig. 6.1   *Automatic indexing in the SMART retrieval project*

a multidimensional space.[12] The essence of cluster hypothesis is that similar documents tend to be relevant to the same queries, and that therefore a clustering method should provide a way of bringing together the relevant documents for a query, thereby producing high precision results.

Clustering

This is a method of automatic generation of document clusters around which all similar documents are available. A clustered file provides efficient file access by limiting the searches to those document clusters that appear to be similar to the corresponding queries. Association between documents, measured by document–document similarity coefficients, conveys information about the joint relevance of documents to queries in a collection.

Salton[1] suggests that two main strategies can be adopted for generating hierarchical clustering:

1   a complete list of all pairwise item similarities can be constructed, in which case it is necessary to employ a grouping mechanism capable of assembling into common clusters of items with sufficiently large pairwise clusters, and
2   heuristic methods can be used that do not require pairwise item similarities to be computed.

The following are the basic steps involved in a hierarchical agglomerative clustering method:[1]

1   compute pairwise document–document similarity $[N(N-1)/2]$ coefficients
2   place each of the N documents into a cluster of its own
3   form a new cluster by combining the most similar pair of current clusters (i and j); update the similarity matrix by deleting the rows and columns corresponding to i and j; calculate the entries in the row corresponding to the new cluster $i+j$
4   repeat step 3 if the number of cluster left is greater than one.

There are two strategies for searching clusters, the *top-down approach* and *bottom-up approach*. In the top-down approach, the query is first compared with the highest level centroids, and the search proceeds downwards in the cluster tree until eventually some individual items in the lowest level clusters are chosen for retrieval. In the bottom-up approach, only the lowest level centroids are stored, i.e. those containing only the specific items of the collection, and the higher-level cluster structure is disregarded. Starting with the low-level centroids, the best clusters (those with the highest query–centroid similarity) are identified, and some of the documents located in these clusters are then retrieved.

In term clustering, inter-term similarities are calculated on the basis of the numbers of documents in which pairs of terms co-occur. The use of term co-occurrence data would provide a simple and direct way of identifying semantic relationships between terms, and hence of constructing a thesaurus.[12] Several researchers have used term clustering techniques for building associative thesauri that may be used to help users in query expansion.

Co-word analysis is a study that counts and analyses the co-occurrences of key-words in the publications of a given subject. Many researchers have used co-word analysis as an important method of exploring the concept network in different subjects; for example, in software engineering (Coultern, Monarch and Konda[13]), polymer chemistry (Callon, et al.[14]), neural network research (Noyons and van Raan[15]), medicine (Rikken, Kiers and Vos[16]), biology (Looze and Lemarie[17]), information retrieval (Ding, Chowdhury and Foo [18]), and so on. Ding, Chowdhury and Foo[19] show how keyword clustering based on co-word analysis can be used to generate an associative thesaurus. This study took information retrieval as the domain and compared the associative thesaurus against information retrieval terms extracted from three different vocabulary control tools; it commented that the associative thesaurus was better in coverage than the three sources combined.

Index file organization

The elementary units of a text retrieval system are the document records. Each document record comprises a number of fields and subfields, each one of which contains a particular unit of information – author's name, publisher's name, title, keyword(s), class number, ISBN, and so on. The document record may also contain an abstract or full text of the document concerned. A text retrieval system is designed to provide fast access to the records through any of the sought keys or access points. This means that there should be a mechanism for fast access to the document records. What should the basic mechanism be for accessing the document records through some key values – by chosen keyword(s), or by author's name, say? To answer this question, we should first understand how document records are physically stored in the computer.

Document records are stored one after another in the computer memory: this is actually the *virtual structure* of the database file. Imagine a text database that stores a few, say ten, document records. Now, suppose a user wants to check if there is a document in the database that is written by F. W. Lancaster; another user wants to know if there is a book on telecommunication. What would the user's approach be? The simplest way would be to open each document record one after another and to check each and every field; if there is a match then retrieve that document. This process continues until all the document records have been checked. It may be a very simple approach, but one can very well imagine that this will be an extremely slow process even for a faster computer when the text database is relatively large, and will be an impossible proposition for a database that has some hundreds or thousands of document records or more.

What is the solution then? How can we retrieve the desired document records? Let's take a common example. What do we do when we want to locate a particular term or phrase, say the word 'computer', or the phrase 'information retrieval', in a book? Do we start from the first line in the first page and continue up to the last line in the last page of the book? No: we use a simple tool – the back-of-the-book index.

What is such an index? It is a simple alphabetical list of all the potential index terms, drawn from the text of the book, each having a pointer showing the occurrence(s) of the terms. Thus, we look into the index file with the required search term, locate it and then move to the page(s) indicated for the actual information. A similar approach is taken in a text retrieval system: an index file is created that contains all the potential index terms arranged alphabetically. This index file is called an *inverted file*. Users looking for particular information are required to consult the inverted file first, which then leads to the main database where the document records are stored.

Inverted file

In an inverted file system of text retrieval, each database consists of two files. One is the text file, which contains what we would expect to find, that is the document records in their normal form – the form in which they are entered into the database. The other is the inverted file, which contains all the index terms, drawn automatically from the document records according to the indexing technique adopted for the purpose. Each index term in the inverted file is associated with a pointer which shows the record number in which the index term occurs.

The indexing technique, i.e. the technique adopted to draw index terms from the records, determines the order in which index terms will appear in the index file. Different techniques may be required for the purpose: for example, index entries may be required for:

- each and every term occurring in a given field, for example, all the words occurring in the title field. However, there is a risk; some unwanted terms, like 'a', 'an', 'and', 'the', etc., occurring in the document titles may also be indexed. To avoid this problem, text retrieval systems usually incorporate a stop-word file which prevents unwanted terms from being indexed
- the whole field as it is, for example, the full title as it occurs in the document record
- each occurrence of a repeatable field, for example, names of all the authors
- some selected words or phrases from a field or subfield, for example, some terms and phrases occurring in the title field, etc.

Thus, for each significant index term in the database the inverted file contains an entry along with a reference list which specifies position(s) in the database where that term appears. Therefore, in an inverted file system, the searcher first consults the index file, which then refers to the position in the main text database where the desired record appears. The inverted file system is thus an example of *indirect file access*. If the terms are arranged alphabetically in the inverted file, then the file represents an example of *indirect sequential file organization*. Figure 6.2 presents a very simple example of such an inverted file which will help us understand the basic concept of an inverted file. However, as discussed later in this section, in reality the structure of an inverted file looks much more complex than this. As shown in Figure 6.2, index entries are drawn from all four sample document records for the author, title, publisher, and

(a) Document records

Document no. 1
Author: Cunningham, M.
Title: File structure and design
Publisher: Chartwell   -Bratt
Year: 1985
Keywords: File structure; File organization

Document no. 2
Author: Tharp, A.
Title: File organization and processing
Publisher: John Wiley
Year: 1988
Keywords: File structure; File organization

Document no. 3
Author: Ford, N.
Title: Expert systems and artificial intelligence
Publisher: Library Association
Year: 1991
Keywords: Expert systems; Artificial intelligence; Knowledge-based systems

Document no. 4
Author: Charniak, E.; McDermott, D.
Title: Introduction to artificial intelligence
Publisher: Addison   -Wes ley
Year: 1985
Keywords: Artificial intelligence; Expert systems

(b) Index file

4 40 1 1 ADDISON-WESLEY
3 60 1 2 ARTIFICIAL INTELLIGENCE
4 60 1 1 ARTIFICIAL INTELLIGENCE
4 20 1 1 CHARNIAK,E.
1 40 1 1 CHARTWELL-BRATT
1 20 1 1 CUNNINGHAM, M.
3 60 1 1 EXPERT SYSTEMS
4 60 1 2 EXPERT SYSTEMS
3 30 1 1 EXPERT SYSTEMS AND ARTIFICIAL INTELLIGENCE
1 60 1 2 FILE ORGANIZATION
2 60 1 2 FILE ORGANIZATION
2 30 1 1 FILE ORGANIZATION AND PROCESSING
1 60 1 1 FILE STRUCTURE
2 60 1 1 FILE STRUCTURE
1 30 1 1 FILE STRUCTURE AND DESIGN
4 30 1 1 INTRODUCTION TO ARTIFICIAL INTELLIGENCE
3 60 1 3 KNOWLEDGE-BASED SYSTEMS
3 40 1 1 LIBRARY ASSOCIATION
4 20 1 2 MCDERMOTT, D.
2 20 1 1 THARP, A.

Fig. 6 .2   *Sample document records and sample index*

keyword fields. Titles have been indexed as they are, while each occurrence of the author and the keyword field in the document records has been indexed.

Figure 6.2 shows the essence of an inverted file approach. However, an inverted file may contain a lot of other information along with each entry, such as the number of occurrences of the term in a given record or position information, such as the field in which the term/phrase occurs, where the term/phrase occurs in a given sentence/paragraph, and so on.

The field tag is used to denote the field where the given term/phrase occurs. This information is used in field-specific searches (discussed in Chapter 9). Similarly, the position information is used for proximity or adjacency searching (discussed in Chapter 9). Other types of information may also be stored along with each entry, and each such item of information facilitates a particular type of search. Nevertheless, the more such information is added to each entry, the more bulky the inverted file becomes, and therefore takes more storage space and processing time. In this example, a user looking for a term 'expert systems' will retrieve two records, document numbers 3 and 4 from the database, while another user looking for a book written by 'Tharp, A.' will retrieve book number 2. A complex query with search terms combined by Boolean operators will follow the same path. For example, a user with a query 'expert systems OR file organization' will retrieve all four document records, while the query 'artificial intelligence AND knowledge-based systems' will retrieve document record number 3. In the first example, as the search terms are joined by the logical operator 'OR', the system will consult the inverted file for each term and then will merge the document numbers retrieved in each case, while in the second case, because the terms are joined by the logical operator 'AND', the retrieved document numbers for both terms will be matched to locate the common document numbers, that is the ones where both terms are present.

Figure 6.2 shows that an index term may occur in several document records, and in each case, several items of information, such as its frequency of occurrence, field(s) in which it has occurred, position information, and so on, have to be stored in the index file. Thus, conceptually the structure of an inverted file may look like the one shown in Figure 6.3.

Figure 6.3 shows that each term may occur in a number of documents (for example, Term 1 occurs in Doc1, Doc5), and in each case we need to store information on the number of occurrences (O), field of occurrence (F), position information (P), and so on. Thus, for a large number of terms, the index file may be quite large and complex. In order to avoid this, in the inverted file organization, information about index terms is stored in two different files. Let us take a simple example: suppose, we have a file of 10,000 documents for which there are 1000 index terms. Two different files can be created to store information about the index terms. The first file may be quite short containing, only 1000 entries, each entry having only three fields: where field 1 contains the index term, field 2 contains the frequency of occurrence (this information is used for a number of purposes in a search), and field 3 contains the address of the block containing the addresses of documents whose document profiles include the descriptor from field 1. Such an index file can easily fit into the primary storage where a fast search for a required search term can be performed. The second file con-

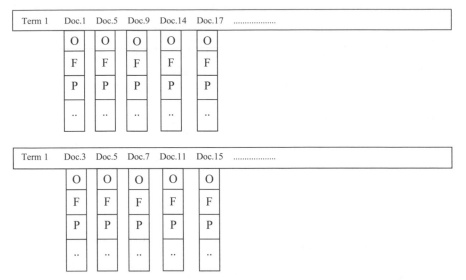

Fig. 6.3 *A simple view of an entry in an inverted file*

sists of a number of blocks where each block contains the addresses and other associated information of those documents where the given search term occurs. The second file may be quite large because each index term may have occurred in a number of records, and therefore, some blocks may contain several lists of addresses. This is handled by linked lists and pointers. Figure 6.4 shows such an index file.

Figure 6.4 shows that for the Term49, we need to store only the address for the first record where it occurs, which in this case is 105. Thus, a pointer from the first file points to an address block where the document and the associated information is stored. Here, after the information about the first document, there is again a pointer that leads to address block 612, and next one to the address block 911, and finally there is a null pointer ($\wedge$) indicating that it is the end of the list. Thus, we need only one address for each descriptor in the index file. This is the address of the first block

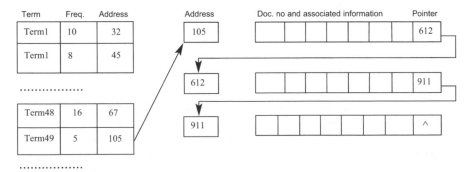

Fig. 6.4 *Index file and linked list*

containing the address of document indexed by the given descriptor, which may lead to the subsequent address blocks each containing the document number and other associated information.

Access to inverted files

The user may pose a single key query or a multiple key query. In the former case, the value of a single search key (say the name of the author) is used as the retrieval criterion, whereas in a multiple key search a number of search keys (say the name of the author, subject name, date of publication, and so on, as in the query 'papers written by Salton on information retrieval systems between 1980 and 1990'). For single key searches, the whole file can be maintained in an order according to the value of the given single set of keys. In a telephone directory, for example, users search through the names of subscribers and therefore the names of subscribers are arranged in alphabetical order. File access in multikey searches is complicated by the fact that it is not possible to order the file simultaneously in accordance with the values of the different search keys. For example, a users' file in a library can be arranged according to the name of the user, occupation or specialization, address or department, and so on, and in each case the resulting arrangement of the records within one field will be different from the other.

In the case of a multikey search, a principal key is to be identified and the file can be ordered in accordance with the values of that key. When the principal key is used as part of a search statement, the subsection of the file corresponding to the given principal key value can then be isolated and subjected to a separate search based on the values of any secondary keys also included in the search query. A catalogue of a library can be considered as a multikey file, where the keys are the author, title, publisher, subject, etc. In such a file, the principal key is usually the author, i.e. the file is ordered in accordance with the name (surname) of the authors. From each record in the main file there may be a number of pointers giving access to secondary keys, like publisher, title, etc. A simple file of authors and publishers can be ordered according to the author's name as the principal key, with a sparse index giving access to a chain of pointers for each publisher name. Documents published by a given publisher can be found by following the pointer chain. Pointer chains can be provided for all secondary keys in addition to the primary keys attached to the records; each given record can be traced through the pointer chain for any of the keys. This type of record organization is known as a multilist.[20]

Multilist organization, however, becomes too time-consuming when each query key is attached to a large number of records. One solution to this might be to use large indexes that provide one pointer for each record exhibiting a given key value. Such an index is called an inverted index or an inverted file. Inverted files are widely used in operational information retrieval situations. The advantage of using inverted files is that such files allow extremely rapid search and retrieval operations, based only on the information provided in the index rather than on data from the main record file.[21]

One important issue for the inverted file system is the size of the index file. If each and every term occurring in the document database is indexed, then size of the index file will be quite large, equal to that of the main document database. Therefore, in order to facilitate fast searching, we need to have a method that allows fast access to the terms/phrases in the inverted file. In other words, we need to have an efficient file organization technique. The rest of this chapter discusses file organization techniques with particular reference to those that are used in information retrieval systems. The discussion begins with the simple sequential file access techniques which is followed by more sophisticated techniques, such as binary and B-tree organization, and to direct access methods such as hashing and text signature.

Sequential access

As mentioned earlier, the easiest approach to consult an inverted file is the sequential access method, that is, looking for each index term one after another from the beginning until:

- either the sought term is found, or
- a key with a higher key value is reached, or
- the end of the index file is reached.

However, the time taken for a sequential search depends on two factors:

1   the key value of the sought key, because the placement of the key will be based on its key value, and
2   the length of the index file.

Sedgewick[20] mentions that a sequential search has two major properties:

1   sequential searches in an unordered file use $N+1$ comparisons (N is the number of records in the file) for an unsuccessful search and an average of $N/2$ comparisons for a successful search
2   sequential searches in an ordered file use about $N/2$ comparisons for both successful and unsuccessful searches.

In an unordered file, each record must be examined to decide whether the record with a given key is present or absent in the file. When no match is found for a given search key, the search is called an unsuccessful search. For a successful search, if we assume that each record in the file is equally likely to be sought, then the average number of comparisons is:

$$1/N \ (1+2+3 \ ... \ +N) = (N+1)/2.$$

The search operation may be simplified if the records in the file are ordered in a particular sequence. In that case, a search can be terminated unsuccessfully when a record with a key higher than the search key is found, and thus the rest of the file need not be searched. The stored order is easy to maintain because a new record can easily be inserted into the file at the point where the unsuccessful search terminated. However, for a larger file, a sequential search can be time-consuming, even if the file is appropriately ordered.[20]

Therefore, a sequential search through a large inverted index file is a very slow process. In an ordered sequential file, an average $N/2$ (N denoting the total number of index terms in the file) searches are to be conducted to accomplish a successful or an unsuccessful search. Thus the number of search probes increases with an increase in the value of N. The sequential method of file access is, therefore, not adopted in inverted file-based text retrieval systems. A number of different methods have been developed to reduce the number of search probes, thereby reducing the search time in a text database.

Alphabetic chain

One way to reduce the number of search probes in an ordered sequential file organization is to use an alphabetic chain.

What is an alphabetic chain? Let's take a simple example. What do we do when we look for a term in a dictionary? Let's suppose that we are looking for the term 'psychology'. We don't start from the beginning of the dictionary but from the letter P, thereby skipping the other letters. Within p we skip terms beginning 'pa', 'pb', etc., and start looking for words beginning 'ps', and then search for the word sequentially. Thus when we use the index we skip some part of the index file so as to reduce the number of words to be searched.

Let us take another example, this time from a library catalogue. What would we do if we had to look for the term 'telecommunication' in a manual library catalogue? We would start our search in the drawer holding those cards that start with the letter t. Then we would follow other tags, if any, to skip some parts of the catalogue file, and select the one where we would expect to find the sought term, the range with a tag 'te–tr', say. Thus there is a mechanism for filing catalogue cards to facilitate the process of searching. The mechanism is an alphabetic chain which leads us to particular blocks, one after another, until we reach a probable location for the sought term.

In an alphabetic chain, if you are looking for a term beginning with 'a', then you take the first block; if it begins with 'b', then you begin with the second block, and so on. For example, if you are looking for the term 'cat', you take the third pointer from the first list, and then the first one from the list that is pointed to, and so on. Thus you would continue down the chain of pointers until the sought term is found or a term is reached whose key value is higher than the term sought, in which case the search term does not occur in the index file; in this process you avoid searching a large part of the index file, thereby greatly reducing the search time.

One problem with the alphabetic chain is that in a subject field many terms occur whose key values or alphabetic positions are very close to one another, e.g. computation, computations, computational, computer, computers, computerization, etc. These terms are said to be in the *densely populated* area of the alphabet. The trouble is that if most words are in the densely populated area of the alphabet, most of the searches take six or seven probes to locate the sought term.[1, 2] The problem could be solved if we had some means to spread the densely populated parts of the alphabet, so that all the terms could be accessed in more or less the same time.

Binary search

We have already seen that for a large index file the sequential search is quite a time-consuming process. An improvement would be a reduction in the number of probes required in conducting a search. If we have an ordered file of index terms, we can reduce the number of probes needed to retrieve an index term by applying a binary search technique.

As the term binary suggests, the basic mechanism followed is to divide the search file automatically into two parts at successive levels and thereby reduce the number of search probes.

A binary search compares a key of the sought term with the middle record, which is identified automatically, then either the sought term is located or half of the file is eliminated for further consideration. The process of elimination is governed by a simple logic – if the sought term comes before the middle term then the right half is eliminated and a further search is conducted with the left half; similarly, if the sought term comes after the middle term, then the first half is discarded and the second half is considered for a further search; this process continues until the sought term is found or only one term in the file is left, in which case the search is an unsuccessful one. Figure 6.5 presents an algorithm for the binary search mechanism.

Let's take a simple example to show how the binary search principle works. Suppose we have a list of ten keywords as follows:

communication   computation   computational   computer   data
dictionary   information   informetrics   network   software

Now, suppose we are looking for the term 'network'. In a simple sequential search we have to make nine search probes to locate the term. Let's see how many probes will be required in a binary search.

```
Begin
    lower = 1; upper = n;
    while lower <= upper do
        begin
            middle = (upper + lower) div 2;
            if key_sought = key [middle] then term is found
            else
            if key_sought > key [middle] then lower := middle + 1
            else
            upper := middle – 1;
        end;
End;
```

Fig. 6.5   *Binary search algorithm*

Step 1

To begin with, lower = 1 and upper = 10. Hence the middle is (1 + 10)/2 = 5 (fractions are not considered). So first we match our search term with that in the fifth position in the list, i.e. 'data':

> communication   computation   computational   computer   **data**
> dictionary   information   informetrics   network   software

Our search term, i.e. 'network', has a key value above that of the middle term. Hence, we discard the first half and the 'lower' now becomes 6 (see the algorithm: lower = middle + 1).

Step 2

Having discarded the first half of the file we concentrate on that half having five terms beginning with the term 'dictionary'. The middle term now is the one in position 8 (middle = (lower, i.e. 6, + upper, i.e.10)/2), which is 'informetrics':

> dictionary   information   **informetrics**   network   software

Again the search term has key value above that of the middle term, and so the left half is discarded and the search is conducted on the right side of the file.

Step 3

'Lower' is now the term in position 9, i.e. 'network' (lower – middle + 1, i.e. 8 +1 =9). The middle term is now 'network' (middle = (lower, i.e. 9+ upper, i.e. 10)/2 = 9):

> **network**   software

Here we note that the search term matches the middle term, and therefore the search ends successfully.

Thus, we have required three searches to locate the search term as compared to nine searches required in a sequential search. The number of searches to be conducted in a binary search is of the order $O(\log_2 n)$, where n denotes the total number of index terms in the file.[21, 22]

Binary search tree

One problem with the binary search technique is that at each stage the system has to determine the middle term and then only can it continue to search. This could be avoided if there was a mechanism by which all the terms in the index file could be organized according to their key values in such a way that at each stage only two options would be available, and the system could proceed by making only one comparison. In fact, the binary search is most commonly conducted by using a tree structure of records. A tree structure consists of nodes or vertices containing node information, together with pointers giving access to additional nodes of the tree.[1] The defining property of a tree is that every node is pointed to by only one other node, called the parent.[20] A tree organization supports operations such as searching for a record, inserting new records, and deleting records. Tharp[21] defines a binary search tree as a binary tree in which the nodes are used both to store information and to provide direction to other nodes. In binary search trees information is organized in such a manner that all the key values smaller than that of the current node are stored in its left tree and those that are larger are in its right tree.

A tree search is performed by comparing the search key with the key values attached to certain nodes of the tree, starting with the root of the tree. If the search key is not equal to the current node key, then the left or right path is chosen from that node depending upon whether the search key is smaller or larger than the current node key. The point wherefrom a tree originates is called the *root node*. This is the *parent node* which gives pointers to the two *child nodes*. Each of these child nodes again points to its child nodes. Thus, the tree bifurcates from the root and continues until the values of all the child nodes become empty. An empty node is called the *leaf node*. The maximum number of searches to be conducted in a binary tree search is equal to the longest path from the root to a leaf of the tree.

In a binary tree each node carries information pertaining to a particular record, and in each case two pointers give access to two new nodes. The defining property of a binary tree is that each node has a left and a right link. In order to find a record with a given key in a binary search, first it is to be compared against the root, if it is smaller then the left subtree is to be followed, if it is equal then the search stops, and if it is larger then the right subtree is followed. This method is applied successively. The procedure stops either when a record with the given key is found or a current subtree becomes empty, in which case the record is not available. Figure 6.6 provides a simple example of a binary search tree organization.

It may be noted that the structure of a binary search tree is dependent on the order of insertion of index terms. As the number of terms increases, the depth of the tree also increases and therefore a greater number of searches are required to locate a particular term, especially if it happens to occur at the bottom part of the tree. In fact, the maximum number of key comparisons needed to conduct a binary tree search is equal to the longest path from the root to a leaf of the tree.

The insertion of a new term other than in a leaf node (that is a blank space suitable for an insertion) and deletion of a term from the tree sometimes requires a major reshuffle of the tree. In fact, node deletion in a binary tree is more complicated than node searching or node addition because the proper tree structure must be preserved when a node is deleted.

In order to insert a key in a binary tree, first an unsuccessful search is conducted and then the node is inserted at the empty node where the search had terminated. Deletion of a node in a binary tree is quite a cumbersome job. Salton[1] suggests the following steps for the deletion of a node from a binary tree.

1   If the node to be deleted is the leaf of the tree, then the corresponding node is simply deleted.

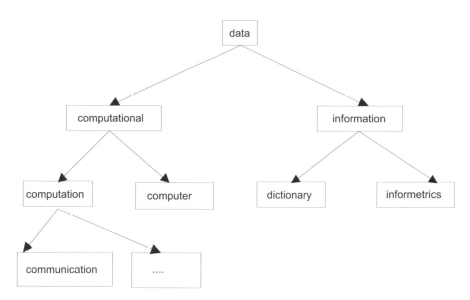

Fig. 6.6 *Sample binary search tree*

2   If the node to be deleted has only one child, that is either the left or the right node of this is empty, then the node to be deleted may be replaced by the only available child node.

3   If the deleted node has two children, then the deleted node information is replaced by the node with the smallest key value in the right subtree.

Balanced tree (B-tree)

A B-tree or a balanced tree, in contrast with a binary tree, is a multiway search tree. A binary tree has a branching factor of two, whereas a balanced tree does not have a theoretical limit to branching factors. A binary tree grows downwards as new terms are added, whereas a B-tree grows upwards with increase in size.

The structure of a B-tree organization looks like a multi-branched tree; at each branch point there is a list of index terms, each one with an accompanying pointer. Thus, with this organization, you find the word that occurs soonest after the one you are searching for in the alphabet. You then follow the corresponding pointer which leads to the next block down in the tree, and there again a pointer is met. Thus after a few moves you reach the bottom (leaf) node where you find the reference list for the sought term; if the sought term is not found there then it does not occur in the index file and therefore it leads to an unsuccessful search. Figure 6.7 provides a simple illustration of a B-tree.

The composition of a B-tree node is similar to a bucket or a block in that it also contains multiple entries. The number of records that may be stored depends on its capacity order, which is specified in the formal definition of the B-tree. Typically the capacity order of a B-tree is between 50 and 200.[21] Each node contains a key value

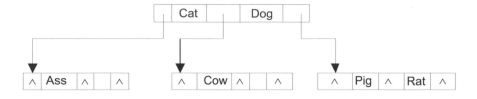

Fig. 6.7   *B-tree of order one*

with two associated pointers. The left pointer indicates a key of a lower key-value, while the right pointer indicates a key of a higher key-value. Since leaf nodes do not have any offspring, they are associated with a null pointer (∧). A B-tree of capacity order one has nodes with one or two keys and two or three pointers.[13, 15]

Suppose, we want to conduct a search for the index term 'rat'. We first compare it with the root word, that is 'cat'. Since the key value of the search term is higher than that of the node, we then compare the search term with the term placed to its right, that is 'dog'. We do not find a match but we get a pointer to another term with a key value 'pig'. Upon comparison we find that the search term has a key value that is higher than this term, and thus we move to the right of the term already searched, where we find another term with a key value 'rat'. Here we find a match and thus come to the end of a successful search.

Figure 6.8 shows another example of a B-tree where one term has been added to that represented in Figure 6.7. Let's consider how is it inserted. We start with the B-tree shown in Figure 6.7. We want to insert the term with a key value 'goat'. We follow the same route as we did in conducting a search. We begin with a comparison with the first key in the root, that is 'cat'. As our term has a higher key value, we move to the right and make a comparison with the key 'dog'. Here we find a pointer that leads us to the key 'pig'. Our term has a lower key value than that met here. Thus, the term 'goat' maps to the leaf node with 'pig' and 'rat'. Because that node is full, we have to split it. The key with the term 'pig' is elevated to the root level, and one leaf node is split into two nodes. Now since the root node is full (the one with the key values 'cat' and 'dog') there is no room for the elevated record 'pig'. Thus that root node

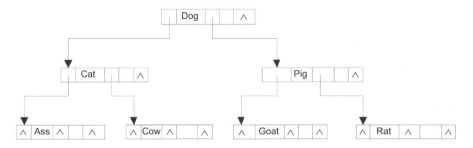

Fig. 6.8   *B-tree of order one (after insertion of the key 'goat')*

is split into two, whereby the key value 'dog' is elevated to the root node, having two leaf nodes accommodating two key values – the lower one with 'cat' takes the left path, whereas the key with 'pig' takes the right path. The B-tree thus formed is shown in Figure 6.8.

The advantage of the B-tree mechanism is that the number of times it is necessary to access a file to reach a reference list is the number of levels in the tree. Because the blocks are always split, rather than new branches being added at the bottom of the tree, new levels are not created until it is absolutely necessary. This actually helps reduce the average retrieval time.

TRIES

Trie is a data structure that was first implemented by Fredkin in 1960.[24] The term 'trie' is taken from the word 're*trie*val' because it is used for data retrieval. The major contribution of trie is that it allows keywords to be represented in a character-by-character format. The trie thereby allows better management of non-numeric, variable-length keywords, and provides a simple way of mapping keywords to storage addresses. It is especially useful for alphabetic keywords because no transformation to a numeric representation (*hashing* – this will be discussed later) is needed, because the alphabetic key is used directly to build or search it.[21]

Of the several representations of the trie, the primary ones are the sequential and linked tries. When the linked trie is converted to a binary linked trie, it becomes a more manageable data structure.[24] Figure 6.9 contains a binary linked trie for the keywords *gallop, gel, gentle, giant, giraffe, glorious, grape, grass,* and *graze*. The first level of the binary trie is searched through the right links for the first character in the keyword. On a match, a down branch is taken to the next level, and the process repeats.

The binary linked trie provides a mechanism for capturing the environment of keyword substrings. At any position in a trie, keywords with the same prefix as a target can be located.[21] This capability enhances prefix searching and approximate string matching.

One concern in using the binary linked trie is the amount of storage that it requires, because both a right and down link field must be stored for each node. The less storage a structure consumes, the faster it can be streamed from the disk into primary memory, and more of it can be held there at a given time.

All the text retrieval systems support some form of B-tree for the inverted file organization. B-tree organization provides faster access to the inverted file and therefore the overall retrieval process becomes faster. Several improvements have taken place in the creation and maintenance of inverted files using B-trees which are discussed in the literature (see for example, Frakes and Baeza-Yates,[25] Nelson,[26] Moffat and Bell.[27])

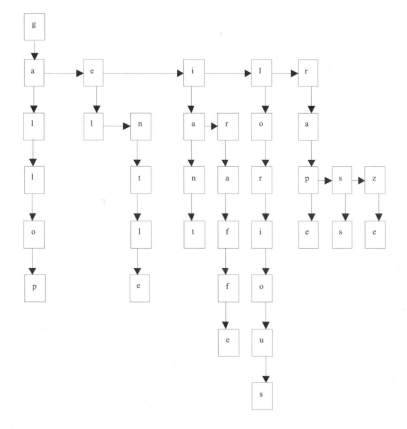

Fig. 6.9 *Binary linked trie*

Alternative text retrieval structures

Inverted file technique is the example of an indirect file access where a search term is first looked for in the inverted file, and if a match is found then the main document database is consulted to retrieve the corresponding record(s). While this is an established practice in information retrieval environment, one major difficulty here relates to the creation and maintenance of the inverted file. This may be avoided in a direct access method where the search term is directly matched with the document records, instead of going through an index.

The easiest way to search a term in a text database might be to compare the given term with each and every term in the text file taking one at a time. For example, if we want to search for the term (called 'pattern' in this context) 'computer' within the text string 'problem solving is a common paradigm of computer science', we have to compare the first symbol of the pattern with the first symbol of the string. If the first symbol matches then we try to match the second symbol of the pattern with the second symbol of the string, and continue to do so if we find a match again. Here the first symbols do not match, and therefore we advance the pattern by one position to the right and try to match with the corresponding symbol of the string. It may be noted that in this example, we have to make 50 matches in order to confirm that the pattern matches the corresponding term in the string.

Although this process seems straightforward it is not possible in practice, because in the worst case the number of matches could be of the order $O(mn)$, where m is the length of the pattern and n is the length of the string.[21] The inverted file system has been designed to deal with this problem. With the alphabetic chain or tree searching technique access to the inverted file may be easier and less time-consuming, but these methods have other problems. Major difficulties arise when the database needs updating. A number of changes need to be made in file access methods whenever any new term needs to be incorporated in or deleted from the alphabetic chain or the tree. In the case of simple serial scanning, this problem would not appear because any new term could be appended to the existing ones without hampering the existing structure. However, the time required for serial scanning remains problematic.

The introduction of parallel processing systems has brought much hope to the text retrieval world. The scanning of large text files can now be performed with parallel processors, which reduces the search time and increases the efficiency. Clayworth[22] mentions that by using parallel processing techniques we can improve the retrieval performance of a serial scanning database to the point where it is comparable to an inverted file database.

In addition to this, some sophisticated methods for search techniques have been developed over the last two decades. Pattern matching algorithms of Boyer and Moore[28] and Aho and Corasick[29] have given rise to quite fast searching techniques. While both of these methods achieve efficiencies in operation by reducing the number of characters in each document that need to be matched against the query patterns, the text signature approach to serial text scanning tries to eliminate some of the documents *in toto* from the pattern matching search.[1,21,23,30]

String matching

The string searching problem can be defined as follows: 'Given two strings $p_1 p_2 p_3 \ldots p_m$, called a pattern, and $a_1, a_2, a_3 \ldots a_n$, called a text, find all indices j with $a_j a_{j+1} \ldots a_{j+m-1} = p_1 p_2 \ldots p_m$.[31]

Knuth, et al.[32, 33] present an algorithm that solves this problem, which runs in time $O(n)$. Aho and Corasick[21] have shown how it can be extended to the multiple pattern problem. In their method, a finite state machine is built which simultaneously recognizes all occurrences of the patterns in a single pass through the text. Such a finite state machine is called a *pattern matching machine*. The running time in the Aho and Corasick method is also $O(n)$. Both these methods (called KMP and AC algorithms respectively) scan the patterns from left to right.

The Boyer and Moore technique of pattern matching

Boyer and Moore[28] developed a method that scans the patterns from right to left. This is contrary to established left-to-right methods, but the Boyer and Moore process has its own merits because it helps reduce the number of search probes significantly. According to this method:[28]

1   if the rightmost symbol of the pattern does not match the corresponding symbol of the string and the symbol does not appear in the pattern, the pattern is moved to the right beyond its current position
2   if the symbol does not match but the symbol (in the string) does appear somewhere in the pattern, the pattern is moved so that the rightmost occurrence of this comparison symbol in the pattern is aligned with the comparison symbol in the string
3   if the rightmost symbol in the pattern matches the corresponding symbol in the string, then the previous (to the left) symbol in the pattern is matched with the corresponding symbol in the string, and the process is continued until a complete match is found or a mismatch between the symbols (in the pattern and in the string) occurs, as shown in the following example.

```
      Problem solving is a common paradigm of computer science
1     computer
2            computer
3                computer
4                  computer
5                    computer
6                       computer
7                          computer
```

We begin by matching the rightmost symbol, r, of the pattern ('computer') with the corresponding symbol, [space], in the string. Here there is no match, and as there is no space character in the pattern, we therefore shift the pattern to its right (step 2). We continue this way until we reach step 3, where we find that the symbol m does not match the pattern symbol r, but note that m does occur in the pattern. Therefore, we align the pattern with the string such that m matches the leftmost m in common. After this, we note that the rightmost symbol r in the pattern does not match the corresponding symbol, which is p. However, p does occur in the pattern, and therefore we align the pattern with the string such that p matches the p in paradigm. After this, we note that the rightmost symbol r in the pattern does not match the corresponding symbol in the string, which is d. We therefore shift the pattern to its right. Here again, we see that the rightmost symbol in the pattern r does not match the corresponding symbol in the string, which is c. However, c does occur in the pattern, and therefore we align the pattern with the string such that the c in the pattern matches the c in computer in the string. Here, we find that the rightmost symbol r in the pattern matches the symbol r in the string. We then match the next character to the left which is e with the corresponding symbol in the string. Here again we find a match, and we continue along this line. After a total of 14 matches we find a complete match. Thus we are making only 14 comparisons in contrast with 50 comparisons required in a naive string search process.

However, for a large amount of text, even the Boyer-Moore (BM) algorithm may require a large number of searches. We may be able to reduce the number of search probes if we can somehow filter the text and reduce the amount of text to be searched. When searching a group of articles, rather than looking at the entire text of each article, one could look only at the abstract in order to asses which of the articles might be of interest, and then search a smaller subset of the articles for the required information. This could be applied to the process of searching by producing what is known as 'text signatures' (discussed in the following section).

It is accepted that the BM algorithm is a fast algorithm for a single pattern.[31] To characterize the efficiency of a string searching algorithm we use the probe rate, which can be defined as the ratio between the total number of references to the text and the length of the text:

$$probe\ rate = \frac{total\ no.\ of\ references\ to\ the\ text}{length\ of\ the\ text}$$

The running time of the BM algorithm is *sublinear*, which means that the probe rate is less than one; for the AC algorithm the probe rate is exactly one, both on an average and in the worst cases.[23]

By combining the AC and BM algorithms, Uratani and Takeda[31] have developed a new string searching algorithm for multiple patterns. For a single pattern it runs faster than the BM algorithm. Moreover, the construction of this algorithm (called the PMM algorithm) requires only linear time proportional to the sum of the lengths of the patterns, like the AC algorithm. The PMM algorithm is the most suitable when all patterns are sufficiently long and the alphabet size is large, but the number of patterns is not very large.[31]

The PMM algorithm

The basic idea of the BM algorithm, as mentioned above, is to match the pattern from right to left. The PMM algorithm uses this idea in the multiple pattern problem as shown in the following example.

Suppose that the collection of patterns {trace, artist, smart} is to be matched with a text string 'the-greatest-artist...'. First, the right ends of the patterns are aligned, which gives rise to:

```
trace
artist
 smart
```

1   Since the length of the shortest pattern is five, the matching is started at the fifth character (in the figures below * denotes a success and x denotes a mismatch):

```
        trace
      artist
       smart
      the-greatest-artist...
           x
```

2   Since g does not occur in any of the patterns in the given position, the patterns can be shifted to the right by five (i.e. the length of the shortest pattern):

```
        trace
      artist
       smart
    the-greatest-artist...
            x*
```

3   The current character e in the text matches the corresponding character in the pattern trace. Therefore, we shift the pointer to the text to the left by one, and we have a mismatch (the character t in the text, against c in the pattern trace).

4   Since the checked substring te of the text does not occur in any pattern, the patterns can again be shifted to the right by five positions (move the pointer to the right by six). Then we have the following:

```
         trace
       artist
        smart
    the-greatest-artist...
            x
```

The current character is a mismatch.

5   So, we align this r with the r in the pattern smart; we shift the patterns to the right by one, giving rise to the following:

```
         trace
       artist
        smart
    the-greatest-artist...
            x***
```

From right to the left, we can see a matching of three characters – t, r, and a – and a fail at the next character, i.e. -.

6   Now we consider the occurrences in the patterns for checking the string -art. In order to do this, we align art with the art in artist by shifting the patterns to the right by three positions (and move the pointer to the right by six). Now we have the following:

```
              trace
             artist
              smart
the-greatest-artist...
           ******
```

This time the characters of the pattern artist match the corresponding characters in the text. It may be noted that we made only 14 references to the text string of 19 characters, and 6 steps were required to confirm the final match. The PMM algorithm consists of three functions: *goto, output,* and *failure*; the *goto* and the *output* functions are nearly the same as the AC algorithm: they form a *trie*, which represents the set of the reversed pattern, and the failure function is used to shift the patterns to the right when a mismatch occurs.[31]

Hashing: a mechanism for directly accessing search terms

The process of searching can be very fast if a bit pattern for each item (here, term) can be generated. Now the question is how can these bit patterns be formed? Remember that the basic objective is to use a mechanism by which key values can be converted to key addresses so that while searching for a given key, a particular location in the computer memory can be accessed to find that key. This technique is known as *hashing*, a method for directly referencing records in a table by doing arithmetic transformations on keys into table addresses (see below). If we know that the keys are distinct integers from 1 to N, then we can store the record with key i in table position i, which can be readily accessed with the key value. Hashing is a generalization of this trivial method for typical searching applications when we don't have such specialized knowledge about the key values.[20]

The first step in a search using hashing is to compute a hash function that transforms the search key into a table address. This is an arithmetic computation having properties similar to random number generation. What is needed is a function that transforms keys (usually integers or short character strings) into integers in the range $[0..M-1]$, where M is the number of records that can fit into the amount of memory available. An ideal hash function is one that is easy to compute and approximates a random function.[20]

The *output* of a hashing function generates a *probable* address for a given key. Several hashing functions are available. One of the most popular is:

Hash (key) $\longrightarrow$ Probable address

$f(key) = key \bmod N$

According to this formula, the hashing function for 27 would be:

27 mod 8 = 3 ($N = 8$, i.e. 8-bit byte)

Another common hashing function is the truncation method. If we have say 123-45-6789 as the key, we may decide to use only three-digits to represent the address.

Folding is another hashing function. Suppose we have a key 123456789. Imagine that the number was divided into three units and the units were written on a piece of paper and then folded, i.e. superimposed. We may then add columns to produce:

```
 3  2  1
 4  5  6
 9  8  7
16 15 14
```

If the superimposed codes were added together without carry we would then obtain the probable address of 654. This process of folding is known as folding by boundary. There are some other folding techniques among the other hashing techniques avalable (for example, see Sedgewick[20]).

All the hashing functions described here required integer arguments. However, this does not mean that we cannot generate a hashing function for alphabetic keys: alphabetic and alphanumeric key values can be input into a hashing function. High level languages provide facilities for interpreting a character string as an integer. For example, in Pascal the construct of *variant records* can be used whereby a field is referred to by multiple names, and in the declaration for the records an association is made as to what data type or interpretation goes with each name. In this way a field can be a character when it is printed and an integer when it is hashed.

Let us take an example to see how hash functions work for a simple text string: 'now is the time to read some books'. We can generate a hash function for each word simply by adding up the lexicographic value of each letter in the words, whereby we would get the following result:

Word	value	word	value
now	52	to	35
is	28	read	28
the	33	some	54
time	47	books	41

Although this is a very simple method, here we will need up to 54 locations (or buckets) to accommodate only 8 words. This may be reduced if we use some other technique to generate the hash functions. Suppose we divide each word value with a prime number, say 19, and take the remainder. In this method we shall get the contents of the buckets as follows:

Word(s)	bucket
books	7
is, time, read	9
now, the	14
to, some	16

Here, we can accommodate all the eight words in four buckets only. However, there is a problem, which occurs when more than one word maps onto one bucket. For example, the words 'is time' and 'read' map onto bucket 9 whereas the two buckets 14 and 16 contain only two words each. This is a typical problem of hashing. Here we have used a very simple measure to generate the hash functions. However, better measures may be taken to spread the words more uniformly into buckets.

Ideally, different keys should map to different addresses, but due to the imperfection of the hash function, two or more different keys can hash to the same table address resulting in, what is known as a *collision*. The second part in the hashing is thus a *collision resolution* process, the most simple one being to build for each table address a linked list of the records whose keys hash to that address. As the keys that hash to the same table position are kept in a linked list, they can be kept in an ordered form as well.

There are several methods by which N records can be stored in a table of size $M > N$, relying on empty places on the table to settle collision resolution, known as open addressing hashing methods.[13] One of the simple open addressing methods is called *linear probing*, whose working principle may be summarized as follows:[20, 22]

When there is a collision, then probe the next position in the table, i.e. compare the key in the record there against the search key. There are three possibilities in such a case: if the keys match then the search terminates successfully; if there is no record in that position then the search terminates unsuccessfully; or the process of probing continues to the next position until either the search key or an empty table position is found. If a record containing the search key is to be inserted following an unsuccessful search, then it can simply be placed in the empty table position which terminated the search.

Text signature

This is yet another method for direct access in which a block of text can be accessed directly. In adding the text signatures to the records of a file we have to preprocess the data so that the search time is reduced.[13] The use of signatures acts as a filtering device. It allows us to quickly filter out those records that cannot possibly contain what we are searching for, thereby reducing the total search time.

A record or text signature is an encoding of the contents of records or lines of text to characterize its essence.[13] A text signature is a function that transforms text words into integers in the range $[0, 2^b-1]$, where b corresponds to the number of bits of the signature; it is important that the transformation function spreads the signatures uniformly in the given interval.[34]

The text signature method works by dividing the file into blocks, each of which contains no more than some fixed number of words. Associated with each block, in a separate file, is a bit pattern that is also of fixed size. In its implementation, a text signature contains bits of information; its length is usually a multiple of the computer word size to allow efficient processing. In adding text signatures to the records of a file we actually preprocess the data so as to minimize the retrieval time. Thus, when we look for information, we generally match the bit pattern of the sought term(s) with the text signatures (Figure 6.10).

Signatures	Text records
| 01101010 |	...............................|
| 10000101 |	...............................|
| 10010101 |	...............................|
| 01101010 |	...............................|
| 10001110 |	...............................|
| 11101110 |	...............................|
| 00100011 |	...............................|
| 11000110 |	...............................|
| 10101001 |	...............................|
| 00010011 |	...............................|

Fig. 6.10 *Text file with signature added*

If the subscript of an array element is considered to be its unique identifier, then a straightforward formula exists to determine its address when the records are stored in contiguous locations:[21]

Location A[i] = ... + m × s

where A = an array of any dimension; i = the typical element; ... = the location of the first element in the array; m = the number of elements preceding the ith element according to a standard ordering, such as lexicographic order; and s = the size (in address units) of an element of the array.

By applying this formula only a single probe is necessary to locate an element of an array. However, this technique has a shortcoming in the sense that a large amount of space has to be kept for storing the key values, much of which might be wasted because the range of acceptable values of keys is much grater than the actual number of keys. In order to avoid this, one may use a function to map the wider range of key values into the narrower range of address values. There are some *hashing functions* that can map multiple key values into a singe address value.[13]

Thus, in producing the text signature, a hashing algorithm produced for each word is used to generate a bit pattern in which a certain fixed number of bits are set. Now, for each block the pattern of set bits is generated by combining together the bit patterns for the words in that block, using the Boolean OR function. Suppose the bit patterns for some index terms have been generated as follows:

Bananas	00100010
Apples	00100100
Nuts	01000100
Sugar	01000010
Ice cream	01000001
Chocolate	10000100
Vanilla	10000010

By superimposing the codes for the terms we can generate text signatures as follows:

Ice cream	01000001
Chocolate	10000100
Chocolate ice cream	11000101

Ice cream	01000001
Vanilla	10000010
Vanilla ice cream	11000011

Apples	00100100
Bananas	00100010
Nuts	01000100
Mixed fruits	01100110

Now, out of these three signatures if we want to know in which 'chocolate' is a component, we have to take the bit pattern of 'chocolate' and compare with the text signatures to check if we have 1s in the same positions in any of the signatures as that of 'chocolate'. 'Chocolate' has a 1 in the first and sixth positions and thus we would retrieve 'chocolate ice cream' because it too has a 1 in the first and sixth positions.

What happens when we are looking for 'nuts'? The code for this term has a 1 in the second and sixth positions. Therefore, we would obviously retrieve 'mixed fruits', because its signature too has a 1 in the second and sixth positions. However, at the same time we would also retrieve 'chocolate ice cream' for the same reason. Similarly, while looking for the term 'sugar', we would have a hit for 'vanilla ice cream' because it has a 1 in the first and seventh positions, though none of the three signatures contain the sought term. These are called *false drops*.

Why do we have false drops? It is because when we condensed the coded information, we lost something; we no longer have the exact information. In other words, as the number of words in the text is generally much bigger than the number of possible integers that can be generated by the hash function, different words may be transformed to the same signature causing the possibility of false drops. This problem, however, can be controlled by the signature length h, i.e. by increasing the code size from 8 to 16 bits.[34, 35]

Signature matching is a very fast process because we are basically matching bits of information. All computers have special built-in mechanisms for processing entire bit strings in a single operation. The compaction factor is also an important issue because by developing text signatures we reduce the size of text files to a significant extent. Typically a text signature file is about 10% of the size of the actual text file that it represents (compare this with inverted index files, which are about the same size as the text files, i.e. 100%), and the probability of false drops in a good text signature method is less than 1%.[14] Thus, with the help of the text signature, the search time can be reduced to 10%, because the time to search a file is proportional to the amount of text to be read.

Discussion

Inverted file techniques are used in all the major information retrieval systems, including online and CD-ROM databases, available today. However, this is nothing new. As Frants, Shapiro and Voiskunskii[36] report, the ideas underlying the creation of inverted files have been known since the 1960s. However, as the sophistication of information retrieval systems increased, several improvements took place in the organization and access to the inverted files. The impact of some search techniques, commonly available in information retrieval systems, on the organization of inverted files, particularly the B-tree organization, have been discussed in Chapter 9, along with the search techniques concerned. In fact, indexing and file organization has drawn much attention of researchers since the introduction of computers in information retrieval about four decades ago,[37–39] and with the recent developments in the Internet and World Wide Web (discussed in Chapter 18), a number of researchers are now engaged in developing improved indexing and file organization techniques for managing digital information resources. Some of these research activities are discussed in Chapters 18 and 22.

References

1   Salton, G., *Automatic text processing: the transformation, analysis, and retrieval of information by computer*, Reading, MA, Addison Wesley, 1989.
2   Borko, H. and Bernier, C. L., *Indexing concepts and methods*, New York, Academic Press, 1978.
3   Salton, G., 'Automatic indexing and abstracting'. In Willett, P. (ed.), *Document retrieval systems*, London, Taylor-Graham, 1988, 42–80.
4   Harter, S. P., 'Statistical approaches to automatic indexing'. In Willett, P. (ed.), *Document retrieval systems*, London, Taylor-Graham, 1988, 81–98.
5   Luhn, H. P., 'A statistical approach to the mechanical encoding and searching of literary information', *IBM journal of research and development*, 1 (4), 1957, 309–17.
6   Sparck Jones, K., 'A statistical interpretation of term specificity and its application in retrieval', *Journal of documentation,* 28 (1), 1972, 11–21.
7   Salton, G. and Yong, C. S., 'On the specification of term values in automatic indexing', *Journal of documentation*, 29 (4), 1973, 351–72.
8   Salton, G. and McGill, M. J., *Introduction to modern information retrieval*, New York, McGraw-Hill, 1983.
9   Croft, W. B., 'Boolean queries and term dependencies in probabilistic retrieval models', *Journal of the American Society for Information Science*, 37 (2), 1986, 71–7.
10   Lancaster, F. W., Elliker, C., and Colonell, T. H., 'Subject analysis'. In M. E. Williams (ed.), *Annual review of information science and technology*, 24, 1989, 35–84.
11   van Rijsbergen, C. J., *Information retrieval*, 2nd edn, London, Butterworth, 1979.
12   Sparck Jones, K. and Willett, P., 'Techniques'. In Sparck Jones, K. and Willett, P. (eds.), *Readings in information retrieval*, San Francisco, Morgan Kaufmann, 1996, 305–12.

13   Coulter, N., Monarch, I., and Konda, S., 'Software engineering as seen through its research literature: a study in co-word analysis', *Journal of the American Society for Information Science*, **49** (13), 1206–1223.

14   Callon, M., Courtial, J. and Laville, F., 'Co-word analysis as a tool for describing the network of interaction between basic and technological research: the case of polymer chemistry', *Scientometrics*, **22** (1), 1991, 155–205.

15   Noyons, E. and van Raan, A., 'Advanced mapping of science and technology', *Scientometrics*, **41** (1–2), 1998, 61–7.

16   Rikken, P., Kiers, H. and Vos, R., 'Mapping the dynamics of adverse drug reactions in subsequent time periods using INDSCAL', *Scientometrics*, **33** (3), 1995, 367–80.

17   Looze, M. and Lemarie, J., 'Corpus relevance through co-word analysis: an application to plant proteing', *Scientometrics*, **39** (3), 267–80.

18   Ding, Y., Chowdhury, G. and Foo, S., 'Bibliometric cartography of information retrieval research by using co-word analysis', *Information processing and management*, **37** (6), 2001, 817–42

19   Ding, Y., Foo, S. and Chowdhury, G., 'Incorporating the results of co-word analyses to increase search variety for information retrieval', *Journal of information science*, **26** (6), 2000, 429–52.

20   Sedgewick, R., *Algorithms*, 2nd edn, Reading, MA, Addison Wesley, 1988.

21   Tharp, A., *File organization and processing*, New York, Wiley, 1988.

22   Clayworth, D., 'File structures for text retrieval'. In Gillman, P. (ed.), *Text retrieval: the state of the art*, London, Taylor-Graham, 1990, 141–58.

23   Cunningham, M., *File structure and design*, Chichester, Chartwell-Bratt, 1985.

24   Cooper, L. K. D. and Tharp, A. L., 'Multi-character tries for text searching', *Information processing and management*, **29** (2), 1993, 197–207.

25   Frakes, W. B. and Baeza-Yates, R. (eds.), *Information retrieval: data structures and algorithms*, Englewood Cliffs, NJ, Prentice Hall, 1992.

26   Nelson, M. J., 'A prefix trie index for inverted files', *Information processing and management*, **33** (6), 1997, 739–44.

27   Moffat, A. and Bell, T. A. H., 'In situ generation of compressed inverted files', *Journal of the American Society for Information Science*, **46** (7) 1995, 537–50.

28   Boyer, R. S. and Moore, J. S., 'A fast string searching algorithm', *Communications of the ACM*, **20** (10), 1977, 762–72.

29   Aho, A. V. and Corasick, M. J., 'Efficient string matching: an aid to bibliographic search', *Communications of the ACM*, **18** (6), 1975, 333–40.

30   Ashford, J. and Willett, P., *Text retrieval and document databases*, Chichester, Chartwell-Bratt, 1988.

31   Uratani, N. and Takeda, M., 'A fast string-searching algorithm for multiple patterns', *Information processing and management*, **29** (6), 1993, 775–91.

32   Knuth, D. E., Morris, J. H. and Pratt, V. R., *Fast pattern matching in strings*, Technical Report CS-74-440., Stanford, CA, Stanford University, 1974.

33   Knuth, D. E., Morris, J. H. and Pratt, V. R., 'Fast pattern matching in strings', *SIAM journal on computing*, **6** (2), 1977, 323–50.

34   Knuth, D. E., *The art of computer programming*, vol. 3: *Sorting and search-*

ing, Reading, MA, Addison Wesley, 1973.

35   Macleod, I. A., 'Storage and retrieval of structural documents', *Information processing and management*, **26** (2), 1990, 197–208.

36   Frants, V. J., Shapiro, J. and Voiskunskii, V. G., *Automated information retrieval: theory and methods*, San Diego, Academic Press, 1997.

37   Frakes, W. B., 'Introduction to information storage and retrieval systems'. In Frakes, William B. and Baeza-Yates, Ricardo (eds.), *Information retrieval: data structures & algorithms*, Englewood Cliffs, NJ, Prentice Hall, 1992, 1–27.

38   Meadow, Charles T., *Text information retrieval systems*, San Diego, Academic Press, 1992.

39   Sparck Jones, K. and Willett, P., 'Overall introduction'. In Sparck Jones, K. and Willett, P. (eds.), *Readings in information retrieval*, San Francisco, Morgan Kaufmann Pub. Inc., 1997, 1–7.

Chapter 7

Vocabulary control

Introduction

Vocabulary control is one of the most important components of an information retrieval system. As we have noted from its simple model given in Chapter 1, an information retrieval system tries to match user queries with the stored documents (document surrogates) and retrieves those that match. In order to match the contents of the user requirements (the search terms) with the contents of the stored documents (the document records), one must follow a vocabulary that is common to both. In other words, user requirements need to be translated and put to the retrieval systems in the same language (using the same terms, for example) as was used to express the contents of the document records. This leads us to the concept of using a standard or controlled vocabulary in an information retrieval environment.

Davis and Rush[1] define the term vocabulary control in a simple way that can be reproduced as follows. Indexing may be thought of as a process of labelling items for future reference. Considerable order can be introduced into the process by standardizing the terms that are to be used as labels. This standardization is known as vocabulary control, the systematic selection of preferred terms.

According to Lancaster[2] the process of subject indexing involves two quite distinct intellectual steps: the 'conceptual analysis' of the documents and 'translation' of the conceptual analysis into a particular vocabulary. The second step in any information retrieval environment involves a 'controlled vocabulary', that is a limited set of terms that must be used to represent the subject matter of documents. Similarly, the process of preparing the search strategy also involves two stages: conceptual analysis and translation. The first step involves an analysis of the request (submitted by the user) to determine what the user is really looking for, and the second step involves translation of the conceptual analysis to the vocabulary of the system.

A number of vocabulary control tools have been designed over the years: they differ in their structure and design features, but they all have the same purpose in an information retrieval environment. Availability of vocabulary control helps both the indexers, i.e. people who are engaged in creating document records, particularly those who create subject representation for the documents (by using keywords, in a post-coordinate system, for example), as well as the end-users in the formulation of their search expressions. A large number of software packages are now available that allow the record creator to automatically switch to one or more chosen online vocabulary control tools in order to select appropriate terms for representing the document in hand. This helps in a number of ways – the document records do not only contain a number of terms that are representative of the contents of the document, but these are also standardized (in terms of their usage, spelling, form, and so on) and are likely to be chosen by the user for searching purposes. Similarly, there are programs available by which end-users may go to the appropriate page of a particular online vocabulary control tool in order to choose the most appropriate term(s) for preparing the search expression. Vocabulary control tools also help end-users modify their previously formulated search expressions by either widening or narrowing down the search expressions.

Lancaster[2] identifies two major objectives of vocabulary control in an information retrieval environment:

1   to promote the consistent representation of subject matter by indexers and searchers, thereby avoiding the dispersion of related materials. This is achieved through the control (merging) of synonymous and nearly synonymous expressions and by distinguishing among homographs
2   to facilitate the conduct of a comprehensive search on some topic by linking together terms whose meanings are related paradigmatically or syntagmatically.

Lancaster adds that indexing tends to be more consistent when the vocabulary used is controlled, because indexers are more likely to agree on the terms needed to describe a particular topic if they are selected from a pre-established list than when given a free hand to use any terms they wish. Similarly, from the searcher's point of view, it is easier to identify the terms appropriate to information needs if these terms must be selected from a definitive list. Thus controlled vocabulary tends to match language of indexers and searchers.

A large number of documents have appeared covering the details of various vocabulary control tools. There are also standards such as BS 5723,[3] BS 6723,[4] ISO 2788,[5] ISO 5964,[6] and UNISIST guidelines.[7, 8] In this chapter, we shall try to understand what a vocabulary control tool is and how it controls the vocabulary in an information retrieval environment. We shall also learn about the various vocabulary control tools, their characteristic features, mechanisms of development, and so on. Finally we shall look into the creation, maintenance and usage aspects of online vocabulary control devices.

Controlled vs natural indexing

Controlled indexing languages are those in which both the terms that are used to represent subjects and the process whereby terms are assigned to particular documents are controlled or executed by a person.[9] Normally there is a list of terms, a subject headings list or a thesaurus, that acts as the authority list in identifying terms that may be assigned to documents, and indexing involves the assignation of terms from this list to specific documents. The searcher is expected to consult the same controlled list during formulation of a search strategy. In natural language indexing, any term that appears in the title, abstract or text of a document record may be an index term. There is no mechanism to control the use of terms for such indexing. Similarly, the searcher is not expected to use any controlled list of terms.

Svenonius[10] divides the debate concerning natural and controlled vocabulary into three eras, which Rowley[9] modified, as shown in Table 7.1.

Table 7.1 *The four eras of debate on controlled vs. natural language indexing*

Era one – controlled vocabulary

Era two – comparisons of natural and controlled language: major experimental studies noted that natural language can perform as well as controlled vocabulary, but other factors, such as the number of access points, are also significant.

Era three – many case studies of limited generalizability. Searching online databases was considered. It was noted that the best performance can be achieved by a combination of controlled and natural language; the number of access points was reaffirmed to have a significant effect; full-text and bibliographic databases were noted to have produced different results

Era four – new advances in user-based systems including OPACs. The value of controlled vocabulary in the context of user-friendly interfaces and the development of knowledge bases were noted.

Aitchison and Gilchrist[11] provide a comparison of natural and controlled language indexing, which is shown in Table 7.2. Rowley[9] mentions that despite much debate extending over more than a century, together with a range of research projects, information scientists have failed to resolve the issue concerning the relative merits and demerits of controlled and natural language. However, practice and tested research have suggested that controlled language and natural language should be used in conjunction with one another.

Table 7.2 *Comparison between controlled and natural language*

Natural language	Controlled language
High specificity gives precision. Excels in retrieving 'individual' terms – names of persons, organizations, etc.	Lack of specificity, even in detailed systems
Exhaustivity gives potential for high recall (does not apply to title-only databases)	Lack of exhaustivity. Cost of indexing to the level of natural language is prohibitive. Also terms may be omitted in error by indexers
Up-to-date. New terms are immediately available	Not immediately up-to-date. Time lag while terms are added to thesaurus
Words of author used – no misinterpretation by indexer	Words of author liable to be misconstrued. Errors in indexing terms can cause losses

(continued)

Table 7.2 *(continued)*

Natural language words used by indexer as well as the searcher	Artificial language has to be learnt by the searcher
Low input costs	High input costs
Easier exchange of material between databases – language incompatibility removed	Incompatibility a barrier to easy exchange
Intellectual effort placed on searcher. Problems arise with terms having many synonyms and near-synonyms	Eases the burden of searching: – controls synonyms and near synonyms and leads to specific preferred terms to broaden search – qualifies homographs – provides scope notes – displays broader, narrower and related terms – expresses concepts elusive in free text
Syntax problems. Danger of false drops through incorrect term association	Overcomes syntax problems with compound terms and other devices
Exhaustivity may lead to loss of precision	At normal levels of indexing, avoids precision loss through over-exhaustivity (i.e. retrieval of minor concepts of peripheral interest)
An asset in numerical databases and multilingual systems	

Vocabulary control tools

As the name suggests, these are the tools used to control the vocabulary of indexing and retrieval. These are natural language tools, meaning that these tools contain natural language terms that can be used for indexing and retrieval purposes. What an indexer and an index user need is a set of guidelines for the proper selection of terms. Syndetic structures are devices that provide these guidelines by showing the relationships among terms or concepts, and they fall into two major categories: (1) classification schemes, and (2) subject heading lists and thesauri.[1] Classification schemes, being tools for organizing knowledge, could be of great help for vocabulary control but the main body of classification schemes is organized in an artificial language, whereas for vocabulary control we need natural language representation. Indexes to classification schemes could serve the role of vocabulary control but here terms appear alphabetically and thus the logical (semantic) organization of knowledge is not available. Some attempts have been made to combine the features of the main arrangement in classification schemes with those that appear in the index to the classification scheme to generate some kind of faceted or classified thesaurus (see below for discussion).

Both subject heading lists and thesauri contain alphabetically arranged terms with necessary cross references and notes that can be used for indexing or searching in an information retrieval environment. However, there is a difference. Subject heading lists were initially developed to prepare entries/headings in a subject catalogue that could replicate the classified arrangement of document records. Therefore, they include rather broader subject terms or headings. On the other hand thesauri have been developed on specific subject fields with a view to bringing together the various representations of terms (synonyms, spelling variants, homonyms, etc.) along with an indication of a mapping of that term in the universe of knowledge by indicating the broader (superordinate), narrower (subordinate), and related (coordinate and collateral) terms. However, this distinction has gradually faded and the latest Library of Congress subject headings list indicates the terms' features as shown in normal thesauri.

The following sections discuss different kinds of vocabulary control tools, including subject headings lists, thesauri, the thesaurofacet and the classaurus. However, emphasis will be given to the concept, development, use, etc., of the thesaurus.

Subject headings lists

The subject headings used in the dictionary catalogues of the Library of Congress (LCSH) are the most important and broadest general list of subject headings covering all known subjects. *Sears list of subject headings* is a smaller work designed for small to medium-sized libraries.

The LCSH contains a complete entry vocabulary of the Library of Congress catalogues. It is available in various formats including hard copy, CD-ROM, microfiche, and so on. The latest edition is the twentieth, published in 1997. LCSH is the most widely used tool for assigning subject headings to manual and machine-readable catalogues. It is also now being used to control vocabulary in the virtual library environment (see for example, INFOMINE, an academic virtual library located at the University of California, Riverside, at **http://lib-www.ucr.edu**). The approved subject headings, in LCSH, are set in bold face while those in the entry vocabulary only, e.g. synonyms, appear in normal type face. Each entry may be accompanied by all or some of the following:

1   a scope note showing how the term may be used
2   a list of headings to which *see also* references may be made
3   a list of headings from which *see* references may be made, and
4   a list of headings from which *see also* references may be made.

The following are examples of a typical entry in LCSH. Each preferred term (appearing in bold face) is followed by an LC class number. There may also be some scope note, as appears under **Computer software**, which delineates the scope of the term/phrase. UF (used for) denotes the non-preferred headings for the given term/phrase, while NT, BT and RT denote narrower, broader, and related terms, respectively. SA (see also) provides hints as to where related materials may be found. Some headings can be further subdivided geographically and this is indicated by the phrase '*May Subd Geog*' immediately after the heading. A preferred heading may further be subdivided to generate an appropriate preferred heading: two levels of subdivision are shown in Figure 7.1, e.g. 'Computer software—Accounting', and 'Computer software—Accounting—Law and legislation'.

Computer software
    [QA76.755]
    Here are entered general works on computer programs along with documentation such as manuals, diagrams and operating instructions, etc. Works limited to computer programs are entered under Computer programs

    UF   Software, Computer
    RT   Computer software industry
           Computers
           Programming (Electronic computers)
    SA   *subdivisions* Software *and* Juvenile *software under subjects for actual software items*
    NT   Application software
           CLEMMA (Computer system)
           Communications software
           Computer programs
           Computer viruses
           Electronic data processing documentation
           Free computer software
           Integrated software
           Interactive media
           Master graphics software
           PFS software
           Shareware (Computer software)
           Systems software
        – Accounting
           [HF5681.C57]
         – – Law and legislation
           (*May Subd Geog*)
        – Catalogs
           UF   Computer programs— Catalogs
        – Development
           [QA76.76D47]

    UF   Development of computer software
          Software development
    RT   Computer programming management
    NT   POLYP (Computer system)
– Human factors
    [QA76.76.H85]
    UF   Computer software ergonomics
          Human factors in computer software
          Software ergonomics
    BT   Human engineering
– Law and legislation (*May Subd Geog*)
– Products liability
    USE Products liability— Computer software
– Reusability
    [QA76.76.R47]
    UF Reusability of software
         Reusable code (Computer programs)
         Software reusability
– Taxation (*May Subd Geog*)
– – Law and legislation
    (May Subd geog)
– Validation (*May Subd Geog*)
    [QA76.76.V47]
    UF Software validation
         Validation of software
– Verification (*May Subd Geog*)
    [QA76.76V47]
    UF Software verification
         Verification of software

Fig. 7.1   *Sample LCSH entry*

LCSH provides all the reciprocal entries for USE/UF, NT/BT, BT/NT and RT/RT relations. For example, the heading **Computer software** has *Computer programs* as one of the NTs. Now if we look at the entry under **Computer programs** (Figure 7.2), we shall find the heading *Computer software* shown as the Broader Term.

Sears list of subject headings is smaller in scope than LCSH, but is used extensively, particularly in smaller libraries, for the purpose of assigning subject headings. This tool prescribes, as a general rule: *enter a work under the most specific term, i.e. subject heading, that accurately and precisely represents its content.* For example, '*a work on 'Bridges' should be entered under 'Bridges' and not under a broader heading 'Engineering'.* However, there are a number of rules that have been formulated in this list in order to resolve conflict between alternative headings. A typical entry in the Sears' *List* would look like the following:

Skis and Skiing
 see also **Water Skiing**
 x *Skiing, Snow*
 xx Winter Sports

An entry beginning with '*see also*' indicates that reference entries from the general heading are to be made to the specific headings (appearing after '*see also*'). An entry beginning with '**xx**' indicates that *see also* references are to be made from the specific heading to the general heading (appearing after '**xx**'). An entry beginning with '*x*' indicates that *see* reference entries from the unused heading (appearing after '*x*') are to be made to the used heading.

Sears now uses thesaurus-type cross-references (BT, NT, RT, SA, USE, and UF), and detailed explanations concerning these relations and the previously used *see* and *see also* references appear at the beginning of the list.[12] Detailed discussions on LCSH and Sears appear in a number of publications (see for example Foskett[13] and Rowley[14]).

Computer programs
 Here are entered works limited to computer programs.
 General works on computer programs along with documentation
 such as manuals, diagrams and operating instructions, etc. are entered
 under Computer software.
    UF   Computer program files
           Files, Computer program
           Program files, Computer
           Programs, Computer
    BT   Computer files
           Computer software
    SA   *subdivision* Computer programs *under subjects.*
        ...

Fig. 7.2 *Sample LCSH entry*

Thesauri

Thesauri appeared in the late 1950s. They were designed for use with the emerging post-coordinate indexing systems of that time, which needed simple terms with low pre-coordination, which was not provided by existing indexing languages.[15] These tools represent a popular method of ordering combinatory documentary languages, and thus a priori relationships between concepts are made explicit. Guinchat and Menou[16] define thesauri as tools consisting of a controlled set of terms linked by hierarchical or associative relations, which mark any needed equivalence relations (synonyms) with terms from the natural language and concentrate on a particular area of knowledge. Rowley[14] defines a thesaurus as a compilation of words and phrases showing synonyms and hierarchical and other relationships and dependencies, the function of which is to provide a standardized vocabulary for information storage and retrieval systems. The major objective of a thesaurus is to exert terminology control in indexing, and to aid in searching by alerting the searcher to the index terms that have been applied.

According to Aitchison,[15] recognition of the thesaurus as a widely-used form of indexing tool came with the first international standard for the construction of monolingual thesauri in 1974. Since then the processes of developing and maintaining thesauri have been standardized. There are international (ISO 2788[5] and ISO 5964[6]), British (BS 5723[3] and BS 6723[4]) and UNISIST standards (called UNISIST Guidelines.[7, 8]) BS 5723 defines a thesaurus in terms of its purpose and its structure:

(a) *Purpose*: A thesaurus serves four major purposes, such as:
1   to control the term used in indexing, providing a means of translating the natural language authors, indexers and enquirers into the more constrained language used for indexing and retrieval;
2   to ensure, through the provision of a controlled language, consistent practice between different indexers, employed by the same agency, or between indexers employed by different agencies in a cooperative network;
3   to limit the number of terms that need to be assigned to a document. The terms assigned to a document should represent, as specifically as possible, the concepts described by the author, but they need not include terms of broader connotation and other related terms if these are implied by normal frames of reference and can therefore be displayed effectively in a thesaurus; and
4   to serve as a search aid in retrieval, including retrieval from free-text systems.
(b) *Structure*: A thesaurus displays, through its structure, the synonymous, hierarchical and other relationships between their terms which together comprise an indexing language.

There are three major features of a thesaurus – vocabulary control, thesaural relationships, and thesaurus display.[15]

Vocabulary control through a thesaurus

In thesauri concepts are represented by indexing terms, which are either preferred or non-preferred terms. Preferred terms are used for indexing and searching, whereas non-preferred terms function as lead-ins to the preferred terms. According to BS 5723,[3] there are two principal means for achieving vocabulary control in a thesaurus:

1   Terms are deliberately restricted in scope to selected meanings. Each term in a thesaurus is restricted to whichever single meaning best serves the needs of an indexing system. The structure of a thesaurus, notably its display of hierarchical relationships, frequently indicates the meaning of a term. If this is not sufficiently explicit, a definition or scope note has to be appended to the term which should state the chosen meaning, and may also indicate meanings which are recognized in natural language but which have been deliberately excluded for indexing purposes.

2   When the same concept can be expressed by two or more synonyms, one of these terms is usually selected as the *preferred term*, which is then used consistently in indexing. Reference to the preferred term should be made from any synonym which might also function as a user's access point. In some systems a language independent symbol functions as the preferred term, and references to this symbol are made from the natural language terms which denote that concept.

One of the most difficult aspects of developing a thesaurus relates to the choice of terms. According to Aitchison[15] some of the issues covering the form of terms are: the use of noun or noun form, choice of singular or plural, treatment of abbreviations, scientific and popular names, slang words and trade names. According to BS 5723[3] indexing terms may denote the following kinds of concepts:

1   *classes of things and their properties*, including names which indicate the form of the documents to which indexing terms are assigned, for example, cars, penguins, thickness, micro forms, etc.

2   *classes of activities and events*, such as sewing, hurricanes, etc., and

3   *individual entities or class-of-one*, usually expressed as proper nouns, such as, France, British Standards Institution, etc.

Standards prescribe a number of rules that help indexer in choosing the appropriate forms of terms for inclusion in a thesaurus. BS 5723 recommends that an indexing term should preferably consist of a noun or a noun phrase, and when a noun phrase begins with an adjective, the noun from which the adjective was derived should be considered as a candidate term in the thesaurus. Similarly it is recommended that:

1   adverbs such as 'very', 'highly', etc., should never be used as indexing terms, unless they have acquired a special meaning in a technical environment

2   verbs expressed as infinitives or participles should not be used alone as indexing terms

3   activities should be represented by nouns or verbal nouns

4   abbreviations and acronyms should not be used as preferred terms except when

they are widely used and readily understood; the full form of the name should be used as the preferred term with a reciprocal reference from the acronym

5   names of countable objects that are subject to the question 'how many?', but not 'how much?', should be expressed as plurals

6   names of abstract concepts, such as systems of belief, activities and disciplines, etc., should be expressed in their singular forms

7   if the singular and plural forms of a term denote different things, then both should be entered in the thesaurus, with the meaning written as qualifying term, written within parenthesis

8   if the spelling of a singular and plural form of a term differs to such an extent that the terms might be far apart in the alphabetical sequence (in the file), then a reference is to be made from the non-preferred term

9   the most widely used spelling of a word is to be accepted

10   homographs are to be supplemented by meaning written in parenthesis

11   if a newly emerging concept is expressed as slang or jargon then it has to be accepted as the preferred term; but if slang/jargon is used as an alternative to an established term, then the established term is to be used as the preferred term

12   when a suitable common name exists for a product, the common name is to be used in place of the trade name, and

13   while choosing between popular and scientific names, preference is to be given to the form most widely used in the literature being indexed.

Establishment of procedures for dealing consistently with compound terms is one of the most difficult jobs of an indexer. The standards deal with this subject in detail. Use of the compound term as it appears has been suggested in the following situations where:[3]

1   the compound term denotes a proper name, such as 'British Museum'

2   the compound term has become familiar in common use, such as 'information retrieval'

3   the term has lost its original meaning, such as 'trade winds'

4   syntactical factoring would lead to a loss of meaning or would introduce ambiguity, such as 'oil transformers'

5   the term contains a difference which suggests a resemblance, as a simile, to an unrelated thing or event, such as 'fountain pens'

6   the term cannot be defined without the use of an extra noun which is present in the compound only as an implication, such as 'fire escapes'

7   the term contains syncategorematic adjectives, such as 'paper flowers', and

8   the term consists of a noun modified by a participle, such as 'washing machines'.

Similarly, there are guidelines for the factoring of compound terms. The following are cases where compound terms are to be factored into separate components, each of which is then entered as a noun or a noun phrase in the thesaurus:[3]

1   if the *focus* (that noun component of a compound term which identifies the broader class of things or events to which the term as a whole refers, e.g. 'rooms' in the compound term 'dining rooms') refers to a part or property and the *difference* (that part of a compound term which refers to a characteristic, or logical difference, which narrows the connotation of the focus by specifying a subclass of the broader concept represented by the focus, e.g. 'dining' in 'dining rooms') represents the whole or possessor of that part or property, such as 'turbine blades'

2   the name of a transitive action should not be modified by the name of the patient on which the action is performed, such as 'house painting'

3   the name of an intransitive action should not be modified by the performer of the action, such as 'bird migration'.

Relationships between terms in a thesaurus

According to Aitchison[15] there are two types of relationships in a thesaurus: (1) the macro-level, which is the arrangement of the whole domain of the thesaurus with its subject fields and subfields containing sets of hierarchically and associatively related terms, and (2) the inter-term relationships. Three general classes of fundamental thesaural relationships have been established:

1   the equivalence relationship
2   the hierarchical (or whole–part) relationship, and
3   the associative relationship.

Equivalence relationships

The equivalence relationship denotes the relationship between preferred and non-preferred terms in an indexing language. This is denoted by *USE* (the prefix used for the preferred terms) and the *UF* (used for, the prefix used for non-preferred term). This general relationship covers two kinds of term: synonym and quasi-synonym.

Synonyms are terms whose meaning can be regarded as the same in a wide range of contexts, so that they are virtually interchangeable.[3] There could be several cases of synonymity, for example,

1   terms with different linguistic origin, such as polyglot/multilingual
2   popular names and scientific names, such as allergy/hypersensitivity
3   variant spellings, such as encyclopaedia/encyclopedia
4   terms from different cultures, such as flats/apartments
5   abbreviations and full names, such as PVC/polyvinyl chloride
6   the factored and unfactored forms of a compound term, such as coal mining/coal & mining.

Quasi-synonyms are terms whose meanings are generally regarded as different in ordinary usage, but which are treated as synonyms for indexing purposes, for example, hardness and softness.

Hierarchical relationships

The hierarchical relationship is the basic relationship that distinguishes a systematic thesaurus from other organized lists of terms (subject heading lists). Pairs of terms are represented in their superordinate or subordinate status, the superordinate term representing the whole and the subordinate term representing a member or a part. The superordinate term is represented by *BT* (broader term), and the subordinate term by *NT* (narrower term). In a thesaurus a pair of superordinate and subordinate terms are represented reciprocally as follows:

CAPITAL MARKETS
BT Financial markets

FINANCIAL MARKETS
NT Capital markets

BS 5723 identifies three relational situations representing hierarchical relationships:

1   the generic relationship
2   the hierarchical whole–part relationship, and
3   the polyhierarchical relationship.

The *generic relationship* identifies the relationship between a class or category and its member species. This relationship has a 'hierarchical force', that is, whatever is true of a given class is also true of all classes subsumed under it.[15]

The *hierarchical whole–part relationship* covers a limited number of classes of terms in which the name of the part implies the name of the whole regardless of the context, so that the terms can be organized as logical hierarchies. There are only four situations when the whole–part relationship may be considered hierarchical; otherwise, it is an associative relationship.[15] These four cases are:

1   systems and organs of the body, such as
        GASTROINTESTINAL SYSTEMS
            BT Digestive systems
            NT Intestines
            NT Stomach
2   geographic locations, such as
        INDIA
            BT Asia
            NT West Bengal
            NT Calcutta
3   disciplines or fields of discourse, such as
        CHEMISTRY
            BT Science
            NT Physical chemistry
            NT Thermodynamics

4   hierarchical social structures, such as
CHURCH OF ENGLAND
NT Dioceses
NT Parishes

The *polyhierarchical relationship* occurs when a concept belongs to more than one category, for example,

PRINTING EQUIPMENT   COMPUTER PERIPHERAL EQUIPMENT
NT Computer printers   NT Computer printers

COMPUTER PRINTERS
NT Computer peripheral equipment
NT Printing equipment

Associative relationships

An *associative relationship* denotes the relationship between terms that is neither hierarchical nor equivalence, yet the terms are mentally associated to such an extent that the link between them should be made explicit in the thesaurus, and would reveal alternative terms that could be used in indexing or in retrieval. This relationship is reciprocal and is represented by *RT*. This relationship is the most difficult one to define and therefore to determine between a pair of terms. BS 5723 provides a general guideline that states that one of the terms should always be implied, according to the common frames of reference shared by the users of an index, whenever the other is used as an indexing term.

This standard further identifies two broad categories of terms that can be bound by the associative relationship:

1   *terms belonging to the same category*: this usually refers to siblings with overlapping meanings, such as 'ships' and 'boats', which can be precisely defined, yet they are sometimes used loosely and almost interchangeably, and
2   *terms belonging to different categories*: this usually refers to such terms that satisfy the requirement that one of the terms should be implied when the other is used in indexing, for example:[3]
(a) a discipline or field of study and the objects or phenomena studied, e.g. entomology and insects
(b) a process or operation and its agent or instrument, e.g. illumination/lamps
(c) an action and the products of the action, e.g. programming/software
(d) an action and its patient, e.g. harvesting/crops
(e) concepts related to their properties, e.g. poisons/toxicity
(f) concepts related to their origins, e.g. India/Indians
(g) concepts linked by causal dependence, e.g. diseases/pathogens
(h) a thing and its counter agent, e.g. insects/insecticides
(i) syncategorematic phrases and their embedded nouns, e.g. model buses/buses.

Display of terms in a thesaurus

Terms and their relationships can be displayed in a number of ways in a thesaurus. However, there are three basic methods:

1   alphabetical display, with scope notes and relationships indicated at each term
2   systematic display with an alphabetical index, and
3   graphic display with an alphabetical index.

Alphabetical display

In this form of display all indexing terms, whether preferred or non-preferred, are organized in a single alphabetical sequence. Ancillary information, such as scope notes and references to other related terms, should be listed under each preferred term in the following order:[3]

1   scope note or definition
2   UF references to non-preferred equivalent terms
3   TT references to top terms
4   BT references to broader terms
5   NT references to narrower terms
6   RT references to related terms.

Non-preferred terms are accompanied only by references (e.g. USE) to the preferred terms. Thus the display in an alphabetical thesaurus looks like the following:

> PREFERRED TERM
>   SN Scope note
>   UF Use for
>   BT Broader term
>   NT Narrower term
>   RT Related term
>
> Non-preferred term
>   Use PREFERRED TERM

However, a multilevel hierarchical display, like the following, is also possible:

> PREFERRED TERM
>   SN Scope note
>   UF Use for
>   BT1 Broader term 1
>   BT2 Broader term 2
>   BT3 Broader term 3
>   NT1 Narrower term 1
>   NT2 Narrower term 2
>   NT3 Narrower term 3
>   RT related term

The alphabetical form of thesaurus is the easiest to develop. However, there is a short-coming of this form of thesaurus from the user's point of view, as all the broader and narrower terms that constitute a hierarchy in an alphabetical thesaurus cannot be surveyed at a single position. Extra relational information can be added to an alphabetical display, for example, the top term in the hierarchy to which a specific concept belongs. Similarly, as shown above, the level of subordination and superordination can also be shown using BT1, BT2, NT1, NT2, etc. A sample alphabetical thesaurus is shown in Figure 7.3.

```
        Aerodynes USE HEAVIER-THAN-AIR AIRCRAFT
        AERONAUTICS
            SN  the design, manufacture and operation of aircraft
            NT  Aviation
            RT  Aircraft
        AEROPLANES
            SN  fixed-wing powered heavier-than-air aircraft
            BT  Heavier-than-air aircraft
            NT  Freight aeroplanes
                Jet aeroplanes
                Passenger aeroplanes
                Propeller-driven aeroplanes
..........
..........
..........

        AVIATION
            SN the operation of heavier-than-air aircraft
            BT Aeronautics
            NT Gliding
            RT Heavier-than-air aircraft
........
........
........


        HEAVIER-THAN-AIR AIRCRAFT
            UF Aerodynes
            BT  Aircraft
            NT  Aeroplanes
                Gliders
                Helicopters
                Man-powered heavier-than-air aircraft
            RT  Aviation
..........
..........
```

Fig. 7.3 *Sample alphabetical thesaurus*

Systematic display

A thesaurus that is organized systematically should have two parts:

1   categories or hierarchies of terms arranged according to their meanings and logical relationships, and
2   an alphabetical index that directs the user to the appropriate part of the systematic section.

The link between these two parts is maintained through notation. The systematic display is helpful both for indexers and searchers, for it gives a bird's-eye view of the topic and puts it into the context of the whole subject field.[15] In a systematic thesaurus, the systematic part is regarded as the main part of the thesaurus (the part that carries the most relational information) and the alphabetical index is regarded as a secondary component. Figure 7.4 shows some sample blocks from the macrothesaurus, developed by the OECD.

Graphic display

Graphic display shows the indexing terms and their relationships in the form of two-dimensional figures, which are supplemented by alphabetical sections. Many types of graphic display are found in thesauri, but there are two major types of graphic display:[3]

1   tree structures and
2   arrowgraphs.

The advantage of graphic display is that it provides an immediate overall view of the environment of the concepts; a disadvantage is that it does not show equivalent terms or scope notes, nor does it distinguish between hierarchical and associative relationships. All the details are given in the alphabetical section. Moreover, in the printed form, graphic display may be bulky and not always easy to consult.[15]

Thesaurofacet

Thesaurofacet is a specialized kind of retrieval language with both a thesaurus-type and a classification-type display, each containing some term unique to itself and not found in the other.[17] Lancaster[2] and Lancaster et al.[18] describe the features of a thesaurofacet in the following example, a hypothetical thesaurofacet in library science (Figure 7.5).

The figure shows that the two parts complement one another: while the faceted component takes care of the hierarchical relationship, all the other relationships appear in the thesaurus component. The thesaurus component shows the notation for each term, which acts as the link between the thesaurus display and the faceted display. According to Lancaster[2] the obvious advantage of the thesaurofacet is that: 'It can be used for arranging books on the shelves of a special library as well as for indexing the items in a database. Moreover, shelf arrangement and database will be fully compatible.'

MANAGEMENT
GESTION / ADMINISTRATION – 12.04.00
SN   USE IN CONNECTION WITH
THREE MAIN TASKS:
SUPERVISION OF AND
RESPONSIBILITY FOR THE
WORK OF OTHERS;
ALLOCATING LABOUR,
MATERIAL AND CAPITAL TO
PRODUCE A HIGH RETURN;
AND DECISION MAKING.
NT   AGRICULTURAL MANAGEMENT
BUSINESS MANAGEMENT
COLLEGE MANAGEMENT
CRISIS MANAGEMENT
ENVIRONMENTAL MANAGEMENT
EQUIPMENT MANAGEMENT
FINANCIAL MANAGEMENT
HOUSING MANAGEMENT
INDUSTRIAL MANAGEMENT
INFORMATION MANAGEMENT
ISSUES MANAGEMENT
OFFICE MANAGEMENT
PERSONNEL MANAGEMENT
RESOURCES MANAGEMENT
SCHOOL MANAGEMENT
SCIENTIFIC MANAGEMENT
SELF-MANAGEMENT
WASTE MANAGEMENT
WATER MANAGEMENT
RT   MANAGEMENT CONSULTANTS
MANAGEMENT DEVELOPMENT
MANAGEMENT INFORMATION
SYSTEMS
MANAGEMENT TECHNIQUES
MANAGERS
MANAGEMENT DEVELOPMENT
FORMATION A LA GESTION / CAPACIT-
ATION DE EMPRESARIOS – 12.04.00
SN   DEVELOPING MANAGERIAL
SKILLS THROUGH MEETINGS,
SEMINARS, INFORMATION
DISSEMINATION, ETC.
UF   MANAGEMENT EDUCATION
MANAGEMENT TRAINING
TT1 TRAINING
TT2 EDUCATIONAL SYSTEMS
BT   TRAINING
VOCATIONAL EDUCATION
RT   ENTREPRENEURS

MANAGEMENT
MANAGEMENT CONSULTANTS
MANAGEMENT INFORMATION
SYSTEMS
SYSTEMES D'INFORMATION DE
GESTION / SISTEMAS DE INFORMACION
ADMINISTRATIVA – 12.04.00
SN   SYSTEMS IN WHICH DEFINED
DATA ARE COLLECTED,
PROCESSED AND COMMUN-
ICATED TO ASSIST THOSE
RESPONSIBLE FOR THE USE
OF RESOURCES.
TT1 INFORMATION SYSTEMS
BT   INFORMATION SYSTEMS
RT   MANAGEMENT
MANAGEMENT TECHNIQUES
TECHNIQUES DE GESTION / TECNICAS ADMIN-
ISTRATIVAS – 12.04.00
UF   ORGANIZATION AND METHOD
NT   LINEAR PROGRAMMING
MANAGEMENT BY OBJECTIVES
NETWORK ANALYSIS
OPERATIONS RESEARCH
RT   DECISION MAKING
ECONOMIC MODELS
EFFICIENCY
MANAGEMENT
RESOURCE ALLOCATION
SCIENTIFIC MANAGEMENT
MANAGEMENT ATTITUDES
ATTITUDES PATRONALES / ACTITUDES DE LA
DIRECCION – 13.06.00
UF   EMPLOYER ATTITUDES
TT1 ATTITUDES
BT   ATTITUDES
RT   EMPLOYERS
MANAGERS
MANAGEMENT BY OBJECTIVES
DIRECTION PAR OBJECTIFS / DIRECCION POR
OBJETIVOS – 12.04.00
SN   SETTING TARGETS WITHIN AN
ORGANIZATION IN ORDER TO
ACHIEVE GREATER EFFICIENCY.
TT1 MANAGEMENT TECHNIQUES
BT   MANAGEMENT TECHNIQUES
MANAGEMENT EDUCATION
USE MANAGEMENT DEVELOPMENT
MANAGEMENT TRAINING
USE MANAGEMENT DEVELOPMENT

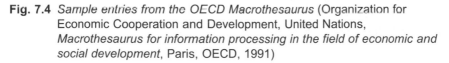

Fig. 7.4 *Sample entries from the OECD Macrothesaurus* (Organization for
Economic Cooperation and Development, United Nations,
*Macrothesaurus for information processing in the field of economic and
social development*, Paris, OECD, 1991)

In the thesaurofacet, the thesaurus part replaces the alphabetical subject index that is
available in a conventional faceted classification scheme. On the other hand, the
faceted classification part replaces the usual hierarchical structure of a thesaurus

Faceted display	Thesaurus display
L Libraries	City libraries Ldc
La Academic libraries	UF Municipal libraries
Lac College libraries	RT City government Qp
Lah University libraries	
Ld Public libraries	Industrial libraries Li
Ldc City libraries	BT (A) Industrial information services rj
Ldf Rural libraries	
Li Industrial libraries	
Lk Government libraries	Municipal libraries
	USE City libraries Ldc

Fig. **7.5** *Examples from a hypothetical thesaurofacet*

through the BT/NT relationships. Since the development of the first thesaurofacet by Jean Aitchison et al. in 1969, a number of vocabulary control tools have appeared based on the same idea, e.g. the Unesco Thesaurus (1977), ROOT thesaurus (1981), etc.

Classaurus

The Classaurus is a vocabulary control tool, developed by Bhattacharyya and used for POPSI, the pre-coordinate indexing system also developed by Bhattacharyya.[19] It is a category-based (faceted) systematic scheme of hierarchical (organizing) classification incorporating all the essential features of a conventional retrieval thesaurus, i.e. control of synonyms, quasi-synonyms, and antonyms in extended senses.[19-21] The application of a scheme of this type calls for a complementary alphabetical index giving the address of each term occurring in the systematic part. A classaurus can be designed either before starting the indexing work or along with the indexing work. But in all cases, its designing warrants both a priori and pragmatic approaches. The structure and style of presentation of a classaurus have been illustrated by Bhattacharyya[19] as follows:

    A SYSTEMATIC PART
        A1 Common Modifiers
            A11 Form Modifiers
            A12 Time Modifiers
            A13 Environment Modifiers
        A2 Inter-subject Relation Modifiers
        A3 Disciplines and Subdisciplines
        A4 Entities
            A41 Part entities
            A42 Type entities
        A5 Properties
        A6 Actions

Field: AGRICULTURE AND RELATED SCIENCE AND TECHNOLOGY

Disciplines and sub-disciplines
SOIL SCIENCE
AGRICULTURE
   AGRICULTURE MACHINERY (Study of)
      = Agricultural tool
      = Farm machinery
      = Machinery, Agricultural
      = Machinery, Farm
      = Tool, Agricultural
   AGRICULTURAL STRUCTURE (Study of)
      FIELD CROP (Culture of)
         HORTICULTURE
            FRUIT CULTURE
            VEGETABLE CULTURE
      FLORICULTURE
      FORESTRY
   ANIMAL HUSBANDRY
         VETERINARY MEDICINE
   DAIRY TECHNOLOGY
   FISHERY AND FISH CULTURE
   MOLLUSC CULTURE
      CRUSTACEAN CULTURE
      INSECT CULTURE
         APICULTURE
         SERICULTURE
Etc.

Note: The basic consideration for creating disciplines and sub-disciplines is the purpose of bringing all information pertaining to an area (denoted by a concept/term) together.

For discipline: FIELD CROP
(Culture of)
Entities
Parts
ROOT
STEM
LEAF
FLOWER
FRUIT
SEED
Etc.

Wholes (types)
CEREAL
  RICE
  WHEAT
  OAT
  RYE
  CORN
  BARLEY
  MILLET
ROOT CROP
  TUBER CROP
SUGAR CROP
  ALCOLOIDAL CROP
  FIBRE CROP
  FORAGE CROP
Etc.

Properties
INJURY
  ENVIRONMENTAL INJURY
DISEASE
  BACTERIAL DISEASE
  FUNGUS DISEASE
  VIRAL DISEASE
DAMAGE
  DAMAGE (by) PEST
  DAMAGE (by) INSECT PEST
  DAMAGE (by) PARASITE
  DAMAGE (by) WEED
GROWTH
Etc.

Actions
CULTIVATION
  TILLAGE
BREEDING
DEVELOPING
HARVESTING
  MOWING
  REAPING
  STACKING
  THRESHING
  HUSKING
  SHELLING
  CLEANING
  WINNOWING
  GRADING
  STORING
  PACKING
DRY FARMING
DRAINING
IRRIGATION
MANURING
CONTROL
Etc.

Fig. 7.6 *Sample classaurus entries*

The arrangement in the systematic part is governed by the following rules:

1   each term in the systematic part under each category is enumerated by displaying its 'COSCO (Coordinate–Superordinate–Subordinate–Collateral) relationships' in a hierarchy of arrays

2   for each term in the systematic part the following order is followed vertically:
    (a) definition/scope note, and
    (b) synonyms, quasi-synonyms and antonyms
3   no non-hierarchically related terms are enumerated for any term in a classaurus because of its category-based (faceted) structure, and because POPSI itself takes the responsibility of revealing this relationship as precisely as possible
4   each array in the classaurus is open and discontinuous, and
5   each term in the systematic part is assigned a unique address, which, if desired, can also be a class number.

The alphabetical index part contains each and every term, including synonyms, quasi-synonyms, and antonyms, occurring in the systematic part, along with its address. The address refers to the systematic part where all synonyms, etc., superordinates, subordinates, coordinates, and collaterals of the term concerned are found to occur. Figure 7.6 shows an example of a classaurus, along with the necessary notes, etc., which has been used by Bhattacharyya himself.[19]

Guidelines for developing a thesaurus

All the available standards[3–8] provide guidelines for the compilation of thesauri. First it must be decided how the thesaurus is to be displayed (in alphabetic, systematic or graphic form) and how the terms are to be collected.

There are two approaches to the latter: the *deductive method* and the *inductive method*.[3] In the deductive method, terms are extracted from the literature during a preliminary indexing stage, but no attempt is made to control the vocabulary or to determine the relationships between terms until a sufficient number of terms has been

Thesaurus form	Class number
Term	
UF	Definition
RT	
	Scope note:
BT	Source:
NT	Date:

Fig. 7.7   *Sample thesaurus form*

collected. With the inductive method, on the other hand, new terms are admitted into the thesaurus as soon as they are encountered in the literature, each term being designed as a member of one or more categories established on an ad hoc basis during the indexing process. However, a combination of both the inductive and deductive methods may be applied. The necessary steps are as follows:

1   *recording of terms*: each term is recorded on a form (for example as shown in Figure 7.7). The record for a term should indicate the source, the date of inclusion, and references to synonyms, scope notes, and broader, narrower, and related terms
2   *term verification*: each term should be verified before it is included in the thesaurus. There are various sources that can be consulted for the purpose, such as standard technical dictionaries and encyclopedias, existing thesauri, classification schemes, indexes to technical journals, indexes to abstract bulletins, current textbooks and handbooks, and subject specialists
3   *deciding the specificity*: the use of specific terms should be restricted to the core area of the subject field concerned
4   *admission and deletion of terms*: the job of inclusion of terms along with all their relationships into the thesaurus, and their display in the chosen form, can be very difficult. However, a number of software packages are now available that can arrange all the sets of terms automatically in the chosen format. At this stage some terms may need to be added or deleted
5   *review*: once the thesaurus has been compiled, it has to be reviewed by subject experts and modified as necessary
6   *maintenance*: development of a thesaurus is a continuous process as subjects are constantly changing their nature, connotations, and consequently vocabularies. New terms and new relationships appear constantly, and these changes are to be incorporated into the thesaurus on a regular basis.

Criteria for evaluating a thesaurus

Davis and Rush[1] propose the following criteria to be employed for evaluating a thesaurus.

1   *Terminology*: is it appropriate for the field, up-to-date and accurate?
2   *Scope*: is it too broad or too narrow to cover the field adequately?
3   *Subdivisions*: are there reasonable subdivisions?
4   *Definitions and notes*: are enough included for clarity?
5   *References*: are they adequate in both number and form?
6   *Format*: is it legible?
7   *Classification numbers*: is the listing keyed to any kind of classification scheme, if appropriate?

Use of thesauri in online information retrieval

Vocabulary control, particularly in an electronic information environment, has been an interesting area of research. Rowley[9] has summarized several studies arguing for and against the need for vocabulary control. Recent developments in the world wide web (discussed in Chapter 18) and digital libraries (discussed in Chapter 22) have given rise to new research projects related to vocabulary control. For example, Shapiro and Yan[28] suggest that vocabulary control is essential in digital libraries, while Milstead[29] comments that thesauri will be used in an information retrieval environment quite differently as they will be blended into systems of machine-aided indexing and text retrieval systems, and they will be used more in helping users define search terms. Glassel and Walls[30] report on the Scout Report Signpost (**http://www.signpost. org/**), which demonstrates that internet resources can be catalogued, classified and arranged using existing taxonomies such as the Library of Congress Classification and Subject Headings. Further discussions relating to the use of vocabulary control tools in digital libraries appear in Chapter 22.

The growing application of online or electronic versions of domain-specific thesauri for query formulation and expansion can be traced back to late 1970s when a number of information retrieval researchers began to develop prototype systems in order to explore ways of enabling users to search within information retrieval systems. The development of expert system and artificial intelligence technologies in the 1980s provided the grounds for a growing interest in applying thesauri as the knowledge bases of a number of expert systems and intelligent front-ends. Efthimiadis[31] provides a detailed review of these thesaurus-enhanced systems, most of them using expert system techniques, which were designed and developed to assist users in formulating and expanding queries in one way or another. Many of these systems embedded thesauri as part of their search facilities, which provided users with a choice of search terms. Some of these systems used mapping techniques for matching user submitted terms with their thesaurus knowledge base and displayed hierarchical structures associated with the entered term. Most of these expert and intermediary systems used standard thesauri such as MeSH and INSPEC to provide either thesaurus browsing or thesaurus mapping capabilities.

The selection of search terms for query formulation and expansion in the context of online information retrieval has been studied from a range of perspectives. These studies can be broadly divided into two groups based on the algorithmic and human approaches.[32] The focus of the algorithmic approach is to develop and evaluate different types of algorithms for selecting, weighting and/or ranking search terms in the process of query formulation or expansion to improve information retrieval. Several instances of research of this type have been reported in the literature.[33–40] The human approach, in contrast, is concerned with studying and evaluating the ways in which users choose terms for formulating, expanding or modifying their queries during the search process. It deals with cognitive and behavioural models and issues that affect the selection of search terms by users. Research has focused on user-centred variables such as those relating to information needs, user intentions, personal characteristics, and different user information-seeking profiles, and investigates their relationship to term selection in the search process (see for example, Fidel[41] and Bates[42]).

Query expansion using thesauri

Several studies have reported the construction and use of different types of thesauri as aids to the query expansion process. In general, thesauri within information retrieval systems can be categorized as belonging to one of three main types: standard manually constructed thesauri, searching thesauri and automatically constructed thesauri.

Standard thesauri with hierarchical, equivalence and associative relationships have been widely used for search term selection and query expansion purposes. Much of the research in this area has focused on comparing the performance and effectiveness of controlled vocabularies versus free text terms in information retrieval.[43-49] These types of thesauri have also been incorporated as knowledge bases or interface components in several prototype expert and intelligent systems to assist users in the process of search terms selection and query expansion.[31]

Searching thesauri, also referred to as end-user thesauri, are defined as a category of thesauri enhanced with a large number of entry terms that are synonyms, quasi-synonyms or term variants, which assist end-users to find alternative terms to add to their search queries.[44, 50-52] A number of searching thesauri have been designed and developed[53, 54] and have been evaluated in query expansion research.[55-57]

The design and testing of several types of automatically constructed thesauri has also been extensively reported in the literature. A number of researchers have constructed co-occurrence-based thesauri to evaluate the performance of thesaurus-based query expansion.[58, 59] Using a laboratory environment and the TREC test collections, these studies resulted in a slight improvement in retrieval performance. General-purpose thesauri such as WordNet have also been evaluated in the query expansion process but have demonstrated little difference in retrieval effectiveness.[60] Thesauri constructed automatically using a linguistic approach have also demonstrated a marginal improvement in retrieval performance.[61] Combining different types of thesauri for query expansion has shown better retrieval results than using only one type of thesaurus.[62]

Automatically constructed thesauri have also been evaluated in user-oriented environments.[63-65] In addition some researchers have found that the integration of automatically and manually constructed thesauri has a positive effect on the query expansion process.[68, 69]

Subject headings lists and thesauri in the organization of internet resources

Although the subject heading lists were devised to assign subject headings in catalogues, many researchers have used these tools for organising internet resources. Examples of some of these are given below.

INFOMINE

INFOMINE is a service providing access to several thousand web resources comprising databases, electronic journals, guides to the internet for most disciplines, textbooks and conference proceedings. It began in January of 1994 as a project of the

Library of the University of California, Riverside.[70] INFOMINE uses the Library of Congress Subject Headings (LCSH) for indexing the information resources. Users can simply select a discipline and enter the search terms or phrases to conduct a search. The catalogue can also be browsed by author, title, keyword and subject. If the option for browsing by subject is chosen, users are taken to an alphabetical list of subjects created by LCSH.

Scout Report

The Scout Report Signpost was a US National Science Foundation funded research project from 1996 to 2000.[71] The primary goal of this project was to demonstrate that internet resources could be catalogued, classified and arranged using existing controlled vocabularies and taxonomies such as the Library of Congress Classification (LCC) Scheme and the Library of Congress Subject Headings together with the Dublin Core metadata standard (discussed later in this chapter). The project ended in 2000 and the materials are now available in the Scout Report Archives, which is a searchable and browseable database containing 12,711 critical annotations of selected internet sites and mailing lists. Here users can conduct a search or browse the database by using the LCSH.

SOSIG

SOSIG, the Social Science Information Gateway, is an internet service that provides access to selected, high quality internet information for students, academics, researchers and practitioners in the social sciences, business and law.[72] SOSIG uses the Humanities and Social Science Electronic Thesaurus (HASSET).[73] The home page of SOSIG allows users to select a subject category to browse. Users can conduct a simple or an advanced search for materials on the SOSIG catalogue. They can also choose a thesaurus for selection of search terms. Three thesauri are available: General Social Science; Government, Politics and Anthropology; and Social Work and Welfare. Users can select a thesaurus and can then look for a search term in the thesaurus. For example, a search for the term 'economics' in the 'General Social Science' thesaurus revealed a number of terms. The user can select a particular term by clicking on it to get the thesaurus entry for the chosen term, or can select it as a search term by checking the corresponding box and clicking on the 'Search' button, which prompts a search on the chosen term.

As well as searching the whole SOSIG catalogue, users can select an option to restrict their search to a subject section of SOSIG. Selection of a broad subject category will lead the users to the corresponding sub categories, and this will continue until the end of the hierarchy is reached. At each stage, a list of items corresponding to the currently chosen category will be displayed. In addition to this provision for searching within a specific section of the SOSIG collection, there is also an option for browsing a specific collection. Here the user has first to select a region – world, Europe or UK – and then a SOSIG subject heading(s) to get information on the topic filtered by region.

BIOME

BIOME offers access to a searchable catalogue of internet sites and resources covering the health and life sciences.[74] Users can choose to search BIOME for internet resources in the field of the health and life sciences, or can choose one of the five subject-specific gateways OMNI, VETGATE, BIORES, NATURAL and AGRIFOR. In addition to searching, users can also browse the BIOME database by keyword or by classification scheme.

Since each gateway uses slightly different indexing and classification tools, the user has first to select one of the five subject gateways before browsing. There are two methods of browsing: by keyword and by classification scheme. All records in BIOME are indexed using keywords from one of several thesauri. Users can browse AgriFor and VetGate using terms from the CAB thesaurus; BioResearch, OMNI and NMAP using MeSH keywords; and NMAP using the Royal College of Nursing (RCN) thesaurus. As well as being able to browse resources using keywords, it is also possible to browse by classification scheme. Users can browse VetGate using the Library of Congress Classification Scheme; AgriFor using the Dewey Decimal Classification Scheme (DDC); and OMNI and BioResearch using the National Library of Medicine (NLM) classification scheme.

Figure 7.8 shows the options that a user gets for browsing the collection using the OMNI gateway – browse by NLM subject headings, or browse by MESH2000 headings. If the user chooses to browse by subject headings, then an alphabetical list of headings appear; otherwise, if the user chooses to browse according to the MeSH headings, then another alphabetical list appears. Selection of any heading from either list takes the user to the items indexed by the chosen heading.

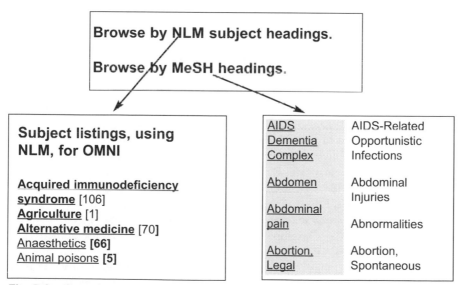

Fig. 7.8 *Browsing options in OMNI*

References

1   Davis, C. H. and Rush, C. L., *Guide to information science*, Westport, CT, Greenwood, 1979.
2   Lancaster, F. W., *Vocabulary control for information retrieval*, 2nd edn, Arlington, VA, Information Resources, 1986.
3   BS 5723:1987 *Guidelines for the establishment and development of monolingual thesauri*, London, British Standards Institution.
4   BS 6723:1985 *Guidelines for the establishment and development of multilingual thesauri*, London, British Standards Institution.
5   ISO 2788:1986 *Guidelines for the establishment and development of monolingual thesauri*, Geneva, International Organization for Standardization.
6   ISO 5964:1985 *Guidelines for the establishment and development of multilingual thesauri*, Geneva, International organization for Standardization.
7   *UNISIST guidelines for the establishment and development of multilingual thesauri*, rev. edn, Paris, Unesco, 1980.
8   *UNISIST guidelines for the establishment and development of monolingual thesauri*, 2nd edn, Paris, Unesco, 1981.
9   Rowley, J. E., 'The controlled versus natural indexing languages debate revisited: a perspective on information retrieval practice and research', *Journal of information science*, **20** (2), 1994, 108–19.
10 Svenonius, E., 'Unanswered questions in the design of controlled vocabularies', *Journal of the American Society for Information Science*, **37** (5), 1986, 331–40.
11 Aitchison, J. and Gilchrist, A., *Thesaurus construction: a practical manual*, 2nd edn, London, Aslib, 1987.
12 Miller, J. (ed.), *Sears list of subject headings*, 15th edn, New York, H. W. Wilson, 1994.
13 Foskett, A. C., *The subject approach to information*, 5th edn, London, Library Association Publishing, 1996.
14 Rowley, J. E., *Organizing knowledge: an introduction to information retrieval*, 2nd edn, Aldershot, Gower, 1992.
15 Aitchison, J., 'Indexing languages and indexing'. In Dossett, P. (ed.), *Handbook of special librarianship and information work*, 6th edn, London, Aslib, 1992, 191–233.
16 Guinchat, C. and Menou, M., *General introduction to the techniques of information and documentation work*, Paris, Unesco, 1983.
17 Townley, H. M. and Gee, R. D., *Thesaurus-making: grow your own wordstock*, London, André Deutsch, 1980.
18 Lancaster, F. W., Elliker, C., and Colonell, T. H., 'Subject analysis', *Annual review of information science and technology*, **24**, 1989, 35–84.
19 Bhattacharyya, G., 'Classaurus: its fundamentals, design and use', *Studien zur Klassifikation*, **11**, 1982, 139–48.
20 Devadasan, F. J., 'Online construction of alphabetical thesaurus: a vocabulary control and indexing tool', *Information processing and management*, **21**, 1985, 11–26.

21 Fugmann, R., 'An interactive classaurus on PC', *International classification*, **17** (3/4), 1990, 133–7.

22 Chowdhury, G. G., Neelameghan, A. and Chowdhury, S., 'Vocabulary control online in MicroIsis databases: a Pascal interface', *First International Congress of CDS/ISIS*, Columbia, May 22–26, 1995, unpublished.

23 Chowdhury, G. G., Neelameghan, A. and Chowdhury, S., 'VOCON: vocabulary control online in MicroIsis databases', *Knowledge organization*, **22** (1), 1995, 18–22.

24 Chowdhury, G. G., Neelameghan, A. and Chowdhury, S., 'Vocabulary control online in MicroIsis databases: a Pascal interface', *ASTINFO newsletter*, **9** (3), 1994, 11–18.

25 Chowdhury, G. G., Neelameghan, A. and Chowdhury, S., 'Vocabulary control online in MicroIsis databases: a Pascal interface', *Microcomputers for information management*, **11** (4), 1994, 295–305.

26 Ritzler, C., 'Comparative study of PC-supported thesaurus software', *International classification*, **17** (3/4), 1990, 138–47.

27 Ganzman, J., 'Criteria for evaluation of thesaurus software', *International classification*, **17** (3/4), 1990, 148–57.

28 Shapiro, C.D. and Yan, P.-F., 'Generous tools: thesauri in digital libraries'. In: Williams, M. E. (ed.), *Proceedings of the 17th National Meeting 1996, Information Today Inc., New York, 14–16 May, 1996*, Medford, NJ, Information Today Inc., 1996, 323–32.

29 Milstead, J. L., 'Invisible thesauri: the year 2000', *Online & CDROM review*, **19** (2), 1995, 93–4.

30 Glassel, A. D. and Wells, A. T., 'Scout Report Signpost: design and development for access to cataloged Internet resources', *Journal of internet cataloging*, **1** (3), 1998, 15–45.

31 E. N. Efthimiadis, 'Query expansion'. In: Williams, M. E. (ed.), *Annual review of information science and technology*, **31**, Medford, NJ, Information Today, 1996, 121–87.

32 Spink, A. and Saracevic, T., 'Interaction in information retrieval: selection and effectiveness of search terms', *Journal of the American Society for Information Science*, **48** (8), 1997, 741–61.

33 Sparck Jones, K., 'Search term relevance weighting given little relevance information', *Journal of documentation*, **35** (1), 1979, 30–48.

34 Van Rijsbergen, C. J., Harper, D. J. and Porter, M. F., 'The selection of good search terms', *Information processing and management*, **17** (2), 1981, 77–91.

35 Salton, G. and Buckley, C., 'Term-weighting approaches in automatic text retrieval', *Information processing and management*, **24** (5), 1988, 513–23.

36 Robertson, S. E., 'On term selection for query expansion', *Journal of documentation*, **46** (4), 1990, 359–64.

37 Efthimiadis, Efthimis N. A user-centred evaluation of ranking algorithms for interactive query expansion. In: Korfhage et. al., *SIGIR93: Proceedings of the Association for Computing Machinery Special Interest Group on Information Retrieval (ACM/SIGIR) 16th Annual International Conference on Research*

and Development in Information Retrieval, New York, ACM, 1993, 146–59.

38   Robertson, S., Walker, S. and Beaulieu, M., 'Laboratory experiments with Okapi: participation in the TREC programme', *Journal of documentation*, **53** (1), 1997, 20–32.

39   Magennis, M. and Van Rijsbergen, C. J., 'The potential and actual effectiveness of interactive query expansion'. In: *SIGIR97: Proceedings of the Association for Computing Machinery Special Interest Group on Information Retrieval (ACM/SIGIR) 20th Annual International Conference on Research and Development in Information Retrieval, 27–31 July*, Philadelphia, ACM, 1997.

40   Text REtrieval Conference (TREC) proceedings. Available at **http://trec.nist.gov**.

41   Fidel, R., 'Searchers' selection of search keys: II. Controlled vocabulary or free-text searching', *Journal of the American Society for Information Science*, **42** (7), 1991, 501–14.

42   Bates, M. J., 'Information search tactics', *Journal of the American Society for Information Science*, **30** (4), 1979, 205–14.

43   Markey, K., Atherton, P. and Newton, C., 'An analysis of controlled and free-text search statements in online searches', *Online review*, **4** (3), 1980, 225–36.

44   Perez, E., 'Text enhancement: controlled vocabulary vs. free text', *Special libraries*, **73**, 1982, 183–92.

45   Svenonius, E., 'Unanswered questions in the design of controlled vocabularies', *Journal of the American Society for Information Science*, **37** (5), 1986, 331–40.

46   Dubois, C. P. R., 'Free text vs controlled vocabulary: a reassessment', *Online review*, **11** (4), 1987, 243–53.

47   Cousins, S. A., 'Enhancing access to OPACs: controlled vs natural language', *Journal of documentation*, **48** (3), 291–309.

48   Rowley, J., 'The controlled versus natural indexing languages debate revisited: a perspective on information retrieval practice and research', *Journal of information science*, **20** (2), 1994, 108–19.

49   Muddamalle, M. R., 'Natural language versus controlled vocabulary in information retrieval: a case study in soil mechanics', *Journal of the American Society for Information Science*, **49** (10), 1998, 881–7.

50   Piternick, A., 'Searching vocabularies: a developing category of online searching tools', *Online review*, **8** (5), 1984, 441–9.

51   Bates, M. J., 'Subject access in online catalogs: a design model', *Journal of the American Society for Information Science*, **37** (6), 1986, 357–76.

52   Cochrane, P. A., 'Indexing and searching thesauri, the Janus or Proteus of information retrieval'. In: Williamson, N. J. et al. (ed.), *Classification research for knowledge organization*, FID, 1992, 161–78.

53   Anderson, J. D. and Rowley, F. A., Building end-user thesauri from full-text. In: Kwasink, B. H. and Fidel, R., *Advances in classification research, proceedings of the 2nd ASIS SIG/CR Classification Research Workshop*, Medford, NJ, Learned Information, 1991, 1–13.

54 Knapp, S. D., Cohen, L. B. and Judes, D. R., 'A natural language thesaurus for humanities', *Library quarterly*, **68** (4), 1998, 406–30.

55 Kristensen, J. and Jarvelin, K., 'The effectiveness of a searching thesaurus in free text searching of a full-text database', *International classification*, **17** (2), 1990, 77–84

56 Kristensen, J. and Jarvelin, K., 'The impact of query structure and query expansion on retrieval performance'. In: Croft, W. B., Moffat A., van Rijsbergen, C. J., Wilkinson R. and Zobel, J. (eds), *SIGIR'98: Proceedings of the Association for Computing Machinery Special Interest Group on Information Retrieval (ACM/SIGIR) 21st Annual International ACM SIGIR Conference on Research and Development in Information Retrieval*, Melbourne, New York, NY, ACM Press, 1998, 130–7.

57 Kristensen, J., 'Expanding end-users' query statements for free text searching with a search-aid thesaurus', *Information processing and management*, **29** (6), 1993, 733–44.

58 Qiu, Yoggang and Frei, H. P. 'Concept-based query expansion'. *SIGIR'93: Proceedings of the Association for Computing Machinery Special Interest Group on Information Retrieval (ACM/SIGIR) 16th International ACM SIGIR Conference on Research and Development in Information Retrieval*, 27 June–1 July, Pittsburgh, PA, 1993, 160–9.

59 Schutze, H. and Pedersen, J., 'A co-occurrence-based thesaurus and two applications to information retrieval', *Information processing and management*, **33** (3), 1997, 307–18.

60 Voorhees, E. M., 'Query expansion using lexical-semantic relations'. In: Croft, W. B. and Rijsbergen, C. J. (eds), *SIGIR'94 Proceedings of the Association for Computing Machinery Special Interest Group on Information Retrieval (ACM/SIGIR) 17th Annual International Conference on Research and Development in Information Retrieval*, Berlin, Springer-Verlag, 1994, 61–9.

61 Jing, Y. and Croft, W. B., 'An association thesaurus for information retrieval'. *RIAO '94: Intelligent Multimedia Information Retrieval Systems and Management*, Paris, CID, 1994, 146–60.

62 Mandala, R., Tokunaga, T. and Tanaka, H., 'Combining multiple evidence from different types of thesaurus for query expansion'. *SIGIR'99: Proceedings of the Association for Computing Machinery Special Interest Group on Information Retrieval (ACM/SIGIR) 22nd Annual International Conference on Research and Development in Information Retrieval*, New York, ACM, 1999, 191–7.

63 Chen, H. and Dhar, V., 'Cognitive process as a basis for intelligent retrieval systems design', *Information processing and management*, **27** (7), 1991, 405–32.

64 Chen, H., Yim, T., Fye, D. and Schatz, B., 'Automatic thesaurus generation for an electronic community system', *Journal of the American Society for Information Science*, **46** (3), 1995, 175–93.

65 Chen, H. and Ng, T. D., 'A concept space approach to addressing the vocabulary problem in scientific information retrieval: an experiment on the worm

community system', *Journal of the American Society for Information Science*, **48** (1), 1997, 17–31.

66   Chen, H. and Ng, T., 'An algorithmic approach to concept exploration in a large knowledge network (automatic thesaurus consultation): Symbolic Branch-and-Bound search vs. connectionist Hopfield net activation', *Journal of the American Society for Information Science*, **46** (5), 1995, 348–69.

67   Schatz, B. R., Johnson, E. H., Cochrane, P. A. and Chen, H., 'Interactive term suggestion for users of digital libraries: using subject thesauri and co-occurrence lists for information retrieval', *Proceedings of the 1st ACM International Conference on Digital libraries*, 1996, 126–33.

68   Chen, H., Martinez, J., Kirchhoff, A., Ng, T. D. and Schatz, B. R., 'Alleviating search uncertainty through concept associations: automatic indexing, co-occurrence analysis, and parallel computing', *Journal of the American Society for Information Science*, **49** (3), 1998, 206–16.

69   Ding, Y., Chowdhury, G. G. and Foo, S., 'Incorporating the results of co-word analyses to increase search variety for information retrieval', *Journal of information science*, **26** (6), 2000, 429–51.

70   Mitchell, S. and Mooney, M., 'INFOMINE: a model web-base academic virtual library', *Information technology and libraries*, **15** (1), 1996, 20–5.

71   Scout Report Signpost, 2000. Available at **http://www.ilrt.bris.ac.uk/ mirrors/scout/addserv/signpost/help.html#01**.

72   Social Science Information Gateway. Available at **http://www.sosig.ac.uk**.

73   Schwartz, C., *Sorting out the web: approaches to subject access*, Westport, Ablex Publishing, 2001.

74   Welcome to BIOME: Your guide to quality internet resources in the health and life sciences. Available at **http://www.biome.ac.uk**.

Chapter 8

Abstracts and abstracting

Abstracts

According to Webster's dictionary[1] an abstract is a summary or an epitome of a book, scientific article, or legal document. Ranganathan[2] defines an abstract as a summary, usually by a professional, other than the author, of essential contents of a work, usually an article in a periodical, together with the specification of its original. Ashworth[3] defines the term abstract as a precis of information, which in its narrower sense now usually refers to the information contained in an article in a periodical, short pamphlet, or serial publication. According to the ISO,[4] the term abstract signifies an abbreviated, accurate representation of a document without added interpretation or criticism and without distinction as to who wrote the abstract. Lancaster[5] defines an abstract as a brief but accurate representation of the contents of a document. Rowley[6] defines an abstract as a concise and accurate representation of the contents of a document in a style similar to that of the original document. She adds that an abstract covers all the main points made in the original document, and usually follows the style and arrangement of the parent document. Guinchat and Menou[7] mention that abstracts, as documentary products, usually take the form of quite short texts either accompanying the original document or included in its surrogate.

An abstract is different from an extract, an annotation or a summary. An extract is an abbreviated version of a document created by drawing sentences from the document itself, whereas an abstract, though it may include words occurring in a document, is a piece of text created by the abstractor rather than a direct quotation from the author.[5] An annotation is a note added to a title or other bibliographic element of a document by a way of comment or explanation, and a summary is a restatement within a document (usually at the end) of the document's salient findings and conclusions.[8]

Types of abstract

Abstracts may differ according to their writer, purpose, and style. Guinchat and Menou[7] suggest that the various types of abstract can be distinguished by:

- *their length*, which normally ranges from a few dozen to several hundred words, and is occasionally over a thousand
- *the amount of detail*, certain abstracts (known as *indicative abstracts*) simply provide a brief summary, whereas others (known as *informative abstracts*)

include a varying number of points that are likely to interest the user

- *the inclusion of judgements or critical analysis*, which may amount to some form of evaluation of the document
- *whether the indexer deals with the whole document* or only with aspects that are likely to interest the user (known as slanted abstracts)
- *whether the author of the abstract is the author of the original document* or some other person, and
- *the language used*, which may be a natural language or a more formalized (artificial) language.

Different criteria have been used by other information scientists to categorize the different kinds of abstracts, as discussed in the following sections.

Abstract by writer

Abstracts may be written by authors, by subject experts, or by professional abstractors. Thus, we may categorize them as: *author-prepared abstracts*, *expert-prepared abstracts*, and *professional-prepared abstracts*.

Articles in professional journals are usually accompanied by author-prepared abstracts. While these abstracts, being written by the authors of the articles themselves, should contain the most sought-after information, they usually lack a professional style. Expert abstractors are usually the choice of abstracting journals. They are trained in abstracting and are also expert in the subject field. Thus, their abstracts should be accurate, comprehensive, lucid, and terse. These abstracts are usually very prompt and are well written, though sometimes may be expensive. Professional abstractors abstract for a living, and may be employed to handle work in more than one language.

Abstracts by purpose

Abstracts are written with certain purposes in mind, and therefore there may be different abstracts to serve different purposes. Borko and Bernier[8] have identified four different types of abstracts: the *indicative abstract*, *informative abstract*, *critical abstract*, and *special purpose abstract*.

An *informative abstract* is intended to provide readers with quantitative and qualitative information as presented in the parent document. Informative abstracts may include information on purpose, scope, and methods, as well as the results and findings. Informative abstracts are often longer and are difficult to write, but they often save the user the time necessary to consult the original work.

An *indicative abstract* simply indicates what the parent document is all about. They are also called descriptive abstracts, because they usually describe what can be found in the original document. Indicative abstracts may contain information on purpose, scope or methodology, but not on results, conclusions or recommendations. Thus, an indicative abstract is unlikely to serve as a substitute for the original document.

A *critical abstract* contains some kind of critical comments or review by the abstractor. For indicative and informative abstracts, abstractors usually function as impartial reporters, whereas in a critical abstract, the abstractor deliberately includes his/her own opinion and interpretations. Preparation of critical abstracts requires subject expertise and is a time-consuming job.

Some abstracts may have been written to serve a special purpose or with a specific category of users in mind. Such abstracts are called *slanted* or *special-purpose abstracts*. Depending on the nature of the target user group, an abstractor may stress some part of the abstract (with more emphasis on informativeness) at the expense of some other part(s) (leading to an indicative abstract for that part). Some abstracts may have a slant towards some part of the subject dealt with in the original document; these are particularly useful for mission-oriented works rather than in discipline-oriented works.

Borko and Bernier[8] and Lancaster[5] suggest that another category of abstract can be identified in this group, called the *modular abstract*. Here an abstractor is expected to prepare different kinds of abstracts – indicative, informative, critical, and so on – any one of which may be used depending on the requirement of the abstracting agency. In fact, the abstractor writes various modules of abstract at the same time. Modular abstracts are intended as full content descriptions of current documents in five parts: a citation, an annotation, an indicative abstract, an informative abstract, and a critical abstract. The prime purpose of modular abstracts is to eliminate the duplication and waste of intellectual effort in the independent abstracting of the same documents by several services, without any attempt to force 'standardized' abstracts on services whose requirements may vary considerably as to form and subject slant.[5]

Abstracts by form

Three other kinds of abstract can also been identified, the *structured abstract*, *mini abstract*, and *telegraphic abstract*. A structured abstract may have a frame and slots that are to be filled in with information taken from the original document. This type of abstract is valuable in the compilation of handbooks summarizing a large number of studies performed in a particular field.[5] The term *mini abstract* refers to a highly structured abstract designed primarily for searching by computer. In fact, it is a cross between an abstract and an index and can be called a 'machine-readable-index-abstract'.[5] The term *telegraphic abstract* refers to an abstract that contains brief statements (as opposed to complete sentences), and thus the resulting abstract looks like telegraphic text.

Qualities of abstracts

An abstract must be brief and accurate and it must be presented in a format designed to facilitate the skimming of a large number of abstracts in a search for relevant material.[8] Guinchat and Menou[7] suggest that an abstract should possess the following qualities:

1   *concision*: however long the abstract is, care should be taken to avoid expressions or circumlocutions that can be replaced by single words, but this should

not be done at the expense of precision

2   *precision*: one should use expressions that are exact and as specific as possible without exceeding the abstract's requested length

3   *self-sufficiency*: the description of the document should be complete in itself and fully understandable without reference to any other document

4   *objectivity*: there must not be any personal interpretation or value judgment on the part of the abstractor (obviously this does not apply to critical abstracts).

Borko and Bernier[8] give the following basic qualities of abstracts:

1   *brevity: o*ne of the essential characteristics of abstracts is their brevity: they are much shorter than the documents from which they are derived. Brevity saves the user's time, and it lowers the cost of producing abstracts. However, it must be remembered that, while redundancy is to be avoided, there should not be any loss of novelty when trying to achieve brevity

2   *accuracy*: abstracts should be accurate and errors avoided as far as practicable. Errors may occur at many stages in the production of abstracts: in understanding the document's content and presentation, in the citation, and in typing, printing, and so on.

3   *clarity:* while an abstract should be brief and accurate, it must also be clearly written, avoiding all sorts of ambiguities.

A good abstract should also have the following qualities:[9]

1   it should be a self-contained unit, a complete report in a miniature form; it should be intelligible without reference to the original document

2   it should enable its users to (a) identify the basic contents of a work quickly and accurately, (b) determine its relevance to their interests, and (c) decide whether or not to read the original document in its entirety

3   it should be capable of being used as a secondary source of information

4   it should be impersonal

5   it should not take a critical form (except for critical abstracts)

6   it should be as up to date as possible

7   it should be able to be used as a retrieval aid in an automated information retrieval environment

8   it should not repeat the information that is obvious from the title or is well known to the user

9   it must avoid redundancy and repetition

10   it should be written in a clear and natural language and should avoid using abbreviations.

Uses of abstracts

Borko and Bernier[8] comment that without surrogates, such as abstracts, search through the accumulated literature would be impossible. In fact, there are a number of uses of abstracts, and that is why abstracting journals (in hard copy and/or on CD-ROM) have existed in almost all subject fields all over the world. Guinchat and Menou[7] identify three major functions of abstracts:

1 dissemination of information
2 selection of information by the end-user, and
3 retrieval of information, especially in computerized information retrieval systems.

The following are some of the major uses of abstracts:

1 they promote current awareness: abstracts repackage the information contained in the original document into a more condensed form and therefore are less time-consuming to read and to keep up-to-date
2 they save reading time: abstracts are much smaller in size in comparison to the original document, and yet can provide as much information as the user needs without going into the full text
3 they facilitate selection: in an information retrieval environment one may retrieve a large number of items, reading the full texts of which may be impossible or very time-consuming. In such cases the user may consult the abstracts of the retrieved items in order to be selective
4 they help overcome the language barrier: most abstracting journals cover more than one language, and therefore the user can find out what studies and research have been published in languages that he or she cannot read, which would have been impossible otherwise even if the original documents were available
5 they facilitate literature searches: without indexed abstracts, searches of open and classified literature would be impossible due to the huge volume of material available
6 they improve indexing efficiency, as they can be indexed much more rapidly than can the original documents. The rate of indexing can be improved by a factor of two to four, and the cost of preparing the index is reduced with little or no reducton in quality[8]
7 they aid in the preparation of reviews and can be of much help in the preparation of bibliographies and so on.

The art of abstracting

The art of preparing abstracts is called abstracting. As already mentioned, there are professionals and subject experts engaged in preparing abstracts for various abstracting journals. There are a number of documents providing guidelines for the preparation of good abstracts (see for example, Lancaster,[5] Borko and Bernier,[8] and Bhattacharyya[9]). Lancaster[5] suggests that the shorter the abstract, the better, as long as the meaning remains clear and there is no sacrifice of accuracy. Superfluous words, such as 'the author states', 'the article has', etc., should be left out. Abbreviations, other than that are standardized and used frequently, should be defined in the abstract.

Borko and Bernier[8] suggest that an adequate abstract of a research article must cover the purpose, method, results, conclusions, and specialized content, if any. They have also suggested some guidelines for writing indicative and informative abstracts:

Informative abstract	*Indicative abstract*
Use active voice	Use passive voice
Use past tense	Use present tense
Discuss the research	Discuss the article that discusses the research

Weil et al.[10] have recommended a list of dos and don'ts for abstractors. They suggest that an abstractor should:

1 scan the document purposefully for key facts
2 slant the abstract to the audience
3 tell what was found
4 tell why the work was done
5 tell how the work was done
6 place findings early in the topical sentence
7 put details in succeeding sentences
8 place general statements last
9 separate relatively independent subjects
10 differentiate experiment from hypothesis
11 be informative but brief
12 be exact, concise and unambiguous
13 use short, complete sentences
14 use short, simple, familiar words
15 avoid unnecessary words
16 use generic expressions when possible
17 employ normal technical English
18 use direct statements
19 describe conclusions in the present tense
20 use abbreviations sparingly
21 avoid using unusual words or phrases
22 cite bibliographical data completely.

They suggest that an abstractor should not:

1 change the meaning of the original
2 comment on or interpret the document
3 mention earlier work
4 include detailed experimental results
5 discuss details of conventional apparatus
6 mention future work
7 begin abstracts with stock phrases
8 use uncommon or rare phraseology

9 use questionable jargon
10 waste words by stating the obvious
11 say the same things in two ways
12 use noun forms of verbs
13 overuse synonyms
14 use a choppy, telegraphic style.

Bhattacharyya[9] proposes the following steps to be followed by abstractors in their task. It should be noted that, when working under time constraints, these steps can be an ideal working method.

1 Read the whole document at least once to obtain a clear idea about its essential contents and special features, such as tables, illustrations, and list of references.
2 After reading, examine the original document carefully with emphasis on the author abstract, if any, the first and the last paragraphs, and the key sections, such as the introduction, purpose, conclusion, summary and recommendations. Also take note of the footnotes, if any.
3 Underline, if necessary, the key phrases and sentences, while reading and examining the original document.
4 Write the abstract in the style and the manner in which you feel most comfortable and efficient of course being consistent with the principles and rules formulated for the purpose.
5 Initially, prepare a rough draft of the abstract.
6 Make use of the author abstract, if it exists, to work out the draft abstract.
7 Choose, if suitable, direct excerpts from the original document to work out the draft abstract.
8 Make references to directly related abstracts in earlier issues and in the same issue of the compilation. The different subject categories in which one and the same abstract falls are also deemed to be directly related.
9 Revise and edit the draft abstract to prune redundancy and improve quality before finalizing the abstract.
10 Put your initials at the end of the abstract.

There are a number of guidelines devised by commercial abstracting services for use by their abstractors. Borko and Bernier[8] discuss the essential guidelines from three manuals of instructions for abstractors, *Directions for abstractors*, published by the Chemical Abstracts Service; *Policies and procedures* by the American Biographic Center, which publishes *Historical abstracts*; and *Guidelines for reviewers*, prepared by *Applied mechanics reviews*. Lancaster[5] also refers to various guidelines, such as the *Abstracting guidelines* published by the Defense Documentation Center. Fidel[11] has analysed the abstracting instructions prepared by as many as 36 producers of databases and has prepared a summary of instructions, which have been reproduced by Lancaster.[5] Figure 8.1 presents some general guidelines for selection of terms and use of language in abstracts.

Selection of terms

- Use important concepts and terms that will help readers understand the content of the host document, and that will also be useful for retrieval of the document concerned by an information retrieval system.
- Use terms that are identical to the assigned descriptors; and also use those that complement the descriptors (e.g. more specific terms, geographic or proper names, etc.).
- Avoid using negative words.
- Use complementary words (e.g. use a company name to specify a product, or a place name to specify a company).

Language

- Write clear and short sentences rather than long and complex ones.
- Avoid using the exact words used by the author(s).
- Use standard vocabulary (as opposed to jargon), and well-accepted terms.
- Do not use slang or colloquial language.
- Follow the language practices of the target user group(s), e.g. American or British spellings.
- If abbreviations are used, give their full form.
- Avoid using repetitive words.
- Follow a consistent style.

Fig. 8.1   *Guidelines for abstractors*

In addition, a number of standards have come out over the years to guide abstractors in their work and also to keep control over the process of preparing abstracts. In the United States a significant step toward the standardization of abstracting was taken by the Armed Services Technical Information Agency (ASTIA) with the publication of the *ASTIA Guidelines for cataloguing and abstracting* in 1962. ASTIA was renamed the Defense Documentation Center (DDC) and another set of guidelines for abstracting was developed by the DDC in 1968. In 1970 the American National Standards Institute (ANSI) brought out a standard for abstracting that defines an abstract, types of abstracts, and related terms designating terse writings. The ANSI standard also prescribes the various points that are to be covered in an abstract, such as purpose, methods, results, conclusions, collateral, and other information. The ISO (International Standards Organization) brought out recommendations concerning abstracts and synopses in 1961, and another standard concerning abstracts in 1974. UNESCO published a *Guide for the preparation of author's abstracts for publication* in 1968.

Automatic abstracting

In 1979 Davis and Rush[12] mention eight significant studies in computer-based abstracting that had been described in the literature:

1   the Luhn study

2   the ACSI-Matic study conducted by IBM
3   Oswald's study
4   word-association research
5   the TRW studies conducted by Edmundson and Wyllys
6   the Earl study
7   the Rush, Salvador, and Zamora study, and
8   the Russian work, led by Skorokhod'ko.

Davis and Rush[12] suggest that a computer-based abstracting system must:

1   read the document to be abstracted
2   analyse the document
3   apply a set of selection/transformational rules to produce the abstract
4   format the resulting abstract, and
5   print the abstract.

According to Salton[13] the most widely used simplified abstracting method consists of computing a value, or weight, for each sentence of an original document, based on the types of words and phrases included in the sentences, and then using the most highly weighted sentences to generate an abstract. This was the basic principle, sometimes called the sentence-scoring technique, of the pioneering work of Luhn[14] on automatic abstracting. Luhn's procedure involved some simple operations, which have been nicely presented by Lancaster.[5]

1   A stoplist eliminates all the nonsubstantive terms from further processing.
2   Occurrences of all remaining words are counted and the words ranked by frequency of occurrence.
3   All words occurring more than x times are defined as 'high frequency' or 'significant' words.
4   Sentences containing concentrations of these high frequency words are located. Two words are considered related within a sentence if there are no more than four intervening words.
5   A 'significance factor' for each sentence is calculated, as follows:

   (a) the number of 'clusters' in the sentence is determined (a cluster is the longest group of words bounded by significant words in which the significant words are not separated by more than four intervening words);
   (b) the number of significant words in the cluster is determined and the square of the number is divided by the total number of words within the cluster;
   (c) the significance factor for the sentence can be defined either as the value of the highest cluster or the sum of the values of all the clusters in the sentence.

According to this procedure the sentences having the highest significance factors are selected and are printed out, in the sequence in which they occur in the text, to form the abstract. Most of the studies that followed, except those based on natural language processing techniques (see further for discussion), are some kind of modifications or improvements of Luhn's work.

Salton[13] outlines a typical automatic abstracting system based on a sentence extracting system (see Figure 8.2). This system distinguishes between words occurring in the text body and those occurring in titles, captions, and section headings. Words occurring in the body of the text may be subjected to a standard term-weighting process, whereas terms occurring in the title, captions, and section headings may receive some kind of special treatment based on the location of the terms in the specific document.

After individual text words are identified, a term weighting system can assign term weights as a function of the frequency of occurrence of the words in the texts and the number of documents in the collection to which the terms are assigned. It may be noted that a high order of indexing performance is obtained by using a term weight that varies directly with the frequency of occurrence of the terms in individual documents and inversely with the number of documents in which the terms occur (*tdf.idf* weight).[13] Phrase weights can also be generated in the same way. Term phrases may be generated consisting of groups of words that occur in the sentences of the texts, and phrase weights can be assigned, for example, as the average weights of the component terms.[13]

Once term and phrase weights have been computed, a composite *sentence score* can be computed as the average weight of the included single words and phrases; alternatively, the term phrases may receive extra weight, or extra importance may be assigned to sentences in which many highly weighted terms and phrases are close together.

The last step of sentence extracting consists of choosing a number of highly scoring sentences, or choosing a certain proportion of text sentences exhibiting the highest sentence score.

A document extract constructed according to this system is likely to contain a large number of sentences that indicate the document's content; at the same time it is difficult to maintain readability and coherence among the sentences. Salton[13] mentions that there are three important factors that should also be considered along with this text extraction process. These are:

1   Certain cue words or cue phrases in text sentences may indicate a sentence's importance regardless of the actual sentence or word scores. Sentences containing such phrases as 'our work', 'this paper', 'the present research', and so on, might automatically be used for abstracting purposes.

2   Syntactic-coherence considerations suggest that sentences referring to earlier passages already used in the abstract should also be included. For example, sentences containing passages such as 'presented earlier', and 'stated above' could be included in the abstract if the preceding text had already been chosen.

3   The location of a sentence in a text may be used to adjust the normal sentence score. For example, the first sentence of a paragraph may be chosen automatically regardless of the computed sentence score.

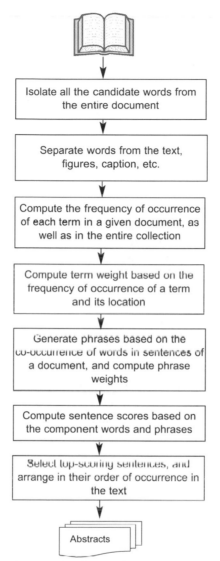

Fig. 8.2 *A simple sentence extracting system*

Edmundson[15, 16] identifies four possible methods for the creation of automatic abstracts:

1   The *key method* is similar to the method of word frequency criteria of Luhn. In this method sentences are given weight that is the sum of the weights of the component words.
2   The *cue method* is based on some cue words that determine the significance of a given sentence within a text. In this method a 'cue dictionary' includes a list

of words that receive a positive weight and another list of words with a negative weight. The significance value of a sentence is the sum of the value of the component words.

3   The *title method* is based on the assumption that words occurring in titles and subheads are good indicators of the content. Sentences are given a significance value based on the number of title and subhead words that they contain.

4   The *location method* weight is given to a sentence on the basis of where it appears in a document. Sentences appearing in certain sections of the text are assumed to be more indicative of content than others.

Rush et al.[17] developed a method that takes into account 'contextual criteria' for the selection of significant sentences. Their 'word control list' includes two sets of words – a larger list that includes words that, if present in a sentence, will automatically reject the sentence from being selected, and another short list of words whose presence in a sentence will mark it as a significant one. Frequency criteria is used to modify the weights associated with the positive and negative cues in the word control list. Once the significant sentences, based on the weight, are chosen, the second step is to select those sentences that may be related to the chosen sentences, using what is termed 'inter-sentence reference'. Each selected sentence is scanned to identify certain cues (such as 'hence', 'therefore', etc.) that would indicate that a previous sentence would be related to the given sentence. Thus the final abstract would be composed of sentences chosen on the basis of 'contextual influence' and 'inter-sentence reference'.

Automatic abstracting systems based on contextual clues of sentence importance have been developed by Paice.[18] In this method some typical word class types (such as 'introduces', 'examines', 'investigates', 'developed', and so on) are identified and sentence templates having some typical words and permissible word distances (in terms of number of words) between a pair of selected words are developed. When a particular sentence fits into the prescribed sentence templates, a complete sentence score is computed by adding up the prescribed weights for the sentence components that match the corresponding template specifications. After having completed the task of sentence scoring, an extract of the prescribed length can be constructed by choosing high-scoring sentences from the original paper together with adjacent text sentences that are related to the chosen excerpts by appropriate exophoric references, i.e.. reference words or phrases that point to text portions outside the immediate context, for example, 'hence', 'besides', and so on.

A substantial lack of coherence among the sentences in the abstract produced by the method developed by Paice may still persist. Salton[13] suggests that a better method of preparing automatic abstracts than the extraction method may be to choose one or more complete paragraphs from the texts of original documents. The identification of interesting passages in particular documents can be used not only to abstract these documents, but also to retrieve them.[13] These systems are called passage retrieval systems.[19] However, automatic abstracting systems, which are based on the sentence/passage extraction methods mentioned above, cannot produce abstracts in natural language. Expert systems and natural language processing techniques have been used to produce abstracts based on text understanding and summarization. Some automatic systems that can produce abstracts by text understanding, such as TOPIC, FRUMP, and so on, are discussed later in this book.

Recent works on text summarization

Automatic abstracting and text summarization are now used synonymously to describe systems that generate abstracts or summaries of texts. In simple abstracting or summarization systems, parts of text – sentences or paragraphs – are selected automatically based on some linguistic and/or statistical criteria to produce the abstract or summary. More sophisticated systems may merge two or more sentences, or parts thereof, to generate one coherent sentence, or may generate simple summaries from discrete items of data.

Interest in automatic abstracting and text summarization is reflected by the huge number of research papers that have appeared in a number of international conferences and workshops at the beginning of the 21st century. Some of these works have been reviewed by Lancaster,[20] Gaizauskas and Wilks[21] and Lancaster and Warner.[22] Several techniques are used for automatic abstracting and text summarization. Goldstein et al.[23] use conventional IR methods and linguistic cues for extracting and ranking sentences for generating news article summaries. A number of studies on text summarization have been reported. Silber and McCoy[24] claim that their linear time algorithm for calculating lexical chains is an efficient method for preparing automatic summarization of documents. Chuang and Yang[25] report a text summarization technique using cue phrases appearing in the texts of US patent abstracts. Jin and Dong-Yan.[26] propose a method of automatic abstracting that integrates the advantages of linguistic and statistical analysis in a corpus. They propose a methodology for generating automatic abstracts that provides an integration of the advantages of methods based on linguistic analysis and those based on statistics. Aristotle builds an automatic medical data system that is capable of producing a semantic representation of the text in a canonical form.[27]

SALOMON (Summary and Analysis of Legal texts for Managing Online Needs) automatically summarizes legal texts written in Dutch.[28] The system extracts relevant information from the full texts of Belgian criminal cases and uses it to summarize each decision. A text grammar represented as a semantic network is used to determine the category of each case. The system extracts relevant information about each case, such as the name of the court that issues the decision, the decision date, the offences charged, the relevant statutory provisions disclosed by the court, as well as the legal principles applied in the case.

RAFI (resume automatique a fragments indicateurs) is an automatic text summarization system that transforms full text scientific and technical documents into condensed texts.[29] RAFI adopts discourse analysis technique using a thesaurus for recognition and selection of the most pertinent elements of texts. The system assumes a typical structure of areas from each scientific document, such as previous knowledge, content, method and new knowledge.

TEXTNET is a software designed to provide assistance to abstractors. Arguing that purely automatic abstracting systems do not always produce useful results, Craven[30–33] proposes a hybrid abstracting system in which some tasks are performed by human abstractors and others by an abstractor's assistance software called TEXNET.

Discussion

With the rapid increase in the availability of full-text and multimedia information in digital form, the need for automatic abstracts or summaries as a filtering tool is becoming extremely important. Consequently areas such as automatic abstracting and text summarization and automatic information extraction have drawn much research interest. However, the performance of many automatic abstracting and information extraction systems has not justified commercial applications. For example, recent experiments on the usefulness of the automatically extracted keywords and phrases from full texts by TEXNET in the process of abstracting by human abstractors showed some considerable variation among subjects, and only 37% of the subjects found the keywords and phrases to be useful in writing their abstracts.[30] Some recent works on information extraction and text mining are discussed in Chapter 21.

References

1   *Webster's third new international dictionary of the English language*, Springfield, MA, Merriam-Webster, 1961.
2   Ranganathan, S. R., *Classified catalogue code*, 5th edn, Bombay, Asia Publishing House, 1964.
3   Ashworth, W., 'Abstracting'. In Ashworth, W. (ed.), *Handbook of special librarianship and information work*, 3rd edn, London, Aslib, 1967, 453–81.
4   ISO 214:1976. *Documentation: abstracts for publication and documentation*, Geneva, International Standards Organization, 1976.
5   Lancaster, F. W., *Indexing and abstracting in theory and practice*, 3rd edn, London, Facet Publishing, 2003.
6   Rowley, J. E., *Organizing knowledge: an introduction to information retrieval*, 2nd edn, Aldershot, Gower, 1992.
7   Guinchat, C. and Menou, M., *General introduction to the techniques of information and documentation work*, Paris, Unesco, 1983.
8   Borko, H. and Bernier, C. L., *Abstracting concepts and methods*, New York, Academic Press, 1975.
9   Bhattacharyya, G., *Abstracts and abstracting for information service professionals*, Bangalore, DRTC, March 1989 [Mimeographed].
10 B. Weil et al., 'Technical-abstracting fundamentals', *Journal of chemical documentation*, **3**, 1963, 86–9, 125–36.
11 Fidel, R., 'Writing abstracts for free-text searching', *Journal of documentation*, **42**, 1986, 11–21.
12 Davis, C. H. and Rush, J. E., *Guide to information science*, Westport, CT, Greenwood Press, 1979.
13 Salton, G., *Automatic text processing: the transformation, analysis and*

retrieval of information by computer, Reading, MA, Addison-Wesley, 1989.

14 Luhn, H. P., 'The automatic creation of literature abstracts', *IBM journal of research and development,* **2** (2), 1958, 159–65.

15 Edmundson, H. P., 'Problems in automatic abstracting', *Communications of the ACM,* **7** (4), 1964, 259–63.

16 Edmundson, H. P., 'New methods in automatic extracting', *Journal of the Association for Computing Machinery,* **16**, 1969, 264–85.

17 Rush, J. E., Salvador, R. and Zamora, A., 'Automatic abstracting and indexing, II: production of indicative abstracts by application of contextual inference and syntactic coherence criteria', *Journal of the American Society for Information Science,* **22** (4), 1971, 260–74.

18 Paice, C. D., 'Automatic generation of literature abstracts: an approach based on the identification of self indicating phrase'. In: Oddy, R. N., Robertson, S. E., van Rijsbergen, C. J. and Williams, P. W. (eds.), *Information retrieval research,* London, Butterworths, 1981.

19 O'Connor, J., 'Passage retrieval by text searching', *Journal of the American Society for Information Science,* **32** (4), 1980, 227–39.

20 Lancaster, F. W., *Indexing and abstracting in theory and practice,* 2nd edn, London, Library Association Publishing, 1998.

21 Gaizauskas, R. and Wilks, Y., 'Information extraction: beyond document retrieval', *Journal of documentation,* **54** (1), 1998, 70–105.

22 Lancaster, F.W. and Warner, A., *Intelligent technologies in library and information service applications,* ASIST Monograph Series, Medford, NJ, Information Today Inc., 2001.

23 Goldstein, J., Kantrowitz, M., Mittal, V. and Carbonell, J., Summarizing text documents: sentence selection and evaluation metrics. In: *Proceeding of the 22nd Annual International Conference on Research and Development in Information Retrieval,* ACM, 1999, 121–8.

24 Silber, H. G. and McCoy, K. F., Efficient text summarization using lexical chains In: H. Lieberman (ed.), *Proceedings of IUI 2000 International Conference on Intelligent User Interfaces,* 9–12 Jan. 2000, New Orleans, LA, New York, ACM, 2000, 252–5.

25 Chuang, W. and Yang, J., Extracting sentence segments for text summarization: a machine learning approach. In: *Proceedings of the 23rd Annual International ACM SIGIR Conference on Research and Development in Information Retrieval,* ACM, 2000, 152–9.

26 Jin, S. and Dong-Yan, Z., 'Study of automatic abstracting based on corpus and hierarchical dictionary', *Journal of software,* **11**, 2000, 308–14

27 Roux, M. and Ledoray, V., 'Understanding of medico-technical reports', *Artificial intelligence in medicine,* **18**, 2000, 149–72

28 Moens, M.-F. and Uyttendaele, C., 'Automatic text structuring and categorization as a first step in summarizing legal cases', *Information processing and management,* **33**, 1997, 727–37.

29 Lehmam, A., 'Text structuration leading to an automatic summary system: RAFI', *Information processing and management,* **35**, 1999, 181–91.

30   Craven, T. C., 'Abstracts produced using computer assistance', *Journal of the American Society for Information Science*, **51**, 2000, 745–56.
31   Craven, T. C., An experiment in the use of tools for computer-assisted abstracting. In: *ASIS'96: Proceedings of the 59th ASIS Annual Meeting 1996. Baltimore, MD, October 21-24, 1996*, Vol. 33, Medford, NJ, Information Today, 1996, 203–8.
32   Craven, T. C., 'A computer-aided abstracting tool kit', *Canadian journal of information science*, **18**, 1993, 19–31.
33   Craven, T. C., 'Text network display editing with special reference to the production of customized abstracts', *Canadian journal of information science*, **13**, 1988, 59–68.

Chapter 9

Searching and retrieval

Introduction

We have already seen in Chapter 1 that the searching subsystem is one of the major subsystems of an information retrieval system. In this subsystem, users' queries are received and interpreted, appropriate search statements are formulated, and the actual search (i.e. matching queries with the document profile or database) is conducted with a view to retrieving the required information. All these tasks can be performed manually, as used to be done in the earlier systems, or can be automated. The development of cheaper direct-access mass storage devices, magnetic disks and drums, the associated software, and advancements in electronic communication systems brought about the possibility of more dynamic searching via online methods. The concept of online searching has occupied a large and significant area in the study and research of modern information retrieval. However, a user often faces difficulties in approaching an online search system, especially in formulating an appropriate search statement. The cost of searching a database, whether in-house or external, can be reduced significantly if an appropriate strategy for searching is followed. The search strategy helps the user select the optimum path for searching a file or a database. This involves a number of measures that are to be taken before and during a search. This chapter discusses the basic concepts of the search strategy and describes the actual searching process in the context of information retrieval systems. Features of online searching are discussed later.

The search strategy and its prerequisites

The search strategy encompasses several steps and levels of work in information retrieval. Meadow and Cochrane[1] mention that the search strategy includes at least three decision points that a searcher has to reach. There are many issues that need to be considered while formulating an appropriate search statement. These are:

1   the concepts or facets to be searched and their order
2   the term(s) that appropriately represent(s) the search concept
3   the feature(s) of the retrieval system concerned, and
4   the measures to be taken in revising a search statement.

Developing a good search strategy requires knowledge about the nature and organization of target database(s) and also the exact needs of the user. Knowledge of the user's exact requirement can greatly affect the actual search and retrieval process. In some cases, the user may want only a few relevant items on a given topic, in which case the task of searching will obviously be limited. Conversely, the user may wish to obtain all the relevant items (obviously with as small a number of non-relevant items as possible), in which case the search must be exhaustive. Thus, there could be three kinds of search:[1]

1   *high recall search*: when the user needs to find out all the relevant items on the stated topic
2   *high precision search*: when the user needs only relevant items, i.e. as small a number of non-relevant items as possible, and
3   *brief search*: when the user wants only a few relevant items as opposed to all the relevant items.

The pre-search interview

The results of a search depend heavily upon the correct understanding of the users' precise needs. This understanding can be developed through a pre-search interview.[2] This is crucial if the client is not to be present during the actual search.

A pre-search interview is a conversation that takes place between a user and member of the information staff regarding the actual information requirement of the user. Somerville[3] lists the following skills that the successful pre-search interviewer should possess:

•   ability to conduct personal communication
•   conceptual skills
•   analytical skills
•   knowledge of file organization
•   understanding of indexing policy and vocabulary control, and
•   subject knowledge.

It may be noted that the concept of pre-search interview presupposes the existence of a search intermediary. This concept was developed to get a better understanding of the search requirements of a user in an online search environment. As discussed later in this book, the concept of pre-search interview, although very important in a mediated search process, has very little relevance in the context of information retrieval from the the world wide web (discussed in Chapter 18) and digital libraries (discussed in Chapter 22), since these systems are designed to be used by end users without any direct involvement of human intermediaries. Nevertheless, an understanding of the process involved in a search interview process may be quite useful for designers of information retrieval systems in the web and digital library environment.

The searching process

A database may comprise controlled or uncontrolled vocabulary. Cleverdon[4] mentions that a user searching a database that has controlled index languages must perform the following:

1 decide the words that might be used by the authors of the relevant documents
2 decide which particular database(s) is/are to be searched
3 use the thesaurus of the chosen database in order to translate the query terms in the appropriate way
4 guess which of the chosen terms (or concepts) might have been used by the database indexer
5 coordinate the terms (often using Boolean operators) to formulate the search statement
6 input the search statement
7 repeat steps 5 and 6 until a desirable output is obtained or the search fails altogether, and
8 identify the actual relevant items from among those retrieved.

One major task in the searching process relates to the coordination of terms (step 5 above) in order to formulate the actual search statement. The result of the search depends largely on how adequately the search terms are combined. Boolean search techniques have been used widely since the beginning of mechanized information retrieval.

Retrieval models

Since the early days of information retrieval research, efforts have been made to develop formal theory-based approaches to model various aspects of information retrieval systems. An advantage of adopting a model-based approach is that each model, although different from another, is based on set of principles and assumptions, and, while theory drives experiment in suggesting new ways and means of carrying out tests, at the same time experiment drives theory by either justifying or improving the model.

Information retrieval models can broadly be classified into two groups: user-centred or cognitive models, and system-centred models. Cognitive models take a holistic view of information retrieval, by taking into account not only the retrieval mechanisms used in matching the queries with stored information, but also the following:

• the ways in which the user's information need can be formulated as a query
• the human–computer interactions that take place during the search process
• the social and cognitive environments in which the process takes place
• how the information is used by the user to meet a specific information need.

These models are very different in their nature, and in their disciplinary bases, when compared with the system-centred models, which provide an explicit statement of the workings of the information search and retrieval mechanism (Sparck Jones and

Willett [5]). User-centred information retrieval models have been discussed in Chapter 11. This chapter provides an overview of classical (system-centred) information retrieval models. These include: the Boolean search model, which compares Boolean query statements with the term set used to represent document contents; the probabilistic retrieval model, which is based on the computation of relevance probabilities for the documents of a collection; and the vector processing model, which represents both documents and queries by term sets and compares global similarities between queries and documents. Several models have been developed on the basis of the classical information retrieval models, not all of which have been discussed in this book, but appropriate references have been provided for interested readers. While classical retrieval models are based on logical and mathematical principles, some alternative models of information retrieval have also been developed over the past few years. Two prominent alternative types of retrieval model, viz. the hypertest model and the natural language processing model, are also discussed in this chapter, and later on in the book.

Boolean search model

George Boole (1815–1864) devised a system of symbolic logic in which he used three operators, viz. +, x, and –, to combine statements in symbolic form. John Venn later expressed Boolean logic relationships through what are known as Venn diagrams. The three operators of Boolean logic are the *logical* sum (+), *logical product* (x), and *logical difference* (–). Information retrieval systems allow the users to express their queries by using these operators.[5]

Logical product or *AND logic* allows the searcher to specify the coincidence of two or more concepts. For example, in order to ask for information on 'computers and information retrieval' the user may formulate the search statement as

(COMPUTERS) AND (INFORMATION RETRIEVAL).

Logical sum or *OR logic* allows the searcher to specify alternatives among search terms (or concepts). For example, with the query statement

(COMPUTERS) OR (INFORMATION RETRIEVAL)

the searcher indicates that items on either of these two topics, or both, will serve the purpose.

Logical difference or *NOT logic* provides facilities to exclude items from a set. For example, with the search statement

(INFORMATION RETRIEVAL) AND NOT (DBMS)

the user narrows his subject, in this case specifying that he or she does not require information on DBMSs.

These three operators may be combined in one search statement, e.g.

(INFORMATION RETRIEVAL OR INFORMATION SCIENCE) AND (ONLINE OR COMPUTERS) AND (DEVELOPING COUNTRIES OR THIRD WORLD) AND NOT (DBMS)

However, when the operators are combined, the resulting search statement can become quite complex. Venn diagrams (Figure 9.1) can be helpful in demonstrating Boolean logical relationships.

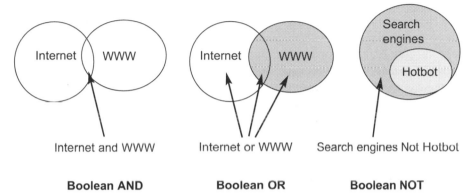

| Boolean AND | Boolean OR | Boolean NOT |

Fig. 9.1 *Boolean searches*

Because of its simplicity, the Boolean retrieval model has formed the basis of most database management and information retrieval systems. All information retrieval systems, including online public access catalogues, CD-ROM and online databases, web search engines, digital libraries, etc., make extensive use of Boolean search operators.

Limitations of Boolean searching

Despite its popularity, the Boolean search model has certain limitations. The first relates to the formulation of search statements. It has been noted that users are not able to formulate an exact search statement by the combination of AND, OR, and NOT operators, especially when several query terms are involved. In such cases either the search statement becomes too narrow or too broad. Boolean searching, therefore, often calls for a trained intermediary.

The second limitation relates to the number of retrieved items. It has been noted that users cannot predict a priori exactly how many items are to be retrieved to satisfy a given query. If the search statement is broad, the number of retrieved items may sometimes be several hundreds and thus it may be quite difficult to find out the exact information required. On the other hand, a given search may retrieve very few items, if the search statement is too narrow, in which case the user may miss some relevant items.

The third limitation of Boolean searching is that it identifies an item as relevant by finding out whether a given query term is present or not in a given record in the database. Thus, all retrieved items are considered to be of equal importance, however, a given concept may be discussed in different documents with differing emphasis or weight: there is no mechanism available in Boolean searching to determine this. In other words, the retrieved items cannot be ranked in decreasing order of relevance, for example.

It is therefore necessary to pay more attention to the provision of facilities that enable the end-user to search in a more effective manner. Two different methods have been suggested for this purpose. First there are systems based on the fuzzy set model, that reduces the strict class membership characteristics of Boolean logic and thereby allows the retrieval of partially matched items (Bookstein[6]). There are also other systems that use Boolean searches but, with the help of front-end systems or interfaces, provide guidance to the users in conducting the search in an effective manner. These systems often allow the user to put the query in natural language, and are therefore called natural language interfaces.

Probabilistic retrieval model

Probability theory has been used as a principal means for modelling the retrieval process in mathematical terms. In conventional retrieval situations a document is retrieved whenever the keyword set attached to the document set appears similar in some sense to the query keywords. In this case, the document is considered relevant to the query. Since the relevance of a document with respect to a query is a matter of degree, it can be postulated that when the document and query vectors are sufficiently similar, the corresponding probability of relevance is large enough to make it reasonable to retrieve the document in response to the query.[7]

The basic underlying tenet of the probabilistic approach to retrieval is that, for optimal performance, documents should be ranked in order of decreasing probability of relevance or usefulness to the user.[8] Probabilistic approaches, therefore, attempt to estimate or calculate, in some way, the probability that a document will be relevant for a particular user. Several models based on probabilistic approaches have been advocated; here we shall briefly look into three such models.

Maron and Kuhns[9] proposed a model for probabilistic retrieval as early as in 1960. They advocated that the probability that a given document would be relevant to a user can be assessed by a calculation of the probability, for each document in the collection, that a user submitting a particular query would judge that document relevant. Thus, for a query consisting of only one term (B), the probability that a particular document (Dm) will be judged relevant is the ratio of users who submit query term (B) and consider the document (Dm) to be relevant in relation to the number of users who submitted the query term (B). Adopting this approach, one has to employ historical information to calculate the probability of relevance: the number of times that users who submitted a particular query term (B) judged a document (Dm) relevant compared with the total number of users who submitted that particular query term (B). However, in the absence of such information, it is the job of the indexer to judge the relevance of the documents in respect of a particular query. Thus, the PRP (probability ranking principle), as represented in Maron's and Kuhns's model, can be represented as the probability that users submitting a particular query term (B) will judge an individual document (Dm) to be relevant.

A different approach to determining the probability of relevance of a document was developed by Robertson and Sparck Jones.[10] The essence of this approach is that the probability of relevance can be calculated not for a set of users employing a particular query term in relation to a given document, but for a set of documents having a particular property in relation to a given user. They propose that given an individual searcher and a set of documents having the property D, the probability that the user will judge the document as relevant can be calculated as the ratio of the number of documents that have the property D. This approach therefore suggests the use of binary (unweighted) indexing and the probabilistic weighting of query terms; the probability of relevance would be interpreted as the probability that an individual user would judge a document having the property D as relevant.

The model suggested by Salton and McGill[7] (see also Salton[12]) takes a different approach. The essence of this model is that if estimates for the probability of occurrence of various terms in relevant documents can be calculated, then the probabilities that a document will be retrieved, given that it is relevant, or that it is not, can be estimated. Several experiments have shown that the probabilistic model can yield good results. However, such results have not been sufficiently better than those obtained using the Boolean or vector space model.

This approach is based on two basic parameters:

1   The probability of relevance – $Pr_{(rel)}$
2   The probability of non-relevance – $Pr_{(non-rel)}$.

If relevance is considered as a binary property then

$$Pr_{(non-rel)} = 1 - Pr_{(rel)}$$

However, there are two cost parameters associated with the process of retrieval:

a_1 – the loss associated with the retrieval of a non-relevant record
a_2 – the loss associated with the non-retrieval of a relevant record.

Because of the fact that retrieval of a non-relevant record carries a loss of $a_1[1-Pr_{(rel)}]$, and the rejection of a relevant item has an associated loss factor of $a_2 Pr_{(rel)}$, the total loss for a given retrieval process will be minimized if an item is retrieved whenever

$$a_2 Pr_{(rel)} \geq a_1[1 - Pr_{(rel)}]$$

Equivalently, a retrieval function (g) or a discriminant function (*DISC*) may be defined, and an item may be retrieved whenever the value of g and *DISC* is greater than or equals zero, where

$$g \text{ or } DISC = \frac{P_{(\text{rel})}}{1 - Pr_{(\text{rel})}} - \frac{a_1}{a_2}$$

The relevance properties of a record must be related to the relevance properties of various terms attached to the records. The probabilities that a document is relevant and not relevant, given that it has been selected, are defined by $P_{(\text{rel}|\text{selected})}$ and $P_{(\text{non-rel}|\text{selected})}$ respectively.

Bayes's theorem from probability theory allows us to invert conditional probabilities:

$$P\,(A|B) = \frac{P_{(B|A)}\,P_{(A)}}{P_{(B)}}$$

Assuming that the factor of loss parameters is insignificant, we get the following expression:

$$g\,(\text{selected}) = \frac{P_{(\text{rel}|\text{selected})}}{P_{(\text{non-rel}|\text{selected})}} = \frac{P_{(\text{selected}|\text{rel})}\,P_{(\text{rel})}}{P_{(\text{selected}|\text{non-rel})}\,P_{(\text{non-rel})}}$$

Note that the last portion of the formula, i.e. $P_{(\text{rel})}/P_{(\text{non-rel})}$, is constant for a given query and document database, independent of any particular document.

Applications of probabilistic models for information retrieval have been demonstrated in the OKAPI system (Sparck Jones and Willett[5]). The Inference Network model, based on the probabilistic model, ranks documents in order of decreasing probability, so that they satisfy the user's information need rather than being relevant to the query, as is done in the basic probabilistic model (Turtle and Croft[11]).

The vector processing model

The vector processing model assumes that an available term set, called *term vectors*, is used for both the stored records and information requests.[12, 13] Collectively the terms assigned to a given text are used to represent text content.

Consider a collection of documents in which each document is characterized by one or more index terms. Thus, the documents are the objects in the collection each of which is represented by a number of properties (here index terms). The similarity between two objects is normally computed as a function of the number of properties that are assigned to both objects; in addition, the number of properties that is jointly absent from both the objects may also be taken into account.[7] Substantially similar methods can be used for determining collection structure (by comparing pairs of text vectors with each other and identifying text pairs found to be sufficiently similar), and for retrieving information (by comparing the query vectors with the vectors representing the stored items and retrieving items that are found to be similar to the queries).[13]

Consider two documents – DOC_i and DOC_j. Let $TERM_{ik}$ represent the weight of the (property) term k assigned to document i. One may assume the value of $TERM_{ik}$ as zero or one (in the case of a binary system), or the weight may vary from zero to a maximum value (say four or six, or so). Now the two document vectors may be represented as

$$DOC_i = (TERM_{i1}, TERM_{i2}, TERM_{i3} \dots TERM_{it})$$
$$DOC_j = (TERM_{j1}, TERM_{j2}, TERM_{j3} \dots TERM_{jt})$$

Where t terms (i.e. properties) have been assigned to characterize each document (i.e. object).

The following vector functions are to be considered to compute the similarity between the two given vectors:[7]

(1) $$\sum_{k=1}^{t} TERM_{ik}$$

which denotes the sum of the weights of all the properties included in a given vector;

(2) $$\sum_{k=1}^{t} TERM_{ik} \cdot TERM_{jk}$$

which denotes the component by component vector product, consisting of the sum of the products of the corresponding term weights for two vectors;

(3) $$\sum_{k=1}^{t} \min(TERM_{ik} \cdot TERM_{jk})$$

which denotes the sum of the minimum component weights of the components of the two vectors; and

(4) $$\sqrt{\sum_{k=1}^{t} (TERM_{ik})^2}$$

which denotes the length of the property vector (here, for the document DOC_j), when the property vectors are considered as ordinary vectors.

These functions can be illustrated with the following example. Suppose the two document vectors are represented as

$$DOC_i = (3,2,1,0,0,0,1,1)$$
$$DOC_j = (1,1,1,0,0,1,0,0)$$

where each document is assigned eight index terms. The four vector functions will then be:

(1) $$\sum_{k=1}^{t} TERM_{ik} = (3+2+1+0+0+0+1+1) = 8$$

(2) $$\sum_{k=1}^{t} TERM_{ik} \cdot TERM_{jk} = (3.1)+(2.1)+(1.1)+(0.0)+(0.0)+ (0.1)+(1.0)+(1.0)=$$
$$(3+2+1+0+0+0+0+0) = 6$$

(3) $$\sum_{k=1}^{t} \min(TERM_{ik}, TERM_{jk}) = \min(3,1)+\min(2,1)+\min(1,1)+\min(0,0)$$
$$+\min(0,0)+\min(0,1)+\min(1,0)+\min(1,0)$$
$$= 1+1+1+0+0+0+0+0 = 3$$

(4) $$\sqrt{\sum_{k=1}^{t} (TERM_{ik})^2} = \sqrt{(3.3)+(2.2)+(1.1)+(0.0)+(0.0)+(0.0)+(1.1)+(1.1)} = 4$$

The ordinary vector product (expression 2) and the sum of the minimum components (expression 3) could be used directly to measure the similarity between the vectors.[7] However, in order to keep the similarity coefficients within a certain bound, e.g., 0 to 1 or -1 to +1, it is customary to include normalizing factors. Several coefficients for similarity measures can be used; Salton and McGill[7] show five such coefficients, which are shown below:

1   *The dice coeffiient*

$$SIM(DOC_i, DOC_j) = \frac{2\left[\sum_{k=1}^{t} (TERM_{ik} \cdot TERM_{jk})\right]}{\sum_{k=1}^{t} TERM_{ik} + \sum_{k=1}^{t} TERM_{jk}} = \frac{2(6)}{8+4} = 1$$

2   *The Jaccard coefficient*

$$SIM(DOC_i, DOC_j) = \frac{\sum_{k=1}^{t} (TERM_{ik} \cdot TERM_{jk})}{\sum_{k=1}^{t} TERM_{ik} + \sum_{k=1}^{t} TERM_{jk} - \sum_{k=1}^{t} (TERM_{ik} \cdot TERM_{jk})} = \frac{6}{8 + 4 - 6} = 1$$

3   The *cosine coefficient*, which is a measure of the angle between two *t*-dimensional object vectors in a space of *t* dimensions:

$$SIM(DOC_i, DOC_j) = \frac{\sum_{k=1}^{t} (TERM_{ik} \cdot TERM_{jk})}{\sqrt{\sum_{k=1}^{t} (TERM_{ik})^2 \cdot \sum_{k=1}^{t} (TERM_{jk})^2}} = \frac{6}{8} = 0.75$$

4   The *overlap coefficient*:

$$SIM(DOC_i, DOC_j) = \frac{\sum_{k=1}^{t} (TERM_{ik} \cdot TERM_{jk})}{\min\left(\sum_{k=1}^{t} TERM_{ik}, \sum_{k=1}^{t} TERM_{jk}\right)} = \frac{6}{4} = 1.5$$

5   The *asymetric coefficient*:

$$SIM(DOC_i, DOC_j) = \frac{\sum_{k=1}^{t} \min (TERM_{ik}, TERM_{jk})}{\sum_{k=1}^{t} TERM_{ik}} = \frac{3}{8} = 0.375$$

All similarity measures exhibit one common property, namely that their value increases when the number of common properties (or the weight of the common properties) in two vectors increases. The *Jaccard expression* and the *Cosine expression* measures have similar characteristics, ranging from a minimum of 0 to a maximum of 1 for non-negative vector elements. These measures are easy to compute and they appear to be as effective in retrieval as other more complicated functions. Both these measures have been widely used for the evaluation of retrieval functions.[7]

Sparck-Jones and Willett[5] comment that, apart from Boolean logic, the information retrieval model that has had the most significant influence on the operational information retrieval environment is the Vector processing model.

Best match searching and relevance feedback model

Best match searching is designed to produce ranked output. It therefore requires a method to measure the relative importance of the retrieved items, which again requires some method of weighting the search terms. A similarity measure comprises two major components: (1) a term weighting scheme that reflects the importance of a term by allocating numerical values to each index term in a query or document; and (2) a similarity coefficient which uses the these weights to calculate the similarity between a document and a query. Of these, the term weighting scheme is the most important, and, as Sparck Jones and Willett[5] comment, it is the single most important factor in determining the effectiveness of an information retrieval system.

A best match search matches a set of query words against the set of words corresponding to each item in the database, calculates a measure of similarity between the query and the item, and then sorts the retrieved items in order of decreasing similarity with the query. Cleverdon[4] suggested the so-called coordination level to measure the relative importance of the retrieved items. According to this theory, the documents that have most terms in common with the query will be on the top of the ranked list.[14]

A best match search can be implemented very efficiently using an inverted file searching technique.[14] The user in a best match search environment can put the query in simple natural language, in the form of a sentence, say. The terms representing the query or a document are then identified, and measures are taken to overcome the variations due to spelling, synonyms, antonyms, etc. There is thus the need for a conflation algorithm, a computational procedure that reduces the variants of a word to a single form for retrieval purposes. The most common automatic conflation procedure uses a stemming algorithm, which reduces all the words with the same root to a single form by stripping the root of its derivational and inflectional affixes; in most cases only suffixes are stripped.[14, 15]

Best match searching involves some quantitative measure of similarity between the query and each of the items in the file, and the ranking is formed on the basis of these similarities. The most important component of a similarity measure is the term weighting scheme (discussed in Chapter 6) which allocates numerical values to each index term in a query or a document to indicate their relative importance. Salton and Buckley[16] summarize the results of a detailed comparison of a number of weighting schemes, the findings of which have subsequently been supported by other studies (see for example, Al-Hawamdeh and Willett.[17] These studies show that the weighting schemes that use term frequency, collection frequency, and vector length normalization tend to produce the best results. According to these studies, the document term weights and the query term weights can be computed by the following formula:

$$Document\ term\ weight = \frac{tf. \log \dfrac{N}{n}}{\sqrt{\Sigma \left(tf_i \log \dfrac{N}{n_i} \right)^2}}$$

$$Query\ term\ weight = \left(0.5 + \frac{0.5\ tf}{\max\ tf} \right) \log \frac{N}{n}$$

Where N is the total number of documents in the database, n is the number of documents containing the ith term, i.e. the number of hits and tf is the term frequency within the document or the query. A similarity measure is then used to rank the retrieved documents in descending order of their similarity with the query.

The relevance feedback process, introduced in the mid-sixties, is a controlled, automatic process for query reformulation, where the basic idea consists of choosing important terms attached to certain previously retrieved items that have been identified as relevant by the user, and of enhancing the importance of these terms in the new query formulation (Salton and Buckley[18]). When relevance feedback is to be used, an initial search is carried out to produce a ranked list of output, and the user inspects a few top-ranking documents to ascertain their relevance to the given query. The user's relevance data enables the system to calculate a new set of weights that should reflect the importance of each query term more accurately. One of the classic experiments on relevance ranking was conducted by Salton and Buckley.[18] They evaluated relevance feedback methods by using six document collections in various subject areas. Initial searches were conducted on each set using the vector match of the query and the document vectors. The term weights used for the documents and the queries were computed as the product of the term frequency multiplied by an inverse collection frequency.

In this experiment the first 15 items retrieved in the initial search were judged for relevance. Twelve different relevance feedback methods were used for evaluation purposes with the six collection sets, including six vector modification methods and six probabilistic feedback runs. The results demonstrated that relevance feedback improves retrieval performance. Thus the authors concluded that 'the relevance feedback process provides an inexpensive method for reformulating queries based on previously retrieved relevant and non-relevant documents' (Salton and Buckley[18]).

Alternative information retrieval models

All the approaches to automatic searching and retrieval discussed above are mainly based on statistical or probabilistic calculations of term occurrences. Present-day working commercial indexing systems are mostly based on statistical analysis.[19] In addition to the three classical models discussed above, two alternative models, viz. the natural language processing model and hypertext model, have become quite popular.

Natural language processing model

The fundamental difference of this model with others is that it aims to consider not only query and document terms, but sentences and discourse. In other words, natural language processing models process and match query and document sentences, keeping in view the context or the domain, resulting in more relevant information retrieval.[20] Building systems that can process natural language texts and queries involve three levels of processing:

1   Syntactic analysis, that is required to understand the structure of a given sentence. It generally includes a lexicon containing words with associated information, such as parts-of-speech, categories and syntactic markers/grammars, etc.
2   Semantic analysis, that deals with the meaning of the words and the sentence, is usually stored in a knowledge base. It is used to derive meaning, and to resolve ambiguities that cannot be resolved by only structural considerations.
3   Pragmatic analysis that takes into consideration the specific domain and the context. Pragmatic knowledge, i.e. the knowledge about a specific situation, allows the system to eliminate the ambiguities and complete the semantic interpretations.

While natural language processing systems propose alternative approaches to information retrieval, these systems require huge processing power and system resources, hence their use in commercial information retrieval has been rather limited. However, with recent improvements in computer storage and processing power, natural language processing systems are beginning to be popular in certain areas of information processing and retrieval. Recent developments and trends in natural language processing have been discussed in Chapter 21.

Hypertext model

Conventional documents are written in a linear fashion, and users are expected to read the text sequentially from the beginning towards the end. While this convention has been followed for preparing documents for centuries, this linear approach has an inherent problem. It does not make provision for navigation within and among a collection of documents. The hypertext model allows users to navigate within the different parts of a text, and among different texts in a collection. The term 'hypertext' is used to describe a computer program that allows a person to browse a document by deliberately jumping from one text block to another (Rada[21]). A hypertext model is an interactive navigational structure that allows users to browse text non-sequentially; it consists basically of nodes which are correlated by direct links in a graph structure.

While the hypertext model provides great flexibility over the linear model, the user's flow of navigation is controlled by the intended design of the hypertext by the creator. Hence the design of a hypertext is an important task, and it should take into account the domain as well as the nature of the text and the intended users. The hypertext model can be extended to allow users to navigate within and among multimedia documents. Hypertext provided the basis for the conceptual design of HTML (hypertext markup language) and HTTP (hypertext transfer protocol), the technology that controls the world wide web and digital libraries. Details of HTML and its use in web information retrieval are discussed in Chapters 17 and 18.

Search facilities offered by most text retrieval systems

So far we have looked at the theoretical issues of various retrieval models. Now, let's see how some of these are introduced in text retrieval software available in the market. Such software packages are characterized by the availability of a wide variety of search and retrieval provisions. However, most software is limited to Boolean and proximity searching, though some offers relevance feedback, and so on. The following are the common search facilities available in all text retrieval packages.[22, 23] This section does not provide an exhaustive review of the chosen packages; rather, it illustrates how the software packages vary in terms of accepting the search expressions, search operators, and so on.

With the introduction of the world wide web (WWW), a number of retrieval systems, called web search engines or simply search engines, have been developed that help users search and retrieve information from the WWW. A number of web search engines are now available, and several publications describe their features; see, for example, Poulter, Tseng and Sargent[24] and Sonnenreich and Macinta.[25] Details of the world wide web and common features of web search engines appear in Chapter 22.

Boolean query formulation

A text retrieval system should provide for query formulation by using the Boolean

AND, OR, and NOT operators, and also provide nested Boolean searching. Boolean search facilities allow a user to combine search terms in a given search prescription, with certain conditions imposed. These conditions specify whether more than one search term should simultaneously be present in the desired records, whether any one of some chosen words should be present, or whether one or more terms should be present while another term should not be present in the desired records, and so on. Nested Boolean search facilities allow more complex conditions to be imposed along with the search terms.

The following are some examples of Boolean search in different information retrieval systems and web search engines:

Dialog: (digital **or** electronic) **and** libraries (to retrieve items on either or both on digital libraries and electronic libraries)

Altavista: computers **and** libraries (to retrieve items containing both the search terms: computers and libraries)

+databases +searching -indexing (to retrieve items on database and searching, but not indexing)

Let us try to understand how a Boolean search takes place from a file organization point of view:

- For Boolean OR queries, the system first finds hits for each search term and them matches the output sets to find out those records that contain both or either of the search terms.
- For Boolean AND queries, the system produces one set for each term is produced and then the results are matched to find out those record numbers that are common in each set.
- For Boolean NOT queries, a set(s) is produced with the search term(s) and another for the NOT term(s), and then the items which appear in the former set but not in the NOT set are retrieved.

However, as a number of sets are to be produced by the retrieval system, complex Boolean search expressions comprising a number of search terms combined with appropriate Boolean operators, may be quite time-consuming.

Proximity searching

In a text retrieval system there should be provision for adjacency/proximity searching, the purpose of which is to refine search statements by permitting the searcher to specify the context in which a term must occur. This search facility allows the user to specify whether two search terms should occur adjacent to each other, whether one or more words occur in between the search terms, whether the search terms should occur in the same paragraph irrespective of the intervening words, and so on.

The following are some examples of proximity searches in Dialog:

- Information (w) system (specifies that the the two terms should appear in the given order next to each other in the retrieved items)
- Information (2n) system (specifies that there may be at most two intervening terms between the two search terms in the retrieved items)
- Information (F) system (specifies that the search terms should appear in the same field in the retrieved items)

Proximity searching is a common feature of most information retrieval systems, including online and CD-ROM databases and web search engines. Different types of proximity search facilities are available, ranging from distance between two search terms to the location of one or more search terms in a given sentence, a given paragraph, and so on. Conceptually, the simplest way to implement a query specification containing a proximity search parameter is to process the query as Boolean AND search and then to discard those items that do not match the specified criteria set by the proximity operator. The later part is performed by using the location information associated with the terms in the inverted file (as discussed in Chapter 6, page 97). This makes it possible to verify the nearness conditions without actually accessing the record information in the main record file. The location information stored in the inverted file, along with a given term, may contain the word number within a sentence (for example the 1st/2nd/3rd . . . word in the sentence), sentence number within a paragraph (for example the 1st/2nd/3rd . . . sentence in a paragraph), the paragraph number within the text (for example 1st/2nd/3rd . . . paragraph within the text), and so on. This is how text retrieval systems, like the one available through Dialog, or the LISA Plus CD-ROM database, allow us to conduct a search by specifying the nearness or word location parameters. However, including term location in inverted index lists expands the size of the indexes to a considerable extent, since each occurrence of each term in the text may have to be separately registered. Nevertheless, the increase in the complexity of the file organization can be justified here because proximity searching is extremely important and is therefore available, with varying degrees of sophistication, in all the major text retrieval systems.

Range searching

Range searching is most useful with numerical information. It is important in selecting records within certain data ranges. The following options are usually available for range searching:

- greater than (>)
- less than (<)
- equal to (=)
- not equal to (/= or <>)
- greater than equal to (>=)
- less than or equal to (<=)

These operators are used to prescribe a precise condition in a given search statement.

Limiting searches

The database in a text retrieval system comprises different fields containing different items of information. The user in his or her query formulation should be able to limit the search in one or more fields, and text retrieval software usually provides this facility. This is also known as field searching, whereby the user can specify that the search terms are to be looked for in one or more fields.

The following are some examples of limiting search features of Dialog:

- Internet/ti,de (restricts the search for the term Internet in the title and descriptor fields)
- Internet/2001:2002 (limits the search to a specified time period; in this case between 2001 and 2002)

Limiting search or field-specific search is a common information retrieval feature available in most information retrieval systems, including search engines. If the system maintains a separate index file for each field, then it will only look for the term in the index file of the specified field and will build the search set(s) accordingly. One the other hand, if the retrieval system maintains only one index file, then it has to have the field information associated with each term in the index file (as shown on page 98). However, in the latter case, the retrieval time will be more because the system first has to produce a set where the search term(s) occur, and then from that set has to select only those items where the specified term occurs in the specified field. Thus, it could be a rather slow process, particularly when a large number of search terms and a number of field specifications are involved.

Truncation

Truncation allows a search to be conducted for all the different forms of a word having the same common root. As an example, the truncated term COMPUT* will retrieve items on COMPUTER, COMPUTING, COMPUTATION, COMPUTE, etc. A number of different options are available for truncation, e.g. right truncation, left truncation, and masking of letters in the middle of the word. Left truncation retrieves all words having the same characters at the right-hand part, e.g. '*hyl' will retrieve words like met*hyl*, 'et*hyl*', etc. Similarly, middle truncation retrieves all words having the same characters at the left and right-hand part. For example, a middle-truncated search term 'colo*r' will retrieve both the terms 'colour' and 'color'. A 'wild card' is used to allow any letter to appear in a specific location within a word.

The following are some examples of truncated searches allowed in Dialog:

- Comput?? (will retrieve records with the word root 'comput', irrespective of the number of characters appearing after the root)
- Wom?n (retrieves records on woman as well as women: here '?'stands for one character)

Let us try to understand how truncated terms are accommodated in the inverted index files. In case of right or suffix truncation, the inverted file organization need not be changed because all the record lists covered by particular truncated terms are adjacent in the index. The problem occurs when we want to make provisions for left or prefix truncation facilities. In principle, prefix truncation can be accommodated analogously by using an inverted index in which the term entries are inversely alphabetized. Thus, the word 'methyl' would be entered into the file as 'lyhtem'; similarly, the word 'ethyl' would appear as 'lyhte'. Now, when we search for '*yl', we actually inverse the search term and look for 'ly*', and this would retrieve both 'lyhtem' and 'lyhtem', i.e., 'methyl' and 'ethyl'.

Therefore, if we want to provide both the prefix and suffix truncation facilities, we shall have to maintain two inverted index files. For word forms exhibiting both prefix and suffix truncation (such as *SYMM*) we have to have inverted index entries that are alphabetized both forward and backward. A much more complex solution is needed to handle infix (or wild card) truncation, such as for 'col*r' (to look both for colour and color) or 'wom*n' (to look both for woman and women). One possible way is to produce lists in the inverted index with entries for all possible rotated word forms. Salton[12] suggests the following method for this:

1 Each term entry $X = x_1, x_2, ..., x_n$ with individual characters x_i is augmented by adding a special terminal character, such as a slash (/).
2 Each augmented term $x_1, x_2, ..., x_n/$ is rotated cyclically by wrapping the term around itself n+1 times. This will produce n+1 different forms $x_1x_2...x_n/$, $/x_1x_2...x_n, x_n/x_1x_2...x_{n-1}$, and so on.
3 Each resulting word form is then augmented by appending a blank character.
4 The resulting file of word forms is then sorted alphabetically, using the sort sequence space, /, a, b,...,z, from the lowest-order to highest-order term.

The resulting dictionary will then carry an entry that accounts for any kind of term truncation. Salton[12] suggests that the following retrieval strategies can be used to obtain the record identifiers corresponding to the various forms of truncated terms:

1 For query term X, representing an untruncated character string, the index entries /X^ or X/^ are picked up from the inverted index; the corresponding record identifiers all relate to term X augmented by the special characters / and ^.
2 For query term X*, look for /X in the index corresponding to all entries with a beginning / followed by a string X, and possibly additional characters.
3 Query term *X corresponds to search term X/; this retrieves list entries $X/^, X/Y_1,...X/Y_n$, representing the original terms $X, Y_1X...Y_nX$ that contain arbitrary prefixes followed by X.
4 For query term *X* the search term is X; this retrieves list entries $XY_1/Z_1,...,XY_n/Z_n$, corresponding to terms $Z_1XY_1,...,Z_nXY_n$, where X is the wanted infix in each case.
5 For the infix truncation, X*Y the search term is Y/X which retrieves entries

$Y/XZ_1,\ldots,Y/XZ_n$, corresponding to terms $XZ_1Y,\ldots,XZ_nY$, where the Z_is represent variable-length infixes.

The permuted dictionary method thus allows truncated terms to be used in query formulations, but at the cost of a substantial increase in index entries.

String searching

String searching is the ability to search on character strings within the body of the text in a record, which is usually available for those fields whose text has not been included in an inverted file, and is, therefore, not pre-indexed. In other words, string searching allows one to search those terms that have not been indexed. However, as the process of string searching matches the search term character by character with the stored records, the search process is tremendously slow for a relatively large database. Typically, text string searching may be used on a subset of the database, that subset having been retrieved by searching on indexed fields. Some text retrieval systems provide a facility for string searching.

Search refinements

The ability to specify a search strategy, and to elicit a response in terms of numbers of postings or records retrieved on the basis of that strategy, is fundamental to most text retrieval systems. This facility supports the narrowing or broadening of search strategies. Once a search statement is formulated, there should be provisions for refining it in a step-by-step fashion so as to arrive at an optimum level of retrieval. The following two examples show how a search can be modified in Dialog and in PubMed online databases.

Suppose we want to search documents on digital libraries. We set up a search using 'digital libraries' and 'electronic libraries' as search terms, since these terms are often used interchangeably in the literature. We want to include both the singular and plural forms of the term 'library', and hence we use a truncation symbol ('$'). Finally we want to limit the search to only 2002. The various search sets are shown below.

It may be noted that in Dialog each search gets an automatic set number; the user can select a specific set number to modify a search statement, and conduct a search on a previously retrieved search set. The examples given here show a Dialog search using the advanced search mode of Dialog (for details see Chapter 15).

Example showing how a search can be refined using a thesaurus in the PubMed database

Suppose we want to conduct a search on SARS (severe acute respiratory syndrome: a disease that appeared recently and spread in different parts of the world like an epidemic).

For this search we want to use PubMed, a service of the National Library of Medicine which provides access to over 12 million MEDLINE citations back to the mid-1960s, together with additional life science journals.[26] We went to the website of

Dialog Search History Database details			
Set	Term Searched	Retrieved Items	
S1	DIGITAL LIBRARIES	381	Display
S2	DIGITAL LIBRAR?	401	Display
S3	ELECTRONIC LIBRAR?	806	Display
S4	(DIGITAL OR ELECTRONIC) (W) LIBRAR?	3497	Display
S5	S4/2002	399	Display

Entrez[27] a text-based search and retrieval system used at NCBI (National Center for Biotechnology Information, National Library of Medicine, USA) for the major databases, including PubMed, Nucleotide and Protein Sequences, Protein Structures, Complete Genomes, Taxonomy, and others. The Entrez interface allows users to select a database and enter a search term to conduct a search. We followed the following steps for our search on SARS:

- We selected the PubMed database and entered the search term 'SARS'.
- The search retrieved 583 records.
- Recognizing that these were too many records, we wanted to narrow the search using the MeSH (Medical Subject Heading) thesaurus.
- We selected the MeSH database and entered the term 'SARS' in the search box.
- It retrieved one entry on SARS as follows:

  SARS virus
  A species of CORONAVIRUS causing atypical respiratory disease (SEVERE ACUTE RESPIRATORY SYNDROME) in humans. The organism is believed to have first emerged in Guandong Province, China, in 2002. Year introduced: 2003

- In order to use this as our search term, we checked the box against the term 'SARS virus' and then clicked on the 'Send to search box' option.
- A search box appeared on the screen with the term 'SARS virus' appearing in it with an option to search the PubMed database. At this stage, the option 'Search PubMed database' was chosen.
- At this stage ten records were retrieved from the PubMed database.

Discussion

IR research has from the beginning concentrated on the development of various retrieval models. The three classical IR models, discussed in this chapter, have given rise to many specific retrieval models. Several alternative models based on hyptertext and natural language processing applications have also been built over the past few years. Some such models are discussed later in this book.

References

1   Meadow, C. T. and Cochrane, P. A., *Basics of online searching*, New York, John Wiley, 1981.
2   Armstrong, C. J. and Large, J. A. (eds.), *Manual of online search strategies*, Aldershot, Gower, 1988.
3   Somerville, A., 'The place of the reference interview in computer searching: the academic setting', *Online*, **1** (4), 1977, 14–27.
4   Cleverdon, C., 'Optimizing convenient online access to bibliographic data-bases'. In: P. Willett (ed.), *Document retrieval systems*, London, Taylor-Graham, 1988, 32–41.
5   Sparck Jones, K. and Willett, P., 'Techniques'. In: Sparck Jones, K. and Willett, P. (eds), *Readings in information retrieval*, San Francisco, Morgan Kaufmann, 1999, 305–12.
6   Bookstein, A., 'Probability and fuzzy-set applications to information retrieval', *Annual review of information science and technology*, **29**, 1986, 117–51.
7   Salton, G. and McGill, M. J., *Introduction to modern information retrieval*, Auckland, McGraw-Hill, 1983.
8   Ellis, D., *New horizons in information retrieval*, London, Library Association, 1990.
9   Maron, M. E. and Kuhns, J. L., 'On relevance, probabilistic indexing and information retrieval', *Journal of the ACM*, **7**, 1960, 216–44.
10   Robertson, S. E. and Sparck Jones, K., 'Relevance weighting of search terms', *Journal of the American Society for Information Science*, **27**, 1976, 129–46.
11   Turtle, H. and Croft, W. B., 'A comparison of text retrieval models', *Computer journal*, **35**, 279–90.
12   Salton, G., *Automatic text processing: the transformation, analysis and retrieval of information by computer*, Reading, MA, Addison-Wesley, 1989.
13   Salton, G., Singhal, A. and Allan, J., 'Automatic text decomposition and structuring', *Information processing and management*, **32** (2), 1996, 127–38.
14   Ashford, J. and Willett, P., *Text retrieval and document databases*, Chartwell-Bratt, 1988.
15   Sedgewick, R., *Algorithms*, 2nd edn, Reading, MA, Addison-Wesley, 1988.
16   Salton, G. and Buckley, C., 'Term-weighting approaches in automatic text retrieval', *Information processing and management*, **24** (5), 1988, 513–23.
17   Al-Hawamdeh, S. and Willett, P., 'Comparison of index term weighting schemes for the ranking of paragraphs in full-text documents', *International journal of information and library research*, **1**, 1989, 116–30.
18   Salton, G. and Buckley, C., 'Improving retrieval performance by relevance feedback', *Journal of the American Society for Information Science*, **41** (4), 1990, 288–97.

19 Korycinsky, C. and Newell, A. F., 'Natural language processing and automatic indexing', *The indexer*, **17** (1), 1990, 21–9.

20 Smeaton, A., 'Natural language processing and information retrieval', *Information processing and management*, **26** (1), 1990, 1–20.

21 Rada, R., Wang, W. and Birchall, A., 'Retrieval hierarchies in hypertext', *Information processing and management*, **29** (3), 1993, 359–71.

22 Chowdhury, G. G., *Text retrieval systems in information management*, New Delhi, New Age International, 1996.

23 Rowley, J., *The electronic library*, Fourth edition of *Computers for libraries*, London, Library Association Publishing, 1998.

24 Poulter, A., Tseng, G. and Sargent, G., *The library and information professional's guide to the world wide web*, London, Library Association Publishing, 1998.

25 Sonnenreich, W. and Macinta, T., *Web developer.com guide to search engines*, New York, John Wiley, 1998.

26 PubMed, **http://www.ncbi.nlm.nih.gov/entrez/query.fcgi?db=PubMed**.

27 Entrez, **http://www.ncbi.nlm.nih.gov/entrez/query.fcgi**.

Chapter 10

Users of information retrieval

Introduction

The user is the focal point of all information retrieval systems because the sole objective of any information storage and retrieval system is to transfer information from the source (the database) to the user. The user subsystem, as shown in Figure 1.1, determines the nature of information to be collected by the system, the nature and level of analysis to be made in order to store the information, and the nature of the user interface to be designed so that users can interact with the system easily in order to search and retrieve the required information. Thus, an understanding of the nature and number of users, their activities vis-à-vis information requirements, information seeking behaviour, etc., will help an information manager develop an appropriate information retrieval system.

Users and their nature

The concept of the user is by no means clear. The type of information user in fact depends on the nature of the information; users may be limited by the organization they work for, by the nature of their work or profession, by age, sex, or other social groups, and so on. Several criteria may be used to identify and categorize users. For example, user categories may be identified by the nature of the libraries they use:

- for an academic library, primary users are students, teachers, researchers, and to some extent administrators
- for special or research libraries, primary users can be determined by the nature of their work or profession, or by attachment to the parent organization; they may be categorized as researchers, planners and policy makers, managers, engineers, doctors, scientists, agriculturists, and so on
- in the public library environment, anyone can be a user – members of the general public, children, students, housewives, adults, the literate, neo-literate and even illiterates, professionals, farmers, artisans, planners and policy makers, and so on.

Pao[1] mentions that the term *users* is quite ambiguous. There are several distinct types of users of an information system. Within the context of an organization, there could be:

1   *actual users*, that is, those who are using the information service at a given time
2   *potential users*, that is, those who are not yet served by the information service
3   *expected users*, that is, those who not only have the privilege of using the information service, but also have the intention of doing so, and
4   *beneficiary users*, that is, those who have derived some benefit from the information service.

Atherton[2] mentions that three important groups of users of a scientific and technical information system are distinguishable according to the kind of activity in which they are engaged:

1   researchers, in basic and applied sciences
2   practitioners and technicians engaged in developmental and/or operational activities in the various fields of technology and industry, agriculture, medicine, industrial production, communication, etc., and
3   managers, planners and decision-makers.

These three user groups are very broadly defined; the categorization is by no means exhaustive. The list does not include some other user groups, such as students and teachers. There is a lot of cross classification of users too. For example, a researcher may be at the same time a manager, planner or policy maker, and so on.

Guinchat and Menou[3] have employed two objective criteria to define users:

•   *objective criteria*, such as the socio-professional category, specialist field, nature of the activity for which information is sought, and reason for using the information system
•   *social and psychological criteria*, such as the users' attitudes and values in regard to information in general and their relation with information units in particular, the reasons behind their particular information-seeking, and their professional and social behaviour.

Guinchat and Menou[3] have identified the following broad categories of user based on the two criteria mentioned above:

1   users not yet engaged in active life, such as students
2   users with a job and whose information needs are related to their work. These users may be classified by the nature of their activity, such as management, research, development, production, services, by activities in a branch and/or specialist field, such as the civil service, agriculture, industry, etc., and by level of education and responsibility, such as professionals, technicians, workers, etc.
3   the ordinary citizen requiring general information for social purposes.

Types of information needs

Information need is often a vague concept. It is often a result of some unresolved prob-

lem(s). It may arise when an individual recognizes that his/her current state of knowledge is insufficient to cope with the task in hand, or to resolve conflicts in a subject
area, or to fill a void in some area of knowledge. Before going to identify the information needs of different categories of users, the following points should be kept in
mind:

1   information need is a relative concept. It depends on several factors and does
    not remain constant
2   information needs change over a period of time
3   information needs vary from person to person, from job to job, subject to sub-
    ject, organization to organization, and so on
4   people's information needs are largely dependent on the environment. For
    example, information needs of those in an academic environment are different
    from those in an industrial, business or government/administrative environment
5   measuring (quantifying) information need is difficult
6   information need often remains unexpressed or poorly expressed
7   information need often changes upon receipt of some information.

We have already seen that information retrieval systems need not be limited to the
four walls of any particular library. There could be information retrieval systems
designed to serve a group of users engaged in a specific kind of activity or mission;
such information systems are often called information support systems or mission-oriented information systems. Users of such systems could be students, academics,
researchers, planners, policy makers, administrators, and so on, the common thread
being that all of them are engaged in a specific area of study/activity, or are joined to
accomplish a particular mission. They could be part of any organization/institution.
For example, in a government information system users may broadly be categorized
in accordance with the nature or area of activity, like education, energy, trade and
commerce, and so on. In an industrial environment, users may be corporate, industri-
alists, professionals like engineers, managers, accountants, and so on. The same is true
for business and commercial information systems. These information systems may
have their own home-grown databases as well as access to one or more CD-ROM
and/or online resources.

    Thus, we can see that the concept of the user depends on the context in which the
information retrieval system is viewed. For instance, in the context of a library environment, we have an idea of the nature and category of users, though their nature,
number, nature of activities, and consequently the nature of their information requirements constantly change. The design of information retrieval systems to support users
engaged in a specific area of study or activity can be much more challenging. While
much of the information content of the databases contained in a library environment
will be bibliographic/reference or textual in nature, in the context of an information
support system the information content is factual in nature. Factual data are significantly different from bibliographic data. For example, doctors working in a hospital
may need information on patients (related to disease, treatment, tests, medication,
etc.), scientists or policy makers working in a pollution control environment may need

data related to the level of pollution by area, by pollutants, by amount and frequency of emission, and so on; the list may go on and on. In their day-to-day activities, scientists, engineers, doctors, administrators, planners, etc. need information that is factual (not necessarily of a bibliographic or textual type), and when they meet difficulties in carrying out a job, in solving a problem, in taking a decision, and so on, they turn to other kinds of databases containing different kinds of information sources – bibliographic, personal, institutional, and so on.

Some of the most important questions in developing an information retrieval system for supporting users in a specific field of activity, therefore, relate to the identification of actual and potential users of the proposed information retrieval system, the nature of their activities, information requirements, and so on. A user survey can help the information manager to gather information on all these and related points.

An understanding of the users' nature, information needs, information seeking patterns, etc. assists an information manager at different levels. At the macro level this knowledge helps such a manager:

1   to decide whether or not to establish an information system, and if so, why, how, and so on
2   to evaluate an existing information retrieval system when
   •   starting a new service
   •   increasing/decreasing emphasis on one or more existing services
   •   optimizing a service
   •   marketing a service, and so on.

At the micro level this knowledge will help an information manager to

1   determine who are the users of an existing or a proposed information retrieval system
2   determine the information needs of each category of users
3   assess how far the existing system is able to meet the needs of the user
4   identify what information sources are to be possessed by the system
5   determine how the information sources are to be analysed and recorded
6   determine the hardware and software requirements, nature and format of the database(s), approach to database design (centralized or distributed), networking requirements, standards, protocols, etc.
7   determine the communication pattern, user interface, etc.
8   determine the output format(s) required, requirement for repackaging of information, etc.
9   determine the marketing strategies – information products, distribution, pricing, etc., and
10   determine the level of staff training, user orientation/ training, etc.

Information needs in different areas of activity

A number of good publications are available that talk about the information needs of various categories of users. For example, the information needs of users (i) in business and industry in general, (ii) in product planning and development, and (iii) in the establishment as well as in the promotion and management of small-scale industries have been discussed by Neelameghan,[4] while Atherton[2] discusses the needs of users in the field of scientific and technological research and Scott and Wootliff[5] discuss the information needs in business environments.

Information needs in scientific and technological research

Atherton[2] has identified the following seven different stages in scientific and technical research and the corresponding information need:

1　*Overall familiarization with the problem and problem statement*
This stage requires a general acquaintance with the subject for drawing up a plan and provisional terms for the solutions of the problems of primary and secondary importance. At this stage users need general information on the chosen subject to build up an overall idea.
2　*Gathering scientific knowledge about the subject of study*
At this stage the user is engaged in the retrospective searching of the broadest possible scope of the literature without any pronounced critical approach.
3　*Coordination and interpretation of scientific data*
Here the user attempts to make a critical evaluation of the ideas and hypotheses of different authors. The relevance criteria for the information needed are specified at this stage and the volume of information is reduced.
4　*Formulation of the problem*
Statement of the hypothesis and choice of the problem are one of the most important stages in a piece of research. As to the need for information, this is characterized by in-depth analysis rather than broad coverage.
5　*Proving the working hypothesis*
Information requirements at this stage depend on the specifics of the research. The researcher may need a lot of factual data at this stage.
6　*Statement of conclusions and recommendations*
At this stage the user may need to come to a conclusion based on his/her own findings and on those available in the literature. The user may need a good amount of consolidated information at this stage to shed light on precedence and priority aspects.
7　*Description of the research results*
At this stage the user requires information on scientific reporting and documentation. Users may need to check each and every document consulted for bibliographic and other details for the purpose of documentation.

Information needs in business

Scott and Wootliff[5] state that there are three major categories of user in a business environment. The following are those categories of user and indications of the nature of information they need in their day-to-day activities:

1 planners and market analysts, who need information on future trends and potential new markets in industries, and on what competitors are doing in their field, in order to plan future strategies for business

2 service professionals, such as accountants, stockbrokers, bankers, and management consultants, who need information on specific industries, such as
- who are the major players in an industry
- how are they performing
- what are their percentage shares of the market
- what are their major activities, and so on

in order to advise their clients. They also need to understand a client's business. For example, what external factors or forces influence that particular industry sector, such as interest rates, foreign exchange rates, political changes, etc., and what problems are peculiar to that industry. They need to keep track of legislation that is going to affect their own or their client's business, for example company law.

3 corporate finance specialists, who need to identify potential takeover targets in a specific industry and need information on their financial performance.

Types of enquiry that are common in a business information unit include requests for

- information on people, for example, directors of a company
- economic indicators and trends of one or more companies
- country risk reports, or information on how to do business in a country, and so on.

Information needs in enterprises

Neelameghan[4] identifies the following activities involved in the promotion and management of enterprises for which users may need information. These include:

1 formulating objectives of the enterprise
2 formulating major strategies and policies to meet specific objectives
3 preparing long-range plans
4 reporting to the stockholders or to the board of management about the results of the enterprise's operations
5 informing employees about the status and performance of the enterprise
6 providing bases and background so that decisions can be made about specific matters as they arise
7 providing bases for giving pre-action approval
8 building the background for outside contacts, such as legislators, competitors, governments, etc.
9 taking decisions about taxes, etc.
10 keeping abreast of current operations and developments in the business concerned
11 being aware of possible troubles and problems ahead

12 allocating capital resources optimally
13 exercising control over day-to-day operations
14 training staff, and
15 improving personnel management and public relations.

Information needs of persons working on different aspects of product design, development, and production vary, and this has to be borne in mind during the development of an information retrieval system. Neelameghan[4] identifies the information needs of persons concerned with product planning and development, and their respective roles and functions in an enterprise, as follows:

1 *Planning*:
This involves long-range forecasting of developments and profits and providing the overall direction for development.
2 *Research*
This stage involves setting up priorities on products and projects on the basis of available funds and time, trouble-shooting, avoiding side-tracking, advising the termination of a project when it is sensed to be unprofitable, and so on.
3 *Engineering*
This involves drawing up specifications, designing and testing prototypes, manufacturing, making adjustments in the final engineering design and models, advising on and implementing continuous improvements in the process of production on the basis of feedback, and so on.
4 *Production*
This involves scheduling, formulating process and procedures, testing of equipment, materials requirements, pilot runs and tests, quality control, and so on.
5 *Marketing*
This involves market analysis, consumer research, forecasting of market developments, market testing, finding solutions to distribution problems, sales promotion and advertising, and so on.
6 *Public relations*
This involves all public relation activities, co-ordinating responses of the firm to criticisms from outside, building the image of the enterprise, and so on.
7 *Packaging/Merchandizing*
This involves special points of view in regard to consumer requirements, product safety, handling facility, etc.
8 *Finance*
This involves costing, pricing, identifying sources of finance and mobilizing funds, budgeting and budget control, cautioning on over-expenditure, and related matters.
9 *Top management*
This involves coordinating the work of all groups and divisions, taking decisions to move ahead or to drop projects, if necessary, establishing policies, etc., building up contacts with government, external relations, etc., and so on.

Information required to support community development planning

Neelameghan[6] provides a detailed account of the different kinds of information required in the process of community development planning. The following are the main points from Neelameghan's account.

The major categories of information that might be required are:

1 information about the geographical environment;
2 population and demographic information, and
3 socio-economic information.

Such items of information are collected in a number of ways: through surveys, from census data, maps, community profiles, etc. Information about the community may consist of:

1 general information on the area/boundary of a village, population, households, literacy rate, birth and mortality rates, and so on
2 information related to special problems of the community
3 agriculture and livestock pattern, inputs and practices
4 livestock information
5 fisheries information
6 cottage industries information
7 trade information
8 information on community structure and facilities, and so on.

Household level information may comprise:

1 information about members of the household
2 information on employment patterns
3 information on housing conditions and related amenities
4 information on assets such as land, livestock, poultry, equipment, etc.
5 consumer expenditure patterns
6 basic health conditions
7 literacy rate, education pattern, and so on.

The UN Food and Agriculture Organization (FAO) has recommended some basic items of information that may be needed in community development planning. These relate to information on the following points:[6]

1 agricultural (cultivated/harvested) land
2 agricultural area improved by drainage, irrigation, terracing, etc., as a percentage of the total agricultural land
3 production and yield rate of crops
4 intensity of cropping
5 number of livestock species and/or units per economically active person in agriculture

6 institutional and non-institutional loan per household
7 percentage of economically active population in agriculture
8 percentage of economically inactive population in agriculture
9 percentage of areas covered by size of groups of agricultural holdings/holders
10 agricultural labourers as percentage of population economically active in agriculture
11 average wage rate of agricultural labourer
12 percentage of community heads without land
13 percentage of households who own their houses (or sites)
14 percentage of households in dwellings which are in good condition
15 percentage of households with specified facilities , e.g. piped water, sanitation, electricity, etc.
16 primary school enrolment ratio
17 primary school attendance ratio
18 total adult literacy rate, and
19 percentage of adult rural population participating in designing, monitoring, and evaluating agricultural and rural development programmes.

Neelameghan has discussed the information needs in a number of specialized activities, for example, (i) in community development planning,[6] (ii) in government and administration,[7] (iii) in socio-economic development,[8] and so on.

Information seeking behaviour of users

Information seeking behaviour or the pattern of using information systems and centres depends on a number of factors. Some of these are closely related to the personal characteristics and traits of users, whereas some depend on the information centre and the information system concerned. Moreover, the general educational level, awareness of people in a society, etc. are also important determining factors influencing information seeking behaviour. The following are some general points that affect the information seeking behaviour of the user:

1 the user's educational and professional background, livelihood, environment in which he or she has grown up and is presently living, and so on
2 the user's awareness of, and ability to access other sources of information
3 the user's relationship with the information unit concerned
4 the information unit's ease of accessibility
5 the user's working conditions
6 the time available to the user for consulting information system(s)
7 the user's hierarchical status and socio-professional position
8 the user's personal and professional connections
9 how challenging the user's job is
10 the amount of competition that exists in the user's field of activities
11 the user's past experience
12 how much the user already knows

13 how easily the user gets on with people
14 what the general attitude of the user is towards people, organizations, etc.
15 how friendly, knowledgeable, and efficient are the members of the information unit
16 the various products and services of the information unit
17 how the user formulates his/her queries
18 how the user makes use of the information obtained
19 how friendly the information system is
20 how effective the marketing policy of the information system(s) is
21 how effective the 'user education', 'user sensitization', 'user orientation', and 'user assistance' programmes are.

Some of these factors, such as those mentioned towards the first half of the above list, are beyond the control of any given information system/centre, rather they depend on the general social structure, general consciousness among people about the importance of information and communication, and so on. However, there are some other points that are within the control of information centres and information systems personnel. Some of these again are more technical in nature, some are more dependent on policy matters, while others are more behavioural or attitudinal. Moreover, the information seeking behaviour of users is largely dependent on the environment in which the user has been brought up, and the one in which he/she presently lives. Recent developments in the world of information and communication, resulting in the development of the Global Information Infrastructure (GII), will also have a tremendous influence on the user's information seeking behaviour.

What we need to know about users

Our discussions in the previous paragraphs have made it clear that in order to develop an effective and efficient information retrieval system we need to know about the users, their information needs, and so on. The process of finding out about users might take place at three different levels. First, we need to know about the organization/institution that the user is linked with, and this will inform us about different user groups, their activities, information needs, and so on. Finally, we should try to gather information about each individual user. However, before going on to gather information on any of these aspects, the information manager has to be acquainted with the subjects that will constitute the core as well as the fringe areas covered by the proposed information retrieval system. There are established methods of studying a subject that has to be followed, and the necessary guidelines may be obtained from the literature.[9, 10] Guidelines for collecting information about users, their employing organizations, and so on have been discussed in the literature (see, for example, Seetharama[11] and Devadasan and Lingam[12]).

Information about the organization/institution

Approaches to an understanding of the fields of interests of individual users to be served, and of the organization as a whole could begin by acquiring information about the organization/institution/project for which the user works. In order to get adequate information about the organization/institution, we might need to find answers to the following questions.

1 What are the major objectives of the organization/ institution/mission/project? The answer to this question will help us understand the nature of the organization, its objectives, area of activities, and so on.

2 What are the organizations/institutions in the related field? The answer to this will help us identify other institutions that might have similar information retrieval systems or those that might be interested in or linked with the proposed information retrieval system.

3 What are the major divisions/groups in terms of tasks/activities performed?

4 What is the scope of each discernible activity of the various groups?

5 What information does the institution/organization need in general and what information is generated by it? The answers to these questions will give a general understanding of the nature (and perhaps variety and volume) of information required by the user community, and also the nature and amount of information generated, which indicate the kind of information that the users might need to generate that kind of information output.

6 What are the major sources of information? This will shed light upon the various information sources used by the organization/institution: internal sources (through surveys, research, marketing, and so on), external sources, which include documentary sources, personal and institutional sources, and so on.

7 What are the major channels through which information is obtained? This will tell us the various means by which information is collected, and will help us determine whether a networking approach would be appropriate to gather information from various sources, and so on.

8 How much currency and exhaustivity of information are required? Is the available information adequate, on time, reliable, and affordable? Answers to these questions will enable us to set parameters regarding input of information to the system.

9 Is there already a library/information centre? Is it part of a larger information system? This will help determine whether we need to conduct another survey on the nature and facilities of the existing library/information system, and so on.

10 What are the computer resources and networking facilities available? This will help us identify the computer and networking requirements for the proposed information retrieval system.

11 Does the organization/institution belong to any business or institutional (local, regional or international) network? This will help us determine the nature and requirements for networking.

12 Is there a plan to improve the existing library/information system? This will help us plan for the proposed information retrieval system and to fit it with institutional plans.

Information on all these points will help us in a number of ways. For example, it will help us understand:

- the organizational structure
- links with other organizations
- the various activity groups within the organization and their major activities
- the flow of information within the various activity groups in the organization
- the external and internal sources of information used
- the nature of the information generated by the organization, and so on.

Information about user groups

Once we have an understanding of the organization/institution we are dealing with, the next step would be to find out about the various user groups. There are several questions that need to be answered at this stage, such as:

1   Can distinct user groups be identified? What are the major activities of each user group?
    This would help us know about each user group and the nature of the jobs they perform which will, in turn, help us understand the possible kinds of information that they might require.
2   How are the various user groups linked to each other within the organization?
    This will help us determine the possible information flow pattern.
3   How diverse are the information requirements of each group vis-à-vis the objectives, functions, and subject background of the user groups?
    This will help us understand the variety of information services and products that might be required for each identified user group.
4   How much of the required information is available:
    - internally
    - from other organizations/institutions
    - from published/unpublished sources, and so on?
    This information will help us choose the various information sources and possibly select the best possible mode of data input from these sources.
5   What information is generated by each user group?
    This will help us determine the possible information that might be made available to the user group to facilitate their expected output.
6   If the activities of some group are hampered for some reason, how is this going to affect the performance of other user groups?
    This information will help us optimize the system design and will help us draw an optimum information flow pattern.
7   Are there any user-related constraints? For example,
    - is there any need to set priorities for providing services to one or more groups of user?
    - does the composition of one or more user groups change frequently, and if so is there a mechanism for being informed about that?

- is there any restriction relating to access to information?
- is there any distinct difference among the user groups in terms of their status, qualifications, nature of job, and so on?
- what kind of computer resources are available to the user groups and what is the level of IT literacy of the group as a whole?

Information on all these points may be consolidated in order to learn about:

- the various user groups, their composition, nature of activities, and so on;
- the link among the user groups, and the possible flow pattern of information;
- the nature of the information required by the user groups;
- the possible sources of information;
- the possible constraints and priorities in services;
- computer resources and information technology literacy; and so on.

Information about individual users

The next step is to gather information about the individual users. Several guidelines have been provided in the literature for gathering information about users. The following may be taken into account for this purpose:

1 the education, training, experience, etc. of the user
2 the position and nature of the user's job
3 the role of the user in an identified user group and his/her link with other group(s) or group head(s)
4 the subject and associated interests of the user, which include specific subjects, nature of information, type of documents, journals, authors, language, etc., of interest to the user
5 the language preference of the user
6 the kind of information required by the user in order to perform his/her day-to-day activities
7 the level of IT literacy of the user
8 the extent to which IT is used, and what for. Does the user acess any information system or database, internal (home-grown or on CD-ROM) or external (online, through e-mail and/or the internet)? If so, what for, and what has been the past experience
9 the professional bodies of which the user is a member
10 the technical periodicals that the user receives through membership, subscription, etc.
11 the type of reports – external and/or internal – read by the user, and the type of reports generated by the user
12 the types of reports that the user is not currently receiving but would like to receive
13 outside organizations with which the user has academic or professional contacts

14 other libraries/information systems accessed by the user
15 channels of communication between the user and other user(s)/groups
16 frequency of use of the in-house library/information centre; time of the day and duration of time spent in the library/information centre
17 the user's opinion of the existing information retrieval facilities
18 kinds of information sources currently used and preferred by the user, for example, books, journal articles, reports, standards, patents, trade literature, business/company data, legal documents, and so on
19 types of information services currently used/preferred by the user, for example, current awareness services, abstracts, digests, state-of-the-art reports, literature search services (in-house, on home-grown and/or CD-ROM databases: external, via remote database access such as database access and search facilities through electronic communication)
20 the user's access to UseNet
21 the user's special role in the group/organization, such as the information gatekeeper
22 the user's suggestions regarding the proposed information retrieval system's location, accessibility, content, input and output features, and so on.

The collection of information on these points will help the information manager propose changes to an existing information retrieval system or develop a new one.

User studies

Extensive studies on users and their information needs have been conducted over the last three decades. Wilson[13, 14] points out that the theoretical foundation of earlier user studies was very weak, whereas the experimental methods used in the eighties were more refined and the data analysis procedures more sophisticated.

Design

Pao[1] suggests the following steps for making a study of users:

A *Design of research plan*:
 1 identify a problem area or a need to study
 2 conduct an initial literature review
 3 define the research problem
 4 estimate the potential for successful execution of the study
 5 conduct a second literature review
 6 select an appropriate research approach
 7 formulate a hypothesis
 8 formulate data collection methods
 9 formulate and develop data collection instruments
10 design a data analysis plan
11 design a data collection plan
12 identify the population and sample

13 conduct pilot studies of methods, instruments and analysis

B *Implementation of research plan*:
14 implement data collection
15 implement data analysis
16 prepare research report.

C *Implementation of results*:
17 disseminate findings and make further moves for implementation.

Methodology

Various methods have been employed in user studies over the past four decades or so (see, for example, Wilson,[13, 14] Moore,[15] and Gorman and Clayton[16]), such as:

- surveys – questionnaires, interviews, case studies, etc.
- critical incident examination – observation of events, review of diaries, etc., and
- qualitative methods – study of internal processes.

However, the method most commonly used is the survey conducted through one or more data collection tools like the questionnaire, interview, observation, etc.

The questionnaire

The questionnaire is the most popular instrument for collecting data to research library and information activities. Questionnaires can be extremely flexible and can be used to gather information from large or small numbers of people on any topic. However, the task of designing an appropriate questionnaire is not easy and requires a lot of time. It is useful to have a pilot run of the questionnaire among a small subset of users before the final version is distributed. This helps improve the questionnaire by modifying/adding/deleting some of the questions, by avoiding redundancy, and so on.

There are two types of questions that can be asked – closed or open. The closed type of question allows the respondent to answer by choosing between alternatives. The advantage of this type is that the data can be easily collected and analysed and it is easy from the respondent's point of view too. However, sometimes more than one option may have to be chosen to provide the correct answer, the respondent may not always find an appropriate choice from the available alternatives, or the respondent might need to be subjective in his/her reply to certain questions. Sometimes shades of opinion are asked for, and in such cases, respondents may be asked to respond using a rating scale.

Open questions require respondents to formulate the answer in their own words. This is effective when respondents are able to express their answer/opinion succinctly in a written form. Analysis of responses to such questions is likely to be more complex and thus time-consuming. In some cases, a combination of open and closed questions may be helpful.

The major advantages of the questionnaire method of surveying users in an information retrieval environment are:

- it is a cheap and flexible method
- it can provide anonymity
- questions can be presented in a consistent format and style
- it is an impersonal method of research, and
- the survey work can be completed at the respondent's own pace and convenience.

However, there are certain disadvantages to this method:

- it may lead to a lack of qualitative depth
- once the questions have been formulated, they cannot be modified according to the answers received, as is possible in some other methods
- answers can be given only to the questions that are asked (no new question can be added to follow up an answer, as is possible in some other methods)
- answers may be inaccurate, incomplete or distorted.

The following are some basic guidelines that might help an information manager gather information about users by questionnaire:

1 keep the questionnaire short and simple
2 try to put the questions in a logical order
3 use simple words, plain and easy to understand language
4 keep sentences short, and avoid ambiguity
5 use a clear type face that is easy to read and understand
6 pay attention to the layout and design, and
7 decide what exactly it is you want to know, formulate the question, then ask yourself whether you would give an answer to the question that would be appropriate for the research; modify, if necessary.

Sproull[17] provides some guidelines that might help to increase the response rate of mailed questionnaires:

1 include a covering letter that appeals to the respondent's interests, such as 'as a regular user of the internet, you may be aware . . .'
2 mail a reminder card about ten days after the first mailing; every respondent, except those whose responses have already been received, should receive this
3 mail a second questionnaire about a week after the reminder card
4 contact non-respondents by phone (or by e-mail)
5 enclose a token of identity or an introduction from a person of repute along with the questionnaire
6 write clear directions
7 avoid open-ended items, if possible; people are more likely to respond to a for-

mat in which they can simply tick the appropriate answer rather than have to generate an original response

8   structure item responses so that respondents can answer quickly and easily
9   mention how little time is required to complete the questionnaire
10 structure the entire questionnaire so that respondents can complete it easily and quickly. Make placement and sequencing of items logical and easy to follow
11 ensure that the questionnaire is professionally typed and printed so that its appearance gives the impression of credibility and professionalism.

The interview

The interview is another widely used data collection instrument in survey research in the field of library and information science. Interview surveys are similar to questionnaire surveys. An interview schedule is to be prepared that is very similar to the questionnaire. The interview method is a useful means of surveying a representative population sample covering all shades of opinion. The questions asked provide opportunities for qualified answers, and the interviewer may prompt the respondent as necessary. When a number of interviewers are involved in a survey, it is important to ensure that they all understand how the questions are to be put. Prompting should be used to ensure that the respondent has considered all the possibilities while replying to the questions.

An interview may be structured or semi-structured. A structured interview is like an oral questionnaire. Structured interviews help the researcher keep control over the process of the interview, and the responses obtained are easy to analyse and consolidate. Semi-structured interviews provide more scope for discussion and recording the respondent's opinions and views. The interview schedule should be carefully designed and should consist of a number of fairly specific questions, each of which may be expanded upon.

There are a number of advantages of this method of research:

1   it is possible to obtain a complete response from different categories of a sample population
2   more complex information can be collected
3   it is more personal than the questionnaire and often produces better response rates
4   the researcher may have more control over the question sequence and timing
5   some questions can be adjusted in response to the answers given to other questions
6   the researcher can explain some questions to the respondent in case of confusion, and thus can ensure a better response.

However, there are a number of disadvantages too, for example:

1   information obtained through oral discussion may be difficult to analyse
2   data may be qualitative rather than quantitative

3   there may be some inconsistency in the responses, and
4   the respondent may be influenced by the researcher.

The list of disadvantages has been lengthened by Sproull,[17] according to whom the interview method is inefficient because:

1   respondents sometimes do not give a relevant answer; they may misinterpret or try to bypass the actual question
2   respondents often refuse (or feel embarrassed or afraid) to respond to certain questions
3   the recall rate may be poor, because respondents may not remember all the relevant points at a given instance
4   the information provided may be incomplete (half-truth can be misleading), out of ignorance or for deliberate reasons
5   the respondent–researcher interaction may influence the responses to some extent
6   the language and level of communication between the respondent and the researcher may be a barrier
7   respondents, especially senior personnel, may be too busy and therefore it may be very difficult to get their time for the required interview
8   at some points the interview may lead to an argument
9   recording responses may be difficult: some people do not like to be voice-recorded, and some may not feel able to answer freely if they are aware that their responses are being recorded
10 responses may be too personal or subjective in nature.

Observation

Observation is another instrument used in survey research that involves observing and recording events or situations. There are two forms of observation – participant and non-participant. In participant observation the researcher acts as a client or user to see what happens. In the non-participative mode, the researcher simply observes other people working and keeps a record. The observation method needs careful planning. Sometimes it may be difficult to keep track of all the events that are taking place simultaneously, and it may be better to follow another method – auditing – which involves simply watching things happen. This will give a general idea as to what is going on, and would help the researcher select the appropriate method of observation.

There are a number of advantages of this method, such as:

1   it is straightforward
2   it requires little training (of course a familiarization with the organization/institution/activity being observed is quite helpful)
3   it provides direct experience
4   it provides useful insights to the existing system
5   it avoids bias that may occur in other methods of research, and

6   it does not make demands on the user's time.

However, there are certain obvious disadvantages to observation too. For example,

1   it may be quite time-consuming
2   the observer may have to wait for some time to see something happen, which could lead to a waste of the researcher's time
3   sometimes it may be difficult to record events, particularly at busy periods
4   the person being observed may deviate from his or her normal behaviour
5   record keeping may be inconsistent
6   some of the events may not be familiar to the respondent, and therefore he/she may not understand what is happening
7   if more than one observer is involved, the results may be skewed, and
8   the constant attention and involvement of the researcher is needed.

Moreover, it is necessary that the researcher has an understanding of what is going to be recorded and for what purpose, and so on. It would be helpful to have a form prepared for recording data.

Possible sources of information about users

A survey of user information need may involve one or more of the instruments described above, and a number of different sources may have to be consulted to collect the relevant information. Atherton[2] provides the following guidelines which might be useful for collecting information about users.

1   Study the organizational chart of the institution(s) concerned.
2   Study the functional activities chart of the institution(s).
3   Study the annual reports, project reports, and other publications of the institution.
4   Conduct a questionnaire survey in order to gather:
     •   personal details of the users, including their qualifications, experience, interests, etc.
     •   details of day-to-day activities
     •   details of the information accessed by the user, including its nature, source, and so on
     •   details on the problems faced in obtaining the right information at the right time, and
     •   suggestions for improvement.
5   Interview the user community, which may include
     •   interviewing the actual and potential users
     •   interviewing the user's superiors
     •   interviewing the user's subordinates
     •   interviewing the user's coordinates (people at the same rank, and so on).
6   Study the papers, books, etc., published by the user.

7 Attend seminars, workshops, etc., in which the user participates.
8 Observe the user at his/her workplace.
9 Make personal informal contact with the user.
10 Meet users in small and homogeneous groups periodically.
11 Get feedback regarding the existing information retrieval facilities.
12 Get suggestions from users on possible measures for improvements.
13 Attend technical meetings within the institution at which projects and problems may be discussed.
14 Scan correspondence and reports received by the user.
15 Study the type of document that the user requests.
16 Study the queries received from the user.
17 Participate in institutional/work orientation programmes.
18 Get involved in user orientation programmes.
19 Study the subject being dealt with.
20 Liaise with users and see how you can fit into their day-to-day activities by identifying the required information and making it available on time.

Nicholas[18] stresses the need for qualitative assessment of user needs. He identifies 11 major characteristics of information need, viz., subject, level, quality, place of publication or origin, function, viewpoint, date, processing and packaging, nature, quality and speed of delivery. A number of interesting issues related to information seeking and searching in the electronic environments have been discussed in a DELOS workshop.[19] Tenopir[20] suggests that insights into patterns of user information behaviour are best obtained using quantitative analysis, while insights into user motivations are best achieved by qualitative analysis.

Wang,[21] in an ARIST chapter, reviews the methodologies applied in empirical research on user behaviour. Early research using quantitative methods contributed to the understanding of information needs and uses at a macro level, while the adoption of qualitative methods adopted from the 1970s onwards has brought a new level of understanding of users at a micro level. Both qualitative and quantitative methods are now used in user information research, and are complementary to each other. While reviewing the literature on user studies, Wang[21] points out that the following important points, crucial for any user study, are often missing:

- *Time* When was the study conducted? How long was the period of data collection?, etc.
- *Place* Where was the study conducted?
- *Sampling* How were the participants selected?
- *Setting* In what environment was the session carried out?
- *Stimuli* Were the search questions real or artificial?
- *Data collection procedure* Who carried out the interviews?
- *Instrument* What did the questionnaire or the interview guidelines include?
- *Recording techniques* How was the data recorded?
- *Process observed* What was the participants' task?

• *Data analysis techniques* What was the analytical scheme? How was the data coded? What units or parameters were used for measuring?, etc.

Recent research shows that users with a broader problem-at-hand often seek information in stages over extended periods and use a variety of information resources such as online databases, CD-ROM databases, online public access catalogues (OPACs), the web or digital libraries, for answers to the same or evolving problem-at-hand. As users learn or progress in their work, or as they clarify a problem and/or question(s), or as their situation changes, they come back to IR systems of various kinds for more searches (Spink et al.[22]). David Nicholas and his colleagues at City University, London, have conducted extensive studies on users' information behaviour and have noted that in today's web and digital library environment, users are 'powerful', short on attention, 'promiscuous', untrusting and above all are interested in the speed of delivery (Nicholas et al.,[23] Nicholas and Dobrowolski,[24] Nicholas, Huttington and Watkinson[25]). Several models of human information seeking behaviour have been proposed over the past few years, and some of these are discussed in the next chapter.

References

1   Pao, M. L., *Concepts of information retrieval, Englewood*, CO, Libraries Unlimited, 1989.

2   Atherton, P., *Handbook of information systems and services*, Paris, Unesco, 1977.

3   Guinchat, C. and Menou, M., *General introduction to the techniques of information and documentation work*, Paris, Unesco, 1983.

4   Neelameghan, A., *Information for small enterprises,* Bangalore, Sarada Ranganathan Endowment for Library Science, 1992.

5   Scott, J. and Wootliff, V., 'Business and commercial information'. In: Dossett, P. (ed.), *Handbook of special librarianship and information work,* 6th edn, London, Aslib, 1992, 145–69.

6   Neelameghan, A., 'Information for socio-economic development planning: general overview'. In: Evans, J. (ed.), *Information for development: seminar papers and proceedings, Department of Library and Information Studies, University of Papua New Guinea*, 1–3 July, 1992. University of Papua New Guinea, 1992, 5–35.

7   Neelameghan, A., 'Public service administrative information systems: general overview'. In: Evans, J. (ed.), *Information for development: seminar papers and proceedings. Department of Library and Information Studies, University of Papua New Guinea, 1-3 July, 1992,* University of Papua New Guinea, 1992, 36–54.

8   Neelameghan, A., 'Technology acquisition, technology transfer and information'. In: Evans, J. (ed.), *Information for development: seminar papers and proceedings. Department of Library and Information Studies, University of Papua New Guinea, 1-3 July, 1992,* University of Papua New Guinea, 1992, 55–90.

9 Bhattacharyya, G., 'Project on study of subject', *Annals of library science and documentation*, **12** (3), 1975, 65–79.

10 Bhattacharyya, G., *Introduction to information science*, Calcutta, IASLIC, 1980.

11 Seetharama, S., *Guidelines for planning of libraries and information centres*, Calcutta, IASLIC, 1990.

12 Devadasan, F. J. and Lingam, P. P., 'A methodology for the identification of information needs of users', *IFLA journal*, **23**, 1997, 41–51.

13 Wilson, T. D., 'On user studies and information needs', *Journal of documentation*, **37** (1), 1981, 3–15.

14 Wilson, T. D., 'Information needs and users: fifty years of progress?'. In: Vickery, B. C. (ed.), *Fifty years of information progress: a Journal of documentation review*, London, Aslib, 1994. 15–51.

15 Moore, N., *How to do research*, 2nd edn, London, Library Association, 1987.

16 Gorman, G. E. and Clayton, P., *Qualitative research for the information professional: a practical handbook*, London, Library Association Publishing, 1997.

17 Sproull, N. L., *Handbook of research methods*, Metuchen, NJ, Scarecrow, 1988.

18 Nicholas, D., *Assessing information needs*, London, Aslib, 1996.

19 Boehm, K., Croft, W. B. and Schek, H. (eds), *Proceedings of the first DELOS Network of Excellence workshop on information seeking, searching and querying in digital libraries. Zurich. December 11-12*, DELOS, 2000.

20 Tenopir, C., 'Information metrics and user studies', *Aslib proceedings: new information perspectives*, **55** (1/2), 2003, 13–17.

21 Wang, P., 'Methodologies and methods for user behavioural research'. In: Williams, M. E. (ed.), *Annual review of information science and technology*, Vol. 34, Medford, NJ, Information Today Inc., 2001, 53–99.

22 Spink, A., Wilson, T., Ellis, D. and Ford, N., 'Modeling users' successive searches in digital environments: a National Science Foundation/British Library funded study', *D-Lib magazine*, April 1998. Available at: **http://www.dlib.org/dlib/april98/04spink.html**.

23 Nicholas, D., Dobrowolski, T., Withey, R., Russell, C., Huttington, P. and Williams, P., 'Digital information consumers, players and purchasers: information seeking behaviour in the new digital interactive environment', *Aslib proceedings: new information perspectives*, **55** (1/2), 2003, 23–31.

24 Nicholas, D. and Dobrowolski, T., 'Re-branding and re-discovering the digital information user', *Libri*, **50** (3), 2000, 157–62.

25 Nicholas, D., Huttington, P. and Watkinson, A., 'Digital journals, big deals and online searching behaviour: a pilot study', *Aslib proceedings: new information perspectives*, **55** (1/2), 2003, 84–109.

Chapter 11

User-centred models of information retrieval

Introduction

The user of an information retrieval system may be anyone living anywhere in the world. This is especially true for those online information retrieval systems and digital libraries that aim to offer information access to the global audience, for example, Dialog, PubMed (providing access to Medline and other online health databases from the National Library of Medicine, US) the Networked Digital Library of Theses and Dissertations (providing access to electronic theses and dissertations from over 150 universities in the world), Networked Computer Science Technical Reference Library (providing access to electronic collections of computer science and engineering information resources from various universities), and so on. Users of these information retrieval systems vary in terms of their information need, characteristics, capabilities, and so on. Nicholas and Dobrowolski[1] propose a new term, 'information players', to replace the word 'users' or 'end-users' in order to reflect the changing nature of the users in a digital environment. IR is essentially an interactive process. The fact that information behaviour is an integral part of an information retrieval process was already recognized in 1948.[2] Subsequently, several researchers concentrated on the issues of information interaction, user information behaviour, and so on. These studies have given birth to many user-centred IR models. This chapter briefly discusses the features of some such models.

Information seeking

Information needs and information seeking have remained a central theme of research among information and computer science researchers for many years. It is commonly agreed that the process of information seeking begins with a user's information need. Much research on information needs and users' information seeking behaviour has been conducted, and a large volume of literature has been produced over the past three decades (see Bates;[3-8] Belkin, Oddy and Brooks;[9, 10] Case, Borgman and Meadow;[11] Dervin;[12] Ellis;[13] Kuhlthau;[14, 15] Kuhlthau et al.;[16] Marchionini;[17] Marchionini and Komlodi;[18] and Wilson[2, 19-21]). Marchionini[17] comments that information seeking is a fundamental human process that is closely related to learning and problem solving.

According to Borgman[22] a need is a psychological construct, and it cannot be observed by a researcher, a librarian or an intelligent agent; only indicators or manifestations of needs can be observed. The type of information needed by the user, to accomplish a goal – to resolve a problem, to answer a specific question, or to meet a curiosity – may be quick and brief or exhaustive and detailed. Figure 11.1 shows a model of information access. Although it appears to be a very simple model, in essence several complex processes take place throughout the process of seeking information. Some of these processes are technological and related to the information retrieval system, user interfaces, and so on. Other processes relate to the nature and characteristics of the content as well as the individual user. The process may take more or less time, and may become simple or complex depending on the nature of the users – their cognitive abilities, background, exact information need, and so on.

Information seeking is an interactive process that depends on initiatives on the part of the user, feedback from the information system, and the user's decisions about subsequent actions based on this feedback.[17] The details of a user's initial information need may often change. Belkin[23] noted that as the information searcher learns more about the problem that they are investigating, through interactions with information

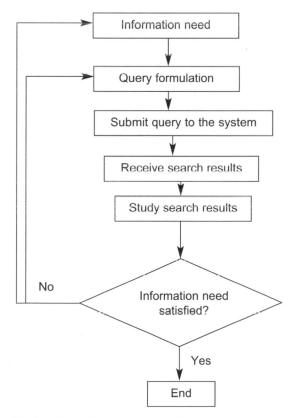

Fig. 11.1 *Basic information access model*

retrieval systems, their information needs are often modified. Hence, the information search process continues till the user gets the information that satisfies their revised information need. Appropriate technology, such as the appropriate information retrieval system and user interface may facilitate the process, but is not the ultimate answer, because the information seeking process depends largely on individual users and their information need as well as on the nature, volume and variety of the content.

Users also learn during the information search process. For example, users may come across some information that influences their information need. The user may also acquire new knowledge about the system, and thus may be able to formulate queries more skilfully and appropriately to retrieve better output.

Human information behaviour models

Information retrieval research can broadly be categorized into two streams: system-centred research that focuses on the systems aspects of information retrieval including retrieval algorithms, indexing, interface design, and so on, and user-centred research that focuses on the human information behaviour (HIB), and user-centred or cognitive approaches to the design of information retrieval systems. The field of HIB is related to the cognitive approach to interactive information retrieval and seeks to investigate the broader issues related to the human processes for information seeking and use.[24] The importance of HIB in the overall information retrieval system has been emphasized by several researchers (for example, Vakkari[25]). Many researchers have proposed interactive models for information search and retrieval that place users in the central role of the information retrieval system. Examples of these models include those proposed by Ingwersen,[26, 27] Belkin et al.,[28] Saracevic,[29, 30] Ellis,[13] Kulthau,[31] Bates,[8] and so on. Two major research papers reviewing the user-centred information retrieval models include those of Wilson[2] and Ingwersen.[32] Some of the most important human information and behaviour models are discussed below.

Wilson's model

Wilson[2] proposes that a model may be described as a framework for thinking about a problem and may evolve into a statement of the relationships among theoretical propositions. He further adds that most models of HIB are of the former variety in the sense that they are statements or diagrams that attempt to describe an information-seeking activity, the causes and consequences of that activity, or the relationship among stages in information-seeking behaviour.

The problem-solving model proposed by Wilson suggests that information seeking arises as a consequence of an information need perceived by the user who, in order to satisfy that need, makes demands upon information sources and services. This results in the success or failure to find relevant information. In this model, the information need of the user is the most factor in originating and driving the entire information retrieval process. However, according to Wilson,[2] a user's information need is not a primary need but a secondary need, which arises out of needs of a more basic type; in order to meet these information needs the user is likely to meet different barriers. The basic need, which in turn generates the information need, may arise from the role of the person in an environment, a life style or a course of work. Wilson identifies three major types of barrier in the context of an information need: personal, role-related and environmental.

While the basic principle and focus remained the same, Wilson[21] developed a new HIB model in 1996 that suggests that information-seeking behaviour is goal directed with the resolution of the problem, and possibly the presentation of the solution, as the goal. In moving through each of the stages of problem identification, problem definition, problem resolution and solution presentation, uncertainty must be reduced through the interactions of the users with the information sources.[33] (See Figure 11.2.)

Dervin's model

The sense-making approach of Dervin[12] posits that users go through different phases in making sense of the world. The first phase establishes the context for the information need, which she calls a *situation*. People find a gap between what they understand and what they need to know in order to make sense of the current situation. These gaps are manifested by formulation of questions. Thus, according to the sense-making approach, the HIB is implemented in terms of four constituent elements:

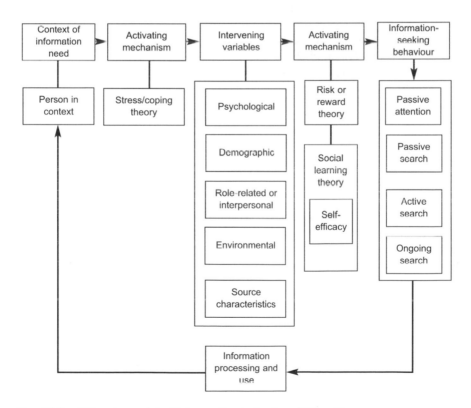

Fig. 11.2 *Wilson's model of information behaviour (Wilson[2])*

- a situation in time and space, which defines the context in which an information problem arises
- a gap, which identifies the difference between the contextual situation and the desired situation
- an outcome, which is the consequence of the sense-making process
- a bridge that is the means of closing the gap between the situation and the outcome.

Marchionini[17] comments that the situation–gap–use model of Dervin applies more to general human conditions than information seeking, but it has been adopted by researchers in information science and communications as a framework for studying the information-seeking process. Wilson[2] comments that the strength of Dervin's model lies partly in the methodological consequences, since in relation to HIB, it can lead to a way of questioning that can reveal the nature of a problematic situation, the extent to which information serves to bridge the gap of uncertainty, and the nature of the outcomes from the use of information.

Ellis's model

According to Ellis,[13] an information-seeking process has the following stages:

- *starting*: beginning the information-seeking process, e.g. when the user asks some knowledgeable colleague
- *chaining*: following links of citations in known material
- *browsing*: comprising some sort of undirected or semi-structured searching for information
- *differentiating*: filterng the information obtained
- *monitoring*: keeping track of developments in the user's field of interest
- *extracting*: selecting the relevant information from a source
- *verifying*: checking the accuracy of information
- *ending*: conducting a final search to complete the process.

Information-seeking processes do not necessarily follow these stages in strict order. According to Ellis[13] the detailed interrelation or interaction of the features in any individual information-seeking pattern will depend on the unique circumstances of the information-seeking activities of the person concerned at the time of looking for the information.

Bates's model

The berry-picking model of information seeking proposed by Bates[8] suggests that as a result of reading and learning from the information retrieved through the search process, users' information needs and queries continually shift. The berry-picking model also suggests that users' information needs are satisfied by a series of selections and bits of information found along the entire information search process, as opposed to the output of any particular search set.

The cascade model proposed by Bates[34] suggests that each layer in an information system interacts with every other design layer, and this cascade of interactions culminates in the interface, where all the prior interactions have either worked to produce effective information retrieval or to produce system elements that work at cross purposes. The cascade model, for operational information retrieval systems, works on the basic proposition that without an integrated design of all the constituent layers of an information retrieval system, the resulting system is likely to be poor. There are four layers in this model:

- The first layer comprises the infrastructure – network, hardware, software and databases.
- The second layer comprises the information or content combined with the metadata structure.
- The third layer represents the information retrieval system – from information in searchable form to interface design supported by the technical infrastructure.
- The fourth layer is the human part of the system, which comprises user searching activities and user understanding and motivation.

Kulthau's model

Kuhlthau[14–16, 31] studied how students search for information as part of their writing process. Based on this, she proposed a model that involves seven stages:

- task initiation
- topic selection
- pre-focus exploration
- focus formulation
- information collection
- search closure or presentation (writing).

Wilson[2] comments that Kulthau's model is more general than Ellis's model in drawing attention to the feelings associated with the various stages and activities. Based on Kulthau's model, Vakkari[35] proposes a task-based model that starts with a focus. Vakkari comments that the finding of a focus, which is comparable to the hypothesis in research, is crucial in any search process. At the beginning, that is at the pre-focus stage, the search remains undirected; once the focus has been constructed, the search for information becomes more directed.

User-centred information search models

The above models are HIB models since they are concerned with the general human behaviour surrounding an information-seeking process, and the broader perspective of the information-search process. A number of user-centred information search models, as opposed to the typical human information behaviour models, have also been proposed in the literature. Some of these are briefly discussed below.

Ingwersen's model

Ingwersen[32] divides research on cognitive approaches to information science into two periods: the period between 1977 and 1991, which can be characterized as use- and intermediary-oriented; and from 1992 onwards that takes a holistic view of all the interactive information retrieval. According to Ingwersen,[32] the following four issues are crucial to information retrieval:

- All interactive communication processes during an information retrieval process can be regarded as processes of cognition, which may occur in all the information-processing components involved.
- The presuppositions and intentionality underlying messages are vital for perception and understanding, but are lost by any transmission system between the sender and the recipient (human or machine).
- Uncertainties and unpredictabilities are inherent in information retrieval interaction and are associated with all acts of interpretation carried out by the sender and the recipient.
- Real information retrieval is possible only by an individual user in context.

Ingwersen's model proposes that information search and retrieval is characterized by:

- an individual user's cognitive space, which is characterized by the work and interests of the user, the current cognitive state of the user, a problem or goal, uncertainty, and information needs and information behaviour
- the social or organizational environment, which is characterized by the domain, strategies or goals of the organization, and tasks and preferences.

Wilson[2] comments that Ingwersen's model has a close family resemblance to the models of information-seeking behaviour, for example the two elements – 'user's cognitive space' and 'social/organizational environment' resemble the elements of 'person in context' and 'environmental factors' in Wilson's model.

Belkin's model

The ASK (Anomalous States of Knowledge) model proposed by Belkin[23] and his associates [9, 10, 28] suggests that an information-seeking process begins with a problem, but initially the actual problem and the information needed to resolve the problem is not clearly understood. Hence, the information seekers need to go through an iterative process to articulate a search request, and the information system should support interactive search processes.

The episode model of Belkin et al.[28] focuses on the actions carried out in an information search from scanning to searching within the framework of 'goal of interaction', 'mode of retrieval' and 'resource considered'. The idea behind this model is that people commonly engage in multiple searching behaviours across a set of information retrieval sessions. According to Belkin's model any single information-seeking strategy can be described according to its location in the four dimensions of 'scanning to searching', 'goal of interaction', 'mode of retrieval' and 'resource considered'.

Saracevic's model

In 1996 Saracevic[29, 30] proposed a stratified interaction model, which he modified in 1997. The basic assumption of the stratified interaction model is that users interact with information retrieval systems in order to use information and the use of information is connected with cognition and situational application.[30] The major elements in the stratified model are users and computer, each with a host of other variables. The interface enables a variety of interactions to be initiated, which can be conceived as a sequence of processes occurring in several connected levels or strata, each involving different elements and/or specific processes. For example, on the human side processes may be physiological (e.g. visual, tactile or auditory), psychological and cognitive; on the computer side they may be physical and symbolic, while the interface provides for an interaction on the *surface* level. The interaction may involve several things, for example,

1   Users may carry out a dialogue by using commands and receiving responses (computer utterances) through an interface. They may also engage in a number of other processes or 'things', above and beyond searching and matching, such as: understanding and drawing out the attributes of a given computer component, or information resource; browsing; navigating within and among information resources, even distributed ones; determining the state of a given process; visualizing of displays and results; obtaining and providing various types of feedback; passing judgements; and so on.
2   Similarly, computers interact with users with given processes and 'understandings' specific to the computer system, and provide given responses in this dialogue; they also may generate requests for responses from the user.

Saracevic[30] comments that investigations of the surface level could concentrate on the observation of:

*   what 'things' users did in order to achieve something
*   what 'things' computers did, with what results
*   how the various things did or did not work together
*   what were the patterns in given situations and how to enhance them.

On the user side the stratified model proposes three different levels: *cognitive, affective* and *situational*:

*   At the *cognitive* level users interact with texts and their representations in the information resources considering them as cognitive structures.
*   At the *affective* level users interact with their intentions, and all that go with

intentionality, such as beliefs, motivation, feelings (e.g. frustration), desires (e.g. for a given degree of completeness), urgency, and so on.

• At the *situational* level users interact with the situation or problem that produced the information need and resulting question. The results of the search may be applied to the resolution or partial resolution of a problem. Users judge the retrieved information according to its usefulness. At this level an information researcher may like to investigate the effects of the retrieved information on tasks or problems at hand, changes in the problem, categorization of problems for interactive decisions, and so on.

Saracevic et al.[36–38] propose a model of information seeking and retrieving, which has been presented in a generalized form by Spink et al.[39] as shown in Figure 11.3.

Event	Variables
Information seeker has an information problem to resolve	Information-seeker pre-search characteristics Cognitive style Problem statement Knowledge level Problem-solving stage Information-seeking stage Uncertainty level
Information-seeking process related to information problem	Information-seeking behaviours Information-seeking models
Information seekers formulate their information problem into a question Pre-search interaction with a search intermediary	Question statement Question analysis Intermediary characteristics
Formulation of the search strategy	Pre-search characteristics of information seeker
Searching activities and interactions	Search strategy Search characteristics Search processes Successive searches
Delivery of responses to the information seeker	Items retrieved Forms delivered
Evaluation of output	Relevance Utility
Information seeker evaluation of impact of search	Information seeker post-search characteristics Problem statement Knowledge level Problem-solving stage Information-seeking stage Uncertainty level

Fig. 11.3   *General model of information seeking and searching*

Discussion

In addition to those mentioned in this chapter, many other models of information seeking and information search have been proposed by researchers, and many of these models are complementary to each other. However, as Ingwersen[32] comments, until very recently the cognitive and user-centred approach to information retrieval has remained a rather low key area in overall information retrieval research. Wilson[2] proposes the following key questions for further research into the information-seeking and searching behaviour of users:

- To what extent are the various models a complete, or reasonably complete, presentation of the reality of the information retrieval process?
- In what ways are the models complementary?
- For information-searching behaviour, how does the knowledge of models of information-seeking behaviour aid our understanding of the actual information search process?

Savage-Knepshield and Belkin[40] comment that during the past four decades we have witnessed a dramatic increase in the amount of interaction between the searcher and the IR system. While these changes can be noticed through developments in the IR system design, and especially through improved user interface designs, many researchers believe that the overall IR system design has been slow to adapt to user-centred IR models.

Reviewing the research on cognitive information retrieval, Ingwersen[32] notes that although the cognitive approaches to information retrieval began in the 1970s, the cognitive view broadened its scope only in the 1990s by seeking to encompass and understand the formal and experimental dimensions of information retrieval. Since then studies have concentrated on the processes of interaction that take place between the complex variety of actors in interactive information retrieval processes.

A number of research papers have appeared reporting on the information-seeking and searching behaviour of users in the large-scale online and web searching environment. Among them, the most prominent one is the multi-part report of a UK–US joint research[24, 33, 39] that has taken into account all the major HIB models and have proposed a new model based on the concept of successive searching. The basic tenet of this model is that problem solving may involve information-seeking activities within which search episodes take place, and within these episodes occur the interactions of various kinds, for instance, the relatively mechanical tasks of entering search terms and pressing keys as well as the mental tasks of selection and relevance judgement formation in response to the retrieved items (Spink et al.[39]). The theoretical framework of this model consists of a set of actions within interactive search episodes over a period of time consisting of the interaction time – the time involved in the online search process – and information-seeking time – the total time spent in seeking information from any source. Another important aspect of this model is the concept of successive searching. Information users with a broader problem often seek information in stages over an extended period of time, and they use a variety of information sources. The process of carrying out repeated searches over a period of time in relation to a given and, possibly, evolving information problem is called successive searching.[39]

Most of the models discussed here are based on, and tend to support, the user information-seeking behaviour in a mediated search environment. However, one of the major impacts of the recent developments in the internet, world wide web and digital libraries is the development of end-user-oriented information retrieval systems where the users are supposed to access and use information without the direct involvement of any human intermediary. While the basic process of information searching remains the same, such information retrieval systems depict somewhat different user information behaviour in terms of information access and use. Recent HIB studies in the context of the web and digital libraries are discussed later in this book.

References

1   Nicholas, D. and Dobrowolski, T., 'The information ''player'': a new and timely term for the digital information user'. In: Scamell, A. (ed.), *Handbook of information management*, London, Aslib, 2001, 513–22.

2   Wilson, T., 'Models of information behaviour research', *Journal of documentation*, **55** (3), 1999, 249–70.

3   Bates, M. J., 'Factors affecting subject catalog search success', *Journal of the American Society for Information Science*, **28** (3), 1977, 161–9.

4   Bates, M.J., 'Information search tactics', *Journal of the American Society for Information Science*, **30** (4), 1979, 205–14.

5   Bates, M. J., 'Search techniques'. In: Williams, M. (ed.). *Annual review of information science and technology*, **16**, New York, Knowledge Industry for ASIS, 1981, 139–69.

6   Bates, M. J., 'The fallacy of the perfect thirty-item online search', *RQ*, **24** (1), 1984, 43–50.

7   Bates, M. J., 'Subject access in online catalogs: a design model', *Journal of the American Society for Information Science,* **37** (6), 1986, 357–76.

8   Bates. M. J., 'The design of browsing and berrypicking techniques for the online search interface', *Online review*, **13** (5), 1989, 407–31.

9   Belkin, N. J., Oddy, R. N. and Brooks, H. M., 'ASK for information retrieval. Part 1. Background and theory', *Journal of documentation*, **38** (2), 1982, 61–71.

10   Belkin, N. J., Oddy, R. N. and Brooks, H. M., 'ASK for information retrieval. Part 2. Results of a design study', *Journal of documentation*, **38** (3), 1982, 145–64.

11   Case, D. O., Borgman, C. L. and Meadow, C. T., 'End-user information-seeking in the energy field: implications for the end-user access to DOE RECON databases', *Information processing and management*, **22** (4), 1986, 299–308.

12   Dervin, B., 'Useful theory for librarianship: communication, not information', *Drexel library quarterly*, **13** (3), 1977, 16–32.

13   Ellis, D., 'A behavioural model for information retrieval system design',

Journal of information science, **15**, 1989, 237–47.

14 Kuhlthau, C., 'Longitudinal case studies of the information search process of users in libraries', *Library and information science research*, **10**, 1988, 257–304.

15 Kuhlthau, C., 'Developing a model of the library search process: cognitive and affective aspects', *RQ*, **28** (2), 1988, 232–42.

16 Kuhlthau, C., Turock, B., George, M. and Belvin, R., 'Validating a model of the search process: a comparison of academic, public and school library users', *Library and information science research*, **12**, 1990, 5–31.

17 Marchionini, G., *Information seeking in electronic environments*, Cambridge, Cambridge University Press, 1995.

18 Marchionini, G. and Komlodi, A., 'Design of interfaces for information seeking'. In: William, M. E. (ed.), *Annual review of information science and technology*, Medford, NJ, Learned Information, **33**, 1998, 89–130.

19 Wilson, T., 'On user studies and information needs', *Journal of documentation*, **37** (1), 1981, 3–15.

20 Wilson, T., 'Information needs and uses: fifty years of progress?' In: Vickery, B. C. (ed.), *Fifty years of information progress: a Journal of documentation review*, London, Aslib, 1994, 15–51.

21 Wilson, T. D. and Walsh, C., *Information behaviour: an interdisciplinary perspective*, Sheffield, University of Sheffield, 1996.

22 Borgman, C., *From Gutenberg to the global information infrastructure: access to information in the networked world*, New York, ACM Press, 2000.

23 Belkin, N. J. 'Anomalous states of knowledge as a basis for information retrieval', *Canadian journal of information science*, **5**, 1980, 133–43.

24 Spink, A., Wilson, T., Ford, N., Foster, A. and Ellis, D., 'Information-seeking and mediated searching. Part 1. Theoretical framework and research design', *Journal of the American Society for Information Science and Technology*, **53** (9), 2002, 695–703.

25 Vakkari, P., 'Task complexity, information types, search strategies and relevance: integrating studies on information seeking and retrieval'. In: Wilson, T. D. (ed.)., *Proceedings of the 2nd International conference on information seeking in context, Aug. 12–15, 1998*, Sheffield and London, Taylor Graham, 1999, 35–54.

26 Ingwersen, P., *Information retrieval interaction*, London, Taylor Graham, 1992.

27 Ingwersen, P., 'Cognitive perspectives of information retrieval interaction: elements of a cognitive IR theory', *Journal of documentation*, **52** (1), 1996, 3–50.

28 Belkin, N., Cool, C., Stein, A. and Theil, S., 'Cases, scripts, and information-seeking strategies: on the design of interactive information retrieval systems', *Expert systems with applications*, **9** (3), 1995, 379–95.

29 Saracevic, T., 'Modeling interaction in information retrieval (IR): a review and proposal', *Proceedings of the Annual Meeting of the American Society for Information Science*, **33**, 1996, 3–9.

30 Saracevic, T., 'Extension and application of the stratified model of information

retrieval interaction'. In: *Proceedings of the Annual Meeting of the American Society for Information Science*, **34**, 1997, 313–27.

31   Kulthau, C., *Seeking meaning: a process approach to library and information services*, Norwood, NJ, Ablex Publishing, 1993.

32   Ingwersen, P., 'Cognitive information retrieval'. In: Williams, M. E. (ed.), *Annual review of information science and technology*, **34**, Medford, NJ, Information Today, Inc., 2001, 3–52.

33   Wilson, T., Ford, N., Ellis, D., Foster, A. and Spink, A., 'Information seeking and mediated searching. Part 2. Uncertainty and its correlates', *Journal of the American Society for Information Science and Technology*, **53** (9), 2002, 704–15.

34   Bates, M. J., 'The cascade of interactions in the digital library interface', *Information processing and management*, **38** (3), 2002, 381–400.

35   Vakkari, P., 'A theory of the task-based information retrieval process: a summary and generalisation of a longitudinal study', *Journal of documentation*, **57** (1), 2001, 44–60.

36   Saracevic, T., Kantor. P., Chamis, A. Y. and Trivison, D., 'A study of information seeking and retrieving. I. Background and methodology', *Journal of the American Society for Information Science*, **39** (3), 1988, 161–76.

37   Saracevic, T. and Kantor. P., 'A study of information seeking and retrieving. II. Users, questions and effectiveness. III. Searchers, searches and overlap', *Journal of the American Society for Information Science*, **39** (3), 1988, 177–96.

38   Saracevic, T. and Kantor. P., 'A study of information seeking and retrieving. III. Searchers, searches and overlap', Journal of the American Society for Information Science, **39** (3), 1988, 197–216.

39   Spink, A., Wilson, T., Ford, N., Foster, A. and Ellis, D., 'Information-seeking and mediated searching. Part 3. Successive searching', *Journal of the American Society for Information Science and Technology*, **53** (9), 2002, 716–27.

40   Savage-Knepshield, P. and Belkin, N., 'Interaction in information retrieval', *Information processing and management*, **50** (12), 1999, 1067–82.

Chapter 12

User interfaces

Introduction

The user interface forms an important component of an information retrieval system since it connects the users to the organized information resources. User interfaces perform two major functions: they allow users to search or browse an information collection and they display the results of a search. They also often allow users to perform further tasks, like sorting, saving and/or printing the search results, modifying the search query, and so on. The user interface is therefore the most important component of an information retrieval system that a user can see and interact with. The success of an information retrieval system depends significantly on the design and usefulness of the user interface. Hence a significant amount of research has taken place in the past few decades on the design, use and evaluation of user interfaces to various kinds of information retrieval systems.

Mitchell[1] observes that the user interface is the means by which information is transferred between the user and the computer and vice-versa; well-designed user interfaces should allow users to find the information that the information system provides access to easily and to exploit it once found. In fact a good user interface greatly enhances the quality of interactions with information systems. This chapter discusses some major characteristics of user interfaces to information retrieval systems.

The four-phase framework for interface design

Information searching is a complex process. It involves a number of stages and at each stage a number of actions are taken and decisions are made. The information retrieval system and the user interface may provide support in performing these actions and in making appropriate decisions. Shneiderman, Byrd and Croft[2] divide the major activities in an information search process into four major phases: formulation, action, review of results and refinement. They propose that this four-phase framework for interface design will provide common structure and terminology for information searching while preserving the distinct features of individual digital library collections and search mechanisms.[3]

Phase 1: Formulation

The first phase – the formulation of a search – is triggered by an information need, and several decisions are made regarding sources, fields, what to search for and the search variants.

Selection of sources (collections and/or databases) is an important step in a search process. In an online IR, users may have access to many collections, and each collection may have one or more databases. Users need to have some idea about the nature and content of the collections or databases and accordingly should make a selection from them. Some online databases and digital libraries show a list of the available collections and allow users to select one particular collection. However, selection of the sources to search is not always an easy task, especially for new and novice users. Some systems provide support for selection of appropriate sources or databases. In this case, users are asked to enter a search expression, and then the system searches across the databases and produces an output of best-matching databases instead of best-matching records. This gives an idea to the user about the content of the collections and thus facilitates the selection of sources. In Dialog the DialIndex option allows users to search across a range of databases to get a list of best matching databases for the chosen search topic.

A search may be conducted against one or more selected fields in a database. A search on specific fields produces more specific search results compared with a search on each complete record. However, it is sometimes difficult for the user to decide which field to search. This calls for a familiarity of the structure of the chosen database and also of the nature and content of the fields. Users may go to the help files, or to some other sources, for example to the blue sheets (pages that contain information on a database including its content, coverage, structure, indexing, and so on) in the case of a Dialog database search. Some systems provide search interfaces (usually in the advanced search mode) with structured fields.

A major challenge for users comes in writing the search statement. A search statement tells the system what to search for in the chosen database(s). Various techniques are available for specifying how the constituent search terms are to be looked for, for example, by using appropriate search operators. The search operators are not always intuitive and are purely dependent on the chosen system. Users need to be familiar with the various operators and the conventions appropriate to the chosen search system.

A search term may be represented in a variety of ways. Users may choose a search term or phrase that may appear in the database records in a variety of ways, for example in singular and/or plural forms, in various synonymous forms, with variant spellings, and so on. It is therefore often very difficult for the user to decide which form or variant of a search term to use. User interfaces of digital libraries often allow users to have control over a number of parameters, for example to allow for case sensitivity, stemming, phonetic variants, synonyms, abbreviations, broader and narrower terms, and stop words.

Phase 2: Action

Usually a search button needs to be pressed to conduct a search. In some cases, the user just needs to press <CR> to activate the search process. Once the search begins, the user is usually expected to wait till the search process is completed. Sometimes this may take a long time and thus may be quite frustrating. In some cases, the interface prompts the user that the search is being processed; it may also tell the user about the progress of the search. A very appealing method of information searching uses 'dynamic queries' where there is no search button; the result set is continuously displayed and updated as phases of the search are changed.[2]

Phase 3: Review of results

Information retrieval interfaces usually offer various choices to the user for viewing results by selecting the size of the display, display format, sequencing of the retrieved items (sorted by author, date, and so on). Some interfaces use different visualization techniques for display of search results. Some interfaces also use helpful messages to explain the results, for example, the degree of relevance. Some digital libraries, for example the California Digital Library, shows results from various different collections separately (see Figure 12.1). Some systems display the relevance ranking of each retrieved item (see for example, output of ABI/INFORM in Figure 12.9).

Fig. 12.1   *Results of a search in CDLIB (showing output from various categories of sources)*

Phase 4: Refinement

Search interfaces provide different facilities for modifying and refining queries. In some cases, users need to reformulate the search statement and conduct a new search, while in others users can refine a search and conduct a new search on the retrieved set. For example, in Dialog search, each search is automatically given a set number, and the user can call any search set and refine the search statement to conduct a search on the previously retrieved set of results. Some IR system provide a thesaurus interface to help users formulate or modify queries (see for example the thesaurus interface of Entrez PubMed search interface in Figures 12.4 to 12.6).

Information seeking and user interfaces

User interfaces to information retrieval systems that support information-seeking processes have been widely discussed in the literature. Interface design encompasses what appears on the users' screen, how they view it, and how they manipulate it. Functional design specifies the functions that are offered to the user, which include selecting parts of a digital object, searching a list or sorting retrieved output, obtaining help and manipulating objects that appear on the screen. Most PCs have a user interface that is based on the style derived at Xerox PARC and made popular on Apple Macs, which use the metaphors of files and folders on a desktop (Arms[4]).

Shneiderman, the Guru of human–computer interaction and user interface design, proposes a number of guiding principles for design of user interfaces.[2, 5]

- Strive for consistency in terminology, layout, instructions, fonts and colour.
- Provide shortcuts for skilled users.
- Provide appropriate and informative feedback about the sources and what is being searched for.
- Design for closure so that users know when they have completed searching the entire collection or have viewed every item in a browse list.
- Permit reversal of actions so that users can undo or modify actions; for example, they should be able to modify their queries or go back to the previous state in a search session.
- Support user control, allowing users to monitor the progress of a search and be able to specify the parameters to control a search.
- Reduce short-term memory load; the system should keep track of some important actions performed by the users and allow them to jump easily to a formerly performed action, for example, to a former query or to a specific result set.
- Simple error-handling facilities to allow users to rectify errors easily; all error messages should be clear and specific.
- Provide plenty of space for entering text in search boxes.
- Provide alternative interfaces for expert and novice users.

Interface design is pivotal to the effective use of an information system, and the application environment of information retrieval systems has its own distinctive needs and characteristics, which need to be understood and addressed in design.

Hearst[6] comments that a user interface designer must make decisions about how to arrange various kinds of information on the screen and how to structure the possible sequences of user-system interactions.

Marchionini[7] provides a description of the essential features of interfaces to support end-user information seeking and suggests five information seeking functions: problem definition, source selection, problem articulation, result examination and information extraction. He argues that much of the interface work has focused on problem articulation (including query formulation) and that other functions need to be investigated in designing information-seeking interfaces. Marchionini and Komlodi[8] discuss the evolution of interfaces and trace research and development in three areas: information seeking, interface design and computer technology. They provide a brief review of interfaces to online information retrieval systems as well as to the online public access catalogues (OPACs). They also discuss the new generation of user interfaces influenced by the emergence of the web. They conclude that interface design has become more user-centred and the trend is toward more mature interfaces that support a range of information-seeking strategies.

Savage-Knepshield and Belkin[9] discuss the trends related to interface design challenges within the context of information retrieval interaction over the last three decades of the 20th century. They suggest three major eras - which they refer to simply as the early years, the middle years, and the later years - to provide a description of the types of interfaces designed in these periods. Command language interfaces provided the main approach in the early years. In the middle years menu-driven and form-fill-in interfaces, which were more appropriate for novices and casual searchers, became the dominant interface type. In the later years, users and their information needs became the focus of the most complex interface design challenges. This period is characterized by use of the natural language and direct manipulation user interfaces. Savage-Knepshield and Belkin note that the degree of interaction between the searcher and the IR system has dramatically increased and much research is still required to meet the challenges in interface design for IR interaction.

Hearst[6] discusses user interface support for the information-seeking process and describes the features of these interfaces that aid such processes as query formulation and specification, viewing results and interactive relevance feedback. She describes a number of graphical user interfaces that provide information seekers with a wide range of approaches to specify, view, analyse and evaluate queries and documents within the context of information retrieval systems. Interfaces that support the formulation of Boolean and natural language queries as well as those providing categorical and subject support are examples of the reviewed interfaces. Hearst points out that there is an increasing interest in taking the behaviours of individuals into account when designing interfaces.

User interfaces and visualization

Since human beings are highly attuned to images, and since visual representation facilitates rapid and easy communication, several visualization techniques have now been applied to the design of user interfaces. Various graphical representation and manipulation techniques are used to represent information on the user screens, though visualization of textually represented information can be challenging.[6]

Users of popular operating systems and common software packages employ a number of visual tools and techniques for day-to-day operations. These include icons, colour highlighting, windows and boxes. The most commonly seen visualization techniques used in interfaces for information access include the following:[6, 10–12]

- *perspective wall*: resembles a grey wall folded into three parts and provides a sort of fish-eye view; the centre panel provides a detailed view and the two wings provide a contextual view; suitable for information that has a linear structure
- *cone tree*: provides a fish-eye view by displaying the closer nodes larger and brighter than the farther nodes; suitable for information that has a hierarchical structure
- *document lenses*: used to focus on one page in a document
- *Hyperbolic Tree Browser*: used to show the hierarchical structure of a collection as a hyperbolic tree (for a demonstration from the Universal Library site see **http://www.ulib.org/webRoot/_hTree/**)
- *brushing and linking*: connects two or more views of the same data such that a change to the representation of one view affects the representation of the other
- *panning and zooming*: mimics the actions of a movie camera, which can scan sideways across a scene, called panning, and can move in for a close-up or back away to get a closer or a wider view, called zooming
- *focus plus context*: one portion of the collection is made the focus of attention by making it larger while shrinking the surrounding objects that form the context.

User interfaces of some information retrieval systems

Information retrieval systems vary in terms of design, objectives, characteristics, contents and users. Consequently, many different types of user interfaces can be found. While some of these user interfaces are quite simple, others are quite sophisticated in terms of design features as well as visualization techniques. In this section we shall look at the user interfaces of some online IR systems.

Interfaces for browsing and searching

The two basic modes of access to information in digital libraries are browsing and searching and most information retrieval systems provide facilities for both.

Browse screens

A browse screen is provided for helping users to browse the entire collection of information in a system. Browsing may be done alphabetically by the title of the collection (as in the browse screen of ABI/INFORM Global, Figure 12.2), or by subject heading (as in BUBL, Figure 12.3). The basic idea is to allow users to select

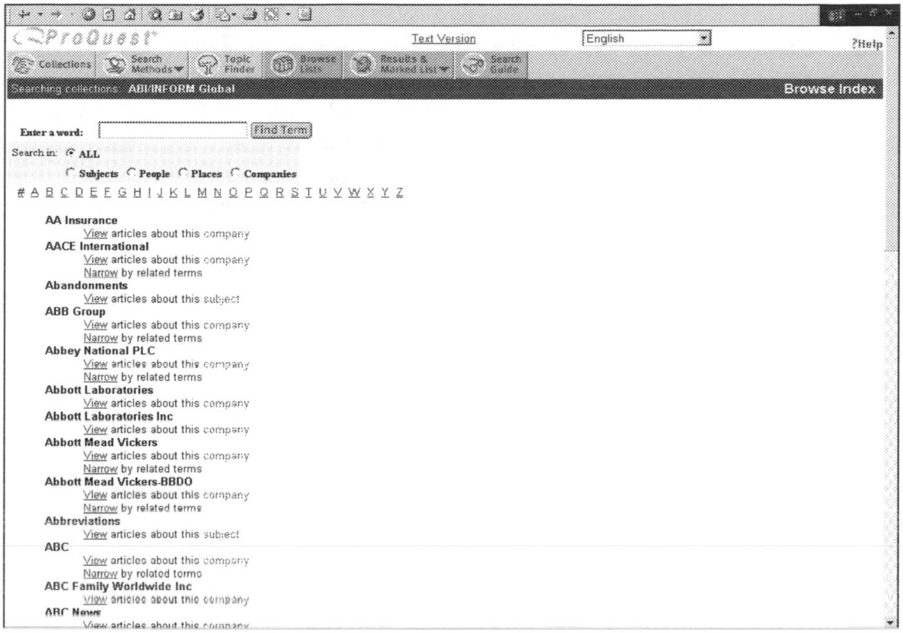

Fig. 12.2 *Browse screen from ABI/INFORM Global*

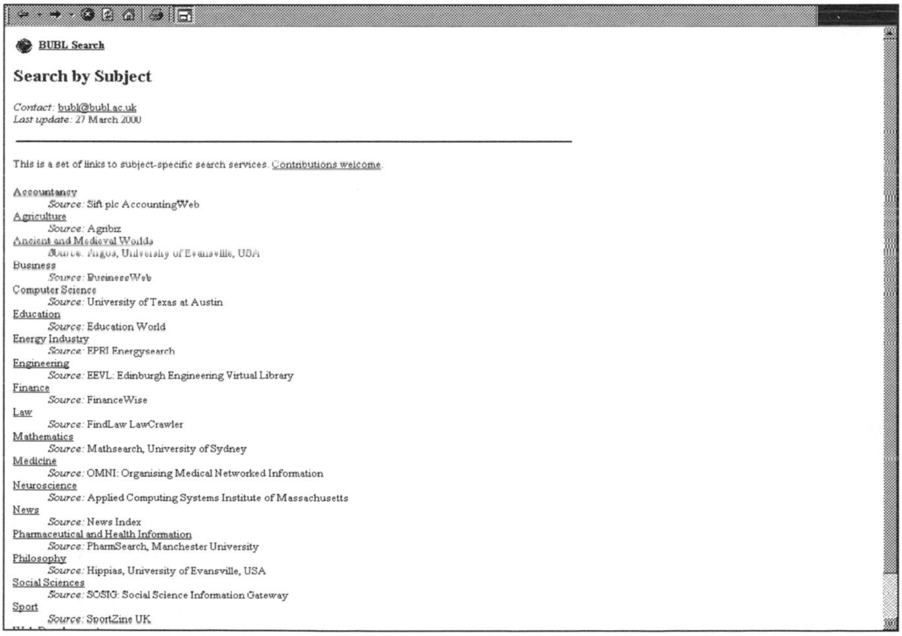

Fig. 12.3 *Browse by Subject in BUBL*

a heading from a given list. Some information retrieval systems provide taxonomy structure for browsing. A typical example is the Entrez Taxonomy Browser (Figures 12.4 and 12.5). Entrez is the text-based search and retrieval system used at NCBI for all the major databases, including PubMed, Nucleotide and Protein Sequences, Protein Structures, Complete Genomes, Taxonomy, OMIM, and many others (**http://www.ncbi.nlm.nih.gov/Database/index.html**). Figure 12.4 shows the main category of the Entrez Taxonomy Browser and Figure 12.5 shows the Taxonomy Browser with difference levels or hierarchy; selection of a specific level from Figure 12.5 will lead the user to the specific hierarchy of the category or heading. At the top of the screen (Figure 12.6) users can see the different levels of the hierarchy, while against each heading two different types of icon are displayed: one leads to the document(s) organized listed under the heading, the other (arrows) lead to the subsequent levels of the hierarchy. Thus, the Entrez Taxonomy Browser allows users to access the hierarchical structure of the subject or topic to browse for the required information from the database. Taxonomy-based search features are also provided by some web search engines such as Kartoo, Vivisimo (Chapter 18), and so on.

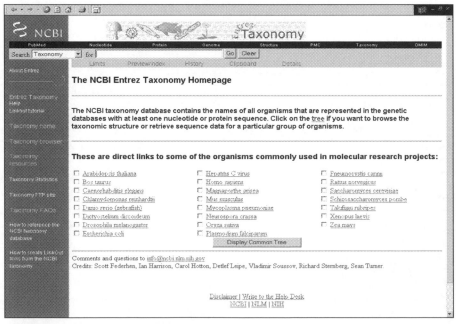

Fig. 12.4 *NCBI Entrez Taxonomy*

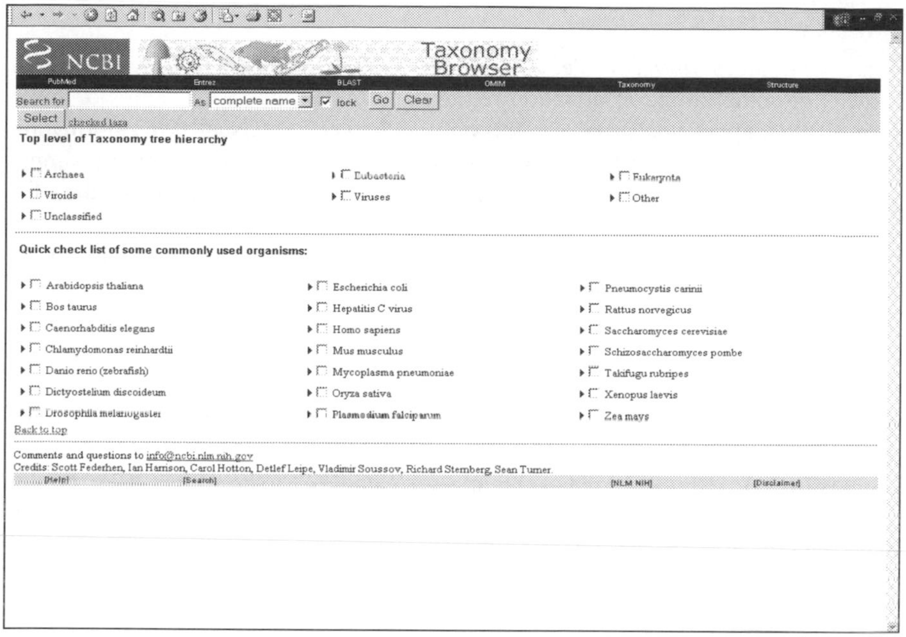

Fig. 12.5 *NCBI Taxonomy Browser (1)*

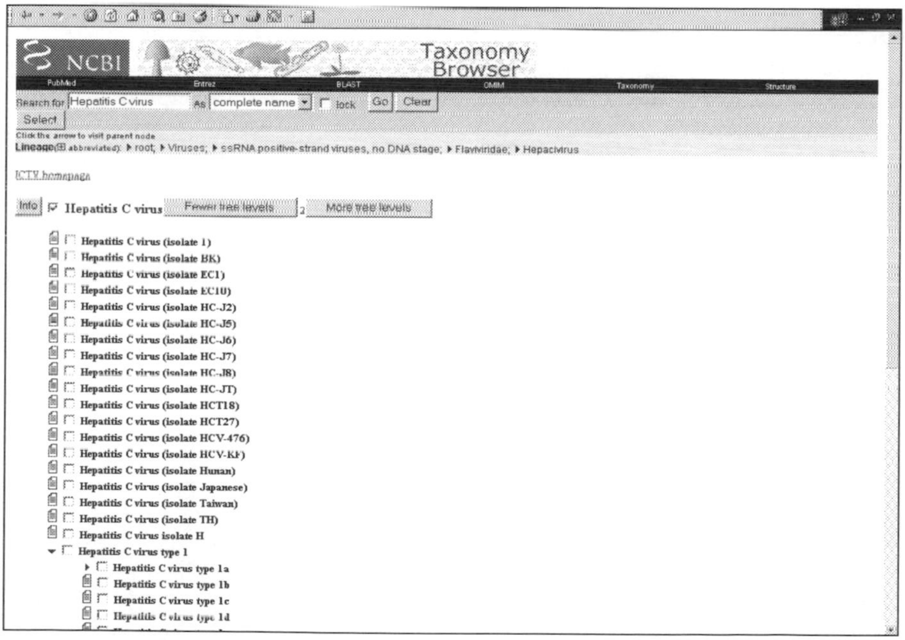

Fig. 12.6 *NCBI Taxonomy Browser (2)*

Search interfaces

Search interfaces vary considerably. In this section we shall look at the search screens of some online information retrieval systems; interface features of some web search engines appear later in this book (Chapter 18). Usually all information retrieval systems have at least two search interfaces: one for conducting a simple search, designed mainly for novice users, or for a quick search; another for advanced search, designed for advanced users and for formulating relatively complex search expressions. While the simple search screen is quite straightforward with a search box and little associate information, the advanced search screens of information retrieval systems, including the web search engines and digital libraries (see Chapters 18 and 22), contain a lot of information for the users and may be complex. The only exception is the command search screen of Dialog, which is designed for advanced users and just contains a search box, with almost no additional information or specific instructions. A quick look at the guided and advanced search screens of ABI/INFORM Global (Figures 12.7 and 12.8) shows that users do not necessarily have to be expert searchers to formulate even quite complex search expressions, since the search screens are self-explanatory and contain a lot of choices and even help.

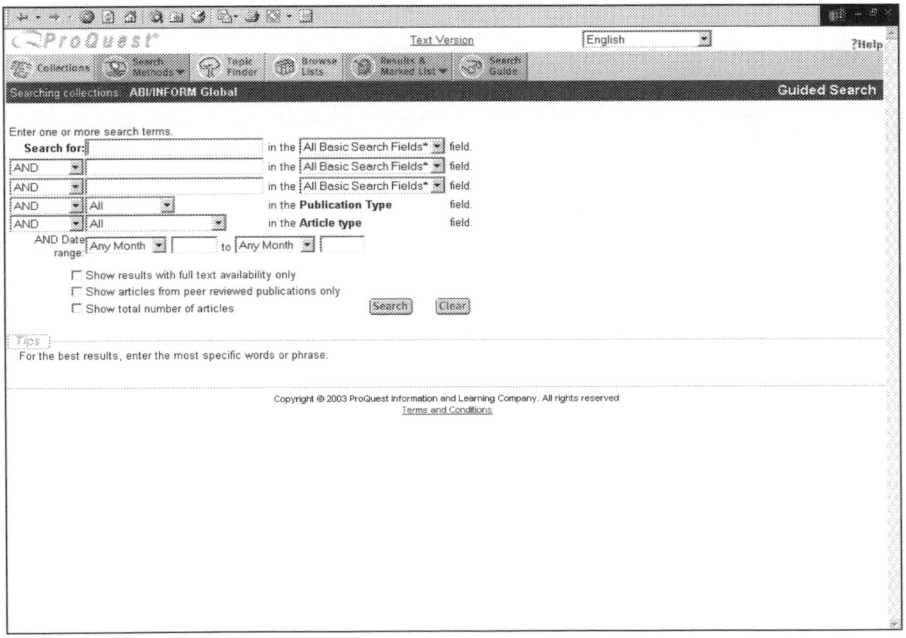

Fig. 12.7   *Guided search screen of ABI/INFORM*

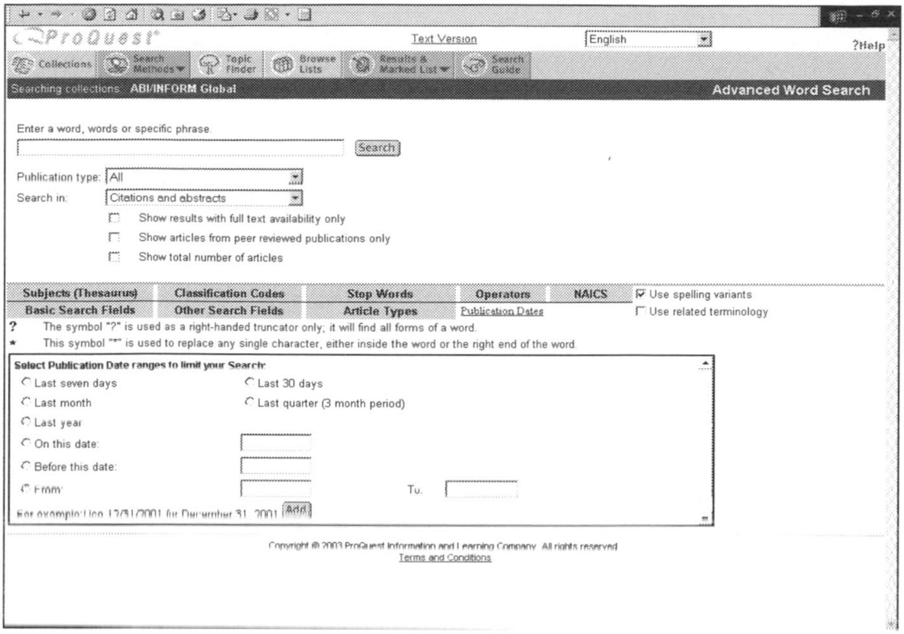

Fig. 12.8 *Advanced search screen of ABI/INFORM*

Interfaces for display of results

Information retrieval systems use different interface design features to allow users to display and view search results. Usually, brief information about each retrieved item appears on the first set of display screens (called Picklist in Dialog), from which the user can select one or more items for detailed display. The display screens also often allow the user to sort the search results further according to a chosen criterion, to choose a format for display of the results and to modify the query. Figure 12.9 shows a results display screen of ABI/INFORM. Some display interfaces also mark the relevance of the records and arrange them in decreasing order of relevance (Figure 12.9). The ABI/INFORM results display interface (shown in Figure 12.9) provides a lot of information to the user, for example, brief information (with links) of each retrieved item, the rank of the retrieved items (marked by asterisks), and the format of the item (shown by different icons, such as text file, text with images, and PDF files). Users can select another option (for instance to start a new search or browse) by selecting an appropriate option from the top of the screen.

Some systems use unique visualization techniques for display of search output. For example, the Kartoo search engine shows the search output (websites) clustered under different subject headings or topics; by moving the cursor to any node the user can see the link of the chosen node with other nodes on the screen and brief information on the chosen node appears on the left side of the screen (see Figures 18.4. and 18.5).

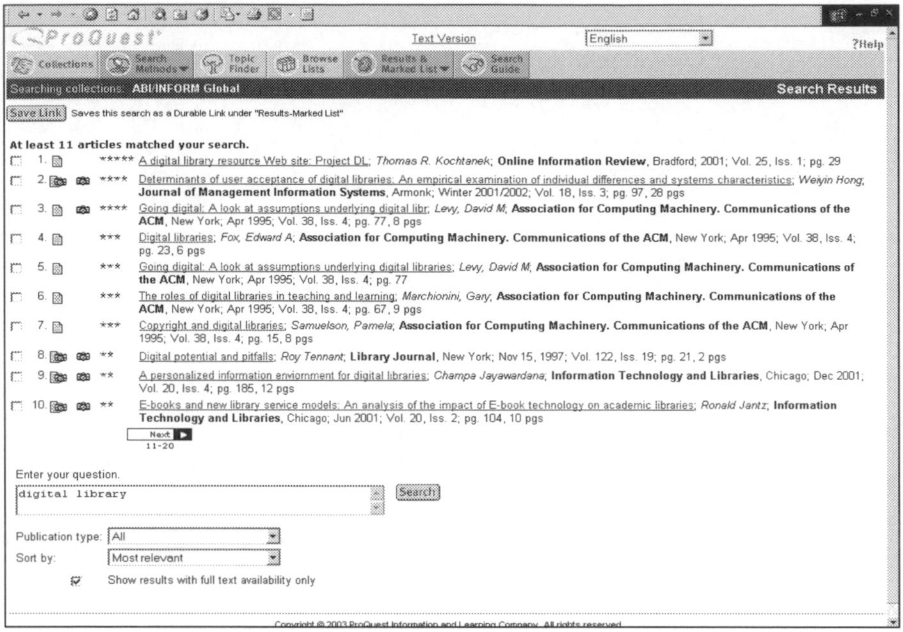

Fig. 12.9   *Results display screen of ABI/INFORM*

User-centred design of interfaces

User-centred design of interfaces has been proposed by many researchers, for example, Marchionini and Komlodi;[8] Fox and Urs;[13] Baldonado;[14] Theng et al.;[15] and Meyyappan, Chowdhury and Foo.[16–18] Several researchers have proposed information access models to support creativity (see for example, Shneiderman[19, 20]).

Shneiderman[19, 20] proposes that user interfaces should be designed such that they support creativity of the users. He proposes the *genex framework*, which supports creativity through four phases:

- *collect*: learn from previous works stored in digital libraries
- *relate*: consult with peers and mentors
- *create*: explore, compose and evaluate possible solutions
- *donate*: disseminate the results and contribute to the digital libraries.

He further describes eight activities that need powerful interfaces to support creative work. In other words, he proposes eight areas that need attention of researchers to make the future digital libraries useful for creative work. These activities are:[20]

1   *Searching and browsing digital libraries*: Users should have more control over searching and browsing so that they can make use of their prior knowledge and can retrieve information that supports their creative activities. Since searching is a part of the entire creative process, users should be able to save the search

results into the appropriate system or software for future use, for example, on a spreadsheet for further manipulation, as a file that can later be used for consultation with peers, or on a personal notebook for later referral.

2   *Consulting with peers*: Users may often consult their peers with new findings or research ideas and information is collected at different stages in the consultation process. Different tools and techniques are also used for consultation. This concerns the design and use of technologies for the interface design, since the appropriate balance of privacy as well as rights to, and ease of, access to information is very important.

3   *Visualizing data and processes*: Interfaces that support visualization of digital library contents are very useful and further works are necessary for smooth integration of the technologies. For example, the interface should allow the user to view the results of a search using appropriate visualization tools that would help them select the most appropriate results. These may then be exported to appropriate packages, for example, to a spreadsheet or to a database, and eventually the processed information may be included into a report or a presentation.

4   *Thinking by free association*: Association of ideas by using related concept is a useful method of thinking and creativity. Thesauri have been used in information retrieval systems to support the association of search terms. Various online tools are now available to associate concepts, for example IdeaFisher,[21] MindManager,[22] and so on. Search interfaces should allow users to use these tools appropriately throughout the search process.

5   *Exploring solutions*: Digital libraries can help users make a decision by making use of the appropriate information and software. Various generic software packages allow uses to explore solutions; one prominent example is the spreadsheet software that has the 'what-if' tools to help users explore the various alternatives. Digital library interfaces may help users run a simulation, save the whole session, and/or send the session to someone for further discussions and explorations. The digital library interface may also allow users to store some excellent sessions to help future researchers build on the best works.

6   *Composing artefacts and performances*: A number of software packages are available that allow users to compose artefacts and performances. Digital library interfaces may integrate the results of a search with such interfaces, for example template and macros for business operations, or Adobe Photoshop Macros for redoing images, music composition programmes with music digital library to help users become more creative.

7   *Reviewing and replaying session histories*: Digital library users may like to replay previous sessions to get some new information, or to begin from there for a new search session. However, as Shneiderman[20] comments, success in this requires careful user interface and software design to ensure that the results are compact, comprehensible and useful.

8   *Disseminating results*: New information may be disseminated to different types of users. The first possible group would be previous and current researchers in the field. Digital libraries should allow users easily find workers in a field of

study. Shneiderman[22] recommends that digital libraries could be conceived of as digital library communities by extensive use of online community software to turn every object into the focus of a discussion group.

Thus research and evaluation are necessary to build systems that would support users in all their activities related to creativity. Other researchers argue that further research into information access and user interfaces is needed so that digital libraries can support more collaborative activities,[23] provide better access to digital video collections,[24] give geographic and spatial information[25] and allow complex interactions.[26] Abdulla, Liu and Fox[27] suggest that comprehensive logs of online information use may be kept for analysing user behaviour, which may provide insights for developing the mechanisms for information access and user interfaces in the future.

References

1   Mitchell, S., 'Interface design considerations in libraries'. In: Stern, D. (ed.), *Digital libraries: philosophies, technical design considerations, and example scenarios*, New York, The Haworth Press, 1999, 131–81.

2   Shneiderman, B., Byrd, D. and Croft, W. B., 'Sorting out searching: a user-interface framework for text searches', *Communications of the ACM*, **41** (4), 1998, 95–8.

3   Shneiderman, B., Byrd, D. and Croft, W. B., 'Clarifying search: a user-interface framework for text searches', *D-lib magazine*, **3** (1), 1997. Available at **http://www.dlib.org/dlib/january97/retrieval/01shneiderman.html**.

4   Arms, W., *Digital libraries*, New York, ACM Press, 2000.

5   Shneiderman, B., *Designing the user interface: strategies for effective human-computer interaction*, 3rd edn, Reading, MA, Addison-Wesley, 1998.

6   Hearst, M., 'User interfaces and visualization'. In: Baeza-Yates, R. and Ribeiro-Neto, B., *Modern information retrieval*, New York, ACM Press, 1999, 257–323.

7   Marchionini, G., 'Interfaces for end-user information seeking', *Journal of the American Society for Information Science*, **43** (2), 1992, 156–63.

8   Marchionini, G. and Komlodi, A., 'Design of interfaces for information seeking'. In: Williams, M. E. (ed.), *Annual review of information science and technology*, Medford, NJ, Learned Information, **33**, 1998, 89–130.

9   Savage-Knepshield, P. A. and Belkin, N. J., 'Interaction in information retrieval: trends over time', *Journal of the American Society for Information Science*, **50** (12), 1999, 1067–82.

10 Kakimoto, T. and Kambayashi, Y., 'Browsing functions in three-dimensional space for digital libraries', *International journal on digital libraries*, **2** (2–3), 1999, 68–78.

11 Robertson, G. G., Card, S. K. and Mackinlay, J. D., 'Information visualization using 3D interactive animation', *Communications of the ACM*, **36** (4), 1993, 57–71.

12   Rao, R., Pedersen, J. O., Hearst, M. A., Mackinlay, J. D., Card, S. K., Masinter, L., Halvorsen, P. and Robertson, G. G., 'Rich interaction in the digital library', *CACM*, **38** (4), 1995, 29–39.

13   Fox, E. A. and Urs, S., 'Digital libraries'. In: Cronin, B. (ed.), *Annual review of information science and technology*, **36**, Medford, NJ, Information Today Inc. on behalf of ASIST, 2002, 503–89.

14   Baldonado, M., 'A user-centred interface for information exploration in a heterogeneous digital library', *Journal of the American Society for Information Science*, **51** (3), 2000, 297–310.

15   Theng, Y. L., Duncker, E., Mohd-Nasir, N., Buchanan, G. and Thimbleby, H. W., *Design guidelines and user-centred digital libraries*, European Conference on Digital Libraries, Paris, Springer, 1999, 167–83.

16   Meyyappan, N. Chowdhury, G. G. and Foo, S., 'Use of a digital work environment (DWE) prototype to create a user-centred university digital library', *Journal of information science*, **27** (4), 2001, 249–64.

17   Meyyappan, N. Chowdhury, G. G. and Foo, S., 'An architecture of a user-centred digital library for the academic community'. In: Chen, C. C. (ed.), *Global digital library development in the new millennium: fertile ground for distributed cross-disciplinary collaboration. NIT 2001 12th International Conference on New Information Technology, Tsinghua University in Beijing, China , May 29-31, 2001*, Beijing, Tsinghua University Press, 2001, 175–82.

18   Meyyappan, N. Chowdhury, G. G. and Foo, S., 'Design and development of a user-centred digital library system: some basic guidelines'. In: Urs, S., Rajashekar, T. B. and Raghavan, K. S. (eds), *Digital libraries: dynamic landscape for knowledge creation, access and management. The 4th International Conference of Asian Digital Libraries, Bangalore, December 10-12, 2001*, 135–48.

19   Shneiderman, B., 'Codex, memex. Genex: the pursuit of transformational technologies', *International journal of human-computer interaction*, **10** (2), 1998, 87–106.

20   Shneiderman, B., 'User interfaces for creativity support tools'. In: *Proceedings of the Third Conference on Creativity and Cognition, Loughborough, New Your, ACM Press, 1999, 15–22.

21   IdeaFisher. Available at **http://www.ideafisher.com**.

22   MindManager. Available at **http://www.mindman.com**.

23   Nicholas, D. and Dobrowolski, T., 'The information "player": a new and timely term for the digital information user'. In: Scamell, A. (ed.), *Handbook of information management*, London, Aslib, 2001, 513–22.

24   Lee, H., Smeaton, A. F., Berrut, C., Murphy, N., Marlow, S. and O'Connor, N., 'Implementation and analysis of several keyframe-based browsing interfaces to digital video'. In: Borbinha, J. and Baker, T. (eds), *ECDL 2000*, Lisbon, Springer, 2000.

25   Oliveira, J. L., Goncalves, M. A. and Medeiros, C. B., 'A framework for designing and implementing the user interface of a geographic digital library', *International journal of digital libraries*, **2** (3), 1999, 190–206.

26   Kovács, L., Micsik, A., Pataki, B. and Zsámboki, I., 'AQUA (Advanced Query User Interface Architecture)'. In: Borbinha, J. and Baker, T. (eds), *Research and advanced technology for digital libraries, proceedings of the 4th European conference, ECDL 2000*, Lisbon, Springer, 2000, 372–5.

27   Abdulla, G., Liu, B. and Fox, E. A., 'Searching the world wide web: implications from studying different user behaviour', *Proceedings of the WebNet98 Conference*, Orlando, FL. Available at **http://www.aace.org/conf/webnet**.

Chapter 13

Evaluation of information retrieval systems

Introduction

An evaluation is basically a judgment of worth. In other words, we evaluate a system in order to ascertain the level of its performance or its value. Lancaster[1] states that we can evaluate an information retrieval system by considering the following three issues:

1   how well the system is satisfying its objectives, that is, how well it is satisfying the demands placed upon it
2   how efficiently it is satisfying its objectives, and finally
3   whether the system justifies its existence.

In the information retrieval environment we may want to assess which of two existing systems performs better, or we may try to assess how the level of performance of a given system can be improved. It is thus quite evident that during an evaluation study we measure the performance of the system under study against some sort of scale. There are two basic parameters for measuring the performance of a system: *effectiveness* and *efficiency*. By effectiveness we mean the level up to which the given system attains its stated objectives. In an information retrieval system, the effectiveness may be a measure of how far it can retrieve relevant information while withholding non-relevant information. By efficiency we mean how economically the system is achieving its objective. In an information retrieval system efficiency can be measured by such factors as at what minimum cost does the system function effectively. The cost factors are to be calculated indirectly. They include such factors as response time, that is time taken by the system to provide an answer: user effort, i.e. the amount of time and effort needed by a user to interact with the system and analyse the output retrieved in order to get the correct information; the financial expenditure involved per search, and so on.

This chapter discusses the major issues related to the evaluation of information retrieval systems. Factors to be taken into consideration for measuring the performance of information retrieval systems are identified and followed by a discussion on the major steps to be followed in designing a programme for evaluation of such a system.

The purpose of evaluation

Evaluation studies investigate the degree to which the stated goals or expectations have been achieved or the degree to which these can be achieved. Keen[2] gives three major purposes of evaluating an information retrieval system:

1   the need for measures with which to make merit comparisons within a single test situation. In other words, evaluation studies are conducted to compare the merits (or demerits) of two or more systems
2   the need for measures with which to make comparisons between results obtained in different test situations, and
3   the need for assessing the merit of a real-life system.

Swanson[3] states that evaluation studies have one or more of the following purposes:

1   to assess a set of goals, a programme plan, or a design prior to implementation
2   to determine whether and how well goals or performance expectations are being fulfilled
3   to determine specific reasons for successes and failures
4   to uncover principles underlying a successful programme
5   to explore techniques for increasing programme effectiveness
6   to establish a foundation of further research on the reasons for the relative success of alternative techniques, and
7   to improve the means employed for attaining objectives or to redefine subgoals or goals in view of research findings.

Evaluation criteria

An evaluation study can be conducted from two different points of view. When it is conducted from managerial point of view, the evaluation study is called management-oriented; conducted from the users' point of view it is called a user-oriented evaluation study. Many information scientists advocate that evaluation of an information retrieval system should always be user-oriented, i.e. evaluators should pay more attention to those factors that can provide improved service to the users. Cleverdon[4] says that a user-oriented evaluation should try to answer the following questions.

1   To what extent does the system meet both the expressed and latent needs of its users' community?
2   What are the reasons for the failure of the system to meet the users' needs?
3   What is the cost-effectiveness of the searches made by the users themselves as against those made by the intermediaries?
4   What basic changes are required to improve the output?
5   Can the costs be reduced while maintaining the same level of performance?
6   What would be the possible effect if some new services were introduced or an existing service were withdrawn?

As with any other system, we expect the best possible performance at the least cost from an information retrieval system. We can thus identify two major factors, performance and cost. Now, if we try to determine how we measure the performance of an information retrieval system we have to go back to the question of its basic objective. We know that the system is intended to retrieve all those documents in a collection that are relevant to a given query while holding back all those documents that are not relevant. The system, therefore, should retrieve relevant and only relevant items. The question of relevance thus becomes an important factor. We shall come to this issue shortly. We also want to assess how economically a system performs. The calculation of costs of an information retrieval system is not easy, as it involves a number of indirect methods of cost calculation.

Lancaster[5] lists the following major factors to be taken into consideration for cost calculation:

1   cost incurred per search
2   users' efforts involved
    * in learning how the system works
    * in actual use
    * in getting the documents through back-up document delivery systems
    * in retrieving information from the retrieved documents, and
3   users' time
    * from submission of query to the retrieval of references
    * from submission of query to the retrieval of documents and the actual information.

A number of studies have been conducted so far to determine the costs of information retrieval systems or subsystems. Detailed discussions on these studies are available in Roberts[6] and are not discussed here. In this chapter, we shall concentrate on the factors relating to the performance of an information retrieval system.

Saracevic[7] mentions that S. C. Bradford was the first person to use the term 'relevance' in the context that it is used today in the field of information science. In the context of the information retrieval system, relevance is a measure of the contact between a source and a destination, i.e. between a document and its user. According to Saracevic, the majority of studies in information science have concentrated on determining

* what factors enter into the notion of relevance and
* what relation the notion of relevance specifies.

Both of these issues require the identification of the performance factors that are the parameters for assessing relevance. In 1997 Mizzaro[8] presented a history of 'relevance' through an exhaustive review of 157 works on the subject: 'it seems clear that the "1959–1976" period is more oriented towards a relevance inherent in document and query: some problems are noted but operationally supposedly negligible. In the "1977–present" period these problems are tackled, and the researchers try to understand, formalize and measure a more subjective, dynamic and multidimensional relevance.' In 1966, Cleverdon[4] identified six criteria for the evaluation of an information retrieval system. These are:

1   *recall*, i.e. the ability of the system to present all the relevant items
2   *precision*, i.e., the ability of the system to present only those items that are relevant
3   *time lag*, i.e. the average interval between the time the search request is made and the time an answer is provided
4   *effort*, intellectual as well as physical, required from the user in obtaining answers to the search requests
5   *form of presentation* of the search output, which affects the user's ability to make use of the retrieved items, and
6   *coverage of the collection*, i.e. the extent to which the system includes relevant matter.

Vickery[9] identifies six criteria, grouped into two sets as follows:

Set 1
1   *coverage* – the proportion of the total potentially useful literature that has been analysed
2   *recall* – the proportion of such references that are retrieved in a search, and
3   *response time* – the average time needed to obtain a response from the system.

These three criteria are related to the availability of information, while the following three are related to the selectivity of output:

Set 2
4   *precision* – the ability of the system to screen out irrelevant references
5   *usability* – the value of the references retrieved, in terms of such factors as their reliability, comprehensibility, currency, etc., and
6   *presentation* – the form in which search results are presented to the user.

In 1971, Lancaster[1] proposed five evaluation criteria:

1   coverage of the system
2   ability of the system to retrieve wanted items (i.e. recall);
3   ability of the system to avoid retrieval of unwanted items (i.e. precision)
4   the response time of the system, and
5   the amount of effort required by the user.

All these factors are related to the system parameters, and thus in order to identify the role played by each of the performance criteria mentioned above, each must be tagged with one or more system parameters. Salton and McGill[10] identified the various parameters of an information retrieval system as related to each of five evaluation criteria:

Evaluation criteria	*System parameters*

Recall and precision

1. Indexing exhaustivity
   Recall tends to increase the exhaustivity of indexing terms.
2. Term specificity
   Precision increases with the specificity of the index terms.
3. Indexing language
   Availability of measures for recognition of synonyms, term relations, etc., which improve recall.
4. Query formulation
   Ability to formulate an accurate search request.
5. Search strategy
   Ability of the user or intermediary to formulate an adequate search strategy.

Response time

1. Organization of stored documents.
2. Type of query.
3. Location of information centre.
4. Frequency of receiving users' queries.
5. Size of the collection.

User effort

1. Accessibility of the system.
2. Availability of guidance by system personnel.
3. Volume of retrieved items.
4. Facilities for interaction with the system.

Form of presentation

1. Type of display device.
2. Nature of output – bibliographic reference, abstract, or full text.

Collection coverage

1. Type of input device and type and size of storage device.
2. Depth of subject analysis.
3. Nature of users' demands.
4. Nature of core subject area.
5. Physical forms of documents.

Some of the performance criteria mentioned above can be measured easily. For example, the parameters related to the collection coverage, and form of presentation are related to policy matters, and thus are defined by the system managers beforehand. Response time and user effort can be measured without much difficulty. However, the two other criteria, recall and precision, cannot be measured so easily. In fact, measurement of these factors often cause a number of problems for the system investigators. Much research effort in the area of the evaluation of information retrieval systems has concentrated on these two factors. The next section is devoted to some detailed discussion of recall and precision.

Recall and precision

The term recall refers to a measure of whether or not a particular item is retrieved or the extent to which the retrieval of wanted items occurs.[5] Whenever a user puts his/her query, it is the responsibility of the system to retrieve all those items that are relevant to the given query. However, in reality it may not be possible to retrieve all the relevant items from a collection, especially when the collection is large. Thus, a system may be able to retrieve a proportion of the total relevant documents in response to a given query. The performance of a system is often measured by recall ratio, which denotes the percentage of relevant items retrieved in a given situation.

For example, if there are 100 documents in a collection that are relevant to a given query and 60 of these items are retrieved in a given search, then the recall is stated to be 60%: in other words, the system has been able to retrieve 60% of the relevant items.

By precision we mean how precisely a particular system functions. It is quite obvious that when the system retrieves items that are relevant to a given query it also retrieves some documents that are not relevant. These non-relevant items then affect the success of the system because they must be discarded by the user, a significant amount of whose time is thus wasted. We have already seen that the basic objective of an information retrieval system is not only to retrieve relevant items but also to hold back non-relevant items. This factor, that is how far the system is able to withhold unwanted items in a given situation, is measured in terms of precision, or precision ratio. For example, if in a given search the system retrieves 80 items, out of which 60 are relevant and 20 are non-relevant, the precision is 75%.

The general formula for calculation of recall and precision may be stated as:

$$Recall = \frac{Number\ of\ relevant\ items\ retrieved}{Total\ number\ of\ relevant\ items\ in\ the\ collection} \times 100$$

$$Precision = \frac{Number\ of\ relevant\ items\ retrieved}{Total\ number\ of\ items\ retrieved} \times 100$$

Recall thus relates to the ability of the system to retrieve relevant documents, and precision relates to its ability not to retrieve non-relevant documents. The ideal system attempts to achieve 100% recall and 100% precision, i.e. it attempts to retrieve all the relevant documents and relevant documents only. However, this is not possible in practice, because as the level of recall increases, precision tends to decrease. The following example shows the relationship between recall and precision of a given search. Let us suppose that in a given situation a system retrieves $a+b$ number of documents, out of which a documents are relevant, and b documents are non-relevant. Say, for example, $c+d$ documents are left in the collection after the search has been conducted. This number will be quite large, because it represents the whole collection minus the retrieved documents. Out of the $c+d$ number, let's say, c documents are relevant to the query but could not be retrieved, and d documents are not relevant and thus have been correctly rejected. For a large collection the value of *d* will be quite large in comparison to *c* because it represents all the non-relevant documents minus those that have been retrieved wrongly (here *b*). Lancaster[5] suggests that these statistics can be represented in a 2 x 2 matrix, as shown in Table 13.1, from which the performance figures can easily be determined.

Table 13.1   *Recall-precision matrix*

	Relevant	Not-relevant	Total
Retrieved	*a* (hits)	*b* (noise)	*a* + *b*
Not retrieved	*c* (misses)	*d* (rejected)	*c* + *d*
Total	*a* + c	*b* + *d*	*a*+*b*+*c*+*d*

It may be noted from Table 13.1 that the system retrieves *a* relevant documents along with *b* non-relevant documents. Following Lancaster[5] it may be stated that *a* denotes the 'hit' whereas *b* denotes the 'noise'. Now, out of the remaining *c*+*d* documents, the system misses *c* documents that should have been retrieved, but it correctly rejects *d* documents that are not relevant to the given query. The recall and precision ratio in this case can be calculated as

$$R = [a/ (a+c)] \times 100$$

$$P = [a/ (a+b)] \times 100$$

The value of recall can be increased by increasing the value of *a*, that is by retrieving a greater number of relevant items, ideally speaking all the relevant ones. This can be achieved by increasing the number of retrieved documents, but as the number of items retrieved increases, so also increases the likelihood of retrieval of non-relevant items, that is *b*, which decreases the value of precision. Lancaster[5] therefore states that recall and precision tend to vary inversely. In a retrieval environment when we want to retrieve more relevant items, we generally broaden our search. For example, in response to a user's query on PRECIS, if we use PRECIS as a search term we are likely to miss some relevant documents, especially those that discuss indexing in general. By using the broader term 'indexing' as the search term, we may retrieve a greater number of relevant documents, but at the same time we may end up retrieving some non-relevant ones (e.g. where PRECIS has not been discussed at all or has been treated too narrowly to serve the user's purpose).

The relationship between recall and precision can be examined by considering searches held at different levels with the same set of documents and requests. Beginning with very general search terms high recall and low precision can be achieved, and as the search terms become more and more specific recall tends to go down and precision tends to go up. In real-life situations, users normally do not want very high recall (except for the patent search, where the user wishes to find out about all the patents existing in his or her area of interest). In general, most users want 'a few' documents in response to a query, which means that a moderate level of recall, say 60%, will serve the purpose. High precision tends to save users' time and effort, and one of the major objectives of an information retrieval system is to achieve this. In most cases information retrieval systems are designed to perform at a moderate level of recall and precision, in the range of 50–60%.

Recently, the theory of the 'inverse relationship between precision and recall' has been questioned by Fugmann.[11, 12] By several examples he has shown that:

1   an increase in precision is by no means *always* accompanied by a corresponding decrease in recall, and
2   an increase in recall is by no means observed to have *always* in its wake a decrease in precision.

These views have however not been accepted by information scientists like Lancaster, who, in his review of Fugmann's book,[11] observes that Fugmann 'completely rejects the inverse relationship between recall and precision'.[12]

Fallout and generality

Investigators have identified some other measures, besides recall and precision, that also reflect the performance of information retrieval systems. We have already noted that while conducting a search, it is quite likely that some non-relevant items are retrieved. One may want to know what proportion of non-relevant items has been retrieved in a given search. This is often termed as the *fallout ratio*. One may also want to know the proportion of relevant documents in the collection for a given query. This factor is called the *generality ratio*. Recall, precision, fallout, and generality ratios have been represented by Salton[13] as shown in Tables 13.1 (p.249) and 13.2.

Salton mentions that the larger the collection, the larger will be the number of non-relevant items for a given query. Hence, an increase in the level of recall will cause a decrease in precision. In practice a cut-off is made through the document collection to distinguish retrieved items from the non-retrieved ones. Taking figures from Table 13.1 the cut-off can be determined by the following formula:[2]

$$Cut\text{-}off = \frac{a+b}{a+b+c+d}$$

However, it is often difficult to assess the relevance of the documents beforehand. It is therefore advisable to use the relevance feedback method, which utilizes user relevance judgments for documents retrieved by an initial search in order to construct an improved query formulation for the final search session.

Van Rijsbergen[14] proposes that recall and precision can be combined in a single measure, called effectiveness, or E, which is a weighted combination of precision and recall where the lower the E value, the greater is the effectiveness.[15] If recall and precision are represented by R and P respectively, the value of E can be measured through the following formula:

$$E = 100 \times [1 - \frac{(1+\beta^2)PR}{\beta^2 P + R}]$$

where β is used to reflect the relative importance of recall and precision to the user ($0 < \beta < \infty$); $\beta = 0.5$ corresponds to attaching half as much importance to recall as precision.

Table 13.2 *Retrieval measures*

Symbol	Evaluation measure	Formula	Explanation
R	Recall	$a/(a+c)$	Proportion of relevant items retrieved
P	Precision	$a/(a+b)$	Proportion of retrieved items that are relevant
F	Fallout	$b/(b+d)$	Proportion of non-relevant items retrieved
G	Generality	$(a+c)/(a+b+c+d)$	Proportion of relevant items per query

Limitations of recall and precision

It may be noted that different users may want different levels of recall. A person going to prepare a state-of-the-art report on a topic would like to have all the items available on that topic and therefore will go for a high recall. Conversely, a user wanting to know 'something' about a given topic will prefer to have 'a few items', and thus will not require a high recall. Some investigators have suggested the use of proportional recall or relative recall, which is expressed in terms of the number of items retrieved over the number of items wanted by the user. However, one major problem in such a measure is that users very often are unable to specify exactly how many items they want to be retrieved.

Another drawback of recall is that it assumes that all relevant items have the same value, which is not always true. The retrieved items may have different degrees of relevance and this may vary from user to user, and even from time to time to the same user. Both recall and precision depend largely on the relevance judgments of the user. In fact after the search session the user has to identify how many of the retrieved items are relevant and how many are not. This judgement is quite subjective and there may be different degrees of relevance of the retrieved output.

A subjective view of relevance considers not only the contents of a document but also the state of knowledge of the user at the time of the search. A document may be regarded as relevant if it deals with the topic of the user's interest but it may not be pertinent if the user is already acquainted with its contents. Therefore, all pertinent items can be said to be relevant, but all relevant items may not be pertinent. This is an example of the weakness of the recall–precision measure of retrieval evaluation. It may also be the case that although the system is capable of retrieving some relevant items these may not be regarded as relevant by a given user at a given point in time. Salton and McGill[10] recommend that if an objective system evaluation is to be accomplished then the relevance assessment of documents to queries is to be obtained from a source external to the retrieval system. In other words, a system is judged to be effective if satisfactory evaluation results are obtained using external relevance criteria.

The steps of evaluation

Lancaster[5] identifies five major steps involved in the evaluation of an information retrieval system, which are

1   designing the scope of evaluation
2   designing the evaluation program
3   execution of the evaluation
4   analysis and interpretation of results, and
5   modifying the system in the light of the evaluation results.

Step 1

An evaluation study is conducted to determine the level of performance of the given system and also to identify those factors that are the reasons for weaknesses of the system. In other words, an attempt is made to find out the different parameters and their interrelations with a view to assessing their contribution towards the overall performance of the system. The first step of an evaluation study entails the preparation of a set of objectives that the given study is going to meet. The purpose and scope of the whole evaluation program are set at this step. How the evaluation study will be conducted is also considered – in a laboratory-type set-up or in a real-life situation, at what level it will be evaluated, i.e. macroevaluation or microevaluation, and so on. The probable constraints – in terms of cost, staff time, etc., are also mentioned at this stage. In fact, a detailed plan is chalked out at this stage that forms the basis of the rest of the programme.

Step 2

Once the basic objectives are set and the proposed plans are outlined, the designer goes on to identify the points on which data are to be collected. At this step the parameters on which data are to be collected are determined, and the methodology is proposed. A detailed plan of action is to be prepared which is to be followed for collection of data. It is also necessary to draw up a plan for the proposed manipulation of data for reaching a conclusion. It may be noted that while conducting an evaluation programme, the designer might need to control some of the paramenters of the system. It is therefore necessary that, while preparing the detailed plan of action, the designer points out which parameters are to be held constant during the study and how this is to be done. In most cases, the detailed design of an evaluation programme is prepared by supervisory staff and systems analysts, while the actual evaluation study is executed by other staff members. It is therefore required that the design should be clear at all points. The design should also mark the major caution points where more care is needed to avoid faults.

Step 3

Execution of the evaluation is obviously the most time-consuming step in an evaluation study. The system personnel collect data in a way prescribed at the design stage. In most cases, a repeated number of observations are required to avoid sampling error and bias. Although the evaluator at this stage has to follow the plan of action thoroughly, he/she may find some interesting features of the system that were not mentioned at the design stage. It is thus important that there should be a communication between the evaluator and the designer at this stage in order to share any interesting observations that might call for redesign of the evaluation programme.

Step 4

The whole fate of the evaluation programme rests upon the method of interpretation of results and its accuracy. On the one hand the evaluator has a set of objectives of the evaluation programme, and on the other the observations, i.e. the data collected on different parameters. Although the methodology for manipulation of the data is determined at the design stage, the evaluator might need to make some changes so as to arrive at a better conclusion. Once the data have been manipulated in a suitable way, the evaluator gets a set of results that is to be interpreted in the light of the set of objectives. The evaluator might need to conduct failure analysis so as to justify the results and also to suggest improvements. Lancaster[5] mentions that the joint use of performance figures and failure analysis should answer most of the questions identified in the objectives of the evaluation.

Step 5

Finally, the retrieval system is modified, if necessary, in the light of the results of the evaluation study.

New retrieval parameters

While the classical information retrieval parameters, such as recall and precision, have been used in information retrieval experiments for over four decades, applying them – especially recall – in the modern day online information retrieval evaluation, is a difficult task. Hence researchers have proposed, and experimented on, new retrieval parameters like relative recall. These are discussed in the following chapter.

References

1   Lancaster, F. W., 'The cost-effectiveness analysis of information retrieval and dissemination systems', *Journal of the American Society for Information*

Science, **22** (1), 1971, 12–27.

2   Keen, E. M., 'Evaluation parameters'. In: Salton, G. (ed.), *The SMART retrieval system: experiments in automatic document processing*. Englewood Cliffs, NJ, Prentice-Hall, 1971, 74–111.

3   Swanson, R. W., 'Performing evaluation studies in information science'. In: King D. W. (ed.), *Key papers in design and evaluation of retrieval systems*, New York, Knowledge Industry, 1978, 58–74.

4   Cleverdon, C. W., 'User evaluation of information retrieval systems'. In: King, D. W. (ed.), *Key papers in design and evaluation of retrieval systems*, New York, Knowledge Industry, 1978, 154–165.

5   Lancaster, F. W., *Information retrieval systems: characteristics, testing and evaluation*, New York, John Wiley, 1979.

6   Roberts, S. A. (ed.), *Costing and economics of library and information services*, London, Aslib, 1984.

7   Saracevic, T., 'Relevance: a review of and a framework for the thinking of the notion in information science'. In: King, D. W. (ed.), *Key papers in design and evaluation of retrieval systems*, New York, Knowledge Industry, 1978, 84–106.

8   Mizzaro, S., 'Relevance: the whole history', *Journal of the American Society for Information Science*, **48** (9), 1997, 810–32.

9   Vickery, B. C., *Techniques of information retrieval*, London, Butterworth, 1970.

10   Salton, G. and McGill, M. J., *Introduction to modern information retrieval*, New York, McGraw-Hill, 1983.

11   Fugmann, R., *Subject analysis and indexing: theoretical foundation and practical advice*, Frankfurt, Indeks Verlag, 1993.

12   Lancaster, F. W., Book review of *Subject analysis and indexing: theoretical foundation and practical advice* by Robert Fugmann, Frankfurt, Indeks Verlag, 1993. In: *Journal of documentation*, **50** (2), June 1994, 149–52.

13   Salton, G., 'The "generality" effect and the retrieval evaluation for large collections'. In: King, D. W. (ed.), *Key papers in design and evaluation of retrieval systems*, New York, Knowledge Industry, 1978, 168–79.

14   van Rijsbergen, C. J., *Information retrieval*, 2nd edn, London, Butterworth, 1979.

15   Al-Hawamdeh, S. and Willett, P., 'Paragraph-based nearest neighbour searching in full-text documents', *Electronic publishing*, **2** (4), 1989, 179–92.

Chapter 14

Evaluation experiments

Introduction

Quite a number of retrieval evaluation studies have been conducted during recent decades. Lancaster[1] mentions that probably the first evaluation study in information retrieval was conducted in 1953. Since then quite a number of attempts have been made in this direction. However, the first significant studies were the Cranfield projects, which in fact brought a new dimension to research in retrieval system evaluation. Sparck Jones[2] provides a nice overview of the evaluation studies conducted between 1958 and 1978. More recent evaluation studies have been discussed in the *Annual review of information science and technology*.[3] Sparck Jones mentions that the first decade of evaluation studies concentrated mainly on the evaluation of indexing systems – manual as well as automatic. The Cranfield projects and the MEDLARS study attempted to evaluate the performance of various indexing systems. However, the most significant contribution of these studies lies in the development of suitable methodology for retrieval evaluation. These studies also attempted to find out the performance criteria of information retrieval systems. The major determinant factors of performance, viz. recall, precision, fallout, etc., were identified through these studies, and the inverse relationship between recall and precision was also established through these studies.

However, there were limitations of these studies too. Sparck Jones[2] mentions that through these studies we learned what happens in information retrieval systems, but it was not quite clear as to why it happens. Evaluation studies conducted during the latter decade concentrated on a number of aspects. Sparck Jones divides these studies into five major groups. The first group of studies concentrated on comparisons of different indexing languages. The second concentrated on indexing exhaustivity and specificity, rather than on indexing languages as such. The third concentrated on another major area of study, search techniques. The fourth emphasized output ranking, term weighting, relevance feedback, etc. The fifth group of studies were mainly concerned with cost effectiveness. However, most of the studies conducted during these decades used the laboratory environment rather than real-life situations. Most were carried out on document surrogates, such as document abstracts rather than full texts. Although research in this area has been going on for more than three decades, there are still controversies regarding the evaluation methodologies, performance measures, relevance judgements, etc.

Experiments on the evaluation of information retrieval got a major boost with the introduction of the TREC (Text Retrieval Conference) series of experiments. TREC was set up in 1991, and since then it has drawn information retrieval researchers from all over the world focusing on design and evaluation of information retrieval systems of different kinds. Although the TREC series of experiments rely largely on the previous evaluation experiments, over the years, many new approaches to evaluation of information retrieval systems have been developed by the TREC researchers. This chapter provides an overview of four early, but major, retrieval evaluation studies followed by a brief discussion on the various TREC experiments.

The Cranfield tests

Cranfield 1

The first extensive evaluation of retrieval systems was undertaken at Cranfield, UK, under the direction of C. W. Cleverdon, and is known as the Cranfield 1 project. The first Cranfield study began in 1957 and was reported by Cleverdon.[4, 5]

Objectives

The project was designed to compare the effectiveness of four indexing systems:

*   an alphabetical subject catalogue based on a subject heading list
*   a UDC classified catalogue with alphabetical chain index to the class headings constructed
*   a catalogue based on a faceted classification and an alphabetical index to the class headings
*   a catalogue compiled by a uniterm coordinate index.

System parameters

The study involved 18,000 indexed items and 1200 search topics. The documents, half of which were research reports and half periodical articles, were chosen equally from the general field of aeronautics and the specialized field of high-speed aerodynamics.

Three indexers were chosen – one with subject knowledge, one with indexing experience, and one straight from library school having neither subject background nor indexing experience. Each indexer was asked to index each source document five times, spending 2, 4, 8, 12, and 16 minutes per document. One hundred source documents thus gave rise to a set of 6000 indexed items (100 documents x 3 indexers x 4 systems x 5 times). Each of these 6000 items was tested in three phases, and therefore the system worked on altogether 18,000 (6000 x 3 phases) indexed items. The test was conducted in three phases with a view to find out whether the level of performance increased with increasing experience of the system personnel.

The project used manufactured queries, i.e. queries were formulated before the beginning of the actual search. Each document was studied by members outside the project and queries were formulated to which the given document would be relevant. Altogether 400 queries were formulated and all processed by the system in each of the three phases. Thus the system worked on a total of 1200 search queries.

Results

1   All four systems were operating with an effectiveness that could be expressed by a recall ratio between 60–90% with an overall average of 80%.

2   The recall ratios for the different systems were as follows:
alphabetical index – 81.5%
faceted classification – 74%
UDC – 76%
uniterm – 82%.

3   Increased time in indexing increased recall, although there was a fall at the 8 minutes level for reasons unknown. Recall ratios for different timings were as follows:

Time, minutes	Recall, %
2	73
4	80
8	74
12	83
16	84

4   No significant difference was noted in retrieving documents indexed by the three different indexers. In other words, there was no significant difference in the performance of the three different indexers.

5   Success rates in retrieving items on general areas of aeronautics were noted to be 4–5% better than those on the high-speed aerodynamics.

6   The success rate in the third group of 6000 items was 3–4% greater than that for the second group.

Failure analysis

Altogether 495 failures were noted. An analysis of these revealed the following figures:

question failures   17%
indexing failures   60%
searching failures 17%
system failures   6%.

It may be noted that 77% of the failures occurred during the searching (17%) and indexing (60%) stages. Of this 77%, 55% were noted to be due to human errors, while the remaining 22% occurred owing to lack of sufficient time for indexing.

Significance

The results of the Cranfield 1 test contradicted the general belief regarding the nature of information retrieval systems in many ways. Firstly, the test proved that the performance of a system does not depend on the experience and subject background of the indexer. Secondly, it showed that systems where documents are organized by a faceted classification scheme perform poorly in comparison to the alphabetical index and uniterm system. Cranfield 1 test was important in two other respects. Firstly it identified the major factors that affect the performance of retrieval systems, and secondly it developed for the first time the methodologies that could be applied successfully in evaluating information retrieval systems.[1] Moreover, it also proved that recall and precision are the two most important parameters for determining the performance of information retrieval systems, and that these two parameters are related inversely to each other. The following findings of Cranfield 1 are significant:[5]

*   indexing times over 4 minutes gave no real improvement in performance
*   a high quality of indexing could be obtained from non–technical indexers
*   the systems operated at a recall rate of 70–90% and precision rate of 8–20%
*   a 1% improvement in precision could be achieved at the cost of 3% loss in recall
*   recall and precision were inversely related to each other
*   all four indexing methods gave a broadly similar performance.

Criticisms

Although Cranfield 1 brought a number of issues to light, it faced a number of criticisms. Swanson[6] argues that the statements made about the performance of the system (as discussed above) are not established by the test, but are products of the design of the test. The major criticism according to Vickery[7] relates to the retrieval queries. The questions used for the test were 'manufactured' from the source documents and it has been argued that such 'manufactured questions' are too closely related to the documents in comparison with real-life questions.[7] Another criticism was that this test identified the level of performance of the indexing systems concerned, but it did not throw any light on reasons for failure of these systems. In fact these questions were taken into consideration in the second Cranfield test.

Cranfield 2

The second Cranfield test was a controlled experiment that attempted to assess the effects of the components of index languages on the performance of retrieval systems. This study tried to assess the effect by varying each factor, while keeping the others constant. Altogether 29 index languages formed by the combination of concepts were tested on 1400 documents.[7]

Test collection

The test was conducted on a collection of 1400 reports and articles collected from the field of high speed aerodynamics and aircraft structures.

Query formulation

About 200 research papers were assembled, each having a number of cited references. Each author of those papers was asked to formulate questions for which he/she had cited the reference(s) in the paper. The authors were also asked to point out the documents that were not cited in their works but might have been relevant for the question they had formulated. The whole set of cited references was scanned and abstracts of those documents were sent to the authors who were asked to assess the relevance of these with the questions they had formulated. The authors identified 1961 papers to be fully or partially relevant to the 279 questions obtained. Finally, 221 questions and 1400 documents were selected for the experiment. The success of the system was calculated by counting how many of the relevant papers thus assessed were retrieved by a given search.

Indexing level

It has already been mentioned that different index languages were formed in this study by different levels of coordination of the index terms. The ways in which these coordinations took place have been discussed by Vickery as follows:

1   Each document was analysed and a series of conceptual phrases used in the documents were collected. These phrases formed one index language. A separate index language was formed when each of these phrases was expanded with synonyms.
2   All the concepts were organized in a hierarchical classification showing superordinate, subordinate and coordinate classes. Expanded index languages were formed by combining the superordinate, subordinate, and collateral concepts along with the given concept.
3   Each concept used in the index language (the conceptual phrases) was isolated into single words. The simple terms formed another index language.
4   Synonyms, quasi-synonyms, and words with a common root for each of the single words were found. Index languages were formed by combining each of these with the original word.
5   All the single terms used in the test indexing were organized into a hierarchical classification and expanded index languages were formulated by combining the superordinate, subordinate, and collateral concepts with the original concept.
6   The concepts corresponding to the concepts used to index each document were translated into the corresponding terms in the EJC (Engineers' Joint Council) thesaurus. This formed an index language that gave rise to four other languages – three languages were formed when each of the broader, narrower, and related terms were attached to the original index term, and one was formed when all of the broader, narrower, and related terms were attached to the original index term.
7   The words from the title of each document formed an index language, which gave rise to another index language when these were expanded to include word forms.
8   The words from the abstract of each document formed an index language, which gave rise to another index language when these were expanded to include word forms.

Searching

Each query was isolated into individual words. These were coordinated and then matched against the coordinated index words. This matching was done at several levels of coordination by dropping one query term at a time, thereby hoping to retrieve some relevant document at each level. The query words and index words were then replaced by the words of the index language that was formed by adding synonyms with the original words (step 4 above). Searches were carried out at different levels of coordination to see what further documents were retrieved. Similar searches were carried out using all the index languages (discussed in the previous section). A record of hits and false drops was maintained for each search.

Results and conclusions

Altogether 221 questions were applied to the collection of 1400 documents. The results of all the searches in each language were summed up and the average recall and precision ratios were calculated (see Table 14.1). Recall and precision ratios for a given index language were defined as follows:

Table 14.1 *Cranfield 2 results*

Level	7	6+	5+	4+	3+	2+	1+
Total hits	12	25	49	88	132	162	189
Total false drops	11	56	251	1039	3979	9811	34,127
Recall ratio	6	13	25	44	67	82	96
Precision ratio	52	31	16	8	3	2	1

$$recall\ ratio = \frac{hits}{C} \times 100$$

where C = total number of documents in the collection relevant to the question set (= 198);

$$precision\ ratio = \frac{hits}{hits + false\ drops} \times 100$$

Recall and precision figures for each level of coordination were plotted in a graph. The following conclusions were reached:

- in the case where concepts were used for indexing, the system performance worsened with the introduction of superordinate, subordinate, and collateral classes along with the original concepts
- in the case of single terms, the inclusion of collateral classes and, in particular, quasi-synonyms worsened the performance
- when broader and narrower terms were included along with the controlled languages of the thesaurus, the performance worsened
- index languages formed out of titles performed better than those formed out of abstracts.

The results of the Cranfield 2 tests were unexpected because the best performing index languages were composed of uncontrolled single words occurring in documents. However, the variables used in the study were subject to criticisms. Each index language consisted of different units of words, phrases, or combinations of both. Both the documents and queries were formed in the same way. Thus the matching of questions to documents would evaluate the relative effectiveness of the languages of different specificity. Vickery[7] comments that the measures used in the second Cranfield project do not adequately characterize those aspects of retrieval performance that are of operational importance.

MEDLARS

Objectives

The performance of the Medical Literature Analysis and Retrieval System (MEDLARS) of the US National Library of Medicine was analysed between August 1966 and July 1967.[1] The test was conducted on the operational database of MEDLARS, a database of biomedical articles, with index entries being drawn from MeSH, a thesaurus of medical subject headings. The objective of the MEDLARS test was to evaluate the existing system and to find out how it could be improved. The document collection available on the MEDLARS service at the time of the test consisted of about 700,000 items.[2]

Twenty-one user groups were selected from the user community that would:

* supply some test questions
* cover all kinds of subjects in the requests
* cover all categories of users.

Methodology

The user group so selected provided 302 search requests. Each query was formulated in terms of MeSH by the system operator and searches were conducted. After completion of a search the sample output was sent to the users for relevance assessment. Photocopies of the articles, rather than the mere references, were supplied for this assessment. The user was asked to mark each retrieved item using the following scale: H1 – of major value; H2 – of minor value; W1 – of no value; W2 – value unknown.

Precision of the searches was then calculated using the following formula:

$$precision\ ratio = \frac{H1 + H2}{L} \times 100$$

where L is the number of sample items retrieved. As the test was conducted on an operational database, it was not easy to determine the total number of items available in the collection relevant to a given query. Therefore, an indirect method was adopted for calculation of recall. Each user was asked to name those items that were relevant to the questions formulated by them. This task was performed prior to the receiving of the search output. The database was then searched to determine whether those items (identified as relevant) were available in the database. The total number of items found through this search was taken as the total number of relevant items available in the collection for the given query, and it was used in the calculation of recall (i.e. $100(H1+H2)/t$, where t is the total number of relevant items).

Results

When the figures for recall and precision for all of the 302 searches were brought together the average overall recall ratio was found to be 57.7% and the precision ratio 50.4%. Over the 302 searches, 797 recall failures and 3038 precision failures were noted. Reasons for the failures were attributed to the principal system components as shown in Table 14.2.

Table 14.2   *Failure analysis in MEDLARS*

System attribute/component	Recall failures (%)	Precision failures (%)
Index language	81 (10.2)	1094 (36)
Indexing	298 (37.4)	393 (12.4)
Searching	279 (35)	983 (32.4)
User-system interaction	99 (25)	503 (16.6)
Others	11 (1.4)	78 (2.5)

The SMART retrieval experiment

Objectives

The SMART system was designed in 1964, largely as an experimental tool for the evaluation of the effectiveness of many different types of analysis and search procedures.[8] Salton[9] characterizes the system through the following steps of its function.
   It is used to:

* take documents and search queries posed in English
* perform a fully automatic content analysis of texts
* match analysed search statements and contents of documents
* retrieve the stored items which are most similar to the queries.

Figure 14.1 provides an overview of the functioning of the SMART retrieval system.[10]
   A number of methods were adopted for automatic content analysis of documents such as:

* word suffix cut-off methods

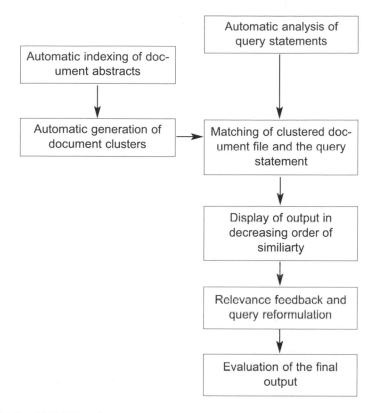

Fig. 14.1 *SMART system overview*

- thesaurus look-up procedures
- phrase generation methods
- statistical term associations
- hierarchical term expansion, and so on.

Evaluation procedures

Though the original SMART experiments were conducted in a laboratory environment, the basic aim was to develop a prototype for a fully automated information retrieval system.[9, 11] Accordingly, a large number of search experiments were performed in which a user environment was simulated by running iterative searches based on user feedback. The evaluation procedures incorporated into the system lent themselves into a pair-wise comparison of the effectiveness of two or more processing methods.[8] A number of evaluation parameters were computed for each of the processing methods under investigation, and then a comparison of the corresponding measures for two or more methods was used to produce a ranking of the methods in decreasing order of retrieval effectiveness.

The following evaluation measures were generated by the SMART system:

- a recall–precision graph reflecting the average precision value at ten discrete recall points – from a recall of 0.1 to a recall of 1.0 in intervals of 0.1
- two global measures, known as normalized recall and normalized precision, which together reflect the overall performance level of the system
- two simplified global measures, known as rank recall and log precision, respectively.

Methodology

A collection of 1268 abstracts in the field of library science and documentation, comprising about 131,500 English text words, was used for this experiment. The collection contained articles mainly published in *American documentation* in 1963 and 1964, and also in other journals in the given subject area.

Eight different persons were asked to generate a total of 48 different search requests in the documentation field. Each person was familiar with the subject field, either as a librarian or as a student of library science, and each was asked to produce six requests that might be asked by library science students. Each query was expected to represent a real information need, and had to be expressed in grammatically correct and unambiguous English.

Following receipt of the query formulations from each of the eight persons, the texts of the document abstracts comprising the collection were distributed, and each person was asked to assess the relevance of each document abstract with respect to each of his or her six queries. A document was considered either as relevant or non-relevant based on the following criterion: 'if it is directly stated in the abstract as printed or can be directly deduced from the printed abstract that the document contains information on the topic asked for in the query, then the document is considered relevant.'[8]

After receiving the relevance judgements, called the 'A judgments', a second and independent set of relevance judgements, called the 'B judgments', was obtained by asking each person in the test group to judge for relevance six additional queries originated by six different people. The same relevance criteria were used for the second relevance judgements as for the original ones; the only difference was that the 'A judgments' were rendered by the query authors, whereas the 'B judgments' were the non-author judgements. In order to preserve independence, the 'B judges' were not informed of the 'A judgments' obtained previously, nor was there any interaction between assessors either before or during the process of judgement.

Thus, for each of the 48 queries, a set of four different document sets became available, each consisting of the items termed relevant by a different set of people as follows:

A set – relevance assessed by the query author
B set – relevance assessed by outside subject expert
C set – relevance asserted by either A or B assessor
D set – relevance asserted by both A and B assessor.

The relevance judgement groupings were as follows:

Group judges	*Function*
A	Original group of query authors. Each person in the A group made relevance judgements for his or her six queries.
B	Non-author judges. Each person in the B group made relevance judgements for six queries corresponding to six different authors from the A group.
C	The document is relevant to a given query if either the A judge or B judge termed it relevant.
D	The document is relevant to a given query if both A and B judges termed it relevant.

Three automatic language analysis procedures included in the SMART system, known as word form, word stem, and thesaurus, are introduced below:

- Word form: texts of document abstracts and queries are reduced by removal of common words and final 's' endings, and weights are assigned to the remaining word forms; the reduced texts are then matched to obtain the document–query correlation coefficient.
- Word stem: texts are treated in the same way as word form, except that complete suffixes are removed from the text words to reduce the texts to weighted word stems; the query–document matching process remains the same.
- Thesaurus: each word stem produced by procedure (2) is looked up in a thesaurus providing synonym recognition, and the resulting weighted concept identifiers assigned to queries and documents are compared (instead of word forms and word stems).

Results

It was found that, under normal circumstances, an evaluation of performance for a variety of processing methods required an examination of the ranking of the corresponding recall–precision curves, rather than a detailed comparison of the actual recall and precision values. From a ranking of the recall–precision graphs obtained from the several processing methods it was noted that

- all four sets of relevance judgements produced the same ranking of the processing methods; in particular the word-form process was found to be less powerful than the two other procedures, and the thesaurus process was slightly better than the word stem match.
- the best results in terms of recall and precision were obtained for the D judgements, which represented the agreements between both the A and B relevance judges; for low recall the precision was about 20% higher for D than for A, B, or C.

It was noted that the SMART evaluation output did not vary with the variations in the relevance judgements. While going on to explain why the recall–precision output was basically invariant for the collection under study, Lesk and Salton[8] mention that, though there may be a considerable difference in the document sets termed relevant by different judges, there was a considerable amount of agreement for those documents that appeared most similar to the queries and were retrieved early in the search process. It was concluded that if the relevance assessments obtained by the query authors used in the SMART study are typical of what can be expected from the general user populations, then 'the resulting average recall–precision figures appear to be stable indicators of system performance which do in fact reflect actual retrieval effectiveness.'[8]

The STAIRS project

In 1985, Blair and Maron[12] published a report on a large scale experiment aimed at evaluating the retrieval effectiveness of a full-text search and retrieval system. This is known as STAIRS (STorage And Information Retrieval System) study.

Methodology

The database examined in the STAIRS study consisted of nearly 40,000 documents, representing roughly 350,000 pages of hard copy text used in the defence of a large corporate lawsuit. The full texts of all the pages were available online texts and could be retrieved where specified words appeared either simply or in Boolean combinations. Users could manipulate their search by using a thesaurus – TLS (thesaurus linguistic system) – by using broader, narrower or related terms. One important feature of STAIRS was that the lawyers who were to use the system for litigation support stipulated that they must be able to retrieve 75% of all the documents relevant to a given request. The major objective of the STAIRS evaluation was to assess how well the system could retrieve all the documents (and only those) relevant to a given request, and measures of recall and precision were used for this purpose.

The lawyers generated a total of 51 general requests, which were translated into formal queries by two paralegals who were familiar with STAIRS. The paralegals searched the database and the documents retrieved were sent to the lawyers who originated the requests. The lawyers evaluated those documents and grouped them into 'vital', 'satisfactory', 'marginally relevant', or 'irrelevant' in relation to the request. Any further changes in the given requests were noted down and further searches were carried out until the user was satisfied (i.e. in his/her judgment at least 75% of 'vital', 'satisfactory', and 'marginally relevant' documents had been retrieved).

Precision was calculated by dividing the total number of 'vital', 'satisfactory', and 'marginally relevant' documents by the total number of documents retrieved. For the calculation of recall, a sampling technique was adopted. Random samples were taken and these were evaluated by the lawyers. The total number of relevant documents that existed in these subsets was estimated.

Results

Out of the 51 requests, values for recall and precision were calculated for 40 and the remaining 11 were used to check the sampling techniques and control for possible bias in the evaluation of retrieved and sample tests. The values of precision ranged in percentage terms from 100% to a minimum of 19.6%, with an average of 79% (standard deviation = 23.2%). The values of recall ranged from a maximum of 78.7% to a minimum of 2.8%, with an average of 20% (standard deviation = 15.9%). These results show that, on average, out of 100 retrieved documents 79 were relevant, but only 20% of the relevant documents in the collection could be retrieved. When the recall and precision values for each of the 40 requests were plotted in a graph, it was noted that in about 50% of cases precision was above 80%, and recall was 20% or less.

In attempting to find out why STAIRS could retrieve only one out of five relevant items in response to a request, Blair and Maron[12] note that it is impossibly difficult for users to predict the exact words, their combinations and phrases, used in all or most of the relevant documents and only in those documents. They also identify the large size of the database, which they call the 'output overload', as one of the reasons for poor recall. They point out that a retrieved set of several thousand documents is impractical to browse on the part of the user, and quite naturally the user in such cases wants to reformulate the query by adding more and more search terms to bring the output size to a manageable limit. However, as the size of the output is narrowed down by adding intersecting terms, the value of recall goes down because of the possibility that some relevant items will be excluded by the use of reformulated queries.

Limitations of early evaluation studies

Early evaluation experiments have produced a number of facts and figures that can be utilized in many ways – in designing a new system, in redesigning a system, in comparing the performance of two or more systems, and so on. However, as was mentioned in the introduction to this chapter, there is still a lot to be learnt. The disagreement in the findings of the different studies is testament to this. The STAIRS study reported retrieval results that are contradictory to the earlier studies. While Salton and Salton and McGill showed (in the SMART system)[9-11] that full-text automatic document retrieval systems perform at a satisfactory level, the STAIRS study observed that they do not. In fact, the report of the STAIRS study provoked much discussion among information scientists. In 1986 Salton[13] published a paper commenting on the study. The major points of objection raised by Salton include the following:

- there is no evidence for 'output overload' in large systems
- previous studies proved that automatic text-based systems are at least competitive with, or even superior to, those systems that are based on intellectual (manual) indexing
- studies where favourable results on automatic indexing were obtained involved indexing of terms collected from abstracts, rather than from full texts.

In 1990 Blair and Maron[14] published a paper replying to Salton's criticisms. They assert that large files are liable to cause 'output overload' because 'as one requests the logical intersection of the sets of documents of the query terms, the probability of retrieving a relevant document drops off drastically'. The effectiveness of automatic indexing mentioned by Salton[13] has been criticized by Blair and Maron,[14] who point out four major methodological problems of the previous studies, viz. small database, unreliable techniques for judging the relevance, lack of a realistic and operational retrieval environment, and unreliable tests of statistical significance to interpret the resulting data. Nevertheless, the most critical issue for information retrieval research is the production of an effective model for the evaluation of large operational systems, the success of which lies in rigorous analysis of the existing problems.

Although research in information retrieval system evaluation has been conducted for some time, some fundamental issues are yet to be solved. Schamber et al.[15] point out that, although relevance judgements are fundamental to the evaluation of information retrieval systems, information scientists have not reached a consensus in defining the central concept of relevance. Another major issue has recently been addressed by Robertson,[16] who comments that, while it is clearly desirable to go beyond highly artificial laboratory experiments, attempting total realism is likely to introduce some unavoidable methodological problems. According to Harman,[17] one major problem in the evaluation of information retrieval systems has arisen because research is becoming increasingly oriented towards user involvement – complete evaluation requires not only evaluation of user interaction with the retrieval system, but also evaluation of the information-seeking experience of the user. Robertson and Hancock-Beaulieu[18] recommend more diagnostic and more operational system tests having a number of evaluation facilities, including an operational environment with real users having real-life problems, one or more live databases, and so on.

Ledwith,[19] in evaluating the applicability of ranked retrieval to searching large scientific files in the STN online services, expresses three major concerns:

1   The first concern is with the size and composition of the collections used for testing in research. There are two major factors to be considered. Firstly, the human component of the retrieval experiment should not be required to review and summarize more data for the larger system than for the smaller, test collections. The second factor deals with the likelihood of unexpected and undesirable combinations of terms appearing within the documents, where unexpected combinations cause non-relevant documents to be ranked as highly relevant ones; even very subtle factors within a test collection environment would translate into significant effects while searching larger files.

2   The second concern is with the nature of the queries used in research collections. For example, looking at the INSPEC test collection of 12,684 documents, if a typical query maps to 33 relevant documents, this would extrapolate to an STN user retrieving and reviewing over 24,000 documents in the Chemical Abstracts database containing 9.5 million documents.

3   The third point raises the issue of whether the performance of a ranked retrieval system is a large enough improvement over the Boolean search model to represent a cost-effective alternative.

Ledwith suggests that the following measures will improve the usefulness of research in the evaluation of information retrieval systems:

1   the use of research collections with larger vocabularies and more records
2   the investigations of retrieval schemes that incorporate proximity information
3   the use of test collections that contain more specific queries
4   the investigation into how the human component of the search system can be made more tolerable, the development of better mechanisms to aid the integration, summary, and display of search results
5   the investigation of retrieval schemes and search languages for accessing primary literature, the potentially valuable creation of new, non-Boolean operators and proximity operators.

Schamber[20] suggests that, although retrieval evaluation research started more than three decades ago, information scientists have failed to reach a consensus in answering the following questions:

•   Behaviour: what factors contribute to human relevance judgements? What processes does relevance assessment entail?
•   Measurement: what is the role of relevance in IR system evaluation? How should relevance judgements be measured?
•   Terminology: what should relevance, or various kinds of relevance, be called?

While addressing these questions Schamber defines relevance as a cognitive, situational, dynamic phenomenon that is integral to a wide range of information-seeking and -use behaviours. Nevertheless, evaluation has become increasingly difficult as information systems are becoming more open and interactive and, unless information scientists have a clear and logical understanding of what users want or expect, any evaluation research is bound to produce the wrong results. Recent evaluation experiments under the TREC (Text Retrieval Conferences) series are discussed below.

TREC

Origin of TREC

As mentioned in the previous section, commercial software or database producers have remained sceptical about employing the results of academic research works on different aspects of information retrieval into their products. Moreover, commercial information retrieval systems have for long chosen to use the classical Boolean retrieval model as the primary means for information retrieval, although experimental results reported in the 1970s have shown that simple natural language query techniques are at least as effective as the Boolean techniques. The major reason for the scepticism of the large scale commercial database systems may be due to the fact that the new retrieval mechanisms were tested on a small data set and their performance in the real-life situation remained unexamined. Researchers in information retrieval have based their research on small test collections like CACM, NPL and INSPEC collections, each containing from only a few hundred to few thousand documents.

A test collection is an abstraction of an operational information retrieval environment that provides a means for the researchers to explore the relative benefits of different retrieval strategies in a laboratory setting.[21] The CACM (Communications of the ACM) collection consists of 3204 articles published between 1958 and 1979. The collection consists of 10,446 terms. The largest test collection, the NPL collection (on electrical engineering), consists of 11,429 documents, whereas the ADI collection (on information science) consists of 82 documents. In brief, the test collections used in information retrieval research are tiny compared with the large-scale online databases, and therefore many information retrieval models and techniques do not scale up to real life situations.

Harman[17] comments that information retrieval research of the last few decades could be accused of being small scale and consequently out of touch with reality. The major problem for the researchers was to get a test collection large enough to match a real-life situation with an infrastructure adequate for conducting tests on them. In 1991, in order to alleviate this difficulty, the US Defence Advanced Research Projects Agency (DARPA), decided to fund the TREC experiments, to be run by the National Institute of Science and Technology (NIST), in order to enable information retrieval researchers to scale up from small collections of data to larger experiments.[2] The goals for the TREC experiments have been to:[22]

- encourage retrieval research based on large test collections
- increase communication among industry, academia, and government by creating an open forum for the exchange of research ideas
- speed the transfer of technology form research labs into commercial products by demonstrating substantial improvements in retrieval methodologies on real-world problems
- increase the availability of appropriate evaluation techniques for use by industry and academia, including development of new evaluation techniques more applicable to current systems.

The TREC series of experiments in information retrieval has drawn much attention since its inception in 1991. A program committee consisting of representatives from government, industry and academia oversee the TREC activities. For each TREC, NIST provides a test set of documents and questions. TREC participants run their own retrieval systems on the data, and return a list of the retrieved top-ranked documents to NIST where the individual results are pooled, the retrieved documents are judged for correctness, and the results are evaluated. The TREC cycle ends with a workshop, which is a forum for participants to share their experiences. So every year there is a TREC workshop and the latest one was the 11th in the series, held at NIST in November 2002.

TREC tracks

Originally two sets of information retrieval activities were recognized by TREC: the main (core in TREC jargon) activity and subsidiary activities (tracks in TREC jargon). The core activity has two types of task: ad hoc (corresponding to retrospective retrieval) and routing or filtering (corresponding to the selective dissemination of information). The prototypical information retrieval scenario where a user conducts a literature search – an unknown item search where the user is not aware of the existence of the expected output, or a known item search where the user know about the existence of the documents and wants to retrieve them – is called an ad hoc retrieval task in TREC terminology. The ad hoc task investigates the performance of systems that search a static set of documents using new questions (called topics in TREC terminology). An ad hoc search – from a database or from the web – usually produces a list of items arranged in a ranked list. In a routing or filtering search, the user's interest remains stable but the document set changes. This is the sort of search that will be needed by researchers who want to keep track of the latest developments in their field of interest, or analysts who wish to monitor a news feed for items of interest on a particular subject. The retrieval system makes a decision whether or not a particular document is of relevance to the user's query, and thus the system's response in the filtering task is an unordered set of documents as opposed to a ranked list.22

In addition to the ad hoc and filtering tasks, TREC series came up with a number of tracks. A track acts as an incubator for a new area of research. The first running of a track usually defines the problem and creates the necessary infrastructure, including test collections, evaluation methodology, and so on, to support research on the specific task. Voorhees22 lists all the TREC tracks, along with the number of research groups that participated in each TREC in the tracks, in the form of a table as shown in Table 14.3.

Table 14.3 *TREC tracks, year of their introduction and number of participants in each year* 22

Track	1992	1993	1994	1995	1996	1997	1998	1999	2000	2001	2002
Ad hoc	18	24	26	23	28	31	42	41	-	-	-
Routing	16	25	25	15	16	21	-	-	-	-	-
Interactive	-	-	3	11	2	9	8	7	6	6	6
Spanish	-	-	4	10	7	-	-	-	-	-	-
Confusion	-	-	-	4	5	-	-	-	-	-	-
Database merging	-	-	-	3	3	-	-	-	-	-	-
Filtering	-	-	-	4	7	10	12	14	15	19	21
Chinese	-	-	-	-	9	12	-	-	-	-	-
NLP	-	-	-	-	4	2	-	-	-	-	-
Speech	-	-	-	-	-	13	10	10	3	-	-
Cross-language	-	-	-	-	-	13	9	13	16	10	9
High precision	-	-	-	-	-	5	4	-	-	-	-
Very large corpus	-	-	-	-	-	-	7	6	-	-	-
Query	-	-	-	-	-	-	2	5	6	-	-
Question answering	-	-	-	-	-	-	-	20	28	36	34
Web	-	-	-	-	-	-	-	17	23	30	23
Video	-	-	-	-	-	-	-	-	-	12	19
Novelty	-	-	-	-	-	-	-	-	-	-	13

Relevance judgements for the old collection and the old topic selection are made available in each subsequent TREC series experiment. The routing task involves using some of the old topics on the new collection; the relevance information from the old collection may be used to help formulate the query or the profile.[18]

It may be noted from Table 14.3 that various new tracks have been introduced in the course of the TREC series of experiments; the latest one to be introduced is the Novelty track in 2002. While research on some tracks has been reported continuously in the TREC workshops, some tracks have only lasted for a few years. Overall, the TREC series of experiments show an evolution of research themes and ideas over a period of time.

TREC collections

The overall goal of the TREC initiative has been to encourage research in information retrieval building and using large-scale test collections. It was hoped that by providing a very large test collection, and encouraging interaction among research teams in a friendly evaluation forum, new momentum in information retrieval would be generated.

The document collection of TREC (also known as the TIPSTER collection) reflects diversity of subject matter, word choice, literary styles, formats, and so on. The primary TREC collections now contain about 2 gigabytes of data with over 800,000 documents, while the document sets used in various tracks have been smaller and larger depending on the needs of the track and the availability of data.[22] The primary TREC document sets consist mostly of newspaper or newswire articles, though there are some government documents such as Federal Register, patent documents and computer science abstracts. Each document is encoded in SGML and is assigned a document number.

TREC topics

In TREC terminology an information need is termed as a topic, and the data structure that is actually submitted to a retrieval system is called a query. In TREC a major objective is to provide topics that would allow a range of query construction methods to be tested. A topic statement generally consists of four sections:[22]

* an identifier, e.g. *<num> Number: R111*
* a title, e.g. *<title> Telemarketing practice in U.S.*
* a description, e.g. *<desc> Description: Find formats which reflect telemarketing practices in the US which are intrusive or deceptive and any efforts to control or regulate against them*
* a narrative, e.g. *<narr> Narrative: Telemarketing practices found to be abusive, intrusive, evasive, deceptive, fraudulent, or in any way unwanted by persons contacted are relevant. Only such practices in the US are relevant. All efforts to halt these practices in the US are relevant. All efforts to halt these practices, including lawsuits, legislation or regulation are also relevant.*

Topic statements are created by the same person who performs the relevance assessment for that topic. In other words the topic creator and the assessor is the same person. Assessors come to NIST with their ideas for topics and search the document collection using the NIST's PRISE system to estimate the number of relevant documents per topic. Thus a set of candidate topics is created from which the final set of topics is selected by the NIST TREC team. From the topic statements participants can formulate their own queries for searching their retrieval system(s). Queries can be fully automatic, purely manual, or partly automatic and partly manual.

Relevance judgements in TREC

TREC uses a binary relevance criterion – either a document is relevant or not relevant. Since the size of the TREC collection is large, it is virtually impossible to assess the relevance of each and every document in the collection in respect of every query. In other words, it is impossible to calculate the absolute recall for each query. In order to assess the relevance of documents in relation to a query, TREC uses a specific method called pooling for calculating relative recall as opposed to absolute recall. In this method of estimating recall, all the relevant documents that occurred in the top 100 documents for each system and for each query are combined together to produce a 'pool' of relevant documents to which each system's retrieved documents for a query or topic could be compared – recall being the proportion of the 'pool' of relevant documents that a single system retrieved for a query or topic. Output lists from each participating research team are sent to NIST where they are merged for evaluation. For each topic, the 100 top-ranking documents from all the participating teams are merged into a single set, which is then given to the assessor for relevance evaluation. This method, called pooling, is adopted for a specific reason. Identifying all the documents relevant to a particular query from a collection of about a million records is almost impossible. Hence, by pooling all the results from all the participating teams, one can expect that most of the relevant documents in the collection have been found. The results for each system are then subjected to a standard analysis for generating the various performance measures. As a consequence of the pooling method for relevance judgement the collection becomes usable for other experiments as a test collection.[18]

The ad hoc tasks in TREC are evaluated using a package called tree_eval, which reports about 85 different numbers for a run, including recall and precision measures at various cut-off points and a single value summary measure from recall and precision.[22] The recall-precision curve (a plot of precision as a function of recall) and mean average precision (mean of the precision obtained after each relevant document is retrieved) are the most commonly used measure to describe TREC results.

The various TRECs

TREC-1

In November 1992, TREC-1 (the first Text REtrieval Conference) was held at NIST. The conference, co-sponsored by DARPA and NIST, brought together information retrieval researchers to compare the results of their different systems when used on a large new test collection (called the TIPSTER collection). The first conference attracted 28 groups of researchers from academia and industry, and generated widespread interest from the information retrieval community. This was the first time that such groups had ever compared results on the same data using different evaluation methods, and represented a breakthrough in cross-system evaluation in information retrieval. It was also for the first time that most of these groups had used such a large test collection, and therefore required a major effort by all groups to scale up their retrieval techniques.

TREC-1 conference demonstrated a wide range of different approaches to the retrieval of text from large document collections. However, due to shortage of time and other factors (particularly scaling), the results have been viewed as preliminary. Most of the works reported was concerned with system engineering: finding reasonable data structures to use, getting indexing routines to be efficient enough to index all the data, finding enough storage to handle the large inverted file and other structures, and so on. Nonetheless, the results showed that the systems did the task well, and the automatic construction of queries from the topics did as well as, or better than, manual construction of queries. Harman[17, 23] reports that the draft results of the TREC-1 experiments revealed the following facts:

- automatic construction of queries from natural language query statements seems to work
- techniques based on natural language processing were no better and no worse than those based on vector or probabilistic approaches; the best of all approaches are all about equal.

Several other observations were also made from the results:[24]

- with one exception all of the 24 groups producing usable results performed at about the same level
- the difference in precision-recall curves was minimal
- the same levels of performance were achieved despite some obvious differences in the experimental designs, for example, some groups generated queries automatically from the topic statements while others generated the queries manually; many systems did not incorporate relevance feedback; the computer platform used ranged from PCs to a supercomputer
- although the precision-recall results were similar, there was a large scatter in the actual documents retrieved.

TREC-2 took place in August 1993. In addition to 22 of the TREC-1 groups, nine new groups took part, bringing the total number of participating groups to 31. The participants were able to choose from three levels of participation: category A, full participation; category B, full participation using one-quarter of the full document set; and category C, for evaluation only (in order to allow commercial systems to protect proprietary algorithms). Two types of retrieval were examined: retrieval using an 'ad hoc' query, such as a researcher might use in a library environment, and retrieval using a 'routing' query, such as a profile to filter some incoming document stream. The test design was based on traditional information retrieval models, and evaluation used traditional recall and precision measures. Additional databases were incorporated in TREC-2; relevance feedback was made a factor in the experiments; the number of documents to be returned was increased from 200 per topic to 1000; and the total database size was increased from roughly 1 gigabyte to 3 gigabytes. TREC-2 demonstrated a wide range of different approaches to the retrieval of text from large document collections. There was a significant improvement in retrieval performance over that seen in TREC-1, especially in the routing task.[26] The availability of large amounts of training data for routing allowed extensive experimentation in the best use of that data, and many different approaches were tried in TREC-2. Harman[23] reports that the automatic construction of queries from the topics continued to do as well, or better than, manual construction of queries, which is encouraging for groups supporting the use of simple natural language interfaces for retrieval systems.

TREC-3 to TREC-5

TREC-3 introduced new topics with shorter descriptions, allowing for more innovative topic expansion ideas.[25] A small group of experiments worked with a Spanish language collection and others dealt with interactive query formulation in multiple databases.

The nature of topics (user queries) in TREC varied in the course of the TREC series of experiments. While the first two TRECs used very long topics (averaging about 130 terms), in TREC-3 they were made shorter by excluding some keywords, and in TREC-4 they were made even shorter to investigate the problems with very short user statements (containing around ten terms).[26] TREC-5 included both short and long versions of the topics with the goal of carrying out deeper investigations into which types of techniques work well on various lengths of topics.[27]

With the maturity of the TREC exercises, variations of the basic ad hoc and routing operations were introduced as specialist tracks. In TREC-4 and TREC-5, some of the tracks were:[28]

- *Multiple database merging*: for distributed information retrieval, a large collection of documents was broken into ten non-overlapping sub-collections, which were indexed and searched independently and the results forming each sub-collection were merged to form one final ranking for the user.
- *Confusion*: the kind of errors created by optical character recognition (OCR) programs were simulated in order to evaluate the effectiveness of ad hoc retrieval on noisy data.
- *Ad hoc information retrieval on non-English languages*: two collections of Spanish and one collection of Chinese documents were used to see whether the techniques that worked well in English language documents also work well on other languages.
- *Interactive usage*: situations where participants were able to employ their own

users to retrieve documents interactively from their systems using the TREC queries.

- *Filtering*: situations where the routing task was varied to allow evaluation using a non-ranking criteria based on a utility measure.

TREC-6

In TREC-6, three new tracks, speech, cross-language and high-precision information retrieval, were introduced. The goal of the cross-language information retrieval track is to facilitate research on systems that are able to retrieve relevant documents regardless of the language of the source documents. Speech, or the spoken document retrieval track, is to stimulate research on retrieval techniques for spoken documents, for example, speeches, radio broadcasts, and so on. The high precision track was designed to deal with tasks in which the user of a retrieval system is asked to retrieve ten documents that answer a given information request within five minutes.

TREC-7

In addition to the main ad hoc task, TREC-7 contained seven tracks out of which two tracks – query track and very large corpus track – were new. The goal of the query track was to create a large query collection. The query track was designed as a means of creating a large set of different queries for an existing TREC topic set, topics 1 to 50. The very large corpus track used a 100 gigabyte document collection in order to explore how well retrieval algorithms scale to large document collections.

TREC-8 to TREC-12

TREC-8 contained seven tracks out of which two – question-answering (QA) and web – tracks were new. The objective of QA track is to explore the possibilities of providing answers to specific natural language queries, as opposed to the traditional retrieval output of documents in response to a query. The web track was introduced to investigate whether and how the traditional information retrieval techniques can be used in web information retrieval. TREC-9 also included seven tracks. A video track was introduced in TREC-10 and a novelty track was introduced in TREC-11. The video track is designed to promote research in content-based retrieval from digital video. The goal of the novelty track is to investigate system's abilities to locate relevant and new information within the ranked set of documents returned by a traditional document retrieval system.[3] TREC-12 (held in 2003) added three new tracks: genome track for research in the domain of genomics; robust retrieval track, the consistency of retrieval technology by focusing on the poorly performing technology; and HARD (Highly Accurate Retrieval from Documents), the effectiveness of ad hoc searches with emphasis on customizing retrieval for individual users by exploiting information about the search context and user interactions.[29]

Benefits of TREC experiments

The TREC series of experiments have brought together researchers from across the world to work on common and specific information retrieval problems. Although initially the goal was to build large test collections of documents and queries with relevance assessment criteria attached to each query, this series of research has produced some very significant and interesting results. Details of the findings of each track, as well as the ad hoc tasks, appear in the TREC overview and specific track reports that appear regularly on the TREC website (**http://trec.nist.gov**). TREC experiments have also become evolutionary in the sense that new tracks have been added as and when new problem areas have been found by researchers. In addition to the TREC publications web pages[29] information about the TREC series of experiments has appeared in many journals, the most prominent ones being *Information processing and management*, *Journal of the American Society for Information Science and Technology* and *Journal of documentation*.

A wide range of information retrieval strategies has been tested through the TREC series of experiments, such as:

* Boolean retrieval
* statistical and probabilistic indexing and term weighting strategies
* passage or paragraph retrieval
* combining the results of more than one search
* retrieval based on prior relevance assessments
* natural language-based and statistically-based phrase indexing
* query expansion and query reduction
* string and concept-based searching
* dictionary-based stemming
* question-answering
* content-based multimedia retrieval, and so on.

All these experiments have shown that significant research results can be achieved through international efforts and collaboration. The TREC series of experiments also have shown that although the first series of information retrieval experiments took place nearly four decades ago, there is still a lot more to learn about evaluation studies. Nevertheless, as Sparck Jones[30] comments, the IR community should be enormously grateful to TREC, because it has revitalized IR research and also demonstrated the importance of text retrieval to wider communities, for example those engaged with natural language processing or artificial intelligence. Commenting on the first few year's of TREC experiments, Robertson, Walker and Beaulieu[31] observe that the state of the art of text retrieval has advanced substantially in the first six years of TREC.

There have been some criticisms of TREC, especially on the methodological issues. For example, Sparck Jones[30] argues that although in the first few years TREC has done a great deal, there are large and important matters that TREC has not yet addressed. She believes that the primary reason for this is that the TREC work has been carried out within the traditional laboratory paradigm, which is hard to relate – as much in modern web browsing as in old-fashioned libraries – to users trying to find their way on the ground. Blair[32] believes that some of the claims for what TREC has accomplished seem to overreach what the tests have actually shown, and this is particularly true when comparing the results demonstrated by the various early TREC experiments. However, Saracevic, Voorhees and Harman[33] note that the use of pooling to produce sample results for human relevance judgements has been extensively studied and found to be more than adequate for the purposes of a test collection. In short, one can conclude that TREC has been a vehicle not only for improving retrieval technology, but also for providing a better understanding of retrieval evaluation.

References

1 Lancaster, F. W., *Information retrieval systems: characteristics, testing, and evaluation*, 2nd edn, New York, John Wiley, 1979.
2 Sparck Jones, K. (ed.), *Information retrieval experiment,* London, Butterworth, 1981.
3 Belkin, N. J. and Croft, W. B., 'Retrieval techniques', *Annual review of information science and technology*, **22**, 1987, 109–45.
4 Cleverdon, C. W., *Report on the first step of an investigation into the comparative efficiency of indexing systems*, Cranfield, College of Aeronautics, 1960.
5 Cleverdon, C. W., *Report on the testing and analysis of an investigation into the comparative efficiency of indexing systems*, Cranfield, College of Aeronautics, 1962.
6 Swanson, D. R., 'Some unexplained aspects of the Cranfield tests of indexing language performance', *Library quarterly*, **41**, 1971, 223–8.
7 Vickery, B. C., *Techniques of information retrieval*, London, Butterworth, 1970.
8 Lesk, M. E. and Salton, G., 'Relevance assessment and retrieval system evaluation'. In: Salton, G. (ed.), *The SMART retrieval system: experiments in automatic document processing,* Englewood Cliffs, NJ, Prentice-Hall, 1971, 506–27.
9 Salton, G., 'The SMART project: status report and plan'. In: Salton, G. (ed.), *The SMART retrieval system: experiments in automatic document processing*, Englewood Cliffs, NJ, Prentice-Hall, 1971, 3–11.
10 Salton, G. and McGill, M. J., *Introduction to modern information retrieval*, Auckland, McGraw-Hill, 1983.
11 Salton, G., 'The SMART environment for retrieval system evaluation: advantages and problem areas'. In: Sparck Jones, K. (ed.), *Information retrieval experiment*, London, Butterworth, 1981, 316–29.
12 Blair, D. C. and Maron, M. E., 'An evaluation of retrieval effectiveness for a full-text document retrieval system', *Communications of the ACM*, **28** (3), 1985, 289–99.
13 Salton, G., 'Another look at automatic text-retrieval systems', *Communications of the ACM,* **29** (7), 1986, 648–56.
14 Blair, D. C. and Maron, M. E., 'Full-text information retrieval: further analysis and clarification', *Information processing and management*, **26** (3), 1990, 437–47.
15 Schamber, L., Eisenberg, M. B. and Nilan, M. S., 'A re-examination of

relevance: toward a dynamic, situational definition', *Information processing and management*, **26** (6), 1990, 755–76.

16 Robertson, S. E., 'On sample sizes for non-matched pair IR experiments', *Information processing and management*, **26** (6), 1990, 739–53.

17 Harman, D., 'Evaluation issues in information retrieval', *Information processing and management,* **28** (4), 1992, 439–40.

18 Robertson, S. E. and Hancock-Beaulieu, M., 'On the evaluation of IR systems', *Information processing and management,* **28** (4), 1992, 457–66.

19 Ledwith, R., 'On the difficulties of applying the results of information research to aid in the searching of large scientific databases', *Information processing and management*, **28** (4), 1992, 451–5.

20 Schamber, L., 'Relevance and information behaviour', *Annual review of information science and technology*, **29**, 1994, 3–48.

21 Voorhees, E. (2001). Overview of TREC 2000. Available at **http://trec.nist.gov/pubs/trec9/papers/**.

22 Voorhees, E. (2002). Overview of TREC 2001. Available at **http://trec.nist.gov/pubs/trec10/t10_proceedings.html**.

23 Harman, D., 'A special conference report: the first text retrieval conference (TREC-1), Rockville, MD, USA, 4–6 Nov. 1992', *Information processing and management*, **29** (4), 1993, 411–14.

24 Korfhage, R. R., *Information storage and retrieval*, New York, John Wiley, 1997.

25 Harman, D., 'Review of TREC', *Information processing and management*, **30**, 1994, 271–90.

26 Harman, D. (ed.), *Overview of the third Text Retrieval Conference (TREC-3)*, Washington DC, 1995, NIST Special Publication, 500–225.

27 Smeaton, A. and Harman, D., 'The TREC experiments and their impact on Europe', *Journal of information science*, **23** (2), 1997, 169–74.

28 Harman, D., *The fourth text retrieval conference (TREC-4)*, Gaithersburg, MD, National Institute of Standards and Technology, 1996, NIST Special Publication, 500–236.

29 TREC. Availble at **http://trec.nist.gov/pubs.html**.

30 Sparck Jones, K., 'Reflections on TREC', *Information processing and management*, **31** (3), 1995, 291–314.

31 Robertson, S. E., Walker, S. and Beaulieu, M., 'Laboratory experiments with OKAPI: participation in TREC programme', *Journal of documentation*, **53** (1), 1997, 8–19.

32 Blair, D. C. (2002), 'Some thoughts on the reported results of TREC', *Information processing and management*, **38** (3), 2002, 445–51.

33 Saracevic, T., Voorhees, E. and Harman, D., 'Letter to the editor', *Information processing and management*, **39** (1), 153–6

Chapter 15

Online and CD-ROM information retrieval

Introduction

Online information retrieval involves searching remotely located databases through interactive communication with the help of computers and communication channels. The database can be accessed by the user directly or via a vendor (supplier of online services); in each case through the computer and communication network. The term online retrieval can thus be used to indicate the information retrieval services available from producers of databases, or vendors of these databases. Although online information retrieval systems have existed for more than three decades, recent developments in the internet and world wide web (discussed in Chapter 18) have brought significant changes and improvements in the online information retrieval environment. This chapter discusses the basic concepts of online information retrieval.

Since its appearance in the 1980s, CD-ROM (Compact Disc Read Only Memory) discs have been used extensively for the production and delivery of large databases. A CD-ROM database has a specially designed search interface and common search interfaces are now available, which allows an operator to use one interface to search many databases produced by the same vendor. Although originally they were used with standalone systems, CD-ROM databases now can run on networks, and users sometimes can search multiple databases. This chapter discusses the key issues of information retrieval from CD-ROM databases.

Online searching

The phrase online searching was originally used to describe the process of directly interrogating computer systems to resolve particular requests for information . Now the phrase is used to denote searches that are conducted by means of a local computer that communicates with a remote computer system containing databases. Users can access the database(s) via an online search service provider (also called vendor). The search process is interactive and user can conduct the search iteratively until a satisfactory result is obtained.

With the advent of the internet and world wide web, the connotation of online searching has changed. Now we can conduct online searches through the world wide web on information sources that are distributed all over the world. For searching these information sources through the web, we can go straight to the web page of the service provider provided we know the URL (uniform resource locator, or the address of the web page). Alternatively, we can try to locate the information source(s) by searching through the web search engines (the retrieval programs that help us search the web) like AltaVista and InfoSeek, or through subject directories or gateways (subject directories that can be navigated to reach a particular information source or a group of similar sources) like Yahoo, SOSIG and Biz/ed.

This chapter discusses the former type of online service, the traditional online service characterized by a remote online database search service offered commercially by a search service provider or vendor. One major advantage of this kind of online searching is that it is designed to be pay-as-you-go, and therefore each search session can be costed. Another advantage of online searching is its speed and the currency of the data retrieved. Originally online search services were very expensive and could be complex, and therefore intermediaries were needed to help end-users conduct an effective and efficient online search. However, over the years online search services have become less expensive and more user-friendly. As a result, they can now be used by end-users themselves.

Development of online searching

The first major online dial-up service was MEDLINE, the online version of MED-LARS, which was followed in 1972 by the offer of commercial online services from Dialog (Lockheed) and ORBIT (SDC).[1] After 1972 many organizations began to offer online databases and search services. By 1975 there were as many as 300 public access databases available from a range of different vendors.[1] Initially, the majority of the online databases were used to provide bibliographic references as the output of search session(s) and these were called bibliographic or reference databases. However, for the past few years, more and more databases are becoming available that retrieve actual information rather than mere bibliographic references. These databases are either full text, where the full texts of documents (including graphics and pictures) are available, or databanks that contain machine readable numerical (often combined with textual and graphical) data.

Rowley[2] identifies three generations of online searching:

1   The first generation, from the beginning to 1981, was characterized by dumb terminals, slow transmission speeds, and mostly bibliographic databases.
2   The second generation, which lasted through the 1980s, was characterized by PCs as workstations, medium transmission speeds, bibliographic as well as full-text databases and interfaces directed at the end-users.
3   The third generation, which started at the beginning of the 1990s, is characterized by multimedia PCs, higher transmission speeds, bibliographic as well as full-text databases, and improved user interfaces, help and tutorial facilities.

To this we can add a new, fourth, generation, which started at the end of the 1990s with web access to online search services. Nowadays, users can go directly to the web address of an online service provider whereby they will get a screen to log in to the service. Web-based online search services, such as DialogWeb, OVID Online, OCLC FirstSearch, provide fast and easy access to online databases with a number of search and retrieval facilities. The qualities of online search services coupled with the advantages of the world wide web have brought significant developments to online search systems and have made online searching more directed towards end-users.

The growth in the database industry can be interpreted in terms of the number of vendors or service providers, database producers, databases, database records and online searches. There are a number of publications that regularly record the growth of online information retrieval; the most prominent publication in this field now is the *Gale directory of databases*[3] and the most prominent author is Martha Williams.

Online search services

There are various components of an online search service:

- information providers or database producers who provide databases to be accessed in an online mode
- a search service provider or vendor, which provides access to the databases and software for conducting the search
- communication links that connect the user with the host and the database(s); nowadays users can communicate with the service providers through the internet
- a local workstation through which the user is linked to the service.

Online search services, or vendors, are those organizations that provide value-added processing to the databases and offer search services. The following are some examples of online search services:

- Dialog (**http://www.dialog.com/about/**): A pioneer in online search services, Dialog provides online access to over 800 million records in 900 databases in different disciplines.
- OCLC FirstSearch (**http://www.oclc.org/firstsearch/**): This provides library users with instant online access to more than 72 databases, including these valuable OCLC databases: OCLC WorldCat, OCLC FirstSearch Electronic Collections Online, OCLC ArticleFirst, OCLC PAIS International, OCLC PapersFirst, OCLC ProceedingsFirst and OCLC Union Lists of Periodicals.
- Ovid (**http://www.ovid.com/site/index.jsp**): Ovid provides access to hundreds of full text journals, renowned textbooks and premier bibliographic databases in various disciplines.
- STN (**http://www.cas.org/stnonline.html**): STN offers current and archival information from over 200 scientific, technical, business and patent databases covering a broad range of scientific fields, including chemistry, engineering, life sciences, pharmaceutical sciences, biotechnology, regulatory compliance, patents and business.

While the above are examples of online search services that provide online access to a large number of databases in various disciplines, the following are examples of some online search services that provide access to the full texts of journals and books:

- EBSCO Information service (**http://www.epnet.com/default.asp**): This provides access to a large collection of full text and bibliographic databases suitable for all kinds of libraries.
- Ingenta (**http://www.ingenta.com/**): Ingenta provides access to the full text of over 5,400 publications from over 230 academic and professional publishers.
- ProQuest (**http://proquest.umi.com/pqdweb**): ProQuest is a resource of electronic collections containing millions of articles originally published in magazines, newspapers and journals.

Details of online search services are available in a number of publications (see for example, Forrester and Rowlands,[4] Large, Tedd and Hartley,[5] and Chowdhury and Chowdhury[6]), as well as in the websites of the respective search services. Various features of, and the steps in carrying out an online search are discussed below, with examples from DialogWeb.

Basic steps in an online search

The steps involved in carrying out an online search vary from system to system. This is because each system has its own custom-built interface, which allows specific types of search and uses specific operators for different search commands. Nevertheless, the graphical user interfaces used in these systems have made the task of searching reasonably straightforward and the process of searching has been simplified further in the web-based interfaces. These are the basic steps that one needs to follow to conduct an online search.

1 Study the search topic and develop a clear understanding of the information requirement. This is a critical step and depends on a number of factors, such as, the nature and requirements of the user, how well the user can express his or her information needs, how much the user already knows, how the user is going to use the information, and so on. This happens before the actual search process begins and is often conducted through a series of dialogues between a searcher and an information intermediary. In the absence of an intermediary, users have to clearly delineate their information requirements for themselves.

2 Get access to an online search service. This can be done through subscription or a licensing agreement. The access right has to be obtained before the search begins.

3 Log on to the service provider. Nowadays this is usually done though the web interfaces of the online search service providers. Users need to know the URL of the online service provider as well as the user ID and password.

4 Select the appropriate database(s) to search. This is a critical and often a difficult task. The success of a search largely depends on the appropriate selection of the databases. Online search services allow users to select one or more data-

bases to search using the same interface. Most search services allow users to browse through the database categories to select appropriate databases(s). Dialog has a unique facility called DialIndex search (details are given later in this chapter), which allows users to see how many times a given search term occurs in a set of chosen databases. This information can guide users to select the appropriate database to conduct the actual search.

5   Formulate search expressions. This is the key part of the job. It may involve a number of activities, the first being the selection of appropriate terms and/or phrases. This may require the user to consult dictionaries and thesauri. Once the appropriate search terms and/or phrases are chosen, the search expression has to be formulated. At this stage the user should have an understanding of the nature, content and structure of the chosen database(s) and to know which fields are indexed and therefore can be searched. The user also needs to know what search facilities are available, such as Boolean search, truncation, field specific search, proximity search, and so on, and the appropriate operators. The search operators and syntax for formulating search expressions vary from one search service to the other. Many search service providers have different interfaces for novice and expert users. If the users want to use the expert search interface, which may be command-driven, they have to have a knowledge of the various search commands and their order of execution.

6   Select the appropriate format for display. Online search services allow users to select an appropriate format, from a number of predefined formats, to display the retrieved records. However, there may be charges for the records displayed. For example, when searching Dialog, charges incurred include output and search time costs, as well as internet charges; prices also vary by database. Therefore, one has to be very careful in deciding which record(s) display and in which format to display them. If the option for the display of the full record(s) is chosen, the process may take some time, depending on the network traffic. However, each online search service provides an option for brief display, which shows the brief details of the output records, and users may select records from this list for a full display.

7   Reformulate your query, if necessary. This may mean going back to step 4 or step 5 and repeating the entire process. Online searches are usually iterative processes, meaning that user conducts several searches, compares the results, modifies a search statement, or conducts a new search in order to get the best results.

8   Select the mode of delivery. You may download all the chosen records online or send an offline request.

Features of an online search service: DialogWeb

DialogWeb is the web interface to the Dialog online search service, one of the oldest and largest online search service providers, which gives easy access to a large number of databases with:

- company information – both directory listings and financial information
- industry information – trends; overviews; market research; specialized industry newsletters and reports; US and international news, including an extensive collection of newspapers and newswires from North America and Asia; and US government news, including public affairs, law and regulatory information
- patents and trademarks – a worldwide collection for research and competitive intelligence tracking
- chemistry, environment, science and technology – technical literature and reference material to support research needs
- social science and humanities including education, information science, psychology, sociology and science, from public opinion, news, and leading scholarly and popular publications
- general reference information – people, books, consumer news and travel.

Users can search and retrieve information from all these different types of information sources using:

- Guided Search mode, which does not require knowledge of the Dialog command language
- Command Search mode, which allows experienced users to use the Dialog command language
- database selection tools, which help users pinpoint the right database for a search
- integrated database descriptions, pricing information and other search assistance
- easy to use forms to create and modify Alerts (current awareness updates).

Dialog search results are available in HTML or text formats. Users have a choice of displaying records or sending search results via email, fax, or postal delivery.

Steps in a DialogWeb search

The first step of a DialogWeb search involves logging in to the system, for which a Dialog account is necessary. The user goes to the DialogWeb site (**http://www. DialogWeb.com**) and must enter the user ID and password. The log-in screen also provides information about DialogWeb and a preview and search tips. After logging in, the user needs to select the mode of search: Guided Search or Command Search. Guided Search is the default search option.

Guided Search

Guided Search is designed for novice to intermediate searchers. The following steps are to be followed for conducting a Guided Search looking for information on digital libraries.

Step 1: Choose database
To begin the Guided Search, the user clicks the New Search button and chooses from the list of main subject categories. Each category is further divided into focused search

topics. For a search on digital libraries, one can select these categories:

> Social Sciences and Humanities > Social Sciences > Library and Information Science

This will lead to a list of databases that cover Library and Information Science.

Step 2: Choose a search option and carry out search
In Guided Search there are two search options:

- *Targeted Search*, which is available in some, but not all, subject categories. It is a ready-made search form with databases pre-assigned to the form.
- *Dynamic Search*, which is available in all the subject categories. The Dynamic Search form is generated based on the category or database that is selected. Dynamic Search has access to many more databases compared than the Targeted Search and is more flexible.

Targeted Search is the easiest type of search to perform. The user can enter the search word or phrase as 'Words in Title' or as the 'Main Subject'.

Dynamic Search is available at various points in the search category selection process or when a user chooses the Quick Functions option in New Search and enters a specific database number. The Dynamic Search capability is available no matter what category or database is picked. In a category with many databases assigned to it, a user can search:

- all of the databases together
- a group of similarly designed databases together
- one of the assigned databases individually.

If a user has chosen the Dynamic Search option and has decided to conduct the search on all the 12 databases under the 'Library and Information Science' category, the 'Dynamic Search' screen is shown. The Dynamic Search forms also offer the following options:

- Navigation – The search category selections display at the top of the form. To return to a category or option, the user clicks the search category or option name.
- Run Saved Strategy – If a user has already saved a search strategy, it can be run against the selected databases by clicking Run Saved Strategy.

A list of the databases used in the search is displayed at the bottom of the form. The info (i) icon gives more information about the database content and pricing.

In the Dynamic Search screen users can enter a search term or phrase and conduct the search on subject, author, descriptor or title field. A search can also be restricted by the year of publication, and the user can browse the list of items by author or year of publication.

Step 3: Display search results
The search results from a Targeted Search or a Dynamic Search will appear on a Picklist page, which provides a quick view of the records. From the Picklist page users can choose to:

- display specific records in more detailed formats or send records via e-mail or fax, or by post
- rearrange the order in which the records are displayed
- refine the search strategy
- remove duplicate records
- view the prices for all format options
- save the strategy for future use
- create an Alert for automatic updates on the search topic.

After the search has finished processing, the Picklist page will appear. Users can choose to view results by selecting one or more items by checking the boxes and then selecting the display button, or can display any one record just by clicking on the hyperlinked title. The format for display is chosen from the 'Format' box and the records are sorted according to a sort criterion chosen from the 'Sort by' box. The search expression can be refined by clicking the 'Back to Search' button, which allows users to edit, add or delete information from the search form.

Command Search

Command Search is designed for intermediate to experienced Dialog searchers. It provides complete command-based access to Dialog's extensive collection of databases. Users are expected to be familiar with the various Dialog commands when using Command Search. Additional features include built-in tools such as Bluesheets (database descriptions) and pricing information, database selection assistance to help pinpoint the right databases for a search and easy to use forms to create and modify Alerts (current awareness updates). The Command Search main page allows users to begin inputting Dialog commands immediately. A Command Search contains:

- a textbox for entering Dialog search commands
- a Submit button that sends the command
- a Previous button that displays your most recent command entries.

The main page has links to the Databases feature, product support information, and Guided Search. Users can move between Guided Search and Command Search. Steps for conducting a Command search can be summarized as follows.

Step 1: Choose database(s)
DialogWeb simplifies database selection by arranging the databases by subject in the Databases feature. Users can select one or more databases by checking in the Database box. However, if users are not sure which database(s) to select, they can choose the

Dialog Index option. This is particularly useful when users do not know which data-bases to search, or when they want to carry out a comprehensive search and cover everything on a topic. Dialog Index is a master index to most of the Dialog databases, and it allows users to compare the number of records retrieved from a group of data-bases.

After selecting a database, users must search the databases to view the records. They can click 'Begin Databases' to enter the files that they have checked and run the same strategy, or may choose the database(s) to search by entering the file numbers and even change their search strategy in the command line.

Step 2: Choose a search option and carry out search
Once the databases are chosen, the Dialog Command Search page appears. It can also appear:

- after log-in if it is set as the default
- when the Command Search link from the main Guided Search page is clicked
- when the Begin Databases button from Databases is clicked for browsing.

The appropriate BEGIN or 'b' command is inserted in the command line automati-cally when a search has been made in Databases and one or more databases have been selected. Users can add the CURRENT command to their BEGIN statement by typ-ing in 'current' after the command. This allows them to search the current year and one year earlier, and narrows the search results at the beginning. Then they click the Submit button or press the ENTER key on the keyboard to start the search.

Any Dialog command followed by the search term(s) should be entered in the search box. The terms when looking for information on digital libraries might be: S digital (w) libraries.

Step 3: Add to a search
The search can be refined by including 'electronic libraries' through the following expression:

S (digital or electronic) (w) libraries

This search statement will retrieve records on electronic as well as digital libraries. The search statement retrieves those records where digital and libraries, or electronic and libraries, occur next to each other in the same sequence. More records are retrieved by truncating the search term libraries as follows:

S (digital or electronic) (w) librar?

Various other modifications may be made by using appropriate search commands, for example, limiting the search to one or more fields or limiting the results to a language, year of publication, and so on.

Step 4: Displaying records

A search history of all of the sets appears and users can view some of the records. It is a good idea to display a few records in 'free' format before displaying the records in the long or full format. To display records users can choose a format from the drop-down list and click Display for the appropriate set. Formats determine the amount of information to be displayed for each record. The Format list box lists the basic format options: free, short, medium, long, full and KWIC. It is possible to indicate the number of records to display; the default is 10 and a maximum of 99 records can be specified. There is an option of using a Type command (see below for details) to display records or From Each together with the Type command, in order to search more than one database.

Dialog search operators

Dialog offers a number of search features, such as Boolean search, proximity search, truncation, field-specific search, limiting search, and so on. The various search features of Dialog and the corresponding operators are shown in Table 15.1.

Table 15.1 *Dialog search operators*

Search operator	Example	Description
Proximity operator (W)	S information (W) system S information (2W) system	Requests adjacent terms in the defined order. You can specify the maximum number of intervening words. In the example there may be at the most two words in between information and systems
Proximity operator (N)	S information (N) system S information (2N) system	Requests adjacent terms in any order. You can specify the maximum number of intervening terms. In the second example, there may be at the most two words in between information and systems
Proximity operator (S)	S solar (S) energy	Requests that terms should be in the same subfield unit
Proximity operator (L)	S solar (L) cell	Requests that terms should be in the same descriptor unit
Proximity operator (F)	S information (F) system	Requests that terms should be in the same field
Open truncation ?	S computer?	This is an open truncation; any number of characters can appear after the root
Truncation operator ? ?	S cat? ?	A maximum of one character can appear after the root
Truncation operator ??	S comput??	As many characters as the number of '?' (in this example two characters)

(continued)

Table 15.1 (*continued*)

Search operator	Example	Description
Internal truncation ?	Wom?n	Will replace the '?' with one character
Field specific search		Suffix codes restrict retrieval to basic index fields.
Suffix code	S internet/ti,de	Prefix codes are used to search the
Prefix code	S au=Chowdhury,G.	additional indexes. From one to seven prefix codes can be used
Limit suffixes	S internet/1999	Used with the select command to restrict the search by a given criteria. Only a few criteria for limit search can be used.
Range searching	S internet/1998:1999	Useful for limiting the search results. A colon (:) is used to indicate a range of sequential entries to be retrieved in a logical OR relationship.
Numeric searching	S EM=100 S EM>1k	It is also available by using the relational operators, such as, $>$, $<$, $>=$, $<=$, $=$. In the first example, the system will retrieve records with employees of 100, and in the second with employees of more than 1000.
Boolean AND	information and internet	Retrieves records with both the terms
Boolean OR	information or internet	Retrieves records with at least one term
Boolean NOT	internet not WWW	Excludes those that contain the search term following the NOT operator

Essential Dialog commands

There are a number of Dialog commands that can be used in Command Search mode. These are for expert users because the user has to remember the commands and they have to be keyed in according to prescribed syntax. Although the list of Dialog commands is long, features offered by many commands, for example, Display, Field, Format, Type, Print, Rates, and so on, are now available as buttons in the DialogWeb interface and users just click on those buttons to perform the corresponding operation. However, some commands are still required to perform an operation and the essential Dialog commands are shown in Table 15.2.

Table 15.2   *Some essential Dialog commands*

Command	Example	Description
Begin or B	B 202 B 1, 202	Opens one or more databases for searching
Current	S 1 current2	Used to narrow the search to records from the most current year(s) within a file. You can specify the number of years.
Find or F	F internet F world wide web	Used in place of the select or s command to conduct a search. The difference with select is that it does not need a proximity operator to search for a phrase
Help or ?	Help field 1	Produces help. For example, the command shown here will show the list of fields for Dialog file 1
Save	Save <name>	Saves the entire search strategy since the last begin command in a file with the given file name
Select or s	S digital libraries	The most essential Dialog command; it is necessary to conduct any search
Select Steps or ss	SS internet and information	Creates a set for each search term/phrase and one for the entire search. This is useful when a multi-word search term is given; later on, you can just call the set with any constituent term to conduct another search
Sort	Sort s1/all/au,ti	Sorts the results of a search set (set1 for the given example) by one or more sort keys (here author and title). Each database has a list of sort keys that can be used. You can click on the 'Sort' button to get a list of sort keys for a given database
Rank	Rank de,id	Conducts a statistical analysis on the existing search set. Dialog extracts the specified fields from the record and lists them in a ranked order

Dialog is a pioneering online information service and many new online search services have better user interfaces and search and retrieval features. Examples of user interfaces and the retrieval features of ABI/INFORM have been discussed in Chapter 12.

CD-ROM databases

Since the early 1960s, the computer industry, being aware of some of the limitations of magnetic storage media, has devoted a great deal of research and development effort to the investigation of alternative high-density recording techniques, particularly optical data storage systems. With magnetic media the presence of dust can cause loss of information, but with holographic storage systems dust or scratching results only in a slight loss of resolution as the data are recorded throughout the entire recording medium. Also, for retrieving data on magnetic media, extreme accuracy is required in the location of the read head, but the holographic system is very tolerant of positional inaccuracies.[7]

CD-ROM is one of a family of compact disc formats, the best known of which is compact disc digital audio (CD-DA, commonly known as the CD), which was jointly developed by the Sony and Philips companies and announced in 1980. The discs have the same physical dimensions and composition. In 1983 Sony and Philips announced a standard for the CD-ROM format, a logical extension of the CD technology, which made it capable of storing textual data. CD-ROMs and audio CDs are both mass-produced using the same physical mastering and replication processes – the main difference between them is that additional error detection and correction features are required for accurate retrieval and representation of data on a computer screen.[8]

Optical storage devices were developed in several parallel tracks geared for different sectors of the market. The range of optical media may be divided into three major functional groups:

* read-only optical media
* write-once optical media, and
* erasable/rewritable optical media.

CD-ROM technology

Compact disc technology owes much of its success to the development of technical standards that have been accepted worldwide. Compact disc standards began with the CD-audio product; the document that specifies the physical and recording characteristics is known as the 'Red Book'.[9] This section discusses some of the basic technological issues related to CD-ROM technology.

Accepted standards

In order for the data stored on a compact disc to be read by any computer operating system and any CD-ROM drive, the data must be stored in a standard form. In 1985 a number of major companies involved in producing CD-ROMs agreed to develop a standard for a logical file structure that would be acceptable to a wide range of operating systems. This became known as the High Sierra Standard (after the name of the hotel High Sierra in Las Vegas, Nevada, where the company representatives met), and was later accepted as ISO 9660.[10]

A CD-ROM file management system, therefore, is designed to allow users to view the disc as a collection of files. A complete CD-ROM file management system comprises three major components:[7]

* the structure or logical format of data
* the software that writes the data in that format (the origination software)
* the software that reads and translates the logical format for use (the destination software).

The logical format of the CD-ROM is concerned with determining where to put the identifying data on the disc, where to find the subdirectories or directories of files on the disc, how the directory is structured, whether subdirectories are supported, how many files can be stored on a CD-ROM, the performance cost of storing a large number of files, how large a file can be, whether files can span multiple volumes and whether files must consist of sequential consecutive sectors.

The logical format is broken into two distinct structures: the volume table of contents (VTOC) and the directory structure. The VTOC contains information about the disc as a whole, including the location of the disc directory. When the file-manager begins reading a disc, it reads the VTOC before anything else. The directory structure specifies the exact locations of the files on the disc.

A number of groups have been involved in the formation of a CD-ROM logical standard, including:[9]

* the High Sierra Group
* the Information Industry Association
* the American Library Association and The Library and Technology Association
* the Optical Disk Forum
* the American National Standards Institution (ANSI)
* the National Information Standards Organization (NISO)
* the International Standards Organization (ISO)
* the European Computer Manufacturer's Association (ECMA).

CD-ROM vs online databases

CD-ROM technology has been in existence since the mid-1980s, while online information retrieval systems have been around for 20 years longer. When CD-ROM technology started becoming popular, many people considered it as an alternative to online information retrieval systems. As an information management tool, CD-ROM offers a potentially attractive and cost-effective alternative to time-sharing systems which provide remote access to databases. Major differences between the CD-ROM and online database options are shown in table 15.3.

Table 15.3   *CD-ROM vs online databases*

Characteristics	CD-ROM	Online databases
Capacity	Limited by the storage capacity of the disc(s), which can be increased by using networked C-ROMs	Several gigabytes of data can be searched at a time
Currency	There is always a time lag; updates may take a long time to reach the user	Updates are available in real time
Costs	Have a fixed price; pay once and use many times	Pay as you go; may prove expensive for frequent and long search sessions
Response time	Depends on the local computers and networks	Depends on the vendor computer, and nowadays more on the network (internet) performance
Cross searching	Possible through networks	Possible and depends on the vendor
Equipment	Can run, although not very efficiently, on a minimum configuration	Depends largely on the reliability of the network and infrastructure

There have been a large number of studies comparing CD-ROM and online information retrieval facilities.[11] Each of these studies suggests that there are several factors
that should be considered in choosing an alternative between an online database and
its CD-ROM counterpart. In fact there are five major issues:

- database content
- software retrieval capabilities
- response time
- indexing
- database segmentation.

Some CD-ROM databases use the same command protocols as online databases,
thereby making it very easy for a user to conduct a search of the database on disc.
Dialog Ondisc and Wilsondisc are examples of this. Some online databases, because
of their large size, need to be segmented when they are published on CD-ROMs. Thus
users may need to swap discs while conducting a search on the whole database.

The number of keystrokes or search steps needed to perform a search can be an
important parameter in the comparison between the CD-ROM and online database
search. For example, 13 separate steps are followed to conduct an author search on the
Science Citation Index compact disc edition and print the retrieved citations; in contrast, the same search would require four steps online. The search software and the

searchable fields are also important factors in the success of the search and retrieval process. CD-ROM databases and their online counterparts sometimes differ in this regard.

It is important to note that setting up a CD-ROM service involves a significant amount of initial investment towards the procurement of an up-to-date computer, a CD-ROM drive along with interface cards, peripherals, and so on, as well as the cost of the CD-ROM database. This expenditure can be justified if the number of searches conducted on the database is fairly high. In contrast, with online search 'pay as you go' pricing, the initial expenditure is considerably less. Saffady[12] proposes a simple formula to calculate the break-even point after which the CD-ROM database will prove less expensive than its online counterpart:

$$N = \frac{C}{T}$$

where N denotes the minimum number of annual searches after which a CD-ROM subscription will prove less expensive than an online search service; C denotes the annual cost of CD-ROM subscription to the given database; and T denotes the combined connect-time, telecommunication, display, printing, labour and other charges for a typical online search session involving the indicated database. This formula was proposed in the pre-internet era, and may now need slight amendment given the different pricing systems of current online databases.

Common search features available in CD-ROM databases

Basic information on CD-ROM discs is available in a number of published documents.[2, 8, 12] The following search features are commonly available in CD-ROM databases though, as we shall see later in this chapter, the search syntax, operators, and so on, may vary from one CD-ROM to another.

1 *Keyword search*: This is the most common search feature of CD-ROM databases whereby a user can conduct search with one or more keywords.
2 *Phrase search*: This allows users to conduct searches on multiple word phrases. Sometimes this is done through subject search facilities while in some CD-ROM databases it can be performed by using proximity operators.
3 *Boolean search*: Three types of Boolean searches, namely Boolean AND, OR and NOT, are available, though the operators used for these searches may vary from one CD-ROM to the other.
4 *Truncation*: Although there are three kinds of truncation, left truncation, right truncation and middle truncation, left truncation is not commonly available in CD-ROM databases. The symbols for truncation and the syntax – how many truncation symbols can be used with what effect on the search term – vary from one CD-ROM to the other, and users have to learn these to conduct an effective CD-ROM search.

5   *Index and/or thesaurus support*: Indexes allow users to select the search term(s) or phrase(s) from the term index, and a thesaurus allows users to get a map of the chosen terms in order to widen or narrow down a given search. CD-ROM retrieval software provides index search facilities so that users can select an index to browse and select terms from the index for searching. There may be one index file, or a separate index file for each searchable field, so that users can choose a field and then browse the corresponding index file. Although index search facilities are commonly available in CD-ROM search systems thesaurus facilities are not always present.

6   *Proximity search*: This search facility allows user to tell the search system how far the chosen search terms should be in the retrieved records. In some cases this is given in terms of the number of intervening words, while in others it may be used to specify whether the search terms should appear in the same sentence, same field, same paragraph, and so on.

7   *Field-specific search*: Most CD-ROM search software allows users to specify one or more fields to search. In fact, users can select a particular field to search and then select the search term from the index file for that field.

8   *Free-text search*: This feature allows users to specify one or more search terms or phrases that are not limited to any particular field. Some CD-ROM search software also provides an index for free-text search terms.

9   *Combining search sets and search refinement*: This allows users to refine a search by adding or dropping search terms or conditions. This may be done by completely rekeying an entire search expression or by calling a previous search set and making modifications to it. In many cases users can save a search statement and then recall it as and when necessary.

10   *Limiting or Range search*: Some CD-ROM search software allows users to limit a search by adding criteria such as language, year of publication or price. In some cases, users may also conduct a search with a range of values added as criteria, such as items published within a certain span of years, and so on.

11   *Searching through retrieved records*: Some CD-ROM search software allows users to select search terms from a record that has been retrieved through a previous search.

The nature of the output depends on a number of factors, such as the type of the database, its content, organization, policies of the publisher, and so on. Some CD-ROM retrieval software automatically displays the output in a different window, in others users have to choose the view/display option to look at the records. Sometimes the system first displays the brief output and users have to select one or more records to view the detailed display. In some cases users can choose from more than one display and print formats. The output is usually not ranked. In some CD-ROM databases the search terms are highlighted in the output.

Summary

In this chapter we have discussed the basic features of online search services and CD-

ROM databases. Though online search services are now accessible through their web interfaces and offer a number of common search and retrieval features, they have some differences in their database coverage, search interface and output features. Points to be considered when evaluating and selecting online search services[2, 4] include:

- databases offered
- search and retrieval facilities
- search interfaces; provision of simple and advanced user interfaces
- database structure and record formats
- cost
- time required for searching
- cross database searching facility
- communication facilities
- support services
- additional facilities such as current awareness services and selective dissemination of information services (like the Dialog Alert service).

Although with the development of web interfaces online search services have become more easy to use, one still needs some training and practice to become an expert online searcher. Users need to be familiarized with the search interface and also to know the various search options. Formulating the most appropriate search expression is not always easy, and one may have to make several attempts, by formulating new search sets and/or modifying search sets, to get the optimum results. Although one can get such results through trial and error, the search session under such circumstances may be expensive, because the longer the user is connected to the system and the more records that are displayed to make a decision about the best results, the more expensive the search will be.

Initially online search services were very expensive. Over the years, more and more flexible pricing systems have been offered to make using online services more feasible.[13] However, price is still a factor and a major concern for the users as well as the service providers. Webber[13] comments that while there are some general trends in online pricing, there seems to be no general solution to the pricing conundrum of online search services. She further argues that complicated multipart pricing system continues, and vendors' increasing sophistication in using price as part of the marketing mix may lead to a wide range of pricing strategies aiming at different market segments; this will eventually make prices of online services more difficult to evaluate and compare.

The introduction and proliferation of the web have brought significant changes in the economy of the information industry, especially the online information search services. While many online search services are still proprietary and users have to register and pay for search sessions as well as for the content that is retrieved, viewed and printed, some services provide searching for free while charging for content. Publishers of online journals provide such services, for instance Ingenta allows users to search and view brief output from a large collection of full text journal articles. At the other extreme, there are some online databases that are freely available, a prominent example being the Pubmed service,[14] which provides free access to Medline and other health information databases.

References

1   Walker, G. and Janes, J., *Online retrieval: a dialogue of theory and practice*, Libraries Unlimited, 1993.
2   Rowley, J., *The electronic library*, 4th edn, London, Library Association Publishing, 1999.
3   *Gale directory of databases. Vol. 1: Online databases 2003. Vol 2: CD-ROM, diskette, magnetic tape, handheld and batch access database products 2003*, Gale 2002.
4   Forrester, W. H. and Rowlands, J. L., *The online searcher's companion*, London, Library Association Publishing, 1999.
5   Large, A., Tedd, L. A. and Hartley, R. J., *Information seeking in the online age: principles and practice*, Bowker-Saur, 1999.
6   Chowdhury, G. G. and Chowdhury, S., *Searching CD-ROM and online information sources*, London, Library Association Publishing, 2001.
7   Hendley, T., 'An introduction to the range of optical storage media'. In: Oppenheim, C. (ed.), *CD-ROM: fundamentals to applications*, London, Butterworths, 1988, 1–38.
8   Hanson, T. and Day, J. (eds), *CD-ROM in libraries: management issues*, London, Bowker, 1994.
9   Heimburger, A., *Guide to CD-ROM* (PGI-88/WS/11), Paris, Unesco/PGI, 1988.
10   ISO 9660:1988, *Information processing: volume and file structure of CD-ROM for information interchange*, International Organization for Standardization.
11   Tedd, L. A., 'The changing face of CD-ROM', *Journal of documentation*, **51** (2), 1995, 85–98.
12   Saffady, W., *Optical storage technology 1992: a state of the art review*, Meckler, 1992.
13   Webber, S., 'Pricing and marketing online information services'. In: Williams, M. E. (ed.) *Annual review of information science and technology*, **33**, Medford, NJ, Information Today Inc., 39–83.
14   PubMed. Available at   **http://www.ncbi.nlm.nih.gov/entrez/query.fcgi?db=PubMed**.

Chapter 16

Multimedia information retrieval

Introduction

Computers have traditionally been used to process numeric as well as textual information. However, although text (including numeric figures, tables, and so on) has been the most commonly used medium, information can be communicated by sound, by picture (graphics), and moving images. Human beings have been communicating information in textual form for centuries and libraries and information centres have been engaged in making this kind of information available to the user community.[1] There are many fields of work that require access to non-textual information. For example, medical professionals need access to X-rays, architects to building plans, ornithologist to bird calls, estate agents to property photographs, car engineers (and buyers as well) need photographs and sound of the car engines, and so on. In these and in many other fields non-textual is at least equally as important as textual information. With the recent advances in quality and reductions in price of display and storage technology, computers are being used more regularly for storage and handling of moving images, animation, and sound, in addition to text and numerals. Thus, it is now possible for information professionals to store and retrieve information that can be textual, audio, and visual. The new systems that have been developed to handle information contained in more than one medium are called *multimedia information systems*.

Multimedia information systems include many different types of media such as text, numeric data, graphics, image, voice and video. This chapter addresses some of the key issues of multimedia information retrieval.

Multimedia information retrieval

Multimedia systems use information and communication technologies for the integrated storage and retrieval of information in the form of numbers, text, images, audio and video. Multimedia information has some specific characteristics that makes it distinct from textual information; thus multimedia information retrieval systems differ from conventional text retrieval systems.

Audio information may include sound, music and speech. Traditionally libraries have catalogued audio information resources similarly to the way they catalogue bibliographic items. Speech retrieval is a special case of information retrieval in which the information is in spoken form. Speech retrieval systems may require explicit formulation of a query; some systems seek to infer the information need from a set of training data. Music information, another major type of audio information, has a number of complex characteristics that makes music information retrieval a complex task.

Digital images are composed of arrays of pixels of different intensities. These pixels do not have any inherent meaning, unlike component words within a text. Text information retrieval systems rely greatly on component words. Most text retrieval systems either look for the presence (or absence) of the query words in the text collection, or try to find the similarity between the query and text vectors. Some, especially the natural language text processing systems, use the syntax (grammar), semantics (meaning), and pragmatics (context) of the text and query languages. It is not possible to do this for image retrieval, especially in those cases where retrieval is based on the content and characteristics of images, rather than the words that describe them. Content-based image retrieval systems try to match the inherent characteristics of images, such as the colour, texture, shape and spatial location. Video information comprises moving images and audio. In addition, digital videos occupy far more storage, and therefore they need more time to process and search than text retrieval systems.

A good multimedia information retrieval system should have the capability to store, retrieve and present heterogeneous data ranging from text to audio, still and moving images, and digital video. Objects in a multimedia database can be two- or three-dimensional black and white or colour images, digitized voice or music, video clips, and so on. The architecture of a multimedia information retrieval system depends on the characteristics of the multimedia data and the kind of operations to be performed on such data.[2] A typical query may be by the content of an image collection, for example, 'show me all the pictures where Prime Minister Tony Blair meets with President George W. Bush', or 'show me all the x-ray images that show a growth of a particular dimension on the bones'. A query may similarly be on the content of an audio clip, a piece of music or a video. Thus the retrieval system should be capable of matching the patterns of the queries and the stored objects in order to retrieve those that match, either fully or partially. Basically the retrieval system can look for a whole match whereby it will retrieve all those objects that match the query, or a sub-pattern match where only part of the query matches the object.

Audio information retrieval

Audio information can be varied from natural sounds to human speech and animal cries, music, and so on. Again, in a collection, some part of the sound or speech may be desirable while others may not, for example the noise within a musical piece. Speech and music retrieval have become prominent areas of research over the past few years.

Speech retrieval

Speech is one of the most commonly used mediums of human communication. The conventional tools for capturing and playing speech and audio information has a common problem: the recorded speech or audio material has to be listened to sequentially. Audio equipment provides mechanisms for going backward and forward in a recorded message, but it is difficult to retrieve a particular segment of a speech from a long recorded voice. Conventional text retrieval techniques may be applied to voice retrieval easily if we could transcribe spoken audio documents. A perfect automatic speech recognition (ASR) system that can efficiently transcribe spoken audio documents would be an ideal solution for speech retrieval. Hidden Markov models (HMM) form the backbone of ASR systems. An HMM is a statistical representation of a speech event like a word.[3] Model parameters are trained on a large corpus of labelled speech data. Once a trained set of HMMs is generated, query speech can be matched to find the most likely model sequence (the recognized words).

This approach has been found successful for large vocabulary recognition systems, as well as for keyword spotting where a speech sequence is searched to identify a specific sequence of words.[3] For large vocabulary recognition systems, a sub-word approach is taken where, instead of building an explicit HMM for every word, a few hundred phonetically based sub-words are used. A language model that defines likely word combinations is also used to facilitate correct word recognition. One of the major problems of ASR systems is their limited accuracy.[3] Another technique used for recognition of words in a speech is called 'word spotting', which involves automatic detection of words or phrases in unconstrained speech. In any case these techniques suffer from serious limitations: in order for a word to be recognized it has to be present in the phonetic dictionary, a language model must be used, and sufficient example texts have to be present. The whole process becomes time-consuming and expensive for processing large volumes of speech. The sub-word indexing approach, which uses sub-word indexing units such as phones or phone clusters, significantly reduces the processing time.

Ideally, a speech recognizer would generate an exact transcription of speech content, regardless of speaking style, vocabulary or the acoustic environment. However, despite recent advances in ASR technology, most ASR systems can recognize vocabularies of many thousands of words. Out-of-vocabulary words, such as proper nouns, which are often important keys for information retrieval, cannot be recognized by many ASR systems. The Video Mail Retrieval project at Cambridge University, in collaboration with Olivetti Research Laboratory (ORL), is developing retrieval methods based on spotting keywords in the audio soundtrack of video messages.[4]

Music retrieval

Although the first published work on music information retrieval appeared long ago,[5, 6] very little research has so far been done on music information retrieval. Byrd and Crawford[7] have reviewed research on music information retrieval and observe that music information retrieval is still a very immature field. Interest in this area has been slow to develop, as is evident from the literature available (Bainbridge et al.;[8] Downie and Nelson;[9] Lemstrom, Laine and Perttu;[10] Tseng;[11] Uitdenbogerd and Zobel;[12] Wiseman, Rusbridge and Griffin[13]).

Music information consists of seven facets:[14]

- *Pitch*: a quality of sound that is related to the frequency
- *Tempo*: information concerning the duration of a musical event
- *Harmony*: related to the attribute of music; a harmony occurs when two or more pitches sound at the same time
- *Timbre*: an attribute related to the tone, which brings about the aural distinction between a note played by two different instruments
- *Editing*: related to the performance instructions such as fingering, ornamentation, articulation, and so on
- *Text*: related to the lyrics, symphonies, and so on
- *Bibliography*: information about the composer, performer, title of the piece, publisher, and so on.

Downie[14] identifies two major types of music information retrieval systems:

- *analytic or production systems*, which are intended for musicologists, music theorists, music composers and music engravers; these systems focus on a number of facets of music
- *locating MIR systems*, which are concerned with access to musical works; in addition to the bibliographic keys, these retrieval systems use timbre and harmonic features of music.

Query-based music retrieval relies on similarity matching between the query and the stored music. Archives of MIDI (Musical Instrument Digital Interface) files, which are score-like representations of music, are used for music retrieval. Most music information retrieval systems, such as those provided by the search engines, use text-based retrieval techniques. For example, AltaVista music search allows users to search by the name of the artist, title of the song, and also by file types, such as MP3, WAV, Windows Media, Real or other file types. Some digital libraries provide access to digital music. One prominent example is the New Zealand Digital Library. Users can search for music in the New Zealand Digital Library that allows music information retrieval by particular notes and keyword and title. Users can search for particular notes and/or words that appear in the music document from the search page.

Music may be monophonic, when only one note sounds at a time, or polyphonic, when multiple notes sound at a time. Several researchers (see for example, Crawford, Iliopoulos and Raman;[15] Smith, McNab and Witten[16]) suggest that partial matching is the solution for music information retrieval. Specialized string matching techniques have been used by researchers (see for example, Downie and Nelson[17]) successfully for the retrieval of monophonic music. Sequential searching, though useful for monophonic music, is not suitable for polyphonic music. Research reported by Lee and Chen[18] on signature-based music information retrieval methods is promising.

Image retrieval

The use of images in human communication began long before modern civilization; paintings carved on the walls of caves and ancient architecture testify to that. The use of computers for processing images can be traced back to 1965 with Ivan Sutherland's Sketchpad project, which was not viable given the limited computing resources and high costs associated with them at that point in time.[19] However, image processing and retrieval activities began in the 1980s, and became an active area of research interest since the creation of the web in the early 1990s.

Areas of application

Image retrieval has many applications in the following major areas:

* crime prevention, in matching fingerprints, matching faces, scanning images from videos, for instance from closed circuit TV
* medicine and health, in analysing images of health and clinical data, such as x-rays, scanned images of various parts of the human body, and so on
* fashion design and graphic arts, for example experiments with various designs, and visual analysis and interpretation of different colours, design, and so on
* publishing and advertising
* engineering and architecture
* historical studies
* trademarks
* science, for instance astronomy, geography
* sports
* defence and military studies
* education and training
* entertainment.

Image retrieval queries

Image retrieval can be based on metadata (such as the creator, date or location), associated text including the human-assigned descriptors, or image characteristics like colour, texture, shape, and so on.

User queries about images may vary depending on the nature and need of the user as well as the nature and content of the image collections they are searching. Typical image queries may include the following:

* display illustrations that may or may not be described properly in words, for example, 'show me all the images of butterflies with a particular [described] texture of colour on the wings' or 'show me a picture of sunset on a golden

beach [of Malaysia, say] where the sky is appears to take a particular colour [golden, say]'

* display all the images of a particular characteristic, for example, 'show all the radiology images of patients with a particular [named] disease'
* display images that show an object from different angles, for example, the interior and exterior of a building or a car
* display an image where a particular event takes place, for example, 'the moment when a space ship is just about to take off' or 'all the pictures where the Queen addresses the British Parliament', or 'those images where Lord Buddha is preaching to his disciples'.

Videos contain images, audio and often some associated text. Hence typical queries about a video may be based on the images (as mentioned above) or a combination of the images and other cues, such as audio and/or text. Typical queries for a digital video collection may be:

* display images related to one section of a particular video, for example, 'show me the last lap of the race of the past few Grand Prix races' or 'show me images of all the free kicks taken by David Beckham in the 2002 World Cup'
* display images that have some particular audio characteristic, for example, 'show me all the images where Prime Minister Tony Blair speaks French' or 'show me all the images where the Secretary General of the UN addresses the Security Council'.

Early image retrieval systems

Institutions like libraries, archives and museums have long been used to handling images. They create catalogue records of images, which are used to provide access to the hard copies of images. Guidelines and tools for creating catalogue records of images have been developed over the years (and are discussed later in this chapter). The main access points for images are through the name of the creator(s), assigned theme or subject descriptors, keywords from abstract or summary, as well as medium, date, size, technical details, and so on.[20] Initial image retrieval systems followed the same principles – the retrieval was either through the common keys like author, or through keywords and descriptors associated with the images. Problems associated with these traditional approaches to image retrieval (as discussed by Enser[21] and Jain[22]) laid the way for improved mechanisms for access through automatically derived features of images, such as colour, texture, shape and content. These retrieval systems are broadly called content-based image retrieval (CBIR) systems.

Keyword-based approaches to image retrieval

Images can be described by associated metadata, such as the creator, location or date, or assigned keyword and descriptors. Standard information retrieval techniques can be used to retrieve images through these keys. However, creating (cataloguc) records for images is more complex than creating records for text documents. Image records should contain information about the creators (such as the artist or photographer, which are not always stated on the image object), and copyright, as well as about the standards and tools used for image capture, storage, and so on. Traditional indexing practices for image and video have been discussed by several researchers (see for example, Rasmussen,[23] Lancaster[24]).

Several tools have been built for assigning index terms to images. The most well-known is the Art and Architecture Thesaurus (AAT)[25] maintained by the Getty Information Institute. The thesaurus contains around 125,000 terms that may be used to describe art, architecture, decorative arts, material culture and archival materials.

Each concept (or record) in AAT is identified by a unique numeric ID and is linked to terms, related concepts, a parent (that is, a position in the hierarchy), sources for the data and notes. Terms for any concept can include the singular or plural form of the term, natural order, inverted order, spelling variants, various forms of speech and synonyms that have various etymological roots. One of the terms is flagged as the preferred term, or a descriptor. The terms are organized into the following seven facets, proceeding from abstract concepts to concrete, physical artefacts:[25]

1 *Associated concepts facet*, which includes abstract concepts and phenomena that relate to the study and execution of a wide range of human thought and activity, including art and architecture in all media. This facet also covers theoretical and critical concerns, ideologies, attitudes, and social or cultural movements.
2 *Physical attributes facet*, which includes the perceptible or measurable characteristics of materials and artefacts as well as features of materials and artefacts that are not separable as components. It includes characteristics such as size and shape, chemical properties of materials, qualities of texture and hardness, and features such as surface ornament and colour.
3 *Styles and periods facet*, which covers the commonly accepted terms for stylistic groupings and distinct chronological periods that are relevant to art, architecture and the decorative arts (such as *French, Louis XIV, Abstract, Expressionist*).
4 *Agents facet*, which contains terms for designations of people, groups of people and organizations, identified by occupation or activity, physical or mental characteristics, or social role or condition (such as *printmakers, landscape architects, corporations, religious orders*).
5 *Activities facet*, which encompasses areas of endeavour, physical and mental actions, discrete occurrences, systematic sequences of actions, methods employed toward a certain end, and processes occurring in materials or objects.
6 *Materials facet*, which deals with physical substances, ranging from specific materials to types of materials designed by their function, such as colorants, and from raw materials to those that have been formed or processed into products that are used in fabricating structures or objects (such as *iron, clay, adhesive, emulsifier, artificial ivory, millwork*).

7   *Objects facet*, which encompasses those discrete tangible or visible things that are inanimate and produced by human endeavour; in other words they are either fabricated or given form by human activity. These range, in physical form, from built works to images and written documents. They range in purpose from utilitarian to the aesthetic. Also included are landscape features that provide the context for the built environment (such as *paintings, amphorae, facades, cathedrals, Brewster chairs, gardens*).

Another tool for assigning subject headings to visual materials is the Thesaurus of Graphic Materials (TGM). TGM I (Thesaurus of Graphic Materials I: Subject Terms[26]) is a thesaurus of over 6,300 terms for indexing visual materials, as well as numerous cross references. TGM I is a companion document of TGM II, a thesaurus of more than 600 terms developed by the Library of Congress Prints and Photographs Division with input from other archival image repositories.[27]

A similar tool for organizing graphic materials is Iconclass,[28] a classification system for iconographic research and the documentation of images. It was developed by Henri van de Waal (1910–72), Professor of Art History at the University of Leiden, and completed by his staff. It is a collection of definitions of objects, persons, events, situations and abstract ideas that can be the subject of an image. Iconclass organizes iconography into ten 'main divisions':

0   Abstract, Non-representational Art
1   Religion and Magic
2   Nature
3   Human Being, Man in general
4   Society, Civilization, Culture
5   Abstract Ideas and Concepts
6   History
7   Bible
8   Literature
9   Classical Mythology and Ancient History.

Of the ten 'main divisions', the divisions 1 to 5 encompass 'general' topics, designed to comprise all the principal aspects of what can be represented. Divisions 6 to 9 accommodate 'special' topics, coherent subject matter of a narrative nature, with an emphasis on the Bible (7) and classical mythology (9). A tenth division, represented by the number 0, was added in 1996 at the request of Iconclass users, to accommodate abstract art. The Iconclass website is now maintained by the Royal Netherlands Academy of Arts and Sciences.

Image retrieval systems

Several commercial image data management systems now store image and video documents in multimedia database management systems. Such systems use retrieval based on metadata and text keywords or assigned descriptors. Some such systems are:

- iBase (**http://www.ibase.com/**), a system that allows data from various different museum systems to be integrated into one central resource
- Index+ (**http://www.ssl.co.uk/indexx/indexx.html**), a software toolkit for creating systems to manage structured and unstructured text, data, still and moving images, sound and video
- Digital Catalogue (**http://www.imageres.com/**)
- Fastfoto (**http://www.picdar.co.uk/Home.mom**), a company dealing with digital asset management (DAM) and web content management (WCM) systems
- FotoWare (**http://www.fotoware.com**), a company that produces digital asset management (DAM) systems ranging from small single user image archives, to enterprise archiving and production solutions
- Signpost (**http://www.signpost.com**), a multimedia services agency that provides various services including design of websites, multimedia libraries, and so on.

Search engines such as Google allow users to search for images by using keywords. In the image search screen of Google users can enter search keywords, and select and click on the thumbnail version of the picture displayed as a result of a text search. The final result displays a larger version of the image, as well as the page on which the original image is located. Addressing the difficulties of assigning appropriate keywords to the images, the Google website (**http://www.google.co.uk/help/faq_images.html**) states that it analyses 'the text on the page adjacent to the image, the image caption and dozens of other factors to determine the image content'.

Several other search engines also provide text-based image search facilities, for instance, the Yahoo Picture Gallery (**http://gallery.yahoo.com/**), Lycos Multimedia Search (**http://multimedia.lycos.com/**), and HotBot advanced search (**http://www.hotbot.com/adv.asp?prov=Inktomi&tab=web**).

Content-based image retrieval

The process of describing images by human indexers is an expensive and time-consuming process, and yet is highly subjective. Moreover, such processes cannot retrieve images based on their visual characteristics. In addition to the basic metadata attached to each object, images may have a number of attributes that can be used for retrieval:[19]

- a combination of colour, texture, shape, and so on
- a specific arrangement of objects in the image
- depiction of a particular event
- presence of one or more persons or objects
- presence of a specific location
- emotions attached to an event or a person, and so on.

All these attributes can be used in what are known as content-based image retrieval (CBIR) systems. CBIR is a technique for retrieving images on the basis of image characteristics such as colour, texture and shape. However, different levels of abstraction are associated with each type of image attribute. Researchers have proposed different groups or types of image retrieval based on the level of these abstractions. Gudivada and Raghavan[29] classify the queries into two major groups: syntactic or textual image retrieval and semantic image retrieval.

Eakins [30–32] proposes three levels of complexity of query types:

- Level 1 comprises retrieval through primitive features such as colour, texture, shape or the spatial features of the images.
- Level 2 comprises retrieval of the derived or logical features of images, for example retrieval of objects of a given type of object or person.
- Level 3 comprises retrieval of images based on their abstract attributes, such as the depiction of specific activity: an emotion, a matter of special significance, and so on.

Challenges of CBIR

Content-based image retrieval systems need to focus on a number of issues, such as:[19]

- understanding the users' information needs and information-seeking behaviour
- finding effective ways of describing image contents
- finding mechanisms for automatic shot and scene detection from digital video
- extracting the desired features from the images
- developing efficient storage mechanisms for large image and video databases
- matching the queries and image or video databases for similarity matching
- finding ways of combining images, audio and text for retrieval from digital video
- developing efficient methods for accessing images or keyframes in a video collection
- building suitable interfaces for user queries and display of output from an image or a video collection.

CBIR techniques

CBIR systems use some sort of similarity matching between the query (the sample image) and the stored objects (images). There are three major issues related to the design of image query languages:

- the interface that determines how the user enters a query
- the search parameters that can be specified by the users
- the matching criteria that will retrieve and rank the output.

Two different types of interface are usually used for querying multimedia objects:[32]

- *Browsing and navigation interface*: Here the user is allowed to browse a collection and navigate through a structured collection of images in order to retrieve the desired image(s).

- *Query interface*: In most cases a query by example approach is followed whereby the user can specify an image from a collection, which is used as a query to search the multimedia database. The problem of this approach is that the system should have a selection of sample objects, with associated attributes, which can be used for querying the database. Some interfaces offer options for selection from a palette or sketch input.

Similarity between a query image and the image objects in a collection is computed and images that fully or partially match the query are retrieved. In a collection of N objects (i.e., $O_1, O_2, O_3 \ldots O_n$), and a query object Q, we want to find those objects that are within a tolerance distance limit of ε from Q. In a whole match the query and the objects are of same type, e.g., 512 x 512 greyscale images; whereas in a partial match, the objects and the query may be different, e.g., the objects may be 512 x 512 greyscale images (such as medical x-rays) and the query may be a 16 x 16 subpattern (such as the typical x-ray of a tumour).[33]

A colour histogram is computed for each image, which shows the proportion of pixels of each colour within the image. The colour histogram for each image is stored in the database, which is searched with the histogram of a sample image that the user chooses to formulate the query. The system retrieves those images whose colour histograms match closely with those of the query. The histogram intersection matching technique developed by Swain and Ballard[34] or its variants (for example, Stricker and Orengo,[35] Stricker and Dimai[36]) are used for retrieval.

Measures of image texture can be represented by the degree of contrast, coarseness, directionality and regularity. Texture queries can be formulated by selecting examples of desired textures from a palette, or by selecting a query image from a sample set. The retrieval is based on similarity measures between the query and stored objects. The retrieval system aims to calculate the relative brightness of selected pairs of pixels from the query and the stored images.

For retrieval of images by shape a number of features related to the shape of objects are computed and stored in the database. The same set of features are computed for the query and objects are retrieved based on the similarity of features. Two main categories of features are used: global features such as aspect ratio, circularity and moment invariants; and local features such as the sets of consecutive boundary segments.[19]

In addition to colour, shape and texture, other characteristics, such as the spatial features (location of an object within an image, say) or retrieval by appearance (for example matching a section of an image) have been used in CBIR.

Video retrieval

Although many of the image retrieval techniques are used in video retrieval, the process is more complex. Videos are usually made up of a number of distinct scenes each of which can be further broken down to individual shots depicting a single view, conversation or action. At first a video is divided into individual scenes, and from each scene a single representative keyframe is selected. All the keyframes are stored in a storyboard, which can be browsed or searched through query by example (sometimes called query by motion example).

Content-based video retrieval may involve text retrieval techniques combined with content-based image retrieval techniques. Content-based indexing of video may involve histogram matching for retrieval based on colour, or texture analysis, image segmentation and pattern recognition. Matching scenes sequentially in a video is very time-consuming, hence various non-sequential browsing techniques are used.

Video retrieval systems are still at an early stage of research and development. Video Mail Retrieval system uses novel techniques for processing video mail messages. Informedia (discussed below) is another good example of content-based video retrieval system.

CBIR systems

A number of software and tools have been developed of digital images and video-for CBIR. Some are available commercially, but most CBIR software was developed as research projects. The following are some examples:

- QBIC (**http://wwwqbic.almaden.ibm.com/**): from IBM, allows users to search large image databases based on visual image content – properties such as colour percentages, colour layout, and textures occurring in the images. Users can combine content-based queries with keywords in order to get powerful retrieval methods for image and multimedia databases.
- Virage (**http://www.virage.com/about/fact_sheet/**): a company based in California, produces video and media communication software. The software allows users to digitize, manage, retrieve and distribute video and other rich media assets.
- Excalibur Visual RetrievalWare (**http://www.aa-lab.cs.uu.nl/cbirsurvey/ cbir-survey/node15.html**): developed by Excalibur Technologies, this is a software developer's kit for building applications for manipulating digital image files and their visual content.
- Informedia (**http://www.informedia.cs.cmu.edu/**): one of the pioneering research systems in content-based digital video retrieval. It originated as a digital library research project, in the first phase of the US Digital Library Initiative, at Carnegie-Melon University in the USA. Informedia-I developed a technology that combines speech, image and natural language understanding to transcribe, segment and index linear video automatically for intelligent search and image retrieval. The second phase of the project, called Informedia-II, seeks to improve the dynamic extraction, summarization, visualization, and presentation of distributed video. It also aims to produce automatically 'collages' and 'auto-documentaries' that summarize documents from text, images, audio and video into one single abstraction.
- VisualSEEK (**http://www.ctr.columbia.edu/VisualSEEk/**): created at the Image and ATV Lab of Columbia University, this is a web tool for searching

for images and videos using visual features.

- Chabot: initiated at the University of California as a project, this is a large image retrieval system that uses content-based image retrieval techniques.[37]
- Photobook (**http://web.media.mit.edu/~tpminka/photobook/**): free software for performing queries on image databases based on image content. It works by comparing features associated with images, such as colour, texture and shape.
- Blobworld (**http://www.aa-lab.cs.uu.nl/cbirsurvey/cbir-survey/node9. html**): a CBIR developed at UC, Berkeley, which allows querying images by colour, texture, location and shape of regions (blobs) and of the background.
- MARS: (**http://citeseer.nj.nec.com/rui97contentbased.html**), a content-based image retrieval system with relevance feedback features.
- Netra (**http://vision.ece.ucsb.edu/netra/**): a prototype image retrieval system that uses colour, texture, shape and spatial location information in segmented image regions to search and retrieve similar regions from the image database.

Some search engines also provide facilities for CBIR, a prominent example being the AltaVista Photo Finder (**http://uk.altavista.com/image/default**).

In addition to the Informedia project, mentioned above, many digital libraries provide access to image resources. The British Library provides access to still images. The UC Berkeley DL allows for image retrieval by image content. DIG-ILIB at the University of Queensland, Australia, also provides access to architectural images. SETIS (Scholarly Electronic Text and Image Service) at the University of Sydney, Australia, provides access to images. New Zealand Digital Library provides access to various image databases.

Standards

A number of standards related to multimedia file formats, information retrieval, markup languages, and metadata description are important for successful multimedia information retrieval. Among these MPEG standards are particularly relevant for multimedia retrieval.

Established in 1988, Moving Picture Experts Group (MPEG) is a working group of ISO/IEC in charge of the development of standards for coded representation of digital audio and video. So far the group has produced several standards, such as:

- MPEG-1 (coding of moving pictures and associated audio for digital storage media at up to about 1.5 MBit/s), the standard on which such products as Video CD and MP3 are based
- MPEG-2 (generic coding of moving pictures and associated audio information), the standard on which products such as digital television set top boxes and DVD are based
- MPEG-4, providing standardized technological elements enabling the integration of the production, distribution and content access paradigms of digital television, interactive graphics applications (synthetic content) and interactive multimedia (world wide web, distribution of and access to content)

- MPEG-7 (Multimedia Content Description Interface), the standard for description and searching of audio and visual content. It is a standard for describing the multimedia content data that supports some degree of interpretation of the information's meaning, which can be passed on to, or accessed by, a device or a computer code for further processing.

Work on the new standard MPEG-21 'Multimedia Framework' started in June 2000 and a technical report and two standards have been produced and three more parts of the standard are at different stages of development (**http://mpeg.telecomitalialab. com/**).

Summary

Multimedia information retrieval has a tremendous potential in different areas. However, multimedia information retrieval, especially content-based retrieval, is a very complex area, and compared with the history of text retrieval, multimedia information retrieval is relatively new. Most current research in this area is concerned with:

- images and audio retrieval – indexing using visual and/or audio features
- speech and music information retrieval, where research is progressing and retrieval systems that are currently available work well up to a certain level of complexity, but further research is needed
- video retrieval – a very complex area since it involves processing a huge volume of audio, speech, natural language and moving images.

Many multimedia retrieval systems are available but most of them are research prototypes. Nevertheless, users can now search for audio and images through many web search engines and digital libraries.

References

1   Dunlop, M. D. and van Rijsbergen, C. J., 'Hypermedia and free text retrieval', *Information processing and management*, **29** (3), 1993, 287–98.
2   Bertino, E., Catania, B. and Ferrari, C., 'Multimedia IR: models and languages'. In: Baeza-Yates, R. and Ribeiro-Neto, B., *Modern information retrieval*, New York, ACM, 1999, 325–43.
3   Foote, J., 'An overview of audio information retrieval', *Multimedia systems*, **7**, 1999, 2–10.
4   Olivetti: Video Mail Retrieval Using Voice. Available at **http://svr-www.eng. cam.ac.uk/research/Projects/vmr/vmr.html**.
5   Kassler, M., 'Toward musical information retrieval', *Perspectives of new music*, **4** (2), 1966, 59–67.
6   Kassler, M., 'MIR – a simple programming language for musical information retrieval'. In: Lincoln, H. B. (ed.), *The computer and music*, Ithaca, NY, Cornell University Press, 1970, 299–327.

7 Byrd, D. and Crawford, T., 'Problems of music information retrieval in the real world', *Information processing and management*, **38** (2), 2002, 249–72.

8 Bainbridge, D., Nevill-Manning, C., Witten, I., Smith, L. and McNab, R., 'Towards a digital library of popular music'. In: *Proceedings of Digital Libraries '99 Conference*, New York, ACM, 1999.

9 Downie, J. S. and Nelson, M., 'Evaluation of a simple and effective music information retrieval system'. In *Proceedings of ACM SIGIR Conference on Research and Development in Information Retrieval*, New York, ACM, 2000.

10 Lemstrom, K., Laine, P. and Perttu, S., 'Using relative interval slope in music information retrieval'. In: *Proceedings of the 1999 International Computer Music Conference*, 1999, 317–20.

11 Tseng, Y. H., 'Content-based retrieval for music collections'. In: *Proceedings of ACM SIGIR Conference on Research and Development in Information Retrieval*, New York, ACM, 1999.

12 Uitdenbogerd, A. L. and Zobel, J., 'Manipulation of music for melody matching'. In: *Proceedings of ACM International Conference on Multimedia*, New York, ACM, 1998, 235–40.

13 Wiseman, N., Rusbridge, C. and Griffin, S., 'The Joint NSF/JISC International Digital Libraries Initiative', *D-Lib magazine*, **5** (6), 1999. Available at **http://www.dlib.org/dlib/june99/06wiseman.html**.

14 Downie, J. S., 'Music information retrieval'. In: Cronin, B. (ed.) *Annual review of information science and technology*, **37**, Medford, NJ, Information Today, 2002, 295–340.

15 Crawford, T., Iliopoulos, C. and Raman, R., 'String-matching techniques for musical similarity and melodic recognition'. In Hewlett, W. and Selfridge-Field, E. (eds), 'Melodic similarity: concepts, procedures, and applications', *Computing in musicology*, **11**, Cambridge, MA, MIT Press, 1998, 73–100.

16 Smith, L., McNab, R. and Witten, I., Sequence-based melodic comparison: a dynamic programming approach. In: In Hewlett, W. and Selfridge-Field, E. (eds), 'Melodic similarity: concepts, procedures, and applications, *Computing in musicology*, **11**, Cambridge, MA, MIT Press, 1998, 101–17.

17 Downie, J. S. and Nelson, M., 'Evaluation of a simple and effective music information retrieval system'. In: *Proceedings of ACM SIGIR Conference on Research and Development in Information Retrieval*, New York, ACM, 2000.

18 Lee, W. and Chen, A. L. P., 'Efficient multi-feature index structures for music data retrieval'. In: *Proceedings of SPIE conference on storage and retrieval for image and video database*, 2000, 177–88.

19 Eakins, J. P. and Graham, M. E., *Content-based image retrieval: a report to the JISC technology applications programme*, 1999. Available at **http://www.unn.ac.uk/iidr/report.html**.

20 Burke, M. A., *Organization of multimedia resources: principles and practices of information retrieval*, Gower, 1999.

21 Enser, P. G. B., 'Pictorial information retrieval', *Journal of documentation*, **51** (2), 1995, 126–70.

22 Jain, R., 'World-wide maze', *IEEE multimedia*, **2** (3), 1995, 3.

23   Rasmussen, E., 'Libraries and bibliographic systems'. In: Baeza-Yates, R. and Ribeiro-Neto, B., *Modern information retrieval*, ACM Press, 1999, 397–413.

24   Lancaster, F. W., *Indexing and abstracting in theory and practice*, 3rd edn, London, Facet Publishing, 2003.

25   *Art and Architecture thesaurus online*, 2000. Available at **http://www.getty. edu/research/tools/vocabulary/aat/**.

26   *Thesaurus of graphic materials I: subject terms*, 1995, Prints and Photographs Division, Library of Congress. Available at **http://www.loc.gov/rr/print/tgm1/**.

27   *Thesaurus for graphic materials II: genre and physical characteristic terms*, 1995, Prints and Photographs Division, Library of Congress. Available at **http://lcweb.loc.gov/rr/print/tgm2/**.

28   Huisstede, Peter van, *A context for the Iconclass system*, 1995. Available at **http://www.iconclass.nl/**.

29   Gudivada, V. N. and Raghavan, V. V., 'Design and evaluation of algorithms for image retrieval by spatial similarity', *ACM transactions on information systems*, **13** (2), 1995, 115–44.

30   Eakins, J. P., 'Design criteria for a shape retrieval system', *Computers in industry*, **21**, 1996, 167–84.

31   Eakins, J. P., 'Automatic image content retrieval – are we getting anywhere?', *Proceedings of Third International Conference on Electronic Library and Visual Information Research (ELVIRA3)*, De Montfort University, Milton Keynes, 1996, 123–35.

32   Eakins, J. P., 'Techniques for image retrieval', *Library and Information Briefings*, **85**, South Bank University, October 1998.

33   Faloutsos, C., 'Multimedia IR: indexing and searching'. In: Baeza-Yates, R. and Ribeiro-Neto, B., *Modern Information retrieval*, New York, ACM, 1999, 345–65.

34   Swain, M. J. and Ballard, D. H., 'Color indexing', *International journal of computer vision*, **7** (1), 1991, 11–32.

35   Stricker, M. and Orengo, M., 'Similarity of color images'. In: Niblack, W. R. and Jain, R. C. (eds), *Storage and retrieval for image and video databases III*, Proc SPIE 2420, 1995, 381–92.

36   Stricker, M. and Dimai, A., 'Color indexing with weak spatial constraints'. In: Sethi, I. K. and Jain, R. C. (eds), *Storage and retrieval for image and video databases IV*, Proc SPIE 2670, 1996, 29–40.

37   Ogle, V. E. and Stonebraker, M., 'Chabot: retrieval from a relational database of images', *IEEE computer*, **28** (9), 1995, 40–8.

Chapter 17

Hypertext and markup languages

Introduction

Conventional documents – books, articles, reports, and so on – whether available in printed form or on computer, prepared with the use of word-processing software, say, are all linear in their presentation. These documents are prepared with the expectation that users start reading from the beginning, from page one or section one, and proceed from there to the end. Users are not usually expected to jump from one part of the document to the other; even if a reader does so, there is no mechanism to do this systematically; moreover, the user may find it very difficult to come back to the place he or she started from. Let's imagine a situation where a person reads a book or an article and comes across a new term that might have been defined elsewhere in the same document or has been taken from another document that has been referred to. In this case, the user wishing to know more about the term (its definition or connotations) has two options before proceeding further:

- to go on searching for the term in the same document, or to jump to the appropriate page or section if it is mentioned
- to get hold of the other document which has been referred to, browse through it till the term is found and the required information about the term is obtained.

In either situation, the user may be referred to one or more places in the same or different document(s) for further information about the term (its origin, application, and so on). If the inquisitive user wants to follow any of the above steps in order to get more information about the term before proceeding further, quite soon he or she will lose track of the path that has been traversed, and will be lost in the 'jungle of information'. However, the situation is quite common in our everyday life.

The problems mentioned above occur due to the linear structure of documents, which does not allow users to navigate freely through different parts of the same or different documents. A non-linear documents/text structure allows the user to jump from one place in the text to another: this non-linear arrangement of textual material is called hypertext, where the term *hyper* means 'extension into other dimensions' converting *text* into a 'multidimensional space'.[1]

Hypertext

The history of hypertext

Since the mid-1980s, there has been an explosion in interest in hypertext, along with the development of a large number of hypertext systems. Indeed, within a span of ten years or so hypertext (and hypermedia) has brought tremendous changes in the handling and dissemination of information. However, the concept of hypertext has not been with us for much longer than 15 years.

Memex

The origin of the basic concept of hypertext and hypermedia goes back more than 50 years. In 1945 Vannevar Bush proposed a non-linear structuring of text that would correspond to the associative nature of the human mind. Although he did not use the term 'hypertext', he described a machine, which he referred to as 'Memex', that could be used to browse and make notes in a voluminous online text and graphics system.[2] Memex would contain a large library of documents, photographs, and sketches. The idea was that Memex would have several screens and a facility for establishing a labelled link between any two points (or nodes) in the library.

At the time of its conception, Memex could not be built, although Bush speculated on how microfiche and technologies of the 1940s could be adapted to the task of constructing such a machine. Today, it is well recognized that hypertext and the modern computer can be used to implement many of the functionalities of Bush's Memex.[2]

NLS

In 1963, while working at the Stanford Research Institute, Englebart was influenced by the idea of Bush's Memex. His ideas eventually resulted in a system called NLS (oN Line System).[2] This was an early hypertext system consisting of files that were organized into segments of 3000 words or fewer that could be linked both hierarchically and non-hierarchically. NLS has since evolved into a hypertext system known as Augment.[2] The Augment system is available commercially and is distributed by the McDonnell Douglas Company.[3]

Xanadu

The term hypertext was coined by Ted Nelson in 1965. Nelson's version of the hypertext concept was more expansive in some senses than that of Engelbart, emphasizing the creation of a unified literary environment on a global scale. The long-term plan of the Xanadu project, Nelson's brainchild, was to place the world's literary sources online and to use hypertext to link them in a way that would facilitate their use. Much of the work of the Xanadu project has been concerned with efficient methods of storing segments of text shared by different documents. Nelson envisaged that Xanadu would permit:[3]

- the allocation of credit for authorship and publishing
- the allocation of payment of royalties based upon readers' use of documents, and
- quotability of any documents with easy tracing to the source of quotations by means of hypertext links.

In 1988, the Xanadu project was taken over by a large software development company, Autodesk.[2]

The intermedia system

Brown University in the US was one of the first organizations to use hypertext for instructional purposes. One of the most notable outcomes of the research of the Institute for Research Scholarship at the university was the development of the intermedia system, an authoring tool that would support the design and development of multimedia and hypermedia documents that were capable of incorporating text, line diagrams, and video disc segments.[3] The system was designed for use by instructors to organize and present materials to students, and by students to prepare reports.

The Knowledge Management System (KMS)

Another significant contributor to the development of hypertext systems was the Carnegie-Mellon University in the US. One of the most significant outcomes of the research team there, known as the ZOG group, was the development of the KMS authoring tool, which is now commercially available.[3]

The NoteCards system

One of the best-known early authoring tools for hypertext development was the NoteCards system devised by Xerox PARC in the US.[3] The NoteCards system provides the user with a network of electronic notecards (the electronic version of 3 x 5 in. notecards), each of which can embed textual or graphical data that can be edited, interconnected by typed links. Thus, the system provides a structure for organizing, storing, and retrieving information with additional facilities for displaying, modifying, manipulating, and navigating through the information networks created by the user.[4]

Hypertext: definition and meaning

In its literal sense, the term hypertext implies extra dimensions to text. In practice, the term is often used to describe a computer program that allows a person to browse a document by deliberately jumping from text block to text block.[5] According to Parsaye et al.,[2] hypertext is a tool for building and using associative structures. While a normal document is linear and is usually read from beginning to end, the reading of hypertext is open-ended: one can jump from one point to another as desired. The nearest thing to a hypertext that most people are familiar with is a thesaurus. It too is not normally read from beginning to end. Each time a thesaurus is consulted, it is entered at a different location based on the word used to initiate the search, and once the sought term is located, there are pointers that lead the user to other parts of the thesaurus to get more information on the terms related to the sought term. Hypertext can be thought of as an enriched thesaurus where, instead of links between words, links between documents and text fragments are available.[2]

According to Barker,[3] the terms hypertext and hypermedia were first introduced by Theodore Nelson, who defined hypertext as being 'computer supported non-sequential writing'.

Hypertext can simply be defined, according to Parsaye et al.,[2] as the creation and representation of links between discrete pieces of data. Thus, any automated retrieval system that enables users to access quantities of text may be called a hypertext system if its components include a database structure in the form of a network and a retrieval mechanism that is navigational and browsing-based.[2, 3]

According to Lucarella and Zanzi:[6]

> Hypertext can simply be defined as a system to manage a collection of information that can be accessed non-sequentially. It consists of a network of nodes and logical links between nodes. The variety of nodes and links that can be defined make hypertext a very flexible structure in which information is provided both by what is stored in each node and by the way the information nodes are linked to each other.

Components of hypertext

Hypertext retrieval systems are the products of an emerging technology that specifies an alternative approach to the retrieval of information from machine-readable full-text documents.

Hypertext systems provide the facility for any relationship existing between two document representations, or nodes, to be represented by a link. Searches are able to retrieve individual nodes successively by activating the links between them. Such links may be created by manual or automatic means.

A document retrieval system may be identified as a hypertext system if its components include the following:[7]

* a structural component, consisting of a database of document representations in which the relationships between documents are explicitly represented, such that the document representations and relationships between them together form a network structure
* a functional component consisting of a *retrieval mechanism* of a type that is,

    — *navigational*, i.e. it allows users to make particular decisions at each stage of the retrieval process as to the object(s) that should be retrieved next
    — *browsing-based*, i.e. it allows users to search for information without their having to specify a definite target.

Although, theoretically speaking, hypertext could be developed without a computer, with a number of documents and references organized around a concept, hypertext reaches its maximum potential when implemented in a computer system, since the computer provides the user with the possibility of moving through a tremendous number of texts, from one topic to another, rapidly and with flexibility. Such movements are accomplished through what is called in hypertext terminology navigation tools, and the memory areas are referred to as labels, nodes or markers.[1]

The use of the word node is derived from an approach to information management in which data are stored in a network of nodes interconnected through common relational space using software specifically designed for a network.

In a hypertext system objects in a database, called *nodes*, are connected to one another by machine-supported *links*. Users can follow these from node to node in order to access the information they contain.[8]

Normally texts may be displayed in a *window* on a computer screen. Such a window can be moved, resized, closed and stored as a window icon. The contents of a node may be scrolled behind the window. Windows can contain any number of *link icons* (also called *targets* or *buttons*). These are words or phrases, usually highlighted, which represent pointers to other nodes in the database. Clicking on the icon with the mouse activates the link and causes the system to open a new window to display the selected node. Users can create new nodes and add new links.

Hypertext systems can be accessed in any one of the following three ways:

- by selecting link icons and following the links from node to node
- by searching the database for some keyword in the normal way
- by *navigating* the database using a browser that displays the network as a *graph*. The sequence of nodes that the user has accessed forms a *path*.

Hypertext reference model

In 1988, with a view to avoiding the inconsistencies of the different approaches to the development of hypertext systems, a workshop was organized at the Dexter Inn in New Hampshire, to achieve a consensus on basic hypertext systems. The workshop came up with a model, called the Dexter hypertext reference model,[9] which provides a set of standard terminology with a formal model of the important abstractions found in a wide range of hypertext systems.[9]

The Dexter model divides a hypertext into three layers:

- the *run-time* layer, which controls the user interface
- the *storage* layer, which is a database containing a network of nodes connected by links
- the *within-component* layer, which is the content structure inside the node.

The main focus of the model has been laid on the storage layer, which consists of a set of components. The interface between the storage and the runtime layers includes the *presentation specification*, which determines how the components are presented at runtime. For example, these specifications might include information on screen location and size of the window. The within-component layer corresponds to individual applications; its interface to the storage layer is via *anchors* which consist of an *identifier*, which can be referred to by *links*, and a *value* that picks out the anchored part of the material. The runtime layer is responsible for handling links, anchors and components at runtime.

Hypermedia systems

Both hypertext and hypermedia systems provide a way of representing and managing information in a flexible non-linear way that is appropriate for many multimedia applications.[4] Hypermedia can simply be defined as the creation and representation of links between discrete pieces of different kinds of data – text, numbers, graphics and/or sound. In other words, in a hypermedia system a node may contain text, graphics, animation, images or sound that can be controlled, presented and edited on a computer.

Arnets and Bogaerts[10] define hypermedia as follows:

- the hyper-representation of textual and non-textual information
- a style of building systems for information representation and management around a network of multimedia nodes connected together by typed links
- a generic approach to constructing non-linear computer-supported materials
- the flexible linking together of similar or different types of information.

The hallmark of any hypermedia system is its capability to link together related forms of information, in a flexible and easily adaptable manner.

There are four ways of working with hypermedia systems:[10]

- hypermedia as a system
- hypermedia as an interface
- hypermedia as an environment
- the dream of Xanadu.

The first three ways of working with hypermedia technology correspond to the use of a computer system as an integrated system, an integrated interface or an integrated environment. In the first case, a single user uses a hypermedia program to obtain multiple views on a very specific type of information. In the second case, multiple users use hypermedia techniques to obtain multiple views on single form of information. In the third case, a single user uses hypermedia technology and principles to obtain a single coherent view on different types of information. The fourth way of working with hypermedia, where one system offers multiple users simultaneous access to all sorts of different information, under a variety of different views, is the vision we find embodied in Ted Nelson's dream of the Xanadu system.

Open hypertext and hypermedia systems

This is a major issue for hypertext research. We have already noted that hypertext provides links among concepts and documents. This facility can be used, in conjunction with *groupware* technology, to create texts with input from different authors at different places or at different points in time. Groupware is software that helps people directly communicate with one another.[11] Groupware and hypertext complement one another in developing what is known as *grouptext*, or *open hypertext*, which allows a group of people to create and access linked text with a provision for communicating directly with one another. The first grouptext computer system was the *augmentation system* of the 1960s.[11] From the 1990s, the concept of the grouptext or open hypertext system is of central importance to researchers: these systems combine simultaneous video, audio and text, and provide decision support.[11, 12]

Some of the major features of grouptext or open hypertext systems are that they:[12]

- are used simultaneously by heterogeneous users, for example members of a research unit, with different read/write permissions and private spaces
- grow steadily in size and interconnectability
- combine different hypertext applications derived from the same hypertext model
- allow access to, and the integration of, external information resources, such as e-mail, online databanks, text and image processing, or any such applications available on the host operating system
- make possible different user-specific views of the global hypertext base.

The opening of hypertext to an arbitrary number of users, to many different applications and to the use of external information sources such as online retrieval systems, has had a tremendous impact on the use and administration of hypertext systems. The major problems that may arise may be characterized as follows:[12]

- the quantity and diversity of information may intensify the disorientation problems already known from conventional hypertext problems
- one standardized interaction strategy for browsing and exploration may not be sufficient for all applications that are to be supported by the hypertext
- some applications need access to structured data, e.g. the address of a person
- new applications need not be permanently integrated in both a semantically controlled and efficient way
- external information sources often do not present their data in ways in which the hypertext applications are designed to handle. Therefore, transformation processes have to take place that are specific to the type and source of information.

Rada et al.[11] have reported a collaborative hypertext system called MUCH (Many

Using and Creating Hypertext). The system was developed at George Washington University and Liverpool University to support collaborative creation and access of semantic nets connected with text blocks. The MUCH system emphasizes connections among concepts and provides opportunities for people to get overviews. The 1991 version of the system was developed on networks of graphic workstations; an extensible editor and window manager constituted the front end, while a relational database management system served as the back end.[11] The system has since been developed to a hypermedia system.

Hammwohner and Kuhlen[12] have described the design of an open hypertext system, called the Konstanz hypertext system (KHS), developed in the Department of Information Science at the University of Konstanz in Germany. The authors report that typed hypertext objects provide the integrating factor, giving special support for different applications within a uniform interaction environment. The KHS research has shown how an elaborate application – supplying more functionality than the standard software – can be integrated into this framework easily. KHS is written in Smalltalk-80 (an object-oriented programming language) and developed on UNIX machines.

The hypermedia extension of existing systems is the field of open hypermedia.[13] The basic idea is to let people to integrate existing applications into hypermedia systems. The classic open hypermedia systems, according to Bouvin[13] are Microcosm, Devise Hypermedia, Hyperdisco, HOSS and Chimera. However, Ggiven the success of the web, there is a doubt whether there is room for further research in open hypertext and hypermedia research. Bouvin[13] argues that this is perhaps the best time to do further research on open hypermedia, since the developments of the web technology have brought many facilities that were not available to the information retrieval researchers before, for instance:

• the availability of standard file formats and protocols
• the availability and use of a limited number of web browsers
• uniform global naming scheme for web resources, and so on
• the huge size and speed of the web in terms of content as well as users, which makes hypermedia application developments more interesting.

Bouvin[13] reviews the work done by the open hypermedia community with special regard to the web.

Hypertext and information retrieval

In text retrieval systems, the relative autonomy of text nodes is emphasized with a system that provides sophisticated techniques for retrieving nodes as answers to user queries. Conversely, in hypertext systems, the semantic link structure is central, with the system providing sophisticated tools for graph traversal and node representation. The former approach emphasizes searching while the latter emphasizes browsing.[6]

The interaction of hypertext and text retrieval systems have brought tremendous developments in the creation and distribution of, and access to, text and multimedia information in a number of ways. Large electronic documents appearing online or on CD-ROMs, for example, dictionaries and encyclopedias, manuals, online help files and databases, are now available in hypertext format, thus making it possible to use the resources in browse as well as search modes. The most obvious application of the hypertext technology has been in the field of the world wide web. Creation of hypertext documents has become easy with the development of the hypertext markup language (HTML), which allows creation of links between text or multimedia elements within a document, or with other documents in the context of the world wide web.

Markup languages

Markup languages help us mark the specific sections of the items with standard codes, which can be interpreted by computer programs in order to take specific measures, for example to take measures for appropriate appearance of the encoded text (in bold or colour, say), or to extract a specific portion of the item, say the title, keywords or abstract, in order to store it in a database for further processing. Several markup languages have been developed to serve different purposes. In this chapter we shall briefly discuss SGML (Standard Generalized Markup Language), HTML (HyperText Markup Language, the language of the world wide web), XML (eXtensible Markup Language) and XHTML (eXtensible HyperText Markup Language).

SGML

SGML was accepted as a standard in 1986 (ISO 8879:1986[14]). This standard was created to provide a set of rules that describe the structure of an electronic document so that it may be interchanged across various computer platforms. SGML also allows users to:

* link files together to form composite documents
* identify where illustrations are to be incorporated into text files
* create different versions of a document in a single file
* add editorial comments to a file
* provide information to supporting programs.

To allow the computer to do as much of the work as possible, SGML requires users to provide a model of the document being produced. This model, called a *document type definition* (DTD), describes each element of the document and formally identifies the relationships between the various elements in the document.

SGML defines data in terms of elements and attributes. A particular unit of an item, such as the title, abstract or section heading, is considered an element. An attribute gives particular information about an element. SGML proposes the use of tags and delimiters to markup elements. For example, the author of a text may be marked as <author>Gobinda G. Chowdhury </author>. In this example, the author name is marked by the tag author; the element between the pair of tags (here author) denotes the content (in this case, the author's name); and the end of an element is denoted by the tag name preceded by a '/'. SGML provides an extensive list of tags and supports many variations. An SGML document consists of three parts:[15]

- the SGML declaration defining the document character set, name lengths for elements, and other basic parameters
- the document type definition (DTD)
- the document instance, i.e., the actual document.

SGML has been used widely in the publishing community and given rise to several applications, especially the TEI (Text Encoding Initiative), EAD (Encoded Archival Description) and XML (eXtensible Markup Language).[15]

HTML

Although SGML provides an extensive mechanism for marking electronic documents, it has some problems. The process of marking up a text is complex and resource-intensive. A simpler markup language called HTML has been developed especially for preparing web documents. It contains a set of markup symbols or codes that are inserted in a file intended for display on a browser page. The HTML markup tells the web browser how to display a web page's content – text, image, and so on – for the user. Each individual markup code is referred to as an element (a tag). Some elements come in pairs that indicate when a display effect is to begin and when it is to end. HTML is a formal recommendation by the World Wide Web Consortium (W3C) and is generally adhered to by the major browsers, Microsoft's Internet Explorer and Netscape's Navigator. Information about HTML activities including the specifications and guidelines for use are available at the W3C web page.[16]

As in SGML, an HTML tag is a code element that will appear as letters or words between a < (less than sign) and a > (greater than sign).

Example: <title>, <body>

To tell the web browser to 'end' doing what you just told it to do, a forward slash is used in the closing tag:

Example: </title>, </body>

Most tags come in matched 'beginning' and 'ending' pairs, but this is not an absolute rule. Any web page will contain the following tags at the start of the page:

- <HTML>: tells the web browser that this is the beginning of an HTML document
- <HEAD>: tells the web browser that this is the header for the page
- <TITLE>: tells the web browser that this is the title of the page
- <BODY>: tells the web browser that this is the beginning of the web page content.

HTML is the *lingua franca* for publishing hypertext on the world wide web.[16] It is a non-proprietary format based upon SGML, and can be created and processed by a wide range of tools, from simple plain text editors – you type it in from scratch – to sophisticated tools like Microsoft Frontpage. The current version of HTML has a wide range of features reflecting the needs of a very diverse and international community wishing to make information available on the web. HTML 4.0, created by W3C, became a recommendation in December 1997 and a revision, HTML 4.01 was published in December 1999.[16]

Originally HTML was designed to be a language for the exchange of scientific and other technical documents, suitable for use by non-document specialists. Thus HTML addressed the problem of SGML complexity by specifying a small set of structural and semantic tags suitable for authoring relatively simple documents. In addition to simplifying the document structure, HTML added support for hypertext and multimedia capabilities.

In a very short space of time, the simplicity of HTML has made it popular. However, since its inception, there has been rapid invention of new elements for use within HTML (as a standard) and for adapting HTML to the specialized user requirements. This plethora of new elements has led to interoperability problems for documents across different platforms. There are many varieties of HTML, and software packages like Microsoft Frontpage use many non-standard codes, which make them proprietary formats. Several programs like Java and Perl have been designed to work with HTML for information processing on the web, but not every browser responds properly to these extended facilities.

XML

While SGML is too complex and resource-intensive to encode and cannot be processed as it is by the web browsers, and HTML is too simple and only tells the browser how to present an element or how to link to another item, XML aims to offer the best of both worlds. XML is a simple and flexible text format derived from SGML (ISO 8879). Originally designed to meet the challenges of large-scale electronic publishing, XML is also playing an increasingly important role in the exchange of a wide variety of data on the web and elsewhere. It contains a set of rules for designing text formats that let users structure their data.[17]

Development of XML started in 1996 and has been a W3C Recommendation since February 1998. The designers of XML simply took the best parts of SGML, guided by the experience with HTML, and produced something that is powerful and vastly more regular and simple to use.

XML is intended for computers to generate data, read data and ensure that the data structure is unambiguous. It is extensible, platform-independent and it supports internationalization and localization. XML was conceived as a means of regaining the power and flexibility of SGML without most of its complexity. Thus XML preserves most of SGML's power and richness, but removes many of the more complex features of SGML that make the authoring and design of suitable software both difficult and costly.[18]

There is a significant difference between HTML and XML. While HTML specifies what each tag and attribute means, and often how the text between them should appear in a browser, XML uses the tags only to delimit pieces of data, and leaves the interpretation of the data completely to the application that reads it. Like HTML, XML files are text files that people shouldn't have to read, but may read when the need arises. XML is a framework that allows users to write application-specific codes along with markup so that the tags become meaningful in terms of data and content, making the XML documents suitable for machine-processing. However, unlike HTML, XML is not fault tolerant and a forgotten tag, or an attribute without quotes, makes an XML file unusable.

The XML family is a growing set of modules that offer a number of useful services to accomplish important and frequently demanded tasks, for example:[17]

- *XML 1.0* is the specification that defines the tags and attributes.
- *Xlink* describes a standard way to add hyperlinks to an XML file.
- *Xpointer* and *XFragments* are syntaxes for pointing to parts of an XML document. An XPointer is a bit like a URL but, instead of pointing to documents on the web, it points to pieces of data inside an XML file.
- *CSS*, the style sheet language, is applicable to XML as it is to HTML.
- *XSL* is the advanced language for expressing style sheets. It is based on XSLT, a transformation language used for rearranging, adding and deleting tags and attributes.
- The *DOM* or document object model, a standard application programming interface for manipulating XML (and HTML) files from a programming language.
- *XML Schemas 1 and 2* help developers precisely define the structures of their own XML-based formats.

XML is believed to have become a universal format not only for business-to-business applications, but also for effective knowledge and information management.[19] It holds a number of promises for improved information access in digital libraries, for example.[20]

- It produces a more precise search by providing additional information in the elements.
- It enables a better integrated search from heteregenous information sources.
- It provides for a powerful search paradigm using structural as well as content specifications.
- It facilitates information exchange to support collaborative research and learning.

XHTML

During 1999, HTML 4 was recast in XML and the resulting XHTML 1.0 became a W3C Recommendation in January 2000. XHTML is the successor of HTML, and a series of specifications has been developed for XHTML. The XHTML family document types are all XML-based and ultimately are designed to work in conjunction with XML-based user agents.

XHTML 1.0 is specified in three 'flavors' (**http://www.w3.org/MarkUp/**):

- *XHTML 1.0 Strict* – to be used to get a clean structural markup, free of any markup associated with layout; this can be used together with W3C's Cascading Style Sheet language (CSS) to get the font, colour and layout effects you want
- *XHTML 1.0 Transitional* – to be used to take advantage of XHTML features including style sheets but making only small adjustments to the markup for the benefit of those viewing the web pages pages with older browsers that can't understand style sheets
- *XHTML 1.0 Frameset* – to be used in order to use frames to partition the browser window into two or more frames.

Users can specify which variant they are using by inserting a line at the beginning of the document. For example, the HTML for a document may start with a line that says that it is using XHTML 1.0 Strict. Each variant has its own DTD, which sets out the rules and regulations for using HTML in a succinct and definitive manner.

According to its developers,[21] the XHTML family is the next step in the evolution of the internet, and by migrating to XHTML today, content developers can enter the XML world with all its attendant benefits, while still remaining confident in their content's backward and future compatibility. The major benefits of migrating to XHTML are:[21]

- The XHTML family can accommodate new and innovative ways of presenting and processing information through XHTML modules and techniques for developing new XHTML-conforming modules (described in the XHTML modularization specification). These modules will permit the combination of existing and new feature sets when developing content and also when designing new user agents.
- The XHTML family is designed with general user agent interoperability in mind, and thus through a new user agent and document profiling mechanism, servers, proxies and user agents will be able to perform best effort content transformation.

Discussion

The hypertext and hypermedia technology, together with the new and evolving standards, HTML, XML and XHTML, have brought a tremendous revolution in the creation and delivery of content, as well as access and processing of information. Hypertext and hypermedia documents allow users to navigate within or across a range of documents located on the same computer, or virtually on any computer on the internet. The various HTML, XML or HTML codes used in preparing the content allow browsers and other software to interpret and process information for different purposes, ranging from presenting the document in the correct format, size, font, and so on on the user's browser, to the automatic processing of data from backend databases, and to the automatic creation of documents and tools and further processing of information.

Documents available on CD-ROM or online databases, web and digital libraries make extensive use of hypertext tools and techniques in order to allow users to navigate within one or among a number of information resources that are conceptually linked through the hypertext links and nodes. As discussed in Chapter 18, web search engines use the links among pages to select information resources from the internet, and also use the information contained in the hypertext nodes or the HTML tags to decide whether and how to index the content associated with them. Some web search engines such as Google, use the link data to rank pages in order of their importance.

Researchers have also used the hypertext links among various web pages for different information retrieval activities. Beeferman and Berger[22] propose a query clustering method based on the click-through data: data relating to user transactions with queries and their corresponding clicks on the hypertext links to discover correlations between queries and the clicked pages. In a similar study, Li et al.[23] combined the indexed terms from the clicked pages to establish the similarities between queries. Some researchers have used the link information among various nodes in web documents to generate a query taxonomy automatically; this is a tree constituted by the concept hierarchies of user requests and categorized query terms.

References

1   Cornejo, J. G., *Hypertext: its use in the documentary treatment of data*, Santiago, Chile, REDUCE-CIDE, 1994.
2   Parsaye, K., Chignell, M., Khoshafian, S. and Wong, H., *Intelligent databases: object-oriented, deductive hypermedia technologies*, New York, John Wiley, 1989.
3   Barker, P., *Exploring hypermedia*, London, Kogan Page, 1993.
4   Jeffcoate, J., *Multimedia in practice: technology and applications*, New York, Prentice-Hall, 1995.
5   Rada, R., 'Focus on links: a holistic view of hypertext', *Knowledge organization*, **18** (1), 1991, 13–18.
6   Lucarella, D. and Zanzi, A., 'Information retrieval from hypertext: an approach using plausible inference', *Information processing and management*, **29** (3), 1993, 299–312.
7   Ellis, D., Furner-Hines, J. and Willett, P., 'On the creation of hypertext links in full text documents: measurement of inter-linker consistency', *Journal of documentation*, **50** (2), 1994, 67–98.
8   Ellis, D., Furner-Hines, J. and Willett, P., 'On the measurement of inter-linker consistency and retrieval effectiveness in hypertext databases'. In: Croft, W. B. and van Rijsbergen, C. J. (eds), *Proceedings of the Seventh Annual*

International ACM-SIGIR Conference on Research and Development in Information Retrieval, Dublin, 3–6 July, 1994, London, Springer-Verlag, 1994, 51–60.

9   Halasz, F. and Schwartz, M., 'The Dexter hypertext reference model', *Communications of the ACM*, **37** (2), 1994, 30–9.

10   Arnets, H. C. and Bogaerts, W. F. L., 'Hypermedia and the user: defining hypermedia by its application areas and its utilization characteristics', *Microcomputers for information management*, **9** (1), 1992, 17–34.

11   Rada, R., Zeb, A., You, G., Michailidis, A. and Mhashi, M., 'Collaborative hypertext and the MUCH system', *Journal of information science*, **17** (4), 1991, 191–6.

12   Hammwohner, R. and Kuhlen, R., 'Semantic control of open hypertext systems by typed objects', *Journal of information science*, **20** (3), 1994, 175–84.

13   Bouvin, N. O., 'Augmenting the web through open hypermedia', *The new review of hypermedia and multimedia*, **8**, 2002, 3–25.

14   ISO 8879:1986, *Information processing: text and office systems: standard generalized markup language (SGML)*, Geneva, International Standards Organization, 1986.

15   Schwartz, C., *Sorting out the web: approaches to subject access*, Westport, Ablex Publishing. 2001.

16   W3C Markup languages. Available at **http://www.w3.org/MarkUp/**.

17   W3C XML. Available at **http://www.w3.org/XML/**.

18   W3C Recommendation 26 January 2000, revised 1 August 2002. Available at **http://www.w3.org/TR/xhtml1/**.

19   Baeza-Yates, R., Carmel, D., Maarek, Y. and Soffer, A., 'Preface to the special topic issue: XML', *Journal of the American Society for Information Science and Technology*, **53** (6), 2002, 413–14.

20   Luk, R. W. P., Leong, H. V., Dillon, T. S., Chan, A. T. S., Croft, W. B. and Allan, J., 'A survey in indexing and searching XML documents', *Journal of the American Society for Information Science and Technology*, **53** (6), 2002, 415–37.

21   *XHTML™ 1.0 The Extensible HyperText Markup Language* (2nd edn), *A reformulation of HTML 4 in XML 1.0*, W3C.

22   Beeferman, D. and Berger, A., Agglomerative clustering of a search engine query log, 2000. Available at **http://citeseer.nj.nec.com/beeferman00agglomerative. html**.

23   Li, W.-S., Candan, K. S., Vu, Q. and Agrawal, D., 'Retrieving and organizing web pages by ''information unit'' '. In: *Proceedings of the Tenth International World Wide Web Conference, WWW 10, Hong Kong, China, May 1–5, 2001*, ACM, 230–44

Chapter 18

Web information retrieval

Introduction

The introduction and growth of the world wide web (WWW or simply the web) have brought significant changes in the way we access information. Simply speaking, the web is a massive collection of web pages stored on the millions of computers across the world that are linked by the internet.[1] The development of the web began in 1989 by Tim Berners-Lee and his colleagues at CERN (European Laboratory for Particle Physics in Geneva). They created a protocol, called the Hyper Text Transfer Protocol (HTTP), which standardized communication between servers and clients. Their text-based web browser was made available for general release in January 1992. The web gained rapid acceptance with the creation of a web browser called Mosaic, which was developed in the USA at the National Center for Supercomputing Applications at the University of Illinois and was released in September 1993.[2] Mosaic allowed people to use the web using the 'point-and-click' graphical manipulations. Subsequently the Mosaic staff started their own company and developed one of the most popular web browsers of today, Netscape Navigator. Another popular browser soon appeared, Internet Explorer from the Microsoft Corporation. Since its inception about a decade ago, the web has grown exponentially. A rough estimation of the size and growth of the web is given later in this chapter.

Traditional information retrieval techniques that have been developed over the past 40 years had to be tested and modified to suit the requirements for indexing and retrieving web documents. This chapter discusses the major issues, techniques and concerns of web information retrieval and highlights some recent studies that shed light on the characteristics of web information retrieval.

Traditional vs web information retrieval

Web information retrieval is significantly different from traditional text retrieval systems. These differences mainly stem from a number of typical characteristics of the web such as its distributed architecture, the variety of information available, its growth, the distribution of information and users, and so on. Several researchers have discussed the uniqueness of web information retrieval (see for example, Bharat and Henzinger;[3] and Rasmussen[4]). This section discusses some of these issues with a view to highlighting the complexities of web information retrieval.

1 *Distributed nature of the web*: Web resources are distributed all over the world, so complex measures are required to locate, index and retrieve them. The fact that the computers that are interconnected have different architecture, and the information resources are created using different platforms, software and standards, makes the matter more complex. Most text retrieval systems deal with a set of information resources that is several times smaller in volume than the web. In addition, text retrieval systems usually deal with a set of documents that have been created using a set of standards – hardware, software and processing standards. When OPACs retrieve distributed information, they use several standards to process it, such as the MARC formats, and to index it, such as Z39.50. No such uniform standard is used for the creation and processing of web information resources.

2 *Size and growth of the web*: The web has grown exponentially from 1994 to 2003. The processes of identifying, indexing and retrieving information become more complex as the size of the web, and hence the volume of information on the web, increases. Conventional text retrieval systems have to be tested and modified to make them suitable for handling the large volume of data on the web.

3 *Deep vs the surface web*: Information resources on the web can be accessed at two different levels. While millions of web information resources can be accessed by anyone, a lot of information is accessible either through authorized accessed (information that is password protected, say) or can be generated only by activating an appropriate program. Researchers call the former the surface web and the latter the deep web, with a note that the deep web is several time larger than the surface web.

4 *Type and format of the documents*: Text retrieval systems deal with textual information only; the web contains a much wider variety, from simple text to multimedia information. Again these information resources appear in a variety of formats thereby making the task of indexing and retrieval more complex.

5 *Quality of information*: Since anyone can publish almost anything on the web, it is very difficult to assess the quality of information resources. As opposed to conventional text retrieval systems, which deal with published information resources that have some quality control, web information retrieval systems have to deal with controlled and uncontrolled information resources.

6 *Frequency of changes*: Web pages change quite frequently. This is in sharp contrast with the input of conventional text retrieval systems, which deal with relatively static information. Once an information resource is added to a text retrieval system it does not change its content; at the most the entire document is removed from the system. Keeping track of the changes in the millions of web pages and making necessary changes in the information retrieval system is a major challenge. Another major problem with the web is that the resources (web pages) often move. This information needs to be tracked by the retrieval system in order to facilitate proper retrieval.

7 *Ownership*: Information resources that are accessible through the web have different access requirements: some information can be accessed and used freely, others require specific permission or access rights, often through payment of fees. Identifying the rights to access is a major challenge for web information retrieval.

8 *Distributed users*: Most text retrieval systems are designed to meet the information needs of a specific user community. Hence text retrieval systems usually have an idea of the nature, characteristics, information needs, search behaviour, and so on of the target user community. Web information is in sharp contrast with this. Ideally the users of an information resource on the web may be anyone, located anywhere in the world. This imposes a significant challenge since the designer of a web information retrieval system will have no idea about the target users, their nature, characteristics, location, information search behaviour, and so on.

9 *Multiple languages*: Since the web is distributed all over the world, the language of information resources as well as users varies significantly. An ideal web information retrieval system should be able to retrieve the required information irrespective of the language of the query or the source information. This diversity of language poses a tremendous challenge for web information retrieval.

10 *Resource requirements*: Massive amount of resources are required to build and run an effective and efficient web information retrieval system. The matter is worsened by the fact that there is no single body who would fund for these resources, and yet everyone wants a good information retrieval system for access to web information resources.

Web information: volume and growth

Measuring the web is a difficult task. However, several researchers have attempted to calculate the size and growth of the web, and the results vary. Two different types of measures may be noticed: the number of websites (all the web pages residing at one particular IP address) and the number of distinct web pages. An OCLC project that measures the growth of the web by counting the number of websites reported that there were 9,040,000 websites in 2002.[5] The findings of this study on the growth of the web, measured by the count of websites, are shown in Tables 18.1 to 18.4. Table 18.1 shows the number of websites from 1998 to 2002; Table 18.2 shows the growth in the number of websites from 1988–9 to 2001–2; Table 18.3 shows the distribution of websites by country of origin in 2002; and Table 18.4 shows the distribution of websites by language in 2002.

Table 18.1　*Distribution of websites from 1998 to 2002*

Year	Websites
1998	2,851,000
1999	4,882,000
2000	7,399,000
2001	8,745,000
2002	9,040,000

Table 18.2 *Growth in the number of websites from 1998–9 to 2001–2*

Year	Growth
1998–9	71%
1999–2000	52%
2000–1	18%
2001–2	3%
Overall growth (1998–2002)	217%

Table 18.3 *Distribution of public websites by country of origin in 2002*

Country	Percentage
US	55%
Germany	6%
Japan	5%
UK	3%
Canada	3%
Italy	2%
France	2%
Netherlands	2%
Others	18%
Unknown	4%

Table 18.4 *Distribution of public websites by language in 2002*

Language	Percentage
English	72%
German	7%
Japanese	6%
Spanish	3%
French	3%
Italian	2%
Dutch	2%
Chinese	2%
Korean	1%
Portuguese	1%
Russian	1%
Polish	1%

The number of pages on the web is difficult to count. One can estimate the figures by looking at the number of pages indexed by various search engines. As of March 2003, Google is reported to be the largest search engines, having indexed over 3.8 billion web pages.[6]

Information on the web can be categorized into two classes: one that can be accessed by web search tools, the other that can only be accessed by activating the appropriate program from a particular web page. Standard web search tools cannot find the latter category of information, which is buried under the websites. The part of the web that is hidden and cannot be easily accessed has been called the 'deep web' as opposed to the part of the web that can be easily accessed, the 'surface web'. Deep web sources store their content in searchable databases, which can only be produced dynamically in response to a direct request. Based on a study conducted in March 2000, BrightPlanet [7] has quantified the size and relevancy of the deep web as follows:

- More than 200,000 deep websites presently exist.
- The deep web contains 7500 terabytes of information compared with 19 terabytes of information on the surface web; 60 of the largest deep websites collectively contain about 750 terabytes of information.
- The deep web contains nearly 550 billion individual documents compared with the one billion of the surface web.
- Public information on the deep web is currently 400 to 550 times larger than the commonly defined world wide web.

It may be noted that the number of pages indexed by the search engines varies significantly. However, the total number of pages on the web will be much more than the highest number of web pages indexed by any one particular search engine, since researchers have noted that only a fraction of the web is actually traced and indexed by the web search tools. A study conducted at the NEC research institute estimates that even the largest search engine can index no more than 16% of the surface web.[7] This study further suggests that since they are missing the deep web when they use such search engines, web searchers are searching only 0.03% – or one in 3000 – of the pages available to them today.

Nevertheless, taking the example of Google, locating, indexing and managing an index of terms from over 3.8 billion pages is a massive task. The size of the document set of any one search engine is thus many times bigger than the largest online database file. In addition to the challenges posed by the huge volume of information on the web, frequent changes in the contents of the web pages also pose major difficulties. Rasmussen[4] comments that the dynamic nature of the web in terms of its growth, and also as a result of changes in the web pages – from additions and deletions to the removal of the entire page – constitutes a major difference between web and traditional information retrieval.

There is another important point on which web information retrieval significantly differs from traditional information retrieval systems, and that is the volume of use. Table 18.5 shows the number of searches handled per day by eight search engines. These figures have been taken from the Searchengine.com site in January–February 2003.[8]

Table 18.5 *Number of searches per day on eight search engines*

Search engine	Searches per day
Google	250 million
Overture	167 million
Inktomi	80 million
LookSmart	45 million
FindWhat	33 million
Ask Jeeves	20 million
AltaVista	18 million
FAST	12 million

It may be noted that no conventional information retrieval system is designed to handle this many searches per day.

Access to information on the web: the tools

A user can get access to any website by entering the URL (uniform resource locator; the address of a web site) on the browser. A web browser, like Netscape Navigator or Microsoft Internet Explorer, is a computer program, an essential tool for getting access to the web. A web browser performs two major tasks:

- It knows how to go to a web server on the internet and request a page so that the browser can pull the page through the network and into your machine.
- It knows how to interpret the set of HTML tags within the page in order to display the page on your screen as the page's creator intended it to be viewed.

Although one could get access to any web page by typing on the browser the URL of a sought website, and then moving into the site through the various links, there are several problems to this approach, especially when the user is interested to get some specific information on a given topic, or find answers to a given question. Problems arose because it is almost impossible for users to know which of the billions of web pages may contain the information they require and which of the millions of websites contains the required web page. In order to solve these difficulties, several web search tools have been developed that assist users in finding the information they need from the right web page with relatively little effort.

There are basically two ways to find information on the web: by conducting a search using what is known as a search engine, or by following the links in a specially designed list called a directory.[1] Search engines allow users to enter search terms – keywords and/or phrases – that are run against a database containing information on web pages collected automatically by programs called spiders. The search engine retrieves from its database web pages that match the search terms entered by the searcher. It is important to note that when a user conducts a search using a search engine, the search engine does not search for the information across the entire web at the given instance. Instead, it searches a fixed database, which is updated at a regular intervals according to specific criteria employed by the search engine, located at the search engine's website and containing information on selected web pages.

How the search engines work

Although all search engines are intended to perform the same task, each goes about doing so in a different way, sometimes with very different results. Factors that influence the search results include the size of the database, frequency of updating it, criteria employed for indexing the chosen web pages, and the search engine's retrieval capabilities. Search engines also differ in their search speed, the design of the search interface, the way in which they display the search results, the amount of help they provide, and in other ways.

Search engines run from special sites on the web and are designed to help people find information stored on other sites. There are differences in the ways search engines work, but they all perform the following three basic tasks:

- They search the internet – or select parts of the internet – according to a set of criteria.
- They keep an index of the words or phrases they find, with specific information such as where they found them, how many times they found them, and so on.
- They allow users to search for words or phrases or combinations of words or phrases found in that index.

There are three main components of a search engine: the spider, the search engine software and interface, and the index.

The spider

To find information on the millions of web pages, a search engine employs special software called a spider or crawler. It is a program that automatically fetches web pages for search engines; it is called a spider because it *crawls* over the web. Spider programs treat the web as a graph and, using a set of URLs as a seed set, traverse the graph to select web pages.[4] The crawler traverses the graph either breadth first (searching all nodes at one level of the tree before going down a level) or depth first (searching the current path as far as possible before backtracking to the last choice point and trying the next alternative path in the tree). Web pages contain links to other pages, and a spider uses these links to move to another page; it visits the page, reads it and then follows links to other pages within the site.

One of the major problems for a spider or a crawler program, and indeed for a specific search engine, is to decide which page to select for indexing. Each search engine aims to index the most important web pages, and therefore aims to prioritize URLs to obtain the best pages. The quality of a web page may be judged in many ways, for instance by measuring its content, by assessing its popularity (by counting the number of visits) or by measuring its connectivity (which other pages link to this page). Spider program metrics based on connectivity have the advantage that they do not require information that is not easily accessible (such as page popularity data), and that they are easy to compute, so they scale well to even very large page collections.[9] Another major issue for a crawler program is to schedule the frequency of revisiting pages. Since web pages keep changing constantly it is important to visit them frequently.

Many researchers have developed crawler programs that take different approaches to crawling the web (see for example Cho, Garcia-Molina and Page;[10] Najork and Wiener;[9] Chakrabarti, Van den Berg and Dom;[11] and Chakrabarti et al.[12]). Search engines do not usually disclose the details of their spider programs.

Search engine software

Search engine software is the information retrieval program that performs two major tasks: it searches through the millions of terms recorded in the index to find matches to a search and it ranks the retrieved records (web pages) in the order it believes is the most relevant. The criteria for selection (or rejection) of search terms and assigning weight to them depend on the policy of the search engine. Similarly, the specific information that is stored along with each keyword – such as where in a given web page it occurred (heading, links, meta-tags or title of the page), how many times it occurred, the attached weight, and so on – depend on the policy of the search engine concerned. Each commercial search engine has a different formula for assigning weight to the words in its index. This is one of the reasons for the fact that a search for the same word on different search engines may produce different results, and the retrieved web pages may be ordered differently.

Google uses the concept 'page rank' to determine the importance of a web page. The idea is based on the principle of citation analysis. A document, according to the basic principle of citation analysis, is considered to be important if it is cited frequently, and thus one can rank a set of documents in order of their importance by counting the number of time each one has been cited. A web page's 'page rank' is an objective measure of its citation importance that corresponds well with people's subjective idea of importance. Page rank is defined by Brin and Page[13] as:

Assuming that page A has pages T1...Tn which point to it (i.e., are citations), the parameter d is a damping factor which can be set between 0 and 1 (usually set to 0.85), and C(A) is defined as the number of links going out of page A, the PageRank of a page A is given as follows:

$$PR(A) = (1-d) + d \ (PR(T1)/C(T1) + ... + PR(Tn)/C(Tn))$$

It may be noted that page ranks form a probability distribution over web pages and therefore the sum of all web pages' page ranks will be one.

Indexing

Early search engines indexed only components of each web page, but increasingly full texts of web pages are indexed (Rasmussen[4]). Specific information on the form and weight of index terms, the techniques for calculating relevance, and so on are usually proprietary. Baeza-Yates and Ribeiro-Neto[14] comment that most search engines use variations of the Boolean and vector space model. Various researchers have proposed different ranking algorithms. For example, Yuwono and Lee[15] have proposed four algorithms: Boolean spreading activation, most cited, the tf.idf vector space model, and the vector spread activation. Kleinberg[16] proposed HITS (Hypertext Induced Topic Search), which depends on the query and considers the set of pages that point to, or are pointed by, pages in the answer.

Although search engines do not usually disclose their secret of ranking pages, some general information is available. Sullivan[17] comments that one of the main rules in a ranking algorithm involves the location and frequency of keywords on a web page. The location of a term on a page is also used as an important criterion. Pages with the search terms appearing in the HTML title tag are often assumed to be more relevant to the topic than others. Pages where the search terms appear near the top of a web page, such as in the headline or in the first few paragraphs of text, are also ranked highly compared with others. Frequency of occurrence is the other major factor used to determine relevance. Pages where the search terms occur frequently are often deemed more relevant than other web pages.

The process

Search engines are usually secretive about their crawling and indexing processes, except for Google, which has made the process public.[13] The following points provided by Brin and Page[13] describe the steps that are used in Google for indexing web pages:

- Web crawling (downloading of web pages) is done by several distributed crawlers.
- A URL server sends lists of URLs to be fetched to the crawlers.
- The web pages that are fetched are sent to the store server, which compresses and stores the web pages into a repository.
- Every web page has an associated ID number called a docID, which is assigned whenever a new URL is parsed out of a web page.
- The indexing function is performed by the indexer and the sorter.
- The indexer reads the repository, uncompresses the documents, and parses them.
- Each document is converted into a set of word occurrences called hits. The hits record the word, position in document, an approximation of font size and capitalization.
- The indexer distributes these hits into a set of 'barrels', creating a partially sorted forward index.
- The indexer also parses out all the links in every web page and stores important information about them in an anchors file; this file contains enough information to determine where each link points from and to, and the text of the link.
- The URL resolver reads the anchors file and converts relative URLs into absolute URLs and in turn into docIDs. It puts the anchor text into the forward index associated with the docID that the anchor points to. It also generates a database of

links, which are pairs of docIDs. The links database is used to compute page ranks for all the documents.

- The sorter takes the barrels, which are sorted by docID, and resorts them by wordID to generate the inverted index. The sorter also produces a list of wordIDs and offsets into the inverted index.
- A program called DumpLexicon takes this list together with the lexicon produced by the indexer and generates a new lexicon to be used by the searcher.
- The searcher is run by a web server and uses the lexicon built by DumpLexicon together with the inverted index and the page ranks to answer queries.

Types of search engine

The results of a web search largely depend on the selection of a search engine, because search engines differ in the way they select, update and index the web as well as in the search and retrieval features that they offer. Search engines can be categorized in a number of ways. Two broad categories are: search engines and meta search engines, the latter term referring to tools that allow users to conduct concurrent searches on more than one search engine. Some people also group search engines according to their characteristics of indexing. For example, Nicholson[18] categorizes search engines as full-text search tools, extracting search tools, subject-specific search tools and meta search tools. Sullivan of Searchenginewatch.com[19] has divided search engines into the following seven categories:

- *Major search engines*, such as Google (**http://www.google.com**), AllTheWeb.com (FAST) (**http://www.alltheweb.com**), MSN Search (**http://search.msn.com**), AOL Search (**http://aolsearch.aol.com**), HotBot (**http://www.hotbot.com**) and AltaVista (**http://www.altavista.com**).
- *News search engines*, such as AltaVista News (**http://news.altavista.com/**), AllTheWeb.com News (**http://www.alltheweb.com/?cat=news**), Yahoo News (**http://news.yahoo.com/**), Daypop (**http://www.daypop.com/**), Net2one (**http://www.net2one.com/**), RocketNews (**http://www.rocketnews.com**) and Ananova (**http://www.ananova.com/**).
- *Speciality search engines*, such as AskJeeves (**http://www.askjeeves.com**) and Web Help (**http://www.webhelp.com**).
- *Kids' search engines*, such as AOL Kids Only (**http://www.aol.com/ netfind/kids/channel/**), KidsClick (**http://sunsite.berkeley.edu/KidsClick!/**) and Yahooligans (**http://www.yahooligans.com/**).
- *Metacrawlers*, such as Dogpile (**http://www.dogpile.com/info.dogpl/**), Metacrawler (**http://www.metacrawler.com/info.metac/dog/index.htm**) and Cnet Search (**http://www.search.com/**).
- *Multimedia search engines*, such as Google Images (**http://images.google.com**), AltaVista Image Search (**http://uk.altavista.com/image/default**), FAST Multimedia Search (**http://multimedia.alltheweb.com/**), Lycos Multimedia Search (**http://multimedia.lycos.com/**), Ditto (**http://www.ditto.com/**) and Speechbot (**http://speechbot.research.compaq.com/**).

*   *Regional and country search engines*, such as European Search Engines (**http:// www.webmasterworld.com/forum18/544.htm**) and Japanese search engines (**http://www.seo-web.com/seo-jpn/japanese-search-engine-relationships. htm**).

Features of each search engine can be learnt by following the help pages. However, there are a number of sources that regularly report on the features and comparisons of web search engines. The most prominent are searchenginewatch.com and the online journal. Chowdhury and Chowdhury[1] have discussed the features of ten popular web search engines and three meta search engines.

Common search and retrieval features of web search engines

Almost all search engines provide basic text search facilities like Boolean search, proximity search, phrase search, truncation, field-specific (often called meta tag) search and limiting search (by language, domain, country, and so on), see Table 18.6. The search operators vary from one search engine to another. However, the search engine interfaces have improved significantly in ease of use compared with the interfaces of many traditional text retrieval systems.

Table 18.6   *General search features of search engines*

Search features	Examples
Boolean search	Usually three different approaches are followed: • combining search terms with AND, OR, NOT (e.g. ANDNOT in AltaVista • using '+' or '–' signs before the search terms • selecting options like 'all of the words' (in Google); or 'any of these words' or 'none of these words' (in AltaVista)
Proximity search	Using an appropriate operator, e.g. 'NEAR' (in AltaVista)
Field search, e.g. title search	Using 'intitle:' or 'all in title:' before the search terms in Google
Phrase search	Entering a phrase within double quotes (available in AltaVista, Google), or by selecting an appropriate option (e.g. 'with all of the words' (in Google), 'this exact phrase' in AltaVista
Limiting search	Limiting by time, date or file type (in AltaVista); by date, file format, language or occurrences (in Google)

It may be noted that one of the major improvements in the web search environment has been in the design of user interfaces that allow users to conduct complex search queries without having to remember or use complex search syntax or operators. A quick look at Figures 18.1 to 18.3 shows that users can formulate comparatively complex search expressions simply by choosing the appropriate options and entering the query terms in the advanced search screens of Google, AltaVista and HotBot. These can be compared with the search interfaces provided by traditional online search services like Dialog. Many advanced search screens also provide enough help information for users to complete their search on the search screen itself (see Figure 18.3 for the HotBot advanced search screen).

In addition to those retrieval features that are common to the traditional text retrieval systems, many search engines provide some unique search facilities that have been designed specifically for web information retrieval. Table 18.7 shows some unique features of search engines and provides examples of search engines where the feature is available.

Fig. 18.1 *Advanced search interface of Google*

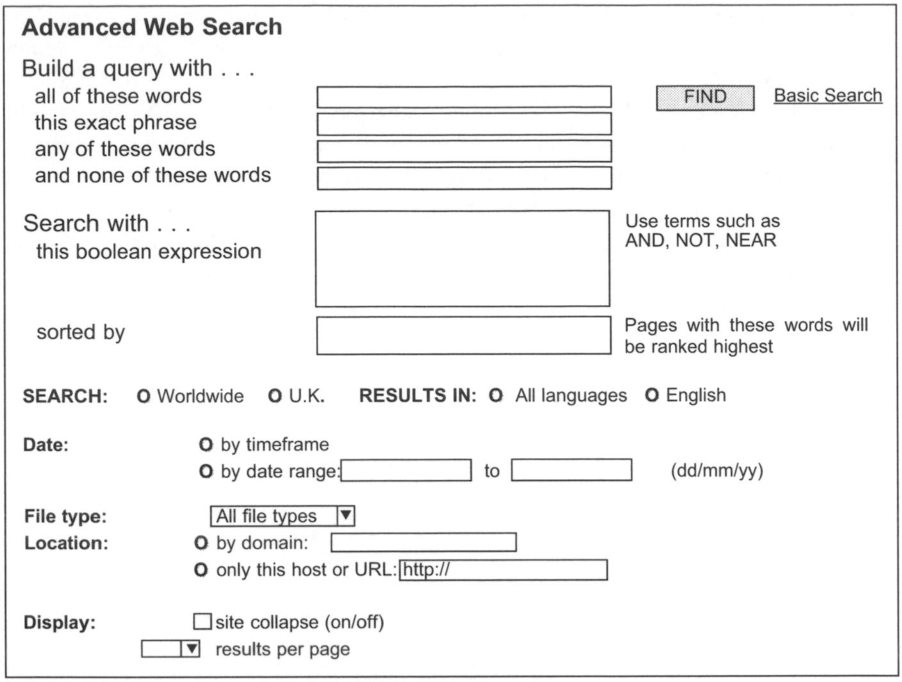

Advanced Web Search

Build a query with . . .

all of these words

this exact phrase

any of these words

and none of these words

| | FIND | Basic Search |

Search with . . .

this boolean expression

Use terms such as
AND, NOT, NEAR

sorted by

Pages with these words will
be ranked highest

SEARCH: O Worldwide   O U.K.   **RESULTS IN:** O All languages   O English

Date: O by timeframe
                   O by date range: [   ] to [   ]   (dd/mm/yy)

File type: [All file types ▼]
Location: O by domain: [   ]
                   O only this host or URL: [http://]

Display: □ site collapse (on/off)
                   [▼] results per page

Fig. 18.2   *Advanced search interface of AltaVista*

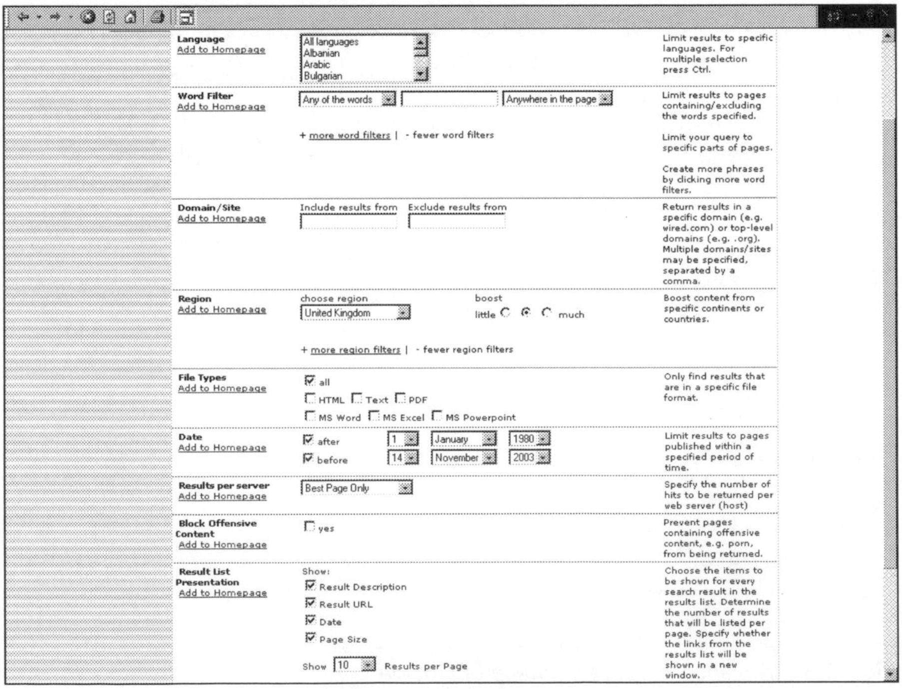

Fig. 18.3   *Advanced search interface of HotBot*

Table 18.7   *Special features of search engines*

Special features	Examples
Host/domain search	In the advanced search screen of AltaVista users can type in a domain name from a list of domain and country codes; in Google, users can type in a domain name (URL) in the search box and select to get or not to get results from the domain
URL scarch: users can search within a site by typing in the top-level URL	In the advanced search screen of AltaVista and Google users can type in a URL in the search box
Link search: a page-specific scarch whereby users can specify a page and ask the scarch engine to retrieve those pages that link to the given page	In the advanced search screen of Google users can type in a URL to find pages that link to the given page
Limiting search: users can restrict the search results by specifying a number of limiting factors	In AltaVista users can limit searches by date, file type and location; in Google a search can be restricted by language, file format, date, occurrences and domain
Find similar: this is a page-specific search whereby the user can specify a web page and ask the search engine to find similar pages; this option is also available in the search output pages of some search engines	In Google, users can enter the URL of a page in the advanced search screen. The 'Similar Pages' option in Google and 'Related Pages' option in AltaVista find pages similar or related to the one selected
Stemming	In the advanced search screen of MSN users can select the 'Enable Stemming' option to search for the variant forms of a word
Search by language	In the advanced search screen of Google and HotBot users can choose a language from a list of languages
Filter: users can choose to activate a filter in order to stop the search engine from retrieving unwanted materials	In the advanced search screen of HotBot users can choose options to block offensive contents; in AltaVista and Google there is an option to activate the filter option in the settings

(*continued*)

Table 18.7   (*continued*)

Special features	Examples
Page content: user can specify the content of a page	In HotBot users can specify the content type of the retrieved pages by selecting options like audio, image, MP3, Word, PDF, audio or video; in the advanced search screen of AltaVista, users can choose a file type: all, HTML or PDF file formats; in MSN users can select the file type or file content type from a list
Page translation	AltaVista and Google options (called 'Translate' in AltaVista and 'Language Tools' in Google) that allow users to enter text in one language and translate it into another language
Sorted by option (in AltaVista)	AltaVista allows users to enter search terms in an appropriate box to tell the search engine to sort the results based on the occurrence of those terms
Results display: users can select the number of output to be displayed on each page	In AltaVista and Google users can select the number from a list

In addition to those mentioned in Table 18.7, some search engines provide further special features to help the searcher. For example,

*   The 'I'm Feeling Lucky™' button in Google takes users directly to the first web page Google returned for a query.
*   Site Collapse in AltaVista shows a maximum of two results per site, allowing the user to look at results from various sites.
*   Google Toolbar (**http://toolbar.google.com**) is a special toolbar for Internet Explorer users that puts a Google search box right into the user's browser.
*   TouchGraph GoogleBrowser: Shows users what the web 'looks like' to the search engine, displaying the links between the user's favourite websites.
*   Yahoo Companion: Allows users to search Yahoo, access Yahoo Mail, checks on stocks and more via a toolbar within the browser.

Specialized search engines

In addition to retrieving text, search engines also provide facilities for retrieving multi-media information. Most current multimedia retrieval is based on text search features and some examples have been given in Chapter 16. A number of specialized search engines provide alternative approaches to query formulation and the display of results.

Natural language queries

Some search engines allow users to enter a query in simple natural language. The idea behind natural language queries is that users can type a question in the same way that they would ask it of a human and therefore they don't need to keep track of Boolean or other search operators or complex query structures. One of the most popular natural language query sites today is AskJeeves.com (**http://www.askjeeves.com**). Users can ask a simple natural language question and AskJeeves comes up with answers and/or a set of related questions, and/or hits from other search tools like AltaVista or Yahoo. One of the unique features of AskJeeves is that it takes users to the page containing the answer to their query. On top of the page an AskJeeves frame appears, which allows users to print the answer, modify the query, and so on. Another unique feature of AskJeeves is that, in addition to the results from various search engines, it comes up with a number of predefined queries related to the question that has been asked by a searcher. The searcher can select any one of them, click on the Ask button, and return the query to AskJeeves. This allows a searcher to pick up the most appropriate query with which to pursue their search. AskJeeves also has a list of popular questions and users can choose any one of them to return it to AskJeeves as a query. AskJeeves processes and categorizes all the queries that it receives, and presents all the related questions on to the screen. In most cases, unlike other search or meta search engines, AskJeeves takes the user directly to the website that contains the answer to their question.

Visualization

A number of search engines allow users to view a visual display of the links among the retrieved web pages on the screen. The TouchGraph GoogleBrowser allows users to view a visual display of links between a chosen website and other sites. Users need to install a program (available free from the Google site) to activate this feature.

Many search engines allow users to enter a search query and produces a visual display of the retrieved output, as opposed to a text page listing the retrieved sites. A typical example of such a search engine is Kartoo (**http://www.kartoo.com**). As shown in Figure 18.4, the search results screen in Kartoo has two parts: on the right-hand side of the screen users can see a display of retrieved sites, under specific topic headings, linked to each other. By moving the mouse to any one node (website) on the screen, the user can see the link of the chosen site with other sites on the screen. On the left-hand side of the screen there is a list of the top sites and a list of topics that are related to the search term entered. Users can choose any of the listed topics to modify the search.

Another interesting search engine is Vivisimo (**www.vivisimo.com**), which shows search results clustered under different topics related to the search term(s) (Figure 18.5). This does not use a visual display of the results like Kartoo, but the search output screen has two parts: on the left results are displayed under various related topics, and on the right there is a set of pages retrieved by the search term(s). Wisenut (**http://www.wisenut.com**) also shows results retrieved by the search term(s) together with a cluster of web pages on related topics.

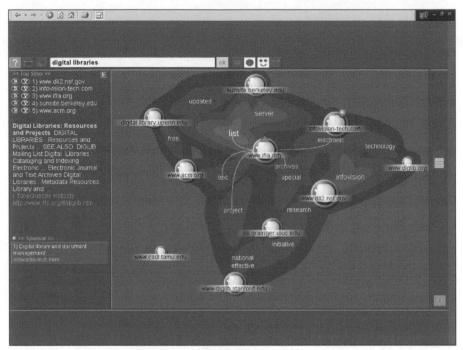

Fig. 18.4   *Search results screen of Kartoo*

Fig. 18.5   *Search results screen of Vivisimo*

Web information retrieval: evaluation studies

The traditional online IR services were designed to work primarily on structured text databases and they were designed with a target user community in view. Information retrieval services on the web deal with text as well as multimedia information resources that are linked with other documents, and there is no target user community as such. A different context for IR emerges from this environment, representing a more 'popular' use of IR, characterized by a broader audience, different document collections and different search models.[20] Researchers have noted that the retrieval characteristics of web information services are designed for the general audiences, and they are different from the features of the traditional IR systems[21, 22]).

Search engine logs are used to study the web search behaviour of users. Silverstein et al.[23] studied the transaction logs of AltaVista for six weeks with over a billion search requests, and noted that an average query size was 2.35 terms. They also noted that most search sessions were short: in 77% of the sessions only one search request was made and in 63.7% of the sessions only one query was entered and one result screen viewed.

When analysing about 16 million queries from the German search engine Fireball, Hoelscher[24] noted that only 2.6% queries used Boolean operators and over 54% queries had only one search term. Gordon and Pathak[25] compared the retrieval effectiveness of eight search engines (Yahoo, Excite, Magellan, HotBot, AltaVista, Lycos, Infoseek and Open Text) and noted that there were no statistical differences in the retrieval effectiveness of them for recall, though there were for precision. Although this study talks about the performance of the selected search engines, some observations are very important as far as the question of precision in digital library searching is concerned. It shows that in general the web search engines lack precision and their performance varies significantly. This could be a good lesson for digital library designers since precision is an important determining factor for the performance of digital libraries.

Jansen and Pooch,[21] and Jansen, Spink and Saracevic[22, 26] studied user search behaviour on the web. Overall their observations show the rather poor state of end-user searches. For example, users input on an average two terms per web search query, only about 8% of search queries contained Boolean operators, 9% were advanced search queries and 54% of searchers viewed ten or fewer retrieved items. Table 18.8 shows the results of these studies and suggests that there is some interesting searching behaviour by users across the three search systems studied.

Similar observations have been made by another study conducted by Spink et al.[22] They analysed over one million web queries to discern how the public searches the web and had some astonishing findings, which may be very useful for digital library designers:

Table 18.8   *User search patterns in different online search environments*

Issues	Web search systems	Traditional IR systems	OPAC search systems
Queries per user per session	1–2	7–16	2–5
Terms per query	2	6–9	1–2
Relevant documents viewed per session	10 or fewer	approx. 10	fewer than 50
Queries containing advanced options	9%	9%	8%
Queries containing Boolean operators	8%	37%	1%
Queries improperly formatted	10%	17%	7–9%

- A great majority of web queries are short, not much modified, and very simple in structure.
- Very few queries incorporate advanced search features, and when they do so, half of them are mistakes.
- Despite gathering a large number of websites as answers to their queries, users do not view beyond the first or the second page of results.
- Web users are not much interested in relevance feedback.

Another study[27] reveals some interesting findings, which may be good lessons for digital library researchers, particularly those who deal with information retrieval issues. Cooper analysed the usage of the Melvyl web catalogue at the University of California at Berkeley. During the 479 day study period users conducted about 2.5 million search sessions, during which about 7.4 million search statements were executed. The findings of this study reveal that:

- The length of time research searchers spent at a session grew from 6 to 10 minutes during the 16 months study period.
- During the study period about 7.4 million database selections were made, out of which Catalogue Database accounted for 32% (about 2.4 million uses), Medlars for 22%, Magazine Database 10%, Periodicals Database 8%, Inspec 4% and Current Contents 4%.
- The time users spent on each database also varied; for instance about 3 minutes per search in the Medlars database and 2.2 minutes for the catalogue database.
- Users displayed about 4–5 citations for each search they performed.
- The length of time users spent displaying results was 30–40 seconds.

Ford, Miller and Moss[28] conducted a study with the AltaVista search engine to test the link between web search strategies with relevance judgements in order to discover whether Boolean or other advanced features are less effective than best match or combined (Boolean and best match) search strategies. They noted that:

- Boolean only searches were associated with poor retrieval.
- Boolean only searches performed worse than best match and combined searches.
- Combined searches performed worse than best match alone searches.
- There was no evidence that these results were related to errors, choice of term or any interaction between them, in Boolean as opposed to best match or combined searches.

The evaluation studies reported above reveal that:

- Users find it difficult to formulate their questions.
- In general users spend very little time on searching a given web search tool or database.
- In most cases users formulate very short and simple queries with one or two search terms and very few search operators.
- Users spend very little time in looking at and deciding the usefulness or relevance of retrieved items.
- Very few queries contain advanced search features.

Further studies are required to produce a clearer picture of web retrieval tasks and user search behaviour that will help researchers build improved web search tools.

References

1   Chowdhury, G. and Chowdhury, S., *Information sources and searching on the world wide web*, London, Library Association Publishing, 2001.
2   Poulter, A., Hiom, D. and Tseng, G., *The library and information professionals guide to the internet*, 3rd edn, Library Association Publishing, 2000.
3   Bharat, K. and Henzinger, M. R., 'Improved algorithms for topic distillation in a hyperlinked environment'. In: Croft, W.B., Moffat, A., Rijsbergen, C. J., Wilkinson, R. and Zobel, J. (eds), *Proceedings of the 21st Annual International ACM SIGIR Conference on Research and Development in Information Retrieval* (SIGIR'98), ACM, New York, 1998, 104–111.
4   Rasmussen, E., 'Indexing and retrieval for the web'. In: Cronin, B. (ed.), *ARIST*, **37**, Medford, NJ, Information Today Inc., 2002, 91–124.
5   OCLC, *Size and growth*. Available at **http://wcp.oclc.org/stats/size.html**.
6   Personal communication with the Google team, 29 March, 2003.
7   Bergman, M. K., *The deep web: surfacing hidden value*. Available at **http://www.brightplanet.com/deepcontent/tutorials/DeepWeb/index.asp**.
8   Sullivan, D., *Searches per day*. Available at **http://www.searchenginewatch.com/reports/perday.html**.
9   Najork, M. and Wiener, J. L., 'Breadth-first search crawling yields high-quality pages'. In: *10th International World Wide Web Conference, WWW10, Hong Kong, May 1–5, 2001*. Available at **http://www10.org/cdrom/papers/pdf/p208.pdf**.
10 Cho, J., Garcia-Molina, H. and Page, L., 'Efficient crawling through URL

ordering'. In: *Proceedings of the 7th International World Wide Web Conference (WWW7)*, published as Computer Networks and ISDN Systems, **30**, 161–72.

11   Chakrabarti, S., Van den Berg, M. and Dom, B., 'Focused crawling: a new approach to topic-specific web resource discovery'. In: *Proceedings of the 8th International World Wide Web Conference (WWW8)*. Available at **http://www8.org/w8-papers/51-search-query/crawling/index.html**.

12   Chakrabarti, S., Dom., B. Raghavan, P., Rajagopalan, S., Gibson, D. and Kleinberg, J., 'Automatic resource compilation by analysing hyperlink structure and associate text'. In: *Proceedings of the 7th International World Wide Web Conference (WWW7)*, published as Computer Networks and ISDN Systems, **30**, 65–74.

13   Brin, S. and Page, L., *The anatomy of a large-scale yypertextual web search engine*. Available at **http://www7.scu.edu.au/programme/fullpapers/1921/com1921.htm**.

14   Baeza-Yates, R. and Ribeiro-Neto, B., *Modern information retrieval,* ACM Press, 1999.

15   Yuwono, B. and Lee, D. L., 'Search and ranking algorithms for locating resources on the world wide web'. In: *Proceedings of the the 12th International Conference on Data Engineering*, New Orleans, Louisiana, Feb. 26–March 1, 1996, 164–71.

16   Kleinberg, J. M., 'Authoritative sources in a hyperlinked environment'. In: *Proceedings of the 9th ACM-SIAM symposium on discrete algorithms*, 1998. Available at **http://www.cs.cornell.edu/home/kleinber/auth.pdf**.

17   Sullivan, D., *How search engines rank web pages*. Available at **http://www.searchenginewatch.com/webmasters/article.php/2167961**.

18   Nicholson, S., 'A proposal for categorization and nomenclature for web search tools'. In: Iyer, H. (ed.), *Electronic resources: use and user behaviour,* Haworth Press, 1998, 9–28.

19   Sullivan, D., Searchenginewatch.com.

20   Wolfram, D. and Xie, H., 'Traditional IR for web users: a context for general audience digital libraries', *Information processing and management*, **38** (5), 2002, 627–48.

21   Jansen, B. and Pooch, U., 'A review of web searching studies and a framework for future research', *Journal of the American Society for Information Science*, **52** (3), 2001, 235–46.

22   Spink, A., Wolfram, D., Jansen, B. J. and Saracevic, T., 'Searching the web: the public and their queries', *Journal of the American Society for Information Science*, **52** (3), 2001, 226–34.

23   Silverstein, C., Henzinger, M., Marais, H. and Moricz, M., *Analysis of a very large web search engine query log*, Digital SRC Technical Note #1998-014, 26 October, 1998. Available at **http://www-cs-students.stanford.edu/~csilvers**.

24   Hoelscher, C., 'How internet experts search for information on the web', paper presented at the *World Conference of the World Wide Web, Internet and Intranet*, Orlando, FL., Association for the Advancement of Computing in

Education, 1998. Available at **http://www.aace.org/pubs**.

25 Gordon, M. and Pathak, P., 'Finding information on the world wide web: the retrieval effectiveness of web search engines', *Information processing and management*, **35** (2), 1999, 141–80.

26 Jansen, B., Spink, A. and Saracevic, T., 'A study of user queries on the web', *Information processing and management*, **36** (2), 2000, 207–27.

27 Cooper, M. D., 'Usage patters of a web-based library catalog', *Journal of the American Society for Information Science and Technology*, **52** (2), 2001, 137–48.

28 Ford, N., Miller, D. and Moss, N., 'Web search strategies and approaches to studying', *Journal of the American Society for Information Science and Technology*, **54** (6), 2003, 473–89.

Chapter 19

Intelligent information retrieval

Introduction

The nations of the world are moving, at varying rates, into the era of the information society. At every moment of our personal and professional life we are information-dependent, i.e. we make use of different kinds of information, sometimes even unknowingly, in the course of our daily lives. As the consumption/use of information has increased, so also has the rate of generation of information increased; this state is reflected by the term 'information explosion'. More and more information, generated in different forms – published or unpublished, in different media, and so on – has caused two major problems. The first one is related to the storage of information, and the second one is related to its effective and efficient retrieval. The growth of computer technology, particularly in terms of the memory and power of computers, has made the problem of storage easier to handle. Now we can store a vast amount of information, the hard copies of which might have occupied a huge space on the shelves, inside a laptop computer. But while doing so we make the retrieval task much more complex. The greater our ability to store information, the more attention must be paid to the problems of organizing it.[1]

From the users' point of view, everyone wants to get the right information at the right time without much effort. But increases in the size and complexity of the storage database pose the user some obvious questions, such as how to approach to the system for retrieval of information, how to conduct the actual search, how to negotiate for ramification of queries once formulated, and so on. The problem could be solved had we an expert assistant ready to extend help to every user at any time. Recent research in the area of artificial intelligence (AI) and expert systems provides promising prospects in this regard. The major area of concern in AI technologies is the development of systems that can behave intelligently, and quite obviously the development of expert systems is one of the major targets of AI research. Recent advances in the area of AI and expert systems have indicated the possibility of developing information retrieval systems that can behave intelligently, or what in other words can be called intelligent retrieval systems. In this chapter we shall discuss the basic concepts of AI and expert systems, and also another major area, natural language processing (NLP). The phases of NLP, the functional aspects of NLP technologies, and the application of NLP technologies in developing natural language interfaces, text processing, and information retrieval systems are discussed in Chapters 20–21.

Intelligent retrieval systems

Sparck Jones[2] defines an intelligent information retrieval system as a computer system with inferential capabilities such that it can use prior knowledge to establish a connection between a user's (probably ill-specified) request and a candidate set of relevant documents. According to Brooks,[3] an intelligent information retrieval system is a system that carries out intelligent retrieval. Brooks further defines intelligent retrieval as the use, by a computer system, of the stored knowledge of its world of documents, users, etc. and of information about the user and his/her problem to infer which documents would enable that particular user to resolve or manage his/her problem in a better way. It has become apparent through different experiments that retrieval cannot be carried out intelligently unless the system 'knows' about its task, world of documents, language, subject domains, etc., as well as the specific requirement of the user. The realization of the need to use knowledge within retrieval systems has led researchers to look at artificial intelligence systems that also aim to incorporate and use knowledge, and one class of these in particular – expert systems.[3] The following sections briefly introduce the concept of artificial intelligence and expert systems.

Artificial intelligence

A somewhat abstract definition of AI has been provided by Charniak and McDermott,[4] according to whom AI is the study of mental faculties through the use of computational models. *The handbook of artificial intelligence*[5] defines AI as a part of computer science concerned with the design of intelligent computer systems, i.e. systems that exhibit the characteristics we associate with intelligence in human behaviour, viz. understanding languages, learning, reliability, reasoning for solving problems, and so on.

Roger Schank (in his introduction to Shwartz[6]) mentions that there are two main goals in AI. The first and foremost is to build an intelligent machine, and the second is to discover the nature of intelligence. Specifically, AI is an area that is concerned with the development of systems that are capable of

- problem solving
- logical reasoning
- understanding natural language, and
- learning.

The major areas of research in AI include

- language understanding
- vision systems
- problem solving

- AI tools and programming languages
- automatic programming, etc.

Garnham[7] observed in 1988 that the kind of intelligent behaviour studied in AI is only possible if an open-ended amount of knowledge about the world is available to the system. With the incorporation of such knowledge into AI programs, a new area of research – expert systems – came into being. Recently, the area of expert systems or knowledge engineering has emerged as a source for the useful applications of AI techniques.

Expert systems

Simply speaking, an expert system can be defined as a computer system that embodies knowledge about a specific problem domain and can solve problems from the domain using its knowledge with a degree of expertise that is comparable to that of a human expert.

Shwartz[6] defines an expert system as a computer program that simulates the reasoning process that a human being would go through in performing a particular task. An idea about the operational aspects of expert systems can be developed from the definition provided by Kemp,[8] according to whom an expert system is a device that allows the identification, retrieval, and application of a particular answer or problem-solution among the many that may be available in appearing to ask the appropriate questions of the users of the system; it also enables and simplifies the entry and validation of the appropriate data. Hays-Roth et al.[9] define an expert system as a computer system that achieves the high levels of performance in task areas that for human beings require years of special education and training. Brachman et al.[10] define an expert system in terms of its various characteristics which may be summarized as:

1   expertise: the system should be able to perform in the same way as an expert human does
2   symbol manipulation: the system should be able to reason by manipulating various underlying symbols
3   intelligence: the system should exhibit an intelligent behaviour
4   complexity: the system should be able to deal with complex problems
5   reformulation: the system should accept a problem stated in any manner and then should be able to convert it according to the system requirements
6   reasoning about self: the system should be able to justify its own decisions, and
7   type of task: the system architecture should be designed in accordance with the problem to be solved or the task to be performed.

From these definitions, it can be stated that expert systems technology provides the capability for capturing human expertise in a computer and making it available for taking decisions and solving complex problems.

From the late sixties onwards, researchers in AI have been concerned with developing intelligent knowledge-based systems in areas which, though very small and highly specific, have on the whole real-world applicability; for example, in medical diagnosis, computer fault finding, chemical structure elucidation, etc. These systems have become known as expert systems.[3]

Kinds of expert systems

Kemp[8] categorizes expert systems as

- advice systems that provide the benefit of expert advice
- decision-support systems intended to aid a human being in arriving at a decision in the same way as a human expert would have done
- intelligent interfaces intended to accept users' queries in natural language and to provide an access to the system, and
- learning systems that can collect information from different systems in the same way as a human being learns about facts.

Components of expert systems

Most expert systems have the following major components:[3, 11]

1   a knowledge base, which embodies the part of the domain knowledge that should be included in an expert system. It consists of facts, relationships and heuristics relevant to the particular domain
2   an inference engine, which processes and combines facts and rules related to a particular problem or a question with the knowledge from the knowledge base in order to come up with answers or recommendations, and
3   the user-interface, which provides communication with the user both in accepting input and providing output.

In addition to these main components, an expert system could have:

4   explanation capability, which shows the line of reasoning leading to the conclusion and informs the user why a particular fact is needed
5   an interface to other systems, such as database management systems and spreadsheets, and
6   a knowledge maintenance module to update the knowledge base.

These components interact with one another to perform a task. These components and their interactions are indicated in Figure 19.1.

The knowledge base

The knowledge base is a vital component of an expert system. It embodies the knowledge that the system uses to solve a problem or to perform a task. The knowledge required in a knowledge base may be represented in a number of ways. The knowledge that needs to be incorporated into an intelligent information retrieval system is

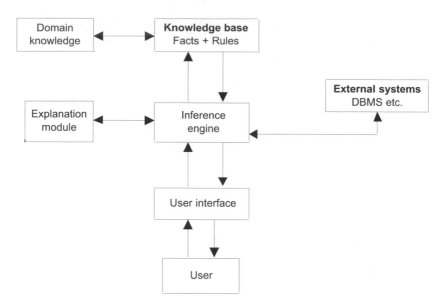

Fig. 19.1 *Basic structure of an expert system*

diverse: it involves many different kinds of knowledge, including knowledge of the relationship between documents and their descriptions, knowledge of the database and its access mechanisms, knowledge of users' problems, and knowledge of the subject domain.[3] The different methods available for knowledge representation are discussed later in this chapter and in Chapter 20.

The inference engine

The inference engine or reasoning mechanism uses and manipulates the knowledge base to arrive at a solution. The form of the inference engine depends on the nature, structure, and size of the knowledge base, but not on its contents. The reasoning mechanism in an intelligent information retrieval system is concerned with inferring a document set that will enable a user to resolve or better manage a particular problem.

User interfaces

Most expert systems require information from the user in order to specify the problem to be solved and to provide an initial set of conditions or observed data.[3] An intelligent information retrieval system will need to communicate with its users in natural language. Interfaces that accept users' queries in natural language and transform it in an internal representation for the purpose of matching with the database are called natural language interfaces. Specific features of these, and the recently developed interfaces in the area of intelligent information retrieval systems are discussed later.

One of the major objectives of expert systems is to allow people to communicate in natural language, which is processed by the system to derive meaning for further action. The processing of natural language input, whether queries or text, for further action by the system is called natural language processing (NLP). A number of AI and expert system technologies have been applied to NLP over the past few years. Brooks[3] says that the great benefit of expert systems research to information retrieval has been that it has stimulated interest in the exploration of what knowledge, in the problem-solving strategies used by human retrieval experts, is required to achieve intelligent retrieval, and in how documents can be represented so that the system knows something about their contents.

Historical development of expert systems

Earlier artificial intelligence (AI) was focused on developing general methods and software for computer processing. A classic example of this research was the GPS (general problem solver). The second half of the 1960s witnessed the emergence of the practical side of AI – expert systems that were the result of the following four interrelated factors.

First, the research approach switched from general to specific or specialist knowledge – the facts and heuristics that are specific to particular problems or domains. As a result of this change, embryonic expert systems such as DENDRAL for determining the chemical structures of molecules, PROSPECTOR for mineral explorations, and MYCIN for medical diagnosis were designed. In 1978 McDermott started developing R1 (later XCON), the first commercially successful expert system, to aid computer configuration at the Digital Equipment Corporation.[11]

Second, the announcement of the Fifth Generation Computer Project in 1981 by the Japanese speeded up research in expert systems and their applications. This in turn stimulated others to take part in the race, mainly in the United Kingdom and the US.

Third, a gradual evolution took place at conceptual and operational levels, from data – through information – to knowledge processing and management.

Fourth, industrial, commercial, educational, and other organizations woke up to the potential of expert systems. In fact, expert systems are currently an AI research area that is quite advanced and has moved out of the research laboratory and into the real world. They are beginning to realize their potential in industrial and commercial applications.[12]

As library and information services became more computerized, they gradually incorporated expert systems technology in the late 1980s. Progress was made in the areas of information retrieval, cataloguing, reference work, indexing and classification, abstracting, thesaurus construction, and training.[13, 14]

Development methodology and approaches

A methodology guides one what to do next, how to do it, and when to do it. It also provides reasons and assumptions for its process. Various methodologies and approaches have been suggested for the development of expert systems, but there is no universal methodology just as there is none for information systems.[15] Except for the unique aspect of knowledge elicitation and representation, which has necessitated a whole new area of software engineering called knowledge engineering, other aspects of expert systems development are similar to those of any information system.[11]

Unstructured and structured methodologies could be used in expert systems development. In the former, the problem is approached randomly and the system developed bit by bit. With a structured methodology the problem is undertaken in structured ways, and mostly the principle of either top-down or bottom-up design is used.

Hilal and Soltan[15] state that at present life cycle (non-prototyping) and prototyping are the two approaches available for expert systems development. No matter which of the two is used, the expert system goes through the following development stages:[11]

1   system analysis, which includes problem identification, domain analysis and modularization, goal identification, communication and expert identification
2   system design, which includes knowledge acquisition as logical design; software selection, hardware selection, user interface design, and physical design of the knowledge base
3   coding, which includes coding the knowledge base and coding the user and system interfaces
4   testing, which includes debugging, verification, validation, and field tests
5   implementation, which includes user training, documentation, and field support, and
6   post-implementation, which includes collecting field reports and statistics, learning new knowledge, and discarding obsolete knowledge.

These stages are applicable in different ways to both the life-cycle and prototyping approaches, as described in the following sections.

The life-cycle approach

In the life-cycle approach the system developer goes through the different stages of expert systems development successively to arrive at the implementation stage and produce the finished product. The strategy is to spend more time specifying and analysing the problem and to postpone all implementation until the detailed study or a complete and correct specification of the required system is ready.

This approach provides an orderly framework for the development of an expert system, which reduces the probability of major errors and pitfalls. However, many authors have indicated that this approach is not suitable for new and unstructured problems in general and for expert systems development in particular. The reason for this is that it is very difficult to achieve detailed specifications when the expertise is hidden in the mind of the expert. As Hilal and Soltan[15] state, spending more time in analysing the hidden knowledge in order to specify it is time-consuming and costly, and could turn out to be fruitless, resulting in piles of useless paper work. Instead, it is better to develop the system prototype without extensive analysis – by the prototyping approach.

Prototyping

Prototyping is an increasingly popular approach in software development for small systems and for new areas. In this approach, a scaled-down version, or prototype, is produced in a short time. This prototype version is delivered to the sponsors and users so that they can see the system's capabilities and limitations, and give their suggestions before allocating resources to the development of a working/final system.[16] Moreover, a prototype need not have to meet the user's requirements in non-critical areas such as completeness or response time, and may exhibit limited functional capabilities, low reliability, and inefficient performance.[16, 17]

Prototyping is a common approach in expert systems because of the novelty and unstructured nature of problems that these systems are trying to solve.[11, 17] Like the life-cycle approach, it follows six stages of system development. However, in prototyping the developer goes through those stages in a quick and incomplete fashion, enhancing each stage in the next iteration of the prototype. Unlike the life-cycle approach, it takes a short time, and hence the development of a prototype expert system is not costly; it allows developers to test and explore their ideas; and it serves as an invaluable focus for feedback from the experts in the application areas and from the users, which is vital for the improvement of the knowledge base and the usability of the system.[17]

Knowledge elicitation and representation methods

Mostly the development of expert systems in general and knowledge acquisition in particular require the involvement of more than one person – e.g. knowledge engineers, domain experts, users, computer programmers, systems analysts, and AI specialists.[11] However, sometimes more than one role is taken by the same person.[18] Prior to the actual knowledge acquisition, the essential tasks are: selection of experts(s) with the recognized expertise and experience in the particular knowledge domain; identification of other sources of knowledge, including printed sources, and the actual process concerned. These all provide input to the knowledge base. In most cases domain experts are the main sources of knowledge, but they may be unable to articulate clearly the nature of their expertise.[16–17] Moreover, in the case of multi-expert knowledge elicitation, issues like organizing the experts and the whole process, and solving conflicting views and opinions about various pieces of knowledge, require decisions.

In order to elicit knowledge by helping experts to articulate their knowledge, there are knowledge acquisition methods that can be used by a knowledge engineer. Basically top-down (or deductive) methods and bottom-up (or inductive) methods are the two knowledge acquisition methodologies. In top-down methods the knowledge engineer organizes acquisition sessions for discovering general concepts, rules, and objects, and then gradually goes into the details of each concept, rule, or object. They comprise questioning methods where the expert is interviewed and/or asked to fill out a questionnaire; object-oriented methods where the expert is asked to discover objects in the domain and explain how the objects are manipulated; quantitative methods to help the expert elicit relations among objects and determine the degree of uncertainty;

i.e. to what extent the relations among the objects remain uniform or unchanged, and methods of invention where the expert is allowed a more active part in the process either as a teacher of the knowledge engineer, as a partner in systematic innovation in which the expert and the knowledge engineer try to identify and resolve contradictory information, or as the knowledge engineer.[11]

In bottom-up methods the knowledge engineer focuses the expert's attention on specific cases in order to help the expert abstract the decision for resolving a specific case to a more generalized rule or concept. In this category are included example-based methods, protocol analysis, and observation of the expert's decision-making process.[11] In example-based methods the knowledge engineer and the expert work on a number of representative cases or examples in the domain. In protocol analysis and observation the knowledge engineer seeks to ascertain the set of actions and responses that the human expert uses. The difference is that in protocol analysis the expert needs to talk through what he or she is doing, which is not necessary in observation.

Once the knowledge is elicited and documented (say using pseudo-code) the next task is to represent it for use in a knowledge base. There are various methods of knowledge representation. The major ones are: Production System (also called Production Rules), Predicate Calculus, Semantic Networks, Case Grammar, Frames, and Conceptual Dependency. These are described in the following chapter under the heading Knowledge Representation. The first two are logic-based methods and the rest are object-based methods.

Inference strategies

One of the main components of an expert system is the inference engine, which uses the knowledge base to come up with a proposed solution or set of alternative solutions. The approach used is the heuristic search for solutions, which is the distinct feature of expert systems and is found to give answers as good as human experts. For this task the two well-known and fundamental methods of inference strategies or search sequences are backward and forward chaining.

The backward chaining inference strategy starts from a goal, i.e. the conclusion in a rule, and then tries to use the knowledge base to get that goal, i.e. it goes back to the condition(s) of the rule. It is goal driven, and preferred when a problem has many premises and few conclusions. In forward chaining, the inferencing starts from a condition and tries to match it to facts obtained from a fact base or a user. If the match succeeds, then the conclusion part is proved and hence the goal is achieved. It is data driven, and preferred when a problem has few premises and many conclusions. It is also possible to combine these two methods of inferencing in order to gain the advantages of each.

End-user modelling and interfaces

A computer-based system is designed for people (users) to accomplish a certain task. Hence the system should be simple and easy to use. This requires thorough consideration of the characteristics and needs of users and then inclusion of these in the design of the system. This can be achieved by establishing an appropriate user model and by developing an appropriate end-user interface. These issues are very important for expert systems, which are intended to provide advice or answers in a variety of situations and are designed to be suitable for inexperienced computer users.

A user model contains knowledge about users of a system. There are the following three main dimensions by which user models can be classified: the canonical model (i.e. the model of a particular type or group of users, such as students, engineers or doctors, vs. models of individual users), explicit models constructed by the user vs. implicit models constructed by the system; and models of long-term, more general information vs. models of short-term, highly specific information.

Depending upon the nature of users and the function of a system, an appropriate approach can be made toward user modelling. Canonical models and individual models are useful for homogeneous and heterogeneous user groups, respectively. Explicit models are not appropriate for systems with naive potential users for whom implicit models are more appropriate. Long-term models are suitable for having an accurate model of some essentially permanent characteristics such as: data/fact about users, their level of expertise with computer systems in general, their expertise with this system in particular, and familiarity with the system's underlying task domain. Short-term models are important in modelling specific and dynamic characteristics, such as preference for type of advice and level of tolerance of the system's response time.

User modelling is still one of the difficult areas in developing an expert system for library and information services. In an academic information centre and in a very narrow domain users tend to be homogeneous, with more or less similar general information needs.

User interfaces have made rapid technological advance. Its main elements are: menus, forms, graphics, symbols and icons, voice, hypertext, and natural language.[11] The first three are relatively common in most software products. Symbols and icons have great significance for an expert system that involves objects.

A natural language interface accepts a user's input in the user's natural language and is able to translate it into system commands. This technology is still young, and so far the systems that have been produced with a natural language user interface are capable of recognizing only a restricted vocabulary concerned with a particular problem domain.[12] The other new and attractive user interface technology is hypertext. Even though this technology for user interfaces is in its early stages, there are expert system shells such as KnowledgePro and LEVEL5 OBJECT which enable the development of expert systems with an integrated hypertext user interface.

Using the latest user interface technology, however, doesn't guarantee a user-friendly interface for a system, because the design of an appropriate interface requires identification of user needs and the type of system user (the user model), and then their incorporation into the interface within resource constraints. The other interface component of an expert system is the systems interface. This allows the expert system to hook onto and communicate with external systems, such as popular database, spreadsheet, and graphics systems.

Development tools

The development tools available for expert systems are:

*   AI programming languages
*   conventional programming languages, and
*   expert system shells.

The early AI programming languages such as LISP (LISt Processing) and Prolog (PROgramming in LOGic) are the most popular. They provide a fully unconstrained development environment, i.e. they have the capability to manipulate arbitrarily complex data structures, and, more importantly, they have an external representation for these structures. However, they are not as suitable for prototyping as shells. On the other hand, any conventional language, such as Pascal C, C++ and BASIC, can be used to program expert systems. They provide run-time efficiency, and also have better interfaces for external application systems, such as databases and graphics systems. But they lack a built-in inference mechanism and hence require code or algorithm to be written to access the data structures.

Expert system shells are expert systems stripped of their domain knowledge.[13] Examples of expert system shells include ADVISOR-2, CRYSTAL, 1st CLASS, KnowledgePro, Xmaster and LEVEL5 OBJECT. The shells available vary from simple ones, with rules and facts constituting the knowledge base, to more sophisticated ones, with frames and inheritance constituting the knowledge base. Unlike programming languages they permit the relatively quick and easy building of a new system, and hence are suitable for prototyping.

Shells have been relatively constrained and inflexible compared to programming languages. But current shells such as KnowledgePro and LEVEL5 OBJECT have built-in procedural languages and interfaces for external programming languages and application systems.

Expert systems for library and information services

Ford[13] suggests that expert systems can be developed for professional tasks in both traditional and non-traditional library and information services and management tasks. These tasks include: indexing, abstracting, thesaurus construction, cataloguing and classification, Boolean text retrieval, non-Boolean text retrieval including reference services, automatic content analysis and knowledge representation, relational database access and management, intelligent documents, training, database selection, and database analysis.

Poulter et al.[18] reviewed the expert systems for LIS over the period 1989 to 1993 by conducting online searches and general searches of the known information science databases within Dialog. From the 195 papers obtained, the development, features, and functions of 139 expert system projects in the LIS domain were reviewed. These systems covered various subdomains, such as online information retrieval (28%); reference work (32%); indexing, cataloguing, or classification (12%); library management applications (7%); abstracting (1%); and others (20%). By function, 69% of the systems were for advisors only, 3% for tutors, 9% for both advisor and tutor, and 19% for other purposes. This review found that:

- some particular LIS domains have received relatively little attention (e.g. abstracting) and others are hardly represented at all (e.g. acquisition). In contrary, some have received great attention (e.g. reference work and online IR)
- the majority of expert systems for LIS are advisory.

Lancaster and Warner[19] provide an excellent review of the applications of expert systems and related intelligent technologies in different areas of library and information science. They note that the major applications of intelligent technologies in the field of library and information science include the following:

- cataloguing
- subject indexing
- collection management
- reference services including:
  — referral of users to appropriate information resources
  — selection of an appropriate database for searching information to meet a specific information need
- text processing including:
  — text categorization
  — text summarization
  — intelligent agents for text processing
  — text mining, data mining and knowledge discovery
- user interfaces.

Examples of applications of intelligent technologies in automatic text processing and user interfaces are discussed later in this book. Some examples of intelligent technologies applied to the other areas of library and information science are discussed below.

Applications in cataloguing

There have been many applications of expert systems in cataloguing, though very few of them have reached the stage of commercial applications. Major experiments in expert systems in cataloging have been:

- Automatic identification of bibliographic elements for cataloguing from electronic versions of title pages. Examples include the works of Jeng,[20, 21] who studied the visual and linguistic cues appearing on the title pages of bibliographic items; and OCLC studies (Weibel et al.;[22] Vizine-Goetz et al.[23]) on developing rule-based systems for identification of various bibliographic elements.
- Automatic determination of the 'main entry' for books. Examples include the studies of Sandberg-Fox[24] and Svenonius and Molto,[25] where the success of the

algorithms varied with the type of books (less successful for scholarly books), and the type of main entry (less successful for corporate body main entry).

Reviews of the applications of expert systems for cataloguing (Sauperl and Saye;[26] Lancaster and Warner[19]) show that:

• Cataloguing rules are not specific and detailed enough to build accurate rules for expert systems; there is enough room for human interpretation of the rules and specific cases
• Visual presentations of title pages of bibliographic items are not uniform enough to allow for the building of accurate rules for expert systems that could be followed for automatic identification of cataloguing elements.

Applications in subject indexing

Lancaster and Warner[19] comment that online machine-aided indexing goes back more than 30 years, and that the systems used vary greatly in terms of their approaches. However, very few of these indexing systems actually use intelligent technologies. Some researchers have developed systems for helping the indexer select appropriate index terms from selected controlled vocabulary tools. For example, CAIN, a system developed to support the European Community's database of ongoing agricultural databases, helps the indexer choose index terms using two vocabulary control tools, viz. AGROVOC and CAB thesaurus (Friis[27]). A similar system has been developed for NASA's Centre for Aerospace Information, which comprises a knowledge base of useful phrases in the aerospace literature used to map to the NASA thesaurus (Silvester et al.[28]). Wright et al.[29] describe how MetaMap, a natural language processing tool, is used to map words and phrases from the full texts of medical documents onto the unified medical language system (UMLS) metathesaurus. Similar systems for automatic indexing based on natural language processing techniques are discussed in Chapter 21.

Applications in collection management

One of the obvious applications of intelligent techniques in collection management has been in the area of automatic selection of booksellers and vendors of library resources, developing an aid in the book selection process. Examples of such systems include:

• The Monographic Acquisitions Consultant developed at Iowa State University to help decide the best vendors to select for the purchase of particular types of monograph (Zager and Smadi;[30] Hawks[31]).
• Systems for the automatic selection of journals, discussed by Rada et al.[32] and Hall[33]; a system developed by Meador and Cline[34] to provide library managers with access to appropriate criteria for selection, etc.; and an agent-based technology for collection management systems developed by McKiernan.[35]

Applications in reference services

As explained by Morris,[14] during the development of most expert systems for reference services the absence of explicit rules for and detailed models of the reference process, the lack of knowledge about user models and the difficulty of deciding exactly what knowledge should be contained within an expert system are the major problems faced by the designer. These problems have not yet been resolved, despite the amount of research devoted to them.

Several expert systems have been developed for reference services,. These include early prototype systems such as REFSEARCH,[36] REFLES,[37] REFLINK,[38] Online Reference System (ORS),[39] and the Information Function (IF).[40]

Some important LIS expert systems were developed in the late 1980s. PLEXUS[41] (see p. 409) is the most ambitious, a demonstration prototype expert referral system with a natural language type interface. It refers users to publications, organizations, databases, and experts in the area of horticulture. Answerman[42] is a small microcomputer-based expert system to point users to a wide variety of agricultural-related reference books and corresponding page numbers for easy access to answers. AquaRef[43] is a working system for providing references to sources of information, answers and advice in response to commonly asked questions in the field of aquaculture. The Information Machine[44] is a menu-driven computer presentation that could also refer users to appropriate reference books or periodical indexes. The Technical Writing Assistant[45] matches the user's request against a database of information sources. Material Librarian[46] is an expert reference advisory system for materials science.

Some of the more recent (early 1990s) LIS expert systems include: Patent Information Assistant,[47] which is a menu-driven expert system assisting users in processing patent information enquiries; ChemRef,[48] a guide to reference sources in chemistry; Expert Reference Advisor for Opera (ORFEO), a system designed to recommend specific sources in answer to questions about opera;[49] and the New Zealand Reference Advisor (NZRef), an expert system to help library assistants answer reference questions about New Zealand by recommending appropriate reference sources.[12]

The approach adopted in developing most of the above expert systems for LIS has been prototyping because of the high level of experimentation required to assemble the knowledge demanded of an expert system. In addition, an unstructured development methodology, which 'is a result of the immaturity of this field and the corresponding uncertainty of researchers in understanding how to deal with the broad base of the LIS profession', has been used.[18]

Regarding knowledge sources and acquisition methods the expert systems in LIS developed so far have used: reviews of printed sources, interviews with experts in the domain, personal experience in the domain, observation, protocol analysis, and/or multidimensional sorting in order of usage frequency.[18] Usually one method is selected as the primary one and supplemented by others. This is the case in most expert reference advisory systems. ORFEO and ChemRef are examples where printed sources (bibliographies, monographs, etc.) of reference information, supplemented by interviews with experienced reference librarians, have been used for knowledge acquisition.

In relation to knowledge representation methods, so far LIS expert systems have used:

- production rules alone, as in Answerman, AquaRef, NZRef and ORFEO
- frames alone, as in Parrott's REFSIM[50]
- semantic nets alone, as in GRANT, developed by Paul Cohen and Rick Kjelsen,[51] which uses a semantic network representing research funding agencies, research topics, and research studies
- predicate calculus, as in CODER,[13] which is a multilayered system for document retrieval, and
- a hybrid of production rules, frames, and/or semantic nets, as in PLEXUS.

Aptagiri et al.[52] have developed a frame-based knowledge representation paradigm for automating the POPSI system (see Chapter 5) developed by Bhattacharyya.[53] This system tackles the different steps in indexing after the formulation of the expressive title, which is the only non-automated step.

Among methods of knowledge representation the production rule is widely used. It is considered an easy means of representing and amending knowledge.[11, 13-14] Moreover, rules are frequently used with other representation methods to select and activate the appropriate method.

So far, the development tools that have been used for developing expert systems for LIS in general and for reference services in particular are: AI programming languages (mainly PROLOG and LISP); expert system shells (mainly 1st-CLASS, KnowledgePro, CRYSTAL, LEVEL5 OBJECT, EXSYS and VP-Expert); and procedural programming languages (mainly BASIC, PASCAL, C and C++). Among these tools, PC-based shells are the most widely used to develop prototype expert systems. The reasons are: they save development time; they are easy to use as they rule out the need for original programming of the inference control mechanism; they offer good 'help' facilities for the developer; they have good user-interface development facilities; and they are comparatively low in cost. However, several developers later choose a programming language for the development of the final system because of the language's flexibility and their unconstrained capabilities.[18]

The features available in the above development tools determine the types of user interface to be created. For both accepting input from a user and for providing output to a user, expert systems developed so far have used dialogue, menus, graphics, and natural languages. Most of the expert systems for reference services described above have used some form of menus and dialogue as their user interface. A few systems, such as PLEXUS, attempt to provide a natural language user interface which has a limited capability and is not mature.[18] However, with the rapid development of graphics and hypertext technology, there is both a great opportunity and the flexibility to have a better user interface. In this respect, the expert system shells KnowledgePro for Windows and LEVEL5 OBJECT are worth mentioning. Both support the WIMP (window, icon, menu and pop-up) and hypertext technologies for developing a user interface.

Compared with other fields only a few expert systems are reported to be operating in LIS, such as: AquaRef, Reference Expert, and ARDIS. A few systems have progressed to commercial availability but have later failed and been withdrawn from the market, like Tome Selector and Tome Searcher.[13]

Evaluation of the systems developed so far indicates that expert systems produce: better results than statistical information retrieval systems; and that users are satisfied with their performance and the answers they provide. For instance, in ChemRef 96% of the evaluators were satisfied with the knowledge ChemRef embodied, and for the same system the answers to a set of questions were compared with that of domain experts and found to be statistically significant.[18]

Discussion

The expert systems that have been developed are largely experimental in nature, and lack integration with other systems. Richardson,[54] while presenting a review of 56 prototype knowledge-based systems for reference services, comments that it is much easier to create a first-generation prototype than it is to put a complete knowledge-based system into operation.

Technological advances, the increasing power of the PC, and the increase in the productivity and simplicity of the software on the one hand and the consistent and continued research for solving the problems in the domain area, user modelling, detailed modelling of the reference process, and lack of standards on the other hand are the driving forces for current research. The trend is towards the integration of expert systems with other application systems, mainly with database, spreadsheet, graphics, multimedia, hypertext, word-processing, statistical, and data communication systems. This is because expert systems, as systems, need to communicate with other systems for various reasons, such as for obtaining data, advanced computations, and quality graphics output. To achieve integration either independent software products that have plugs to other systems or integrated software products that contain all the necessary applications could be used. The former achieve integration through compatibility and the latter through self-sufficiency.[11]

This trend is also prevailing in library and information science in general. For reference services, expert advisory systems are being developed by integrating them with database, multimedia, and hypertext systems. Expert systems are also being networked. Moreover, this integration also includes broader information systems, such as OPACs, CD-ROM, and online databases as well as web-based information retrieval services (see Chapter 18). An example is PlantIt!-CD, a CD-ROM project on ornamental horticulture multimedia that integrates text, images, audio, and an expert advisory system in an interactive hypermedia format.[55] Hanne[56] suggests that the increase in OPAC systems and the development of the Internet and World Wide Web (WWW) will allow us to build a single KBS that would benefit a much larger number of librarians and their clients.

Hayes-Roth and Jacobstein[57] report a number of applications of expert systems, while the reviews by Lancaster[58] and Lancaster and Warner[19] suggest that out of the several thousand expert systems described in literature, only a tiny fraction were ever fully implemented in day-to-day operations. Lancaster[58] further suggests that many of the knowledge-based applications taken place in libraries so far can be referred to as 'solutions in search of a problem'. Lancaster and Warner[19] comment that the expert systems developed in the library field are little more than toys compared with operational systems in use in other environments.

Recent developments in the internet and world wide web (discussed in Chapter 18) have opened up a major area of application of knowledge-based systems that is concerned with the development and management of intelligent search agents (see for example Haverkamp and Gauch.[59])

References

1 Davies, R. (ed.), *Intelligent information systems: progress and prospects*, Chichester, Ellis Horwood, 1986.
2 Sparck Jones, K., 'Intelligent retrieval'. In: Jones, K. P. (ed.), *Intelligent information retrieval: Informatics 7*, London, Aslib, 1983, 136–42.
3 Brooks, H. M., 'Expert systems and intelligent information retrieval', *Information processing and management*, **23** (4), 1987, 367–82.
4 Charniak, E. and McDermott, D., *Introduction to artificial intelligence*, Reading, MA, Addison-Wesley, 1985.
5 Barr, A. and Feigenbaum, A. (eds.), *The handbook of artificial intelligence*, vol.1, London, Pitman, 1981.
6 Shwartz, S. P., *Applied natural language processing*, Princeton, NJ, Petrocelli Books, 1987.
7 Garnham, A., *Artificial intelligence: an introduction*, London, Routledge & Kegan Paul, 1988.
8 Kemp, D. A., *Computer based knowledge retrieval*, London, Aslib, 1988.
9 Hays-Roth, F., Waterman, D. A. and Lenat, D. B., 'An overview of expert systems'. In: F. Hays-Roth, D. A. Waterman, and D. B. Lenat (eds.), *Building expert systems,* Reading, MA, Addison-Wesley, 1983, 3–29.
10 Brachman, R. J., Amarel, S., Engelman, C., Engelmore, R. S., Feigenbaum, E. A. and Wilkins, D. E., 'What are expert systems?'. In: Hays-Roth, F., Waterman, D. A. and Lenat, D. B. (eds.), *Building expert systems,* Reading, MA, Addison-Wesley, 1983, 31–58.
11 Zahedi, F., *Intelligent systems for business expert systems with neural networks*, Boston, MA, Wadsworth Publishing, 1993.
12 Smith, L. C., 'Artificial intelligence and information retrieval'. In: *Annual review of information science and technology*, **22**, 1987, 41–77.
13 Ford, N., *Expert systems and artificial intelligence: an information manager's guide*, London, Library Association Publishing, 1991.
14 Morris, A., 'Expert systems for library and information services: a review', *Information processing and management,* **2** (6), 1991, 713–24.
15 Hilal, D. K. and Soltan, H., 'Towards a comprehensive methodology for KBS development', *Expert systems*, **10** (2), 1989, 75–91.
16 Rauch-Hindin, W. B., *A guide to commercial artificial intelligence: funda-*

mentals and real-world applications, Englewood Cliffs, NJ, Prentice-Hall, 1988.

17 Drenth, H. and Morris, A., 'Prototyping expert solutions: an evaluation of Crystal, Leonardo, GURU and ART-IN', *Expert systems*, **9** (1), 1992, 35–45.

18 Poulter, A., Morris, A. and Dow, J., 'LIS professionals as knowledge engineers', *Annual review of information science and technology*, **29**, 1994, 305–50.

19 Lancaster, F. W. and Warner, A., *Intelligent technologies in library and information science applications*, Medford, NJ, Information Today Inc., 2001.

20 Jeng, L. H., 'Modeling cataloging expertise: a feasibility study', *Information processing and management*, **30** (1), 1994, 119–29.

21 Jeng, L. H., 'The structure of a knowledge base for cataloging rules', *Information processing and management*, **27**, 1991, 97 110.

22 Weibel, S. et al., 'Automated title page cataloguing: a feasibility study', *Information processing and management*, **25**, 1989, 187–203

23 Vizine-Goetz, et al., 'Automating descriptive cataloging'. In: Aluri, R. and Riggs, D. (eds), *Expert systems in libraries*, Norwood, NJ, Ablex Publishing, 1990, 123–34.

24 Sandberg-Fox, A., 'Selection of main entry: a conceptual model'. In: Aluri, R. and Riggs, D. (eds), *Expert systems in libraries*, Norwood, NJ, Ablex Publishing, 1990, 135–54.

25 Svenonius. E. and Molto, M., 'Automatic derivation of name access points in cataloguing', *Journal of the American Society for Information Science*, **41**, 1990, 254–63.

26 Sauperl, A. and Saye, J. D., 'Pebbles for the mosaic of cataloging expertise: what do problems in expert systems for cataloguing reveal about cataloguing expertise?', *Library resources and technical services*, **43** (2), 1999, 78–94.

27 Friis, T., 'Assisted indexing (CAIN)', *IAALD quarterly bulletin*, **37** (1/2), 1992, 35–7.

28 Silvester, J. et al., *Machine-aided indexing from natural language text. Status report*, Linthicum Heights. MD, RMS Associates, 1993 (NASA-CR-4512).

29 Wright, L. et al., 'Hierarchical concept indexing of full-text documents in the Unified Medical Language System information sources', *Journal of the American Society for Information Science*, **50**, 1999, 514–23.

30 Zager, P. and Smadi, O., 'A knowledge-based expert systems application in library acquisitions: monographs', *Library acquisitions: practice & theory*, **16**, 1992, 145–54.

31 Hawks, C. P., 'Expert systems in technical services and collection management', *Information technology and libraries*, **13** (3), 1994, 203–12.

32 Rada, R. et al., 'Computerized guides to journal selection', *Information technology and libraries*, **6**, 1987, 173–84.

33 Hall, G., 'Improving library performance: experimenting with expert systems'. In: *Libraries: the heart of the matter*, DEAKIN, ACT, Australian Library and Information Association, 1992, 126–30.

34 Meador, J. and Cline, L., 'Displaying and utilizing selection tools in a user-

friendly electronic environment', *Library acquisitions: practice and theory*, **16**, 1992, 289–94.

35 McKiernan, G., 'ABCD: agent-based collection development with intelligent agent software at Iowa State University', *Technicalities*, **18** (9), 1998, 8–10.

36 Meredith, J. C., 'Machine-assisted approach to general reference materials', *Journal of the American Society for Information Science*, **22** (3), 1971, 176–86.

37 Bivins, K. T. and Palmer, R. C., 'REFLES: an individual microcomputer system for fact retrieval', *Online review*, **4** (4), 1980, 357–65.

38 Bivins, K. T. and Erikson, L., 'REFLINK: a microcomputer information retrieval and evaluation system', *Information processing and management*, **18** (3), 1982, 111–16.

39 Chisman, H. and Treat, W., 'An online reference system', *RQ*, **23** (4), 1984, 438–45.

40 Diskin, G. M. and Michalak, T. J., 'Beyond the online catalog: utilising the OPAC for library information', *Library hi tech*, **3** (9), 1985, 7–13.

41 Vickery, A. and Brooks, H. M., 'PLEXUS: the expert system for referral', *Information processing and management*, **23** (2), 1987, 99–117.

42 Waters, S. T., 'Answerman: the expert information specialist: an expert system for retrieval of information from library reference books', *Information technology and libraries*, **5**, 1986, 204–12.

43 Haufman, D., 'AquaRef: an expert advisory system for reference support', *Reference librarian*, **23**, 1989, 113–33.

44 Fadell, J. and Myers, J. E., 'The information machine: a microcomputer-based reference service', *Reference librarian*, **23**, 1989, 75–112.

45 Butkovitch, N. J., Taylor ,K. L, Dent, S. H. and Moore, A. S., 'An expert system at the reference desk: Impressions from users', *Reference librarian*, **23**, 1989, 61–74.

46 Carande, R., 'Reference Advisory System (RAS): some practical issues', *Reference services review*, **17**, 1989, 87–90.

47 Ardis, S. B., 'Online patent searching: guided by an expert system', *Online*, March 1990, 56–62.

48 Sarangapan,i C., 'Development and evaluation of a reference expert system in chemistry'. In: Williams, M. E. (ed.), *Proceedings of the 11th National Online Meeting, May 1-3, 1990*, New York, Medford, NJ, Learned Information, 1990, 355–62.

49 Gerber, B., 'ORFEO: an expert reference advisor for opera', *Library software review*, **11** (3); 1992, 8–12.

50 Parrott, J. R., 'Expert systems for reference work', *Microcomputers for information management*, **3** (3), 1986, 155–71.

51 Cohen, P. and Kjelsen, R., 'Information retrieval by constrained spreading activation in semantic networks', *Information processing and management*, **23** (4), 1987, 255–68.

52 Aptagiri, D. V., Gopinath, M. A. and Prasad, A. R. D., 'A frame-based knowledge representation paradigm for automating POPSI', *Knowledge organization*, **22** (3/4), 1995. 162–7.

53 Bhattacharyya, G., 'A general theory of subject indexing languages', PhD thesis, Karnataka University, Dharwad, 1980.

54 Richardson, John V., *Knowledge-based systems for general reference work: applications, problems and progress*, San Diego, Academic Press, 1995.

55 Anderson, J. M., 'The use of expert systems, hypertext and authoring packages to develop reference advisory systems'. In: Ching-Chih Chen (ed.), *Proceedings of the NIT '92: Fifth International Conference on New Information Technology, Hong Kong, Nov. 30 - Dec. 2, 1992*, West Newton, MA, MicroUse Information, 1992.

56 Hanne, D., 'A discussion of knowledge-based systems and librarians: with a selected bibliography from library science and other disciplines', *Public library quarterly*, **16** (2) 1997, 21–44.

57 Hayes-Roth, F. and Jacobstein, N., 'The state of knowledge-based systems', *Communications of the ACM*, **37** (3), 1994, 27–39.

58 Lancaster, F. W., 'Artificial intelligence and expert system technologies: prospects'. In: Raitt, David (ed.), *Libraries for the new millennium: implications for managers*, London, Library Association Publishing, 1997, 27 39.

59 Haverkamp, D., S. and Gauch, S., 'Intelligent information agents: review and challenges for distributed information sources', *Journal of the American Society for Information Science*, **49** (3), 1998, 304–11.

Chapter 20

Natural language processing and information retrieval

Introduction

Natural language processing is an area of research and application that explores how the natural language text entered into a computer system can be manipulated and transformed into a form more suitable for further processing. Automatic natural language processing techniques have been identified as a desirable feature of information retrieval. The aim of an information retrieval system is to retrieve documents in response to a user's request in such a way that the contents of the documents are relevant to the user's requirement. The most comfortable way for a user to express an information need is as a natural language statement or as part of a natural language dialogue. When the documents are retrieved, the users examine the natural language texts and on the basis of this they determine whether the given documents are relevant or not. It is, therefore, no wonder that with the help of sophisticated natural language processing techniques, we should be able to produce representations of documents and queries for efficient retrieval. In a retrieval environment, the users are quite often unsure of what their exact information need are, but they will be able to judge whether a given document is relevant to those needs. The system should, therefore, be able to accept natural language statements as the expression of the users' needs, or it should make provision for a human-machine dialogue through which the system can identify the exact requirement of the user and can take necessary measures for searching. These kinds of systems are known as the natural language interfaces or front-end systems. Most automatic retrieval systems based on natural language processing techniques convert the contents of the document files and user's queries in an internal form, and the task of matching takes place at that level. Systems that take document texts as natural language statements and transform them in an internal form for the purpose of retrieval matching are called text processing systems. Having sketched the possible areas of application of natural language processing in information retrieval, we shall now try to understand how natural language processing systems work.

Natural language understanding

At the core of any natural language processing task there lies an important issue of natural language understanding. The process of building computer programs that understand natural language involves three major problems (Shwartz[1]). The first relates to the thought process, the second to the representation and meaning of the linguistic input, and the third to world knowledge. A natural language processing system requires three kinds of knowledge, *syntactic knowledge*, *semantic knowledge* and *pragmatic knowledge*.

Syntactic knowledge is required to understand the structure of a given sentence. It generally includes a lexicon which consists of words considered as valid in the given domain. The lexicon may also contain syntactic markers or certain categories that can be useful in processing. There is also a need for a grammar that describes the possible word order and different rules of agreement. Semantic knowledge is concerned with meanings of words. Different methods for representing meaning have been developed over the years. However, a given concept may occur in a number of different situations, and to decide which particular meaning is applicable in a given situation the system needs another type of knowledge, called pragmatic knowledge. This type of knowledge is useful because it helps to eliminate ambiguities and supplements the semantic representation.

Liddy[2] and Feldman[3] suggest that, in order to understand natural languages, it is important to be able to distinguish from amongst the following seven interdependent levels, used by people to extract meaning from text or spoken languages:

- phonetic or phonological level – pronunciation
- morphological level – the smallest parts of words that carry a meaning; suffixes and prefixes
- lexical level   meaning of words and analysis of parts of speech
- syntactic level – grammar and structure of sentences
- semantic level – the meaning of words and sentences
- discourse level – the structure of different kinds of text within the document
- pragmatic level – the knowledge that comes from the outside world, i.e., from outside the contents of the document.

A natural language processing system may involve all or some of these levels of analysis.

Syntactic analysis

Syntax deals with the structural properties of texts. Syntactic analysis systems decompose complete utterances into simpler phrases and characterize the structural relations between the components of sentences.[4] Rules of syntax specify the legal syntactic structure for a given sentence.

Context-free grammars

One method to formalize our knowledge is to provide a series of rewrite rules (known as grammar) that will generate the legal sentences of the language[5] Context-free grammars or the type 2 grammars introduced by Chomsky,[6] are the best examples of such systems. They are grammars in which each production must have only a single non-terminal symbol on its left-hand side.[7] Figure 20.1 represents the context-free grammar for a very small sentence. Here the starting point is the *non-terminal node s-maj*. A non-terminal node is one that appears only in the interior of the tree structure for the given sentence (Figure 20.2). Each non-terminal node is replaced by the right-hand side of a rule in which it appears on the left, and this process continues until we have only the *terminal nodes*. These are the nodes that appear in the final sentence.

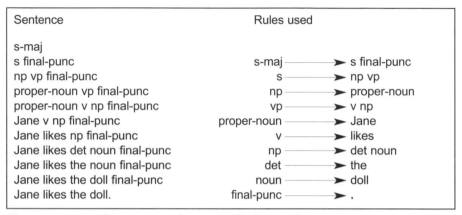

Sentence	Rules used
s-maj	
s final-punc	s-maj ———► s final-punc
np vp final-punc	s ———► np vp
proper-noun vp final-punc	np ———► proper-noun
proper-noun v np final-punc	vp ———► v np
Jane v np final-punc	proper-noun ———► Jane
Jane likes np final-punc	v ———► likes
Jane likes det noun final-punc	np ———► det noun
Jane likes the noun final-punc	det ———► the
Jane likes the doll final-punc	noun ———► doll
Jane likes the doll.	final-punc ———► .

Key: np = noun phrase; v = verb; vp = verb phrase; det = determiner; final-punc = final punctuation.

Fig. 20.1   *A context-free derivation*

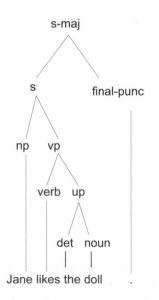

Fig. 20.2   *Context-free derivation tree*

Transformational grammar

The term transformational grammar refers to a theory of language introduced by Chomsky[6] in which an utterance is characterized as the surface manifestation of a 'deeper' structure representing the 'meaning' of the sentence (see Figures 20.3 and 20.4). It was noted that context-free grammars fail to represent subject-verb agreement in all cases. Such a failure called for analysis on a higher level, which is provided by transformational grammars.

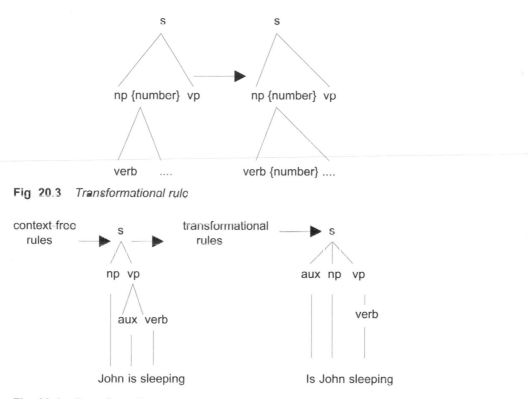

Fig 20.3 *Transformational rule*

Fig. 20.4 *Transformational grammar*

As in the case of context-free grammars, transformational grammars specify the legal sentences of a language by giving rules that generate them. For example, in the rule

s ⟶ np vp

the transformational rule specifies that the verb should be replaced by a verb that has a feature that gives it the same number as the subject of the sentence (Figure 20.3). Transformational grammar starts out with context-free rules to build up the basics of the sentence, but then modifies the basic sentences with the transformational rules.⁵ The tree structure produced by the context-free rules from a basic sentence is called the *deep structure*. After applying the transformational rules to a deep structure, we end up with another tree structure called the *surface structure*.

Parsing

In syntax analysis, valid sentences of a language are recognized and their underlying structures are determined. A central component of the syntactic phase is the *parser*, a computational process that takes individual sentences or connected texts and converts them to some representational structure useful for further processing.⁸ Broadly speaking, parsing is the 'delinearization' of linguistic input, i.e. the use of syntax to determine the functions of the words in the input sentences in order to create a data structure that can be used to get at the meaning of the sentence. The major objective of this phase is to transform the potentially ambiguous input phrase into an unambiguous form. This transposition from some potentially ambiguous phrase to an internal representation is known as parsing, the word parse being derived from the Latin phrase *pars orationis* (part of speech).⁹ The basic parsing techniques are discussed briefly in the following sections.

Top-down and bottom-up parsing

Restricting our attention to context-free grammar for the present moment, there are two basic methods of parsing – top-down and bottom-up. A top-down approach (or hypothesis-driven approach) is one in which the main clause structure and subject-verb-object decompositions are generated at first, and then more refined decomposition of each sub-clause takes place resulting in individual clause components.⁸ A bottom-up (or data-driven) approach is one in which the individual text words are initially considered, and then attempts are made to group them into larger and more comprehensive components.

Bottom-up parsing

The basic idea of bottom-up parsing is to use the rules 'backwards'.⁵ Starting with a given sentence, 'he ate an apple', say, we try to match each part in turn with the right-hand side of some rule. As shown in Figure 20.5 and Figure 20.6, we can match the term 'he' with the right-hand side of the pronoun 'he'. Having done this, we replace the part matched by the left-hand side of the rule, giving rise to the statement 'pronoun ate an apple'. By consistently doing this we generate the complete tree (Figure 20.6).

Top-down parsing

Top-down parsing works in a way opposite to bottom-up parsing. Here we start with an 's node' and replace it with the right-hand side. By repeating this process we finally reach a tree. The process is illustrated with the same example in Figure 20.7.

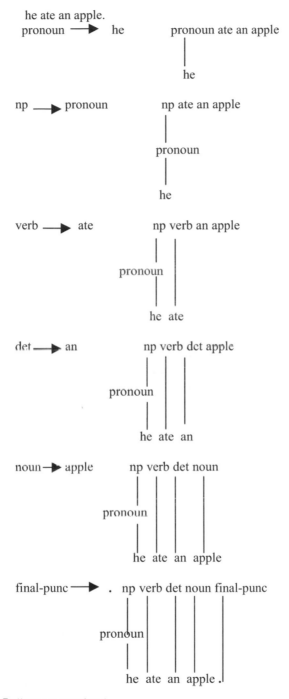

Fig. 20.5   *Bottom-up parsing I*

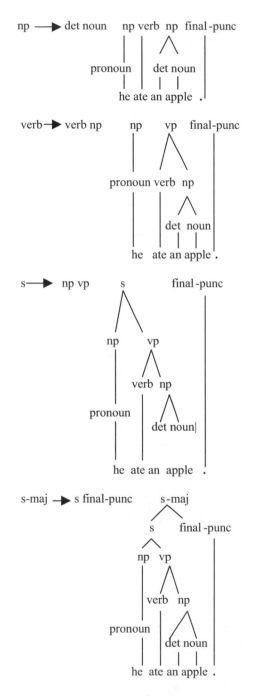

Fig. 20.6   *Bottom-up parsing II*

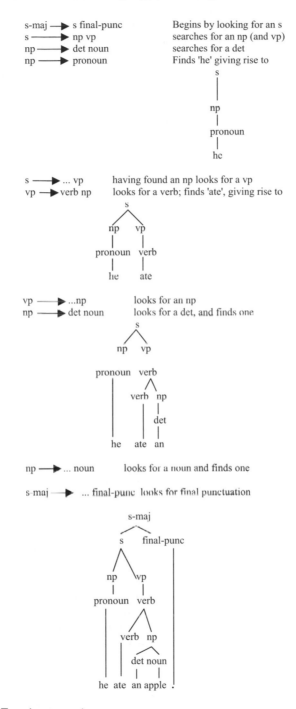

```
s-maj ──▶ s final-punc        Begins by looking for an s
s ──────▶ np vp               searches for an np (and vp)
np───────▶ det noun           searches for a det
np ──────▶ pronoun            Finds 'he' giving rise to

                                        s
                                        │
                                        np
                                        │
                                     pronoun
                                        │
                                        he


s ──────▶ ... vp        having found an np looks for a vp
vp ──▶verb np           looks for a verb; finds 'ate', giving rise to
                              s
                             ╱╲
                           np   vp
                           │    │
                        pronoun verb
                           │    │
                          he   ate


vp ──────▶ ...np             looks for an np
np ──────▶ det noun          looks for a det, and finds one
                            s
                           ╱╲
                         np  vp

                      pronoun verb
                         │      ╱╲
                         │   verb  np
                         │    │    │
                         │    │   det
                         │    │    │
                         he  ate   an


np ──▶ ... noun          looks for a noun and finds one

s-maj ──▶  ... final-punc  looks for final punctuation

                        s-maj
                        ╱╲
                       s   final-punc
                      ╱╲        │
                    np  vp      │
                    │   │       │
                 pronoun verb   │
                    │     ╱╲    │
                    │  verb  np │
                    │   │    ╱╲ │
                    │   │ det noun
                    │   │  │   │
                    he ate an apple .
```

Fig. 20.7 *Top-down parsing*

In practice, none of these approaches is completely satisfactory. A top-down, left-to-right, parsing strategy proves to be inefficient when the initial expectations do not match with the actual sentence components. When an expectation is not met it becomes necessary to abandon the analysis and start over with a new set of expectations. This process is called *backtracking*, i.e. abandoning the current analysis and considering a new path. A bottom-up analysis may also be inefficient because a hypothesis confirmed during a structural analysis may not finally produce a desirable derivation.

Transition network

One important approach to parsing has been to extend the concept of phrase structure rules by adding mechanisms for more complex representations and manipulations of sentences.[7] A typical version of top-down parsing is known as a transition network parser.[3] Let us consider the following two examples:

A   ⟶   B C D   A   ⟶   B C E

In the case of top-down parsing, every time the expectations fail the process of analysis is started afresh, thereby duplicating the process (in this case the parsing of B and C). One solution could be to combine the two rules to indicate the common parts, e.g.

A   ⟶   B C {D / E}

An alternative notation for the process could have been:

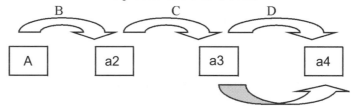

The first node A indicates that this is for parsing an A, while the arcs indicate the next item to be found (B, C, etc.). This means that an arc with the label B on it says that the parser may follow this arc if the next item in the sentence passes the test 'Is this a B?'. From node a3 the parser can follow either of the two paths. A node like a4, which has no arcs leading out of it, is called a 'done node'.

There are two basic ways in which tests on arcs in transition networks take place. If the parser is looking for a part of speech, say 'noun', the test works by looking at the input stream (i.e. checking whether the next symbol is a 'noun'). This may be called a category test and denoted as:

(category terminal-symbol)

Contrarily, if the parser wants to find a non-terminal, like np, it goes to the network and if it finds the np network to a done node then it will have found an np and the test succeeds. This test may be called a parse test and can be represented as:

(parse non-terminal symbol)

Situations where more than one arc comes out of a node of a network are called choice points. If the parser reaches a point where all the outgoing arcs fail, it goes back to a previous choice point and thus a process of backtracking takes place.

Augmented transition network (ATN)

Context-free grammars are not fully suitable for describing languages, and thus the transition networks based on these need to be augmented with transformational rules. The result is the augmented transition network or ATN. This adds the following facilities[5] by:

- remembering what already appeared in the sentence
- manipulating features of constituents, and
- adding and deleting constituents.

Semantic analysis

All syntactic analysis systems must use semantic knowledge to eliminate ambiguities that cannot be resolved by only structural considerations. Now, we shall discuss how a program might go from the syntactic tree to an internal representation. This process is called semantic interpretation, which is based on a *knowledge base* and knowledge/semantic representation schemes. The following sections discuss the basic concepts of knowledge base and knowledge representation followed by some widely used knowledge representation techniques.

Knowledge base

A knowledge base comprises different kinds of knowledge stored within the memory to be used by the program in the course of processing the natural language statements. The amount of knowledge required generally depends on the domain being handled.

A knowledge base can be of declarative or of procedural form.[10] The distinction between declarative and procedural knowledge corresponds to the distinction between a database and a program that acts on the database.[11] In the declarative form an item in the knowledge base does not carry in itself any indications regarding where and how it is to be used. Declarative representations seem more natural than procedural representations to non-programmers because these are like statements of facts, e.g. 'New Delhi is the capital of India'. On the other hand the procedural form means that the datum also includes information on how it is to be used and when, or what is to be done before or after. An example of the declarative form might be 'The article agrees in gender and number with the noun': the equivalent procedural form might be 'On encountering an article, seek the noun it is attached to; check first that the gender of the noun is the same as that of the article, then the number of the noun is the same as that of the article'.[10]

Knowledge representation

Knowledge representation or semantic representation refers to the internal representation created from natural language statements. This internal representation is not limited to the language of the input text, and can be used for further processing, e.g. in matching users' queries in information retrieval, in the creation of a database in one or more languages, in any sort of text processing work, i.e. representing the text in a specific format, etc. Kemp[12] mentions that the two major purposes of knowledge representation are:

- to help people understand the system they are working with, and
- to enable the system to process the representations.

Some of the methods available for knowledge representation are introduced in the following sections.

Production systems

A production system consists of three parts:

- a rule base composed of a set of production rules
- a special, buffer-like data structure, called the context, and
- an interpreter, which controls the system's activity.

A production rule is a statement that can be represented in the form:[7]

IF this condition holds THEN this action is appropriate

The condition may be simple or may be compound (comprising several terms linked by Boolean operators). The IF part of the productions, called the condition part, states the conditions that must be present for the production to be applicable. The THEN part, called the action part, is the appropriate action to take place. The context (also known as the data or the short-term memory buffer) is the focus of attention of the production rules. The left-hand side of each production in the rule base represents a condition that must be present in the context data structure before the production rule can work. The interpreter is a program whose job is to decide what to do next.

Production systems have the following features:

1   the individual productions in the rule base can be added, deleted or changed independently. One rule can be changed without much concern over direct effects on the other rules
2   any information encoded within the rigid structure of production rules can be easily understood

3 production system formalism provides knowledge about what to do in a predetermined situation, and

4 one major disadvantage of production system formalism is the inefficiency of
program execution. The other disadvantage is that it is difficult to follow the
flow control in problem-solving; in other words, the program algorithms are
less transparent.

However, production systems capture, in a manageable representation, a certain
type of problem-solving knowledge. Production systems have been used in systems
like DENDRAL, MYCIN, and PROSPECTOR.[7]

Predicate calculus

Predicate calculus is a logical system invented by the German mathematician and
logician Gottlob Frege.[9] It is used to represent statements about specific objects or
individuals as described in sentences. Statements about individuals, both by themselves and in relation to other individuals, are called predicates.[7]

In predicate calculus, knowledge is represented by statements having two parts –
the first part is the predicate and the second part is the argument.[10] A predicate is
applied to a specific number of arguments and has a value of either TRUE or
FALSE. Predicates can have more than one argument. An example of a two-place
predicate from mathematics is 'greater than'. One very important two-place predicate is 'equals'.[7] Each one-place predicate defines a set (or sort), e.g. for any one-
place predicate P, all individuals X can be sorted into two disjunct groups, with
those objects that satisfy P (i.e. $P(X)$ is TRUE) forming one group and those that
don't forming another.

Sentences or well-formed formulae in predicate calculus are made up from predicates, constant terms, variables, logical connectives, and quantifiers. Predicates
take one or more arguments. For example, 'sleeps (john)' means a person called
John is asleep. Examples of predicates taking more than one argument may be

sees (mary, john)	Mary sees John
sees (mary, brother, john)	Mary sees John's brother

Predicates can also have variables and function applications as arguments, e.g.

left-of (chair, table)	The chair is left of a table

The connectives of a predicate calculus are the one-place connective, which corresponds to 'not', and can be placed in front of a well-formed formula to mean its
negation,[11] e.g.

~ likes (john, mary)	John does not like Mary

and the two-place connectives, which can be introduced by using &, v, and Ý (to
represent 'and', 'or', 'if ... then' respectively), e.g.

made-of (food, vegetables) Ý edible (food)   If the food is made of vegetables
                                              then it is edible

The two quantifiers are the universal for all and the existential for some. A quantifier is always associated with a variable. The quantifier and its variable stand in front of an expression containing instances of that variable, which they are said to bind,[11] e.g.

(for all x) (man (x))   For all x, if x is a man
(for some y) (woman(y)   then there is some woman y, such that
& loves (x,y)) x loves y
                                       i.e. every man loves woman

These are all formation rules. Similarly, there are some inference rules, which show how one formula can be derived from others. One example of such a rule is that from the formula of the form P and P Q, the formula Q can be deduced.[11]

Predicate calculus has been used to represent and manipulate information in many AI projects, particularly in such domains where uniform representations are useful.[11] Kemp[12] points out that predicate calculus has the following advantages:

- once the system has been grasped, it is easy to follow the statements
- a system of inference rules is available that are logically complete and well-defined, and
- it is independent of domains.

However, there are certain disadvantages too. It is not very useful for dealing with special relationships and special cases that are often illogical and occur in particular domains, and it can only provide YES/NO answers and therefore cannot readily cater for certainty factors.[12] Garnham[11] mentions that predicate calculus databases do not readily support the domain specific methods of inference making that can be exploited if non-uniform methods of representation are used. A good domain specific method is one that produces those conclusions that are required in the domain for which it is intended. Semantic networks are one example of such a method.

Semantic networks

Many of the recently developed systems in AI research use a class of knowledge representation formalisms called semantic networks. A semantic network may be described as a drawing in which the hierarchies of all the relevant facets are represented, with lines joining classes and subclasses. The networks are called semantic because they encode information about meaning. The representation formalisms in semantic networks are grouped together because they share a common notation, consisting of nodes (which are drawn as dots, circles or boxes) and arcs (or links drawn as arrows) connecting the nodes.[7] Both the nodes and arcs can have labels. Usually, nodes represent objects, concepts, or situations in the domain, and arcs represent relations between them. Semantic networks provide a non-uniform way of representing information. There were two main ideas behind the semantic network. The first one was the intersecting search, which is a method of finding a connection between two concepts. The second idea was that of an inheritance hierarchy, which is a taxonomy of concepts denoted by common nouns. The hierarchies are called inheritance hierarchies because nodes inherit properties from those above them in the hierarchy.[11]

As linguistic theory, semantic nets offer a convenient formalism for representing such ideas as 'deep structure' or 'underlying semantic structure'.[10] A semantic network represents a structure that contains meanings of language arranged in a network. It generally contains concept nodes interconnected by semantic relations. The simple semantic network shown in Figure 20.8 represents a series of facts embodied within the network, e.g. 'Clyde is a bird' (Clyde is a robin, and robins are birds; hence, Clyde is a bird). Similarly, it represents that 'Clyde owns NEST-1 (which is a NEST) from SPRING to FALL'. Many semantic network systems use sets of case arcs and case-frame structure to inherit expectations about, even for default values (for some slots in the frames, there may be some default values) certain attributes.

Semantic networks are primarily useful tools for those who need to form a conceptual schema of the domain. These can be used to represent not only the relations between concepts but also relations between individuals, and hence facts about the world.[11] Most current work on the representation of knowledge involves elaboration of the basic semantic network idea.[7]

Case grammar

Case grammar is the best known of the relatively shallow, domain-independent approaches to semantic processing.[4] It claims that there is a small fixed number of

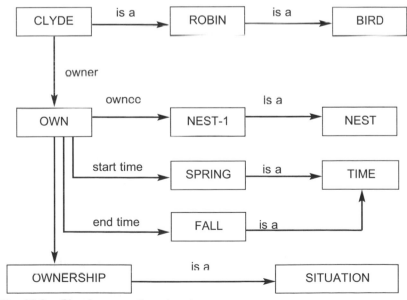

Fig. 20.8 *Simple semantic network*

so called deep cases.[13] The central idea of case grammar is that the proposition embodied in a simple sentence has a deep structure consisting of a verb, which is the central component, and one or more noun phrases. Each noun phrase is associated with the verb in a particular relationship. These relationships are called cases. For example, in the following two sentences:

John opened the door with the key
The door was opened by John with the key

'John' is the agent of the verb 'opened'; the 'door' is the object, and 'the key' is the instrument. Thus although the two sentences have two different surface structures, they are the same in their deep structure. Fillmore[13, 14] proposed the following cases:

Case name	*Case definition*
Agent	The instigator of the event
Counter-agent	The force or resistance against which the action is carried out
Object	The entity that moves or changes or whose position or existence is in consideration
Result	The entity that comes into existence as a result of the action
Instrument	The stimulus or immediate physical cause of an event
Source	The place from which something moves
Goal	The place to which something moves
Experiencer	The entity which receives or accepts or experiences or undergoes the effect of an action.

If we want to identify the case, there are three particular sources of information, viz., the verb, the noun phrase and the preposition.[5] For each verb, we have to indicate which case does it take, how these cases are flagged through prepositions, and whether the case was optional (indicated by { }) or obligatory, e.g.

Jack bought the car from Bill for a thousand pounds

buy	agent	Jack
	patient	the car
	{source}	from Bill
	{cost}	for a thousand pounds

When a case grammar analysis is completed by filling the case-frame slots with appropriate sentence elements, most of the syntactic ambiguities are automatically eliminated.[5]

Frames

One of the widely used schemes for knowledge representation is the frame. The idea of frames was proposed by Minsky[15] as a basis for understanding visual perception, natural language communication, and other complex behaviours. Frames provide a structure, a framework, within which new data are interpreted in terms of concepts acquired through previous experiences.[4] The organization of knowledge facilitates expectation-driven processing by looking for things that are expected according to the context. The representational mechanism that makes possible this kind of reasoning is the slot, the place where knowledge fits within the larger context created by the frame. In a system a frame may carry information about how to use it, what is likely to happen, and what frames are likely to be used in particular circumstances. For example, in an 'employee' frame the different slots may be 'sex', 'age', 'specialization', 'salary', etc. Each of these slots can have a specific value. For example, for a particular employee x, the value of different slots may be:

```
Employee frame
name:            x
age:             40
sex:             male
specialization:  management
salary:          25,000
and so on
```

Sometimes frames are linked in such a way that the value of one slot points towards the new frame to be considered, e.g. the value 'management' in the slot 'specialization' may point towards another frame, like 'responsibility'. In fact, frames are quite easy to use, and for this reason quite a number of systems have used frames for the representation of knowledge. However, Schank and Riesbeck[16] mention that there are two basic problems with the frame hypothesis:

1   often there is no one single frame into which coherent inputs will fit, and
2   there will usually be a number of frames into which a given input can fit, but finding out exactly which is suitable in a given situation is often a difficult job.

Using the idea of frames, Schank and Abelson[17] have developed scripts, which are frame-like structures specifically designed to represent sequences of events. The idea of scripts is discussed along with pragmatic knowledge (p. 390).

Conceptual dependency

Conceptual dependency (CD) is a theory of representation of the meaning of sentences. The basic axiom of the theory may be stated as:[16]

For any two sentences that are identical in meaning, regardless of language, there should be only one representation.
There is a corollary of this axiom:

Any information in a sentence that is implicit must be made explicit in the representation of the meaning of that sentence.

According to the CD theory, the meaning propositions underlying languages are called conceptualizations. A conceptualization can be active or stative. An active conceptualization has the form: Actor *Action Object Direction (Instrument)*. A stative conceptualization has the form: Object *(is in) State (with value)*.

The foundation of Schank's theory of CD is the primitive ACT. Primitives are the basic elements of knowledge representations in AI theories. Schank identified primitive ACTs to capture the meaning of action sentences (see Schank and Riesbeck[16]). He termed these as ACTs to denote that they represent actions rather than categories of verbs.

Primitive ACTs

Physical ACTs	Application of a physical force to an object.
PROPEL	PROPEL is used whenever any force is applied regardless of whether a movement took place or not. *Give, push, pull*, etc., have PROPEL as part of them.
MOVE	Movement of a body part of an animal by that animal, e.g. MOVE *foot* is an instrument to *kick*.
INGEST	The taking in of an object by an animal to the inside of that animal. *Eat, drink, smoke, breathe*, etc. are common examples of INGEST.
EXPEL	The expulsion of an object from the body of an animal into the physical world. Words for excretion and secretion are described by EXPEL (e.g. *sweat, spit*, etc.)
GRASP	The grasping of an object by an actor, e.g. *hold, throw*, etc.

ACTs characterized by resulting state changes	
PTRANS	The transfer of the physical location of an object, e.g. *go* is PTRANS oneself to a place, *put* is PTRANS of an object to a place.
ATRANS	The transfer of an abstract relationship such as possession, ownership or control e.g. *give* is ATRANS something to someone else, *take* is ATRANS to self.

ACTs used mainly as an instrument for other acts	
SPEAK	The actions of producing sounds. The words *say, play music*, etc. involve SPEAK.
ATTEND	The action of attending or focusing a sense organ towards a stimulus, e.g. ATTEND *ear* is *listen*, ATTEND *eye* is *see*, and so on.
Mental ACTs	The transfer of mental information between animals or within an animal.
MTRANS	The three mental locations in the CD scheme are considered as conscious processor (CP), long term memory (LTM), and short term memory (STM). *Tell* is MTRANS between

MBUILD

people, *see* is MTRANS from eyes to CP, and so on.
The construction by an animal of new information from old information. *Decide, imagine, consider,* etc. are common examples.

Each primitive ACT is a frame that organizes a set of slots (e.g. actor, object, from, to, etc.) that are filled by some nominal value (e.g. a person, animal, place, or object). Schank's theory (see Schank and Abelson[17]) also provides for a representation of states. Each state can be measured in a scale of –10 to 10. Some examples of the states of CD are given on the following page.

Many sentences require a conceptualization consisting of more than one ACT. Five ACTs, viz., GRASP, SPEAK, MOVE, ATTEND, and EXPEL are mainly used in the INSTRUMENT slots of the ACTs. According to Schank and Riesbeck,[16] the sentence 'John read a book' can be represented as follows:

actor:	John	
action:	MTRANS	
object:	information in a book	
	direction TO:	CP (conscious processor) of John
	FROM:	book
	instrument:	
	actor:	John
	action:	ATTEND
	object:	eyes
	direction TO:	book
	FROM:	unknown

In his earlier work, Schank[16] claimed that the primitive ACTs of CD, together with a set of possible states of objects were sufficient to represent the meaning of any English verb, but later it became clear that additional mechanisms would be needed for a general purpose language understanding system. Schank[18] developed several new devices, e.g. scripts, plans, and goals, for his representational system in order to reflect the purposive aspects of actions as well as their physical descriptions. These issues are discussed in the following section.

States	*Examples*	*Value*
HEALTH	dead	–10
	gravely ill	–9
	sick	–9 to –1
	under the weather	–2
	all right	0
	tip-top	7
	perfect health	10

FEAR	terrified	−9
	scared	−5
	anxious	−2
	calm	0
ANGER	furious	−9
	angry	−5
	upset	−2
	calm	0
	catatonic	−10
	depressed	−5
	upset	−3
MENTAL STATE	OK	0
	pleasant	2
	happy	5
	ecstatic	10
HUNGER	starving	−8
	ravenous	−6
	hungry	−3
	no appetite	0
	satisfied	3
	full	5
	stuffed	8

Pragmatic knowledge

Shwartz[1] mentions that our ability to understand language is a function of the quantity and quality of the information (knowledge) that we have about the domain of the discourse as well as our ability to make reasons (or inferences) based on this information. We have already seen how syntactic knowledge helps to determine the structure of sentences, and how semantic knowledge helps to derive the meaning. However, in natural language, a given statement may have more than one meaning, and sometimes the sentences are in a sense incomplete. Pitrat[10] mentions that to understand a text, more is needed than knowledge merely of grammar and meaning of words. We use specific knowledge to interpret and participate in events we have been through many times. This is pragmatic knowledge. Specific detailed knowledge about a situation allows us to do less processing and wondering about frequently experienced events.[17] Pragmatic knowledge is useful because it helps to eliminate ambiguities and complete semantic interpretation. Methods like scripts, plans, and goals have been developed for representing pragmatic knowledge about everyday life. Scripts, plans, and goals are knowledge structures that are useful for organizing knowledge concerning how people deal with the environment they live in, for organizing one's own episodic memory of life's events, and for understanding linguistic utterances that refer to these episodes.[1]

Scripts

Roger Schank (see Schank and Abelson[17]) devised the method of representing pragmatic knowledge about everyday life, which he called scripts. A script is a structure that describes appropriate sequences of events in a particular context.[17] Scripts serve to organize the knowledge that people must have in order to understand. A script is made up of slots and requirements about what can fill those slots.

In fact, a script is a predetermined, stereotyped sequence of actions that defines a well-known situation. Understanding a story that relies upon scripts requires first deciding what script is being referred to. This is called script instantiation. Next, the script is used to fill in the important details in the causal chain being built. This process is called script application. Script application fills in the gaps in a causal chain between two seemingly unrelated events.

Every script has associated with it a number of roles. When a script is instantiated, the actors in the story assume the roles within the script. If an actor has not been specifically mentioned in a story when a particular script is being used, his presence is assumed.[16] There are scripts for eating in a restaurant, riding a bus, watching and playing a football game, participating in a birthday party, and so on.[17] A script must be written from one particular role's point of view. A customer sees a restaurant in one way, while a cook sees it in another way. Schank and his colleagues at Yale University have built a system called SAM (script application mechanism), which understands simple stories about script-based situations.[16, 17] Figure 20.9 is a sketch of one track of the restaurant script (the coffee shop track) from the point of view of the customer. The actions of the scripts are described in terms of the underlying events that take place. The primitive ACT is the core of each event in the chain of events being effected. In the story

John went to a restaurant. He ordered a sandwich and a coffee. He paid the bill and left

the first sentence describes the first action of scene 1 of the restaurant script; sentence 2 refers to the crucial action of scene 2; and sentence 3 to the last two actions of scene 4. The final interpretation of the story would contain a chain through the restaurant script that included all the principal actions (or MAINCONS for main conceptualization) needed to connect the events. To define when a script should be called into play, script headers are necessary. The headers for the restaurant script are concepts having to do with hunger, restaurants, and so on in the context of a plan of action for getting food.[17] Shwartz[1] mentions that the theory of script and script application is fairly complex. The theory provides for optional components in scenes, different tracks on a script, rules for when and in how much detail a script is activated during the understanding process, script deviations, interactions between scripts, scriptal ambiguity, and differences in scripts due to different sets of life experiences.[1]

Scripts are very suitable for completing the semantic representation, and they are especially suitable for summarizing programs. We can initially mark each action in a script with a grade (e.g. essential, very important, important, secondary, minor, etc.) and then we are able to make longer or shorter summaries by determining when the importance exceeds a certain threshold. Scripts can also be useful for a robot that has to achieve an objective that corresponds to a script.[10]

Plans and goals

Scripts are not sufficient to capture all of the diverse kinds of information about the world. They are intended to account for the specific knowledge that people have. But it is not practicable to foresee all sorts of events and encode them into scripts. Human knowledge can cope with more than stereotyped sequences of actions for solving problems. A computer understanding system must be able to understand stories that describe new or unexpected situations. To do this it is necessary to connect pieces of information by means other than scripts.[17] Schank has proposed plans to provide computer programs with this sort of capability. Plans enable the understanding of the relationships between the various actions that serve to achieve a goal. A plan is made up of general information about how actors achieve goals. Plans can help to solve new problems or can deal with unexpected information. They describe the set of choices that are available to a person when he or she sets out to accomplish a goal. A plan is not composed of actions alone; some of its stages are goals which in turn call for other plans in order to be realized. A plan for eating could be as follows:

Goal 1: find out where there is some food
Goal 2: go to the place where this food is
Goal 3: take control of the food
Goal 4: the food must be put into consumable form
Action: eat the food.

Each of these goals can be achieved in a number of ways. For example, to take control of food one may buy it, one may steal it, may exchange something for it, and so on. This implies having a set of methods that we are aware will realize a goal, or at least being able to recognize the actions of an individual as a possible method for realizing a goal. Methods for realizing goals involve chains of instrumental goals, i.e. necessary partial accomplishments along the path to the main goal.[17] Some instrumental goals can be pursued without further planning; they involve fixed steps that can be achieved by simple instrumental scripts. The simple and stereotyped instrumental goals are called I-goals. The general goal of getting somewhere can be characterized as a change in the state of proximity of something. Similarly, other general goals can be characterized as changes in the other common states. These goals are called 'delta goals', abbreviated as D-goals. The D-goal of changing proximity is labelled as D-PROX. A D-goal has no value in and of itself. D-goals are usually subordinate to higher-level main goals. There can be many possible main goals (and I-goals), but there is only a rather small set of D-goals.[16] Schank and Abelson[17] state that the process of understanding plan-based stories is as follows:

- determine the goal
- determine the D-goals that will satisfy that goal, and
- analyse input conceptualizations for their potential realization of one of the planboxes that are called by one of the determined D-goals. A planbox has a set of preconditions, or states of the world, that must be true in order to use the given planbox. It also has an ACT associated with it and a goal that a successful planbox will fulfil (see Schank and Riesbeck.[16])

There is a fine line between the point where the scripts leave off and plans begin. Many predictions come from an understanding that an individual has certain goals

```
Script:  RESTAURANT
Track:   coffee shop
Roles:   S – customer
Props:   tables          W - waiter
         menu            C - cook
         F - food        M - cashier
         Cheque          O - owner
         money

Entry conditions:  S is hungry       Results: S has less money
                   S has money                O has more money
                                              S is not hungry
                                              S is pleased (optional)
```

Scene 1: Entering
S PTRANS S into restaurant
S ATTEND eyes to tables
S MBUILD where to sit
S PTRANS S to table
S MOVE S to sitting position

Scene 2: Ordering
(menu on table) (W brings menu) (S asks for menu)

S PTRANS menu to S	S MTRANS signal to W
W PTRANS W to table	S MTRANS 'need menu' to W
W PTRANS W to menu	W PTRANS W to table
W ATRANS menu to S	
S MTRANS food list to CP(S)	*S MBUILD choice to F
S MTRANS signal to W	W PTRANS W to table
S MTRANS 'I want F' to W	W PTRANS W to C
W MTRANS (ATRANS F) to C	C MTRANS 'noF' to W
C DO (prepare F script)	W PTRANS W to S to Scene 3
W MTRANS 'no F' to S	

       (go back to*) or
       (go to Scene 4 at no pay path)

Fig. 20.9 *Restaurant script*   *(continued)*

Scene 3: Eating
C ATRANS F to W
W ATRANS F to S
S INGEST F
(optionally return to Scene 2 to order more; otherwise go to Scene 4)

Scene 4: Exiting
S MTRANS to W
W MOVE (write cheque)
W PTRANS W to S
W ATRANS cheque to S
S ATRANS tip to W
S PTRANS S to M
S ATRANS money to M
(no pay path): S PTRANS S to out of restaurant

Fig. 20.9   *(continued)*

and is likely to want to effect actions to carry out those goals. Main goals cause D-goals and I-goals. These goals make predictions about actions and the preconditions for those actions. The actions can come either from scripts or from planboxes. Scripts and planboxes have the same status in the overall scheme of goal realization.[17] They tell the actor what to do next. When a script is available for satisfying a D-goal, it is chosen; otherwise a planbox is chosen.

A goal covers all the possible sequences of actions that could cause it to be attained. However, we are obliged to give much more detail, so that the reader can choose the outcome from amongst a multitude of possibilities. In the case of a script, the sequence of actions is automatic, and thus very little guidance is needed. With plans, however, little information is needed to specify the goals, but much detail must be given in order to indicate how to achieve each goal.

Goals may not always be given explicitly. Schank[18] introduces themes, which are ways of discovering implicit goals. If we know that 'John loves Mary', and 'Mary is in danger', then we also know that John will have a goal to rescue Mary. The author need not make it explicit: knowledge associated with the theme' includes the fact that an individual who loves another will try to rescue him/her from danger.

The mechanism of comprehension is thus based on three new elements: plans, goals, and themes. Each goal is linked to a certain number of plans. A plan comprises a sequence of goals and/or actions. When a goal is perceived, the presence of a plan linked to this goal is predicted. The unfolding of this plan is attempted through the constituent goals or actions. Sometimes the text does not provide the goal, but suggests the presence of a theme that leads to the unfolding of the plan.

References

1   Shwartz, S. P., *Applied natural language processing*, Princeton, NJ, Petrocelli Books, 1987.

2 Liddy, E., 'Enhanced text retrieval using natural language processing', *Bulletin of the American Society for Information Science*, **24**, 1998 14–16.

3 Feldman, S., 'NLP meets the jabberwocky', *Online*, **23**, 1999, 62–72.

4 Salton, G., *Automatic text processing: the transformation, analysis and retrieval of information by computer*, Reading, MA, Addison-Wesley, 1989.

5 Charniak, E. and McDermott, D., *Introduction to artificial intelligence*, Reading, MA, Addison-Wesley, 1985.

6 Chomsky, N., *Aspects of the theory of syntax*, MIT Press, 1965.

7 Barr, A. and Feigenbaum, A. (eds.), *The handbook of artificial intelligence*, Vol. 1, London, Pitman, 1981.

8 Warner, A. J., 'Natural language processing'. In: Williams, M. E. (ed.), *Annual review of information science and technology*, **22**, Elsevier, 1987, 79–108.

9 Obermeier, K. K., 'Natural language processing: an introductory look at some of the technology used in this area of artificial intelligence', *Byte*, **12** (4), 1987, 225–32.

10 Pitrat, J., *An artificial intelligence approach to understanding natural language*, trans. Harding, E. F., London, North Oxford Academic, 1988.

11 Garnham, A., *Artificial intelligence: an introduction*, London, Routledge & Kegan Paul, 1988.

12 Kemp, D. A., *Computer-based knowledge retrieval*, London, Aslib, 1988.

13 Fillmore, C., 'The case for case'. In: Bach, E. and Harms, R., *Universals in linguistic theory*, New York, Holt, Reinhart and Winston, 1968, 1–68.

14 Fillmore, C., 'Types of lexical information'. In: Steinberg, D. and Jakobovits, L., *Semantics*, Cambridge University Press, 1971, 370–92.

15 Minsky, M., 'A framework for representing knowledge'. In Pinston, P. H. (ed.), *The psychology of computer vision*, New York, McGraw-Hill, 1975, 211–77.

16 Schank, R. C. and Riesbeck, C. K. (eds.), *Inside computer understanding: five programs plus miniatures*, Hillsdale, NJ, Lawrence Erlbaum, 1981.

17 Schank, R. C. and Abelson, R. P., *Scripts, plans, goals and understanding: an inquiry into human knowledge structures*, Hillsdale, NJ, Lawrence Erlbaum, 1977.

18 Schank, R. C., *Conceptual information processing*, Amsterdam, North-Holland, 1975.

Chapter 21

Natural language processing systems

Introduction

Information retrieval is largely concerned with designing, implementing and maintaining effective and efficient information systems for practical use. One of the most important aspects of information retrieval concerns how the documents (or other records) in a system are represented. The fastest computer or the most sophisticated search techniques cannot overcome the problems caused by poorly represented documents. There are a potentially unlimited number of ways in which a given document can be represented in an information retrieval environment. The success of the retrieval system depends significantly on the way the documents in the database are represented. According to Blair,[1] the process of representing documents for retrieval is fundamentally a linguistic process, and the most important problem relates to how language is used.

The linguistic problem of information retrieval can be viewed from two angles. From the point of view of input, the problem lies in the fact that the documents are represented (indexed) by people who have little or no idea of the terms that the users will select. From the user's point of view, the tasks for which the user wants information determine what index terms he or she would like to use, and the terms actually used in the search will determine the nature of the final result.

Traditional theories of document indexing or representation consider two aspects: the context and the subject. Contextual information is represented in a number of ways, including name of author, type of document, source of origin, date of publication, and so on. Subject descriptions are used to represent the 'intellectual content' of a document. This is usually done by selecting a small number of subject terms which are supposed to represent what the given document is 'about'. This is an important task in document representation, and much information may be lost owing to inappropriate choice of content-bearing words. Blair[1] suggests that the use of subject description to represent the intellectual content of a document is a linguistic act, and that to understand and improve the process one must look at this linguistic act.

For many years results of the application of NLP techniques to different areas of information retrieval were in general not very encouraging.[2] In consequence, most systems for automatic content analysis of texts were based on statistical models, which involve frequency counts of document terms, clustering methods based on term association factors, or probabilistic relevance measures. All these approaches mostly provide keyword-level analyses of texts. The methods are inadequate, given the rich information potential inherent in full texts and the requirement to make knowledge embodied in the texts directly available.[3] Blair[1] maintains that linguistic approaches are appropriate to account for structural aspects of sentence analysis, which are further supplemented by knowledge-based analysis to derive the underlying meaning of a text for further information retrieval tasks.

Research in NLP began in the late 1960s,[4] and automatic NLP techniques were regarded as desirable for the information retrieval environment. However, owing to the complexities of natural language, the complexity of its processing and the overall complexity of texts, the initial results of automatic language processing tasks, particularly the attempts in machine translation, did not produce encouraging results. With the developments of new NLP techniques, new artificial intelligence and expert systems technologies, and with the rapid developments in computational power and techniques over the last few years, considerable attention has been paid to explore the potential of NLP in different areas of information retrieval.

Considerable current interest can be seen in the development of natural language text processing systems that allow structuring of large bodies of textual information with a view to retrieving particular information or to deriving knowledge structures that may be used in accessing information from the texts.[5, 6]

Literature on natural language processing systems

Natural language processing techniques have been applied to a number of fields of studies, such as machine translation, natural language text processing and summarization, user interfaces, multilingual and cross language information retrieval (CLIR), speech recognition, artificial intelligence and expert systems, and so on. Research on natural language processing systems have appeared in several volumes of the *Annual review of information science and technology* (ARIST) (see for example, Chowdhury,[7] Haas[8], Grishman[9] and Warner[10]. Reviews of literature on large-scale NLP systems, as well as the various theoretical issues have also appeared in a number of publications (see for example, Jurafsky and Martin;[11] Manning and Schutze;[12] Mani and Maybury;[13] Sparck Jones[14] and Wilks[15]). Smeaton[16] provides a good overview of the past research on the applications of NLP in various information retrieval tasks. Several ARIST chapters have also appeared on areas related to NLP, such as machine-readable dictionaries,[17, 18] speech synthesis and recognition[19] and cross-language information retrieval.[20]

Research on NLP is regularly published in a number of conferences such as the annual proceedings of ACL (Association of Computational Linguistics) and its European counterpart EACL, biennial proceedings of the International Conference on Computational Linguistics (COLING), annual proceedings of the Message Understanding Conferences (MUCs), Text Retrieval Conferences (TRECs) and ACM-SIGIR (Association of Computing Machinery – Special Interest Group on Information Retrieval) conferences. The most prominent journals reporting NLP research are *Computational linguistics* and *Natural language engineering*. Articles reporting NLP research also appear in a number of information science journals such as *Information processing and management, Journal of the American Society for Information Science and Technology* and *Journal of documentation*. Several researchers have also conducted domain-specific NLP studies and have reported on them in journals specifically dealing with the domain concerned, such as the *International journal of medical informatics* and *Journal of chemical information and computer science*.

This chapter provides an overview of various applications of NLP systems in information processing, access and related areas.

Natural language text processing systems

General studies on natural language information retrieval and text processing systems have been amply discussed in the literature.[21–24] Early studies on automatic database generation in some specialized subject areas have been reported by Sager,[25] Kittredge and Lehrberger,[26] and Lyttinen and Gershman.[27] Features of some natural language text processing systems are briefly described in this section.

Automatic abstracting and text summarizing

Automatic abstracting and text summarization are now used synonymously to describe research that aims to generate abstracts or summaries of texts. This area of NLP research is becoming more common in the web and digital library environment. Some applications of NLP in automatic abstracting and text summarization have been discussed in Chapter 8. Features of some more NLP applications are discussed below.

FRUMP

FRUMP (Fast Reading Understanding and Memory Program) is a newspaper skimming program developed at the Yale Artificial Intelligence Project to skim and summarize news articles.[28] It uses a data structure called a 'sketchy script' to organize its knowledge about the world. A script is a structure that describes appropriate sequences of events in a particular context. The semantic schema in FRUMP provides ready-made frameworks for representing objects, ideas, events or activities that are typical of the domain. Semantic analysis of texts is then greatly assisted because the 'semantic shape' of the concepts that will be encountered is largely predictable. Each domain is characterized by a special repertoire of carefully constructed schemas, one of which is selected to represent each discourse concept.

Conceptual analysers

Gershman[29] describes a framework for natural language processors, called conceptual analysers, which take natural language texts as input and produce conceptual dependency representations of their meaning at a certain level of detail. The main idea behind this framework is the application of predictive understanding to language analysis. The analyser goes through the sentence from left to right trying to find a conceptualization that forms the backbone of the meaning representation for the sentence. Once the conceptual frame of the sentence is found, the analyser uses the predictions that come with the frame to analyse the rest of the sentence in a top-down fashion. Conceptual analysis is dictionary-based. The dictionary entry for each word contains information about what this word means and how it is used. The knowledge is stored in the form of special routines that generate the conceptual frame of the sentence being built. Depending on the connotation of the given word, the slots of the frame with semantic expectations are generated. Once the backbone of the meaning representation is formed, the analyser will use the expectations associated with the conceptualization slots to interpret the rest of the sentence.

The stock market report generator

An example of automatic text generation is the stock market report generator, which takes simple facts contained on stock exchange ticker tape as input and produces natural language reports.[30] This module uses lexical, syntactic and rhetorical constraints to determine syntactic structure, usage of pronouns and other anaphoric referents, verb-tense specifications, and other criteria of text structure.

RUBRIC

RUBRIC is an example of a production rule-based full-text retrieval system.[31] A production rule is usually represented in the form – 'if CONDITION then CONSEQUENCE'; the condition may be simple or compound, and the consequence may take a number of forms. The indexing base of this system contains positional information about words in the texts, which allows positional controls on words while processing queries. The performance of the system is strongly dependent on the way the query is presented. Knowledge about retrieval requests is encoded in RUBRIC as a collection of rules with uncertainty values. It is an example of a production system that can perform evidential reasoning: the text of the document is the evidence on which the system can determine the relevance of that document to the retrieval request in question. The implementation of the system is divided into two modules: the preprocessor module and the system module. The preprocessor module takes the free-format text of a collection of documents and builds the database, which primarily represents an inverted structure of the word stems occurring in the collection of documents. Each word has one entry in the structure and is accompanied by contextual information, such as in which document and in which position it occurs. The system module includes the user interface, the toolbox, and the retrieval subsystems.

The CODER project

The CODER project was proposed as a means of systematically investigating the use of knowledge-based approaches for handling the complex task of analysis and retrieval of composite documents.[32, 33] The plan for CODER was to use blackboard-based expert system methods. A blackboard is a continually changing information store; the experts are able to see the overall situation at all times and respond as and when the state of the knowledge on the blackboard is appropriate to their own unique expertise. NLP is supported, in this system, through a dictionary. The knowledge representation is organized by a 'knowledge administration complex', which allows the creation and manipulation of document types for elementary object frames and relations. One blackboard for the retrieval function and another blackboard for the document analysis task are used to allow maximum flexibility and to ease integration of the components.

SCISOR

SCISOR (System for Conceptual Information Summarization) is an information retrieval system that reads news stories about mergers and acquisitions from a news wire source (online financial news from Dow Jones), extracts information from the stories, and answers questions in English pertaining to what it has read.[34, 35] In order to overcome one significant drawback of NLP systems, i.e. the inability of the lexicon to cover all the words and phrases in texts, Rau[34] adopted two methods in SCISOR: to apply a text processing strategy that is tolerant of unknown words and gaps in linguistic knowledge, and to acquire lexical information automatically from the texts. The system combines a bottom-up full parser TRUMP (Transportable Understanding Mechanism Package) and a top-down skimming partial parser.[35] TRUMP is a suite of natural language processing tools, which includes a parser, a semantic interpreter and a set of lexical acquisition tools. The TRUMP parser combines words into phrases and sentences, checks specific constraints, and instantiates linguistic relations. It also incorporates a top-down mode that offers the benefit of being able to 'skim' texts for particular pieces of information, passing over unknown words or constructs and ignoring some of the complexities of the language. The combination of top-down and bottom-up processing allows this text processing system to make use of all sources of information it may have in the understanding of texts in a domain.[35] A test result shows that out of one day's total of 729 stories, SCISOR achieved over 90% averaged recall and precision in its determination of which stories were about mergers and acquisitions. It correctly identified the target and suitor in 90% of all the stories. When dollar-per-share values were present in the stories, SCISOR extracted this quantity in 79% of the cases, and the total value of the offer in 82% of cases.[36]

SIMPR

SIMPR (Structured Information Processing and Management: Processing and Retrieval) is a project that includes research on text and language analysis, automatic indexing, automatic classification, machine learning, and domain and task modelling.[37, 38] Research on automatic language processing aspects of SIMPR has been carried out by the Research Unit for Computational Linguistics at the University of Helsinki. An important part of the SIMPR project is the morpho-syntactic analysis phase. This phase is, however, preceded by another, called the mark-up processing phase, which identifies the word boundaries, punctuation marks, etc., in the input text, and passes it on for spelling-error detection. The morphological analysis is based on a lexicon (containing about 29,000 entries) and an analyser that identifies the legal inflectional forms of lexical entries and retrieves the proper base form of words when they are inflected in texts. The analyser also provides the parts of speech and other grammatical properties of input words to aid in syntactic analysis. The morphological analysis phase generates a list of lexical interpretations for each input token, out of which a single acceptable interpretation is chosen by applying a set of disambiguation and syntax rules. The syntactic analysis is then carried out with a parser, which determines the clause, boundaries, and syntactic functions of the token by generating a dependency syntax that will identify whether an input token is a head or a modifier, and if a modifier, which one is its head. Thus the syntactic analysis phase finally generates a database of tree-structured analytics (TSAs) for each clausal or sentential unit of the texts, which is matched against the TSAs generated from users' queries in the same way. The matching of the 'related phrases' is thus based on morpho-syntactic analysis, not on semantic analysis. The system of this linguistic morpho-syntactic analysis is, however, ongoing and further refinements are likely to take place.[38]

COP

Metzler et al.[39, 40] developed COP (the Constituent Object Parser), which is designed to produce simple hierarchical descriptions of the syntactic structures of phrases and sentences for use in matching queries and documents in IRS (Information Retrieval System) and similar text matching situations. The first step in parsing a sentence, according to Metzler et al.,[40] is to create a token for each word using information from the lexical dictionary. Each token thus isolated comprises the word, its position in the sentence, its lexical category and its number, and tense and feature fields. COP matches these structural descriptions to estimate the similarity between the query phrase and body or content of the texts. It is also possible to determine the relationship between any two terms occurring in a phrase by considering the items of information associated with each token. COP uses two basic data structures – a control stack which points to the tokens, and a general chart or blackboard-like area which keeps track of all the tokens. This system is based on the premise that much of the information conveyed by the syntactic structure of natural language entities can be represented in the form of binary trees, which indicate which branch contains the dominant concept and which acts in the role of a modifier.

SILOL

SILOL[41] (the Simple Logical Linguistic document retrieval system) introduces a simple means of semantic translation of natural language in a document retrieval system. The semantic translation technique is based on the Simple Montague Grammar (SMG), which is a type of categorical grammar. Document texts and query phrases are translated into sets of first-order predicates, which are used as their content indicators.

Information extraction

Knowledge discovery and data mining have become important areas of research over the past few years and a number of information science journals have published special issues reporting research on these topics (see for example, Benoit;[42] Qin and Norton;[43] Raghavan, Deogun and Server;[44] Trybula[45] and Vickery[46]). Knowledge discovery and data mining research use a variety of techniques in order to extract useful information from source documents. Information extraction (IE) is a subset of knowledge discovery and data mining research that aims to extract useful bits of textual information from natural language texts.[47] A variety of IE techniques are used and the extracted information can be used for a number of purposes, for example to prepare a summary of texts, to populate databases, fill in slots in frames, identify keywords and phrase for information retrieval, and so on. IE techniques are also used for classifying text items according to some predefined categories. An earlier example of text categorization system is CONSTRUE, developed for Reuters, which classifies news stories.[48] The CONSTRUE software was subsequently generalized into a commercial product called TCS (Text Categorization Shell). An evaluation of five text categorization systems has been reported by Yang and Liu.[49]

PROMETHEE

PROMETHEE is a system that extracts lexico-syntactic patterns relative to a specific conceptual relation from technical corpora.[50] Bondale et al.[51] suggest that IE systems must operate at many levels, from word recognition to discourse analysis at the level of the complete document. They report an application of the Blank Slate Language Processor (BSLP) approach for the analysis of a real life natural language corpus that consists of responses to open-ended questionnaires in the field of advertising.

MITA

Glasgow et al.[52] report on a system called MITA (Metlife's Intelligent Text Analyzer), which extracts information from life insurance applications. Ahonen et al.[53] propose a general framework for text mining that uses pragmatic and discourse level analyses of text. Sokol et al.[54] report research that uses visualization and NLP technologies to perform text mining. Chang, Ko and Hsu[55] argue that IE systems are usually event-driven (based on domain knowledge built on various events) and propose an event detection driven intelligent information extraction by using the neural network paradigm. They use the backpropagation learning algorithm to train the event detector, and apply NLP technology to aid the selection of nouns as feature words that are supposed to characterize documents appropriately. These nouns are stored in ontology as a knowledge base and are used for the extraction of useful information from e-mail messages.

Problems in information extraction research

Cowie and Lehnert[56] reviewed the earlier research on IE and commented that the NLP research community is ill-prepared to tackle the difficult problems of semantic feature-tagging, co-reference resolution, and discourse analysis, all of which are important issues of IE research. Gaizauskas and Wilks[47] reviewed the IE research from its origin in the artificial intelligence world in the 1960s and 1970s through to the 21st century. They discussed the major IE projects undertaken in different sectors: academic research, employment, fault diagnosis, finance, law, medicine, military intelligence, police, software system requirements specification, and technology or product tracking.

Owei[57] and Chowdhury[58] review works on information extraction and text mining. Chowdhury[58] identifies various template mining techniques in the extraction of proper names from full text documents, extraction of facts from press releases, abstracting scientific papers, summarizing new product information, extracting specific information from chemical texts, and so on. He also discusses how some web search engines use templates to facilitate information retrieval. He recommends that if each web author is given a template to complete in order to characterize his or her document, then eventually a more controlled and systematic method of creating document surrogates can be achieved. However, he warns that a single all-purpose metadata format will not be applicable for all authors in all the domains and further research is necessary to come up with appropriate formats for each.

Sublanguage analysis

Some natural language processing systems have been built to process texts using particular small sublanguages to reduce the size of the operations and the nature of the complexities.[10] As noted earlier, these domain-specific studies are largely known as 'sublanguage analyses'. Some of these studies are limited to a particular subject area and others deal with a specific type of document, such as patent texts. Some of these sublanguage analysis studies are described briefly below.

SINTESSI (Integrated System for Italian Text) is a prototype system for the interpretation of Italian texts on automobile research (texts produced at the Fiat Research Centre, Torino, Italy). The system analyses descriptive technical texts and extracts information for generating search keys for a full-text database.[59] The performance of a prototype system that extracts information from patient discharge summaries sentences in a restricted medical domain – thyroid cancer care – has been reported by Zweigenbaum and Cavazza.[60] COTEM is a prototype system designed to acquire knowledge from financial news in the Spanish language with a view to integrating new information into the financial knowledge base.[61] Liddy, et al.[62] developed a prototype system for processing free-text comments on life insurance applications for evaluation by an underwriting expert system.

Some typical investigations in the application of NLP in specific fields with particular reference to chemical and patent information retrieval are briefly discussed below.

Sublanguage analyses in chemical information retrieval

Zamora and Blower[63, 64] attempt to generate automatically reaction information forms (RIFs) from the descriptions of syntheses of organic chemicals in the journals of the American Chemical Society. These contain the reactants and reagents of a chemical reaction, along with their quantities (scale) and reaction conditions. This project uses a word-expert approach during the lexical and syntactic phases. Discourse structure analysis and a frame approach are used to obtain a representation of the meaning of the paragraphs during the semantic phase. The initial pass (lexical phase) consists of a simple word look-up or morphological analysis of words and numeric strings. A secondary stage (syntactic phase) analyses superficial sentence structure on the basis of parts of speech and punctuation. A third (semantic) stage identifies sentences to be processed or skipped and provides a suitable representation for those to be processed. Finally, a detailed analysis of the sentences describing the synthesis is performed to extract information for compilation of the RIFs. The techniques explored in the semantic phase of this project include the use of a case grammar and frames to map the surface structure of the text into an internal representation from which the RIF can be formed. The system was tested on 40 synthetic paragraphs from the experimental sections of the *Journal of organic chemistry*, 36 of which were processed satisfactorily.[64]

Ledwith[65] describes a project that attempts to develop a concept-oriented database to be used in online retrieval systems. The goal of this project was to develop a database having explicit, detailed conceptual information associated with each document in the database. The data selected were *Chemical abstracts* (vol. 105), containing 238,000 document citations. The input text is first broken into a sequence of tokens, where each token represents a word or punctuation character. The tokens are then installed in a memory resident token pool, and entries in a hash list are set to point to their corresponding tokens in the pool. Each token within the input data is then replaced by its corresponding address in the token pool. The token pool contains over 150,000 unique tokens. In addition to the token pool, another memory resident pool is maintained, where each entry represents the name of a concept, together with a sequence of one or more token pointers. The name list contains 570,000 entries. The semantic patterns are formalized into prototypical frames, where slots of the frame refer to known concepts within the system. The knowledge base is constructed using object-oriented programming techniques. The concept objects are loaded in the knowledge base and form the basis of a semantic network, which is augmented by the names and synonyms of the concepts. A parser processes the index entries to create instantiated frames. The frames are then linked into the augmented semantic network. This project has thus constructed an object-oriented system with an initial semantic network of 956,000 objects.

Using the work of Zamora and Blower[63, 64] as a model, Ai, Blower and Ledwith[66] have developed a system that generates a summary of all preparative reactions from the experimental section of the *Journal of organic chemistry* papers. The processing is divided into four stages. The first stage preprocesses the primary journal file with a view to extracting the experimental section; translating the text into ASCII (American Standard Code for Information Interchange) format; marking word, sentence, and paragraph boundaries; and building a LISP data structure for the text. The second stage performs the task of token classification through dictionary look-up and word morphology. The third stage transforms the text into a sequence of frames representing meaning. Altogether, a sequence of seven events has been identified in the text of the experimental section: combine reactants/reagents, allow reaction to proceed under a stated condition, quench reaction, isolate product, purify product, report yield, and report characterization data. The frame representation is designed to mimic these events. Phase I of this semantic processing searches each sentence for important sentence fragments describing actions, substances and reaction conditions using ATN parsing. The major objective of this phase is to divide the experimental paragraph into a sequence of clauses.

Phase II of the semantic processing converts the series of clauses produced by phase I into event frames. The fourth stage of processing takes a sequence of unorganized event frames from the third phase, organizes reaction information, and creates a synthesis frame for each preparation described in the experimental section. For simple synthesis paragraphs the program produces successful results in 80–90% of cases, which falls to 60–70% for complex paragraphs.[66]

Postma et al.[67, 68] developed a system called TICA, which extracts information from abstracts in the domain of inorganic titrimetric analysis. TICA uses a parallel approach to sentence analysis where the morphological, syntactic and semantic analyses are performed concurrently during the analysis of sentences. The parsing program follows an expectation-based approach: words or groups of words expect other words or concepts to appear. The expectations are implemented in what is known as 'requests', which are basic modules consisting of tests and actions linked to words. The semantic analysis which acts on the output of the parser, is a combination of the conceptual dependency theory and the case structure. After semantic analysis of the input sentences the 'script' approach is used to interpret the meaning of the sentences. After the instantiation of the input of each sentence the system tries to link them with the 'episodes' of the 'titration script'. The frames that contain the information that is useful as output are marked, and at the end the information is written to a database. The result of an analysis of 40 abstracts from *Analytical abstracts* (1988/9) shows that performance of the system varied between 98% and 37% depending on the item of information it attempted to extract – in 98% of cases it identified the main reagent, in 52% of cases it identified the method performance figures, whereas in only 37% of cases was it able to identify the detection limit.[68]

A system, related to natural language text processing but mostly based on morphological analysis, has been designed for analysing the syntax and semantics of IUPAC (International Union of Pure and Applied Chemistry) systematic nomenclature.[69-74] The project uses a combination of both top-down and bottom-up parsing. The grammar developed for this project comprises 444 terminal symbols representing about 350 morphemes, which are manipulated by 233 production rules. In the lexical analysis phase the input string is split into valid fragments and corresponding syntactic tokens (in parsing, a syntactic unit, such as identifiers or an operator, is referred to as a token) are fed to the syntax analysis phase. The syntactic phase uses a simple LR (left to right) parser generator or SLR.

The parsing process depends upon the ability to determine which terminal symbol corresponds to each morpheme of the input string and to identify those morphemes. Where the parser successfully reaches the end of the input name, and indicates that the name is acceptable, the sequence of terminal symbols identified for the name is recorded as a syntactically valid interpretation, and the semantic processing then begins. Semantic information is held within the grammar alongside each appropriate morpheme. After the parsing and semantic analysis are over, a concise connection table is generated, which represents the molecular structure of the corresponding name that can further be converted into full atom-by-atom connection tables. This study initially attempted to build grammar and related techniques for dealing with hydrocarbon nomenclature, which were then extended to the more complex area of steroid nomenclature.[48] Work related to the translation of chemical nomenclature dates back to the early 1970s[75, 76] and 1980s.[77, 78] Work on automatic translation of structure diagrams into IUPAC nomenclature has given rise to AUTONOM software: the structure of the given substance is input via the graphic interface, and the software analyses the structure and generates the name on the basis of the resulting connection table.[79, 80]

Sublanguage analyses in patent information retrieval

Some studies that have been carried out on the application of NLP techniques to the processing of patent texts are briefly discussed in this section.

A semi-automatic method for extraction of information from patent-claim sentences and summaries of technical papers written in English and Japanese has been reported by Nishida and Takamatsu[81] and Nishida, Takamatsu and Fujita.[82] The information to be extracted is first designated by a 'specification table', which consists of several sub-frames for each specific field; each sub-frame has a case structure and each case is filled by a normalized term if a corresponding term exists in the text. In case of ambiguity, the system asks the user to correct dependency relations among terms. Each input text sentence is parsed using a precise verb pattern and an internal form is constructed. After the parsing, the internal expression is normalized into a form similar to the specification. The specified information is extracted by scanning the normalized internal expressions of the text, where the system first picks up the main term and its corresponding sub-frames and case labels followed by verb, and so on, and the process is repeated until the end of the text is reached. The extracted information in the form of specification tables is transformed into relational tables and inverted files. A relational table is constructed for each sub-frame of the specification table, and each case label in a sub-frame is inherited as an attribute name of a relational table. An inverted file is also constructed for each descriptor appearing in the specification table. Each entry in the inverted file consists of both the sub-frame label and the case label of the descriptor as well as the source document number.

RESEARCHER[83] is related to earlier investigations of natural language understanding, for instance supporting the capability of reading and understanding newspaper stories on a particular topic. It is intended to accept information presented in natural language, in particular, patent abstracts. It analyses the abstracts and creates a knowledge representation of the information they contain; it can search for similarities between different patents and it answers questions about the information in the memory. RESEARCHER uses scripts for knowledge representation and creates a hierarchical representation of the information contained in patents.[83] The generalization of the hierarchical representations allows the system to learn about a wide range of complex objects and build up a memory, which is used in text processing, primarily for disambiguation, to achieve what is claimed to be 'a robust performance'.[84]

The TINA (Text-Inhalts-Analyse: text content analysis) project, developed at the Siemens Corporate Research Laboratories in Germany, aims at developing natural language processing software for information retrieval, free-text searching and indexing, automatic abstracting, thesaurus building, and natural language search question input for textual databases. The application areas are commercial free-text databases on mainframes as well as the field of text handling on a personal computer.[2, 85, 86]

The TINA project started in the mid-1980s, and was based on more than five years of previous research and development work in information and documentation. TINA software has been tested by the US Department of Commerce for patent search and indexing.[86] TINA research and development work is focused on syntactical analysis for full-text documents and large free-text databases. The syntactic analysis in TINA first isolates noun phrases in a text. A number of syntactic rules help to build the dependency structure of the isolated noun phrases. The syntactic processing of texts thus results in structures where dependency relations between words are made explicit. By evaluating these relations for all the words of a database statistically, each text word is correlated with all other words by which it is determined or specified or which it determines or specifies itself. This exercise helps in building the syntactic tables for the database words, which can be used for searching and indexing purposes for free-text databases. TINA can also be used in order to match multi-word expressions against full-text documents. The user of this system submits phrases to the text and gets more and more detailed ideas about the content of the full-text document. The syntactic analysis is done by an automatic search and indexing system called COPSY (Context OPerator SYntax), which performs a number of functions: automatic noun phrase recognition, noun phrase selection, noun phrase normalization, noun phrase matching and automatic document ranking on the basis of syntactic criteria.[86] The rules that determine the syntactic links are formulated in terms of various syntactic categories like noun, adverb and preposition. The processing of 195,000 abstracts from the US PTO (United States Patent and Trademark Office) resulted in 140 megabytes of dependency structures.[2] The TINA evaluation was performed on the basis of 50 PTO abstracts that were not involved in rule development and belonged to different patent domains. The syntactic analysis resulted in 85% recall and 84% precision.[2]

A basic linguistic approach has been adopted in the LEXITRAN (LEXIcon TRANslation) project,[87, 88] which attempted to apply natural language processing techniques to build technological lexicons for indexing patent documents that are classified in the IPC (International Patent Classification) system. The objective of the project was to use the results of the automatic indexing to create a 'natural language gateway to the IPC'.

The template mining approach can be used in extracting valuable information from natural language texts. Lawson et al.[89] describe a natural language processing technique of template mining used to extract data from full texts of chemical patents. When text matches a template, the system extracts data according to the instructions associated with that template. Gaizauskas and Wilks[47] have reviewed several research works that have used template mining approach for extraction of different types of information from the full texts of digital documents.

Natural language user interfaces

A considerable amount of research has taken place on natural language interfaces that make the task of communicating with the information source easier, allowing a system to respond to a range of inputs to produce more customized output. Older systems of natural language interfaces have been discussed.[90–92]

A natural language interface is one that accepts query statements or commands in natural language and sends data to a system, typically a retrieval system, which then results in appropriate responses to the commands or query statements.[90] 'Front-end' or 'gateway' is sometimes used synonymously with interface. Kemp[93] defines a natural language interface as one that allows the entry of the enquiry statement and performs the conversion into the search statement to be used by the retrieval system. Brooks[91] establishes the major aim of natural language interfaces as the understanding of the user and his or her problem on the one hand, and understanding of the documents and document descriptions that are essential for the system's functioning on the other. Therefore, a natural language interface must be able to translate natural language statements into appropriate actions for the system.[91] Kemp[93] suggests that interfaces have different degrees of 'naturalness'. The unnatural end of the interfaces allows the use of only some recognizable words, while the natural end allows normal sentences, as used in everyday life. Researchers are more interested in the latter area and as a result a number of projects have aimed at the development of suitable natural language interfaces for information retrieval. An intelligent interface is one that makes use of some kind of knowledge base and is adaptive to new or unprecedented situations. The first task of an interface is to isolate and translate the terms of the queries posed by the users.[1] Different features of natural language interfaces have been widely discussed in the literature.[90–92] Specific features of the more recent studies are discussed below with an emphasis on the technical aspects.

CANSEARCH

Pollitt[94] reports an investigation into the possibility of computer searching carried out directly by a user using an interface. The program to provide the intermediary was given the title CANSEARCH, a name that has since been used to refer to the whole system. The main objective of the experiment was to determine whether the CANSEARCH approach to document retrieval by naïve end users was feasible. The CANSEARCH program design is based on sets of rules that carry out matching functions on user selections and internal messages, and perform actions appropriate to the conditions signified by the match. The rules represent the knowledge of search statement formation for the retrieval of references related to cancer therapy from the MEDLINE database. The internal messages and eventually the actual MEDLINE search terms are written to working storage areas, called the blackboards, where each board is concerned either with some facet of the query or with an element of control. The system is designed to use a touch terminal where the user can directly select a term by touching the screen of the terminal, with a finger, pen or pencil.

The terminology of the subject domain is encoded in MeSH (Medical Subject Headings), which is a hierarchical thesaurus used for indexing documents in MED-LINE. The system is based on the premise that searchers may not know exactly what search terms they should use, but they will recognize them once they see them displayed on the screen. Appropriate subsets of the thesaurus are displayed and users are allowed to choose those terms that apply to their query. The user specifies a choice by touching a screen location and a frame is then presented. In all, there are 41 frames in the hierarchy, arranged into seven levels, out of which three or four are typically needed for the specification of a search.

PLEXUS

The PLEXUS project was designed as a prototype of a tool to be used in public and academic libraries, where it is intended to assist the reference librarian in answering user queries.[95, 96] Terms are organized according to the BSO (broad system of ordering).[97] The dictionary holds a list of all the words known to the system, each entry comprising a term name (stemmed), a semantic category (altogether there are 11 categories, which may be divided into subcategories), a BSO pointer and a semantic net number. PLEXUS embodies about 1000 rules, which are specific to particular subtasks for generating the knowledge base.

Users' queries are analysed into words: insignificant words are screened out by matching against a stopword list, and the remaining words are stripped of common suffixes by using a stemming algorithm. The word sequence in the original input is maintained. PLEXUS tries to infer the meaning of a query by imposing a framework or context on it. A particular context is defined as a template specified by the categories associated with these stems and the number of stems in a particular semantic category that are present. Once a context has been imposed on the query, a model of the query is built consisting of one or more interconnected frames, where each frame represents a significant term in the query and has a particular form and structure specific to a particular concept class.[96, 98]

The design criteria for the user interface were as follows:

*   The user should be able to operate the system without recourse to a manual or human adviser. Input should be through natural language statements and menu-driven.
*   The system should not crash or present the user with a failed message after the first message.
*   The system should be able to accept statements from users in any form – a single word, a list of words, phrases or grammatical sentences.
*   The interface must be able to deal intelligently with terms it cannot recognize.

The different menu-based screens were devised for different purposes. At the outset the system gives an introduction of the system to the user. Through some of the following screens it attempts to develop a user model and then allows the user to input the problem statement, which is clarified and searched in the dictionary. The next task is the filling of slots and initializing the search query that leads to the actual search and conclusion.

IOTA

IOTA (the Intelligent System for Information Retrieval)[99] is a procedural expert system meant for the processing of queries in French. The task of query processing is performed through several steps involving both expert and non-expert tasks. Queries are parsed by syntactic pattern-matching methods and valid query terms are generated at this stage. Two dictionaries are used during query analysis – one of inflected words and one of lemmatized words (or canonical representations of words). The knowledge is coded in the form of production rules that allow procedure calls (the procedure that is called when the 'IF' part of the rule is satisfied) on their right-hand side. The resulting data structure may be considered as a general interface acting like a blackboard (a common data structure). At the retrieval stage the Boolean operators are used in the final search equation. Though limited in scope this experiment shows encouraging results.[99]

IRUS

The IRUS system is designed for processing heterogeneous databases through natural English language queries.[100] In this system queries are first translated into a general formalism (meaning representation language) and then translated again into the particular database query language. This translation is performed using a morphosyntactical parser, based on an ATN,[101] a semantic processor that solves syntactical ambiguities and generates first-order logic expressions fitting that query.

I³R

The Intelligent Intermediary for Information Retrieval (I³R) developed by Croft[102, 103] consists of a set of expert systems managed by a scheduler. Each expert system manages a specific part of the query processing and these independent components communicate by means of a blackboard. Each blackboard contains a knowledge base containing documents and their semantic representation, a user model containing users' specific knowledge, and domain knowledge stored in a frame-like formalism.

Fuzzy set systems

A natural language interface based on fuzzy set techniques has been proposed by Biswas et al.[104, 105] Fuzzy sets represent one facet of an area of study called fuzzy mathematics. In a normal set the boundary of the set is distinct and the membership of the items is determined by the yes/no criteria. Whether an item is a member or not depends on whether it is inside or outside the boundary of the set. In the case of a fuzzy set the boundary is not clearly distinguishable and each item can be assigned a degree of membership. The interface designed by Biswas et al.[104, 105] identifies three components in a natural language query: the concept-querycomponent, which includes all the concepts the user is interested in; the time-query component, which indicates the publication period the user is interested in; and the quantity-query component, which relates to the number of documents the user wants the system to retrieve.

The system uses ATN techniques and a semantic grammar approach to analyse user queries and produce an unambiguous intermediate form for the inferencing mechanism. A dictionary incorporates all the phrases, terms and qualifiers that the system recognizes. This permits the ATN parser to match words and phrases in the input text with the current category for which a match is being sought. The presence of a 'nil' value in the expression term indicates that the word that matches the specific category should be ignored. The interface accomplishes its task through a two-step process. First the query is analysed structurally using an ATN parser with a set of semantic categories to represent the components of the sentence. This results in a derivation tree corresponding to the three main parts of a sentence. The second step accomplishes the semantic interpretation using a set of operators and parenthesizing rules to understand the concept-query component part of the request and produce an unambiguous intermediate representation for it. This step also uses fuzzy set theory to produce an intermediate form for the other two parts of the query. The prototype implementation has a knowledge base with about 200 subject domain concepts on topics in knowledge representation, and a document database with about 40 document descriptors.[104, 105]

Recent research on natural language interfaces

Much of the effort in natural language interface design to date has focused on handling rather than on software to deal with simple natural language queries, but a number of question-answering systems are now being developed that aim to provide answers to natural language questions directly rather than through documents containing information related to the question. Such systems often use a variety of IE and IR operations using NLP tools and techniques to get the correct answer from the source texts. Breck et al.[106] report a question-answering system that uses techniques from knowledge representation, information retrieval and NLP. The authors claim that this combination enables domain independence and robustness in the face of text variability, both in the question and in the raw text documents used as knowledge sources.

Research reported in the Question Answering (QA) track of TREC (Text Retrieval Conferences) shows some interesting results. The basic technology used by the participants in the QA track included several steps. First, cue words or phrases like 'who' (as in 'who is the prime minister of Japan'), or 'when' (as in 'when did the Jurassic period end') were identified to guess what was needed and then a small portion of the document collection was retrieved using standard text retrieval technology. This was followed by a shallow parsing of the returned documents to identify the entities required for an answer. If no appropriate answer type was found then the best matching passage was retrieved. This approach works well as long as the query types recognized by the system have broad coverage and the system can classify questions reasonably accurately.[107] In TREC-8, the first QA track of TREC, the most accurate QA systems could answer more than two-thirds of the questions correctly. In the second QA track (TREC-9), the best performing QA system, the Falcon system from Southern Methodist University, was able to answer 65% of the questions (Voorhees[108]). These results are impressive in a domain-independent question-answering environment. However, the questions were still simple in the first two QA tracks. In the future more complex questions requiring answers to be obtained from more than one document will be handled by QA track researchers.

Problems of NLP have been discussed at length at the various Message Understanding Conferences[109]. Owei[57] argues that the drawbacks of most natural language interfaces to database systems stem primarily from their weak interpretative power, which is caused by their inability to deal with the nuances in human use of natural language. The author further argues that the difficulty with NL database query languages (DBQLs) can be overcome by combining concept based DBQL paradigms with NL approaches to enhance the overall ease of use of the query interface.

Internet, web and digital library applications of natural language processing systems

The internet and the web have brought significant improvements in the way we create, look for and use information. A huge volume of information is now available through the internet and digital libraries. However, these developments have made some problems related to information processing and retrieval more prominent. According to a survey in 2001 by Global Reach,[110] 55% of internet users are non-English speakers and this figure is increasing rapidly, thereby reducing the percentage of net users who are native English speakers. However, about 80% of the internet and digital library resources available today are in English.[111] This calls for an urgent need to establish multilingual information systems and CLIR facilities.

Several issues are involved in the question of how to manipulate the large volume of multilingual data. At the user interface level, there has to be a query translation system that should translate the query from the user's native language to the language of the system. Various approaches have been proposed for query translation. The dictionary-based approach uses a bilingual dictionary to convert terms from the source language to the target language. Coverage and currency of the bilingual dictionary is a major factor here. The corpus-based approach uses parallel corpora for word selection, where the problem lies with the domain and scale of the corpora. Bian and Chen[111] propose a Chinese–English CLIR system on the web called MTIR, which integrates the query translation and document translation. They also address a number of issues of machine translation on the web, such as the role played by the HTML tags in translation, the trade-off between the speed and performance of the translation system and the form in which the translated material is presented.

Staab et al.[112] describe the features of an intelligent information agent called GET-ESS, which uses semantic methods and NLP capabilities in order to gather tourist information from the web and present it to the human user in an intuitive, user-friendly way. Ceric[113] reviews the advancements of web search technology and mentions that, among others, NLP technologies will have very good impact on the success of the search engines. Mock and Vemuri[114] describe the Intelligent News Filtering Organizational System (INFOS), which is designed to filter out unwanted news items from a usenet. INFOS builds a profile of user interests based on user feedback. After users browse an article, INFOS asks them to rate the article and uses this rating as a criterion for selection (or rejection) of similar articles next time round. News articles are classified by a simple keyword method, called Global Hill Climbing (GHC), which is used as a simple quick-pass method. Articles that cannot be classified by GHC are passed through a WordNet knowledgebase through a case-based reasoning (CBR) module, which is a slower but more accurate method of classifying them. Very small-scale evaluation of INFOS suggests that the indexing pattern method – mapping of the words from the input text into the correct concepts in the WordNet abstraction hierarchy – correctly classified 80% of the articles; the major reason for errors is the weakness of the system to disambiguate pronouns.

One of the major stumbling blocks of providing personalized news delivery to users over the internet is the problem involved in the automatic association of related items of different media type. Carrick and Watters[115] describe a system that aims to determine to what degree any two news items refer to the same news event. This research focused on determining the association between photographs and stories by using names. The algorithm developed in the course of this research was tested against a test data set as well as new data sets. The pair of news items and photos generated by the system were checked by human experts. The system performed similarly on the new data sets as it did on the training set in terms of recall, precision and time.

Because of the volume of text available on the web, many researchers have proposed to use the web as the testbed for NLP research. Grefenstette[116] argues that although noisy, web text presents language as it is used, and statistics derived from the web can have practical uses in many NLP applications.

Machine translation and cross-language information retrieval

With the proliferation of the web and digital libraries, multilingual information retrieval has become a major challenge. There are two concerns in this area: the recognition, manipulation and display of multiple languages; and cross-language information search and retrieval.[117] The former relates to the enabling technology that will allow users to access information in whatever language it is stored; while the latter implies permitting users to specify their information needs in their preferred language while retrieving information in whatever language it is stored. Text translation can take place at two levels: translation of the full text from one language to another for the purpose of search and retrieval and translation of queries from one language to one or more different languages. The first option is feasible for small collections or for specific applications, as in meteorological reports (Oudet[118]). Translation of queries is a more practicable approach and promising results have been reported in the literature (discussed below).

Oard[119] comments that users seeking information from a digital library could benefit from the ability to search large collections only once using a single language.

Furthermore, if the retrieved information is not available in a language that the user can read, some form of translation will be needed. Multilingual thesauri such as EUROVOC help to address this challenge by facilitating controlled vocabulary search using terms from several languages and services such as INSPEC produce English abstracts for documents in other languages. However, as Oard[119] mentions, fully automatic multilingual thesauri are presently neither sufficiently fast nor sufficiently accurate to support interactive cross-language information seeking on the web and in digital libraries adequately. Fortunately, an active and rapidly growing research community has coalesced around these and other related issues, applying techniques drawn from several fields – notably IR and NLP – to provide access to large multi-lingual collections.

Borgman[120] comments that we have hundreds (and sometimes thousands) of years worth of textual materials in hundreds of languages, created long before data encoding standards existed. She illustrates the multi-language digital library challenge with examples drawn from the research library community, which typically handles collections of materials in about 400 different languages.

Ruiz and Srinivasan[121] investigate an automatic method for CLIR that uses the multilingual Unified Medical Language System (UMLS) Metathesaurus to translate Spanish natural-language queries into English. They conclude that this method is at least equivalent to, if not better, than multilingual-dictionary-based approaches. Dan-Hee, Gomez and Song[122] observe that there is no reliable guideline on how large machine-readable corpus resources should be compiled to develop practical NLP software package and/or complete dictionaries for humans and computational use. They propose a new mathematical tool: a piecewise curve-fitting algorithm, and suggest a way of determining the tolerance error of the algorithm for good prediction using a specific corpus.

Two Telematics Application Program projects in the Telematics for Libraries sector, TRANSLIB and CANAL/LS, were active between 1995 and 1997.[119] Both these projects investigated cross-language searching in library catalogs, and each included English, Spanish and at least one other language: CANAL/LS added German and French, while TRANSLIB added Greek. MULINEX, another European project, is concerned with the efficient use of multilingual online information. The project aims to process multilingual information and present it to the user in a way that facilitates finding and evaluating the desired information quickly and accurately. TwentyOne, started in 1996, is a EU-funded project that is developing a tool for efficient dissemination of multimedia information in the field of sustainable development. Details of these and CLIR research projects in the USA and other parts of the world have been reviewed by Oard and Diekama.[20]

Magnini et al.[123] report two projects where NLP has been used for improving the performance in the public administration sector. The first project, GIST, is concerned with automatic multilingual generation of instructional texts for form filling. The second project, TAMIC, aims to provide an interface for interactive access to information.

A number of companies now provide a machine translation service, for example (McMurchie[124]):

- Berlitz International Inc. offers professional translation service in 20 countries.
- Lernout & Hauspie has an internet translation division.
- Orange, California-based Language Force Inc., has a product called Universal Translator Deluxe.
- IBM MT services has a product called WebSphere Translation Server.

A large number of research papers are available that discuss various research projects dealing with MT and CLIR with reference to specific languages. These works have been discussed in the recent ARIST chapter by Chowdhury.[7]

Summary

Arguing that IR has been the subject of research and development and has been delivering working solutions for many decades, whereas IE is a more recent and emerging technology, Smeaton[16] comments that it is of interest to the IE community to see how a related task, perhaps the most-related task, IR, has managed to use the NLP base technology in its development so far. Commenting on the future challenges of IE researchers, Gaizauskas and Wilks[47] mention that the performance levels of the common IE systems, which stand in the range of 50% for combined recall and precision, should improve significantly to satisfy information analysts. A major stumbling block of IE systems development is its cost. Portability and scalability are also two big issues for IE systems. Since they depend heavily on the domain knowledge, a given IE system may work satisfactorily in a relatively small text collection, but it may not perform well in a larger collection or in a different domain. Alternative technologies are now being used to overcome these problems.

Several NLP software packages for information handling have been designed over the past few years that use NLP techniques.[124] Adams[125] discusses the merits of the NLP and the wrapper induction technology in information extraction from web documents. In contrast with NLP, wrapper induction operates independently of specific domain knowledge. Instead of analysing the meaning of discourse at the sentence level, the wrapper technology identifies relevant content based on the textual qualities that surround desired data. Wrappers operate on the surface features of document texts that characterize training examples. A number of vendors such as Jango (purchased by Excite), Junglee (purchased by Amazon) and Mohomine employ wrapper induction technology.[125]

Zadrozny et al.[126] suggest that in an ideal information retrieval environment users should be able to express their interests or queries directly and naturally, by speaking, typing and/or pointing; the computer system then should be able to provide intelligent answers or ask relevant questions. However, they comment that even though we build natural language systems, this goal cannot be fully achieved owing to limitations of science, technology, business knowledge, and programming environments. The specific problems include:

- limitations of NL understanding
- managing the complexities of interaction (for example, when using natural

language on devices with differing bandwidth)
* lack of precise user models (for example, knowing how the demographics and personal characteristics of a person should be reflected in the type of language and dialogue the system is using with the user)
* lack of middleware and toolkits.

Historically one of the major stumbling blocks of NLP research, as in areas like information retrieval, has been the absence of large test collections and reusable experimental methods and tools. Fortunately, the situation has changed over the past few years. Several national and international research groups are now working together to build and reuse large test collections and experimental tools and techniques. Since the origin of the Message Understanding Conferences, group research efforts have proliferated and there are regular conferences and workshops, for example, the TREC series and other conferences organized by NAACL (North American Chapter of the Association for Computational Linguistics), EACL (European ACL), and so on. Such group research helps researchers share their expertise by building reusable NLP tools, test collections and experimental methodologies.

References

1   Blair, D. C., *Language and representation in information retrieval*, New York, Elsevier, 1990.
2   Ruge, G., Schwarz, C. and Warner, A. J., 'Effectiveness and efficiency in natural language processing for large amounts of text', *Journal of the American Society for Information Science*, **42**, 1991, 450–6.
3   Lancaster, F. W., *Indexing and abstracting in theory and practice*, 3rd edn, London, Facet Publishing, 2003.
4   Grosz, B. J., Weber, B. L. and Sparck Jones, K. (eds.), *Readings in natural language processing*, New York, Morgan Kaufmann, 1986.
5   Obermeier, K. K., 'Natural language processing: an introductory look at some of the technology used in this area of artificial intelligence', *Byte*, **12**, 1987, 225–32.
6   Jacobs, P. S. and Rau, L. F., 'Natural language techniques for intelligent information retrieval'. In: *Eleventh International Conference on Research and Development in Information Retrieval*, New York, ACM, 1988, 85–99.
7   Chowdhury, G. G., 'Natural language processing'. In: Cronin, B. (ed.), *Annual review of information science and technology*, **37**, Medford, NJ, Information Today Inc., 2003, 51–89.
8   Haas, S. W., 'Natural language processing: toward large-scale robust systems'. In: Williams, M. E. (ed.), *Annual review of information science and technology*, **31**, Medford, NJ, Learned Information Inc. for the American Society for Information Science, 1996, 83–119.
9   Grishman, R., 'Natural language processing', *Journal of the American Society for Information Science*, **35**, 1984, 291–6.
10   Warner, A. J., 'Natural language processing'. In: Williams, M. E. (ed.), *Annual*

review of information science and technology, **22**, Amsterdam, The Netherlands, Elsevier Science Publishers B.V. for the American Society for Information Science, 1987, 79–108.

11 Jurafsky, D. and Martin, J. H., *Speech and language processing: an introduction to natural language processing, computational linguistics and speech recognition*, Upper Saddle River, NJ, Prentice Hall, 2000.

12 Manning, C. D. and Schutze, H., *Foundations of statistical natural language processing*, Cambridge, MA, MIT Press, 1999.

13 Mani, I. and Maybury, M. T., *Advances in automatic text summarization*, Cambridge, MA, MIT Press, 1999.

14 Sparck Jones, K., 'What is the role for NLP in text retrieval'. In: Strzalkowski, T. (ed.), *Natural language information retrieval*, Kluwer, 1999, 1–25.

15 Wilks, Y., 'Natural language processing', *Communications of the ACM*, **39**, 1996, 60.

16 Smeaton A. F., 'Using NLP or NLP resources for information retrieval tasks'. In: Strzalkowski, T. (ed.), *Natural language information retrieval*, Kluwer Academic Publishers, 1999, 99–111.

17 Amsler, R. A., 'Machine-readable dictionaries'. In: Williams, M. E. (ed.), *Annual review of information science and technology*, **19**, White Plains, NY, Knowledge Industry Publications Inc. for the American Society for Information Science, 1984, 161–209.

18 Evans, M., 'Computer readable dictionaries'. In: Williams, M. E. (ed.), *Annual review of information science and technology*, **24**, Amsterdam, The Netherlands, Elsevier Science Publishers B.V. for the American Society for Information Science, 1989, 85–117.

19 Lange, H., 'Speech synthesis and speech recognition: tomorrow's human-computer interfaces? In: Williams, M. E. (ed.), *Annual review of information science and technology*, **28**, Medford, NJ, Learned Information Inc. for the American Society for Information Science, 1993, 153–85.

20 Oard, D. W and Diekama, A. R., 'Cross-language information retrieval'. In: Williams, M. E. (ed.), *Annual review of information science and technology*, **33**, Medford, NJ, Learned Information Inc. for the American Society for Information Science, 1998, 223–56.

21 Grishman, R. and Kittredge, R. (eds) *Analyzing language in restricted domains: sublanguage descriptions and processing*, London, Lawrence Erlbaum Associates, 1986.

22 Doszkocs, T. E., 'IR, NLP, AI and UFOS: or IR, relevance, natural language problems, artful intelligence and user-friendly online system'. In: Rabitti, F. (ed.), *Proceedings of the Ninth International Conference on Research and Development in Information Retrieval*, New York, ACM, 1986, 49–53.

23 Smeaton, A. F., 'Information retrieval and natural language processing'. In: Jones, K. P. (ed.), *Prospects for intelligent retrieval – Proceedings of Informatics 10, Cambridge, March 1989*, Aslib, London, 1990, 1–14.

24 Burton, A. and Steward, A. P., 'Domain modelling for intelligent natural language interfaces'. In: *Twelfth BCS IRSG Research Colloquium on Information*

Retrieval, 1990, 123–34.
25   Sager, N., 'Natural language information formatting: the automatic conversion of texts to structured data base'. In: Yovits, M. C. (ed.), *Advances in computers*, **17**, New York, Academic Press, 89–162.
26   Kittredge, R. and Lehrberger, J. (eds), *Sublanguage studies of languages in restricted semantic domains*, Berlin, Walter DeGruyter, 1982.
27   Lyttinen, S. and Gershman, A., 'ATRANS: automatic processing of money transfer messages'. In: *Proceedings of the Fifth International Conference on Artificial Intelligence*, Philadelphia, 1986.
28   DeJong, G., 'An overview of the FRUMP System'. In: Lehnert, W. G. and Ringle, M. H. (eds), *Strategies for natural language processing*, Hillsdale, NJ, Lawrence Erlbaum, 1982, 149–76.
29   Gershman, A. V., 'A framework for conceptual analysers'. In: Lehnert, W. G. and Ringle, M. H. (eds), *Strategies for natural language processing*, Hillsdale, NJ, Lawrence Erlbaum, 1982, 177–97.
30   Kukich, K., 'Design of a knowledge-based report generator'. In: *Proceedings of the 21st Annual Meeting of the Association of Computational Linguistics*, 1983, 145–50.
31   Tong, R. M., Applebaum, L. A., Askman, U. N. and Cunningham, J. F., 'Conceptual information retrieval using RUBRIC'. In: Yu, C. T. and van Rijsbergen, C. J. (eds), *Proceedings of the Tenth Annual International ACM/SIGIR Conference on Research and Development in Information Retrieval*, New York, ACM, 1987. 247–53.
32   Fox, E. A., 'Composite document extended retrieval: an overview'. In: *Proceedings of the Eighth International Conference on Research and Development in Information Retrieval*, New York, ACM, 1985, 42–53.
33   Fox, E. A., 'Development of the CODER system: a testbed for artificial intelligence methods in information retrieval', *Information processing and management*, **23**, 1987, 341–66.
34   Rau, L. F., 'Knowledge organisation and access in a conceptual information system', *Information processing and management*, **23**, 1987, 269–83.
35   Rau, L. F. and Jacobs, P. S., 'Integrating top-down and bottom-up strategies in a text processing system'. In: *Proceedings of the Second Conference on Applied Natural Language Processing*, 1988, 129–35.
36   Jacobs, P. S. and Rau, L. F., 'SCISOR: extracting information from on-line news', *Communications of the ACM*, **33**, 1990, 88–97.
37   Smeaton, A., 'SIMPR: Using natural language processing techniques for information retrieval'. In: Pollitt, A. S. (ed.), *Twelfth BCS IRSG Research Colloquium on Information Retrieval*, 1990, 152–61.
38   Smeaton, A. and Sheridan, P., 'Using morpho-syntactic language analysis in phrase matching'. In: Lichnerowicz, A. (ed.), *Intelligent text and image handling: proceedings of the RIAO'91 Conference*, 1991, 414–30.
39   Metzler, D. P., Stephanie, W. H., Cosic, C. L. and Wheeler, L. H., 'Constituent object parsing for information retrieval and similar text processing problems', *Journal of the American Society for Information Science*, **40**, 1989, 398–423.

40   Metzler, D. P., Stephanie, W. H., Cosic, C. L. and Weise, C. A., 'Conjunction, ellipsis, and other discontinuous constituents in the constituent object parser', *Information processing and management*, **26**, 1990, 53–71.

41   Sembok, T. M. T. and van Rijsbergen, C. J., 'SILOL: a simple logical-linguistic document retrieval system', *Information processing and management*, **26**, 1990, 111–34.

42   Benoit, G., Data mining. In: Cronin, B. (ed.), *Annual review of information science and technology*, **36**, Medford, NJ, Information Today for ASIS, 2001, 265–310.

43   Qin, J. and Norton, M. J. (eds), 'Introduction [to] special issue: Knowledge discovery in bibliographic databases', *Library trends*, **48**, 1999, 1–8.

44   Raghavan, V. V., Deogun, J. S. and Server, H. (eds), 'Special topical issue: Knowledge discovery and data mining', *Journal of the American Society for Information Science*, **49** (5), 1998, 397–402.

45   Trybula, W. J., 'Data mining and knowledge discovery'. In: Williams, M. E. (ed.), *Annual review of information science and technology*, **32**, Medford, NJ, Learned Information Inc. for the American Society for Information Science, 1997, 197–229.

46   Vickery, B., 'Knowledge discovery from databases: an introductory review', *Journal of documentation*, **53**, 1997, 107–22.

47   Gaizauskas, R. and Wilks, Y., 'Information extraction: beyond document retrieval', *Journal of documentation*, **54**, 1998, 70–105.

48   Hayes, P., 'Intelligent high-volume text processing using shallow, domain-specific techniques'. In: Jacobs, P. S. (ed.), *Text-based intelligent systems*, Hillsdale, NJ, Lawrence Erlbaum, 1992, 227–41.

49   Yang, Y. and Liu, X., 'A re-examination of text categorization methods'. In: SIGIR '99 *Proceedings of the 22nd Annual International ACM SIGIR Conference on Research and Development in Information Retrieval*, ACM, 1999, 42–9.

50   Morin, E., 'Automatic acquisition of semantic relations between terms from technical corpora'. In: Sandrini, P. (ed.), *TKE '99. Terminology and Knowledge Engineering. Proceedings Fifth International Congress on Terminology and Knowledge Engineering*, Innsbruck, Austria, 23–27 Aug 1999, Vienna, TermNet, 1999, 268–78.

51   Bondale, N., Maloor, P., Vaidyanathan, A., Sengupta, S. and Rao, P. V. S., 'Extraction of information from open-ended questionnaires using natural language processing techniques', *Computer science and informatics*, **29**, 1999, 15–22.

52   Glasgow, B., Mandell, A., Binney, D., Ghemri, L. and Fisher, D., 'MITA: an information-extraction approach to the analysis of free-form text in life insurance applications', *AI magazine*, **19**, 1998, 59–71.

53   Ahonen, H., Heinonen, O., Klemettinen, M. and Verkamo, A. I., 'Applying data mining techniques for descriptive phrase extraction in digital document collections', *IEEE International Forum on Research and Technology. Advances in Digital Libraries – ADL '98*, 22–24 April 1998, Santa Barbara,

CA. Los Alamitos, CA, IEEE Computer Society, 1998, 2–11.

54　Sokol, L., Murphy, K., Brooks, W. and Mattox, D., 'Visualizing text-based data mining'. *Proceedings of the Fourth International Conference on the Practical Application of Knowledge Discovery and Data Mining, 11–13 April 2000, Manchester*, Blackpool, Practical Application Company, 2000, 57–61.

55　Chang, H.-H., Ko, Y.-H. and Hsu, J.-P., 'An event-driven and ontology-based approach for the delivery and information extraction of e-mails', *Proceedings International Symposium on Multimedia Software Engineering, 11–13 Dec. 2000, Taipei, Taiwan*, Los Alamitos, CA, IEEE Computer Society, 2000, 103–9.

56　Cowie, J. and Lehnert, W., 'Information extraction', *Communications of the ACM*, **39**, 1996, 80–91.

57　Owei, V., 'Natural language querying of databases: an information extraction approach in the conceptual query language', *International journal of human-computer studies*, **53**, 2000, 439–92.

58　Chowdhury, G. G., 'Template mining for information extraction from digital documents', *Library trends*, **48**, 1999, 182–208.

59　Ciravenga, F., Tarditi, R., Campia, P. and Colognese, A., 'Syntax and semantics in a text interpretation system'. In: Lichnerowicz, A. (ed.), *Intelligent text and image handling: proceedings of the RIAO'91 Conference*, New York, Elsevier, 1991, 684–94.

60　Zweigenbaum, P. and Cavazza, M., 'Extracting implicit information from free-text technical reports'. In: Lichnerowicz, A. (ed.), *Intelligent text and image handling: proceedings of the RIAO'91 Conference*, New York, Elsevier, 1991, 695–706.

61　Castell, N. and Verdezo, M. F., 'Automatic extraction of factual information from text and its integration in a knowledge'. In: Lichnerowicz, A. (ed.), *Intelligent text and image handling: proceedings of the RIAO'91 Conference*, New York, Elsevier, 1991, 718–37.

62　Liddy, E. D., Jorgenson, C. L., Sibert, E. and Yu, E. S., 'Sublanguage grammar in natural language processing for an expert system'. In: Lichnerowicz, A. (ed.), *Intelligent text and image handling: proceedings of the RIAO'91 Conference*, New York, Elsevier, 1991, 707–17.

63　Zamora, E. and Blower, P. E., 'Extraction of chemical reaction information from primary journal text using computational linguistics techniques. 1. Lexical and syntactic phases', *Journal of chemical information and computer sciences*, **24**, 1984, 176–81.

64　Zamora, E. and Blower, P. E., 'Extraction of chemical reaction information from primary journal text using computational linguistics techniques. 2. Semantic phase', *Journal of chemical information and computer sciences*, **24**, 1984, 181–8.

65　Ledwith, R., 'Development of a large concept-oriented database for information retrieval'. In: *Eleventh International Conference on Research and Development in Information Retrieval*, New York, ACM, 1988, 651–61.

66　Ai, C. S., Blower, P. E. and Ledwith, R. H., 'Extraction of chemical reaction information from primary journal text', *Journal of chemical information and computer sciences*, **30**, 1990, 163–9.

67 Postma, G. J., Van Der Linden, B., Smits, J. R. M. and Kateman, G., 'TICA: a system for the extraction of data from analytical chemical text', *Chemometrics and intelligent laboratory systems*, **9**, 1990, 65–74.

68 Postma, G. J., Van Der Linden, B., Smits, J. R. M. and Kateman, G., 'TICA: program for the extraction of analytical chemical information from texts'. In: Karjalainen, E. J. (ed.), *Scientific computing and automation (Europe)*, Amsterdam, Elsevier, 1990, 407–14.

69 Cooke-Fox, D. I., Kirby, G. H. and Rayner, J. D., 'Computer translation of IUPAC systematic organic chemical nomenclature, 1. Introduction and background to a grammar', *Journal of chemical information and computer sciences*, **29**, 1989, 101–5.

70 Cooke-Fox, D. I., Kirby, G. H. and Rayner, J. D., 'Computer translation of IUPAC systematic organic chemical nomenclature, 2. Development of a formal grammar', *Journal of chemical information and computer sciences*, **29**, 1989, 106–12.

71 Cooke-Fox, D. I., Kirby, G. H. and Rayner, J. D., 'Computer translation of IUPAC systematic organic chemical nomenclature, 3. Analysis and semantic processing', *Journal of chemical information and computer sciences*, **29**, 1989, 112–18.

72 Cooke-Fox, D. I., Kirby, G. H. and Rayner, J. D., 'Computer translation of IUPAC systematic organic chemical nomenclature, 4. Concise connection tables to structure diagrams', *Journal of chemical information and computer sciences*, **30**, 1990, 122–7.

73 Cooke-Fox, D. I., Kirby, G. H. and Rayner, J. D., 'Computer translation of IUPAC systematic organic chemical nomenclature, 5. Steroid nomenclature', *Journal of chemical information and computer sciences*, **30**, 1990, 128–32.

74 Kirby, G. H., Lord, M. R. and Rayner, J. D., Computer translation of IUPAC systematic organic chemical nomenclature, 6. (Semi)automatic name correction', *Journal of chemical information and computer sciences*, **31**, 1991, 153–60.

75 Vander Stouw, G. G., Elliot, P. M. and Isenberg, A. C., 'Automated conversion of chemical substance names to atom bond connection tables', *Journal of chemical documentation*, **4**, 1974, 187–93.

76 Vander Stouw, G. G., Gustafson, C., Rule, J. D. and Watson, C. E., 'The Chemical Abstracts Service chemical registry system, IV. Use of the registry system to support the preparation of index nomenclature', *Journal of chemical information and computer sciences*, **16**, 1976, 213–18.

77 Garfield, E., 'An algorithm for translating chemical names to molecular formulas'. In: *The awards of science and other essays*, Philadelphia, ISI Press, 1985, 463–4.

78 Garfield, E., Revesz, G. S., Granito, C. E., Dorr, H. A., Calderon, M. M. and Warner, A., 'Index Chemicus registry system: pragmatic approach to substructure chemical retrieval', *Journal of chemical documentation*, **10**, 1970, 54–8.

79 Goebels, L., Lawson, A. J. and Wisniewski, J. L., 'AUTONOM: system for

computer translation of structural diagrams into iupac-compatible names, 2. Nomenclature of chains and rings', *Journal of chemical information and computer sciences*, **31**, 1991, 216–25.

80   Wisniewski, J. L., 'AUTONOM: system for computer translation of structural diagrams into iupac-compatible names. 1. General design', *Journal of chemical information and computer sciences*, **30**, 1990, 324–32.

81   Nishida, F. and Takamatsu, S., 'Structured-information extraction from patent-claim sentences', Information processing and management, 18, 1982, 11–13.

82   Nishida, F., Takamatsu, S. and Fujita, Y., 'Semiautomatic indexing of structured information of text', *Journal of chemical information and computer sciences*, **24**, 1984, 15–20.

83   Lebowitz, M., 'An experiment in intelligent information systems: RESEARCHER'. In: Davies, R. (ed.), *Intelligent information systems: progress and prospects*, Chichester, Ellis Horwood, 1986, 127–49.

84   Davies, R., 'Information retrieval'. In: Davies, R. (ed.), *Intelligent information systems: progress and prospects*, Chichester, Ellis Horwood, 1986, 79–81.

85   Schwarz, C., 'Content based text handling', *Information processing and management*, **26**, 1990, 219–26.

86   Schwarz, C., 'Automatic syntactic analysis of free text', *Journal of the American Society for Information Science*, **41**, 1990, 408–17.

87   Turner, W. A., Buffet, P. and Laville, F., 'LEXITRAN for an easier public access to patent database'. In: Lichnerowic. A., (ed.), *Intelligent text and image handling: proceedings of the RIAO '91 Conference*, New York, Elsevier, 1991, 320–36.

88   Turner, W. A., Buffet, P. and Laville, F., 'LEXITRAN for an easier public access to patent database', *World patent information*, **13**, 1991, 81–90.

89   Lawson, M., Kemp, N., Lynch, M. F. and Chowdhury, G. G., 'Automatic extraction of citations from the text of English language patents: an example of template mining', *Journal of information science*, **22** (6), 1996, 423–36.

90   Smeaton, A. F., 'Information retrieval: still butting heads with natural language processing?' In: Pazienza, M. T. (ed.), *Information Extraction. A Multidisciplinary Approach to an Emerging Information Technology International Summer School, SCIE-97*, 14–18 July 1997, Frascati, Italy. Berlin, Springer-Verlag, 1997, 115–38.

91   Brooks, H. M., 'Expert systems and intelligent information retrieval', *Information processing and management*, **23** (4), 1987, 367–82.

92   Davies, R. (ed.), *Intelligent information systems: progress and prospects*, Chichester, Ellis Horwood, 1986.

93   Kemp, D. A., *Computer-based knowledge retrieval*, Aslib, London, 1988.

94   Pollitt, S., 'CANSEARCH: an expert systems approach to document retrieval', *Information processing and management*, **23** (2), 1987, 119–38.

95   Vickery, A., Brooks, H. M. and Vickery, B. C., 'Central information service. An expert system for referral: the PLEXUS project'. In: Davies, R. (ed.), *Intelligent information systems: progress and prospects*, Chichester, Ellis Horwood, 1986, 154–83.

96 Vickery, A. and Brooks, H. M., 'PLEXUS: the expert system for retrieval', *Information processing and management*, **23** (2), 1987, 99–118.

97 Coates, E., Lloyd, G. and Simandl, D., *BSO: broad system of ordering, schedule and index*, The Hague, FID, 1978.

98 Ashford, J. and Willett, P., *Text retrieval and document databases*, Bromley, Chartwell–Bratt, 1988.

99 Chiaramella, Y. and Defude, B., 'A prototype of an intelligent system for information retrieval: IOTA', *Information processing and management*, **23** (4), 1987, 285–303.

100 Bates, M. and Bobrow, B.J., Information retrieval using a transportable natural language interface. *Proceedings of the ACM SIGIR Conference*, New York, ACM, 1983.

101 Charniak, E., 'A parser with something for everyone'. In: M. King (ed.), *Parsing natural language*, London, Academic Press, 1983.

102 Croft, W. B., 'An expert assistant for a document retrieval system'. In: *Recherche d'Informations Assistee par Ordinateur: Actes de la Conference RIAO 85, Grenoble, France*, Grenoble, IMAG, 1985, 131–49.

103 Croft, W. B., 'User-specified domain knowledge for document retrieval'. In: Rabiitti F. (ed.), *Proceedings of the Ninth International Conference on Research and Development in Information Retrieval, Pisa, Italy, 1986*, Washington, ACM, 1986, 201–6.

104 Biswas, G., Bezdek, J. C., Marques, M. and Subramanian, V., 'Knowledge-assisted document retrieval. I. The natural language interface', Journal of the American Society for Information Science, 38 (2), 1987, 83–96.

105 Biswas, G., Bezdek, J. C., Marques, M. and Subramanian, V., 'Knowledge-assisted document retrieval. II. The retrieval process', *Journal of the American Society for Information Science*, **38** (2), 1987, 97–110.

106 Breck, E., Burger, J., House, D., Light, M. and Mani, I., 'Question answering from large document collections'. *Question Answering Systems. Papers from the 1999 AAAI Fall Symposium*, 5–7 Nov. 1999, North Falmouth, MA, Menlo Park, CA, AAAI Press, 1999, 26–31.

107 Voorhees, E., The TREC-8 question answering track report, 1999. Available at **http://trec.nist.gov/pubs/trec8/papers/qa-report.pdf**.

108 Voorhees, E., The TREC-9 question answering track report, 2000. Available at **http://trec.nist.gov/pubs/trec9/papers/qa-report.pdf**.

109 Chinchor, N. A., Overview of MUC-7/MET-2. Available at **http://www.itl.nist.gov/iaui/894.02/related_projects/muc/proceedings/ muc_7_proceedings/overview.html-92**.

110 Global Reach, Global Internet Statistics (by language), 2001. Available at **http://www.euromktg.com/globstats/**.

111 Bian, G.-W. and Chen, H.-H., 'Cross-language information access to multilingual collections on the internet', *Journal of the American Society for Information Science*, **51**, 2000, 281–96.

112 Staab, S., Braun, C., Bruder, I., Dusterhoft, A., Heuer, A., Klettke, M., Neumann, G., Prager, B., Pretzel, J., Schnurr, H.-P., Studer, R., Uszkoreit, H. and

Wrenger, B., 'GETESS-searching the Web exploiting German texts', *Cooperative Information Agents III. Third International Workshop, CIA'99 Proceedings, 31 July–2 Aug. 1999*, Uppsala, Sweden; Berlin, Springer-Verlag, 1999, 113–24.

113 Ceric, V., 'Advancements and trends in the World Wide Web search'. In: Kalpic, D. and Dobric, V. H. (eds), *Proceedings of the 22nd International Conference on Information Technology Interfaces, 13–16 June 2000*, Pula, Croatia, SRCE University Computer Centre, Univ. Zagreb, 2000, 211–20.

114 Mock, K. J. and Vemuri, V. R., 'Information filtering via hill climbing, wordnet and index patterns', *Information processing and management*, **33**, 1997, 633–44.

115 Carrick, C. and Watters, C., 'Automatic association of news items', *Information processing and management*, **33**, 1997, 615–32.

116 Grefenstette, G., 'The world wide web as a resource for example-based machine translation tasks', *Translating and the Computer 21. Proceedings of the Twenty-first International Conference on Translating and the Computer 10–11 Nov. 1999*, London, Aslib/IMI, 1999, 12.

117 Peters, C. and Picchi, E., 'Across languages, across cultures: issues in multi-linguality and digital jibraries, *D-lib magazine*, 1997. Available at **http://www.dlib.org/dlib/may97/peters/05peters.html**.

118 Oudet, B., 'Multilingualism on the internet', *Scientific American*, **276** (3), 1997, 77–8.

119 Oard, D. W., 'Serving users in many languages: cross-language information retrieval for digital libraries', *D-lib magazine*, 1997. Available at **http://www.dlib.org/dlib/december97/oard/12oard.html**.

120 Borgman, C. L., 'Multi-media, multi-dultural, and multi-lingual digital libraries: or how do we exchange data in 400 languages?', *D-Lib magazine*, 1997. Available at **http://www.dlib.org/dlib/june97/06borgman.html**.

121 Ruiz, M. E. and Srinivasan, P., 'Cross-language information retrieval: an analysis of errors', *Proceedings of the 61st ASIS Annual Meeting, Pittsburgh, PA, October 25–29*, 1998, 153–65.

122 Dan-Hee, Y., Gomez, P. C. and Song, M., 'An algorithm for predicting the relationship between lemmas and corpus size', *ETRI journal*, **22**, 2000, 20–31.

123 Magnini, B., Not, E., Stock, O. and Strapparava, C., 'Natural language processing for transparent communication between public administration and citizens', *Artificial intelligence and law*, **8**, 2000, 1–34.

124 McMurchie, L. L., 'Software speaks user's language', *Computing Canada*, **24**, 1998, 19–21.

125 Adams, K. C., 'The web as a database: new extraction technologies and content management', *Online*, **25**, 2001, 27–32.

126 Zadrozny, W., Budzikowska, M., Chai, J. and Kambhatla, N., 'Natural language dialogue for personalized interaction', *Communications of the ACM*, 43, 2000, 116–20.

Chapter 22

Information retrieval in digital libraries

Introduction

There are several definitions of digital libraries, many formulated in the course of digital library research projects. Consequently these definitions have been influenced by the people involved in the projects, by their understanding of the concept of libraries vis-à-vis electronic databases and also by the nature of the research project. Borgman[1, 2] analyses a number of definitions of digital libraries and concludes that there are two major classes of definitions: those coming from digital library researchers – who in the US context are mostly computer scientists and engineers – and those coming from library and information professionals. The most comprehensive definition of a digital library, which emphasizes both the technical and the service aspects of digital libraries, was given during the March 1994 Workshop:[3]

> A digital library is an assemblage of digital computing, storage, and communications machinery together with the content and software needed to reproduce, emulate, and extend the services provided by conventional libraries based on paper and other material means of collecting, cataloguing, finding, and disseminating information. A full service digital library must accomplish all essential services of traditional libraries and also exploit the well-known advantages of digital storage, searching, and communication.

A number of researchers believe that for the foreseeable future we shall live in the world of, what they call hybrid libraries, which will integrate traditional libraries with the emerging digital libraries (see for example, Oppenheim and Smithson,[4] Pinfield et al.[5] and Rusbridge[6]). Rusbridge[6] suggests that a hybrid library brings a range of technologies from different sources together, and it integrates systems and services in the electronic and print environments. He further argues that 'the name hybrid library is intended to reflect the transitional state of the library, which today can neither be fully print nor fully digital'. Pinfield et al.[5] have the same views and comment that a hybrid library is on a continuum between the conventional and digital library.

Information resources in digital libraries

Digital libraries provide access to different types of information sources in a variety of formats. For example, a digital library may contain simple metadata or catalogues of information resources, like OPACs, or may contain the full text of documents, images, audio and video materials. The information resources may be available in different formats, and they may have been produced by using different types of hardware and software. For example, the text may be in MS Word, PDF or HTML format; images may be available in GIF or JPEG file formats. These information resources may reside on a number of different servers – local as well as remote – and they may have been indexed differently. All these issues make the information retrieval process very complex. Today, users of a digital library may have access to a variety of textual information resources. The following list represents the common choices of format that a user may have today in a digital library:[7]

*   OPACs
*   electronic databases (online search services or CD-ROM databases)
*   e-journals
*   other digital libraries (local or remote)
*   web resources.

Each information system, mentioned above has its own characteristics. Since a user can get access to all or many of the above information systems through a digital library, it is necessary to have a basic idea of the characteristic features of these systems. Users may select any of them and may get the appropriate user interface to interact – search, browse, and so on – with the item in question. However, as discussed later in this chapter, some libraries, for example California Digital Library, allow users to conduct a search across a range of information resources and services. In such cases, users need not move from one service to another, and consequently from one interface to another, in order to conduct a search. The system conducts a search of all the different services and provides the results for the user.

The basic design of a digital library

Providing access to a variety of information resources residing on different computer systems in several parts of the world to a number of users of differing natures and needs is a major challenge for digital library designers. Digital libraries, especially hybrid libraries, aim to work as the 'one stop shop' for all kinds of information resources. This involves a number of complex issues related to integration and seamlessness.

Figure 22.1 shows the basic design of a digital library. As this figure shows, users of a digital library may have access to a range of information resources and there are two basic modes of getting access to them. One possibility is for users to go through a custom-built interface that will allow them to select a particular type of resource, at which point the corresponding search interface opens for them to interact with it. Some digital libraries follow this model. A typical example is the

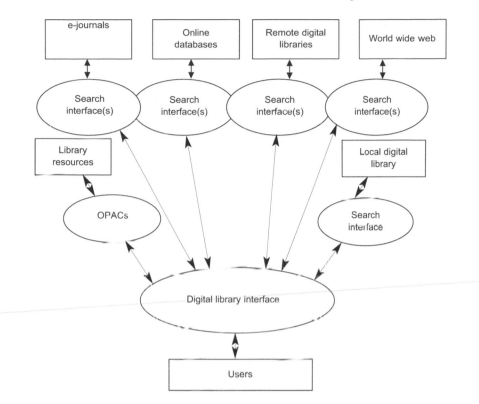

Fig. 22.1 *Conceptual design of a digital library*

Greenstone Digital Library, which allows users to select a particular type of resource or collection; then the interface of the corresponding resource is opened allowing the user to browse or search. The major problem of this model is that the user has to search or browse each collection separately.

Alternatively, users may choose one or more resources or collections and then formulate just one query, which is passed on to the various resources or collections by the digital library interface; results are brought back after the search is carried out. The user does not need to search the resources one by one, so this is a better approach from the user's perspective because he or she formulates only one search query and gets results from all the different resources. The SearchLight option in the California Digital Library is a typical example of this way of retrieving information. However, technologically this approach is more challenging and a number of technical issues need to be considered in order to build this model.

In both the approaches mentioned above users need to select one or more resource type and have to formulate one or more queries in order to conduct a search. However, selection of a suitable resource type may be a difficult task for many users even in subjects that are familiar to them. Formulating a suitable query in an unknown area of study is even more difficult.

Interoperability

One of the major problems facing digital libraries is the issue of interoperability – how to get a wide variety of computing systems to work together and/or to talk to one another for access to and retrieval of information (Arms[8]). Interoperability and standardization are the most important considerations for digital library designers. There are different types of interoperability, such as systems interoperability, software interoperability or portability, semantic interoperability, linguistic interoperability, and so on. Interoperability among digital library systems can be achieved by a number of means, such as through adopting.[8, 9]

- common user interfaces
- uniform naming and identification systems
- standard formats for information resources
- standard metadata formats
- standard network protocols
- standard information retrieval protocols
- standard measures for authentication and security, and so on.

Information retrieval features of selected digital libraries

Information retrieval services are at the heart of digital libraries.[10, 11] Since a hybrid library can provide access to one or more of the information resources mentioned above, users may search each system separately using the search interface of each respective system. Alternatively, there may be a single search interface to allow users to conduct searches across all the systems with just one query.

In the following sections we shall discuss the basic information retrieval facilities provided by some digital libraries. In order to facilitate our discussion, we have selected one digital library representing each one of the following loosely defined groups:

- *Type 1*: fully fledged digital libraries that contain a variety of information distributed among a number of systems and platforms; however, users would like to use only one interface and get results from all the different systems by submitting only one query; although this poses a major challenge, some digital libraries provide such cross-database search facilities; California Digital Library is a prominent example
- *Type 2*: digital libraries that provide access to some specific type of data, for example the Alexandria Digital Library, which provides access to spatial data
- *Type 3*: digital libraries that provide access to a variety of information resources through different interfaces, e.g. New Zealand Digital Library
- *Type 4*: digital libraries that provide access to only one type of material, but allow a single or a multiple-site (federated) search, e.g. Networked Digital Library of Theses and Dissertations

- *Type 5*: digital libraries that provide access to all the different types of publications from a given publisher, e.g. ACM DL.

Type 1: California Digital Library

From the main webpage of California Digital Library (CDL; **http://www.cdlib.org**), users can click on the 'Select a QuickLink' option, whereby they'll get a list of the various collections of CDL. The options 'Browse the CDL directory' or 'Search the CDL directory' can be chosen to browse or search for a specific collection, such as electronic journals, databases or reference texts. The following steps may be followed to browse the directory collections:

- Select a broad topic.
- Select a format (electronic journal, database, and so on).
- Select a campus of interest (or no limit by campus).
- Browse by title or narrower topic(s).

Table 22.1 shows the search and retrieval features of CDL.

Table 22.1 *Search and retrieval features of CDL*

Features	Explanation
Browse by selecting a topic	Users can select a topic (or 'all the topics', which is the default) from a list of subjects, such as General Interest & Reference, History and Social Science, to browse. Browsing can be limited by format: electronic journals, databases, reference texts, etc., and library holdings
Search options: 'Search collections' and 'Search'	Users can search the CDL Directory or can choose the SearchLight option. In the CDL Directory search option, a search can be conducted by keyword or by 'the exact beginning of the title'. A search can be limited to a specific format, and/or to a specific library collection. In the SearchLight option users have to first select a collection – Science and Engineering or Social Sciences and Humanities – and can then enter the search terms in the search box
Boolean search	Boolean OR and NOT operators are not supported by the SearchLight; AND is implied between each word. Phrase search is not supported by the SearchLight search engine
Proximity search	Not supported by SearchLight
Truncation	Not available in SearchLight

(*continued*)

Table 22.1   *(continued)*

Features	Explanation
Limiting search by format or the library holdings	Users can check one or more formats, and can select a particular library (the default is all the libraries) in the UC system. Users can search by Exact Beginning of Title if they know the exact beginning of the title of the resource they are looking for
Other features • query refinement	Users can go to the bottom of the search results page and revise a search by entering a new term(s) and/or changing the selected subject categories
• Output size can be specified. • Results can be sorted. • Output format can be selected.	SearchLight results are categorized according to the source (databases, journals, e-texts, etc.). Output is ranked by the number of hits under each category. Each record contains brief details of the document concerned and two options: 'more info' and a hyperlink. The 'more info' option shows the details of the record with metadata information. By clicking on the number of hits, users can get to another output window containing brief information on each output record with a hyperlink to the full document or the summary in PDF or HTML. The source hyperlink takes users to the particular collection (the URL) where they can enter a search expression in the search interface of the source. The search can be modified by choosing the appropriate options on the same output screen.

Search results are presented under various categories: books, journal indexes, electronic journals, e-texts and documents, reference resources and web directories. On the output page, users can:

- link directly to a given resource by clicking the 'Go to it now' button under a given entry
- view a page with more information by clicking on the 'more information' link under a given entry for more complete information such as creator or publisher, dates of coverage and links to tutorials where available
- examine and change the browse or search conditions.

Type 2: Alexandria Digital Library

The Alexandria Digital Library (ADL) has a collection of geographically referenced materials such as maps, images and texts and datasets in multimedia form in earth and social sciences. The ADL Catalog provides geospatial data and metadata in digital and hard copy. Users can enter a place name for a quick search or browse through ADL Gazetteer, ADL Catalog (containing cartographic works, maps, photographs, aerial photographs and remote-sensing images), or ESSW AVHRR (Earth System Science Workbench: AVHRR imagery). Table 22.2 shows the search and retrieval features of the ADL search interface. The following steps can be followed by users:

* Select a collection to search from those that are available.
* Choose a geographic location either by orienting the Map Browser or typing in co-ordinates.
* Enter search words or phrases.
* Select specific types that you want to find.
* Select specific formats that you want to find.
* Choose between available methods of ranking the results.
* Specify the maximum number of hits.
* Start search.

Table 22.2 *Search and retrieval features of ADL*

Features	Explanation
Map browser	Allows users to pan and zoom a two-dimensional map of the world to locate their area(s) of interest; then they can select an area to query
Search options	Allows users to search by geographic names, latitude and longitude, resource types (maps, photographs, etc.) and formats (online, offline, paper, etc.)
Search options: by originators, assigned terms, identifiers, geographical locations and free-text	Users can search by originators: authors, publishers, etc.; assigned terms: subject headings and index terms assigned by the indexers; or free-text search: titles, abstracts, themes and place names in the metadata. Selection of 'Search on geographical locations' shows the geographical location (the latitude, longitude, etc.) of the place in the query box. 'Identifier search' can be searched by URL, ISBN, ADL control number, etc.
Boolean search	The Any of the Above Words option finds items with one or more of the words in the box (equivalent to the Boolean OR operator); All of the Above Words will find items with all the words (equivalent to the Boolean AND operator); Exact Phrase will look for the exact phrase entered
Thesaurus	For the ADL Catalog, there is the Object Type Thesaurus, and for the ADL Gazetteer, there is the ADL Feature Type Thesaurus

(continued)

Table 22.2 (*continued*)

Features	Explanation
Search results	Results of a query are displayed in the lower right hand frame. Each item is represented by a short descriptive entry containing title (or name), type, format, date, and collection ID. For each result, users can select the following options: • Highlight in Map will display the location (footprint) of the item in the Map Browser. • Complete Description will display the full metadata record of the item in the same frame. • Access/Download will display the access and download information in the same frame. For online items, hyperlinks are included for accessing the data; for offline items, contact information is provided. At the end of each listing of results, a report is included describing the query, the date, and the time it took the system to return the results.

Type 3: New Zealand Digital Library

The Greenstone Digital Library (GDL) software, which is available for free from the New Zealand Digital Library (NZDL) team, is used to provide search and browsing facilities for all the collections. Users need to select a specific collection; each collection has a different set of searching and browsing facilities. Table 22.3 shows the search and retrieval features available in NZDL.

Table 22.3 *Search and retrieval features of GDL software at NZDL*

Features	Explanation
Browsing	Each collection has a different set of criteria for browsing, e.g., the computer science reports collection can be browsed from a list of ftp sites; the women's history collection can be browsed by titles, and so on
Search options: different for each collection	For each collection, there is a different set of search options, which vary from keyword search to searching through the 'Melody Index' search. Depending on the search collection, users can limit a search by title, full text, photos, interviews, sections, paragraphs, and so on. Users can click on a bookshelf icon for books on that subject. The simple or the advanced search option can be selected

(*continued*)

Table 22.3 (*continued*)

Features	Explanation
Boolean search	In the advanced search mode, search terms can be combined using Boolean AND, OR, NOT operators and parentheses. Alternatively, one can choose 'All the Words' or 'Some Words' option
Truncation	The preferences button on top of the page may be chosen to set an option for stemming
Other features: changing preferences	Users can change the preferences by clicking on the 'Preferences' button. The search parameters including the language and interface format can be changed by the user
Ranked output	If the user specifies only one term, documents will be ordered by the frequency of occurrence of that term

NZDL provides two facilities for searching for music. The first is a melody indexing service that allows users to search a database of tunes by melody. The second option is an optical music recognition service, available in a demonstration mode only. In addition to the melody indexing, the text-based indexing service provides access to a collection of MIDI files of over 100,000 tunes including pop, rock, jazz and classical.

Type 4: Networked Digital Library of Theses and Dissertations

Users accessing the Networked Digital Library of Theses and Dissertations (NDLTD) website can search for theses and dissertations that are available in any participating institution by searching the NDLTD Union Catalog. This serves as a repository of theses contributed by a number of member institutions from around the world. Users can search for words or exact phrases anywhere in the theses and dissertation catalogue record, or can specify a field such as author, title, subject or name of a thesis committee member to narrow the search. The Expert search function allows the use of Boolean operators in a command mode.

The option 'Browse through collections at members' sites' can be chosen from the NDLTD web page to get the list of electronic theses and dissertations (ETD) sites of the participating members, including the Virginia Tech site. There is also an option for a federated search to retrieve information on theses and dissertations from all the participating institutions. The thesis collection in the Virginia Tech ETD collection can be browsed by author or searched through the InfoSeek search engine. Users browsing by author go through an alphabetical list of authors; the titles of their theses are also listed alphabetically. There are two search interfaces for ETD – simple and advanced. Table 22.4 shows the various search and retrieval features of ETD. While searching, users can select a specific collection or conduct searches across all the collections. However, if all the collections are chosen in which to carry out a search, the number of hits may be high. The search interfaces for the ETD digital libraries of the participating institutions vary.

Table 22.4 *Search and retrieval features of ETD at Virginia Tech*

Features	Explanation
A particular DL can be selected to search, or a federated search can be conducted	Once the user selects a particular site, say Virginia Tech., the collection can be browsed or searched
Search options: specific collection or federated search, simple and advanced search, field search, search with InfoSeek or browse by author	The InfoSeek search engine can be used to search the ETD site. Users can select a collection: Electronic Journals, Virginia Tech Spectrum, Special collections, VT ETD collection or WDBJ7 Script Archives. In the simple search mode, users enter words and phrases (within double quotes); a search can be restricted to the title field only. In field search, users select a field from a list. In the Virginia Tech collection, users have the choice to conduct a search with InfoSeek or browse by author
Boolean search	Users can use '+' to indicate that a search term must occur, and '−' to indicate that a search term must not occur in the result(s). In the advanced search mode, there are the 'should contain', 'must contain' and 'must not contain' options. Users can select one of the two options to specify whether the output 'should' or 'must' contain the search terms/phrase
Proximity search	No special operator; users can enter a phrase within quotes
Limiting search by time	Users can limit their search by the date of approval; the limiting options are: days, weeks, months, year
Other features: phrase and name search	Users can select to search for a word, a phrase or a name
Output is ranked. Number of hits and output format can be specified. Output can be sorted.	Users can specify the number of records to be retrieved, and also the nature of output, i.e., results with or without the summary. Output can be sorted by relevance, date or title. Each output record contains title and brief information. Once a title is chosen, another page gives the details of the thesis such as author, department, abstract, etc., as well as information on the files (number and format) and availability information, e.g. access restrictions

Type 5: American Computing Machinery Digital Library

The American Computing Machinery Digital Library (ACM DL; **http://portal. acm.org**) contains bibliographic information, abstracts, reviews and the full-text of articles published in ACM periodicals and proceedings since its foundation in 1947, together with selected works published by affiliated organizations.

From the main page of the ACM portal users can select a particular collection, such as journals, magazines, transactions, proceedings, newsletters, publications by affiliated organizations or special interest groups. Upon selection of a particular collection, users get a simple search screen, which allows them to browse the various titles or issues of the chosen publication type or to conduct a simple search on the entire collection. From this screen users can also choose the advanced search option if they want to formulate a complex search. The different information retrieval features of the ACM Digital Library are shown in Table 22.5.

Table 22.5　*Search and retrieval features of ACM Digital Library*

Features	Explanation
Browsing	Users can browse the collection by journals, magazines, transactions, proceedings, newsletters, etc.
Simple and advanced search options	Users can enter a search term or a phrase in the search box and conduct a simple search. Alternatively the advanced search option may be chosen
Boolean search	All words are automatically ANDed. Other Boolean operators can be used. Users can choose one of the three options: 'must have all', 'must have any' or 'must have none' to indicate how the entered search terms or phrases are to be treated by the retrieval engine
Proximity search	The NEAR operator finds pages matching specified search terms within close proximity. The closer the search terms are to each other, the higher the document appears in the ranked results list. The SENTENCE and PARAGRAPH operators are used to specify a search within a sentence and paragraph
Truncation	Search terms can be truncated with '*' (for any number of characters), or '?' (for specified number of characters; each '?' represents one character)
Field search	A search can be restricted in a field – author, title, abstract, ISBN, etc.
Limiting search by time	Users can limit their search by the publication date, conference date, conference location, etc.
Phrase search	Phrases are to be entered in double quotes
Subject search	Subject searches can be conducted by the CCS subject code, subject descriptors or keywords

(continued)

Table 22.5   *(continued)*

Features	Explanation
Output is ranked. Output format can be specified and output can be sorted	Results are ranked and a '%' sign shows the relevance. Users can choose the short or long display format. Results can be sorted by title, publication type or publication date

Common features of information retrieval in digital libraries

Meyyappan, Chowdhury and Foo[12] reviewed the general features and Chowdhury and Chowdhury[13] reviewed the information retrieval features of some selected digital libraries. Their major observations were as follows:

- Users can access the collections of a digital library by either browsing or searching.
- While most digital libraries allow users to search the local digital library collections, some digital libraries, e.g. NDLTD, provide facilities for federated search or search across a number of digital libraries.
- Boolean, proximity and truncation search facilities are commonly available search options in digital libraries, though the operators vary. Some digital libraries provide options like 'also must contain', 'or may contain', 'but not contain', 'should contain', 'must contain' and so on, to activate a Boolean search.
- Keyword and phrase search are the common facilities of digital libraries, though the techniques for conducting a phrase search differ. In some cases, for example in BUILDER, users can enter a phrase in the 'Phrase Search Box', while in others, for example DIGILIB (at University of Queensland, Australia; **http://www.architect.uq.edu.au/digilib/**), NCSTRL (Networked Computer Science Technical Reference Library; **http://www.ncstrl.org**), a search phrase has to be entered within double quotes.
- Right truncation and wild card search facilities are common in many digital libraries, and a variety of operators, such as '%', '*', '@' and '?' are used for the purpose. However, some digital libraries provide specific truncation search facilities. For example, in THOMAS and American Memory, the 'include word variants' option is used for truncation.
- Many digital libraries support proximity search differently. Basically, there are two options: one is through the use of proximity operators, but the operators vary, for instance 'Near', 'Nearby', 'Sentence', 'Paragraph', and so on.
- Most of the chosen digital libraries allow users to conduct a search on specific fields.
- While most digital libraries allow users to specify the maximum number of hits, the output is not always ranked, except in a few like NDLTD.
- In some cases, for example in ACM digital library, users can sort the results of a search using chosen keys.

- Usually the system comes up with a brief output that can lead to the full records. However, in many cases an output format can be chosen by the user.

Special IR Features in DLs

In addition to the common features mentioned above, some digital libraries have special information retrieval features.[13] For example:

- *ACM DL* has some unique search features, such as Stem expansion, Fuzzy expansion (spelled like) and Sounds Like search.
- *DeLiver* (outcome of a DLI1 project at the University of Illinois) offers some unique search features. It allows users to search and view specific parts of an article, such as the figures or references. Thus users can 'fine tune' a search and get more relevant results.
- *GEMS* (Nanyang Technological University, Singapore, digital library; presently called iGEMS) allows users to set up their own profile for future searches and for obtaining SDI services. It also allows instant opening of a CD-ROM and provides access to an online journal or database.
- *HEADLINE* (a hybrid library project in the UK, **http://www.headline.ac.uk**) is unique in two respects:
  - It automatically creates an information page, called the Subject Page, on the subject of interest of the user. The necessary information is gathered from the user's log-in screen.
  - It allows the user to customize the Subject Page to create his/her own subject page.
- *IEL* allows users to choose options to match similar subjects, or to search for the latest additions to IEL. Search interface allows users to browse and select search terms from the displayed list. Superscript, subscript and special characters can be searched.
- *GDL* has developed digital library software and it makes it freely available.
- *NDLTD* uses the *InfoSeek* search engine, and therefore a number of good search features are available. Users can search a specific site search or can conduct a federated Search across the digital libraries that are member of the NDLTD Federation.
- *THOMAS* uses a probabilistic information retrieval system called 'InQuery'
- *The UC Berkeley DL* uses *Cha-Cha* and *ChesireII* search systems and has two unique features:
  - Natural language search facilities.
  - Image retrieval by image content.
- *The Universal Library* (at Carnegie-Mellon University; **http://www.ul.cs.cmu.edu/**) has a unique feature called the *hyperbolic tree* that has a unique visualization effect and user search the collection through this hyperbolic tree.

Problems and prospects

Information retrieval in digital libraries involves a number of challenges. There are a number of issues that need to be taken into consideration in order to develop efficient information retrieval systems for digital libraries. Some issues, that influence information retrieval issues in digital libraries are discussed below.

Problems caused by large databases

Digital libraries have to deal with a number of databases that are huge in size. Blair[14] argues that the scaling problem is the central to document retrieval, and performance decreases rapidly as the size of the document databases is multiplied. He further argues that the success of a text retrieval system is strongly influenced by three factors: (1) the size of the document collection, (2) the type of search – exhaustive search, where the user wants everything, or almost everything available; or sample search, where the user does not need all of the useful items in the collection, and (3) the determinacy of document representation, which means how accurately the documents are represented (indexed) in the collection. Blair[14] proposes a two-stage search process based on the use of identifiable partitions of large document collections. Sornil and Fox[15] propose an inverted index partitioning scheme to support searching for information in a large-scale digital library. They report some encouraging results based on some simulation experiments on the *Hybrid Partitioned Inverted Index* on a terabyte of text.

Problems caused by cross-database searching

Designing systems to support cross-database searching is a major challenge. ANSI Z39.50 is a protocol designed for the exchange of bibliographic data. It is often seen as the most likely solution to the problem of integration. The standard specifies an abstract information system with a rich set of facilities for searching, retrieving records, browsing term lists, etc. The essential power of this standard is that it allows diverse information resources to look and act in the same way to the individual user; it also allows each information system to have a different interface to suit the user needs (Hammer and Favaro[16]). The eLib phase 3 'Clumps' projects were designed to 'kick start' the use of Z39.50 in the UK higher education sector and it was noted that the major problems of implementation of Z39.50 stem from the inconsistencies of implementation of MARC in library OPACs (Pinfield[17]). Many local variations are made by libraries at their local sites, which leads to inconsistencies in the exchange of data.

Metadata is used heavily in building software for cross-database searching among various text databases. However, use of various metadata formats such as MARC (for libraries), ISADG (for archives), and Dublin Core (for web sites) make the task of interoperability quite difficult. Hence, searching descriptions of collections of material may be a useful preliminary to searching at the item level (Pinfield[18]). The Collection Development Focus (**http://www.ukoln.ac.uk/cd-focus/**) studies under the UKOLN, and the research Support libraries Programme (**http://www.rslp.ac.uk/**) are working towards this end.

A number of information retrieval software packages have been developed recently that support cross-database searching in digital libraries. These include Ex

Libris' SFX (**http://www.sfxit.com/**) and MetaLib (**http://www.exlibris.co.il/**), WebExpress/ iPort from OCLC (**http://www.oclc.org/webexpress**), and Fretwell Downing's VDX/Agora product (**http://www.fdgroup.com/fdi/vdx**). The last of these is of course partly based on work carried out on eLib projects, particularly the Agora hybrid library project (**http://hosted.ukoln.ac.uk/agora/**). The SearchLight software, developed by the California Digital Library team uses the Z39.50 protocol for cross-database searching among the University of California OPACs and various online databases. Researchers at Virginia Tech are working on software for federated search across a range of ETD (Electronic Theses and Dissertations) sites (Fox et al. [19,20]). Myaeng et al.[21] report research, done in Korea, that makes heavy use of metadata for federated search and retrieval. Their approach, as opposed to that of Stanford, is based on a relatively simple mechanism by which various metadata are collected and passed on to the integrator. In exchanging the metadata, including queries and search results, the system requires that an XML be used so that the metadata exchange format can be described by a DTD (document type definition) and can be extended, if necessary (Myaeng et al.[21]).

One interesting alternative to cross-database searching that has recently emerged is the Open Archives Initiative (OAI) protocol (**http://www.openarchives.org**). Rather than dynamically searching across different databases in response to a command from a user, the OAI protocol allows metadata to be harvested from OAI-compliant databases which can subsequently be collected into a single searchable database. Pinfield[17] comments that it is difficult to predict at this stage how widely this technology will be adopted but it has potential; adoption may partly depend on whether a formal metadata schema for OAI-compliant datasets can be worked out in detail.

Problems of multilingual IR

Borgman[22] argues that digital libraries should support searching and display in multiple languages. She illustrates the multi-language challenge of digital libraries with examples drawn from the research library community, which typically handles collections of materials in about 400 different languages. She further suggests that a fundamental challenge of building a global digital library system is to provide access to the collections regardless of the language of the content and the language of the information seeker (Borgman[23]). The importance of multilingual information retrieval in the web and digital library environment has also been emphasized by other researchers (see for example, Large and Moukdad[24]). Even if a digital library contains materials in only one language, the content needs to be searchable and displayable on computers in countries speaking other languages. We also need to exchange data between digital libraries, whether in a single language or in multiple languages. Hence multilingual search and display in digital libraries should be a critical area of research.

Multilingual information retrieval in digital libraries involves two major issues: (1) recognition, manipulation and display of multiple languages, and (2) cross-language information search and retrieval (Peters and Picchi[25]). The first set of issues relates to the enabling technology that will allow users to access information in whatever language it is stored; while the second set implies permitting users to specify their information needs in their preferred language while retrieving information in whatever language it is stored. Text translation can take place at two levels: (1) translation of the full text from one language to another for the purpose of search and retrieval, and (2) translation of queries from one language to one or more different languages. The first option is feasible for small collections or for specific applications, as in meteorological reports (Oudet[26]). Translation of queries is a more practicable approach and promising results have been reported in the literature. Oard[27] comments that seeking information from a digital library could benefit from the ability to query large collections once using a single language. Furthermore, if the retrieved information is not available in a language that the user can read, some form of translation will be needed. Multilingual thesauri such as EUROVOC help to address this challenge by facilitating controlled vocabulary search using terms from several languages. Services such as INSPEC produce English abstracts for documents in other languages (Oard[27]). However, as Oard mentions, fully automatic machine translation is presently neither sufficiently fast nor sufficiently accurate to adequately support interactive cross-language information seeking in the web and digital libraries. Fortunately, an active and rapidly growing research community has coalesced around these and other related issues, applying techniques drawn from several fields – notably information retrieval and natural language processing – to provide access to large multilingual collections.

Sugimoto[28] reports on a number of research projects, that are being carried out in Japan, for multilingual information access in digital libraries. Fox and Powell[29] describe a federated search system, called *SearchDB-ML Lite*, for searching heterogeneous multilingual theses and dissertations collections through NDLTD. A markup language, called *SearchDB*, was developed for describing the characteristics of a search engine and its interface, and a protocol was built for requesting word translations between languages. A review of the results generated from querying over 50 sites simultaneously revealed that in some cases more sophisticated query mapping is necessary to retrieve results sets that truly correspond to the original query.

Need for design integration

In order to design an effective and efficient information retrieval system for digital libraries, several layers of information system design need to be properly integrated. In short, the information retrieval system, in a digital library, aims to match the user requirements with the contents using the appropriate computer and networking technologies. However, different layers of work involving the organization and processing of information, user interfaces, networking, standards and protocols, and so on, are involved in the process. All these different layers of work need to be properly integrated in order to develop a successful global digital library. Bates warns that (Bates[30]):

> all layers of the system for accessing and displaying digital library information should be simultaneously designed with knowledge of what is going forward in the other layers. It takes only one wrongly placed layer to thwart all the clever work

done at every other layer. For effective information retrieval to occur, all layers of a system must be designed to work together, and the people doing the designing must genuinely communicate.

Need for interactive question-answering systems

Most information retrieval systems of today retrieve documents or parts of one or more documents in response to a user query. However, ideally users would like to have specific answers to their questions. Building digital libraries that are capable of providing answers in an interactive question-answering mode is a real challenge. It needs expertise from a number of fields including information retrieval, natural language processing, human-computer interactions, expert systems, and so on.

A number of experimental question-answering systems are now being developed that aim to provide answers to natural language questions, as opposed to documents containing information related to the question. Such systems often use a variety of information extraction and retrieval operations using natural language processing tools and techniques to get the correct answer from the source texts. Breck et al.[31] report on a question answering system that uses techniques from knowledge representation, information retrieval, and natural language processing. The authors claim that this combination enables domain independence and robustness in the face of text variability, both in the question and in the raw text documents used as knowledge sources. Research reported in the Question Answering (QA) track of TREC (Text Retrieval Conferences; **http://trec.nist.gov**) shows some interesting results. At the moment the experimental systems can provide answers to simple 'who' questions like 'Who is the prime minister of Japan?', and 'when' questions like 'When did the Jurassic period end?'. The experimental systems work well as long as the query types recognized by the system have broad coverage, and the system can classify questions reasonably accurately (Voorhees[32]). In TREC-8, the first QA track of TREC, the most accurate QA systems could answer more than 2/3 of the questions correctly. In the second QA track (TREC-9), the best performing QA system, the Falcon system from Southern Methodist University, was able to answer 65% of the questions (Voorhees[33]). These results are quite impressive in a domain-independent question answering environment. However, the questions were still simple in the first two QA tracks. In the future more complex questions requiring answers to be obtained from more than one documents will be handled by QA track researchers.

Summary

Information retrieval is one the most fascinating, and yet challenging, areas in digital libraries. While years' of research in text information retrieval are available to the researchers, the problems are multiplied by the volume, variety, format and language of information resources coupled with the problems of the widely varying nature and requirements of users, and of information producers. Users of digital libraries should be familiar with the basics of information search techniques as well as with the information retrieval features of those systems that are accessible through the modern digital libraries. A number of working digital libraries provide reasonably good information retrieval features, especially for textual information retrieval. Results of experimental studies on multimedia and multilingual information retrieval are promising, and one can expect to see their applications in the future digital libraries.

References

1   Borgman, C., 'What are digital libraries? Competing visions', *Information processing and management*, **35** (3), 1999, 227–43.

2   Borgman, C., *From Gutenberg to the global information infrastructure: access to information in the networked world*, New York, ACM Press, 2000.

3   Gladney, H. H., Fox, E. A., Ahmed, Z., Asany, R., Belkin, N. J. and Zemankova, M., 'Digital library: gross structure and requirements: report from a March 1994 Workshop', 1994. Available at **http://www.csdl.tamu.edu/ DL94/paper/fox.html**.

4   Oppenheim, C. and Smithson, D., 'What is the hybrid library?', *Journal of information science*, **25** (2), 1999, 97–112.

5   Pinfield, S., Eaton, J., Edwards, C., Russell, R., Wissenburg, A. and Wynne, P., 'Realizing the hybrid library', *D-lib magazine*, October 1998. Available at **http://www.dlib.org/dlib/october98/10pinfield.html**

6   Rusbridge, C., 'Towards the hybrid library', *D-lib magazine*, 1998. Available at **http://www.dlib.org/dlib/july98/rusbridge/07rusbridge.html**

7   Chowdhury, G. and Chowdhury, S., *Introduction to digital libraries*, London, Facet Publishing, 2003.

8   Arms, W., *Digital libraries*, Cambridge, MA, MIT Press, 2000.

9   HyLife, 'The hybrid library toolkit. Interoperability', 2002. Available at **http://hylife.unn.ac.uk/toolkit/Interoperability.html**

10   Fox, E. and Sornil, O., 'Digital libraries'. In: Baeza-Yates, R. and Ribeiro-Neto, B., *Modern information retrieval*, ACM Press, 1999, 415–32.

11   Fox, E. A. and Urs, S., 'Digital libraries'. In: Cronin, B. (ed.), *Annual review of information science and technology*, **36**, Medford, NJ, Information Today Inc., on behalf of ASIST, 2002, 503–89.

12   Meyyappan, N., Chowdhury, G. G. and Foo, S., 'A review of twenty digital libraries', *Journal of information science*, **26** (5), 2000, 331–48.

13   Chowdhury, G. G. and Chowdhury, S., 'An overview of the information retrieval features of twenty digital libraries', *Program,* **34** (4), 2000, 341–73.

14   Blair, D. C., 'The challenge of commercial document retrieval. Part I: major issues, and a framework based on search exhaustivity, determinacy of representation and document collection size', *Information processing and management*, **38** (2), 2002, 273–91.

15   Sornil, O. and Fox. E. A., 'Hybrid partitioned inverted indices for large-scale digital libraries'. In: Urs, S., Rajashekar, T. B. and Raghavan, K. S. (eds), *Digital libraries: dynamic landscapes for knowledge creation, access and management. The 4th International Conference on digital libraries,* Bangalore, Dec. 10–12, 2001, 192–207.

16   Hammer, S. and Favaro, J., 'Z39.50 and the World Wide Web', *D-lib maga-*

zine, 1996. Available at **http://www.dlib.org/dlib/march96/briefings/03indexdata.html**.

17 Pinfield, S., 'Beyond eLib: Lessons from Phase 3 of the Electronic Libraries Programme', 2001. Available at **http://www.ukoln.ac.uk/services/elib/papers/other/intro.html#elib-evaluation**.

18 Pinfield, S., 'Managing electronic library services: current issues in UK higher education institutions', 2001. Available at **http://www.ariadne.ac.uk/issue29/pinfield/**.

19 Fox, E. A., Suleman, H., Atkins, A., Gonçalves, M. A., France, R. K., Chachra, V., Crowder, M. and Young, J., 'Networked digital library of theses and dissertations: bridging the gaps for global access – Part 1, Mission and progress', *D-lib magazine*, 2001. Available at **http://www.dlib.org/dlib/september01/suleman/09suleman-pt1.html**.

20 Fox, E. A., Suleman, H., Atkins, A., Gonçalves, M. A., France, R. K., Chachra, V., Crowder, M. and Young, J., 'Networked digital library of theses and dissertations: bridging the gaps for global access – Part 2, Services and research', *D-lib magazine*, 2001. Available at **http://www.dlib.org/dlib/september01/suleman/09suleman-pt2.html**.

21 Myaeng, S., Jeong, C.-H., Lee, J.-H., Lee, H.-S., Kim, P., Yang, M.-S., Seo, J.-H. and Kim, H., 'A protocol-based architecture for federated searching in digital libraries'. In: Urs, S., Rajashekar, T. B. and Raghavan, K. S. (eds), *Digital libraries: dynamic landscapes for knowledge creation, access and management. The 4th International Conference on digital libraries,* Bangalore, Dec. 10–12, 2001, 116–24.

22 Borgman, C., 'Multi-media, multi-cultural and multi-lingual digital libraries: or how do we exchange data in 400 languages', *D-lib magazine,* June 1997, Available at **http://www.dlib.org/dlib/june97/ 06borgman.html**.

23 Borgman, C., 'Digital libraries and the continuum of scholarly communication', *Journal of documentation,* **56** (4), 2000, 412–30.

24 Large, A. and Moukdad, H., 'Multilingual access to web resources: an overview', *Program,* **34** (1), 2000, 43–58.

25 Peters, C. and Picchi, E., 'Across languages, across cultures: issues in multilinguality and digital libraries', *D-lib magazine,* 1997. Available at **http://www.dlib.org/dlib/may97/peters/05peters.html**.

26 Oudet, B., 'Multilingualism on the internet', *Scientific American,* **276** (3), 1997, 77–8.

27 Oard, D. W., 'Serving users in many languages: cross-language information retrieval for digital libraries', *D-lib magazine,* 1997. Available at **http://www.dlib.org/dlib/december97/oard/12oard.html**.

28 Sugimoto, S., 'Helping infrmation access across languages using simple tools: multilingual projects at ULIs and lessons learned'. In: Urs, S., Rajashekar, T. B. and Raghavan, K. S. (eds), *Digital libraries: dynamic landscapes for knowledge creation, access and management. The 4th International Conference on digital libraries,* Bangalore, Dec. 10–12, 2001, 16–29.

29 Fox, E. A. and Powell, J., 'Multilingual federated searching across heteroge-

neous collections', *D-lib magazine*, 1998. Available at **http://www.dlib.org/dlib/september98/powell/09powell.html**.

30   Bates, M. J., 'The cascade of interactions in the digital library interface', *Information processing and management*, **38** (3), 2002, 381–400.

31   Breck, E., Burger, J., House, D., Light, M. and Mani, I., 'Question answering from large document collections', *Question Answering Systems. Papers from the 1999 AAAI Fall Symposium,* North Falmouth, MA, 5–7 November, Menlo Park, CA, AAAI Press. 1999, 26–31.

32   Voorhees, E., *The TREC-8 question answering track report*, 1999. Available at **http://trec.nist.gov/pubs/trec8/papers/qa-report.pdf**.

33   Voorhees, E., *The TREC-9 question answering track report*, 2000. Available at **http://trec.nist.gov/pubs/trec9/papers/qa-report.pdf**.

Chapter 23

Trends in information retrieval

Introduction

As we have already noted through the preceding chapters, information retrieval covers a vast area of study, and it is therefore difficult to keep track of the latest developments and consequently the trends in research in this field. Thousands of research papers are published every year in a number of research journals, in seminar, conference and workshop volumes, on different areas of library and information science, computer science, electronic engineering, expert systems and artificial intelligence, linguistics, psychology, and so on. Leading library and information science journals that regularly report research in information retrieval include: *Journal of documentation, Information processing and management, Journal of the American Society for Information Science, Journal of information science, Online information review, Library and information science research*, and so on. This chapter aims to highlight some of the important research issues in information retrieval and is not meant to be exhaustive.

Before we consider the latest developments in this field, it is better to take a quick look at what has taken place in the past. Mechanization of information storage and retrieval using computer technology has a history that is about as long as that of the computer itself. Probably the first person to think about computer-aided solutions of information retrieval problems was Robert Fairthrone who, in the early 1950s, investigated the use of punched card equipment for the retrieval of bibliographic information.[1] In the early 1960s people proposed techniques, systems and models for information retrieval but most of this research did not produce fruitful results because the computational power available then was not adequate for all these tasks. A substantial amount of scientific work was done in the late 1960s and early 1970s experimenting on a number of information retrieval problems.[1] In the 1970s a number of mathematically sophisticated information retrieval models were developed, such as vector space and probabilistic models for retrieval. These experimental investigations yielded concrete evidence that relevance feedback was an effective way of enhancing retrieval. The developments in both theoretical and experimental research continued into the 1980s. During that decade it was realized that retrieval methods such as string searching, keyword searching or searches using keyword frequency information can be computationally efficient but they may not always produce the desired results.[2] So interest shifted back to examining natural language processing techniques as a way of improving retrieval performance when the stored information is largely textual.

Information retrieval research, which has expended so much effort over 30 years or so developing statistical and keyword-based approaches, has now started to use NLP approaches to the processing of texts constructively.[2] These techniques are currently used in many applications, as described here (Chapter 21) and elsewhere. For instance, Joscelyne[3] reports machine translation in the METAL system and Ruge[4] reports on an NLP system called REALIST, which can perform syntactic analysis on 130 megabytes of text in 18 hours on a 4.5 MIPs (million instructions per second) machine – in other words, at a rate of about 300 words per second.

One of the simplest applications of NLP in information retrieval has been in indexing based on some normalized or derived form of individual words occurring in input texts. Lexical level language analysis for the generation of automatic indexes was given much impetus with the arrival of machine-readable dictionaries. These dictionaries, such as the large ones available on CD-ROM (such as the *Oxford English dictionary*), include a definition for each sense of a term, usually including syntactic category, morphology and perhaps semantic information like restrictions on verb arguments or subject classifications. These dictionaries therefore help to produce more accurate descriptions of concepts in a text.

Humphrey and Miller[5] produced a frame-based 'index aid system' as part of the Automated Classification and Retrieval Program (ACRP) undertaken at the Computer Science Branch of the US National Library of Medicine. Frames are used to represent indexable knowledge entities, in the domain of medical science, for processes, procedures, biological structures and chemical substances. The TIS (Topic Identification System) of Reuters, reported by Weinstein,[6] uses artificial intelligence techniques to build rules that define the news topics; stories are categorized, indexed and entered into the database at the rate of three per second.

The first reported experiment on automatic abstracting took place in 1957–8 by H. P. Luhn.[7, 8] This and further work in the 1970s attempted to produce document extracts and did not consider the linguistic aspects of texts. As a result, the abstracts produced had a lack of cohesion and lack of balance. More recent work attempted to apply NLP techniques to avoid these problems. DeJong[9] produced a system that analyses newspaper articles using frame–based techniques; the articles are scanned and data are automatically put into frames; scripts are then used to generate summaries of the information held in the relevance frames. SCISOR, produced by Jacobs and Rau,[10] is a system that carries out a detailed linguistic analysis of text and then generates a semantic graph. Work in automatic abstracting was carried out in the 1990s by Black at the University of Manchester Institute of Science and Technology and Paice at Lancaster University.[11, 12] Paice[12] had been experimenting with automatically producing abstracts or text summaries by building frames or templates for these summaries, with slots like 'aim of paper', 'purpose of study', 'results', 'conclusions', and so on. Processing an input text will only partially fill some of these frames, but all frame slots need not always be filled. When the text is analysed, a coherent abstract can be generated automatically. However, one of the major difficulties of this sort of approach is handling discourse level phenomena like anaphora and ellipses. Further work by Paice and Black has concentrated on the development of a system that uses Prolog rules to improve its ability to sort out the linguistic problems encountered in automatic abstracting.[13]

An ideal information retrieval system should make provision for conceptual information retrieval. This usually requires semantic and pragmatic level language processing, often restricted to a narrow domain. Smeaton[2] suggests that semantic level language processing does not scale up to information retrieval size dimensions because of the robustness of the supporting knowledge base, and this looks like being the case for the foreseeable future.

The following sections attempt to highlight some of the recent research in different areas of information retrieval with a view to indicating the research trends in the subject globally.

Evaluation of information retrieval systems

Evaluation of information retrieval systems in a laboratory environment has a history of about 40 years. The basic ideas were originally established in the Cranfield tests set up in the late 1950s, while the major experimental programme of recent years has been TREC. The tradition that began with Cranfield and is now represented by TREC has formed a powerful paradigm for a wide range of information retrieval research.[14] As Sparck Jones observes,[15] one of the greatest benefits of the TREC series of experiments is that it has also brought a large number of information retrieval researchers from around the globe together on a common platform to share their research experience. There is still scope for TREC to refine its methods and extend its range to various types of information retrieval systems in different languages.

However, one important issue has been ignored, or not given due importance, in many retrieval evaluation experiments, even until very recently by TREC. This relates to the user component of information retrieval systems and many researchers have emphasized the need for user-centred design and evaluation of information retrieval systems (see for example[16, 17]) Robertson and Beaulicu[17] argue that every document, every query, every person, every term is unique, and yet in order to design information retrieval systems we have to consider generalities, gross classes that conceal many individual differences. So, the question is how to deal with the individual variations and how to measure this. The answer is not readily available, and yet this matter must be addressed in order to develop effective information retrieval systems. Bates[18] argues that evaluation of information retrieval systems will continue to be a problem since:

- Information retrieval systems involve language and cognitive processing.
- They involve serious scalability problems.
- User needs vary according to time, subject domain, and a number of other factors that call for special indexing and retrieval mechanisms.

Evaluation studies have become more important and more complex in the web and digital library environment for several reasons:

- Web search engines are mostly systems-driven rather than user-driven: they have been designed by systems personnel and are not backed up by systematic studies of user needs, behaviour, and so on.
- User communities are not defined in the web environment and virtually anyone can be a user; therefore conducting a systematic evaluation involving end-users is extremely difficult.
- The volume of information on the web rapidly, making it very difficult to conduct a study on a representative document sample.
- It is extremely difficult to use traditional evaluation measures such as recall because no one knows how many relevant documents are available on a given topic.

However, some researchers have been trying to resolve some of these issues. Discussing the problems of measuring the classic information retrieval parameter of recall in the web and digital library environment, Clarke and Willett[19] propose the use of a relative recall measure by using the technique of pooling used in the course of the TREC experiments (discussed in Chapter 14). Bates[20] argues that information retrieval problems in a digital library environment will be more acute because the human, domain and user factors will still operate in a digital library. Nicholas et al.[21] have characterized web information users as powerful, short on attention, promiscuous and untrusting. They note that users are very much interested in the speed of delivery. This has also been the finding of many other evaluation studies on the web, where it has been noted that users spend very little time looking at search results.

Developments related to the input subsystem

There have been several studies concerned with improving ways of providing input to any information retrieval system. Some of these studies are mentioned below.

Database creation

Several attempts have been made by information scientists to develop methods for designing databases as part of information retrieval systems. For example, Neelameghan[22] discusses a new approach to database development in which the postulates, principles and techniques formulated by Ranganathan within the framework of his general theory of knowledge classification are applied at various stages in the design and development of specialized databases, such as the conceptualizing, structuring and organizing of information, as perceived by specialist users, and the preparation of databases therefrom.

Traditionally, most of the databases in an information retrieval environment have been bibliographic or referral in nature. There are now integrated approaches combining text, audio, images and video information. Thus modern information retrieval systems have become more complex since they have to deal with the problems of text as well as content-based audio, image and video retrieval.

Vocabulary control

A sublanguage is the language used in a restricted or specialized domain or field, such as computer science. Information about the vocabulary and structure of a sublanguage is used in any domain-related NLP application. However, such information is very time-consuming to gather and much of it must be found and organized manually. On the other hand, information retrieval strategies using lexical information depend on finding the appropriate dictionary entry for general and technical words. The ability to identify terms belonging to a sublanguage automatically could aid in these and other applications. Hass and He[23] have reported research that has developed a method for automatic identification of sublanguage vocabulary words as they occur in abstracts.

Authors and searchers can express the same concepts in many different ways, which causes problems in free text searching in text databases. Thus a switching tool connecting the different names of the same concept is needed. Kristensen[24] reports a study that aimed at testing the effectiveness of a thesaurus as a search aid in free-text searching of a full-text database. The thesaurus constructed for this research contained the usual relationships of a thesaurus – equivalence, hierarchical and associative relationships. The effect of the test thesaurus on improving recall was substantial: twice as many relevant documents were retrieved with the union search (which included basic terms and all the alternative terms given by the thesaurus) as with the basic search (which included the terms of the search statements only). As discussed in Chapter 7, many information retrieval systems now provide access to online thesauri for expansion and modification of queries. While the term thesaurus has remained a well understood and used concept in the field of information science and information retrieval, the terms taxonomy and ontology are less widely recognized. Taxonomy means systematic classification and has been used within information science for a very long time. Nowadays taxonomy is used more in the context of the organization of internet information resources. Gilchrist[25] notes that the word taxonomy has been used with at least five different meanings, for example to denote:

- web directories
- taxonomies to support automatic indexing
- taxonomies created by automatic categorization
- front end filters
- corporate taxonomies.

Gilchrist[25] comments that taxonomies use both classification and thesaurus techniques.

An ontology can be defined as a formal, explicit specification of a shared conceptualization. Gilchrist[25] notes that Vickery was one of the first in the LIS field to draw attention to the emergence of the term ontology in knowledge engineering and information science. Two of the oldest and most widely known ontologies are WordNet and CYC. WordNet, a lexical tool, was developed by the Cognitive Science Laboratory at Stanford University, and contains some 100,000 word meanings organized in a taxonomy (Fellbaum[26]; **www.wordnet.com**). These are grouped into five categories: nouns, verbs, adjectives, adverbs and function words, and the meanings are related by synonymy, antonymy, hyponymy (the is-a relation), meronymy (part-of relationship between concepts) and morphological relations between word forms. WordNet is available free on the internet and has been used by a number of commercial organizations, including vendors of taxonomy software. The CYC ontology[27] provides a foundation for common sense reasoning by developing ontologies for a wide variety of domain-specific applications. A large number of domain-specific ontologies have been built for applications such as machine translation, enterprise modelling, knowledge reuse and information retrieval. Overviews of some of these projects, and the tools used by them can be found in Ding,[28] Ding and Foo[29] and Fensel.[30]

Searching and retrieval

Several research studies have been undertaken that aim to improve the process of searching and retrieval in an information retrieval environment. Some of them are discussed briefly below.

Knowledge-based searching

How would users access an 'ideal' computer-based information retrieval system? What strategies would they use in seeking information if they had access to a truly expert knowledge base that could respond effectively to any kind of questioning, phrased in any way? Ford and Ford[31] argue that no such system exists. However, they have reported a study that they claim as the next best thing – a computer system that allows unlimited access to genuinely expert knowledge. The results of this experiment reveal a number of different information accessing strategies linked to individual user characteristics and retrieval effectiveness.

Shute and Smith[32] have developed a model for knowledge-based searching that describes certain ways in which human intermediaries use their subject-specific knowledge to help end-users refine their searches. In this model suggestions for topic refinements are generated by applying certain knowledge-based tactics to a specific type of knowledge structure (frames). The insights gained in this research have potentially important implications for the design of computerized intermediary systems, as well as for the training of human intermediaries. The study suggested that one possibly important role for a computerized intermediary system would be to generate suggestions for topic refinement that the information seeker can then assess for relevance. Such a computational system can be based in part on the application of knowledge-based search tactics to domain knowledge represented as frames. Such systems now exist and work reasonably well; a typical example is AskJeeves, which uses knowledge-based techniques to provide users with a set of predefined queries on a specific topic or question. Kartoos is another example, where the user has a visual representation of links among various clusters of documents retrieved in response to a user query, and also various topics that are related to the user query; and the user can select any of them – either the retrieved items shown in clusters or a term from the topic map – to access the required information.

Searcher performance

Several measures, such as recall, precision, term overlap and efficiency, have been used to evaluate searching in bibliographic databases. When applied to searches for specific facts in a full-text database, these measures seem less appropriate.[32] For example, recall is reduced to a binary measure reflecting the success or failure of the search to retrieve the desired fact; the lack of precision may simply reflect the searcher's unwillingness to expend further effort in narrowing a search. Wildemuth et al.[33] conducted a study to evaluate 21 measures of performance on factual searches of a full-text database. The measures included: two measures of recall, two measures of precision, seven measures of search term overlap, seven measures of improvement in search term overlap and three measures of efficiency. Each of these measures was calculated for the searches performed by each of 26 first-year medical students, at the University of North Carolina at Chapel Hill, USA, on INQUIRER, a database of facts and concepts in microbiology. This study shows that the construct of searcher performance is made up of three types of behaviours:[33]

- those related to the selection of terms and the results of those selections (precision, recall and term overlap)
- those related to the searcher's use of feedback from the system to improve the selection of terms (improvement in term overlap)
- those related to the efficiency with which the search is executed by the searcher (time and number of search cycles).

A large number of research papers have appeared recently reporting on the searcher behaviour, performance, and so on in the web and digital library environment and some of these studies have been discussed earlier in this book. In general it has been noted that the searcher's performance is affected by a number of factors, including their digital literacy and information search skills, their status, their subject knowledge, information overload caused by the availability of too much information and speed of retrieval. Current research (see Wilson et al.[34]) also shows that the performance of the searcher improves in the course of carrying out a successful search, which is a common search pattern among subject experts.

Retrieval mechanism

Most commercial text retrieval systems employ inverted files to improve retrieval speed. Wong and Lee[35] have reported research conducted at the Ohio State University concerned with the implementation of document ranking based on inverted files. This research has studied three heuristic methods for implementing the $tf \times idf$ weighting strategy. The basic idea of the heuristic method is to process the query terms in an order such that as many high frequency documents as possible can be identified without having to process all the query terms. The first heuristic studied in this research was proposed by Smeaton and van Rijsbergen[36] and was used as the basis for comparison with the two other heuristic methods proposed by the authors. These three heuristics were evaluated and compared by experimental runs based on the number of disk accesses required for partial document ranking, in which the returned documents contain some of the requested number of top documents. The study by Wong and Lee showed that their two heuristic methods performed better than that proposed by Smeaton and van Rijsbergen[36] in terms of retrieval accuracy, which is used to indicate the percentage of top documents obtained after a number of disk accesses. Recent research on formal information retrieval models have been reported in journals, especially in *Information processing and management* and *Journal of the American Society for Information Science and Technology* (*JASIST*), with a special issue of *JASIST* (Vol. 54, No. 4, 2003) exclusively on the mathematical, logical and formal methods in information retrieval. Several novel retrieval mechanisms have been developed and tested in course of the TREC experiments. Brown[37]comments that currently we have a plethora of retrieval tools, each representing a point on a spectrum of information retrieval. The future surely lies in making these tools work together in a seamless way and making each tool cover a wider part of the spectrum. The ubiquitous adoption of a read–write interface (an interface with a program that allows users to make notes or edit; by looking at user's manipulations, the system understands better what users are interested in) would improve the smooth running of the tools. Brown[37] proposes two tools, SUPERIR and SUPERIF, to cover a wider part of the spectrum. Each knows some information in advance and this offers a chance for a practical and efficient implementation, which caters for document collections of a realistic size.

User studies and user modelling

Ingwersen[38] comments that information retrieval R&D has developed into three fundamental approaches; classical or traditional, user-oriented and cognitive. Ellis[39] observes that two conceptual approaches have dominated the field: the first, which he called the archetypal approach, derives from the comparative tests of indexing languages; the second derives from interest in cognitive research that can be traced back to the mid-1970s. Ellis stresses that the archetypal approach tends to focus on the artefacts or surface representations of knowledge recorded in physical documents, while the cognitive approach focuses on people and modelling of human knowledge structures. Information retrieval has always had a close relationship with database research, and researchers have made frequent attempts to develop models and build systems that will deal efficiently with structured and unstructured data. The traditional, system-oriented approach has dominated information retrieval research. Fortunately, people have now begun to realize that the user component of information retrieval is equally, if not more, important. As a result, the user-oriented approach to the development of information systems and services is regaining its importance, and the concept of relevance in the context of evaluation of information retrieval systems is being looked into from the end-users' point of view rather than entirely from the system's point of view. This is not easy, though, particularly in a digital library scenario where there is no limiting boundary to users; they could be anybody anywhere in the world. In fact:

- In a web environment there is no closeness at all between designer or creator of information and the potential user.
- There is a lack of clear understanding on the part of most searchers as to what course is taken by the search engines in the course of searching for a particular piece of information.
- The more distant the users are in characteristics and information needs from the types of user conceived of by the creators of information, the more likely there are to be problems in accessing information.
- The problem of providing easy access to information is compounded when the user is unknown.

Kafai and Bates[40] report on the SNAPdragon Project, which was created to investigate how children at elementary school can interact with the internet and the world wide web. Hill[41] reports on a study that focuses on the methods that people use for extracting information from the web and concludes that cognitive strategies are important for successful searching. He and Jacobson[42] report on a survey, conducted by the State University of New York at Albany Library, which indicated that users have high expectations of searching capabilities and feel disappointed with browsing.

The constant growth in the number of end-users who are deprived of the help of an intermediary is a source of substantial problems, which must be solved at different levels of communication between the human and the computer system. Several studies have been undertaken to develop user interfaces based on user modelling. Danilowicz[43] describes a model that solves many problems related to end-user searching by introducing additional user information by means of 'profiles',

Research on human information behaviour (HIB) has become easier to some extent with the availability of new technology and tools. One can now use easily collected information about every movement of a user in an information search process by using appropriate tools. Earlier it was a difficult and cumbersome job to collect information on every movement a user made in an information search process. The researcher had to spend time in minute observation and note taking, and the very presence of an observer could prove counterproductive or intimidating for the information user. Now this can be avoided, and every detail of a user's actions can be captured by using software like MouseClick. Nowadays, user search behaviour – right from the formulation of a search to its modification, viewing of the retrieved records, the time taken for each activitiy, and so on – can be captured through log analysis.

Researchers have used these tools for capturing information about the online search behaviour of users. However, many aspects of HIB have yet to be studied. For example, Foster and Ford[44] note that the role of serendipity when users carry out a search (when they make accidental but useful discoveries) has not been studied in the course of HIB research. During an experiment with researchers from different subject fields, Foster and Ford observed that serendipity was widely experienced among inter-disciplinary researchers, though perceptions of the extent to which serendipity could be induced was mixed.

User interfaces

There are three major choices available for a library or information manager to choose from when considering how to satisfy the information requirements of the user com-munity: online (including web) sources, CD-ROM sources and home-grown or locally produced databases or OPACs. However, there may be hundreds of separate databases each with its own user interface causing problems for the end-user. Thus provision of a single, standard interface to access a wide range of databases is high on the list of desirable features of interfaces in the future.[45] There have been attempts to design and promote the notion of a standard interface, such as the Common Command Language, which would be made available to all hosts, but the main focus is now on the idea of making the choice of interface entirely a matter for local decision.

User interfaces have been largely standardized by the use of common browser fea-tures. Many user interfaces now have attractive visualization features, for example the interfaces of search engines like Kartoos and Vivisimo (see Chapter 18). In general, online search services and search engine interfaces have improved significantly; they have become more intuitive and less demanding. Most advanced search interfaces allow users to formulate fairly complex search queries without having to learn the typ-ical search syntax. An exception is the expert search interface of Dialog.

Some search engines provide unique help facilities to users for formulating queries. A very good example is AskJeeves, which allows users to ask natural language queries. A unique feature of AskJeeves is that in addition to the results it provides from various search engines it comes up with a number of predefined queries related to the question that has been asked by a searcher. Many of these predefined questions are displayed with small boxes and a list of queries; the searcher can select one of them and click on the Ask button to put the query to AskJeeves. This is a very good feature and allows a searcher to pick up the most appropriate query. AskJeeves also has a list of popular questions and users can click on one of them to put it to AskJeeves.

Information retrieval standards and protocols

The notion of interoperability between different database systems is so attractive that it has generated many different attempts to achieve standards. These aim to enable machines and information systems to be able to communicate with one another by sharing and exchanging data and to enable users to have access to more than one infor-mation system (OPACs, databases, and so on) using the same techniques and inter-face. As discussed in Chapters 3 and 4, libraries have long recognized the need for appropriate standards to ensure interoperability among various library and informa-tion systems. Examples of these standards include MARC, MARC21, AACR2 and various metadata standards that allow library catalogues to exchange data. For ensuring interoperability among OPACs, libraries use the ANSI Z39.50 standard. Subsequently information retrieval systems have benefited from various markup languages – SGML, HTML, XML and XHTML.

American National Standard (ANSI/NISO) Z39.50, the information retrieval service definition and protocol specifications for library applications, is a standard that came out first in 1988, with subsequent versions in 1992 and 1994. Its main purpose is to encode the messages required to communicate between two computer systems for the purpose of information searching and retrieval. The protocol is defined to serve as a search and retrieval service that is completely independent of the underlying structure of data. In fact, it is designed to allow searching on remote systems without prior knowledge of the other system's syntax, strategies or data content.[46] The user interacts with only the local system's interface, while the implemented computer system acts as an intermediary between the user and the other system despite possible differences in hardware or software. This standard has equivalent international standards, ISO 10162 and ISO 10163 (known as ISO SR).

Iltis[46] reviews some Z39.50 implementations by universities, vendors and information services for different purposes. Payette and Rieger discuss this standard in the context of a common user interface for searching bibliographic resources and the ability to search multiple resources simultaneously.[47] This study concluded that in order to satisfy user requirements for the presentation of results from a multi-database search, the system will have to support merged result sets, compression of duplicates, and cross-database relevance ranking; if these capabilities are not available in an existing Z39.50 client, or cannot be effectively developed in a custom-made client, libraries may introduce multi-database searching in a limited manner. Lynch[48] observes that the Z39.50 standard has raised some false expectations and, in support of this statement, highlights the limitations of this standard, both as a protocol and as deployed in current implementations.

Search engines make extensive use of mark-up languages for selection of search terms and creation of indexes as well as for relevance judgements. As discussed in Chapter 18, many researchers have also used the HTML anchors for creating associative thesauri and concept maps to provide support for query modification and expansion.

Information retrieval in the context of web and digital libraries

Information retrieval in the context of web and digital libraries is characterized by three major factors:

- heterogeneity of information resources in terms of structure, content, format and source
- the variety of hardware, software and standards used to create the documents
- the distributed nature of the information as well as the users.

As discussed in Chapter 18, each one poses a number of challenges and information seeking and human information behaviour have become focal areas of research on web information retrieval. There have been some interesting and promising results. Several recent studied have been reported in the literature, and have been discussed in different chapters in this book. A special issue of *JASIST* (Vol. 53, No. 4, 2002) contained six very interesting papers discussing methods for studying information needs, information seeking, information use, and so on in the digital information environment. Nicholas et al.[49] have noted that today's online information users are demanding, and yet they don't want to spend much time on search and retrieval. Similar findings have been reported by other researchers too (see Chapters 18 and 22). Marchionini[50] comments that in order to achieve the goals of universal access to information, we must find ways to bring together data, people, technology and organizations.

Spink and Ozmultu[51] identified four types of web user queries: keyword, Boolean, question and request. Based on their study of user information search behaviour on the web they propose that future research on the web should focus on:

- whether question format queries or non-question format queries contain more significant terms and how the structure of question or request format queries can be improved for more effective retrieval
- whether the user's gender, communication style or interaction style affects the question and request query construction
- whether there are any similarities and differences that occur when users interact with different types of structured and unstructured data over different types of retrieval systems, such as online public access catalogues, web search engines, IR systems and databases.

The retrieval services of the web do not generally have the same level of search and display features found in traditional IR systems used to access bibliographic databases.[52] Researchers have noted that the search characteristics of these systems catering to general audiences are different from traditional IR.[53, 54] A different context for IR emerges from this environment, representing a more 'popular' use of IR, characterized by a broader audience, different document collections and different search models.[52]

In the introduction to a special issue of *JASIST* on web research, Spink[55] notes that web IR research can be classified into three main groups:

- web searching research that develops models of user behaviour and analyses trends using large-scale user data
- web page and system research that focuses on the development and testing of new algorithms, agents, web page design, interfaces and systems
- social and organizational impacts and aspects of the web.

In the editorial of a special issue of *Information processing and management* called 'Context in IR', Cool and Spink[56] comment that the future of research on IR context lies in its increasing depth and integration:

- We need a deeper understanding of the important contextual elements that encompass IR processes and generalizeable process models across situations.
- We need further integration of IR and information-seeking models within the broader human information behavior context.
- Integrative models will work to help people develop their information seeking behaviours into effective searches, involving query formulation and reformulation, and to formulate relevance judgements effectively.
- A relatively new area of research with respect to context focuses on deriving contextual information from user queries themselves. Work in this area has been conducted primarily in the web environment, but it has general application to interactive IR more generally and we can expect more work in this area in future studies.

The first few years of digital library research have focused especially on the systems issues of information retrieval to deal with the information architecture, design, formats, standards, protocols, and so on (for detailed discussions see Chowdhury and Chowdhury[57]). However, the success of digital libraries will largely depend on how digital libraries are best equipped to meet the information needs and search behaviour of their users. This aspect of digital libraries and information retrieval has been considered more important recently as evidenced by the digital library research activities under the DLI-2 (Digital Library Initiatives, phase 2) in the USA, under the eLib programme in the UK, and in many other parts of the world. Research into information retrieval in digital libraries has been discussed by Chowdhury and Chowdhury,[57] who conclude that digital libraries are not properly integrated at present. For example, one may have to use a number of digital libraries, one at a time, to get different types of information on a given topic. Digital library research and development activities should be properly integrated to meet users' needs most efficiently.

Intelligent information retrieval

Traditional information retrieval systems based on Boolean logic suffer from two inherent problems: inaccurate or incomplete query representation and inconsistent indexing. Although many researchers have demonstrated that neural networks can deal with the former, the inconsistent indexing problem still remains unsolved. Several researchers have used NLP and expert systems techniques to develop better information reteival systems. Cortez et al.[58] have developed a hybrid methodology of an intelligent and inductive learning technique with a neural network (connectionist model) in order to solve inconsistent indexing and incomplete query problems.

Automatic text summarizing/abstracting

As a result of the transition to full-text storage, multimedia and networking, information systems are becoming more efficient but at the same time more difficult to use. This is because users are confronted with volumes of information that increasingly exceed the processing capacities of the individual user. Consequently, there is an increase in demand for user aids such as summarizing techniques.[59] Against this background, the interdisciplinary seminar Summarizing Text for Intelligent Communication, held in Dagstuhl, Germany, in December 1993, outlined the state of the art with regard to summarizing (abstracting) and proposed future directions for research and systems development.

According to Endres-Niggemeyer[59] and Sparck Jones and Endres-Niggemeyer[60] the process of automatic text processing and summarizing or abstracting demands a multi- or interdisciplinary approach drawing on ideas and experience from several different subject areas. They add that research into automatic summarizing so far can supply information about the value or limitations of shallow techniques, particularly those exploiting statistical information or surface text cues, and about the utility of tightly constrained approaches designed for individual applications and relying on sharply defined domain models. A number of questions involved in the process of automatic text summarizing were raised at the Dagstuhl seminar:

- Can effective summaries be obtained with purely linguistic strategies?
- How general purpose can summarizing strategies be?
- How well do automatic summarizing techniques capture large-scale text structure?
- What specific aspects of human summarizing are best candidates for automation?
- What discourse properties are the most important for summarizing?
- What user features and tailoring techniques can we most usefully exploit in summarizing?
- How can current sentence processing methods help identify significant text content?

This was followed by a special issue of *Information processing and management* (Vol. 31, No. 5, 1995) on summarizing text, which reported eight important studies in this area. This set of papers shows that significant computational work in the process of automatic text summarizing is already being done. According to Endres-Niggemeyer:[59]

> Research in automatic text summarizing and abstracting is currently shifting its attention from text summarizing to summarizing states of affairs. Recycling solutions are put forward in order to satisfy short-term needs for summarization products. In the medium and long term, it is necessary to devise concepts and methods of intelligent summarizing which have a better formal and empirical grounding and a more modular organization.

Nonetheless, we have a long way to go in writing programs capable of interpreting, as opposed to generating, extended text, of recognizing large-scale text structure, and of identifying important source content using discourse as well as domain information. Craven's study with TEXNET[61] shows a limited success (only 37%). Gaizauskas and Wilks[62] mention that the performance levels of the common IE systems stand in the range of 50% for combined recall and precision. Such low success rates are not acceptable in large-scale operational information systems.

Evaluation of natural language processing systems

Some recent evaluation studies on NLP applications show promising results. Very small-scale evaluation of INFOS suggests that the indexing pattern method – mapping of the words from the input text into the correct concepts in the WordNet abstraction hierarchy – correctly classified 80% of the articles.[63] Some large-scale experiments with NLP also show encouraging results. For example, Kwok et al.[64] and Kwok, Grunfield and Chen[65] report that their PIRCS system can perform the tasks of English–Chinese query translation with an effectiveness of over 80%. Strzalkowski et al.[66] report that by using the algorithm of automatic expansion of queries using NLP techniques they obtained a 37% improvement of average precision over a baseline where no expansion was used. There are conflicting results too. For example, Elworthy[67] reports that the NLP system, using the Microsoft product NLPWin, performed much more poorly in the TREC-9 test set than in the TREC-8 test set. While trying to find out the reasons for this discrepancy, Elworthy[67] comments that an important challenge for future work may be to look at how to build a system that merges definitive, pre-encoded knowledge and ad-hoc documents of unknown reliability.

Natural language interfaces

Smith[68] suggests that there are two possible scenarios for future relations between computers and humans: in the user-friendliness scenario, computers become smart enough to communicate in natural language, and in the computer-friendliness scenario humans adapt their practices in order to communicate with, and make use of, computers. He further argues that the use of computer-friendly encoding of natural language texts on the web is symptomatic of a revolutionary trend toward the computerization of human knowledge. Petreley[69] raises a very pertinent question about natural language user interfaces: 'Will the natural language interface have to wait until voice recognition becomes more commonplace?' This question appears to be legitimate when we see that although a large number of natural language user interfaces were built, most at the laboratory level and a few at the commercial level (see Chowdhury[70]), natural language user interfaces are still not very common. The impediments to progress in developing natural language interfaces are various and include language issues. Zadrozny et al.[71] mention that, except for very restricted domains, we do not know how to compute the meaning of a sentence based on the meaning of its words and its context. Another problem is caused by the lack of precise user models. Zadrozny et al.[71] also maintain that even assuming that we could have much more detailed information about a person, we would not know how we could use this knowledge to make the person's interaction with a dialogue system most effective and pleasant.

Machine translation

Machine translation (MT) involves a number of difficult problems, mainly because human language is at times very ambiguous, full of special constructions and exceptions to rules. Despite that there has been a steady development in this subject and MT research has now reached the stage where the benefits can be enjoyed by people. A number of web search tools – AltaVista, Google, Lycos and AOL – offer free MT facilities of web information resources. A number of companies also provide MT services commercially. For example, the IBM WebSphere Translation Server for Multiplatforms is a machine translation service available commercially for translating web documents in a number of languages, such as English, French, Italian, Spanish, Chinese, Japanese and Korean. In June 2001, Autodesk, a US software company began to offer MT services to its European customers at a cost that is 50% less than human translation services.[72] Though machine translations are not always perfect and do not produce as good translations as human translators would, the results and evidence of interest in improving the performance level of MT systems are very encouraging.

Question-answering systems

One area of application of NLP that has drawn much research attention, but where the results are yet to reach the general public with an acceptable level of performance, is the natural language question-answering system. While some systems, as reported in this chapter, produce acceptable results, there are still many failures and surprises. Results of systems reported under the QA track of TREC (see Chapter 22) show promising results with some simple natural language queries. However, these systems are still at the experimental stage, and much research is needed before robust QA systems can be built that are capable of accepting user queries in any form of natural language and producing natural language answers retrieved form a number of distributed information resources. Scalability and portability are the main challenges facing natural language text processing research. Adams[73] argues that current NLP systems establish patterns that are valid for a specific domain and particular task only; as soon as the topic, context or user changes, entirely new patterns need to be established. Sparck Jones[74] rightly warns that advanced NLP techniques such as concept extraction are too expensive for large-scale NLP applications. The research community continues to study the subject, however. The reason for not having reliable NLP systems, which work at a high level of performance and with a high degree of sophistication, may largely be not because of the inefficiency of the systems or researchers, but a result of the complexities and idiosyncrasies of human behaviour and communication patterns.

Spink and Ozmultu[51] reported on a study examining queries in question format submitted to two different Web search engines – AskJeeves, which explicitly encourages queries in question format, and the Excite search service, which does not. This study noted that:

- 50% of AskJeeves queries and less than 1% of Excite queries were in question format.
- Most users entered only one query in question format with little query reformulation.

- There is a limited range of formats for queries in question format – they are mainly 'where', 'what', or 'how' questions.
- The most common question query format was 'Where can I find . . .' for general information on a topic.
- Non-question queries may be in request form.

Conclusions

To sum up, information retrieval research has gradually become more confident and has established strong links with a number of related fields such as artificial intelligence, expert systems, human–computer interaction, psychology and cognitive science. A recent trend, in addition to those mentioned earlier in this chapter, is towards the development of intelligent knowledge-based systems in a global information infrastructure. Intelligent search agents are now available in information retrieval, particularly in the internet environment. Some researchers (such as Haverkamp and Gauch)[75] predict that in future people will hardly interact with the web directly; instead they will use agents to take care of all their searching and arranging of schedules through the network. However, there are certain issues that need to be solved before this can be achieved. One major problem is how to start and keep running an agent for every database in the world, and perhaps a user-agent for every user. The other question is how to ensure that each agent communicates effectively with others. Researchers are actively engaged in solving these problems and are also working on new standards for agent communications and knowledge transfer. Nevertheless, information professionals with their rich experience in organizing and searching for information, and identifying user needs should work together with software professionals in making the concept of the global digital library a reality.

Crestani et al.[76] comment that future research in information retrieval should focus on:

- increasing the integration between different formal approaches to information retrieval
- capturing user modelling and the issues of context in information retrieval
- exploring links with other disciplines such as mathematics, logic and engineering.

Nicholas, Huttington and Watkinson[49] recommend that we need to take the following actions to lead the web and digital libraries to success:

- track and evaluate digital user (or consumer) needs as a matter of course
- (information vendors and providers) engage in the same process as all other providers of goods and services and put customer relationship management at the centre of their activities.

It is interesting to note that internet and web developments have brought significant changes to the economics of the information industry, from which end-users are largely benefiting. Some such developments include the following:

- Search tools are built competitively and most are available for free.
- Content is also available freely or on payment of a fee; for instance medical literature, including MEDLINE, can be accessed freely through PubMed.
- A number of question-answering systems are now available without charge.
- Significant improvements have taken place to user interfaces, visualization, and so on, the benefits of which are enjoyed freely by end-users (for details see Chapter 12).

Although a significant amount of money is being spent on developing technology and infrastructure for information retrieval, some significant changes are taking place behind the scenes that may affect its future. Nicholas et al.[21] observe that current trends in cyberspace suggest that it is not content developers or providers who are making real profits out of the digital information revolution; much money now goes to telecom companies and internet service providers. They provide a nice simile of this trend: imagine that we are living in a world where supermarkets are giving away everything for free, but the councils who build and maintain roads for access to the supermarkets are charging the customers. In these circumstances, the objectives of the IR community will be to find ways and means to help users to cut short their journey, so that they get the same amount of material with minimal costs. Research on various fronts of IR, as reported in different chapters in this book, aim to achieve this goal, and undoubtedly the results so far are encouraging.

References

1   Van Rijsbergen, C. J. and Agosti, M., 'The context of information', *The computer journal*, **35** (2), 1992, 193.
2   Smeaton, A. F., 'Progress in the application of natural language processing to information retrieval tasks', *The computer journal*, **35** (2), 1992, 267–78.
3   Joscelyne, A., 'Pedal to the METAL', *Electronic world*, **17**, 1990, 33–8.
4   Ruge, G., 'Experiments in linguistically based term associations', In: Lichenerowicz, A. (ed.), *Intelligent text and image handling: Proceedings of the RIAO'91 Conference, Barcelona, April 2–4, 1991*, New York, Elsevier, 528–45.
5   Humphrey, S. M. and Miller, N. E., 'Knowledge-based indexing of the medical literature: the indexing aid project', *Journal of American Society for Information Science*, **38** (3), 1987, 184–96.
6   Weinstein, P., 'The use of expert systems for end-user interfaces', In: *Proceedings. of the Fourth Annual Conference on Computers in Libraries, London, February 1990*, 96–9.
7   Luhn, H. P., 'A statistical approach to the mechanical encoding and searching literary information', *IBM journal of research and development*, **1** (4), 1957, 309–17.
8   Luhn, H. P., 'The automatic creation of literature abstracts', *IBM journal of*

research and development, **2** (2), 1958, 159–65.

9   DeJong, G., 'An overview of the FRUMP system', In: Lehnhert, W. G. and Ringle, M. H. (eds), *Strategies for natural language processing*, Hillsdale, NJ, Lawrence Erlbaum, 1982, 149–76.

10 Jacobs, P. S. and Rau, L. F., 'SCISOR: extracting information from online news', *Communications of the ACM*, **33** (11), 1990, 88–97.

11 Morris, A., 'Expert systems for library and information services: a review', *Information processing and management*, **27** (6), 1991, 713–24.

12 Paice, C. D., 'Constructing literature abstracts by computer: techniques and prospects', *Information processing and management*, **26** (1), 1990, 171–86.

13 Black, W. J., 'Applications of expert systems to abstracting', In: *Proceedings of the Fourth Annual Conference on Computers in Libraries*, London, February 1990, 100–3.

14 Robertson, S. E., Walker, S. and Beaulieu, M., 'Laboratory experiments with OKAPI: participation in TREC programme', *Journal of documentation*, **53** (1), 1997, 20–34.

15 Sparck Jones, K., 'Reflections on TREC', *Information processing and management*, **31** (3), 1995, 291–314.

16 Ingwersen, P., 'Cognitive perspectives of information retrieval interaction: elements of a cognitive IR theory', *Journal of documentation*, **52** (1) 1996, 3–50.

17 Robertson, S. E. and Beaulieu, M., 'Research and evaluation in information retrieval', *Journal of documentation*, **53** (1), 1997, 51–7.

18 Bates, M., 'Indexing and access for digital libraries and the Internet: human, database and domain factors', *Journal of American Society for Information Science*, **49** (13), 1998, 1185–205.

19 Clarke, S. J. and Willett, P., 'Estimating the recall performance of web search engines', *Aslib proceedings*, **49** (7), 1997, 184–9.

20 Bates, M. E., 'The internet: part of a professional searcher's toolkit', *Online*, **21** (1), 1997, 47–50.

21 Nicholas, D., Dobrowolski, T. Withey, R., Russell, C., Huttington, P. and Williams, P., 'Digital information consumers, players and purchasers: information seeking behaviour in the new digital interactive environment', *Aslib proceedings: new information perspectives*, **55** (1/2), 2003, 23–31.

22 Neelameghan, A., 'Application of Ranganathan's general theory of knowledge classification in designing specialized databases', *Libri*, **42** (3), 1992, 202–26.

23 Hass, S. W. and Hc, S., 'Toward the automatic identification of sublanguage vocabulary', *Information processing and management*, **29** (6), 1993, 721–32.

24 Kristensen, J., 'Expanding end-user's query statements for free text searching with a search-aid thesaurus', *Information processing and management*, **29** (6), 1993, 733–44.

25 Gilchrist, A., 'Thesauri, taxonomies and ontologies – an etymological note', *Journal of documentation*, **59** (1), 2003, 7–18.

26 Fellbaum, C. (ed.), *WordNet, an electronic lexical database*, Cambridge, Mass, MIT Press, Wordnet, 1998. Available at **www.wordnet.com**.

27 Cycorp. Available at **www.cyc.com**.

28   Ding, Y., 'A review of ontologies with the semantic web in view', *Journal of information science*, **27** (6), 2001, 377–84.

29   Ding, Y. and Foo, S., 'Ontology research and development. Part 1 – a review of ontology generation', *Journal of information science*, **28** (2), 2002, 123–36.

30   Fensel, D., *Ontologies: a silver bullet for knowledge management and electric commerce*, Berlin, Springer, 2001.

31   Ford, N. and Ford, R., 'Towards a cognitive theory of information accessing: an empirical study', *Information processing and management*, **29** (5), 1993, 569–85.

32   Shute, S. J. and Smith, P. J., 'Knowledge-based search tactics', *Information processing and management*, **29** (1), 1993, 29–45.

33   Wildemuth, B. M., Bliek, R. D. and Friedman, C. P., 'Measures of searcher performance: a psychometric evaluation', *Information processing and management*, **29** (5), 1993, 533–50.

34   Wilson, T., Ford, N., Ellis, D., Foster, A. and Spink, A., 'Information seeking and mediated searching. Part 2. Uncertainty and its correlates', *Journal of the American Society for Information Science and Technology*, **53** (9), 2002, 704–15.

35   Wong, W. Y. P. and Lee, D., 'Implementations of partial document ranking using inverted files', *Information processing and management*, **29** (5), 1993, 647–69.

36   Smeaton, A. F. and van Rijsbergen, C. J., 'The nearest neighbour problem in information retrieval: an algorithm using upper bounds', *Proceedings of the ACM SIGIR Conference, Oakland, California, 1981*, New York, ACM, 83–7.

37   Brown, P. J., 'From information retrieval to hypertext linking', *The new review of hypermedia and multimedia*, **8**, 2002, 231–55.

38   Ingwersen, P., *Information retrieval interaction*, London, Taylor Graham, 1992.

39   Ellis, D., *Progress and problems in information retrieval*, 2nd edn, London, Library Association Publishing, 1996.

40   Kafai, Y. and Bates, M. J., 'Internet Web searching in the elementary classroom: building a foundation for information literacy', *School library media quarterly*, **25** (2), 1997, 103–11.

41   Hill, J. R., 'The World Wide Web as a tool for information retrieval: an exploratory study of users' strategies in an open ended model', *School library media quarterly*, **25** (4), 1997, 229–36.

42   He, P. W and. Jacobson, T. E., 'What are they doing with the Internet? A study of user information seeking behaviour', *Internet reference service quarterly*, **1** (1), 1996, 31–51.

43   Danilowicz, C., 'Modelling of user preferences and needs in Boolean retrieval systems', *Information processing and management*, **30** (3), 1994, 363–78.

44   Foster, A. and Ford, N., 'Serendipity and information seeking', *Journal of documentation*, **59** (3), 2003, 321–41.

45   Hanson, T., 'A future for CD-ROM as a strategic technology?', In: Hanson, T. and Day, J. (eds.), *CD-ROM in libraries: management issues*, London,

Bowker-Saur, 1994, 241–53.

46 Iltis, S., 'Z39.50: an overview of development and the future', 1995. Available at **http://www.cqs.washington.edu/~camel/z/z.html**.

47 Payette, S. D. and Rieger, O. Y., 'Z39.50: the user's perspective', *D-lib magazine*, April 1997. Available at **http://www:dlib.org/dlib/april97/cornell/04payette**. html.

48 Lynch, C. A., 'Building the infrastructure of resource sharing: union catalogs, distributed search, and cross-database linkage', *Library trends*, **45** (3), 1997, 448–61.

49 Nicholas, D., Huttington, P. and Watkinson, A., 'Digital journals, big deals and online searching behaviour: a pilot study', *Aslib proceedings: new information perspectives*, **55** (1/2), 2003, 84–109.

50 Marchionini, G., 'Co-evolution of user and organizational interfaces: a longitudinal case study of www dissemination of national statistics', *Journal of the American Society for Information Science and Technology*, **53** (14), 2003, 1192–209.

51 Spink, A. and Ozmultu, H,, 'Characteristics of question format web queries: an exploratory study', *Information processing and management*, **38** (4), 2002, 453–71.

52 Wolfram, D. and Xie, H., 'Traditional IR for web users: a context for general audience digital libraries', *Information processing and management*, **38** (5), 2002, 627–48.

53 Jansen, B. and Pooch, U., 'A review of web searching studies and a framework for future research', *Journal of the American Society for Information Science*, **52** (3), 2001, 235–46.

54 Spink, A., Wolfram, D., Jansen, B. J. and Saracevic, T., 'Searching the web: the public and their queries', *Journal of the American Society for Information Science*, **52** (3), 2001, 226–34.

55 Spink, A., 'Introduction to the special issue on web research', *Journal of the American Society for Information Science and Technology*, **53** (2), 2002, 65–6.

56 Cool, C. and Spink, A., 'Issues of context in information retrieval (IR): an introduction to the special issue', *Information processing and management*, **38** (5), 2002, 605–11.

57 Chowdhury, G. G. and Chowdhury, S., *Introduction to digital libraries*, London, Facet Publishing, 2002.

58 Cortez, E. M., Park, S. C. and Kim, S., 'The hybrid application of an inductive learning method and a neural network for intelligent information retrieval', *Information processing and management*, **31** (6), 1995, 789–813.

59 Endres-Niggemeyer, B., 'Summarizing text for intelligent communication: results of the Dagstuhl seminar', *Knowledge organization*, **21** (4), 1994, 213–23.

60 Sparck Jones, K. and Endres-Niggemeyer, B., 'Automatic summarizing', *Information processing and management*, **31** (5), 1995, 625–30.

61 Craven, T. C., 'An experiment in the use of tools for computer-assisted abstracting'. In: *ASIS'96: Proceedings of the 59th ASIS Annual Meeting 1996.*

Baltimore, MD, October 21–24, 1996, **33**, Medford, NJ, Information Today, 203–8.

62   Gaizauskas, R. and Wilks, Y., 'Information extraction: beyond document retrieval', *Journal of documentation*, **54**, 70–105.

63   Mock, K. J. and Vemuri, V. R., 'Information filtering via hill climbing, wordnet and index patterns', *Information processing and management*, **33**, 1997, 633–644

64   Kwok, K. L, Grunfeld, L., Dinstl, N. and Chan, M., 'TREC–9 cross language, web and question-answering track experiments using PIRCS', *The Ninth Text REtrieval Conference (TREC 9), 2000*. Available at **http://trec.nist.gov/pubs/trec9/t9_proceedings.html**.

65   Kwok, K. L., Grunfield, L. and Chan, M., 'TREC-8 Ad-hoc, query filtering track experiments using PIRCS', *The Eighth text retrieval Conference (TREC-8)*, 1999. Available at **http://trec.nist.gov/pubs/trec8/papers/queenst8.pdf**.

66   Strzalkowski, T., Perez-Carballo, J., Karlgren, J., Hulth, A., Tapanainen, P. and Lahtinen, T., 'Natural language information retrieval: TREC-8 report'. *NIST Special Publication 500-246:The Eighth Text REtrieval Conference (TREC 8)*, 1999. Available at **http://trec.nist.gov/pubs/trec8/papers/ge8adhoc2. pdf**.

67   Elworthy, D., 'Question answering using a large NLP system'. *The Ninth Text REtrieval Conference (TREC 9)*, 2000. Available at **http://trec.nist.gov/pubs/trec9/papers/msrc-qa.pdf**.

68   Smith, D., 'Computerizing computer science', *Communications of the ACM*, **41**, 1998, 21–23

69   Petreley, N., 'Waiting for innovations to hit the mainstream: what about natural language?', *InfoWorld*, **22** (4), 2000 102.

70   Chowdhury, G.G., 'Natural language processing'. In, Cronin, B. (ed.), *Annual review of information science and technology*, **37**, 2002, 51–89.

71   Zadrozny, W., Budzikowska, M., Chai, J. and Kambhatla, N., 'Natural language dialogue for personalized interaction', *Communications of the ACM*, **43**, 2000, 116–120.

72   Schenker, J. L., 'The gist of translation: how long will it be before machines make the web multilingual?', *Time*, **158**, July 16 2001, 54.

73   Adams, K. C., 'The web as a database: new extraction technologies and content management', *Online*, **25**, 2001, 27–32.

74   Sparck Jones, K., 'What is the role for NLP in text retrieval?' In: Strzalkowski, T. (ed.), *Natural language information retrieval*, Kluwer, 1991, 1–25.

75   Haverkamp, D. S. and Gauch, S., 'Intelligent information agents: review and challenges for distributed information sources', *Journal of the American Society for Information Science*, **49** (3), 1998, 304–11.

76   Crestani, F., Dominich, S., Lalmas, M. and Rijsbergen, K., 'Mathematical, logical, and formal methods in information retrieval: an introduction to the special issue', *Journal of the American Society for Information Science and Technology*, **54** (4), 2003, 281–4.

Index

AA Code 45
AACR2 43–8
  entry 46; areas 43–4
  implications for OPACs 47–8
  levels of description 44–5
AAT *see* Art and Architecture Thesaurus
ABI/INFORM 229, 232, 233, 236, 237,
  238, 292
ABNCD+ 27
aboutness 74
abstract
  definition 153
  qualities 155–6
  types 153–5; by form 155; by purpose
    154; by writer 154
abstracting 157–60
  guidelines 158–60
  see also automatic abstracting
ACM DL 429, 434–6
ALA code 43
Alexandria Digital Library 428, 430–32
alphabetic chain 103–4
alphabetical display 136–37
  see also graphic display; systematic display
AltaVista 281, 335, 339, 340, 341, 342,
  343, 344, 347, 348
AltaVista Photo Finder 311
alternative information retrieval models 182–3
  see also hypertext model; natural
    language processing model
American Computing Machinery Digital
  Library *see* ACM DL
AND logic 172
AND operator 184
ANSI Z39.2 32, 455
AOL 460
Art and Architecture Thesaurus 305
artificial intelligence 453–4
AskJeeves 339, 345, 454, 460
associative relationship 135
  see also equivalence relationship;
    hierarchical relationship

asymetric coefficient 180
ATN 381, 411
  parsing 405
audio information retrieval 300–3
  see also music retrieval; speech retrieval
augmented transition network *see* ATN
Autodesk 460
automatic abstracting 160–5, 398–401
  see also text summarization process 165
automatic classification 94–7
  see also clustering
automatic index
  steps 95
automatic indexing
  advantages 91
  definition 91
  process 91–4

balanced tree *see* B–tree
berry-picking model 218
  see also cascade model
best match searching 180–1
Bibliographic Classification 65–6
bibliographic databases 15
bibliographic format
  definition 24; components 25–6;
    content 25; content designators 25;
    physical structure 25
bibliographic item 25
bibliographic record
  definition 25
binary linked trie 109–10
binary search 104–5
  tree 105–7
BIOME 147
BIOSIS 16
Biz/ed 281
Blobworld 311
Boolean
  AND 173
  OR 173
  NOT 173

query formulation 183–4
search; in CD–ROM databases 295;
    limitations 173–4; model 172–4
bottom-up parsing 376
    see also top-down parsing
Boyer-Moore (BM) algorithm 111–13
brief search 170
brushing and linking 232
BT 128,129, 134, 135
    see also NT; RT
B-tree 107–9
BUBL 232, 233
BUBL LINK 66–8

California Digital Library 229, 427, 428,
    429–31
CANSEARCH 408–9
CARIS/FAO 16
cascade model 219
    see also berry-picking model
case grammar 385–6
CA Search 16
catalogue
    code 43
    databases 15
    objectives 42–3
cataloguing 42
    internet resources 48–50
    process 44
CBIR *see* content-based image retrieval
CCF 26, 29, 38–40
CD-ROM databases 292
    common search features 295–6
    technology 292–3
    vs online database 295–6
Chabot 311
Cha-Cha 437
chain indexing 76–8
child nodes 106
classaurus 140–2
classification 58–70
    internet resources 66–70
Classified Catalogue Code 43
clustering 95–6
CODER 366, 399–400
cognitive models of information retrieval   171
collision resolution 117
Colon Classification 57, 58, 59
conceptual analysers 398–9
conceptual dependency 387–8
cone tree 232
content analysis 262
content–based image retrieval 307–9
    challenges 308

standards 311–12
systems 310–11
techniques 308
content-based video retrieval 310–11
context-free grammars 373–4
controlled indexing 124–5
    vs natural language indexing 125
COP 401
COPSY 407
cosine coefficient 179
COTEM 403
Cranfield1 258–8
    criticisms 258
    failure analysis 257
    objectives 256
    results 257
    system parameters 256
Cranfield2 258–61
    indexing 259
    query 258–9
    results 260–61
    searching 259–60
    test collection 258
critical abstract 154
cross-language information retrieval 276, 397,
    413
cut-off 250
CyberDewey 68
CyberStacks 69

data 13
    entry 21; form/worksheet 21
database 13
    definition 13
    design 22
    development 18
    indexing 21
    kinds 15–6
    properties 14–5
    technology 16
DB/Text Works 20
DDC 57, 59–65, 66, 67, 77, 147, 160
    guidelines for classification 60–1
    main class 61–2
    tables 62–5
deep web 334
    see also surface web
DeLiver 437
DELOS 211
Dewey Decimal Classification *see* DDC
DialIndex 228, 284
Dialog 184, 185, 186, 188, 228, 230,
    236, 237, 281, 282, 292, 341
    Alert service 297

commands 290–91
    search operators 289–90
DialogWeb 284–9
    command search 287–8
    guided search 285–7
dice coefficient 179
Digital Catalogue 307
digital images 300
digital library
    common information retrieval features 436
    definition 425
    design 426–7
    design integration 440
    information resources 426
    information retrieval features 428–36
DISCVALUE93
document lenses 232
document retrieval 1
document subsystem 3
DRUGLINE 16
DTD 54, 323, 324, 439
DtSearch 20
Dublin Core 51, 52–4

EAD 52, 53, 324
EBSCO information service 283
ectosystem 11
EELS 69
EEVL 69
endosystem 11
end-user modelling 360–61
ENERGYLINE 16
Entrez 189, 230, 234
Entrez Taxonomy Browser 234–5
ENVIROLINE 16
equivalence relationship 133
    see also associative relationship;
        hierarchical relationship
ERIC 16
ETD 433, 434, 439
    see also NDLTD
Excalibur Visual Retrieval Ware 310
expert systems
    applications; in cataloguing 363–4;
        in collection management 364;
        in reference services 365–7; in
        subject indexing 364
    components 355–7; inference engine
        356; knowledge base 355–6; user
        interfaces 356–7
    development methodology 357–9; for
        library and information services 362–7
    development tools 362, 366
    historical developments 357

fallout 250
Fastfoto 307
FGDC 51
field 14
    separators 29
    tags 14
field-specific search 296
Fine Chemicals Directory 16
focus plus context 232
FOREST 16
FotoWare 307
Foundations Directory 16
frames 360, 386–7, 446
free–text search 296
FRUMP 165, 398
full-text databases 15
fuzzy set systems 410–11

GDL *see* New Zealand Digital Library
GEMS 437
generality 250
generic relationship 134
genex framework 238
goals 392–4
    see also plans
Google 307, 334, 335, 339, 340, 341,
        343, 344, 460
    indexing process 338–9
graphic display 138
    see also alphabetical display;
        systematic display
Greenstone Digital Library 432–33
    see also New Zealand Digital Library
grouptext 321
Guided Search, Dialog 285–7

hashing 115–7
HEADLINE, 437
IIIB *see* human information behaviour
Hidden Markov Models 301
hierarchical relationship 134–5
    see also associative relationship;
        equivalence relationship
high precision search 170
high recall search 170
High Sierra Standard 293
HotBot 307, 339, 341, 342, 347
HTML 183, 285, 323, 324, 325, 326,
        327, 328, 335, 412, 426, 430, 455
HTTP 51, 183, 330
human information behaviour 11
    models 216–9
human–computer interaction 230
hyperbolic tree 232, 437

hypermedia systems 320
hypertext
    components 318–19
    definition 317–18
    history 316–17
    model 183
    reference model 319–20

I³R 410
iBase 307
Iconclass 307
IDIN 26
IEL 437
image retrieval 303–09
    areas of application 303
    content-based 307–9
    keyword-based approaches 304–7
    queries 303–04
Index+ 307
indexing
    manual indexing 74–6; problems 86;
        steps 74–5
    subject indexing 72–4; effectiveness 72;
        exhaustivity 72; specificity 72
    theory 86–7
    see also automatic indexing
indicative abstract 154
    see also informative abstract
indirect file access 97
indirect sequential file organization 97
inference engine 356
inference strategies 360
INFOMINE 127, 145–6
information extraction 401–3
    problems 402–3
information needs 193–200
    in business 196–7
    in community development 199–203
    in enterprises 197–8
    in scientific and technological
        research 196
    types of 193–5
information retrieval
    definition 1
    in the context of web and digital
        libraries 455–7
    models 171–83; alternative models:
        hypertext model 183; natural
        language processing model 182–3;
        classical models: Boolean search
        model 172–4; probabilistic model
        174–6; vector-space model 176–80
    objective 2
    software 19, 20, 438

    types 20
    standards and protocols 454–5
information retrieval system 1, 2
    components 3
    design issues 5–8
    design phases 9–12
    document subsystem 2
    evaluation
        criteria 244–52
        purpose 244
    functions 3
    kinds of 4–5
    purpose 2
    retrieval subsystem 2
    users' subsystem 2
information search behaviour on the
    web 456
information search models
    human information behaviour models
        216–9; Bates's model 218–9;
        Dervin's model 217–8; Ellis's
        model 218; Kulthau's model 219
        Wilson's model 216–7; user-
        centred models 219–222; Belkin's
        model 220–1; Ingwersen's model
        220; Saracevic's model 221–22
information seeking 214–6
    and user interfaces 230–1
information seeking behaviour 200–01
information-systems methodologies 10
informative abstract 154
    see also indicative abstract
Informedia 310
INFOS 413, 459
Infoseek 281
Ingenta 283
Inmagic DB/TextWorks 20
INQUIRER 451
INSPEC 144
integrated database 27–8
intelligent retrieval systems 353
interface design
    the four-phase framework 227–30;
        phase 1 228; phase 2 229; phase 3
        229; phase 4 230
interfaces for browsing and searching 232–7
interfaces for display of results 237–8
intermedia system 317
internet 4, 5, 48, 51, 120, 330, 367
Internet Explorer 334
interoperability 428
interview 208–9
inverse document frequency 92, 93
inverted file 97–110

access 101–110; alphabetic chain 103–4; B-tree 107–9; binary search 104–5; binary search tree 105–7; tries 109–10
IOTA 410
IRUS 410
ISBD 27, 37, 48
ISO 10162 455
ISO 10163 455
ISO 2709 28, 29

Jaccard coefficient 179

Kartoo 234, 237, 345, 346
keyword search 295
keyword–based approaches to image retrieval 308
kids' search engines 339
knowledge base 355–6, 381–2
knowledge elicitation 359–60
Knowledge Management System 317
knowledge representation 359 60
knowledge-based searching 450–1

leaf node 106
Library of Congress Classification 59
Library of Congress Subject Headings 66, 69, 127–9
life-cycle approach 358
limiting searches 186
linear probing 117
logical difference 172
logical product 172
logical sum 172
Lycos 307, 339, 347, 460
Lycos Multimedia Search 307

machine translation 413–5
main class, 63
major search engines 339
manual indexing 74–6, 86
MARC 26, 27, 31–2
MARC 21 32–6
  fields 33–6
  types of 33; format for authority data 33; format for bibliographic data 33; format for classification data 33; format for community information 33; format for holdings data 33
markup languages 323–7
  HTML 324–5
  SGML 323–4
  XHTML 327–7
  XML 325–6
MARS 311

matching subsystem 4
MEDLARS 261–2, 281
MEDLINE 188, 281, 408, 409
Memex 316
MeSH 144
metacrawlers 339
metadata 50–4
  definition 50–1
  types 51–2
  see also Dublin Core; EAD
MetaLib 439
MIBIS 26
MITA 402
modular abstract 155
monophonic music 302
  see also polyphonic music
MouseClick 453
MPEG 311–2
MULINEX 414
multikey search 101
multilingual IR
  problems 439 40
multilist organization 101
multimedia information retrieval 1, 299–300
multimedia search engines 339
multiway search tree 107
music information
  facets 302
music retrieval 301–03
  types 302

NASA 16
natural language indexing 125
  interfaces 411 2, 459
  internet, web and digital library applications 412–3
  processing model 182–3
  queries 345
  text processing systems 402–08
  understanding 372–3
  user interfaces 408–12
NCBI 189, 234
NDLTD 433–4, 436, 437, 440
  see also ETD
NEPHIS 72
nested Boolean search 184
Netra 311
Netscape Navigator 330, 335
Networked Digital Library of Theses and Dissertations *see* NDLTD
New Zealand Digital Library 302, 311, 428, 432–3
  see also Greenstone Digital Library
news search engines 339

NLS 316
non-preferred term 131
NOT logic 172
NOT operator 184
NoteCards 317
NT 128, 129, 134–5
    see also BT, RT
null pointer 108
numeric databases 15

observation 209–10
OCLC FirstSearch 36, 282
Olivetti Research Laboratory 301
OMNI 147
online information retrieval 4, 144, 214,
    231, 236
online search
    services 282–3
    steps 283–4
online searching 280–82
    development 281–2
    generations 281
OPAC 48, 54, 212, 348, 367
    generations 47
open hypertext and hypermedia 321–2
Open Text 347
optical coincidence 85–6
OR logic 172
OR operator 184
organization of internet resources 145–6
output format 22
overlap coefficient 179
Ovid 282
Ovid Online 282

panning and zooming 232
parent node 106
parsing 376–80
Peek-a-boo 85–6
perspective wall 232
Photobook 311
phrase search 295
picklist 237
PIRA ABSTRACTS 16
pixels 300, 309
plans 392–4
    see also goals
PLEXUS 409–10
PMM algorithm 113–18
polyphonic music 302
    see also monophonic music
POPSI 57, 72, 75, 83–4
pragmatic analysis 182
pragmatic knowledge 182, 390

PRECIS, 57, 72, 76, 80–3
    main entry 82
    primary operators 80
    role operators 80–1
    secondary operators 80
precision 73, 246, 247, 248–50, 251
    limitations 251–52
    see also recall
pre-coordinate indexing 76–84
predicate calculus 383–4
preferred terms 131
pre-search interview 170
primary keys 101
primitive ACTs 388
probabilistic retrieval model 174–6
probability ranking principle 175
Production systems 382–3
PROMETHEE 402
ProQuest 283
prototyping 359
proximity search 184–5
PTS Forecasts 16
PubMed 188, 189, 214, 234, 298, 462

QA track of TREC 460
QBIC 310
quasi-synonyms 133
query expansion 145
query-based music retrieval 302
question-answering 276, 411, 441, 460–1
questionnaire 206–8

RAFI 165
range search 185, 296
reaction information forms 403
recall 73, 246, 247, 248–50, 251–2
    limitations 251–2
    see also precision
record 14
    identifier 29
    label 29
    structure 28
referral databases 15
regional and country search engines 340
relational indexing 57, 78–80
relevance feedback model 180–82
relevance judgements 273
retrieval mechanism 451–2
reverse rendering 77
root node 106
RT 128
    see also BT, NT
RUBRIC 399

SALOMON 165
SCI SEARCH 16
SCISOR 400, 446
Scorpion 68–9
Scout Report 69
scripts 390, 391–2
search engine 183, 307
   common search and retrieval features
      340–2; components 336–7;
      software 337–9; software indexing
      337–8; spider 336–7
   definition 335
   how they work 336–9
   special search and retrieval features 343–4
   types 343
search refinements 188–90
search strategy 169–70
SearchDB 440
searching subsystem 3
SearchLight 427, 429, 430, 439
   see also reference 128
semantic analysis 182, 381
semantic knowledge 373
semantic networks 384–5
sequential access 102–3
SFX 439
SGML 272, 323–4, 455
Signpost 307
SILOL 401
SIMPR 400–01
SLR 405
SMART retrieval 94
   experiment 262–6
SNAPdragon project 453
SOCIAL SCISEARCH 16
SOSIG 281
source databases 15
speciality search engines 339
special–purpose abstracts 154
specificity 72–4
speech retrieval 301
spider 336–7
STAIRS project 266–9
STN 268, 282
stock market report generator 399
string matching 111
   Boyer Moore techniques 111–13
   PMM algorithm 113–5
subfield 14
subject analysis 70
subject heading lists 127–29
   see also Library of Congress Subject
      Headings
subject indexing 72

   definition 72
   problems 59
   process 72
sublanguage analysis 403–8
   in chemical information retrieval 403–6
   in patent information retrieval 406–8
subordinate term 134
superordinate term 134
surface web 334
   see also deep web
synonym 133
synonymity 133
syntactic analysis 182, 373
syntactic knowledge 373
system
   definition 5
   design 5
systematic display 139
   see also alphabetical display; graphic
      display
system-centred models 171
   see also user-centred information
      retrieval models

TAMIC 414
TEI 52, 324
TEXNET 165, 458
text signature 117–19
text summarization 165–6
text-numeric databases 15
TGM I 306
TGM II 306
thesaurofacet 138–40
thesaurus 130–38
   display 136–8; alphabetical 136–7;
      graphic 138; systematic 138
   evaluation criteria 143
   features 130
   purpose 130
   relationship between terms 133–5
   structure 130
   use in online information retrieval 143–44
   use in query expansion 145
Thesaurus of Graphic Materials 306
   see also TGM I, TGM II
THOMAS 436, 437
TICA 405
TINA 407
TIS 446
top-down parsing 376–8
   see also bottom-up parsing
TOXLINE 16
transformational grammar 375–6
transition network 380–1

TRANSLIB 414
TREC 269–78
    collections 272
    origin 269–70
    topics 272–3
    tracks 270–2
    relevance judgements 273
TREC-1 273–5
TREC-10 276
TREC-11 276
TREC-12 276
TREC-2 274–5
TREC-3 275
TREC-4 275
TREC-5 275
TREC-6 276
TREC-7 276
TREC-8 276
TREC-9 276
TRIES 109–10
TRUMP 400
truncation 186–8, 289, 290

UDC 57, 58
UF 133, 128–9
UKMARC 32
Ulrich's International Periodicals Directory 16
Unified Medical Language System 414
UNIMARC 26, 27, 36–8
    record components 37
Uniterm 72, 84–5
Universal Decimal Classification *see* UDC
URL 281, 335, 336, 338
USE 129, 13
user-centred designed of interfaces 238–40
user-centred information retrieval models   171
user-centred information search models 219–22
user interfaces
    and information seeking 230–1
    and visualization 231–2
    design, four phase famework 227–30
    for browsing and searching 232–7
    for display of results 237–8
    user-centred design 238–40
users 192
    information about individual user 204–5
    information about organization 201–3
    information about user groups 204–5
    information sources about users 205–210
    modelling 361, 452–4

studies; design 205–6; methodology
    206–210; interview 208–9;
    observation 209–10; questionnaire
    206–8
    see also information needs; information
        seeking behaviour
USMARC 32

VDX/Agora 439
vector processing model 176–80
video retrieval 309–11
Virage 310
visualization 345–6
VisualSEEK 310
Vivisimo 234, 345, 454
vocabulary control 8, 11 75
    definition 123
    objectives 124
    tools 126–38
    see also subject heading lists; thesaurus
vocabulary subsystem 3

web 4, 5, 120
    see also world wide web
web browser 324, 330, 335
    see also Internet Explorer; Netscape
        Navigator
web information
    growth 332–5
web information retrieval
    complexities 331
    evaluation studies 347–9
    vs traditional information retrieval
        330–2
WebExpress/iPort 339
WebSphere Translation Server 460
WordNet 459
world wide web 4, 5, 75, 123, 328, 333,
        354, 371, 427, 447, 468
    see also web
WWW *see* world wide web

Xanadu 316–7
XHTML 323, 326–7
XML 54, 323, 325–6

Yahoo! 281
    Companion 344
    Picture Gallery 307